International Criminal Justice Series

Volume 11

Series editors

Gerhard Werle, Berlin, Germany
Lovell Fernandez, Bellville, South Africa
Moritz Vormbaum, Berlin, Germany

Series Information

The *International Criminal Justice Series* aims to create a platform for publications in the whole field of international criminal justice. It, therefore, deals with issues relating, among others, to:

- the work of international criminal courts and tribunals;
- transitional justice approaches in different countries;
- international anti-corruption and anti-money laundering initiatives;
- the history of international criminal law.

The series concentrates on themes pertinent to developing countries. It is peer-reviewed and seeks to publish high-quality works emanating from excellent scholars, in particular from African countries.

Editorial Office

Prof. Dr. Gerhard Werle
Humboldt-Universität zu Berlin
Faculty of Law
Unter den Linden 6,
10099 Berlin, Germany
gerhard.werle@rewi.hu-berlin.de
moritz.vormbaum@rewi.hu-berlin.de

More information about this series at http://www.springer.com/series/13470

Kinga Tibori-Szabó · Megan Hirst
Editors

Victim Participation in International Criminal Justice

Practitioners' Guide

ASSER PRESS

Springer

Editors
Kinga Tibori-Szabó
Kosovo Specialist Chambers
The Hague
The Netherlands

Megan Hirst
Doughty Street Chambers
London
UK

ISSN 2352-6718 ISSN 2352-6726 (electronic)
International Criminal Justice Series
ISBN 978-94-6265-176-0 ISBN 978-94-6265-177-7 (eBook)
DOI 10.1007/978-94-6265-177-7

Library of Congress Control Number: 2016963158

Published by T.M.C.ASSER PRESS, The Hague, The Netherlands www.asserpress.nl
Produced and distributed for T.M.C.ASSER PRESS by Springer-Verlag Berlin Heidelberg

Printed on acid-free paper

This T.M.C. Asser Press imprint is published by Springer Nature
The registered company is Springer Science+Business Media B.V.
The registered company address is: Van Godewijckstraat 30, 3311 GX Dordrecht, The Netherlands

Foreword

The participation of victims in criminal justice has fluctuated and changed throughout history. Although victims were once instrumental in bringing their offenders to justice, the prevailing practice in recent history has been to relegate victims' interests to the sidelines in favour of the interests of society as a whole. However, contemporary international criminal justice has been turning its focus to elevating and legitimising victim participation, and to recognising the need to better take into account the restorative dimension of the international criminal process.

As this book demonstrates, this shift in focus has resulted in the acceptance of victim participation as integral to modern international criminal justice processes. Yet no consensus exists among practitioners or academics around the precise form this participation should take at the international level. Reflecting the diversity of perspectives on the issue, the frameworks and rules currently in place at international courts and tribunals differ in important ways from one another, and no one model replicates any particular national approach. We thus find ourselves in a place where both theories and the actual practice of victim participation continue to evolve.

With their experience to date, international courts and tribunals, in addition to already achieving a measure of justice for victims, have served as laboratories for the benefit of future endeavours. This book, through its comprehensive coverage of and thoughtful commentary on that experience, is an essential contribution to the international discussion. It makes clear that victim participation is a work in progress and reminds us that critical questions for the international justice community concerning effectiveness, expeditiousness and cost remain. Part of the book's significant value will be to stimulate debate that is necessary for progress.

It will also have immediate utility in proceedings. Victim participation at the international level is multifaceted and challenging. Among the issues that arise are the right to participate, how such participation is determined, the timing and manner of participation, victims' well-being and compensation. As the first practitioners' guide for victim participation work at international courts and tribunals, and one grounded not only in theory and the existing rules but also in the now extensive record of practice, this book will enable victims' interests to be better represented and heard through international criminal justice efforts, as well as enlighten other judicial and non-judicial actors with responsibilities pertinent to victims.

Her Honourable Judge Ivana Hrdličková
President of the Special Tribunal for Lebanon

Acknowledgements

This book is the product of three years of research and cooperation of an ensemble of enthusiastic practitioners working in or familiar with the field of victim participation in international criminal justice.

The editors express their gratitude to all contributing authors, who, besides preparing their own chapters, have also helped reviewing and improving each other's contributions and provided invaluable information to fellow authors on topics within their specialised knowledge.

In addition, the editors owe thanks to all practitioners who agreed to be interviewed for this book, namely Alice Banens, Hélène Cissé, Eleonor Fernandez, Paolina Massidda, Brianne McGonigle Leyh, Fiona McKay, Carine Pineau, Virginie Roche, Helena Vranov Schoorl, Luc Walleyn, Marten Youssef, as well as those who preferred to be referred to solely by their positions within the relevant organisations.

Special thanks go to Christoph Sperfeldt who dedicated a lot of his time and energy in supplementing and reviewing information regarding the Extraordinary Chambers of the Courts of Cambodia.

The editors are also grateful to Thomas Pinto Vasconcelos for his dedicated editing work.

This book would not have been finalised without the meticulous and thorough review work of Kiat Wei Ng, to whom the editors are especially grateful.

The Hague, The Netherlands
November 2016

Contents

Editors and Contributors

About the Editors

Kinga Tibori-Szabó is a legal officer for the Chambers' Legal Support Unit at the Kosovo Specialist Chambers. Dr. Tibori-Szabó is a qualified attorney and has nine years of professional experience in the field of international criminal law. Between 2012 and 2016, she worked as a legal officer for the Legal Representatives of Victims at the Special Tribunal for Lebanon. Before that, she was the legal assistant of the Pandurević Defence at the International Criminal Tribunal for the former Yugoslavia. Dr. Tibori-Szabó's doctoral monograph was awarded the 2012 Francis Lieber Prize of the American Society of International Law. She also teaches and publishes on various topics of international criminal law, international humanitarian law and public international law.

Megan Hirst is an Australian lawyer currently practising as a barrister at Doughty Street Chambers in London. She has worked in the areas of international human rights and transitional justice since 2005. She has particular experience working in East Timor, where she advised the national truth and reconciliation commission and was later employed by the International Center for Transitional Justice. From 2009 to 2015, she worked in the Registries of the International Criminal Court and the Special Tribunal for Lebanon in the respective sections of those courts which oversee victims' participation. She is part of the external legal team representing participating victims before the International Criminal Court in the case of *Prosecutor v. Dominic Ongwen.*

Contributors

Barbara Bianchini is the psychologist of the Victims and Witnesses Unit at the Special Tribunal for Lebanon. Ms. Bianchini worked as staff counsellor for the UN Assistance Mission in Afghanistan (2011–2014), and she was a training expert for the United Nations Interregional Crime and Justice Research Institute (2009–2011). In 2008, she cooperated with the European Commission in developing interviewing protocols for Khmer Rouge survivors in Cambodia. Specialised in traumatic disorders and mental health support during emergencies and critical incidents, and licensed to practise as clinical psychologist, she also worked as trauma expert with sexually abused children as well as alcohol and substance abuse specialist for governmental hospitals in Italy (2004–2008).

Heloise Dumont, B.C.L, LL.B., has practised as a litigation lawyer in Canada and has also worked for the International Committee of the Red Cross. She is currently an associate legal officer at the Registry of the International Criminal Court.

Mélissa Fardel is a Ph.D. candidate at the Law Faculty, University of Geneva (Switzerland). She has worked as a teaching and research assistant at the University of Geneva (Law Faculty — Department of Public International Law and International Organization) and at the Geneva Academy of International Humanitarian Law and Human Rights. She has also worked as a legal intern for the Victims' Participation Unit of the Special Tribunal for Lebanon.

Carla Ferstman is the director of REDRESS. She was called to the bar in British Columbia, Canada, in 1994 and practised there as a criminal law barrister. Also prior to joining REDRESS, she worked with the UN High Commissioner for Human Rights in post-genocide Rwanda, with Amnesty International's International Secretariat as a legal researcher on trials in Central Africa and as Executive Legal Advisor to Bosnia and Herzegovina's Commission for Real Property Claims of Displaced Persons and Refugees (CRPC). In 2012/2013, while on sabbatical from REDRESS, she was a Jennings Randolph Senior Fellow at the United States Institute of Peace. She has also been a visiting professional with Australian National University in Canberra. She obtained an LL.B. from the University of British Columbia, an LL.M. from New York University and DPhil at the University of Oxford.

Peter Haynes is Legal Representative of Victims in the *Ayyash* et al. case at the Special Tribunal for Lebanon. He is a British barrister and Queen's Counsel (QC) with over 30 years of experience in domestic and international criminal proceedings, including at the International Criminal Tribunal for the former Yugoslavia and the International Criminal Court.

Rianne Letschert is rector magnificus of the University of Maastricht. In March 2011, Dr. Letschert was appointed full professor of the new chair of victimology and international law at Tilburg University. From April 2010 to August 2010, she was a visiting research fellow at the Lauterpacht Centre for International Law at the University of Cambridge (UK) and research fellow of Clare College, Cambridge, where she was offered a lifelong membership. In 2014, she was a visiting professor at the University of Barcelona. In May 2015, she was awarded a Vidi grant by the Netherlands Organisation for scientific research on the impact of international tribunals on societies and individuals that have been confronted with serious human rights violations and international crimes. She is an expert consultant for the Legal

Representative for Victims in the *Ayyash* et al. case before the Special Tribunal for Lebanon. Apart from her position as professor, she served as director of the International Victimology Institute Tilburg (INTERVICT). In 2012, Letschert joined De Jonge Akademie (Young Academy) of the Royal Netherlands Academy of Arts and Sciences of which she became chairperson in April 2015. Dr. Letschert has authored and edited several book publications and articles in national and international journals.

Mariana Pena is a legal officer with the Open Society Justice Initiative. She has been working for civil society and donor organisations, in the field of human rights and international justice since 2005. Her most prominent areas of expertise include victims' involvement in accountability processes and the role of NGOs in international justice. She is a lawyer and has been admitted to the bar in her native country, Argentina. She holds two master's degrees from Paris I and Uppsala universities.

Yaiza Alvarez Reyes is the legal officer of the Victims and Witnesses Unit at the Special Tribunal for Lebanon. She has been a member of the Madrid Bar since 2002 and has a master's degree in International Humanitarian Assistance from the Université Catholique de Louvain, Belgium. She worked for the Registry of the International Tribunal for the former Yugoslavia from 2005 until 2012, providing legal advice within the Court Management and the Victims and Witnesses Section of the Registry. Ms. Alvarez is often involved in projects regarding capacity building and training of investigators, prosecutors and judges concerning the protection of victims and witnesses, both in relation to prosecution of war crimes and terrorism cases. Ms. Alvarez also presents lectures and seminars about victims' and witnesses' rights.

Daniella Rudy is a legal officer in the Office of the President of the Mechanism for International Criminal Tribunals (MICT). Prior to joining the MICT, Ms. Rudy served as an associate legal officer at the International Criminal Tribunal for the former Yugoslavia and the International Criminal Tribunal for Rwanda for several years and as an assistant co-prosecutor and a legal advisor for Civil Party Group 1 at the Extraordinary Chambers in the Courts of Cambodia. Before that, Ms. Rudy worked as an associate at Proskauer Rose LL.P. in New York for several years.

Anushka Sehmi practises as a lawyer and worked in the past as a legal assistant and case manager for the Legal Representative for Victims in the case of *The Prosecutor v. Uhuru Muigai Kenyatta* before the International Criminal Court. She was also field officer for the Victims Participation and Reparations Section at the International Criminal Court.

Ellie Smith is an international lawyer, researcher, consultant and trainer specialising in medicolegal and psychological issues affecting victims of international crimes within the justice process. Dr. Smith holds a degree in law from Cambridge University and a master's degree in international law from the London School of Economics. She has worked with survivors of international crimes for 15 years, including for eight years as a senior researcher with the Medical Foundation for the Care of Victims of Torture (now "Freedom from Torture").

Silke Studzinsky is the head of the Victims' Participation Office at the Kosovo Specialist Chambers. Ms. Studzinsky was a legal adviser to the Trust Fund for Victims at the International Criminal Court (2013–2015) and an international civil party lawyer before the Extraordinary Chambers in the Courts of Cambodia (2008–2012). She worked as criminal lawyer (victims' representation and defence) in Germany from 1990 to 2007.

Elizabeth A. Turchi is a legal officer with the United Nations in New York serving within the peacekeeping headquarters with a focus on victims' assistance and the United Nations' response to sexual exploitation and abuse in conflict and post-conflict states.

Nuria Vehils Olarra is an external relations and cooperation officer at the Registry of the International Criminal Court. She has also worked as a legal intern for the Victims' Participation Unit of the Special Tribunal for Lebanon.

Caroline Walter is a legal officer at the Office of Public Counsel for Victims at the International Criminal Court where she has been working since 2007. Before moving to The Hague, she lived in Montreal and worked on various projects with the International Clinic for the Defense of Human Rights (CIDDHU), the Centre d'études sur le droit international et la mondialisation (CEDIM) and the Groupe de réflexion en droit pénal International et humanitaire (GRÉPIH).

Other Contributors

Kiat Wei Ng is the case manager for the Legal Representative of Victims at the Special Tribunal for Lebanon. He previously assisted in various cases at the International Criminal Tribunal for the former Yugoslavia (Prosecution and Defence) and was a legal consultant in other major international cases. He graduated with a first-class honours LL.B. degree at Multimedia University, Malaysia, in 2009 and obtained his LL.M. (Distinction) from University College London (UCL) in 2010, specialising in Public International Law. Since he graduated from UCL, he has worked as a writer and researcher at various non-governmental organizations in the fields of international criminal law, women's rights and refugees' rights.

Christoph Sperfeldt is a Ph.D. scholar at the School of Regulation and Global Governance (RegNet), Australian National University. He has also been deputy director at the Asian International Justice Initiative, a joint programme of the East–West Center and the WSD Handa Center for Human Rights and International Justice, Stanford University, where he has supported human rights and rule of law capacity-building efforts in Southeast Asia. Prior to this, Mr. Sperfeldt was senior advisor with the Gesellschaft für Internationale Zusammenarbeit (GIZ) in Cambodia. In this capacity, he worked from 2007 to 2010 as an advisor to the Cambodian

Human Rights Action Committee and, from 2010 to 2011, as advisor to the Victims Support Section of the Extraordinary Chambers in the Courts of Cambodia.

Thomas Pinto Vasconcelos is an emergency planning officer at the Belgian Federal Crisis Center. Thomas Pinto Vasconcelos was a legal assistant at the Special Tribunal for Lebanon between 2015 and 2016.

Abbreviations

ADHOC	Cambodian Human Rights and Development Association
ASP	Assembly of State Parties
AU	African Union
BMZ	Federal Ministry for Economic Cooperation and Development (of Germany)
CDP	Cambodian Defenders Project
CLR	Common Legal Representative
CPLCL	Civil Party Lead Co-Lawyer
CSS	Counsel Support Section
DC-Cam	Documentation Center of Cambodia
DRC	Democratic Republic of the Congo
ECCC	Extraordinary Chambers at the Courts of Cambodia
GIZ	Deutsche Gesellschaft für Internationale Zusammenarbeit (German Corporation for International Cooperation)
ICC	International Criminal Court
ICCPP	International Criminal Court Protection Programme
ICTR	International Criminal Tribunal for Rwanda
ICTY	International Criminal Tribunal for the Former Yugoslavia
IR	Internal Rules
IRA	Individual Risk Assessment
IRCT	International Rehabilitation Council for Torture Victims
IRS	Initial Response System
KID	Khmer Institute of Democracy
LRV	Legal Representative(s) of Victims
NGO	Non-governmental Organization
OPCV	Office of Public Counsel for Victims
OTP	Office of the Prosecutor
PIDS	Public Information and Documentation Section
PIOS	Public Information and Outreach Section
PTSD	Posttraumatic Stress Disorder
RPE	Rules of Procedure and Evidence

SCSL	Special Court for Sierra Leone
STL	Special Tribunal for Lebanon
TPO	Transcultural Psychosocial Organisation
VPP	Victim Participating in the Proceedings
VPRS	Victims Participation and Reparations Section
VPU	Victims' Participation Unit
VSS	Victims Support Section
VWS	Victims and Witnesses Section
VWU	Victims and Witnesses Unit
WESU	Witness/Experts Support Unit

Chapter 1
Introduction: Victim Participation in International Criminal Justice

Kinga Tibori-Szabó and Megan Hirst

Abstract This introductory chapter sets out the purpose and structure of this book. It contends that victim participation in international criminal justice is a novel concept with a practice that is still evolving. It also states that the purpose of this book is to offer a guide to the law and practice of victims' roles before the ICC, ECCC and STL. It is a book written mainly by practitioners and it is addressed to those who work or wish to work in the field. The last sections of this introductory chapter explain the structure and the terminology used.

Keywords Formally recognised victim participants · Practice · *Ad hoc* victim engagement · Terminology

Contents

Kinga Tibori-Szabó is a legal officer for the Kosovo Specialist Chambers. She has previously worked for the Legal Representative of Victims at the Special Tribunal for Lebanon. Megan Hirst is a barrister at Doughty Street Chambers in London and a member of an LRV team in *Prosecutor v. Dominic Ongwen*. She has previously worked on victims' participation in the Registries of the ICC and the STL. The views expressed herein are those of the authors and do not necessarily reflect the views of the employing organisations.

K. Tibori-Szabó (✉)
The Hague, The Netherlands
e-mail: kingatibori@gmail.com

M. Hirst
London, UK
e-mail: m.hirst@doughtystreet.co.uk

K. Tibori-Szabó and M. Hirst (eds.), *Victim Participation in International Criminal Justice*, International Criminal Justice Series 11,
DOI 10.1007/978-94-6265-177-7_1

1.1 Preliminary Remarks

Victim participation in international criminal justice is a novel concept. The last two decades have seen a clear shift as regards the roles victims of mass crimes can play when the perpetrators accused of such crimes are prosecuted internationally.[1] The first international criminal tribunals did not provide victims an independent role in their proceedings. The Nuremberg and Tokyo Tribunals as well as the *ad hoc* tribunals for the former Yugoslavia and Rwanda acknowledged victims in their process only as witnesses. While the outreach efforts of the two *ad hoc* tribunals involved victims' issues, this was done in the context of legacy-building within the relevant societies.[2]

A right of victims to participate in the criminal justice process was internationally recognised for the first time in the 1985 United Nations Declaration of Basic Principles of Justice for Victims of Crime and Abuse of Power.[3] This possibility was later acknowledged in the creation of a new generation of international criminal courts and tribunals. Victims' role as independent participants in proceedings was thus included in the statutory documents of the International Criminal Court (ICC), and subsequently in the founding documents of the Extraordinary Chambers in the Courts of Cambodia (ECCC) and the Special Tribunal for Lebanon (STL).[4] Victims were also allowed to participate and obtain reparations at the Extraordinary African Chambers in the Courts of Senegal.[5] More recently, the law establishing the Kosovo Specialist Chambers and the Specialist Prosecutor's Office also adopted victim participation.[6]

While a lot has been written on the development, significance and impact of victims' participation schemes at the ICC, ECCC and STL, no comprehensive guide to the practical implementation of these schemes has been put forward. One reason for this may be the still developing nature of the field, which means that the actual practice of victim participation before international criminal courts continues to evolve rapidly.

It is the purpose of this book to offer a guide to the law and practice of victims' roles before the ICC, ECCC and STL. It is a book written mainly by practitioners and addressed to those who work or wish to work in the field. The book is thus not envisaged as a historical overview of the development of the concept and various

---

[1] Bonacker and Safferling 2013, pp. 1–7; McGonigle Leyh 2011, pp. 493–495.

[2] Bonacker and Safferling 2013, p. 2.

[3] United Nations Declaration of Basic Principles of Justice for Victims of Crime and Abuse of Power, Resolution (40/34), adopted by the General Assembly of the United Nations on 29 November 1985, UN Doc. A/RES/40/34.

[4] Article 68(3) of the ICC Statute; Rule 23 of the Internal Rules of the ECCC; Article 17 of the STL Statute.

[5] Statute of the Extraordinary African Chambers within the Courts of Senegal, Articles 14 and 27.

[6] Article 22 of the Law on Specialist Chambers and Specialist Prosecutor's Office, Law No.05/L-053, 2015.

schemes of victim participation in international criminal justice. Nor is it a review of the ample literature on the significance, advantages and challenges of victim participation. Instead, the various chapters focus on the relevant provisions at the three courts and the case-law interpreting and applying those provisions. Where relevant literature is nevertheless reviewed, it is done complementarily to the analysis of the pertinent jurisprudence.

The book's principal focus is the role accorded to formally recognised victim participants: in other words, those victims who submit written applications for the ongoing status of victim participants and who, if successful, are recognised and legally represented before the court. By contrast, the book does not purport to address the various ancillary methods in which victims can engage with international criminal institutions. For example, at all international courts, victims—like other persons—can put information concerning a crime before prosecutors, for the purpose of requesting an investigation. At the ECCC, special forms and procedures exist by which victims can make complaints.[7] At the ICC, victims are also provided with various other opportunities to be heard before the court through less stringent procedures than those involved in formal participation, and sometimes without the aid of a lawyer. For example, where the ICC prosecutor requests the opening of an investigation *proprio motu*, victims may make representations on this question to the Pre-Trial Chamber.[8] This has occurred in the situations in Kenya, the Ivory Coast and Georgia, with the Registry collecting and reporting on victims' representations.[9] Victims are also permitted to submit observations in ICC proceedings on jurisdiction or admissibility under Article 19 of the ICC Statute,[10] although this has been understood as restricted to those victims who have at least applied for formal participation in the case.[11] A similar provision exists in respect

---

[7] ECCC, Practice Direction 02/2007/Rev.1, Victim Participation, Article 2.

[8] ICC Statute, Article 15(3); ICC RPE, Rule 50.

[9] ICC, *Situation in the Republic of Kenya*, Victims Participation and Reparations Section, Public Redacted Version of Corrigendum to the Report on Victims' Representations (ICC-01/09-17-Conf-Exp-Corr) and Annexes 1 and 5, ICC-01/09-17-Corr-Red, 29 March 2010; ICC, *Situation in the Republic of Côte D'Ivoire*, Registry, Report on Victims' Representations, ICC-2/11-11-Red, 29 August 2011; ICC, *Situation in Georgia*, Registry, Report on the Victims' Representations Received Pursuant to Article 15(3) of the Rome Statute, ICC-01/15-11, 4 December 2015.

[10] ICC Statute, Article 19(3); ICC RPE, Rule 59.

[11] For example: ICC, *Prosecutor v. Joseph Kony, Vincent Otti, Okot Odhiambo, Dominic Ongwen*, Pre-Trial Chamber II, Decision initiating proceedings under Article 19, requesting observations and appointing counsel for the Defence, ICC-02/04-01/05-320, 21 October 2008, p. 7; *Prosecutor v. Callixte Mbarushimana*, Pre-Trial Chamber I, Decision requesting observations on the "Defence Challenge to the Jurisdiction of the Court", ICC-01/04-01/10-377, 16 August 2011, pp. 3–4; ICC, *Prosecutor v. William Samoei Ruto, Henry Kiprono Kosgey and Joshua Arap Sang,* Pre-Trial Chamber II, Decision on the Conduct of the Proceedings Following the Application of the Government of Kenya Pursuant to Article 19 of the Rome Statute, ICC-01/09-01/11-31, 4 April 2011, para 12; *Prosecutor v. Francis Kirimi Muthaura, Uhuru Muigai Kenyatta and Mohammed Hussein Ali*, Pre-Trial Chamber II, Decision on the Conduct of the Proceedings Following the Application of the Government of Kenya Pursuant to Article 19 of the Rome Statute, ICC-01/09-02/11-40, 4 April 2011, para 12.

of proceedings under Article 53 of the Statute to review a decision by the Prosecutor not to investigate.[12] A question remains as to what other roles the ICC might afford to victims who have not been formally recognised, for example pursuant to Rule 93 of the Rules of Procedure and Evidence.[13]

However, these avenues for *ad hoc* victim engagement have in practice been substantially overshadowed by the possibility for victims to obtain formal recognition and thereby ongoing standing and legal representation in international criminal proceedings. It is on that form of ongoing role, and its various aspects before the ICC, ECCC and STL, which this book is focused. Such participation exists in varying forms at the three tribunals. At the ECCC, it has its roots in the French civil law tradition, with "civil parties" having the expressly stated purposes of supporting the Prosecution and seeking reparations.[14] At the ICC, which attempts to blend different legal traditions in its procedural law, a *sui generis* approach to victim participation was created, which was subsequently followed in the texts of the STL. Its guiding principle is based on the 1985 UN Declaration's reference to allowing 'the views and concerns of victims to be presented and considered at appropriate stages of the proceedings where their personal interests are affected.'[15] This model has created a slightly different approach to victim participation, where victims are not treated as "parties", but rather as "participants" in the proceedings. In some ways this can limit victims' roles, however, in other ways it enables victims to engage with proceedings for purposes other than to support the Prosecution or to seek reparations. Indeed, it could be argued that victim participation at the ICC has been most meaningful and effective where—rather than seeking to support the Prosecution—it has held the Prosecution accountable to the victims' interests.[16] Nonetheless, the differences

---

[12] Article 53, ICC Statute; Rule 92(2), ICC RPE; ICC, *Situation on the Registered Vessels of the Union of the Comoros, the Hellenic Republic and the Kingdom of Cambodia*, Pre-Trial Chamber I, Decision on Victims' Participation, ICC-01/13-18, 24 April 2015, paras 8–10.

[13] This rule allows a chamber to seek the views of victims 'participating pursuant to rules 89–91', but additionally permits it to 'seek the views of other victims, as appropriate'. In the *Mbarushimana* case Pre-Trial Chamber I rejected a proposal made by the Registry for Rule 93 to be used where insufficient time remained to process victim applications before the confirmation of charges hearing: ICC, *Prosecutor v. Callixte Mbarushimana*, Pre-Trial Chamber I, Decision on the "Proposal on victim participation in the confirmation hearing", ICC-01/04-01/10-229, 10 June 2011.

[14] ECCC Internal Rules, Rule 23(1).

[15] United Nations Declaration of Basic Principles of Justice for Victims of Crime and Abuse of Power, Resolution (40/34), adopted by the General Assembly of the United Nations on 29 November 1985, UN Doc. A/RES/40/34, para 6(b).

[16] See for example the following steps taken by victims' lawyers in the *Kenyatta* case: ICC, *Prosecutor v. Uhuru Muigai Kenyatta*, Common Legal Representative of Victims, Victims' response to Prosecution's application for an adjournment of the provisional trial date, ICC-01/09-02/11-879-Red, 13 January 2014, paras 25–31, 58–61; ICC, *Prosecutor v. Uhuru Muigai Kenyatta*, Legal Representative of Victims, Request for access to filings which may relate to steps taken to identify, trace, freeze or seize assets of the accused, ICC-01/09-02/11-899, 29 January 2014 (reclassified as public on 11 December 2014); ICC, *Prosecutor v. Uhuru Muigai Kenyatta*, Legal Representative of Victims, Victims' response to the 'Prosecution's notice of withdrawal of the charges against Uhuru Muigai Kenyatta', ICC-01/09-02/11-984, 9 December 2014.

between the ECCC's civil party system and the model of victim participation established at the ICC and STL should not be overstated. Perhaps the most fundamental similarity is a key limitation on victims' potential roles, and a source of common frustration experienced by them: before all the three courts, victims have an extremely limited ability to influence prosecutors' selection of cases. Other than presenting complaints and information, victims have been allowed a minimal role in this area. At the ICC, despite initially confusing jurisprudence, the Appeals Chamber eventually clarified that although victims can participate in *judicial proceedings* which occur in respect of a "situation" (as opposed to a specific case against identified individuals), a prosecutorial investigation is itself not a judicial proceeding.[17] As a result victims have very limited rights to seek review of prosecutorial policy or decisions implementing it. A similar situation prevails at the ECCC and the STL.

Similarities also exist in more mundane aspects of the practice and jurisprudence of the three courts, numerous examples of which are set out in the pages of this book. Many common challenges have arisen in the experience of victims participating before the three institutions, and not infrequently similar practices and legal approaches have been adopted. Unfortunately, mutual learning has often been inhibited by a lack of communication. It is one of the goals of this book therefore, to enable practitioners working before one of these courts to easily identify practice from the others which may be of relevance.

1.2 A Continuously Developing Field

While each chapter of this book strives to give a comprehensive view of the practice of the three courts on particular topics, the book is not an exhaustive compendium of every application of each provision related to victims' participation. Rather, it informs the reader of the principal ways in which the relevant practice is developing, the distinct avenues taken in the application of similar provisions as well as the ensuing advantages and challenges.

The ensemble image that emerges from a brief perusal of the chapters shows a multi-directional evolution process, through which victims' rights have been interpreted and applied in distinct ways, ranging from very strictly defined criteria to poignantly permissive standards.

As discussed in Chap. 2, the three courts analysed herein—and the various chambers within the ICC—have adopted differing approaches to the application process required of victims to partake in the proceedings. While various forms of

[17] ICC, *Situation in the Democratic Republic of the Congo*, Appeals Chamber, Judgment on victim participation in the investigation stage of the proceedings in the appeal of the OPCD against the decision of Pre-Trial Chamber I of 7 December 2007 and in the appeals of the OPCD and the Prosecutor against the decision of Pre-Trial Chamber I of 24 December 2007, ICC-01/04-556, 19 December 2008.

individual written applications are the general rule at all three courts, the ICC has also allowed collective applications or simple registration (as opposed to judicial scrutiny) in certain cases. Moreover, as shown in Chap. 3, the three courts have applied different evidentiary standards in assessing the applications of victims, with the STL's Pre-Trial Judge adopting the strictest approach in this respect.

The roles which third parties (often referred to as "intermediaries") have played in the work of the three courts are also distinct. As indicated in Chap. 4, while the role of third parties at the ECCC has been viewed largely positively, the experience of the ICC with intermediaries is mixed.

While all three courts have opted for schemes of common legal representation for victims, they differ in the manner in which these schemes have been implemented. As Chap. 5 explains, the institutional frameworks set up for the representation of victims and the system for resourcing legal representatives are combined in different ways at the three tribunals. The relative merits and cost implications of internal legal representation versus external counsel are yet to be seen.

Furthermore, the three courts have applied different approaches to protecting the safety and well-being of victims participating in their proceedings. Chapter 6 elaborates on these differences and highlights that while anonymity is accepted at the ICC, the STL Appeals Chamber has rejected it and the ECCC never contemplated it as a protective measure. The same chapter also touches upon a very important, but largely underrated aspect of victim participation: special (psycho-social) measures undertaken to facilitate the testimony of vulnerable victims (and witnesses) and to prevent further traumatisation. While all three courts have set up a basic scheme of such measures, systems to cater for the psychological well-being of non-witness participating victims are still in their infancy.

Victims' access to confidential information is also regulated differently. As elaborated in Chap. 7, civil parties at the ECCC and participating victims at the ICC and STL can only access public information. The trends are dissimilar when it comes to legal representatives' access to information. While the ECCC and STL allows victims' lawyers access to confidential information, the practice at the ICC has been less consistent, although recent decisions seem to be moving in the same direction.

The modalities through which victims' lawyers can represent their clients during proceedings also take different forms at the three courts. Chapter 8 delves into the various modalities for participation as well as the differences and similarities in practice. It shows the scant consistency with which chambers at the three courts have set limitations on victims' lawyers' rights to intervene in the proceedings, such as the different approaches adopted by chambers of the ICC to the scope of questioning witnesses by legal representatives. The three courts have also adopted different approaches in relation to in-person participation of victims in the trial process as well. Chapter 9 focuses on the two main manners in which victims can participate in person in proceedings at the three courts. As the chapter shows, one method, presenting views and concerns, has only been applied at the ICC. The other method, giving evidence, is used at all three courts, although the ECCC only permits civil parties to give unsworn testimony. The book also looks at victim testimony as a source of information and the factors that mainly influence its reliability. While Chap. 10 only focuses on victim testimony in ICC cases, it offers invaluable advice on barriers to and factors negatively influencing testimony of victims. It elaborates on the clinical impact of trauma and the way in which this may prevent victims from producing a complete, coherent and credible account of their experience.

Another difference of practice is highlighted in Chap. 11: while the ECCC and STL have created opportunities for civil parties and participating victims, respectively, to observe proceedings in the courtroom, the ICC has not yet developed a comparable system accommodating victims' observational attendance. Chapter 11 also elaborates on the personal impact such form of attendance has had on participating victims at the STL.

Victims' rights to appeal judicial decisions also differ at the three courts. Chapter 12 explains that while civil parties have relatively broad rights to appeal interlocutory decisions, the STL has allowed the same under limited conditions, whereas the ICC entertains no such possibility. The same chapter also elaborates on the various approaches to victims' participation in interlocutory appeal initiated by (other) parties, as well as on victims' rights as regards appeals against final judgments and sentencing. In particular, while the ECCC does not permit civil parties to appeal a sentence, the Appeals Chamber at the ICC has allowed victims to make observations on sentence in appeal proceedings.

Victims' rights to reparations have also followed different paths at the three courts. Chapter 13 elaborates on the provisions and practice regarding reparations at the ICC and ECCC. The STL does not provide reparations at all. The ECCC enables the grant of (collective and moral) reparations to those victims who were admitted to participate in the proceedings as civil parties, while the ICC treats victims' participation and reparations requests distinctly, but has yet to finalise its first reparations implementation procedure. At the time of writing, the first order on the implementation of a symbolic reparations project has already been issued.[18] The ICC Trust Fund for Victims has emphasised that such a symbolic reparations project was feasible as long as it was not conceived as a stand-alone undertaking, disconnected from the forthcoming service-based reparations awards.[19] Echoing that stance, Trial Chamber II held in its decision that the proposed symbolic reparations project 'provide for an enabling environment to develop and implement service-based collective reparations awards'.[20]

[18] ICC, *Prosecutor v. Thomas Lubanga Dyilo*, Trial Chamber II, Order approving the proposed plan of the Trust Fund for Victims in relation to symbolic collective reparations, ICC-01/04-01/06-3251, 21 October 2016.

[19] ICC, *Prosecutor v. Thomas Lubanga Dyilo*, The Trust Fund for Victims, Public redacted version of the Filing regarding symbolic collective reparations projects, ICC-01/04-01/06-3223-Red, 19 September 2016, para 13.

[20] ICC, *Prosecutor v. Thomas Lubanga Dyilo*, Trial Chamber II, Order approving the proposed plan of the Trust Fund for Victims in relation to symbolic collective reparations, ICC-01/04-01/06-3251, 21 October 2016, para 12.

There is minimal guidance in the texts of the three courts as to the manners in which a victim's participation in the proceedings can be brought to an end. Chapter 14 considers the practice to date on this issue. Notably, it discusses the different consequences the death of a participating victim or civil party can have at the three courts. While at the ECCC, a deceased victim's participation can be continued by a successor, at the ICC the jurisprudence has been inconsistent and this situation has not yet arisen at the STL.

Of crucial importance in the development of victims' participation in international criminal justice is communication between client and lawyer. Chapter 15 looks at the manner and methods of communication with victims in the context of an international criminal trial.

The above examples show how victim participation in international criminal justice is far from being fully developed. At best, it is an assortment of distinct trends and differing practices fuelled by a common drive to involve victims of mass crimes in the proceedings prosecuting the accused perpetrators of those crimes. That being said, the various trends and practices within this process have the ability to become general norms and thus broaden or narrow the interpretation given to victims' rights. The last chapter of this book, Chap. 16, focuses on some of the most important issues that need to be addressed while victim participation in international criminal trials evolves, so as to ensure that the emerging scheme(s) of participation are able to represent meaningfully, efficiently and effectively victims' interests.

1.3 Structure of the Book

Each chapter of this book addresses a particular step or aspect of the participation of victims in international criminal proceedings. The order of the chapters largely follows the logic of participation schemes: from application (Chaps. 2 and 3) and modalities of participation (Chaps. 7–10), to appeal rights (Chap. 12), reparations (Chap. 13), and termination (Chap. 14). Some chapters address issues that relate to the participation of victims throughout the process: involvement of third parties (Chap. 4), legal representation (Chap. 5), protective measures (Chap. 6), observational attendance (Chap. 11), and communication with victims (Chap. 15). Some chapters—like those on application and modalities of participation—will most likely have to be read together. In any case, where relevant, a chapter contains references to other chapters.

The particular step or aspect of victim participation addressed in each chapter is discussed with a view to all three courts and their comparative practice wherever possible. In some cases, however, an issue under discussion is not relevant to the work of one or more of the institutions. For instance, Chaps. 4 and 13 do not address the perspective of the STL, as neither third parties, nor reparations, respectively, are germane to that court.

Each chapter concludes with key points summarising the main issues to remember regarding that particular step or aspect of victim participation. The main purpose of the key points is to highlight the main trends of practice, but also to emphasise the different directions taken by the court and, where pertinent, the challenges lying ahead.

The chapters have been updated to the end of October 2016.

1.4 Notes on Terminology

The term 'victim' is used throughout this book as a common denominator of those persons who have been granted participant status before the ICC and STL, and civil party status before the ECCC. 'Participating victim' is generally used to refer to victims participating before the ICC and the STL, whereas 'civil party' denotes victims before the ECCC. Where it is material that the persons referred to do not (or do not yet) have a participant or party status, that is indicated (as in Chap. 2, where the authors refer to 'applicants').

The term 'victims' lawyers' is used to refer to all counsel representing victims before the three courts. The term 'legal representative of victims' is used in relation to ICC and STL, as this role exists at those two courts. As regards the ECCC, the general term 'lawyers representing civil parties' is employed to refer both to Civil Party Lead Co-Lawyers (CPLCL) and civil party lawyers. The distinction between these latter two roles is elaborated in Chap. 5.

References

Bonacker T, Safferling C (2013) Victims of international crimes: An interdisciplinary discourse. Springer, Berlin/Heidelberg

McGonigle Leyh B (2011) Victim participation at the International Criminal Court. In: Letschert R, Haveman R, De Brouwer A, Pemberton A (eds) Victimological approaches to international crimes: Africa. Intersentia, Antwerp

United Nations Declaration of Basic Principles of Justice for Victims of Crime and Abuse of Power Resolution (40/34), adopted by the General Assembly of the United Nations on 29 November 1985, UN Doc. A/RES/40/34

Chapter 2
The Application Process: Procedure and Players

Mélissa Fardel and Nuria Vehils Olarra

Abstract When a person, having suffered harm as a result of the commission of a crime falling within the jurisdiction of the International Criminal Court, the Extraordinary Chambers in the Courts of Cambodia or the Special Tribunal for Lebanon, wishes to be granted status as a victim before one of these tribunals, he or she usually has to apply to do so. This step opens the door to the so-called application process for victims, a process that may lead to the recognition of the status of victim and the granting of the rights and obligations relating to it. This chapter gives a comprehensive overview of this application process, its procedure and the players involved in it, by focusing on the major issues related to this process.

Keywords Institutional players · Submission of applications · Assistance · Time limits · Assessment · Observations by the parties · Decisions · Appeals

Mélissa Fardel is a Ph.D. candidate at the Law Faculty, University of Geneva (Switzerland). She has worked as a teaching and research assistant at the University of Geneva (Law Faculty - Department of Public International Law and International Organization) and at the Geneva Academy of International Humanitarian Law and Human Rights. She has also worked as a legal intern for the Victims' Participation Unit of the Special Tribunal for Lebanon.
Nuria Vehils Olarra is Associate External Relations and Cooperation Officer at the Registry of the International Criminal Court. She has also worked as a legal intern for the Victims' Participation Unit of the Special Tribunal for Lebanon. The views expressed herein are those of the author and do not necessarily reflect the views of the International Criminal Court.

M. Fardel (✉)
University of Geneva, Geneva, Switzerland
e-mail: melissa.fardel@gmail.com

N. Vehils Olarra
International Criminal Court, The Hague, The Netherlands
e-mail: nuria.vehils@icc-cpi.int

K. Tibori-Szabó and M. Hirst (eds.), *Victim Participation in International Criminal Justice*, International Criminal Justice Series 11,
DOI 10.1007/978-94-6265-177-7_2

Contents

2.1 Introduction

This chapter describes the procedure of application for victims who wish to participate in international criminal proceedings at the International Criminal Court (ICC), the Extraordinary Chambers in the Courts of Cambodia (ECCC) and the Special Tribunal for Lebanon (STL).

It first defines the players involved in the application process, and explains their roles and how they interact with each other (if at all).

Attention will then be paid to the process for the submission of applications by victims who wish to participate in the proceedings at any of the three courts mentioned above. The chapter will examine the assistance provided to these applicants, particularly by whom such assistance is undertaken, and the time frame in which such applications can be submitted.

The chapter further addresses the next steps in the application process, dealing with the receipt and processing of applications, observations that can be made in relation to the applications, protection of victims' identities and, finally, whether appeals can be lodged against decisions made on the applications.

Throughout this chapter, when describing the application process which victims of a crime within the jurisdiction of any of these courts must undergo before being granted the status of participating victims (or civil parties for the ECCC) in the proceedings, victims will be referred to as *applicants* as opposed to *participating victims* in order to reflect the different legal nature of these two statuses.

While this chapter concentrates on the application procedure, the next chapter looks at the substantive requirements to become a victim participating in the proceedings (ICC, STL) or a civil party (ECCC). The two chapters should therefore be read together.

2.2 Players

This section gives a general overview of the most important players involved in the victims' application processes of the ICC, the ECCC and the STL. Many other actors play a key role in these victims' participation systems.[1] However, as they *usually*[2] come into play after an applicant has been granted the status of victim participating in the proceedings (or civil party for the ECCC), they are not directly related to the subject matter of this chapter, and consequently will not be described in this section.

2.2.1 International Criminal Court

Both sections of the Registry described below are involved in the ICC's victims' application process:

- The Public Information and Outreach Section (PIOS)[3]: while PIOS does not assist with the applications as such, it leads the initial approach towards affected communities, through its outreach activities and as a neutral representative of the Court. In the implementation of its functions, this section is helped by intermediaries,[4] such as NGOs who are normally based in the situation country and can help access and communicate with the affected communities in their local languages.[5]
- The Victims Participation and Reparations Section (VPRS): the VPRS plays a central role throughout the victims' application process as it acts as a focal point facilitating access to the Court for potential applicants and is the main section responsible for the collection and processing of applications for victims' participation. The VPRS receives application forms, reviews them, collects any

---

[1] For example, lawyers representing victims, the Office of Public Counsel for Victims (at the ICC) and the respective units entrusted with the protection of victims and witnesses.

[2] The roles of court-appointed lawyers and of the Office of Public Counsel for Victims (OPCV) usually come into play after an applicant has been granted victim status. However, at the ICC, victims can give powers of attorney to private lawyers of their own choosing up until the point when common legal representation is arranged, and these persons are sometimes involved in the application process. In some cases, the OPCV has been appointed as lawyer for unrepresented applicants (see Chap. 5). In this capacity, the OPCV may assist applicants to provide supplementary information, and, while in the field, might also assist other victims to apply for participation where this is requested.

[3] Formerly the Public Information and Documentation Section (PIDS).

[4] For more information on intermediaries, see Chap. 4.

[5] For example, specific directions were given by the Chamber to (then) PIDS regarding its role and the need to coordinate with the VPRS in ICC, *Prosecutor v. Dominic Ongwen*, Pre-Trial Chamber II, Decision Establishing Principles on the Victims' Application Process, ICC-02/04-01/15-205, 4 March 2015, paras 10–13.

missing documents or information, and files them with the respective chamber and to the parties, if necessary in redacted version. The VPRS also enters information from the applications into a database, performs *prima facie* analysis, and extracts reports for the chambers.[6] Additionally, the VPRS is mandated to inform victims of their participation rights and about reparations, to assist them in obtaining legal advice and legal representation, and to provide information related to the application procedure to the Legal Representatives of Victims (LRVs).

It should be mentioned however that, while the VPRS still serves as the focal section handling the victims' application process before the ICC, the Assembly of States Parties (ASP) has mandated the Registry 'to reorganize and streamline the Registry's organizational structure' with the goals of 'eliminating duplication, increasing effectiveness and efficiency, as well as creating synergies.'[7] A proposal made for this reorganisation included restructuring the institutional units working in the victims' participation system.[8] The Registrar proposed establishing a single Victims Office, 'which would consolidate the functions currently performed by the Office of Public Counsel for Victims (OPCV) and the Registry's VPRS, as well as redefining some functions currently being performed by the Counsel Support Section (CSS).'[9] However, the establishment of the proposed Victims Office would require an amendment to the Regulations of the Court and thus the approval of the judges.[10] While the Registrar had hoped for consideration by the judges in 2014 so as to enable implementation in 2015,[11] the 4 May 2015 report on the revision project noted that any recommendations or decisions on, *inter alia*, the OPCV and the VPRS have been postponed, pending the outcome of the discussions on the possible creation of a single Victims Office and a single Defence Office.[12] To date no progress has been made on this proposed reorganisation and it is not clear whether it has any prospects of proceeding.[13]

---

[6] Interview with Fiona McKay, former Head of Victims Participation and Reparations Section, ICC, 3 March 2015, (records on file with the authors).

[7] ICC, Resolution adopted by the Assembly of States Parties, ICC-ASP/12/Res.1 2013, section H, para 3.

[8] ICC Registry *Re*Vision Project: Basic Outline of Proposals to Establish Defence and Victims Offices, 2014b, http://www.uianet.org/sites/default/files/Registry_ReVision_BasicOutline_Defence_Victims_Offices_0.pdf. Accessed 1 March 2015.

[9] Ibid., p. 2.

[10] ICC, Assembly of States Parties, Report on the review of the organizational structure of the Registry, ICC-ASP/13/26, 28 October 2014a, para 19.

[11] Ibid.

[12] ICC, Assembly of State Parties, Report on the review of the organizational structure of the Registry, ICC-ASP/14/18, 4 May 2015, para 6.

[13] ICC, Comprehensive Report on the Reorganisation of the Registry of the International Criminal Court, August 2016. https://www.icc-cpi.int/itemsDocuments/ICC-Registry-CR.pdf. Accessed 4 November 2016, p. 12.

2.2.2 *Extraordinary Chambers in the Courts of Cambodia*

The *Victims Support Section* (VSS)—originally called the Victims Unit—established under Rule 12 of the ECCC Internal Rules[14] is the central contact point between the ECCC and victims. The VSS is mandated to inform victims about their rights relating to participation and reparation and, under the supervision of the Co-Investigating Judges, assist victims in processing their civil party applications. It also assists victims in obtaining legal advice or identifying a lawyer, and supports civil party lawyers. The section maintains contact with victims and their lawyers regarding the status of their applications, and keeps them updated regarding developments in individual cases. In earlier years, lawyers, in close cooperation with NGOs, undertook these tasks until the VSS received enough funding to maintain minimum capacities.[15] The VSS also facilitates visits by civil parties to attend the proceedings of the ECCC in person.[16]

Besides the VSS, the ECCC relies on several intermediary organisations,[17] some of which are based abroad (US, France), which provide support to victims during the application process. Amongst the main intermediary organisations are the Cambodian Human Rights & Development Association (ADHOC), Documentation Center of Cambodia (DC-Cam) for *Case 001*, and the Khmer Institute of Democracy (KID) and Cambodian Defender Project (CDP).[18] These organisations play a key role in facilitating the application process (including making the first contact with potential civil parties, filling in forms, and assisting with client meetings). Without their assistance, the application process would be difficult if not impossible. Notwithstanding this important role of intermediaries, practitioners should always be mindful about which intermediary they choose to work with as it can have a significant impact on their work.[19]

2.2.3 *Special Tribunal for Lebanon*

At the STL, the Victims' Participation Unit (VPU) has been set up within the Registry, in accordance with Rule 51 of the STL Rules of Procedure and Evidence

[14] Rev. 9 (2015) (ECCC Internal Rules).

[15] Written correspondence with Christoph Sperfeldt, Ph.D. Scholar, Australian National University, 20 August 2016 (records on file with the editors).

[16] See further Chap. 11.

[17] For more information on intermediaries, please refer to Chap. 4.

[18] For a list of intermediary organisations, see https://www.eccc.gov.kh/en/victims-support/intermediary-organizations-ios-0. Accessed 1 March 2015.

[19] Interview with Dr. Brianne McGonigle Leyh, former civil party lawyer, ECCC, 26 February 2015 (records on file with the authors). See further Chap. 4.

(STL RPE), to assist victims to participate in the proceedings. Its tasks include, but are not limited to, locating and reaching out to victims,[20] informing victims of their rights, receiving applications, and verifying that applications are complete and transmitting them to the Pre-Trial Judge. Furthermore, the VPU is mandated to provide logistical and administrative assistance to the LRVs ensuring that they provide a good service to their clients. Additionally, the VPU is mandated with keeping a list of highly qualified counsel, and administering the provision of legal aid funds, and monitoring the work of the LRVs.

2.3 First Step of the Procedure: Submission of an Application for Participation to the ICC, the ECCC or the STL

The submission of a written application form is the first step a victim must take in order to participate in court proceedings (Sect. 2.3.1). Assistance is generally provided to the applicant in order to reduce any burdens that may be associated with the submission of an application for participation to the ICC, the ECCC or the STL (Sect. 2.3.2). The chambers of the three courts have developed various practices regarding deadlines for the submission of victims' applications (Sect. 2.3.3).

2.3.1 Submission of Applications

At the ICC, the general principle, as set forth under Rule 89 of the ICC Rules of Procedure and Evidence (ICC RPE), is that an applicant needs to submit an individually completed written application form. A standard individual application form of 7 pages is available on the ICC website in both English and French.[21]

[20] In this task, the VPU has been assisted by the Registry's Outreach Unit that published press releases inviting victims to participate, and facilitated the broadcasting of a video on local and regional television channels with the same purpose. Written correspondence with Marie-Reine Sfeir, former associate liaison officer, Victims' Participation Unit, STL, 2 March 2015 (records on file with the authors).

[21] Applicants are requested to use one of these two languages if at all possible. If an applicant is unable to submit a form in English or French, and would like to submit the application form in another language, it is recommended to first contact the Court or its Field Offices, since the Court does not have translators who can work in all languages and has limited funds for this purpose (Interview with Fiona McKay, former Head of Victims Participation and Reparations Section, ICC, 3 March 2015 (records on file with the authors)).

It is however not compulsory for an applicant to use this specific application form. What matters is the content of the application.[22]

However, in some specific cases particular chambers of the Court have mandated that a modified application process be used. For instance, in *Prosecutor v. Laurent Gbagbo*, a partly collective application process was imposed by Pre-Trial Chamber III.[23] In the Kenya cases, Trial Chamber V determined that victims who did not wish to present their views and concerns individually and directly to the Chamber, but rather to express those views and concerns solely through common legal representation, were not required to submit written applications to participate in the trial. A simple registration by the Registry, with no judicial involvement, was in those cases sufficient in order to be granted victim status.[24] Additionally, in the *Ntaganda* case and in the *Ongwen* case, Pre-Trial Chamber II ordered that a simplified and shortened form be used.[25] A simplified form was also used for applications at the trial stage in the *Ntaganda* case, however Trial Chamber VI established a different procedure for the admission of victims to participate in that trial: the Trial Chamber required the Registry to assess individual victim applications on the basis of clear guidelines outlined by the Chamber, which retained ultimate authority over the process.[26]

---

[22] See for example, ICC, *Situation in the Democratic Republic of Congo*, Pre-Trial Chamber I, Decision on the Applications for Participation in the Proceedings of VPRS 1, VPRS 2, VPRS 3, VPRS 4, VPRS 5 and VPRS 6, ICC-01/04-101-tEN-Corr, 17 January 2006, para 102. At the time of the first six victims to ever apply for participation in ICC proceedings, the VPRS had not yet developed an application form. The forms used by the applicants were therefore forms created by the NGO Fédération Internationale des Ligues des Droits de l'Homme (FIDH) for taking testimonies during fact-finding missions. These forms contained the information required by Regulation 86(2) of the Regulations of the Court and were, therefore, accepted by the Chamber (Interview with Mariana Pena, Legal Officer, Open Society Justice Initiative, 17 November 2014 (records on file with the authors).

[23] ICC, *Prosecutor v. Laurent Gbagbo*, Pre-Trial Chamber III, Decision on Issues Related to the Victims' Application Process, ICC-02/11-01/11-33, 6 February 2012. See also, *Prosecutor v. Laurent Gbagbo*, Pre-Trial Chamber I, Second Decision on Issues Related to the Victims' Application Process, ICC-02/11-01/11-86, 5 April 2012.

[24] ICC, *Prosecutor v. William Samoei Ruto and Joshua Arap Sang*, Trial Chamber V, Decision on Victim's Representation and Participation, ICC-01/09-01/11-460, 3 October 2012, paras 48–55; *Prosecutor v. Francis Kirimi Muthaura and Uhuru Muigai Kenyatta*, Trial Chamber V, Decision on Victims' Representation and Participation, ICC-01/09-02/11-498, 3 October 2012, paras 47–54.

[25] ICC, *Prosecutor v. Bosco Ntaganda*, Pre-Trial Chamber II, Decision Establishing Principles on the Victims' Application Process, ICC-01/04-02/06-67, 28 May 2013, para 21; *Prosecutor v. Dominic Ongwen*, Pre-Trial Chamber II, Decision Establishing Principles on the Victims' Application Process, ICC-02/04-01/15-205, 4 March 2015, paras 14.

[26] ICC, *Prosecutor v. Bosco Ntaganda,* Trial Chamber VI, Decision on Victims' Participation in Trial Proceedings, ICC-01/04-02/06-449, 6 February 2015, paras 20–40.

In general terms, where a special application procedure has not been adopted, all applications must contain certain minimum information in order to be considered complete by a Chamber. This includes most importantly, but not exhaustively, the following:[27]

- the identity of the applicant (with documentary proof attached),
- the harm suffered by the applicant,
- the location and date of the crime,
- the applicant's signature or mark showing his or her consent.

Where an application is missing required information or documents, the VPRS may request supplementary information from applicants, persons acting on their behalf, states, the Prosecution or intergovernmental or non-governmental organisations.[28] In practice, these requests are hardly made to such entities. If anything, requests are made by the VPRS to the victims themselves, persons acting on behalf of victims or intermediaries.[29]

At the ECCC, one standard application form ("Victim Information Form") is used. It is 5 pages long and available on the ECCC website in English, French and Khmer. The applicant is requested to provide personal information about himself or herself, sufficient proof of identity,[30] details of the status as a victim, information about the alleged crime(s), and any evidence of the injury suffered or tending to show the guilt of the alleged perpetrator(s).[31] The applicant is given the option to request to join as a civil party (Part C of the Victim Information Form). For notification purposes, the applicant must also provide an address in Cambodia.[32]

Applicants must use the form provided by the Court and submit their applications in writing.[33] According to the ECCC Practice Direction on Victim Participation all civil party applications shall be submitted to the VSS.[34]

---

[27] For further details, see Sect. 2.4.1 below and Chap. 3.

[28] ICC Regulations of the Court, Regulation 86(4).

[29] Interview with Anushka Sehmi, former legal assistant/case manager for the Legal Representative of Victims in *Prosecutor v. Uhuru Muigai Kenyatta,* ICC, 21 February 2015 (records on file with the authors). See for example, *Prosecutor v. Dominic Ongwen*, Pre-Trial Chamber II, Decision Establishing Principles on the Victims' Application Process, ICC-02/04-01/15-205, 4 March 2015, para 27.

[30] Possible ways to prove identity are listed in the form: identity card (also student or employee card), voting card, letter from Local Authority, driver's license, passport, camp registration card, card from humanitarian agency (such as United Nations High Commissioner for Refugees, World Food Program).

[31] ECCC Internal Rules, Rule 23*bis*(4).

[32] Ibid.

[33] See Article 3.6 of the ECCC Practice Direction on Victim Participation, 02/2007/Rev.1 (2008) (ECCC Practice Direction on Victim Participation); and ECCC Internal Rules, Rule 23*bis*(2).

[34] ECCC Practice Direction on Victim Participation, Articles 3.4 and 3.7.

At the STL, a 9-page application form is used, available on the Tribunal's website in French, Arabic and English. Most importantly, applicants are asked to submit the following information:

- personal information relating to the victim,
- a brief explanation of the events as a result of which he or she became a victim (i.e. the circumstances and the damage, loss or harm),
- documentary proof relating to the victim's identity and the harm suffered.

If an application does not contain all the required information, the VPU is in charge of contacting the applicant to request such information.

The STL may produce an amended form which takes into account Rule changes and jurisprudence since the original form was developed.[35]

2.3.2 *Assistance to Applicants*

At the ICC, according to Regulation 86(9) of the Regulations of the Court, a specialised unit 'shall be responsible for assisting victims and groups of victims.' This unit is the VPRS. However, because of its limited capacity and resources and also because of logistical and security challenges, the VPRS has, since the early cases, relied at least in part on intermediaries to execute this task. This practice has been recognised by Pre-Trial Chamber II in the *Ntaganda* case. Although it considered that '[the] VPRS should be directly involved in assisting the applicants to fill the simplified forms',[36] the Chamber, taking note of observations from the Registry, acknowledged the Court's lack of resources and field presence, while citing considerable security concerns.[37] Therefore, it was affirmed that the VPRS, while retaining control and responsibility for the performance of the tasks, may benefit from the assistance of intermediaries, such as community leaders, *chefs du village* or staff members of local NGOs.[38]

Rule 12*bis* of the ECCC Internal Rules provides that, under the supervision of the Co-Investigating Judges, the VSS is in charge of assisting victims in submitting civil party applications. However, in practice, assistance to victims in collecting their stories and supporting their decisions concerning participation in the proceedings is not coordinated by the ECCC's own services, but rather is

[35] Written correspondence with Megan Hirst, former legal officer, Victims' Participation Unit, STL, 2 March 2015 (records on file with the authors).

[36] ICC, *Prosecutor v. Bosco Ntaganda*, Pre-Trial Chamber II, Decision Establishing Principles on the Victims' Application Process, ICC-01/04-02/06-67, 28 May 2013, para 26.

[37] Ibid., para 27.

[38] Ibid. See also *Prosecutor v. Dominic Ongwen*, Pre-Trial Chamber II, Decision Establishing Principles on the Victims' Application Process, ICC-02/04-01/15-205, 4 March 2015, paras 23–34. See also Chap. 4.

conducted through intermediary organisations. In *Case 002*, 82% of the civil party applications were filed with the assistance of intermediaries.[39]

One challenge that has arisen in the early stages of assisting victims to complete applications for civil party status is the lack of certainty about what the scope of the case would eventually be. This was a particular problem in *Case 002*. Eventually, the Office of the Co-Investigating Judges issued a press release disclosing the scope of the investigation. However, significant work had to be done in order to re-contact applicants to collect additional information required in the light of the scope of the investigation.[40]

At the STL, the VPU is the main contact for assistance in completing application forms. A Liaison Officer assists victims in filling in their applications. This Officer and other relevant staff meet victims, applicants and potential applicants. Moreover, the VPU staff contact an applicant when further information is needed in an application form.

Additionally, some applicants have been assisted by persons other than the VPU staff or Liaison Officer to complete their forms. As an example, some applicants had their own private lawyers who completed the form for them.[41] In some cases, the Tribunal-designated LRVs have assisted applicants in completing the forms and submitting them to the VPU. This has happened where already-participating victims brought their relatives to the LRVs for assistance with completing application forms.[42]

2.3.3 Time Limits in the Application Process

Except for Regulation 86(3) of the ICC's Regulations of the Court, according to which '[v]ictims applying for participation in the trial and/or appeal proceedings shall, to the extent possible, make their application to the Registrar before the start of the stage of the proceedings in which they want to participate', no guidance can be found in the ICC's legal documents regarding deadlines for submission of applications by victims to the Registry or, more precisely, to the VPRS.

The practice of the chambers has not been consistent on this issue. In *Lubanga*, no deadlines were set for the submission of victim applications to the VPRS, or for transmission by the VPRS to the Chamber. Consequently, the section received

---

[39] ECCC, *Case 002*, Office of the Co-Investigating Judges, Closing Order, Case No.002/19-09-2007-ECCC-OCIJ, 15 September 2010, para 11.

[40] Interview with Silke Studzinsky, former civil party lawyer, ECCC, 24 February 2015 (records on file with the authors).

[41] Written correspondence with Megan Hirst, former legal officer, Victims' Participation Unit, STL, 24 January 2015 (records on file with the authors).

[42] Written correspondence with Kinga Tibori-Szabó, former associate legal officer, Legal Representative of Victims, STL, 19 March 2015 (records on file with the authors).

applications on an ongoing basis, throughout the entire proceedings, including at late stages of the trial and during the subsequent appeal.[43]

In some other cases, chambers set a deadline for the submission of victim applications to the VPRS. This deadline concerned particular phases of the proceedings, such as the confirmation of charges hearings or the trial itself.[44] In most cases, however, no deadlines have been set for the submission of applications to the VPRS; instead a deadline is often set for the VPRS to transmit these applications to the relevant chamber.[45] Such deadlines enable the chambers to decide in a timely way on issues related to victim applications, i.e. before the confirmation of the charges or the trial.

The difference between the two types of deadlines (i.e. a deadline set for the submission of application forms to the VPRS, and a deadline set for the VPRS to

---

[43] ICC, *Prosecutor v. Thomas Lubanga Dyilo*, Trial Chamber I, Order on the Applications by Victims to Participate and for Reparations, ICC-01/04-01/06-2838, 27 January 2012, paras 5–6; *Prosecutor v. Thomas Lubanga Dyilo*, Appeals Chamber, Decision on a/2922/11's Application to Participate in the Appeals proceedings, ICC-01/04-01/06-3052-Red, 3 October 2013.

[44] ICC, *Prosecutor v. Germain Katanga et Mathieu Ngudjolo Chui*, Trial Chamber II, Décision relative au traitement des demandes de participation, ICC-01/04-01/07-933, 26 February 2009, para 27; *Prosecutor v. Jean-Pierre Bemba Gombo*, Trial Chamber III, Decision Setting a Time-Limit for the Submission of New Victims' Applications for Participation, ICC-01/05-01/08-875, 7 September 2010, para 9; *Prosecutor v. Jean-Pierre Bemba Gombo*, Trial Chamber III, Corrigendum to the Decision on 401 Applications by Victims to Participate in the Proceedings and Setting a Final Deadline for the Submission of New Victims' Applications to the Registry, ICC-01/05-01/08-1590-Corr, 21 July 2011, para 25; *Prosecutor v. Laurent Gbagbo*, Pre-Trial Chamber I, Second Decision on Issues Related to the Victims' Application Process, ICC-02/11-01/11-86, 5 April 2012, para 37.

[45] ICC, *Situation in the Democratic Republic of the Congo*, Appeals Chamber, Order of the Appeals Chamber on the Date of Filing of Applications for Participation and on the Time of the Filing of the Responses thereto by the OPCD and the Prosecutor, ICC-01/04-480, 29 February 2008, p. 2; ICC, *Situation in the Democratic Republic of the Congo*, Appeals Chamber, Order of the Appeals Chamber on the Date of Filing of Applications for Participation and on the Time of the Filing of the Responses thereto by the OPCD and the Prosecutor, ICC-01/04-481, 29 February 2008, p. 2; *Prosecutor v. Germain Katanga and Mathieu Ngudjolo Chui*, Pre-Trial Chamber I, Decision on the Set of Procedural Rights Attached to Procedural Status of Victim at the Pre-Trial Stage of the Case, ICC-01/04-01/07-474, 13 May 2008, para 189; *Prosecutor v. Jean- Pierre Bemba Gombo*, Pre-Trial Chamber III, Decision on Victim Participation, ICC-01/05-01/08-103-tEN-Corr, 12 September 2008, p. 5; *Prosecutor v. Jean-Pierre Bemba Gombo*, Pre-Trial Chamber III, Decision Concerning the Time Limit for the Submission of New Victim Applications, ICC-01/05-01/08-305, 2 December 2008, para 1; *Prosecutor v. Germain Katanga et Mathieu Ngudjolo Chui*, Trial Chamber II, Décision relative au traitement des demandes de participation, ICC-01/04-01/07-933, 26 February 2009, para 27; *Prosecutor v. Bahar Idriss Abu Garda*, Pre-Trial Chamber I, Decision on the Designation of a Single Judge on Victims' Issues and on the Deadline for the Filing of Applications for Participation, ICC-02/05-02/09-55-RSC, 19 August 2009, p. 6; *Prosecutor v. Callixte Mbarushimana*, Pre-Trial Chamber I, Order Setting a Deadline for the Transmission of Applications for Victims' Participation, ICC-01/04-01/10-78, 15 March 2011, p. 3; *Prosecutor v. Francis Kirimi Muthaura* et al., Pre-Trial Chamber II, First Decision on Victims' Participation in the Case, ICC-01/09-02/11-23, 30 March 2011, para 17; *Prosecutor v. William Samoei Ruto, Henry Kiprono Kosgey and Joshua Arap Sang*, Pre-Trial Chamber II, First Decision on Victims' Participation in the Case, ICC-01/09-01/11-17, 30 March 2011, para 17.

transmit these applications to the judges) is significant because sometimes applications have been received by the VPRS before a deadline for transmission to the chamber, but without sufficient time to be processed and transmitted by the VPRS before the deadline.[46] This can be problematic as victims do not have certainty as to when they have to submit their applications in order for them to be processed and transmitted in time.

In the case of the ECCC, Internal Rule 23*bis*(2) makes it clear that when a victim wishes to be joined as a civil party, he or she shall submit such application in writing no later than fifteen days after the Co-Investigating Judges notify the parties of the conclusion of the judicial investigation.

This deadline was inserted in the ECCC Internal Rules in September 2009,[47] and has been applied in *Cases 002*, *003*, and *004*. For *Case 001*, the deadline for submitting applications was ten working days before the initial hearing.[48]

In *Case 001*, the Trial Chamber rejected an application submitted after the deadline, because the applicant could not demonstrate exceptional circumstances preventing him from applying within the deadline.[49]

The STL legal documents do not provide a deadline for the submission of applications for victims' participation.[50]

In *Ayyash* et al., the Pre-Trial Judge considered it necessary to set a deadline during pre-trial proceedings, before which applications had to be received by the

[46] See for example, ICC, *Prosecutor v. Callixte Mbarushimana*, Registrar, Proposal on Victim Participation in the Confirmation Hearing, ICC-01/04-01/10-213, 6 June 2011, paras 1–6; and *Prosecutor v. Callixte Mbarushimana,* Pre-Trial Chamber I, Decision on the "Proposal on Victim Participation in the Confirmation Hearing", ICC-01/04-01/10-229, 10 June 2011, especially at p. 5 where the Judge noted that 'applicants whose Applications have not been submitted by [the deadline] will not be permitted to participate in the proceedings related to the confirmation hearing'.

[47] See Rule 23(3) of the ECCC Internal Rules, Rev. 4 (2009).

[48] See Rule 23(4) of the ECCC Internal Rules, Rev. 3 (2009).

[49] ECCC, *Case 001*, Trial Chamber, Decision on Request to Extend Deadline for the Filing of Civil Party Applications, Case No.001/18-07-2007-ECCC/TC 10 March 2009. In this case, an application was filed two days late by a victim, for the reason that the victim was unaware of the filing deadline and acted as soon as he became aware of it. The Chamber considered this reason insufficient to grant an extension of the deadline to the victim, particularly in light of the efforts that had been made by the Court to inform the public of the deadline. The Chamber ruled, in particular, that '[a]lthough, pursuant to Rule 23(4) [revision 3 of the Internal Rules], the President may alter deadlines for the filing of civil party applications, the exercise of this discretion must be supported by cogent reasons. Further, it must ensure equal treatment of all victims and avoid the appearance of individual dispensation. Consequently, an extension of this deadline for one civil party applicant shall either result in an extended deadline for all applicants or, where requested only in relation to one particular applicant, may be granted only in exceptional circumstances.' (para 9). See also ECCC Internal Rules, Rule 39(1) and (4).

[50] Rule 86(A) of the STL RPE specifies that the Pre-Trial Judge must have confirmed an indictment under Rule 68 before a person claiming to be a victim of a crime within the Tribunal's jurisdiction may request the status of victim participating in the proceedings.

VPU.[51] However, the Pre-Trial Judge also made it clear that applications submitted after the deadline would be considered as long as valid reasons explaining the delay could be provided.[52] In practice the Pre-Trial Judge has accepted a variety of reasons including fear of applying to participate as a victim in the proceedings,[53] or a lack of awareness or misunderstanding of victims' rights at the time of the initial deadline.[54] To date no applications submitted after the deadline have been rejected for that reason.[55]

2.4 Procedure Once an Application for Participation Has Been Submitted to the ICC, the ECCC or the STL

This section examines the detailed procedure that follows once an application for participation has been received by the VPRS (at the ICC), the VSS (at the ECCC) or the VPU (at the STL), and up until a decision on it is taken by the relevant chamber. An overview of this procedure will first be provided before explaining the following important related issues:

- *Parties' observations*: Are the Defence and the Prosecution entitled to make observations on the applications for participation?
- *Protection*: How is any information identifying the applicants protected if the applications are provided to the parties?
- *Appeals*: Are the Defence, the Prosecution and/or the applicants able to appeal decisions taken by a chamber on applications for participation?

2.4.1 Assessment of Victims' Applications

Once the ICC's VPRS has received applications for participation, it is then responsible for verifying the completeness of these documents.[56] This verification should be carried out within any time limit set by the relevant chamber. Where information

---

[51] STL, *Prosecutor v. Salim Jamil Ayyash, Mustafa Amine Badreddine, Hussein Hassan Oneissi and Assad Hassan Sabra ('Ayyash* et al.*')*, Pre-Trial Judge, Scheduling Order Regarding the Deadline for Filing Applications to Participate in the Proceedings as a Victim, STL-11-01/I/PTJ, 8 September 2011, para 4.

[52] Ibid., para 7.

[53] STL, *Prosecutor v. Ayyash* et al., Pre-Trial Judge, Second Decision on Victims' Participation in the Proceedings, STL-11-01/PT/PTJ, 3 September 2012, para 11.

[54] STL, *Prosecutor v. Ayyash* et al., Pre-Trial Judge, Fifth Decision on Victim's Participation in the Proceedings, STL-11-01/T/PTJ, 18 July 2014, para 11; STL, *Prosecutor v. Ayyash* et al., Pre-Trial Judge, Sixth Decision on Victims' Participation in the Proceedings, STL-11-01/T/PTJ, 6 November 2014, paras 3 and 11.

[55] Ibid. See also, STL, *Prosecutor v. Ayyash* et al., Pre-Trial Judge, Second Decision on Victims' Participation in the Proceedings, STL-11-01/PT/PTJ, 3 September 2012, para 11.

[56] ICC Regulations of the Court, Regulation 86(4).

or documentation is missing, the VPRS is required to request it before the application is submitted to the relevant chamber. The practice of the chambers however differs where those requests prove to be unsuccessful within a reasonable period of time. While some chambers will still require the VPRS to present incomplete applications to them for consideration,[57] some others have instructed the VPRS not to transmit those incomplete applications to the relevant chamber at all.[58]

In practice, applications are considered complete when they contain the following:[59]

[57] ICC, *Situation in the Democratic Republic of the Congo*, Pre-Trial Chamber I, Decision on the Requests of the Legal Representative of Applicants on Application Process for Victims' Participation and Legal Representation, ICC-01/04-374, 17 August 2007, paras 8–11; ICC, *Prosecutor v. Jean-Pierre Bemba Gombo*, Pre-Trial Chamber III, Fourth Decision on Victims' Participation, ICC-01/05-01/08-320, 12 December 2008, para 80; ICC, *Prosecutor v. Germain Katanga and Mathieu Ngudjolo Chui,* Trial Chamber II, Décision relative au traitement des demandes de participation, ICC-01/04-01/07-933, 26 February 2009, paras 26–27.

[58] ICC, *Prosecutor v. Jean-Pierre Bemba Gombo,* Pre-Trial Chamber III, Decision on Victim Participation, ICC-01/05-01/08-103-tENG-Corr, 12 September 2008, para 8; ICC, *Prosecutor v. Jean-Pierre Bemba Gombo*, Trial Chamber III, Decision Defining the Status of 54 Victims who Participated at the Pre-Trial Stage, and Inviting the Parties' Observations on Applications for Participation by 86 Applicants, ICC-01/05-01/08-699, 22 February 2010, paras 35 and 37; ICC, *Prosecutor v. Bosco Ntaganda*, Pre-Trial Chamber II, Decision Establishing Principles on the Victims' Application Process, ICC-01/04-02/06-67, 28 May 2013, para 29.

[59] ICC, *Situation in the Democratic Republic of the Congo,* Pre-Trial Chamber I, Decision on the Requests of the Legal Representative of Applicants on Application Process for Victims' Participation and Legal Representation, ICC-01/04-374, 17 August 2007, para 12; ICC, *Prosecutor v. Germain Katanga and Mathieu Ngudjolo Chui*, Pre-Trial Chamber I, Public Redacted Version of the "Decision on the 97 Applications for Participation at the Pre-Trial Stage of the Case", ICC-01/04-01/07-579, 10 June 2008, para 44; ICC, *Prosecutor v. Jean-Pierre Bemba Gombo,* Pre-Trial Chamber III, Fourth Decision on Victims' Participation, ICC-01/05-01/08-320, 12 December 2008, para 81; ICC, *Prosecutor v. Germain Katanga and Mathieu Ngudjolo Chui,* Trial Chamber II, Décision relative au traitement des demandes de participation, ICC-01/04-01/07-933, 26 February 2009, para 28; ICC, *Prosecutor v. Bahar Idriss Abu Garda,* Pre-Trial Chamber I, Decision on the 34 Applications for Participation at the Pre-Trial Stage of the Case, ICC-02/05-02/09-121, 25 September 2009, para 7; ICC, *Prosecutor v. Jean-Pierre Bemba Gombo,* Trial Chamber III, Decision Defining the Status of 54 Victims who Participated at the Pre-Trial Stage, and Inviting the Parties' Observations on Applications for Participation by 86 Applicants, ICC-01/05-01/08-699, 22 February 2010, para 35; ICC, *Prosecutor v. William Samoei Ruto, Henry Kiprono Kosgey and Joshua Arap Sang*, Pre-Trial Chamber II, First Decision on Victims' Participation in the Case, ICC-01/09-01/11-17, 30 March 2011, para 19; ICC, *Prosecutor v. Francis Kirimi Muthaura* et al., Pre-Trial Chamber II, First Decision on Victims' Participation in the Case, ICC-01/09-02/11-23, 30 March 2011, para 19; ICC, *Prosecutor v. William Samoei Ruto, Henry Kiprono Kosgey and Joshua Arap Sang,* Pre-Trial Chamber II, Decision on Victims' Participation at the Confirmation of Charges Hearing and in the Related Proceedings, ICC-01/09-01/11-249, 5 August 2011, para 57; ICC, *Prosecutor v. Francis Kirimi Muthaura* et al., Pre-Trial Chamber II, Decision on Victims' Participation at the Confirmation of Charges Hearing and in the Related Proceedings, ICC-01/09-02/11-267, 26 August 2011, para 71; ICC, *Prosecutor v. Laurent Gbagbo*, Pre-Trial Chamber I, Corrigendum to the Second Decision on Victims' Participation at the Confirmation of Charges Hearing and in the Related Proceedings, ICC-02/11-01/11-384-Corr, 6 February 2013, para 36; ICC, *Prosecutor v. Bosco Ntaganda,* Pre-Trial Chamber II, Decision on Victims' Participation at the Confirmation of Charges Hearing and in the Related Proceedings, ICC-01/04-02/06-211, 15 January 2014, para 60; ICC, *Prosecutor v. Dominic Ongwen*, Pre-Trial Chamber II, Decision Establishing Principles on the Victims' Application Process, ICC-02/04-01/15-205, 4 March 2015, para 28.

- the identity of the applicant,
- the date and location of the crime(s),
- a description of the harm suffered as a result of the crime(s),
- proof of identity,
- the express consent of the victim, if the application is made by a person acting on behalf of a victim with the victim's consent,
- proof of kinship or legal guardianship, if the application is made by a person acting on behalf of a victim who is a child,
- proof of legal guardianship, in the case of a victim who is disabled,
- a signature or thumb-print of the applicant on the document.[60]

Once verified as complete, the applications are sent by the VPRS, together with a report thereon, to the relevant chamber for consideration.[61] The report contains an initial assessment of the requirements of Rule 85 of the ICC RPE. In addition, chambers generally ask the VPRS to include an assessment as to which applications might be accepted, rejected, or raise difficult issues, and may also request a one-paragraph summary for each victim which reflects the information contained in the application analysed in respect of each of the requirements of Rule 85.[62] While the chamber may be guided by the VPRS's initial assessment, it remains for the chamber itself to determine whether the victim should be permitted to participate in the proceedings or not.

The VPRS also provides a copy of the applications to the Prosecution and the Defence, who are entitled to reply within a time limit to be set by the chamber (see further below Sect. 2.4.3 regarding the redaction of the applications provided to the parties).[63] Initially the VPRS's reports to the chambers were not provided to

---

[60] See Chap. 3.

[61] ICC Regulations of the Court, Regulation 86(5).

[62] ICC, *Situation in Uganda*, Pre-Trial Chamber II, Decision on Victim's Participation in Proceedings Related to the Situation in Uganda, ICC-02/04-191, 9 March 2012, para 27; ICC, *Prosecutor v. William Samoei Ruto, Henry Kiprono Kosgey and Joshua Arap Sang*, Pre-Trial Chamber II, First Decision on Victims' Participation in the Case, ICC-01/09-01/11-17, 30 March 2011, para 21; ICC, *Prosecutor v. Francis Kirimi Muthaura* et al., Pre-Trial Chamber II, First Decision on Victims' Participation in the Case, ICC-01/09-02/11-23, 30 March 2011, para 21; ICC, *Prosecutor v. Bosco Ntaganda,* Trial Chamber VI, Decision on Victims' Participation in Trial Proceedings, ICC-01/04-02/06-499, 6 February 2015, para 24; ICC, *Prosecutor v. Dominic Ongwen*, Pre-Trial Chamber II, Decision Establishing Principles on the Victims' Application Process, ICC-02/04-01/15-205, 4 March 2015, paras 29–30.

[63] ICC RPE, Rule 89(1). For an example, see ICC, *Prosecutor v. Dominic Ongwen*, Pre-Trial Chamber II, Decision Establishing Principles on the Victims' Application Process, ICC-02/04-01/15-205, 4 March 2015, para 31.

the parties and participants.[64] However this approach has since changed before at least some chambers.[65]

Like the VPRS at the ICC, the ECCC's VSS is responsible, after having received applications for civil party status, for verifying their completeness. To be considered complete, applications must contain[66]:

- details allowing verification of the applicant's status as victim, including, if available, a copy of an identity card or any other form of identification,
- a contact address in Cambodia,
- a description of the alleged criminal acts,
- any evidence of the injury suffered or tending to show the guilt of the alleged perpetrator or accomplices, and
- the signature or thumbprint of the applicant.

Once applications have been verified as complete, the VSS transmits them to the *Greffier* of the Office of the Co-Investigating Judges.[67] This is to be done within the time limit determined by the latter.[68]

At the STL, once the VPU has received applications for participation, it verifies their completeness and then transmits the documents to the Pre-Trial Judge.[69]

To verify whether or not an application is complete, the VPU focuses its assessment on Rule 86(B)(i) of the STL RPE, i.e. on whether the applicant has provided *prima facie* evidence that he or she is a victim as defined in Rule 2 of the STL

---

[64] ICC, *Prosecutor v. Thomas Lubanga Dyilo,* Trial Chamber I, Decision on the implementation of the reporting system between the Registrar and the Trial Chamber in accordance with Rule 89 and Regulation of the Court 86(5), ICC-01/04-01/06-1022, 9 November 2007, paras 21–27; ICC, *Situation In the Democratic Republic of the Congo,* Pre-Trial Chamber I, Decision on the Requests of the Legal Representative of Applicants on application process for victims' participation and legal representation, ICC-01/04-374, 17 August 2007, paras 32–38; ICC, *Situation in Darfur, Sudan,* Pre-Trial Chamber I, Decision on the Requests of the OPCD and the Legal Representatives of the Applicants Regarding the Transmission of the Report of the Registry under rule 89 of the Rules of Procedure and Evidence, ICC-02/05-93, 21 August 2007.

[65] ICC, *Prosecutor v. Bosco Ntaganda,* Trial Chamber VI, Decision on Victims' Participation in Trial Proceedings, ICC-01/04-02/06-499, 6 February 2015, para 24 (iv); ICC, *Prosecutor v. Dominic Ongwen*, Pre-Trial Chamber II, Decision Establishing Principles on the Victims' Application Process, ICC-02/04-01/15-205, 4 March 2015, para 31.

[66] ECCC Practice Direction on Victim Participation, Article 3.5; ECCC Internal Rules, Rule 23*bis*(4).

[67] ECCC Practice Direction on Victim Participation, Articles 3.4 and 3.7. Note that in *Case 001*, applications were transmitted to the Trial Chamber after the case file was submitted. However, the competence to decide on civil party admissibility is now vested only in the Co-Investigating Judges.

[68] ECCC, *Case 002*, Office of the Co-Investigating Judges, Interoffice memorandum, Deadline for Supplementary Information, Case No. 002/19-09-2007-ECCC/OCIJ, 9 April 2010; ECCC, *Case 002*, Office of the Co-Investigating Judges, Interoffice memorandum, Deadline for Filing Supplementary Information, Case No. 002/19-09-2007-ECCC/OCIJ, 29 April 2010.

[69] STL RPE, Rule 51(B)(iii).

RPE.[70] More particularly, the VPU concentrates on whether the applicant has provided: '(a) particulars of how the victim meets the definition of 'victim' in Rule 2; and (b) evidence in support of those particulars.'[71] Regarding the criteria listed in Rule 86(B)(ii) to (x), the VPU does not treat them as 'issues needing to be addressed in order for an applicant to be considered complete. However, where, in the process of its review for completeness, information relevant to the latter considerations has been identified, it is brought to the attention of the Pre-Trial Judge in the relevant Application Summary.'[72]

The VPU generally sends the application forms altogether with an executive summary of each individual application.[73] These documents are filed as confidential and *ex parte*. They are not provided to either the Defence or Prosecution as they contain information identifying the applicants.[74] The application forms and the executive summaries of successful applicants are however provided to the LRVs, once the status of participating victim has been granted.

Neither the STL's RPE nor its case-law gives the VPU a timeframe for transmitting new applications to the Pre-Trial Judge after they have been received. In practice, the VPU transmits such applications on a rolling basis to the Pre-Trial Judge.[75] Applications may sometimes be held for several weeks if this will facilitate the filing of a group of applications together, and applications will also be held pending attempts to gather further documentation to complete the application. Subject to these considerations, applications are transmitted as soon as possible after they have been received and processed by the VPU.[76]

---

[70] STL, *Prosecutor v. Ayyash* et al., Victims' Participation Unit, Transmission of Applications for the Status of Victim Participating in the Proceedings, STL-11-01/PT/PTJ, 9 February 2012, para 14.

[71] Ibid., para 15.

[72] Ibid., para 9.

[73] In its first transmission of 9 February 2012, the VPU also submitted to the Pre-Trial Judge an overview summarising the procedures employed by the VPU in the receipt and administration of applications, as well as some features of the applicants and their applications. STL, *Prosecutor v. Ayyash* et al., Victims' Participation Unit, Transmission of Applications for the Status of Victim Participating in the Proceedings, STL-11-01/PT/PTJ, 9 February 2012, para 9.

[74] STL, *Prosecutor v. Ayyash* et al., Victims' Participation Unit, Transmission of Applications for the Status of Victim Participating in the Proceedings, STL-11-01/PT/PTJ, 9 February 2012, paras 5 and 9. See also, STL, *Prosecutor v. Ayyash* et al., Pre-Trial Judge, Decision on Defence Motion of 17 February 2012 for an Order to the Victims' Participation Unit to Refile its Submission *Inter Partes* and Inviting Submissions on Legal Issues Related to Applications for the Status of Victim Participating in the Proceedings, STL-11-01/PT/PTJ, 5 April 2012.

[75] STL, *Prosecutor v. Ayyash* et al., Pre-Trial Judge, Transmission of Applications for the Status of Victim Participating in the Proceedings, STL-11-01/PT/PTJ, 9 February 2012; STL, *Prosecutor v. Ayyash* et al., Pre-Trial Judge, Sixth Transmission by the VPU pursuant to Rule 51(B)(iii), STL-11-01/T/PTJ, 27 June 2014; STL, *Prosecutor v. Ayyash* et al., Pre-Trial Judge, Seventh Transmission by the VPU pursuant to Rule 51(B)(iii), STL-11-01/T/PTJ, 28 October 2014.

[76] Written correspondence with Megan Hirst, former legal officer, Victims Participation Unit, STL, 1 March 2015 (records on file with the authors).

2.4.2 Observations by the Parties

Under Rule 89(1) of the ICC RPE, the Registrar shall provide a copy of the applications to the Prosecution and to the Defence, 'who shall be entitled to reply within a time limit set by the Chamber.' Observations on applications for participation can then be made by the parties.[77]

Such observations are frequently made by the Defence on a diverse range of issues. These have included, for example, questions such as who has the legal standing to submit applications,[78] the timing of the application,[79] the completeness of the application forms, the anonymity of the applicants,[80] the required identification documents,[81] the redactions made on the applications,[82] the harm allegedly suffered by the applicant,[83] and the question of a link between the harm suffered and the crimes with which the defendant is charged.[84] These observations

[77] See Sect. 2.4.3 of this chapter for details on redactions made to victim applications.

[78] For example, in the *DRC Situation*, the Defence argued that FIDH (Fédération Internationale des Ligues des Droits de l'Homme) had no standing to file any document on behalf of victims. The Pre-Trial Chamber rejected that view. ICC, *Situation in the Democratic Republic of Congo*, Pre-Trial Chamber I, Decision on the Applications for Participation in the Proceedings of VPRS 1, VPRS 2, VPRS 3, VPRS 4, VPRS 5 and VPRS 6, ICC-01/04-101-tEN-Corr, 17 January 2006, para 104.

[79] ICC, *Prosecutor v. Jean-Pierre Bemba Gombo*, Defence, Defence Observations on the "Fourth Transmission to the Parties and Legal Representatives of Redacted Versions of Applications for Participation in the Proceedings", ICC-01/05-01/08-968, 22 October 2010, paras 5–6.

[80] ICC, *Prosecutor v. Germain Katanga,* Defence, Defence Response to the Legal Representatives of Victims Requests to Participate in the Appeal Proceedings, ICC-01/04-01/07-3491, 13 June 2014, para 10.

[81] ICC, *Prosecutor v. Jean-Pierre Bemba Gombo*, Defence, Defence Observations on the "Fourth Transmission to the Parties and Legal Representatives of Redacted Versions of Applications for Participation in the Proceedings", ICC-01/05-01/08-968, 22 October 2010, paras 25 and 28.

[82] ICC, *Prosecutor v. Laurent Gbagbo*, Defence, Observations de la Défense du Président Gbagbo concernant les 57 demandes individuelles et les 6 demandes collectives de participation des victimes, ICC-02/11-01/11-133, 28 May 2012, para 18; ICC, *Prosecutor v. Jean-Pierre Bemba Gombo*, Defence, Defence Observations on the "Fourth Transmission to the Parties and Legal Representatives of Redacted Versions of Applications for Participation in the Proceedings", ICC-01/05-01/08-968, 22 October 2010, paras 7–12.

[83] ICC, *Prosecutor v. Laurent Gbagbo*, Defence, Observations de la Défense du Président Gbagbo concernant les 57 demandes individuelles et les 6 demandes collectives de participation des victimes, ICC-02/11-01/11-133, 28 May 2012, paras 51–55.

[84] ICC, *Prosecutor v. Jean-Pierre Bemba Gombo*, Defence, Defence Observations on the "Fourth Transmission to the Parties and Legal Representatives of Redacted Versions of Applications for Participation in the Proceedings", ICC-01/05-01/08-968, 22 October 2010, para 22.

generally tend to reflect the Defence's opposition to the victims' applications, and frequently include a request for rejection of at least some applications.[85]

The Prosecution also submits observations on victim applications. Prosecution observations have focused, for example, on whether the harm suffered by the applicant resulted from a crime with which the defendant is charged.[86]

Applicants are not entitled to respond to these observations.[87]

Time limits to file observations are established by the relevant chamber when requesting such observations, following a transmission of applications by the Registry to the chamber.

Since addressing such observations adds a considerable amount of time to the proceedings, including the time required by the Registry to redact the application forms prior to transmission and the time required by the parties to review such applications and, if appropriate, file observations,[88] it has been suggested that parties' rights to file observations on victim applications should be limited.[89] Some of the advantages identified in adopting this approach would be: time and resource saving for the Registry, protection of victims' identities, time saving for the parties (and thus a reduction in legal aid expenditures on Defence work), expedition of decision-making on victim applications, and expedition of the judicial proceedings in general.[90] However, concerns about this approach have also been identified: the right of the Defence to be heard could be undermined, it might not represent a time saving approach in the long-term (if submissions on the victim applications

---

[85] For example, in the *Bemba* case, the Defence requested the rejection of 176 applicants. ICC, *Prosecutor v. Jean-Pierre Bemba Gombo*, Defence, Defence Observations on the "Fourth Transmission to the Parties and Legal Representatives of Redacted Versions of Applications for Participation in the Proceedings", ICC-01/05-01/08-968, 22 October 2010, para 30.

[86] ICC, *Prosecutor v. Jean-Pierre Bemba Gombo,* Prosecutor, Prosecution's Observations on the Applications for Participation in the Proceedings of 24 Applicants, ICC-01/05-01/08-206-Red, 4 November 2008, para 35.

[87] ICC, *Situation in Uganda*, Pre-Trial Chamber II, Decision on the request by the Office of Public Counsel for Victims dated 21 October 2008, ICC-02/04-162, 23 October 2008; ICC, *Prosecutor v. Joseph Kony, Vincent Otti, Okot Odhiambo, Dominic Ongwen*, Pre-Trial Chamber II, Decision on the request by the Office of Public Counsel for Victims dated 21 October 2008, ICC-02/04-01/05-322, 23 October 2008.

[88] Indeed, the Defence have often complained that these steps entail a great amount of time and resources. See for example: ICC, *Prosecutor v. Jean-Pierre Bemba Gombo*, Defence, Defence Response to the Third Transmission of Victims' Applications for Participation in the Proceedings, ICC-01/05-01/08-945, 11 October 2010, para 5; ICC, *Prosecutor v. Jean-Pierre Bemba Gombo*, Defence, Defence Observations on the "Fourth Transmission to the Parties and Legal Representatives of Redacted Versions of Applications for Participation in the Proceedings", ICC-01/05-01/08-968, 22 October 2010, paras 5–6; ICC, *Prosecutor v. Jean-Pierre Bemba Gombo*, Defence, Defence Observations on the "Seventh Transmission to the Parties and Legal Representatives of Redacted Versions of Applications for Participation in the Proceedings", ICC-01/05-01/08-1053, 26 November 2010, para 5.

[89] ICC, Report of the Court on the Review of the System for Victims to Apply to Participate in Proceedings, ICC-ASP/11/22 2012, paras 58–63.

[90] Ibid.

are made at a later stage) and it could moreover be disadvantageous for victims themselves, if it meant they would lack certainty regarding their status.[91]

In the *Ntaganda* case, Trial Chamber IV required the Registry to group applications into three categories: those which clearly qualified, those which clearly did not qualify, and those on which the Registry was unable to make a clear determination.[92] Only applications in the latter category were sent to the parties for their observations, following which individual determinations were made by the Chamber.[93] In respect of the former two categories the Chamber stated that it would ratify the Registry's assessment unless it involves a 'clear and material error.'[94] This appears to be a step forward in efficiency, as the VPRS already undertakes an assessment of the victim applications and is sufficiently trained for the task. A modified version of this system was adopted in the *Ongwen* case by the first Single Judge (Judge Ekaterina Trendafilova) of Pre-Trial Chamber II (although she required transmission to the parties for possible observations not only of applications on which a determination could not be made, but also those which the Registry considered as clearly qualifying).[95] However, before any applications had been submitted this approach was replaced by a different approach as decided by the new Single Judge (Judge Cuno Tarfusser). According to his decision, the VPRS transmitted to the Chamber and parties all applications considered by the Registry to be complete and to fall within the scope of the case, however without an applicant-by-applicant assessment.[96]

At the ECCC, under Internal Rule 23*bis*, and subject to the provisions in the Internal Rules relating to the protection of victims, the Co-Investigating Judges must notify the Co-Prosecutors and the Charged Person(s) of civil party applications. However, the ECCC Internal Rules are silent as to whether the parties may submit comments or observations.

At the STL, under Rule 86(C)(i) of the RPE, before deciding on requests for the status of a victim participating in the proceedings, the Pre-Trial Judge may seek submissions from the parties and the VPU on the relevant legal issues.[97] This enables the parties to file observations if requested by the Pre-Trial Judge. As explained in Sect. 2.4.1, in the *Ayyash* et al. case, victims' application forms were

---

[91] Ibid.

[92] ICC, *Prosecutor v. Bosco Ntaganda*, Trial Chamber VI, Decision on victims' participation in trial proceedings, ICC-01/04-02/06-449, 6 February 2015, paras 20–40.

[93] Ibid., para 24(v)–(viii).

[94] Ibid., para 24(vii).

[95] ICC, *Prosecutor v. Dominic Ongwen*, Pre-Trial Chamber II, Decision Establishing Principles on the Victims' Application Process, ICC-02/04-01/15-205, 4 March 2015, paras 29–32.

[96] ICC, *Prosecutor v. Dominic Ongwen*, Pre-Trial Chamber II, Decision concerning the procedure for admission of victims to participate in the proceedings in the present case, ICC-02/04-01/15-299, 3 September 2015, paras 4–5.

[97] See STL, *Prosecutor v. Ayyash* et al., Pre-Trial Judge, Decision on Defence Motion of 17 February 2012 for an Order to the Victims' Participation Unit to Refile its Submission *Inter Partes* and Inviting Submissions on Legal Issues Related to Applications for the Status of Victim Participating in the Proceedings, STL-11-01/PT/PTJ, 5 April 2012, paras 27 and 37.

not disclosed to the parties, so the observations made by the parties were in the abstract, without an opportunity to comment on particular applications.

To date, the Pre-Trial Judge has only sought observations from the parties in relation to the first batch of victim applications transmitted to him.[98] Observations were sought and filed concerning various legal issues, such as the concept of the harm suffered by the applicants, the required proximity between the direct and indirect applicants claiming victim status, and the notion of the personal interest of the victim being affected.[99]

After the parties have made their observations (if permitted to do so), the Pre-Trial Judge makes a decision granting or denying the status of victim participating in the proceedings to each applicant, or occasionally defers a decision on victim status pending the collection of further documentation.[100]

2.4.3 Protection of Victim Identities During the Application Process

As is further described in Chap. 6, before the ICC, most victims remain anonymous throughout the proceedings, meaning that their identity is not known to the parties, or at least to the Defence. While some victims will have their anonymity lifted for various reasons,[101] the default assumption is anonymity, and for this reason, in most cases measures are imposed during the application process to protect the identity of applicants from the parties.

According to Article 43(6) of the ICC Statute, it is the responsibility of the Victims and Witnesses Section (VWS) (formerly known as the Victims and Witnesses Unit) to provide the necessary protective measures to victims who appear before the Court.[102] It would nonetheless be too costly and time-consum-

98 STL, *Prosecutor v. Ayyash* et al., Pre-Trial Judge, Decision on Defence Motion of 17 February 2012 for an Order to the Victims' Participation Unit to Refile its Submission *Inter Partes* and Inviting Submissions on Legal Issues Related to Applications for the Status of Victim Participating in the Proceedings, STL-11-01/PT/PTJ, 5 April 2012. paras 2 and 57.

99 STL, *Prosecutor v. Ayyash* et al., Prosecutor, Prosecution's Submission in Response to the Pre-Trial Judge's Decision of 5 April 2012, STL-11-01/PT/PTJ, 23 April 2012, paras 5–16.

100 For example, the Pre-Trial Judge deferred ruling on the application submitted by V079, stating that some required information was missing. STL, *Prosecutor v. Ayyash* et al., Pre-Trial Judge, Fifth Decision on Victim's Participation in the Proceedings, STL-11-01/T/PTJ, 18 July 2014, para 14.

101 See Chap. 6.

102 See ICC, *Prosecutor v. Thomas Lubanga Dyilo*, Trial Chamber I, Decision on Victims' Participation, ICC-01/04-01/06-1119, 18 January 2008, paras 136 and 137, in which the Chamber recalled Article 43(6) of the ICC Statute and decided that the notion of 'victims who appear before the Court' also applies to victim applicants. Therefore, once an application to participate is received by the Court, Article 43(6) of the ICC Statute is engaged and the VWS must take appropriate protective measures.

ing for a chamber to require the VWS to carry out an individual risk assessment for each of the applications received, especially knowing that some of these applications would ultimately not be deemed to meet the requirements of Rule 85(a).[103] For these reasons, ICC chambers routinely adopt redactions as an appropriate protective measure at the application stage.[104] Such redactions shall be made in accordance with the principle of proportionality enshrined in Article 68(1) of the ICC Statute and it is said that they shall not amount to an unnecessary restriction of the rights of the Defence.[105]

In practice, any information that might possibly reveal the identity of the victim, if put together with other information, is redacted from the version of the

[103] ICC, *Prosecutor v. Thomas Lubanga Dyilo,* Trial Chamber I, Decision Inviting the Parties' Observations on Applications for Participation of a/0001/06 to a/0004/06, a/0047/06 to a/0052/06, a/0077/06, a/0078/06, a/0105/06, a/0221/06, a/0224/06 to a/0233/06, a/0236/06, a/0237/06 to a/0250/06, a/0001/07 to a/0005/07, a/0054/07 to a/0062/07, a/0064/07, a/0065/07, a/0149/07, a/0155/07, a/0156/07, a/0162/07, a/0168/07 to a/0185/07, a/0187/07 to a/0191/07, a/0251/07 to a/0253/07, a/0255/07 to a/0257/07, a/0270/07 to a/0285/07, and a/0007/08, ICC-01/04-01/06-1308, 6 May 2008, para 23.

[104] ICC, *Prosecutor v. Joseph Kony* et al., Pre-Trial Chamber II, Decision on Legal Representation, Appointment of Counsel for the Defence, Protective Measures and Time-Limit for Submission of Observations on Applications for Participation a/0010/06, a/0064/06 to a/0070/06, a/0081/06 to a/0104/06 and a/0111/06 to a/0127/06, ICC-02/04-01/05-134, 1 February 2007, para 20; ICC, *Prosecutor v. Thomas Lubanga Dyilo,* Trial Chamber I, Decision Inviting the Parties' Observations on Applications for Participation of a/0001/06 to a/0004/06, a/0047/06 to a/0052/06, a/0077/06, a/0078/06, a/0105/06, a/0221/06, a/0224/06 to a/0233/06, a/0236/06, a/0237/06 to a/0250/06, a/0001/07 to a/0005/07, a/0054/07 to a/0062/07, a/0064/07, a/0065/07, a/0149/07, a/0155/07, a/0156/07, a/0162/07, a/0168/07 to a/0185/07, a/0187/07 to a/0191/07, a/0251/07 to a/0253/07, a/0255/07 to a/0257/07, a/0270/07 to a/0285/07, and a/0007/08, ICC-01/04-01/06-1308, 6 May 2008, para 24.

[105] ICC, *Prosecutor v. Joseph Kony* et al., Pre-Trial Chamber II, Decision on Legal Representation, Appointment of Counsel for the Defence, Protective Measures and Time-Limit for Submission of Observations on Applications for Participation of a/0010/06, a/0064/06 to a/0070/06, a/0081/06 to a/0104/06 and a/0111/06 to a/0127/06, ICC-02/04-01/05-134, 1 February 2007, para 24; ICC, *Prosecutor v. Thomas Lubanga Dyilo,* Trial Chamber I, Decision Inviting the Parties' Observations on Applications for Participation of a/0001/06 to a/0004/06, a/0047/06 to a/0052/06, a/0077/06, a/0078/06, a/0105/06, a/0221/06, a/0224/06 to a/0233/06, a/0236/06, a/0237/06 to a/0250/06, a/0001/07 to a/0005/07, a/0054/07 to a/0062/07, a/0064/07, a/0065/07, a/0149/07, a/0155/07, a/0156/07, a/0162/07, a/0168/07 to a/0185/07, a/0187/07 to a/0191/07, a/0251/07 to a/0253/07, a/0255/07 to a/0257/07, a/0270/07 to a/0285/07, and a/0007/08, ICC-01/04-01/06-1308, 6 May 2008, para 25; ICC, *Prosecutor v. Francis Kirimi Muthaura, Uhuru Muigai Kenyatta and Mohammed Hussein Ali,* Pre-Trial Chamber II, Decision on the Defence Requests in Relation to the Victims' Applications for Participation in the Present Case, ICC-01/09-02/11-164, 8 July 2011, para 18; ICC, *Prosecutor v. Francis Kirimi Muthaura, Uhuru Muigai Kenyatta and Mohammed Hussein Ali*, Pre-Trial Chamber II, Decision on Victims' Participation at the Confirmation of Charges Hearing and in the Related Proceedings, ICC-01/09-02/11-267, 26 August 2011, para 39; ICC, *Prosecutor v. Laurent Gbagbo*, Pre-Trial Chamber I, Corrigendum to the Second Decision on Victims' Participation at the Confirmation of Charges Hearing and in the Related Proceedings, ICC-02/11-01/11-384-Corr, 6 February 2013, para 34; ICC, *Prosecutor v. Charles Blé Goudé*, Pre-Trial Chamber I, Decision on Victims' Participation in the Pre-Trial Proceedings and Related Issues, ICC-02/11-02/11-83, 11 June 2014, para 43.

application form which is transmitted to the parties. Where a crime is very specific, many of the details of the crime will be redacted, as well as many of the personal details of the applicant. Parties, particularly the Defence, have complained, as a result, that there is little useful information left unredacted in the form, thus 'compromis[ing] the receiving party's ability to investigate them and/or make meaningful submissions.'[106]

The practice of the chambers is divided on whether the victim applications are to be provided in redacted form to both the Defence and the Prosecution, or only to the Defence (with the Prosecution receiving unredacted versions of the forms). For some chambers, the need to preserve the equality of arms between the Prosecution and the Defence requires that redacted copies of the applications be transmitted to both parties.[107] Other chambers ordered the Defence to be provided with applications in redacted form, while unredacted versions of the victim

---

[106] ICC, *Prosecutor v. Bosco Ntaganda*, Trial Chamber VI, Decision on Victims' Participation in Trial Proceedings, ICC-01/04-02/06-499, 6 February 2015, para 28. See also: ICC, *Prosecutor v. Jean-Pierre Bemba Gombo*, Defence, Defence Observations on the "Fourth Transmission to the Parties and Legal Representatives of Redacted Versions of Applications for Participation in the Proceedings", ICC-01/05-01/08-968, 22 October 2010, paras 7-12; ICC, *Prosecutor v. William Samoei Ruto, Henry Kiprono Kosgey and Joshua Arap Sang,* Pre-Trial Chamber II, Defence, Response on Behalf of Mr. William Samoei Ruto and Mr. Joshua Arap Sang to the First Transmission to the Parties and Legal Representatives of Redacted Applications to Participate in the Proceedings, with Confidential Annex, ICC-01/09-01/11-102, 3 June 2011, paras 8–10; ICC, *Prosecutor v. Laurent Gbagbo*, Chambre préliminaire I, Observations de la Défense du Président Gbagbo concernant les 57 demandes individuelles et les 6 demandes collectives de participation des victimes, ICC-02/11-01/11-133, 28 May 2012, para 18; ICC, *Prosecutor v. Laurent Gbagbo*, Defence, Observations de la défense portant sur les cinquante-neuf demandes de participation de victimes transmises par le Greffe le 18 décembre 2012 en version expurgée (ICC-02/11-01/11-366), ICC-02/11-01/11-382, 5 February 2013, paras 24–26.

[107] ICC, *Prosecutor v. Joseph Kony* et al., Pre-Trial Chamber II, Decision on Legal Representation, Appointment of Counsel for the Defence, Protective Measures and Time-Limit for Submission of Observations on Applications for Participation a/0010/06, a/0064/06 to a/0070/06, a/0081/06 to a/0104/06 and a/0111/06 to a/0127/06, ICC-02/04-01/05-134, 1 February 2007, para 25; ICC, *Prosecutor v. Thomas Lubanga Dyilo*, Trial Chamber I, Decision Inviting the Parties' Observations on Applications for Participation of a/0001/06 to a/0004/06, a/0047/06 to a/0052/06, a/0077/06, a/0078/06, a/0105/06, a/0221/06, a/0224/06 to a/0233/06, a/0236/06, a/0237/06 to a/0250/06, a/0001/07 to a/0005/07, a/0054/07 to a/0062/07, a/0064/07, a/0065/07, a/0149/07, a/0155/07, a/0156/07, a/0162/07, a/0168/07 to a/0185/07, a/0187/07 to a/0191/07, a/0251/07 to a/0253/07, a/0255/07 to a/0257/07, a/0270/07 to a/0285/07, and a/0007/08, ICC-01/04-01/06-1038, 6 May 2008, para 30; ICC, *Prosecutor v. Jean-Pierre Bemba Gombo*, Pre-Trial Chamber III, Second Decision on the Question of Victims' Participation Requesting Observations from the Parties, ICC-01/05-01/08-184, 23 October 2008, paras 12–14; ICC, *Prosecutor v. Germain Katanga and Mathieu Ngudjolo Chui*, Trial Chamber II, Décision relative au traitement des demandes de participation ICC-01/04-01/07-933, 26 February 2009, para 53; ICC, *Prosecutor v. Jean-Pierre Bemba Gombo,* Trial Chamber III, Decision Defining the Status of 54 Victims who Participated at the Pre-Trial Stage, and Inviting the Parties' Observations on Applications for Participation by 86 Applicants, ICC-01/05-01/08-699, 22 February 2010, para 32.

applications were transmitted to the Prosecution.[108] Amongst the various justifications advanced for this approach was the Prosecution's obligation to respect the interests and the personal circumstances of victims,[109] the Prosecution's status as an organ charged with protecting victims[110] or the fact that applications might contain exculpatory information that may be relevant for the Prosecution's investigative duties.[111] An additional difficulty can arise where the approach of sending unredacted applications to Prosecution and redacted ones to Defence occurs at pre-trial but is changed at trial. In some cases, this has created an anomalous outcome whereby the Prosecution has access to the victims' application forms that were submitted during pre-trial but not those submitted at trial.

A certain number of civil party applicants requested protective measures at the beginning of the work of the ECCC. However, their general fears dissipated as the number of applicants increased and no reprisals were experienced by them.[112] As a consequence, almost no requests for protective measures have been submitted to the ECCC.[113]

---

[108] Unredacted application forms had been transmitted to the Office of Public Counsel for Defence in the past, although this practice appears to be discontinued. See, for instance: ICC, *Situation in the Democratic Republic of the Congo*, Pre-Trial Chamber I, Decision on the Requests of the Legal Representative of Applicants on application process for victims' participation and legal representation, ICC-01/04-374, 17 August 2007, p. 23.

[109] ICC, *Prosecutor v. Callixte Mbarushimana*, Pre-Trial Chamber I, Decision Requesting the Parties to Submit Observations on 14 Applications for Victims' Participation in the Proceedings, ICC-01/04-01/10-181, 24 May 2011, p. 5; ICC, *Prosecutor v. Bosco Ntaganda*, Pre-Trial Chamber II, Decision Establishing Principles on the Victims' Applications Process, ICC-01/04-02/06-67, 28 May 2013, para 44; ICC, *Prosecutor v. Dominic Ongwen*, Pre-Trial Chamber II, Decision Establishing Principles on the Victims' Application Process, ICC-02/04-01/15-205, 4 March 2015, para 35.

[110] ICC, *Prosecutor v. Bahar Idriss Abu Garda*, Pre-Trial Chamber I, Decision Ordering the Parties to Submit their Observations on the 52 Applications for Victims' Participation in the Proceedings, ICC-02/05-02/09-106, 16 September 2009, p. 5; ICC, *Prosecutor v. Bosco Ntaganda*, Pre-Trial Chamber II, Decision Establishing Principles on the Victims' Applications Process, ICC-01/04-02/06-67, 28 May 2013, para 44; ICC, *Prosecutor v. Dominic Ongwen*, Pre-Trial Chamber II, Decision Establishing Principles on the Victims' Application Process, ICC-02/04-01/15-205, 4 March 2015, para 35.

[111] ICC, *Prosecutor v. William Samoei Ruto, Henry Kiprono Kosgey and Joshua Arap Sang*, Pre-Trial Chamber II, Decision on the Defence Requests in Relation to the Victims' Applications for Participation in the Present Case, ICC-01/09-01/11-169, 8 July 2011, para 13; ICC, *Prosecutor v. Laurent Gbagbo*, Pre-Trial Chamber I, Second decision on issues related to the victims' application process, ICC-02/11-01/11-86, 5 April 2012, para 42; ICC, Prosecutor *v. Bosco Ntaganda*, Pre-Trial Chamber II, Decision Establishing Principles on the Victims' Applications Process, ICC-01/04-02/06-67, 28 May 2013, para 44; ICC, *Prosecutor v. Dominic Ongwen*, Pre-Trial Chamber II, Decision Establishing Principles on the Victims' Application Process, ICC-02/04-01/15-205, 4 March 2015, para 35.

[112] Interview with Silke Studzinsky, former civil party lawyer, ECCC, 24 February 2015 (records on file with the authors).

[113] Ibid., For details on protective measures regarding civil parties at the ECCC, see Chap. 6.

The provision of redacted civil party applications to the Prosecution and the Defence is not provided for in any legal instruments or in the case-law of the ECCC.

Applications containing a request for protective measures are classified as strictly confidential, i.e. only accessible for the respective chamber(s) and such other persons, who require access in the discharge of their duties, expressly given access by the Court.[114] However, the number of such applications is very low in practice.[115]

At the STL in the *Ayyash* et al. case victim applications have so far maintained their classification as confidential and *ex parte*, and as a result the need for redacted versions of those documents has not yet arisen.

2.4.4 Decisions on Victim Applications

At the ICC, after the completion of the above-mentioned steps, the relevant chamber decides whether or not each applicant is a victim according to the requirements of Rule 85 of the ICC RPE,[116] and grants the status of victim participating in the proceedings to any successful applicants. In accordance with Regulation 86(8) of the ICC Regulations of the Court, this status shall apply throughout the proceedings in the same case, subject to modification by the chamber.[117] The chamber's decision shall be notified to the applicant. In particular, the reasons for which an application was rejected shall be notified to the unsuccessful applicant in order to enable him or her to re-apply where appropriate.[118]

At the ECCC, from *Case 002* onwards, the Co-Investigating Judges have been required to decide on the admissibility of each of application for civil party status.[119] The conditions of admissibility are detailed in Chap. 3. The decision of the

[114] ECCC Practice Direction on Classification and Management of Case-Related Information, Rev. 2 (2014), Articles 2(d)(iii), 6(a) and 7.3.

[115] Interview with Silke Studzinsky, former civil party lawyer, ECCC, 24 February 2015 (records on file with the authors).

[116] For a comprehensive analysis of these requirements, see Chap. 3.

[117] See Chap. 14 on the circumstances in which the status may be terminated.

[118] ICC, *Situation in the Democratic Republic of the Congo*, Pre-Trial Chamber I, Decision on the Requests of the OPCV, ICC-01/04-418, 10 December 2007, para 17.

[119] ECCC Practice Direction on Victim Participation, Article 3.8. The competence to decide on civil party admissibility is only vested in the Co-Investigating Judges as this power was removed from the Trial Chamber in September 2009 with Revision 4 of the ECCC Internal Rules. The Trial Chamber is therefore not competent to receive any civil party applications or to decide on their admissibility. See: ECCC, *Co-Prosecutors v. Kaing Guek Eav*, Supreme Court Chamber, Appeal Judgment, Case No. 001/18-07-2007-ECCC/SC, 3 February 2012, para 511.

Co-Investigating Judges is notified to the applicant[120] and must be duly justified, particularly when an application is rejected.[121]

At the STL, to decide on applications for participation, the Pre-Trial Judge considers whether the applicant satisfies the four mandatory and cumulative requirements of Rule 86(B)(i) to (iv). In addition, the Pre-Trial Judge may also take into account the six non-mandatory criteria set out in Rule 86(B)(v) to (x). These requirements are detailed in Chap. 3. In his decisions on victim status, the Pre-Trial Judge has set specific deadlines by which the VPU must notify victims of the decisions on their requests for participation.[122]

2.4.5 Appeals Against Decisions on Victim Applications

At the ICC, an applicant has no standing to appeal (or request leave to appeal) a decision of the relevant chamber which has rejected his or her application for participation.[123] However, Rule 89(2) of the ICC RPE clarifies that an unsuccessful applicant may file a fresh application.

By contrast, the parties may be granted leave to appeal a decision on a victim's application, provided that the conditions of Article 82(1)(d) of the ICC Statute are fulfilled. This means that the decision of the relevant chamber must involve an issue that would significantly affect the fair and expeditious conduct of the

[120] This requirement can be deduced from Internal Rules 23*bis*(3) and 77*bis*(2).

[121] ECCC, *Case 002*, Pre-Trial Chamber, Decision on Appeals against Order of the Co-Investigating Judges on the Admissibility of Civil Party Applications, Case No. 002/19-09-2007-ECCC/OCIJ (PTC76, PTC112, PTC113, PTC114, PTC115, PTC142, PTC157, PTC164, PTC165 and PTC172), 24 June 2011, paras 37–40.

[122] STL RPE, Rule 51(B)(v) and 86(C)(i). See also, STL, *Prosecutor v. Ayyash* et al., Pre-Trial Judge, Decision on Victims' Participation in the Proceedings, STL-11-01/PT/PTJ, 8 May 2012, p. 42; STL, *Prosecutor v. Ayyash* et al., Pre-Trial Judge, Second Decision on Victims' Participation in the Proceedings, STL-11-01/PT/PTJ, 3 September 2012, p. 5; STL, *Prosecutor v. Ayyash* et al., Pre-Trial Judge, Third Decision on Victims' Participation in the Proceedings, STL-11-01/PT/PTJ, 28 November 2012, p. 5; STL, *Prosecutor v. Ayyash* et al., Pre-Trial Judge, Fourth Decision on Victims' Participation in the Proceedings, STL-11-01/PT/PTJ, 2 May 2013, para 31; STL, *Prosecutor v. Ayyash* et al., Pre-Trial Judge, Fifth Decision on Victims' Participation in the Proceedings, 18 July 2014, STL-11-01/T/PTJ, para 15; STL, *Prosecutor v. Ayyash* et al., Pre-Trial Judge, Sixth Decision on Victims' Participation in the Proceedings, STL-11-01/T/PTJ, 6 November 2014, para 14.

[123] ICC, *Situation in the Democratic Republic of the Congo*, Pre-Trial Chamber I, Decision on the Requests of the OPCV, ICC-01/04-418, 10 December 2007, para 16.

proceedings or the outcome of the trial, and for which an immediate resolution by the Appeals Chamber may materially advance the proceedings.[124]

Civil party applicants at the ECCC have a right to appeal decisions of the Co-Investigating Judges declaring their applications inadmissible.[125] This appeal shall be filed before the Pre-Trial Chamber by the applicant.[126]

As required by Internal Rule 23*bis*(2) and (3), an appeal of this kind is an expedited one. This means that the appeal must be filed within 10 days of the decision in question and no extension of time shall be granted.[127] This may create substantial practical difficulties for lawyers representing civil parties where a large number of applications are rejected in a single decision or within a short space of time. For example, in *Case 002*, the Office of the Co-Investigating Judges issued several orders on admissibility of civil party applications within approximately three weeks during August and September 2010.[128] These orders decided upon the bulk of the nearly 4000 civil party applications and a great number of those applications

---

[124] ICC, *Situation in the Democratic Republic of the Congo*, Pre-Trial Chamber I, Decision on the Prosecution's Application for Leave to Appeal the Chamber's Decision of 17 January 2006 on the Applications for Participation in the Proceedings of VPRS 1, VPRS 2, VPRS 3, VPRS 4, VPRS 5 AND VPRS 6, ICC-01/04-135-tEN, 31 March 2006; ICC, *Situation in the Democratic Republic of the Congo,* Appeals Chamber, Judgment on the Prosecutor's Application for Extraordinary Review of Pre-Trial Chamber I's 31 March 2006 Decision Denying Leave to Appeal, ICC-01/04-168, 13 July 2006; ICC, *Prosecutor v. Thomas Lubanga Dyilo*, Trial Chamber I, Decision on the Defence and Prosecution Requests for Leave to Appeal the Decision on Victims' Participation of 18 January 2008, ICC-01/04-01/06-1191, 26 February 2008; ICC, *Prosecutor v. Joseph Kony* et al., Appeals Chamber, Judgment on the Appeals of the Defence against the Decisions Entitled "Decision on Victims' Applications for Participation a/0010/06, a/0064/06 to a/0070/06, a/0081/06, a/0082/06, a/0084/06 to a/0089/06, a/0091/06 to a/0097/06, a/0099/06, a/0100/06, a/0102/06 to a/0104/06, a/0111/06, a/0113/06 to a/0117/06, a/0120/06, a/0121/06 and a/0123/06 to a/0127/06" of Pre-Trial Chamber II, ICC-02/04-01/05-371, 23 February 2009.

[125] ECCC Internal Rules, Rule 74(4)(b).

[126] Ibid., Rule 23*bis*(2).

[127] Ibid., Rule 77*bis*(2).

[128] The Office of the Co-Investigating Judges issued the orders of admissibility per province. See, for example: ECCC, *Case 002*, Order on Admissibility of Civil Party Applicants from Current Residents of Rattanakiri Province, 26 August 2010 (approx. 17 admissible and 16 inadmissible applications); Order on Admissibility of Civil Party Applicants from Current Residents of Mundulkiri Province, 26 August 2010 (approx. 31 admissible and 27 inadmissible applications); Order on Admissibility of Civil Party Applicants from Current Residents of Stung Treng Province, 30 August 2010 (approx. 34 admissible and 37 inadmissible applications); Order on Admissibility of Civil Party Applicants from Current Residents of Koh Kong Province, 30 August 2010 (approx. 41 admissible and 22 inadmissible applications); Order on Admissibility of Civil Party Applicants from Current Residents of Takeo Province, 31 August 2010 (approx. 60 admissible and 13 inadmissible applications); Order on Admissibility of Civil Party Applicants from Current Residents of Preah Sihanouk Province, 2 September 2010 (approx. 45 admissible and 60 inadmissible applications); Order on Admissibility of Civil Party Applicants from Current Residents of Phnom Penh, 6 September 2010 (approx. 109 admissible and 26 inadmissible applications); Order on Admissibility of Civil Party Applicants from Current Residents of Kampong Thom Province, 14 September 2010 (approx. 111 admissible and 97 inadmissible applications).

were found to be inadmissible. A large number of appeals had thus to be filed within the shortened deadline of 10 days by the lawyers representing these applicants.[129] Appeals are decided on the basis of written submissions alone.[130]

Under the ECCC's Internal Rules, the right to appeal decisions of the Co-Investigating Judges on civil party applications is also open to the Co-Prosecutors[131] and, when civil party status has been granted, to the charged person or the accused.[132] Such appeals are subject to the same procedural rules as those applying to applicants' appeals on admissibility decisions.[133]

At the STL, an unsuccessful applicant may appeal the Pre-Trial Judge's decision within seven days of receiving notification from the VPU, and may base such an appeal on questions of fact or of law.[134] The Directive on Victims' Legal Representation permits the designation of a duty counsel for this purpose.[135]

The parties may also appeal a decision of the Pre-Trial Judge concerning an application for victim participation, but only after obtaining certification under Rule 126 of the STL RPE and only on the basis of an error of law.[136]

To date no appeals or requests for certification have been made at the STL against decisions on victim applications.

2.5 Key Points

Institutional players

- At the ICC, the Victims Participation and Reparations Section (VPRS) plays the main role in the victims' application process.
- At the ECCC, the Victims Support Section (VSS) is the central contact point between the Extraordinary Chambers and the victims. The VSS is mandated to inform victims about their rights relating to participation and reparation and, under the supervision of the Co-Investigating Judges, assist victims in processing their civil party applications. It also assists victims in obtaining legal advice or identifying a lawyer, and supports civil party lawyers. Besides the VSS, the ECCC relies on several intermediary organisations, some of which are based abroad, which provide support to victims during the application process.

---

129 Interview with Silke Studzinsky, former civil party lawyer, ECCC, 24 February 2015 (records on file with the authors).

130 ECCC Internal Rules, Rule 77*bis*(1).

131 Ibid., Rule 74(2).

132 Ibid., Rule 74(3)(i).

133 Ibid., Rule 77*bis*(1) and (2).

134 STL RPE, Rule 86(C)(i).

135 STL Directive on Victims' Legal Representation, STL-BD-2012-04-Rev.1-Corr.1, (2012), Article 18.

136 STL RPE, Rule 86(C)(i).

- At the STL, the Victims' Participation Unit (VPU) has been set up within the Registry to assist victims to participate in the proceedings. Its tasks include locating and reaching out to victims, informing victims of their rights, receiving applications, and verifying that applications are complete and transmitting them to the Pre-Trial Judge.

The Application Process

- The submission of a written application form is the first step a victim must take in order to participate in court proceedings.
- At the ICC, a standard individual application form of 7 pages is available on the ICC website in both English and French. It is however not compulsory for an applicant to use this specific application form. What matters is the content of the application. All applications must contain certain minimum information in order to be considered complete by a chamber.
- At the ECCC, one standard application form is used. It is 5 pages long and available on the ECCC website in English, French and Khmer.
- At the STL, a 9-page application form is used, available on the Tribunal's website in French, Arabic and English.
- Assistance is generally provided to the applicant in order to reduce any burdens that may be associated with the submission of an application for participation to the ICC, the ECCC or the STL.
- The chambers of the three courts have developed various practices regarding deadlines for the submission of victims' applications.

Parties' Observations during the Application Process

- Under Rule 89(1) of the ICC RPE, the Registrar provides a copy of the applications to the Prosecution and to the Defence, who are permitted to submit observations within a time limit set by the chamber. Victims are not entitled to respond to these observations.
- At the ECCC, under Internal Rule 23*bis*, the Co-Investigating Judges must notify the Co-Prosecutors and the Charged Person(s) of civil party applications. The ECCC Internal Rules are silent as to whether the parties can submit comments or observations.
- Under Rule 86(C)(i) of the STL RPE, before deciding on requests for the status of a victim participating in the proceedings, the Pre-Trial Judge may seek submissions from the parties and the VPU on relevant legal issues. In the *Ayyash* et al. case, victims' application forms were not provided to the parties, so any observations made by the parties were made in the abstract, without reference to the specific applications.

Protecting applicants during the application process

- Before the ICC, most victims remain anonymous throughout the proceedings, meaning that their identity is not known to the parties (or at least to the Defence). While some victims will have their anonymity lifted for various reasons, the default assumption is anonymity, and for this reason, ICC chambers commonly adopt redactions as an appropriate protective measure at the initial application stage

- At the ECCC, applications containing a request for protective measures are classified as strictly confidential, i.e. only accessible for the respective chamber(s) and such other persons as are given access by the Court in order to discharge their official duties.
- At the STL, victim applications in the *Ayyash* et al. case have so far maintained their classification as confidential and *ex parte*, and as a result the need for redacted versions of those documents has not yet arisen.

Appeals against decisions on victim applications

- At the ICC, an applicant has no standing to appeal a decision of the relevant ICC chamber when his or her application for participation is rejected. However, an unsuccessful applicant may file a new application.
- At the ECCC, civil party applicants have a right to appeal decisions of the Co-Investigating Judges declaring their applications inadmissible. This appeal shall be filed before the Pre-Trial Chamber by the applicant.
- At the STL, an unsuccessful applicant may appeal the Pre-Trial Judge's decision rejecting his or her application for participation, and may do so on a question of law or of fact.

Appendix—Steps in the Application Process

ICC

Steps	Relevant provisions	Main issues to consider
1. Submission	Rule 89 of the ICC RPE	A written application must be submitted. Standard forms are available. Applicants must satisfy the requirements of Rule 85 of the ICC RPE.
	Regulation 86(3) of the ICC Regulations of the Court	Time limit: these are set case-by-case, as per decision of the relevant chamber. In some cases no deadline has been set and applications are accepted continuously.
2. Assessment	Regulation 86(4) of the ICC Regulations of the Court	The VPRS verifies the completeness of applications and prepares an individual report on each application for the chamber.
	Regulation 86(5) of the ICC Regulations of the Court/Rule 89 of the ICC RPE	Applications are sent to the relevant chamber (with the VPRS reports).

Steps	Relevant provisions	Main issues to consider
3. Transmission to the parties	Rule 89 of the ICC RPE	The chamber sets a deadline for the VPRS to transmit the applications (usually with redactions) to the Prosecution and Defence, as well as a deadline for the parties' observations.
		The VPRS transmits copies of the applications to Defence and Prosecution (redacted if necessary). Until some recent decisions, the individual VPRS reports were not disclosed to the parties, but in some cases they are now provided.
4. Observations	Rule 89 of the ICC RPE	Observations can be made by the parties on questions of law and fact concerning the applications within a deadline set by the chamber.
5. Decision	Rule 89 of the ICC RPE Rule 85 of the ICC RPE	The chamber issues a decision on a case-by-case basis examining whether each applicant is permitted to participate in the proceedings.
6. Appeal	Rule 89(2) of the ICC RPE	The applicant is not entitled to appeal the chamber's decision. However, if the application is rejected, the applicant may submit a fresh application.
	Article 82(1)(d) of the ICC Statute	The parties can request leave to appeal a decision on victims' applications within 5 days of the notification of such a decision.

ECCC

Steps	Relevant provisions	Main issues to consider
1. Submission	Rule 23*bis* of the ECCC Internal Rules	Written application is to be made using the standard application form.
	Rule 23*bis*(2) of the ECCC Internal Rules	Time limit: applications must be submitted no later than 15 days after the Co-Investigating Judges notify the parties of the conclusion of the judicial investigation.

Steps	Relevant provisions	Main issues to consider
2. Assessment	Practice Direction on Victim Participation, Article 3.5; Rule 23*bis*(4) of the ECCC Internal Rules	The VSS verifies the applications and sends them to the Office of the Co-Investigating Judges.
3. Observations	–	–
4. Decision	Practice Direction on Victim Participation, Article 3.8	The Co-Investigating Judges decide on the admissibility of each of the applications.
	Rule 23*bis*(1) of the ECCC Internal Rules	
5. Appeal	Rules 23*bis*(2) and 74(4)(b) of the ECCC Internal Rules	Civil party applicants may appeal decisions of the Co-Investigating Judges declaring their applications inadmissible. Also both Prosecution and Defence can appeal. The time limit is of 10 days after notification of the decision.

STL

Steps	Relevant provisions	Main issues to consider
1. Submission	Rule 86(A) of the STL RPE	A standard written form is used.
	Rule 51(B)(iii) of the STL RPE	Time limit: deadlines may be established by the Pre-Trial Judge.
2. Assessment	Rule 51 (B) (iii) of the STL RPE	The VPU verifies the applications and then transmits them to the Pre-Trial Judge.
3. Observations	Rule 86(C)(i) of the STL RPE	Pre-Trial Judge may request submissions from the parties on legal issues.
4. Decision	Rule 86(B)(i) to (iv) of the STL RPE	The Pre-Trial Judge decides on whether to grant each application for the status of victim participating in the proceedings.
5. Appeal	Rule 86(C)(i) of the STL RPE	An unsuccessful applicant may appeal the Pre-Trial Judge's decision. Time limit: appeals must be filed within seven days of receiving notification.
		Parties may request leave to appeal the Pre-Trial Judge's decision on an application for victim participation, but only on an error of law.

References

International Criminal Court (2012) Report of the Court on the Review of the System for Victims to Apply to Participate in Proceedings, Doc. No. ICC-ASP/11/22

International Criminal Court (2013) Assembly of the State Parties, Programme Budget for 2014, the Working Capital Fund for 2014, scale of assessments for the apportionment of expenses of the International Criminal Court, financing appropriations for 2014 and the Contingency Fund, Doc. No. ICC-ASP/12/Res.1

International Criminal Court (2014a) Assembly of States Parties, Report on the review of the organizational structure of the Registry, Doc. No. ICC-ASP/13/26

International Criminal Court (2014b) Registry ReVision Project: Basic Outline of Proposals to Establish Defence and Victims Offices. http://www.uianet.org/sites/default/files/Registry_ReVision_BasicOutline_Defence_Victims_Offices_0.pdf. Accessed 1 Mar 2015

International Criminal Court (2015) Assembly of State Parties, Report on the review of the organizational structure of the Registry, Doc. No. ICC-ASP/14/18

International Criminal Court (2016) Comprehensive report on the reorganisation of the registry of the International Criminal Court, August 2016. https://www.icc-cpi.int/itemsDocuments/ICC-Registry-CR.pdf. Accessed 4 Nov 2016

Chapter 3
Requirements for Victim Participation

Heloise Dumont

Abstract Being recognised as a participating victim at the International Criminal Court (ICC) or the Special Tribunal for Lebanon (STL), or as a civil party at the Extraordinary Chambers in the Courts of Cambodia (ECCC) carries with it a procedural role that is unprecedented in other international jurisdictions. It is therefore unsurprising that the admission of victims to that status has itself been the subject of much jurisprudence. This is particularly true at the ICC, which, in its more than 10 years of existence, has accumulated a considerable amount of jurisprudence on the standards applied regarding who may qualify to participate in the proceedings. The three courts have each adopted a legal definition of who is a 'victim' for the purpose of participation as well as other rules on the requirements that an application for participation or an application to be a civil party must satisfy. The interpretation of these rules and the context in which judges and chambers have applied them have either enabled or limited participation. This chapter aims at describing the different requirements that judges and chambers of the ICC, STL and ECCC have so far applied when deciding on victims' applications to participate, having in mind the practical implications and challenges this has for a practitioner who assists a victim in this process. It thus describes who may be considered as a victim as per the definition of the courts and what information and documents should be submitted in an application to enable the relevant decision-makers to determine an application.

Heloise Dumont is currently Associate Legal Officer at the Registry of the International Criminal Court. The views expressed herein are those of the author and do not necessarily reflect the views of the International Criminal Court.

H. Dumont (✉)
International Criminal Court, The Hague, The Netherlands
e-mail: heloisedumont@hotmail.com

K. Tibori-Szabó and M. Hirst (eds.), *Victim Participation in International Criminal Justice*, International Criminal Justice Series 11,
DOI 10.1007/978-94-6265-177-7_3

Keywords Application form · Harm · Identity documents · Proof of victimisation · Direct and indirect victims · Persons acting on behalf of victims · Deceased victims · Causation of harm · Standard of review

Contents

3.1 Definition of Victims at ICC, STL, ECCC

The three courts discussed in this chapter try crimes of the severest gravity, which usually take place within a context of conflict that has resulted in hundreds or thousands of victims. The victims who eventually participate in the proceedings of these courts form, however, a much narrower category.

This chapter aims at describing the different requirements that judges and chambers of the International Criminal Court (ICC), Special Tribunal for Lebanon (STL) and Extraordinary Chambers in the Courts of Cambodia (ECCC) have so far applied when deciding on victims' applications to participate. The previous chapter addressed the various steps of the application procedure for victims to become participants (ICC, STL) or parties (ECCC) in the proceedings. The two chapters should therefore be read together.

The definitions of victim adopted by the three courts mark an evolution from the definition of victims adopted by the previous international tribunals,[1] and reflect a broad consensus of the international community reflected in documents such as the Declaration of Basic Principles of Justice for Victims of Crime and Abuse of Power,[2] and, later, the Basic Principles and Guidelines on the Right to a Remedy and Reparation for Victims of Gross Violations of International Human Rights Law and Serious Violations of International Humanitarian Law.[3]

[1] See Rule 2 common to the Rules of Procedure and Evidence of the International Criminal Tribunal for the former Yugoslavia (IT/32/Rev. 49, (2013)) and the International Criminal Tribunal for Rwanda (ITR/3/Rev. 1, (2015)) which restricted the definition of victim to 'a person against whom a crime over which the Tribunal has jurisdiction has allegedly been committed', and did not include indirect victims, such as family members and dependents of a direct victim.

[2] UN Doc. A/RES/40/34 1985.

[3] UN Doc. A/RES/60/147 2006 (the 'Basic Principles').

Victims are mentioned throughout the Rome Statute of the International Criminal Court (ICC Statute) in different capacities, such as, for example, persons who send information to the Prosecutor, or victims who make representations in the context of an investigation *proprio motu* initiated by the Prosecutor. For the purpose of victim participation in the proceedings under Article 68(3) of the ICC Statute, applicants need to meet the requirements set by the definition of victim found in Rule 85(a) of the Rules of Procedure and Evidence of the ICC (ICC RPE), i.e. as 'natural persons who have suffered harm as a result of the commission of any crime within the jurisdiction of the Court'. Rule 85(b) of the ICC RPE further specifies that victims can include legal persons, provided that they 'have sustained direct harm to any of their property which is dedicated to religion, education, art or science or charitable purposes, and to their historic monuments, hospitals and other places and objects for humanitarian purposes'. Although the definition of victim is broader than that of the international instruments mentioned above, as will be seen in this chapter, chambers have interpreted it by referring to those international instruments.

At the STL, a victim is defined in Rule 2 of the Rules of Procedure and Evidence (STL RPE) as a 'natural person, who has suffered physical, material or mental harm as a direct result of an attack within the Tribunal's jurisdiction'. A 'victim participating in the proceedings' (VPP) is further defined as a victim who has been granted leave to present his or her views and concerns at one or more stages of the proceedings after an indictment is confirmed. In contrast to the situation at the ICC, legal persons are excluded from participating in the proceedings as victims at the STL.[4]

The glossary of the ECCC Internal Rules[5] defines a victim as a natural person or legal entity that has suffered harm as a result of the commission of any crime within the jurisdiction of the ECCC.[6] The glossary also defines a civil party as 'a victim whose application to become a Civil Party has been declared admissible by the Co-Investigating Judges or the Pre-Trial Chamber in accordance with these I[nternal] R[ules].'

---

[4] Explanatory Memorandum by the Tribunal's President (2010), para 19 cited in STL, *Prosecutor v. Ayyash* et al., Pre-Trial Judge, Decision on Victims' Participation in the Proceedings, STL-11-01/PT/PTJ, 8 May 2012, para 30.

[5] Rev. 9 (2015) (the 'ECCC Internal Rules').

[6] See also Article 3.2(a) of the ECCC Practice Direction on Victim Participation, 02/2007/Rev.1 (2008). This chapter deals only with victims participating as civil parties, whose dual purpose is defined in Rule 23(1) of the ECCC Internal Rules, as: 'a) Participat[ing] in criminal proceedings against those responsible within the jurisdiction of the ECCC by supporting the prosecution; and b) Seek[ing] collective and moral reparations […]'. It will not deal with 'victim-complainants', i.e. victims who file a complaint with the ECCC in order to make the Co-Prosecutors aware of specific crimes (pursuant to Article 2 of the ECCC Practice Direction on Victim Participation). Such 'victim-complainants' do not enjoy further procedural rights: they cannot participate and cannot request reparations.

Usually, in all three courts, a victim who wishes to participate has to apply and be authorised to do so.[7] In all three courts a standard application form for participation has been developed, which allows the applicant to describe and explain how he or she meets the criteria needed to be considered a victim.[8]

Since 2012, alternatives to the standard application form have been proposed by ICC chambers and applied in different cases.[9] The most radical change has been the adoption of the participation and representation scheme by Trial Chamber V for participation of victims in both Kenya cases at the trial stage, which did not involve a formal application process for victims who wish to express their views and concerns through a legal representative.[10]

---

[7] See Chap. 2 for the various application procedures.

[8] For the ICC, see Regulation 86(1) of the ICC Regulations of the Court, ICC-BD/01-03-11 (2011). The language of the text does not make the use of the Standard Application form compulsory, and some chambers have accepted applications not submitted on this support. See ICC, *Situation in the Democratic Republic of Congo*, Pre-Trial Chamber I, Decision on the Applications for Participation in the Proceedings of VPRS 1, VPRS 2, VPRS 3, VPRS 4, VPRS 5 and VPRS 6, ICC-01/04 -101-tEN-Corr, 22 March 2006, para 102; ECCC Practice Direction on Victim Participation, Articles 3.4, 3.6 and 3.7.

[9] A 'partly collective approach' was used alongside the traditional individual application process in the context of participation at the pre-trial stage of *Prosecutor v. Laurent Gbagbo*, see ICC, *Prosecutor v. Laurent Gbagbo*, Pre-Trial Chamber I, Second decision on issues related to the victims' application process, ICC-02/11-01/11-86, 5 April 2012, para 17. The Single Judge in the pre-trial stage of *Prosecutor v. Bosco Ntaganda* introduced a one-page application form for participation in the confirmation of charges hearing, see ICC, *Prosecutor v. Bosco Ntaganda,* Pre-Trial Chamber II, Decision Establishing Principles on the Victims' Application Process, ICC-01/04-02/06-67, 28 May 2013, paras 17–25. Simplified forms have also been ordered to be used since then, see ICC, *Prosecutor v. Dominic Ongwen*, Pre-Trial Chamber II, Decision Establishing Principles on the Victims' Application Process, ICC-02/04-01/15-205, 4 March 2015, para 19; ICC, *Prosecutor v. Bosco Ntaganda,* Trial Chamber VI, Decision on Victims' Participation in Trial Proceedings, ICC-01/04-02/06-449, 6 February 2015, para 24; and ICC, *Prosecutor v. Laurent Gbagbo,* Trial Chamber I, Decision on Victim Participation, ICC-02/11-01/11-800, 6 March 2015, para 50.

[10] Under this system, only those victims who wished to appear in person were required to apply for participation through the regular application process established in Rule 89 of the ICC RPE, and have their applications judicially assessed. All other victims, who wished to express their views and concerns only through a legal representative, did not need to apply for participation, but could register with the Registry by submitting their names, contact information, and information regarding the harm suffered. Moreover, unregistered victims were also to be represented, in a general way, through common legal representation. See ICC, *Prosecutor v. William Samoei Ruto and Joshua Arap Sang*, Trial Chamber V, Decision on Victims' Representation and Participation, ICC-01/09-01/11-460, 3 October 2012, paras 25, 48–50, 52, 56–58; ICC, *Prosecutor v. Francis Kirimi Muthaura and Uhuru Muigai Kenyatta*, Trial Chamber V, Decision on Victims' Representation and Participation, ICC-01/09-02/11-498, 3 October 2012, paras 24, 47–49, 51, 55–57.

3.2 Requirements: Tests Applied by the Courts to Grant Participation or Civil Party Status

The respective Registries of the ICC and the STL and the *Greffier* at the ECCC receive victims' applications, which they then transmit to the appropriate judicial body that will determine the applications.[11]

Regulation 86(2) of the ICC Regulations of the Court describes the information that should be provided in a victim's application, 'to the extent possible', and decisions issued by the ICC chambers commonly enumerate the list of information required for an application to be considered complete.[12] As will be further explained below, aside from providing a copy of an identity document and, when applicable, a proof of relationship, to date no other document is needed to support an ICC application to participate.[13]

At the STL, when assessing whether a victim may participate in the proceedings, the Pre-Trial Judge considers Rule 86(B) of the STL RPE. In his first decision on victims' participation, the Pre-Trial Judge found that the first four criteria indicated in Rule 86(B)(i) to (iv) of the STL RPE were cumulative, and the six further criteria in Rule 86(B)(v) to (x) of the STL RPE were not mandatory requirements but factors that the Pre-Trial Judge may take into account in addition to the mandatory criteria indicated in Rule 86(B)(i)–(iv) of the STL RPE. In short,

[11] Rule 89 of the ICC RPE and Regulation 86(5) and (6) of the ICC Regulations of the Court provide that the ICC Registry transmits applications received to the chamber, along with a report, as well as to the parties; the Victims' Participation Unit of the STL Registry is in charge of the verification of the completeness of the applications received and, subsequently, their transmission to the Pre-Trial Judge, along with a report (see Chap. 2). At the ECCC, applications to join as civil party must be sent to the Victims Unit, which forwards applications received to the *Greffier* of the Office of the Co-Investigating Judges along with a report (Articles 3.4 and 3.7 of the ECCC Practice Direction on Victim Participation).

[12] Commonly these are: (i) the identity of the applicant; (ii) the date of the crime(s); (iii) the location of the crime(s); (iv) a description of the harm suffered as a result of the commission of any crime within the jurisdiction of the Court; (v) proof of identity; (vi) if the application is made by a person acting with the consent of the victim, the express consent of that victim; (vii) if the application is made by a person acting on behalf of a victim, in the case of a victim who is a child, proof of kinship or legal guardianship; or, in the case of a victim who is disabled, proof of legal guardianship; (viii) a signature or thumb-print of the Applicant on the document at the very least on the last page of the application. See, for example, ICC, *Prosecutor v. Bosco Ntaganda*, Pre-Trial Chamber II, Decision Establishing Principles on the Victims' Application Process, ICC-01/04-02/06-67, 28 May 2013, para 30; ICC, *Prosecutor v. Francis Kirimi Muthaura, Uhuru Muigai Kenyatta and Mohammed Hussein Ali*, Pre-Trial Chamber II, Decision on Victims' Participation at the Confirmation of Charges Hearing and in the Related Proceedings, ICC-01/09-02/11-267, 26 August 2011, para 71; ICC, *Prosecutor v. Germain Katanga and Mathieu Ngudjolo Chui,* Trial Chamber II, Decision on the Treatment of Applications for Participation, ICC-01/04-01/07-933-tENG, 26 February 2009, para 28.

[13] ICC, *Prosecutor v. Thomas Lubanga Dyilo*, Trial Chamber I, Redacted Version of the Decision on the Applications by 7 Victims to Participate in the Proceedings, ICC-01/04- 01/06-2764-Red, 25 July 2011, para 23.

applicants are only required to provide *prima facie* evidence that they are victims as per the definition in Rule 2 of the STL RPE, and indicate the reasons why they wish to participate in the proceeding. Evidence regarding the other requirements does not need to be provided if the Pre-Trial Judge can derive sufficient information from the application to rule on whether it complies with them.[14] As will be seen further below, and contrary to ICC practice, applicants at the STL are generally required to provide documentary evidence to support their application to participate, not only for the purpose of proving their identities, but also the harm suffered by the victims.

At the ECCC, Internal Rule 23*bis*(4) states that 'the application must provide details of the status as a Victim, specify the alleged crime and attach any evidence of the injury suffered, or tending to show the guilt of the alleged perpetrator'. The applications should also specify 'the domicile of the Victim, the registered office of the Victims' Association of which he or she is a member, or the address of the lawyer, as appropriate'. In practice, the information and documents provided by victims in support of their applications have ranged from a few pages to more than 50 pages.[15]

While each court has its own practice based on its legal texts and jurisprudence when considering whether a person can be authorised to participate as a victim or, in the case of the ECCC, as civil party in the proceedings, they have in common that they verify that the same three core criteria are met. These are:

- that the applicant's identity as a natural person is established (Sect. 3.2.1);
- that the applicant suffered harm (Sect. 3.2.2);
- that there was a causal link between the harm suffered and the crime(s) charged in the case at hand (Sect. 3.2.3).[16]

[14] Explanatory Memorandum by the Tribunal's President, November 2010, para 19, cited in STL, *Prosecutor v. Ayyash* et al., Pre-Trial Judge, Decision on Victims' Participation in the Proceedings, STL-11-01/PT/PTJ, 8 May 2012, paras 22–25.

[15] Written correspondence with Eleonor Fernandez, Senior legal consultant, Civil Party Lead Co-Lawyers Section, ECCC, 23 and 29 March 2015 (records on file with the author).

[16] ICC: similar tests have been applied by Chambers, albeit with some variations, see for example: ICC, *Prosecutor v. Bosco Ntaganda,* Trial Chamber VI, Decision on victims' participation in trial proceedings, ICC-01/04-02/06-449, 6 February 2015, para 43; ICC, *Prosecutor v. Jean-Pierre Bemba Gombo*, Trial Chamber III, Decision on 772 Applications by Victims to Participate in the Proceedings, ICC-01/05-01/08-1017, 18 November 2010, para 38; ICC, *Prosecutor v. Abdallah Banda Abakaer Nourain*, Trial Chamber IV, Decision on 19 applications to participate in the proceedings, ICC-02/05-03/09-528, 12 December 2013, para 19. See STL RPE, Rule 2; ECCC Internal Rules, Rule 23*bis*(1).

3.2.1 *The Identity of the Applicant as a Natural Person Is Established*

3.2.1.1 The Victim's Identity

The first requirement verified by all three courts is that the victim is a natural person whose identity appears to be duly established. As will be discussed in Sect. 3.3, all three courts have asked that applicants provide documentary means of identification along with their application, often providing a list of what types of documents, either official or non-official, would qualify as such.[17]

At the ICC, where an organisation or institution applies to participate as a victim, the person making the application on its behalf needs to submit documents proving his or her identity and *locus standi* to represent it, as provided by the constitutive documents.[18]

3.2.1.2 Persons Acting on Behalf of Victims

The three courts have allowed for the possibility that a person applies on behalf of a victim, when the latter cannot legally give consent either because this person is disabled or underage.[19] In those cases, the person applying on his or her

[17] See for example, ICC, *Prosecutor v. Jean-Pierre Bemba Gombo*, Pre-Trial Chamber III, Fourth Decision on Victims' Participation, ICC-01/05-01/08-320, 12 December 2008, para 36; ICC, *Prosecutor v. Laurent Gbagbo*, Pre-Trial Chamber I, Corrigendum to the Second decision on victims' participation at the confirmation of charges hearing and in the related proceedings, ICC-02/11-01/11-384-Corr, 6 February 2013 (corrigendum notified on 8 February 2013), para 28; STL, *Prosecutor v. Ayyash* et al., Pre-Trial Judge, Decision on Victims' Participation in the Proceedings, STL-11-01/PT/PTJ, 8 May 2012, para 33. At the ECCC, the Co-Investigating Judges have used a flexible approach when deciding the types of documents accepted to establish the applicant's identity. See for example ECCC, *Case 002,* Pre-Trial Chamber, Decision on Appeals against Orders of the Co-Investigating Judges on the Admissibility of Civil Party Applications, Case No. 002/19-09-2007-ECCC/OCIJ, 24 June 2011, para 95; ECCC, *Case 001*, Trial Chamber, Decision of the Trial Chamber concerning Proof of Identity for Civil Party Applicants, Case No. 001/18-07-2007/ECCC/TC, 26 February 2009, paras 6–8.

[18] ICC, *Prosecutor v. Jean-Pierre Bemba Gombo*, Pre-Trial Chamber III, Fourth Decision on Victims' Participation, ICC-01/05-01/08-320, 12 December 2008, para 53; ICC, *Prosecutor v. Ahmad Al Faqi Al Mahdi,* Trial Chamber VIII, Public redacted version of 'Decision on Victim Participation at Trial and on Common Legal Representation of Victims', ICC-01/12-01/15-97-Red, 8 June 2016, paras 23–25.

[19] See ICC RPE, Rule 89(3). At the STL, an application can be brought by a person acting on the applicant's behalf when he or she is a minor (which, in line with the Lebanese Civil Code, is a person under 18 years of age) or otherwise lacks legal capacity. STL, *Prosecutor v. Ayyash* et al., Pre-Trial Judge, Decision on Victims' Participation in the Proceedings, STL-11-01/PT/PTJ, 8 May 2012, para 31.

behalf needs to provide proof of identity and proof of the relationship with the victim.[20]

ICC chambers typically ask that a kinship, guardianship, or legal guardianship be demonstrated when a person acts on behalf of an applicant.[21] However, Trial Chamber I in the *Lubanga* case found that the RPE have not restricted the types of people who can act on behalf on another, and that it was for the Chamber to decide on the suitability of particular individuals to act on behalf of others on a case-by-case basis. In the case at hand, Trial Chamber I took into account the particular situation of former child soldiers "living in circumstances where they cannot be represented by their parents, other family relatives or a legal guardian," and accepted that they could apply through persons acting on their behalves who are not their next-of-kin or their legal guardians, or who had no documentary proof of the relationship.[22]

Rule 89(3) of the ICC RPE envisages the possibility for a person to act on behalf of a minor, and applications from minors that were not submitted by persons acting on their behalf have been rejected by some chambers.[23] Other chambers granted victim participant status to minors who had submitted their own applications. Such decisions are taken on a case-by-case basis where proof of maturity and power of

[20] See, for example ICC, *Prosecutor v. Jean-Pierre Bemba Gombo*, Pre-Trial Chamber III, Fourth Decision on Victims' Participation, ICC-01/05-01/08-320, 12 December 2008, para 38; ICC, *Prosecutor v. William Samoei Ruto, Henry Kiprono Kosgey and Joshua Arap Sang*, Pre-Trial Chamber II, Decision on Victims' Participation at the Confirmation of Charges Hearing and in the Related Proceedings, ICC-01/09-01/11-249, 5 August 2011, para 43; STL, *Prosecutor v. Ayyash* et al., Pre-Trial Judge, Decision on Victims' Participation in the Proceedings, STL-11-01/PT/PTJ, 8 May 2012, paras 31–32.

[21] ICC, *Prosecutor v. Kony* et al., Pre-Trial Chamber II, Decision on victims' applications for participation a/0010/06, a/0064/06 to a/0070/06, a/0081/06, a/0082/06, a/0084/06 to a/0089/06, a/0091/06 to a/0097/06, a/0099/06,a/0100/06, a/0102/06 to a/0104/06, a/0111/06, a/0113/06 to a/0117/06, a/0120/0, ICC-02/04-01/05-282, 14 March 2008, para 7; ICC, *Prosecutor v. Jean-Pierre Bemba Gombo*, Pre-Trial Chamber III, Fourth Decision on Victims' Participation, ICC-01/05-01/08-320, 12 December 20008, para 38; ICC, *Prosecutor v. Germain Katanga and Mathieu Ngudjolo Chui*, Trial Chamber II, Decision on the treatment of applications for participation, ICC-01/04-01/07-933-tENG, 26 February 2009, para 28.

[22] ICC, *Prosecutor v. Thomas Lubanga Dyilo*, Trial Chamber I, Decision on the Applications by Victims to Participate in the Proceedings, ICC-01/04-01/06-1556-Corr-Anx1, 13 January 2009, paras 67–72.

[23] ICC, *Situation in Uganda*, Pre-Trial Chamber II, Decision on victims' applications for participation a/0014/07 to a/0020/07 and a/0076/07 to a/0125/07, ICC-02/04-172, 21 November 2008, paras 19–20; ICC, *Situation in Darfur, Sudan*, Pre-Trial Chamber I, Corrigendum to Decision on the Applications for Participation in the Proceedings of Applicants a/0011/06 to a/0015/06, a/0021/07, a/0023/07 to a/0033/07 and a/0035/07 to a/0038/07, ICC-02/05-111-Corr, 14 December 2007, paras 32–33.

discernment on the part of the applicant is proved.[24] In the *Lubanga* case, Trial Chamber I decided that if a minor was accepted to participate with a person acting on his behalf, once the minor became an adult, he could continue to be represented by the same person or he could declare that he wished to participate on his own behalf.[25]

At the ICC, a person who is not legally incompetent can also have someone else participate on his or her behalf, provided that consent is expressed.[26] No provision precludes a similar approach at the ECCC, although it has never been used by any applicant so far.[27]

The ECCC legal texts allow for Victims' Associations to act on behalf of their members who are civil parties.[28] In order for a Victims' Association to be authorised to act on behalf of its members it must first be admitted to the list of Victims' Associations approved to act on behalf of civil parties before the ECCC, and provide, *inter alia*, 'documentation showing that it is validly registered or established in the country in which it is carrying out activities' as well as proof that it is authorised to represent its members before the ECCC.[29]

The STL application form only contemplates applications on behalf of minors or disabled persons. The STL RPE is silent on whether applications on behalf of other individuals are permitted.

3.2.1.3 Deceased Victims

At the ICC, the jurisprudence has been inconsistent on the question of whether a deceased victim can participate via a person acting on his or her behalf. Pre-Trial

[24] ICC, *Prosecutor v. Thomas Lubanga Dyilo,* Trial Chamber I, Decision on the Applications by Victims to Participate in the Proceedings, ICC-01/04-01/06-1556-Corr-Anx1, 13 January 2009, para 94; ICC, *Prosecutor v. Germain Katanga and Mathieu Ngudjolo Chui*, Trial Chamber II, Decision on the Treatment of Applications for Participation, ICC-01/04-01/07-933-tENG, 26 February 2009, para 39. See also ICC, *Prosecutor v. Laurent Gbagbo and Charles Blé Goudé*, Trial Chamber I, Decision on victims' participation status, ICC-02/11-01/15-379, 7 January 2016, para 60.

[25] ICC, *Prosecutor v. Thomas Lubanga Dyilo*, Trial Chamber I, Decision on the Applications by Victims to Participate in the Proceedings, ICC-01/04-01/06-1556-Corr-Anx1, 13 January 2009, para 78.

[26] ICC RPE, Rule 89(3). In the Darfur situation a person was denied the possibility to present applications on behalf of members of his family who had disappeared, as the Single Judge found that if these alleged victims were still alive, their express consent had to be given. There is however a possibility for the affected family member to apply for participation on his own behalf. ICC, *Situation in Darfur, Sudan*, Pre-Trial Chamber I, Corrigendum to Decision on the Applications for Participation in the Proceedings of Applicants a/0011/06 to a/0015/06, a/0021/07, a/0023/07 to a/0033/07 and a/0035/07 to a/0038/07, ICC-02/05-111-Corr, 14 December 2007, para 35.

[27] Written correspondence with Eleonor Fernandez, senior legal consultant, Civil Party Lead Co-Lawyers Section, ECCC, 23 and 29 March 2015 (records on file with the author).

[28] ECCC Practice Direction on Victim Participation, Article 5.1.

[29] Ibid., Articles 5.2., 5.5 and 5.8.

Chamber III in the *Bemba* case opined that although a deceased person cannot be a participant in the proceedings, his or her rights can be represented in the proceedings before the Court by his or her successor, provided that the successor is a victim recognised as participant in the proceedings.[30] Trial Chamber III endorsed this approach, finding that 'the death of a victim should not extinguish the opportunity for the Chamber to consider his or her views and concerns'.[31]

The Single Judge of Pre-Trial Chamber I in the *Darfur* situation, on the contrary, found that a deceased person cannot be considered a 'natural person' in the sense of Rule 85(a) of the ICC RPE.[32] Similarly, Trial Chamber II noted in the *Katanga and Ngujolo Chui* case that no provision in the Court's legal texts permits an application for participation to be submitted on behalf of a deceased person, and, in any case, consent of the deceased could not be proven and it would not be conceptually feasible for a person 'to convey the views and concerns of the deceased accurately, in the sense of Article 68(3) of the [ICC] Statute'.[33] In light of this jurisprudence, and to avoid a possible rejection of an application on that basis, it would seem preferable that a family member who alleges having suffered personal harm as a result of the events that led to the death of the direct victim applies on his or her own behalf (rather than on behalf of the deceased victim), and describe personal harm[34] as well as providing documentary evidence of the identity and relationship with the deceased.

---

[30] ICC, *Prosecutor v. Jean-Pierre Bemba Gombo*, Pre-Trial Chamber III, Fourth Decision on Victims' Participation, ICC-01/05-01/08-320, 12 December 2008, paras 44–48; In paras 48–49, the Chamber indicated that 'The successors must clearly indicate in the application form whether they act on their own behalf and on behalf of the deceased person. Further, the applicant must provide the sufficient information on: (i) the identity of the deceased person, (ii) the identity of the successor, and (iii) the kinship between the successor and the deceased.'

[31] ICC, *Prosecutor v. Jean-Pierre Bemba Gombo*, Trial Chamber III, Corrigendum to the Decision on the participation of victims in the trial and on 86 applications by victims to participate in the proceedings, ICC-01/05-01/08-807-Corr, 12 July 2010, paras 78–85.

[32] ICC, *Situation in Darfur, Sudan*, Pre-Trial Chamber I, Corrigendum to Decision on the Applications for Participation in the Proceedings of Applicants a/0011/06 to a/0015/06, a/0021/07, a/0023/07 to a/0033/07 and a/0035/07 to a/0038/07, ICC-02/05-111-Corr, 14 December 2007, para 35.

[33] ICC, *Prosecutor v. Germain Katanga and Mathieu Ngudjolo Chui*, Trial Chamber II, Public Redacted Version of Grounds for the Decision on the 345 Applications for Participation in the Proceedings Submitted by Victims, ICC-01/04-01/07-1491-Red-tENG, 23 September 2009, paras 49–56; See also ICC, *Prosecutor v. Francis Kirimi Muthaura, Uhuru Muigai Kenyatta and Mohammed Hussein Ali*, Pre-Trial Chamber II, Decision on Victims' Participation at the Confirmation of Charges Hearing and in the Related Proceedings, ICC-01/09-02/11-267, 26 August 2011, para 47.

[34] ICC, *Prosecutor v. Laurent Gbagbo*, Pre-Trial Chamber I, Corrigendum to the Second Decision on Victims' Participation at the Confirmation of Charges Hearing and in the Related Proceedings, ICC-02/11-01/11-384-Corr, 6 February 2013 (corrigendum notified on 8 February 2013), para 39; ICC, *Prosecutor v. Bosco Ntaganda,* Trial Chamber VI, Decision on Victims' Participation in Trial Proceedings, ICC-01/04-02/06-449, 6 February 2015, para 48.

Three ICC chambers have allowed someone to take over from a participating victim who died during the proceedings, specifying the conditions to be met for a successor to be authorised to resume the actions initiated by the deceased victim.[35] Although the Appeals Chamber issued a decision appearing to suggest that victims who die before the conclusion of the trial proceedings may not participate in the proceedings through another person,[36] this decision has been interpreted by Trial Chamber III as confined to appellate proceedings and 'without prejudice to any determination on behalf of deceased victims in relation to reparation proceedings'.[37] This issue is considered in more detail in Chap. 14.

The legal framework of the ECCC does not explicitly regulate the question of whether another person can participate on behalf of a deceased victim. However, it is clear that successors can resume participation on behalf of civil parties who die during the proceedings.[38]

At the STL no application has been made to date for any form of participation by a deceased victim.

3.2.2 The Applicant Suffered Harm

3.2.2.1 Type of Harm

The harm recognised by the three courts as being required for the status of victim can for the most part be categorised into three types: physical, psychological and

[35] ICC, *Prosecutor v. Germain Katanga and Mathieu Ngudjolo Chui*, Trial Chamber II, Public Redacted Version of Grounds for the Decision on the 345 Applications for Participation in the Proceedings Submitted by Victims, ICC-01/04-01/07-1491-Red, 23 September 2009, para 30; ICC, *Prosecutor v. Germain Katanga and Mathieu Ngudjolo* Chui, Trial Chamber II, Decision on the applications to resume action submitted by the family members of deceased Victims a/0025/08, a/0051/08, a/0197/08 and a/0311/09, ICC-01/04-01/07-3018-tENG, 14 June 2011, para 20; ICC, *Prosecutor v. Germain Katanga and Mathieu Ngudjolo Chui*, Trial Chamber II, Decision on the application to resume action, submitted by a family member of deceased Victim a/0253/09, ICC-01/04-01/07-3383-tENG, 10 June 2013, para 6; ICC, *Prosecutor v. Bosco Ntaganda*, Trial Chamber VI, Fourth decision on victims' participation in trial proceedings, ICC-01/04-02/06-805, 1 September 2015; ICC, *Prosecutor v. Jean-Pierre Bemba Gombo*, Trial Chamber III, Decision on "Requête relative à la reprise des actions introduites devant la Cour par des victimes décédées", ICC-01/05-01/08-3346, 24 March 2016.

[36] ICC, *Prosecutor v Ngudjolo Chui*, Appeals Chamber, Decision on the Participation of Anonymous Victims in the Appeal and on the Maintenance of Deceased Victims on the List of Participating victims, ICC-01/04-02/12-140, 23 September 2013, paras 25–26.

[37] ICC, *Prosecutor v. Jean-Pierre Bemba Gombo*, Trial Chamber III, Decision on "Requête relative à la reprise des actions introduites devant la Cour par des victimes décédées", ICC-01/05-01/08-3346, 24 March 2016, para 22 citing ICC, *Prosecutor v. Ngudjolo Chui*, Appeals Chamber, Decision on the Participation of Anonymous Victims in the Appeal and on the Maintenance of Deceased Victims on the List of Participating victims, ICC-01/04-02/12-140, 23 September 2013, para 26 footnote 48. See further Chap. 14.

[38] ECCC, *Case 001*, Trial Chamber, Decision on Motion Regarding Deceased Civil Party, Case No. 001/18-07-2007/ECCC/TC, 13 March 2009, paras 10–13. See further Chap. 14.

material. Certain ICC chambers have also recognised as harm the substantial impairment of fundamental rights based on the Basic Principles, which could include, for example, the loss of educational opportunities, or the loss of social status.[39] In *Abu Garda*, the Single Judge referred to victims' claims that they had lost "social status" as a result of having been widowed, however she did not determine whether harm to social standing would suffice for the purposes of Rule 85 in the absence of other forms of harm.[40]

As the ICC Statute does not provide a definition for the concept of harm, the Appeals Chamber ruled in the *Lubanga* case that the word 'harm' in Rule 85(a) of the ICC RPE denotes 'injury, loss or damage', and that material, physical, and psychological harm are all recognised forms of harm if they are suffered personally by the victim.[41] Chambers have recognised, *inter alia*, physical injury as a result of having been shot,[42] emotional suffering and physical suffering related to enslavement and detention,[43] economic loss as a result of pillage,[44] and material harm as a result of forcible transfer.[45] They have also recognised the emotional suffering of a parent as a result of the enlistment of a child,[46] and the financial loss as a result of the death of a relative.[47] The Appeals Chamber considered

[39] ICC, *Prosecutor v. Thomas Lubanga Dyilo,* Trial Chamber I, Decision on Victims' Participation, ICC-01/04-01/06-1119, 18 January 2008, para 92.

[40] ICC, *Prosecutor v. Bahar Idriss Abu Garda*, Pre-Trial Chamber I, Public Redacted Version of "Decision on the 52 Applications for Participation at the Pre-Trial Stage of the Case", ICC-02/05-02/09-147-Red, 9 October 2009, paras 25, 33 and 42.

[41] ICC, *Prosecutor v. Thomas Lubanga Dyilo*, Appeals Chamber, Judgment on the appeals of the Prosecutor and the Defence against Trial Chamber I's Decision on Victims' Participation of 18 January 2008, ICC-01/04-01/06-1432, 11 July 2008, paras 31–32.

[42] ICC, *Prosecutor v. Germain Katanga and Mathieu Ngudjolo Chui*, Pre-Trial Chamber I, Decision on the 97 Applications for Participation at the Pre-Trial Stage of the Case, ICC-01/04-01/07-579, 10 June 2008, para 71.

[43] ICC, *Situation in the Democratic Republic of Congo*, Pre-Trial Chamber I, Decision on the Applications for Participation in the Proceedings of VPRS 1, VPRS 2, VPRS 3, VPRS 4, VPRS 5 and VPRS 6, ICC-01/04-101-tEN-Corr, 22 March 2006, para 147.

[44] ICC, *Prosecutor v. Jean-Pierre Bemba Gombo*, Pre Trial Chamber III, Public redacted version of ANNEX to "Fourth Decision on Victims' Participation", ICC-01/05-01/08-320-Anx-Red, 15 December 2008, 28 May 2013, paras 2–3.

[45] ICC, *Prosecutor v. Francis Kirimi Muthaura, Uhuru Muigai Kenyatta and Mohammed Hussein Ali,* Pre-Trial Chamber II, Decision on Victims' Participation at the Confirmation of Charges Hearing and in the Related Proceedings, ICC-01/09-02/11-267, 26 August 2011, para 29.

[46] ICC, *Prosecutor v. Thomas Lubanga Dyilo*, Appeals Chamber, Judgment on the appeals of the Prosecutor and the Defence against Trial Chamber I's Decision on Victims' Participation of 18 January 2008, ICC-01/04-01/06-1432, 11 July 2008, para 32.

[47] ICC, *Prosecutor v. Abdallah Banda Abakaer Nourain*, Trial Chamber IV, Decision on 19 Applications to Participate in the Proceedings, ICC-02/05-03/09-528, 12 December 2013, para 27.

in the *Lubanga* case that the fact that harm is collective in nature (it has been suffered by a collectivity) does not prevent it from being personal.[48]

Whether a victim has suffered one type of harm or all three, the status as a victim is the same;[49] however the harm needs to be of a certain level to be recognised as such. In the *Banda and Jerbo* case, Pre-Trial Chamber I rejected an application which alleged that the applicant had been frightened and traumatised after hearing about the attack against the camp and the death of the African Union (AU) soldiers (who were not relatives of the applicant). The Chamber found that the harm described did "not attain the level of psychological harm within the meaning and for the purposes of Rule 85(a) of the ICC RPE".[50]

At the STL, the definition of victim set out in Rule 2 of the STL RPE refers to physical, material or mental harm in a way which appears to suggest that these categories are exhaustive rather than inclusive as is the case at the ICC. The Pre-Trial Judge further noted in the *Ayyash* et al. case that the three forms of harm mentioned in Rule 2 of the STL RPE were listed alternatively.[51] As at the ICC, whether a victim has suffered one or multiple forms of harm has therefore no influence on the determination of victim status. As a consequence, where one type of harm has been sufficiently substantiated, the Pre-Trial Judge does not make findings in relations to the other forms of harm possibly alleged by an applicant. Since victims identified in the final judgment may file suit for compensation before national courts,[52] the Pre-Trial Judge has nevertheless been cautious to rule that his *prima facie* findings concerning the harm suffered do not preclude any further recognition of other forms of harm suffered.[53]

The Pre-Trial Judge held in the *Ayyash* et al. case that physical harm 'does not have to be life-threatening or permanent for the purpose of granting the status of participating victim'; 'however, it must be of such nature and gravity as to interfere with the health, well-being or comfort of the victim'.[54] Similarly, while the

---

[48] ICC, *Prosecutor v. Thomas Lubanga Dyilo*, Appeals Chamber, Judgment on the appeals of the Prosecutor and the Defence against Trial Chamber I's Decision on Victims' Participation of 18 January 2008, ICC-01/04-01/06-1432, 11 July 2008, para 35.

[49] ICC, *Prosecutor v. Bosco Ntaganda*, Pre-Trial Chamber II, Decision on Victims' Participation at the Confirmation of Charges Hearing and in the Related Proceedings, ICC-01/04-02/06-211, 15 January 2014, para 33.

[50] ICC, *Prosecutor v. Abdallah Banda Abaker Nourain and Saleh Mohammed Jerbo Jamus*, Pre-Trial Chamber I, Decision on Victims' Participation at the Hearing on the Confirmation of the Charges, ICC-02/05-03/09-89, 29 October 2010, para 39.

[51] STL, *Prosecutor v. Ayyash* et al., Pre-Trial Judge, Decision on Victims' Participation in the Proceedings, STL-11-01/PT/PTJ, 8 May 2012, para 57.

[52] Article 25(4) of the Statute of the Special Tribunal for Lebanon (STL Statute) and STL RPE, Rule 86(G).

[53] STL, *Prosecutor v. Ayyash* et al., Pre-Trial Judge, Decision on Victims' Participation in the Proceedings, STL-11-01/PT/PTJ, 8 May 2012, para 58.

[54] Ibid., para 65.

notion of mental harm 'encompasses harm of emotional, psychological or psychiatric nature',[55] emotional distress must be 'so severe that no reasonable man could be expected to endure it'.[56] As for material harm, it includes 'damage to, or destruction or deterioration of property, loss of income or of means of subsistence and other forms of financial loss.'[57]

Harm is defined in Rule 23*bis*(1)(b) of the ECCC Internal Rules as 'physical, material or psychological injury'. According to the ECCC Supreme Court Chamber, '[p]hysical injury denotes biological damage, anatomical or functional. It may be described as a wound, mutilation, disfigurement, disease, loss or dysfunction of organs, or death. Material injury refers to material objects' loss of value, such as complete or partial destruction of personal property, or loss of income'. The Supreme Court Chamber also found that the injury may be psychological and include mental disorders or psychiatric trauma, such as post-traumatic stress disorder.[58]

3.2.2.2 Direct and Indirect Harm

All three courts have adopted the approach of the UN Basic Principles and Guidelines and the UN Declaration on Justice for Victims, both of which place the connection between the crime and the harm suffered at the heart of the definition of victimhood. This approach allows for the recognition of a wider circle of potential victims as opposed to only the direct victims of crimes.

At the ICC, the Appeals Chamber recognised in the *Lubanga* case that the harm, which can be both personal and collective in nature, does not need to be direct, but it must be personal to the victim.[59] This, however, is not the case for the legal entity, as the drafters of the ICC RPE specifically provided that a victim under Rule 85(b) of the ICC RPE must have suffered direct harm.[60]

The Appeals Chamber further recognised that '[h]arm suffered by one victim as a result of the commission of a crime within the jurisdiction of the Court can give rise to harm suffered by other victims',[61] thereby creating two categories of victims: those whose harm is the result of the commission of the crime (the 'direct

[55] Ibid., para 78.

[56] Ibid., para 78.

[57] Ibid., para 72.

[58] ECCC, *Case 001*, Supreme Court Chamber, Appeal Judgment, Case No. 001/18-07-2007/ECCC/SC, 3 February 2012, para 415.

[59] ICC, *Prosecutor v. Thomas Lubanga Dyilo*, Appeals Chamber, Judgment on the Appeals of the Prosecutor and the Defence against Trial Chamber I's Decision on Victims' Participation of 18 January 2008, ICC-01/04-01/06-1432, 11 July 2008, paras 1 and 35.

[60] ICC RPE, Rule 85(b).

[61] ICC, *Prosecutor v. Thomas Lubanga Dyilo*, Appeals Chamber, Judgment on the Appeals of the Prosecutor and the Defence against Trial Chamber I's Decision on Victims' Participation of 18 January 2008, ICC-01/04-01/06-1432, 11 July 2008, para 32.

victims'), and those who suffered harm as a result of the harm suffered by the direct victims (the 'indirect victims').[62] On that basis, chambers have recognised, for example, the emotional suffering of an applicant as a result of the death of a family member, and the financial loss or material deprivation that accompanies the loss of a person who used to provide for another.[63] Trial Chamber III in the *Bemba* case acknowledged that emotional harm could be claimed on the account of crimes committed against a relative who is still alive, for instance harm suffered by the husband as a result the rape of his wife.[64]

Chambers have also recognised the harm suffered by individuals who had intervened to help direct victims.[65]

Excluded from the category of 'indirect victims', however, are individuals who suffered harm as a result of the subsequent conduct of direct victims: for instance, it was decided in the *Lubanga* case that a person who was attacked by a child soldier would not qualify as an indirect victim because his or her loss was not linked to the harm inflicted on the child when the confirmed offence of conscription, enlistment or use of children to participate actively in hostilities was committed.[66]

At the STL, although Rule 2 of the STL RPE mentions a requirement of 'direct result', the jurisprudence has held that this should not be interpreted narrowly so as to exclude from the definition of victim persons who suffered indirect harm.[67] The Pre-Trial Judge considered that victims could also include persons with sufficiently close relationships to a direct victim where they had experienced harm by virtue of the harm suffered by the latter. He considered that this would encompass not only first degree relatives, for which a presumption of emotional harm exists, but also persons in relationships of like proximity to the direct victim, and other extended family members having a special bond of affection with, or dependence on the direct victim. The Pre-Trial Judge required that proof of this relationship to the

[62] ICC, *Prosecutor v. Thomas Lubanga Dyilo*, Trial Chamber I, Redacted version of "Decision on 'indirect victims'", ICC-01/04-01/06-1813, 8 April 2009, para 44.

[63] ICC, *Prosecutor v. Thomas Lubanga Dyilo*, Trial Chamber I, Redacted version of "Decision on 'indirect victims'", ICC-01/04-01/06-1813, 8 April 2009, para 50; ICC, *Prosecutor v. Abdallah Banda Abakaer Nourain*, Trial Chamber IV, Decision on 19 Applications to Participate in the Proceedings, ICC-02/05-03/09-528, 12 December 2013, para 26.

[64] ICC, *Prosecutor v. Jean-Pierre Bemba Gombo*, Trial Chamber III, Decision on 772 Applications by Victims to Participate in the Proceedings, ICC-01/05-01/08-1017, 18 November 2010, para 44.

[65] ICC, *Prosecutor v. Thomas Lubanga Dyilo*, Trial Chamber I, Decision on the Applications by Victims to Participate in the Proceedings, ICC-01/04-01/06-1556-Corr-Anx1, 13 January 2009, paras 107–111.

[66] ICC, *Prosecutor v. Thomas Lubanga Dyilo*, Trial Chamber I, Redacted version of "Decision on 'Indirect Victims'", ICC-01/04-01/06-1813, 8 April 2009, para 52.

[67] STL, *Prosecutor v. Ayyash* et al., Pre-Trial Judge, Decision on Victims' Participation in the Proceedings, STL-11-01/PT/PTJ, 8 May 2012, para 40.

direct victim must be provided. In practice, of the victims currently participating in the *Ayyash* et al. case, approximately 80% could be described as indirect victims.[68]

At the ECCC, Internal Rule 23*bis*(1)(b) requires the victim to demonstrate that he or she suffered injury 'as a direct consequence' of a relevant crime. However, the term 'direct consequence' has been interpreted as emphasising the link between the crime and the injury suffered rather than the intended target of the criminal act.[69] The Supreme Court Chamber determined in the appeal of *Case 001* that 'the term 'direct victim' [...] is not coterminous with the category of persons who suffered injury as a 'direct consequence' of the crime.'[70] Indeed, since the injury resulting from the crime charged is the only defining, and—equally—limiting, criterion for the admissibility of the civil party applications, indirect victims can also participate as civil parties so long as they 'suffered injury as a direct consequence of the crimes committed against the direct victim(s).'[71] The Supreme Court Chamber further found that the category of indirect victims is not restricted to any specific class of persons such as family members, and 'may encompass common law spouses, distant relatives, friends, *de facto* adopters and adoptees, or other beneficiaries, provided that the injury on their part can be demonstrated'.[72] It provided examples of harm or injury that could be suffered by people who are not direct victims, recognising that 'a wide range of persons' may be affected. The Chamber mentioned, *inter alia*, psychological injury as a result of the injury of a loved one or a caregiver, or resulting from uncertainty and fear about the direct victim's fate or knowledge of their suffering, or the loss of the sense of safety and moral integrity, acknowledging that this psychological harm could lead, in some cases, to physical injury. The Chamber also recognised the possibility of material injury from losing a person who was a breadwinner at the time of the victimisation or, in all probability, would have been a breadwinner in the future, or from damage to the possessions of the family.[73] Among the civil parties in *Case 001*, 11% were direct survivors, and the remaining civil parties made an application on the basis that they were kin or had a close relationship to a person who died as a result of the crimes charged.[74]

68 Written correspondence with Kinga Tibori-Szabó, former associate legal officer, Legal Representatives of Victims, STL, 13 May 2015 (records on file with the author).

69 ECCC, *Case 001*, Trial Chamber, Judgment, Case No. 001/18-07-2007/ECCC/TC, 26 July 2010, para 642.

70 ECCC, *Case 001*, Supreme Court Chamber, Appeal Judgment, Case No. 001/18-07-2007/ECCC/SC, 3 February 2012, para 416.

71 Ibid., paras 415–416.

72 Ibid., para 418.

73 Ibid., para 417.

74 Pham et al. 2011, p. 269.

3.2.3 *Causal Link Between the Harm Suffered and the Crime(s) Charged*

3.2.3.1 Link Between the Harm and a Crime Charged Against the Suspect or the Accused

In all three courts the participation in the proceedings is limited to those victims who have suffered from crimes that have been charged against the suspect or the accused.

At the ICC this means in practice that applications to participate in a case are accepted only if there is a link between the events alleged in the application form and at least one crime contained in the authoritative document that frames the scope of the case at the particular stage of the proceedings, i.e. the warrant of arrest or summons to appear, or, at a later stage in the proceedings, the document containing the charges.[75] Victims' applications for participation will be rejected or victims will no longer be able to participate from one stage of the proceedings to another when the events described in their applications fail to meet one or more of the parameters shaping the case (i.e. the geographical, temporal and material scope). Note however that, before the ICC, victims may also participate in judicial proceedings which arise in the context of a *situation* (as opposed to a *case*),[76] in which circumstances an analogous requirement applies: the harm suffered by the victim must have resulted from a crime which falls within the scope of the situation.

Applicants should provide sufficient information regarding the incidents alleged and the harm suffered. It is however not necessary for applicants to provide a detailed description of the constitutive elements of a particular offence. Pre-Trial Chamber II further specified that it is for the chambers 'to consider whether the event(s) described by the applicants may constitute one of the crimes charged against the suspects'.[77] In practice, some, albeit not all, ICC chambers have been

---

[75] ICC, *Prosecutor v. Francis Kirimi Muthaura, Uhuru Muigai Kenyatta and Mohammed Hussein Ali,* Pre-Trial Chamber II, Decision on Victims' Participation at the Confirmation of Charges Hearing and in the Related Proceedings, ICC-01/09-02/11-267, 26 August 2011, para 60. The status of a victim does not differ depending on whether he or she has been recognised as a victim of one, or more than one, crime allegedly committed by the suspect or accused. See ICC, *Prosecutor v. Bosco Ntaganda*, Pre-Trial Chamber II, Decision on Victims' Participation at the Confirmation of Charges Hearing and in the Related Proceedings, ICC-01/04-02/06-211, 15 January 2014, para 27.

[76] ICC, *Situation in the Democratic Republic of the Congo*, Appeals Chamber, Judgment on victim participation in the investigation stage of the proceedings in the appeal of the OPCD against the decision of Pre-Trial Chamber I of 7 December 2007 and in the appeals of the OPCD and the Prosecutor against the decision of Pre-Trial Chamber I of 24 December 2007, ICC-01/04-556, 19 December 2008.

[77] ICC, *Prosecutor v. William Samoei Ruto, Henry Kiprono Kosgey and Joshua Arap Sang*, Pre-Trial Chamber II, Decision on Victims' Participation at the Confirmation of Charges Hearing and in the Related Proceedings, ICC-01/09-01/11-249, 5 August 2011, para 36.

flexible in that regard, preferring to decide on a case-by-case basis, on the merits of the application's intrinsic coherence and taking into account, *inter alia*, information taken from other applications. For example, in the *Bemba* case, the omission of a precise date of event was not automatically fatal to an application.[78] Likewise, discrepancies in the time and place of a crime within one application were sometimes not seen as fatal to the merits of the application, depending on the overall information presented.[79] In the *Katanga and Ngudjolo Chui* case, despite the fact that applicants only referred to the date of 'February 2003', and not the actual specific date of the attack on Bogoro, Trial Chamber II found that the event described by the applicants corresponded to the scope of the case as defined in the decision on the confirmation of charges.[80]

Practitioners should be particularly careful that applicants provide sufficient information to allow a chamber to conclude, *prima facie*, that he or she has suffered from crimes allegedly committed that are within the scope of the case, since a lack of information in that regard could lead to the application being rejected. For example, Pre-Trial Chamber II in the *Ntaganda* case rejected applications with insufficient information to determine the location where the crimes allegedly took place,[81] and Trial Chamber III in the *Bemba* case rejected applications in which it was not indicated that the crime had started on the territory of the Central African Republic.[82] If the applicant cannot provide such information, the reason for it should be explained, and information regarding the general context should be provided in order to substantiate the allegation that the events occurred within the temporal or geographical scope of the case.

As regards the identification of the suspect or accused person in the application form, Pre-Trial Chamber I in *Mbarushimana* stated that although the identification of the perpetrators of the incidents alleged 'constitutes a facet of the requisite link between the alleged harm and the alleged crimes against the suspect', as per

---

[78] ICC, *Prosecutor v. Jean-Pierre Bemba Gombo*, Trial Chamber III, Decision on 270 applications by victims to participate in the proceedings, ICC-01/05-01/08-1862, 25 October 2011, para 24. See also ICC, *Prosecutor v. Dominic Ongwen*, Pre-Trial Chamber II, Decision on contested victims' applications for participation, legal representation of victims and their procedural rights, ICC-02/04-01/15-350, 27 November 2015, para 13.

[79] ICC, *Prosecutor v. Jean-Pierre Bemba Gombo*, Trial Chamber III, Corrigendum to the Decision on the participation of victims in the trial and on 86 applications by victims to participate in the proceedings, ICC-01/05-01/08-807-Corr, 12 July 2010, para 96.

[80] ICC, *Prosecutor v. Germain Katanga and Mathieu Ngudjolo Chui*, Trial Chamber II, Public Redacted Version of Grounds for the Decision on the 345 Applications for Participation in the Proceedings Submitted by Victims, ICC-01/04-01/07-1491-Red-tENG, 23 September 2009, para 82.

[81] ICC, *Prosecutor v. Bosco Ntaganda*, Pre-Trial Chamber II, Second Decision on Victims' Participation at the Confirmation of Charges Hearing and in the Related Proceedings, ICC-01/04-02/06-251, 7 February 2014, para 29.

[82] ICC, *Prosecutor v. Jean-Pierre Bemba Gombo*, Trial Chamber III, Decision on 772 Applications by Victims to Participate in the Proceedings, ICC-01/05-01/08-1017, 18 November 2010, para 58.

Regulation 86(2)(d) of the ICC Regulations of the Court,[83] it would nevertheless be unfair, at the pre-trial stage, to place on victims the onerous burden of identifying 'in a conclusive way or by providing a precise degree of precisions' those responsible for their suffering. After recalling that the link between the alleged harm and the crimes charged must be established on a *prima facie* basis at that stage of the proceedings, the Single Judge of Pre-Trial Chamber I said she would consider the description made of the perpetrator(s) in light of the overall assessment of the account of events as described in the application, its intrinsic coherence and the parameters and the circumstances surrounding the alleged events, alongside the Chamber's findings regarding the material time and place of the crimes charged.[84]

Moreover, as pointed out by Pre-Trial Chamber I in *Blé Goudé*, nothing precludes victims' applications from being 'relevant' in more than one case. In this particular instance, it authorised the participation of victims who had previously been authorised to participate in the *Gbagbo* case on the basis that the subject-matter of the cases appeared to be the same, and that 'applicants fulfilling the criteria of Rule 85 in one case will in principle satisfy the criteria in the other.'[85] The same principle had been applied to victims participating in *Abu Garda*, who were subsequently authorised to participate in the *Banda and Jerbo* case (a later case containing materially identical charges) without their applications being re-assessed by the Pre-Trial Chamber.[86] Despite this, a different approach was taken by Pre-Trial Chamber II in the *Ntaganda* case. There the Single Judge held that victims must submit a fresh application even if they had already been accepted to participate in the *Lubanga* case in respect of the same crimes.[87]

---

[83] It is to be noted, however, that according to Regulation 86(2)(d) of the ICC Regulations of the Court, the application should contain the identification of the perpetrator 'to the extent possible'.

[84] ICC, *Prosecutor v. Callixte Mbarushimana*, Pre-Trial Chamber I, Decision on the 138 Applications for Victims' Participation in the Proceedings ICC-01/04-01/10-351, 11 August 2011, paras 36–39; See also, ICC, *Prosecutor v. Francis Kirimi Muthaura, Uhuru Muigai Kenyatta and Mohammed Hussein Ali,* Pre-Trial Chamber II, Decision on Victims' Participation at the Confirmation of Charges Hearing and in the Related Proceedings, ICC-01/09-02/11-267, 26 August 2011, paras 32–34. In the same manner, the Trial Chamber in the *Bemba* case decided on a case-by-case basis, taking into account the circumstances, and in the absence of any indication that the alleged crimes were attributable to perpetrators other than those linked to the case. The mere reference to other persons or warring groups in the application would not, as such, automatically serve to exclude the applicant. ICC, *Prosecutor v. Jean-Pierre Bemba Gombo*, Trial Chamber III, Decision on 653 Applications by Victims to Participate in the Proceeding, ICC-01/05-01/08-1091, 23 December 2010, para 27.

[85] ICC, *Prosecutor v. Charles Blé Goudé*, Pre-Trial Chamber I, Decision on victims' Participation in the Pre-Trial Proceedings and Related Issues, ICC-02/11-02/11-83, 11 June 2014, paras 12–18.

[86] ICC, *Prosecutor v. Abdallah Banda Abaker Nourain and Saleh Mohammed Jerbo Jamus*, Pre-Trial Chamber I, Decision on Victims' Participation at the Hearing on the Confirmation of the Charges, ICC-02/05-03/09-89, 29 October 2010, paras 6–10.

[87] *Prosecutor v. Bosco Ntaganda*, Pre-Trial Chamber II, Decision on the "*Demande de participation de neuf victimes admises dans le procès de M. Thomas Lubanga Dyilo*", ICC-01/04-02/06-75, 26 June 2013, paras 13–17.

In order to be a victim in the sense of the definition in Rule 2 of the STL RPE, a person must have suffered harm 'as a direct result of an attack within the Tribunal's jurisdiction'.[88] This use of the term 'attack' that is nowhere defined in the Statute or the RPE, raised an ambiguity, especially where other provisions in the Statute and RPE prefer the formulations 'victims who have suffered harm as a result of the commission of crimes by an accused convicted by the tribunal'[89] or 'victim of a crime within the Tribunal's jurisdiction.'[90] The Pre-Trial Judge resolved this ambiguity in his Fourth Decision on Victims' Participation in the *Ayyash* et al. case, holding that the causal link required a nexus between the harm alleged and a crime specifically charged in the indictment, which in this case was the attack of 14 February 2005 resulting in the death of former Lebanese Prime Minister Rafiq Hariri and in the death or injury of other persons.[91] The Pre-Trial Judge found that this reading was in accordance with the spirit of the Statute and was consistent with the other provisions of the RPE dealing with victims' participation, such as Article 25 of the Statute ('Compensations to victims') which requires a *nexus* between the injury and one of the crimes charged. The Pre-Trial Judge additionally observed that this approach was in line with relevant international law and the jurisprudence of the ECCC and the ICC. In order to establish whether the harm suffered by an applicant who claimed to be a victim was a direct result of the crime, the Pre-Trial Judge assessed whether the context (the place and timing) where the harm was suffered corresponded *prima facie* to that of the events alleged by the Prosecutor.[92]

Internal Rule 23*bis*(1)(b) of the ECCC provides that a civil party applicant shall demonstrate that he or she suffered harm 'as a direct consequence of at least one of the crimes alleged against the Charged Person'. In *Case 001* each civil party had to show that he or she was a victim of crimes committed in the S-21 Security Centre or in the S-24 labour camp, either as a direct victim or as close relative of a direct victim.[93] Victims who could not provide evidence of their detention, or their close relative's detention in S-21 or S-24 were denied civil party status.

On appeal from a decision of the Co-Investigating Judges on the admissibility of victims in *Case 002*, the Pre-Trial Chamber adopted an expansive interpretation based on the nature and legal characterisation of the alleged crimes (as opposed to the alleged *facts*). This interpretation included mass atrocities allegedly committed by the accused by acting in a joint criminal enterprise together and with others

---

[88] See STL Statute, Articles 2 and 25, and STL RPE, Rule 86(G).

[89] STL Statute, Article 25.

[90] STL RPE, Rule 86(A) and (G).

[91] STL, *Prosecutor v. Ayyash* et al., Pre-Trial Judge, Fourth Decision on Victims' Participation in the Proceedings, Public with *ex-parte* annex, STL-11-01/PT/PTJ, 2 May 2013, paras 14–15.

[92] STL, *Prosecutor v. Ayyash* et al., Pre-Trial Judge, Decision on Victims' Participation in the Proceedings, STL-11-01/PT/PTJ, 8 May 2012, para 51.

[93] ECCC, *Case 001,* Trial Chamber, Judgment, Case No. 001/18-07-2007/ECCC/TC, 26 July 2010, para 644.

against the population and 'throughout the country', hence not limited to the area investigated by the Co-Investigating Judges. When the Pre-Trial Chamber considered the appeals of rejected civil party applicants who stated that they had suffered from the implementation of policies associated with the commission of these atrocities, it found that they did not necessarily have to relate their injury to only those areas chosen to be investigated and identified in the factual findings of the Closing Order.[94]

3.2.3.2 Causation Between the Harm and the Crime

ICC chambers have defined in various ways the causal link that must exist between the alleged crime and the harm suffered. In the investigation stage of the *Democratic Republic of Congo (DRC)* situation, Pre-Trial Chamber I applied the standard of *grounds to believe* that the applicant suffered harm as a result of the commission of the crimes, finding it unnecessary, at that stage, 'to determine in any great detail [...] the precise nature of the causal link and the identity of the person(s) responsible for the crimes'.[95] At the pre-trial stage in the *Lubanga* case the Chamber applied the standard of a *sufficient causal link* between the harm [...] suffered and the crimes for which there are reasonable grounds to believe that [the suspect] is criminally responsible;[96] while in the pre-trial phase of both Kenya cases the Single Judge found that the causation between the crime and the harm could not be established with precision *in abstracto*, but would be 'assessed on a case-by-case basis in light of all the circumstances of the events as described in the applications'.[97] In the *Bemba* case, the Single Judge of Pre-Trial Chamber III found that 'the circumstances surrounding the crime(s) must be appropriate to bring about the harm alleged and are not entirely outside the range of expectation or probability, as viewed *ex post* by an objective observer.'[98] The applicant does

[94] ECCC, *Case 002,* Pre-Trial Chamber, Decision on Appeals against Orders of the Co-Investigating Judges on the Admissibility of Civil Party Applications, Case No. 002/19-09-2007/ECCC/OCIJ, 24 June 2011, paras 77–78.

[95] ICC, *Situation in the Democratic Republic of Congo*, Pre-Trial Chamber I, Decision on the Applications for Participation in the Proceedings of VPRS 1, VPRS 2, VPRS 3, VPRS 4, VPRS 5 and VPRS 6, ICC-01/04-101-tEN-Corr, 22 March 2006, para 94.

[96] ICC, *Prosecutor v. Thomas Lubanga Dyilo*, Pre-Trial Chamber I, Decision on the Applications for Participation in the Proceedings Submitted by VPRS 1 to VPRS 6 in the Case the Prosecutor v. Thomas Lubanga Dyilo, ICC-01/04-01/06 -172-tEN, 29 June 2006, p. 6.

[97] ICC, *Prosecutor v. Francis Kirimi Muthaura, Uhuru Muigai Kenyatta and Mohammed Hussein Ali,* Pre-Trial Chamber II, Decision on Victims' Participation at the Confirmation of Charges Hearing and in the Related Proceedings, ICC-01/09-02/11-267, 26 August 2011, para 66 and ICC, *Prosecutor v. William Samoei Ruto, Henry Kiprono Kosgey and Joshua Arap Sang*, Pre-Trial Chamber II, Decision on Victims' Participation at the Confirmation of Charges Hearing and in the Related Proceedings, ICC-01/09-01/11-249, 5 August 2011, para 52.

[98] ICC, *Prosecutor v. Jean-Pierre Bemba Gombo*, Pre-Trial Chamber III, Fourth Decision on Victims' Participation, ICC-01/05-01/08-320, 12 December 2008, paras 76–77.

not need to demonstrate that the alleged incident(s) forming the basis of the charges are the only or substantial cause of the harm he suffered, but only that they could have objectively contributed to such harm.[99]

Practitioners should be aware that for some crimes, specific information may need to be provided in order for a chamber to be able to link the harm suffered to the crime charged against the suspect or accused. In the *Lubanga* case, Trial Chamber I stated that it should be provided with enough information to determine, *prima facie*, that the applicants were under the age of 15 at the time of the events.[100]

Some chambers have rejected applications when the harm alleged appeared to be too remotely connected to the crime charged. As described in Sect. 3.2.2.2, individuals who were victims of the crimes committed by child soldiers were not recognised as victims of the crime of conscription, enlistment or use of children to participate actively in hostilities and were denied victim status for the purpose of participation in the *Lubanga* case. In the *Banda and Jerbo* case, which concerned an attack on the AU mission near the village of Haskanita in Darfur, Pre-Trial Chamber I considered harm allegedly suffered by Haskanita residents as a result of the closure of the AU mission following the attack. The Chamber held that this harm was too remote to fulfil the requirements of Rule 89(a).[101]

The Pre-Trial Judge at the STL did not specify the particular test of causation he applied to determine whether there is sufficient nexus between the crime and the harm. However, the references made to ICC jurisprudence tend to suggest that a similar nexus is required.[102]

3.3 Evidentiary Matters

3.3.1 Standard of Review of Applications

The legal texts and jurisprudence of the three courts have set out a relatively similar standard of review for granting participating victim or civil party status.

---

[99] ICC, *Prosecutor v. Laurent Gbagbo*, Pre-Trial Chamber I, Corrigendum to the Second Decision on Victims' Participation at the Confirmation of Charges Hearing and in the Related Proceedings, ICC-02/11-01/11-384-Corr, 6 February 2013 (corrigendum notified on 8 February 2013), para 32; ICC, *Prosecutor v. Bosco Ntaganda,* Trial Chamber VI, Decision on Victims' Participation in Trial Proceedings, ICC-01/04-02/06-449, 6 February 2015, para 50.

[100] ICC, *Prosecutor v. Thomas Lubanga Dyilo*, Trial Chamber I, Decision on the Applications by Victims to Participate in the Proceedings, ICC-01/04-01/06-1556-Corr-Anx1, 13 January 2009, para 56.

[101] ICC, *Prosecutor v. Abdallah Banda Abaker Nourain and Saleh Mohammed Jerbo Jamus*, Pre-Trial Chamber I, Decision on Victims' Participation at the Hearing on the Confirmation of the Charges, ICC-02/05-03/09-89, 29 October 2010, para 37.

[102] STL, *Prosecutor v. Ayyash* et al., Pre-Trial Judge, Fourth Decision on Victims' Participation in the Proceedings, STL-11-01/PT/PTJ, 2 May 2013, paras 26–27.

At the ICC, the legal texts do not specify the standard of proof that chambers should use to decide on the applications for participation. At the investigation stage in the *DRC* situation, Pre-Trial Chamber I adopted the review standard of *grounds to believe* that the victim meets the criteria set forth in Rule 85 (a) of the ICC RPE.[103] Since then, when assessing applications to participate, ICC chambers at the pre-trial and trial stages have examined whether the requirements established by Rule 85(a) of the ICC RPE are met *prima facie*.[104] Trial Chamber I said that 'it would be untenable for the Chamber to engage in a substantive assessment of the credibility or the reliability of a victim's application before the commencement of the trial.'[105] The ICC chambers have also specified that their assessment of applications will not consist of 'a process of corroboration *stricto sensu*, and will be based on the merits of the applications' intrinsic coherence, taking into consideration all the information available to the Chamber'.[106] Accordingly, chambers have generally not required any evidence additional to the victim applicant's own statement (except in relation to identity) but have decided on a case-by-case basis what evidence provided by the applicant may be sufficient to establish the elements of Rule 85 of the ICC RPE.[107] For instance, they have decided on a case-by-case basis whether an internal contradiction, for example relating to the circumstances in which property was lost,[108] or a contradiction between

[103] ICC, *Situation in the Democratic Republic of Congo*, Pre-Trial Chamber I, Decision on the Applications for Participation in the Proceedings of VPRS 1, VPRS 2, VPRS 3, VPRS 4, VPRS 5 and VPRS 6, ICC-01/04-101-tEN-Corr, 22 March 2006, paras 99–100.

[104] See, for example, ICC, *Prosecutor v. Jean-Pierre Bemba Gombo*, Pre-Trial Chamber III, Fourth Decision on Victims' Participation, ICC-01/05-01/08-320, 12 December 2008, para 31; ICC, *Prosecutor v. Bosco Ntaganda,* Trial Chamber VI, Decision on Victims' Participation in Trial Proceedings, ICC-01/04-02/06-449, 6 February 2015, paras 30, 36 and 44.

[105] ICC, *Prosecutor v. Thomas Lubanga Dyilo*, Trial Chamber I, Decision on Victims' Participation, ICC-01/04-01/06-1119, 18 January 2008, para 99. This principle was applied *mutadis mutandis* at the trial stage. See ICC, *Prosecutor v. Jean-Pierre Bemba Gombo*, Trial Chamber III, Decision on 270 Applications by Victims to Participate in the Proceedings, ICC-01/05-01/08-1862, 25 October 2011, para 27.

[106] See ICC, *Prosecutor v. Laurent Gbagbo*, Pre-Trial Chamber I, Decision on Victims' Participation and Victims' Common Legal Representation at the Confirmation of Charges Hearing and in the Related Proceedings, ICC-02/11-01/11-138, 4 June 2012, para 21; ICC, *Prosecutor v. Jean-Pierre Bemba Gombo*, Pre-Trial Chamber III, Fourth Decision on Victims' Participation, ICC-01/05-01/08-320, 12 December 2008, para 31.

[107] ICC, *Situation in Uganda*, Appeals Chamber, Judgment on the appeals of the Defence against the Decisions entitled "Decision on Victims' Applications for Participation a/0010/06, a/0064/06 to a/0070/06, a/0081/06, a/0082/06, a/0084/06 to a/0089/06, a/0091/06 to a/0097/06, a/0099/06, a/0100/06, a/0102/06 to a/0104/06, a/0111/06, a/0113/06 to a/0117/06, a/0120/06, a/0121/06 and a/0123/06 to a/0127/06" of Pre-Trial Chamber II, ICC-02/04-01/05-371, 23 February 2009, para 2. See also ICC, *Prosecutor v. Dominic Ongwen*, Pre-Trial Chamber II, Decision on contested victims' applications for participation, legal representation of victims and their procedural rights, ICC-02/04-01/15-350, 27 November 2015, para 11.

[108] ICC, *Prosecutor v. Jean-Pierre Bemba Gombo*, Trial Chamber III, Decision on 418 Applications by Victims to Participate in the Proceedings, ICC-01/05-01/08-2011, 15 December 2011, paras 19–20.

applications[109] is fatal in terms of its merits, in view of the overall evidence presented.

According to Rule 86(B)(i) of the STL RPE and its application by the Pre-Trial Judge,[110] persons requesting VPP status are required to provide *prima facie* evidence that they fall under the definition of victim found in Rule 2 of the STL RPE. In practice, the STL Pre-Trial Judge asked that every requirement related to the definition of victims be supported by documentary evidence, something that, aside from identity document and, when applicable, proof of relationship, is not required at the ICC.

At the ECCC, Internal Rule 23*bis*(1) states that the Co-Investigating Judges should be satisfied that the facts alleged in support of the application are *more likely than not to be true*. The Supreme Court Chamber in *Case 001* made a distinction between the standard of review which had been applied at the admissibility level by the Co-Investigating Judges (a *prima facie* standard, which the Supreme Court Chamber found consistent with the international jurisprudence) and the standard of review applied in the determination on the eligibility of the civil parties for reparations by the Trial Chamber, the *more likely than not to be true* standard, assimilated to the 'preponderance of evidence' and 'balance of probabilities' standard.[111] Deciding on the appeal of 1,728 applicants whose applications had been rejected by the Co-Investigating Judges in *Case 002*, the Pre-Trial Chamber found that it should be satisfied that the facts alleged in support of the application are *more likely than not to be true*.[112]

The relatively low standard of proof for admitting victims or civil parties into the proceedings at the ICC and the ECCC has been counterbalanced by the possibility for victims to have their statuses revoked at a later stage. As experienced in the *Lubanga* case, the statuses of participating victims can be withdrawn following evidence submitted during the trial which casts doubt on the veracity of the content of their application forms.[113] At the ECCC, the Trial Chamber in *Case 001*

[109] ICC, *Prosecutor v. Thomas Lubanga Dyilo,* Trial Chamber I, Order Issuing Confidential and Public Redacted Versions of Annex A to the "Decision on the Applications by 7 Victims to Participate in the Proceedings" of 10 July 2009 (ICC-01/04-01/06-2035), ICC-01/04-01/06-2065-Anx2-RSC, 23 July 2009, p. 10; ICC, *Prosecutor v. Thomas Lubanga Dyilo*, Appeals Chamber, Decision on 32 Applications to Participate in the Proceedings, ICC-01/04-01/06-3045-Red2, 27 August 2013, para 166.

[110] STL, *Prosecutor v. Ayyash* et al., Pre-Trial Judge, Decision on Victims' Participation in the Proceedings, STL-11-01/PT/PTJ, 8 May 2012, para 27.

[111] ECCC, *Case 001*, Supreme Court Chamber, Appeal Judgment, Case No. 001/18-07-2007/ECCC/SC, 3 February 2012, para 523.

[112] ECCC, *Case 002*, Pre-Trial Chamber, Decision on Appeals against Orders of the Co-Investigating Judges on the Admissibility of Civil Party Applications, Case No. 002/19-09-2007/ECCC/OCIJ, 24 June 2011, para 94.

[113] ICC, *Prosecutor v. Thomas Lubanga Dyilo*, Trial Chamber, Judgment Pursuant to Article 74 of the Statute, ICC-01/04-01/06-2842, 14 March 2012, paras 484 and 1362. See Chap. 14.

declared a third of the civil parties inadmissible at the reparation stage, based on evidence submitted in the course of the proceedings.[114]

3.3.2 Type of Evidence Required

The main difference between the practices of the three courts when it comes to victims' applications relates to the type of documents required to support an application to participate. Whereas the ICC only requires applicants to provide means of identification and, when relevant, proof of kinship, the requirements at the STL have been much more demanding for the applicants.

3.3.2.1 Identity Documents

As stated earlier,[115] at all three courts applicants are required to provide documentary proof of identification. As the three courts often operate in countries where official documents such as birth certificates or identity cards may not be easily available or reliable, or may have been lost or destroyed, the three courts have shown flexibility in the types of documents which may be used to prove identity.[116]

At the ICC, it is generally in their decision setting out the application process that chambers list the type of documents that will be accepted to prove identity and, in the case of a person acting on behalf of an applicant, to prove the relationship to the victim. Chambers have usually acknowledged the harsh realities faced by victims and the challenges they experience when asked to supply official documents of identification and proof of kinship, and, as one chamber has explained, have tried to 'achieve a balance between the need to establish an applicant's identity with certainty, on the one hand, and the applicant's personal circumstances, on the other.'[117]

---

[114] On appeal, the Supreme Court Chamber found that although the Trial Chamber did not commit an error of law by conducting an evaluation of victimhood based on the Trial Judgment, there 'appeared to have been a fundamental misunderstanding between the Trial Chamber and the Civil Party Appellants as to the merits and legal effect of the initial review of the applications' at an earlier stage, and granted the civil party appellants' motions to submit additional evidence, irrespective of whether such evidence would have been available during the first instance proceedings. ECCC, *Case 001*, Supreme Court Chamber, Appeal Judgment, Case No. 001/18-07-2007/ECCC/SC, 3 February 2012, paras 500–501.

[115] See Sect. 3.2.1.1.

[116] See ICC, *Prosecutor v. Thomas Lubanga Dyilo,* Trial Chamber I, Decision on Victims' Participation, ICC-01/04-01/06-1119, 18 January 2008, para 87.

[117] See ICC, *Prosecutor v. Jean-Pierre Bemba Gombo*, Pre-Trial Chamber III, Fourth Decision on Victims' Participation, ICC-01/05-01/08-320, 12 December 2008, para 36; ICC, *Prosecutor v. Laurent Gbagbo*, Pre-Trial Chamber I, Corrigendum to the Second Decision on Victims' Participation at the Confirmation of Charges Hearing and in the Related Proceedings, ICC-02/11-01/11-384-Corr, 6 February 2013 (corrigendum notified on 8 February 2013), para 28.

For instance, the Trial Chamber in the *Bemba* case took into account the fact that 'numerous [...] citizens [of the Central African Republic], living in rural areas, do not possess any official identity document' and that others 'face difficulties in obtaining identity documents due to e.g. cumbersome administrative procedures, the high costs incurred and a lack of transport means to reach the competent authorities.'[118] In the Kenya cases, the Single Judge at the pre-trial stage took into account the fact that victims may have lost their identity documents during the course of the post-election violence.[119] Chambers have accepted documents such as certificates from local authorities,[120] demobilisation certificates,[121] cards indicating marital status, police records,[122] membership cards,[123] and student identity cards.[124] Chambers have also accepted a signed declaration from two witnesses, accompanied by their proof of identity, attesting the identity of the applicant.[125] Pre-Trial Chamber II, however, asked applicants in the Kenya cases to provide a 'brief explanation' as to why any of the formal identity documents were not available and only less reliable

---

[118] ICC, *Prosecutor v. Jean-Pierre Bemba Gombo*, Trial Chamber III, Decision on 772 Applications by Victims to Participate in the Proceedings, ICC-01/05-01/08-1017, 18 November 2010, para 41.

[119] ICC, *Prosecutor v. Francis Kirimi Muthaura, Uhuru Muigai Kenyatta and Mohammed Hussein Ali,* Pre-Trial Chamber II, First Decision on Victims' Participation in the Case, ICC-01/09-02/11-23, 30 March 2011, para 7; ICC, *Prosecutor v. William Samoei Ruto, Henry Kiprono Kosgey and Joshua Arap Sang*, Pre-Trial Chamber II, First Decision on Victims' Participation in the Case, ICC-01/09-01/11-17, 30 March 2011, para 7.

[120] ICC, *Prosecutor v. Jean-Pierre Bemba Gombo*, Trial Chamber III, Decision on 418 applications by Victims to Participate in the Proceedings, ICC-01/05-01/08-2011, 15 December 2011, para 17.

[121] ICC, *Prosecutor v. Thomas Lubanga Dyilo*, Trial Chamber I, Redacted version of the Decision on the applications by 7 victims to participate in the proceedings, ICC-01/04-01/06-2764-Red, 25 July 2011, para 28.

[122] ICC, *Prosecutor v. Jean-Pierre Bemba Gombo*, Trial Chamber III, Decision on 270 Applications by Victims to Participate in the Proceedings, ICC-01/05-01/08-1862, 25 October 2011, para 25.

[123] ICC, *Prosecutor v. Jean-Pierre Bemba Gombo*, Trial Chamber III, Decision on 418 Applications by Victims to Participate in the Proceedings, ICC-01/05-01/08-2011, 15 December 2011, para 17.

[124] ICC, *Prosecutor v. Jean-Pierre Bemba Gombo*, Trial Chamber III, Corrigendum to the Decision on 401 Applications by Victims to Participate in the Proceedings and Setting a Final Deadline for the Submission of New Victims' Applications to the Registry, ICC-01/05-01/08-1590-Corr, 21 July 2011, para 35.

[125] ICC, *Prosecutor v. Jean-Pierre Bemba Gombo*, Pre-Trial Chamber III, Fourth Decision on Victims' Participation, ICC-01/05-01/08-320, 12 December 2008, para 37; ICC, *Prosecutor v. Francis Kirimi Muthaura, Uhuru Muigai Kenyatta and Mohammed Hussein Ali,* Pre-Trial Chamber II, First Decision on Victims' Participation in the Case, ICC-01/09-02/11-23, 30 March 2011, para 8; ICC, *Prosecutor v. William Samoei Ruto, Henry Kiprono Kosgey and Joshua Arap Sang*, Pre-Trial Chamber II, First Decision on Victims' Participation in the Case, ICC-01/09-01/11-17, 30 March 2011, para 8.

forms of identifications were provided.[126] Practitioners are encouraged to do the same, whether or not they submit an application to the same Chamber.

The reality of the countries where the ICC operates is such that information related to the identity of applicants, such as names and dates of birth, can vary from one identity document to another, based on different spellings, dialects, or because of imprecise or inaccurate records. ICC chambers have decided on a case-by-case basis whether inconsistencies between the information contained in the application form and that featured on the identification document provided cast doubts on the identity of the victim applicant, taking into account the overall coherence of the documents and the information submitted, as well as any explanation provided. The chambers have often adopted a certain degree of flexibility and have considered that minor inconsistencies, such as discrepancies in the spelling of the name, date of birth or ethnicity, and especially those that have explanations, did not affect the credibility or veracity of the overall information provided by an applicant to establish his or her identity.[127] For instance, Trial Chamber III in the *Bemba* case disregarded inconsistencies such as where the date of birth appearing on the application form did not correspond to the date of birth of the applicant, but rather to the date on which the birth was declared.[128] However, in case of 'blatant contradiction', an application could be dismissed.[129] The practitioner should thus be particularly aware of discrepancies and should encourage the applicant to justify them within the application itself.

At the STL, the Pre-Trial Judge listed the documents that are accepted to prove identity in his first Decision on victim's participation.[130] As in the case of the ICC,

---

[126] These are '(i) National ID Waiting Card; (ii) Chief's Identification Letter which provides certain basic information [...]; (iv) Clinic Cards (for minors); (v) Kenya Police Abstract Form (for lost national identity cards or Kenyan passports); (vi) a signed declaration from two witnesses accompanied by their proof of identity—attesting to the identity of the victim applicant.' See ICC, *Prosecutor v. Francis Kirimi Muthaura, Uhuru Muigai Kenyatta and Mohammed Hussein Ali*, Pre-Trial Chamber II, First Decision on Victims' Participation in the Case, ICC-01/09-02/11-23, 30 March 2011, para 9; ICC, *Prosecutor v. William Samoei Ruto, Henry Kiprono Kosgey and Joshua Arap Sang*, Pre-Trial Chamber II, First Decision on Victims' Participation in the Case, ICC-01/09-01/11-17, 30 March 2011, para 9.

[127] ICC, *Prosecutor v. Bosco Ntaganda*, Pre-Trial Chamber II, Decision on Victims' Participation at the Confirmation of Charges Hearing and in the Related Proceedings, ICC-01/04-02/06-211, 15 January 2014, para 23. See also ICC, *Prosecutor v. Jean-Pierre Bemba Gombo*, Trial Chamber III, Decision on 270 Applications by Victims to Participate in the Proceedings, ICC-01/05-01/08-1862, 25 October 2011, para 28; ICC, *Prosecutor v. Bosco Ntaganda*, Trial Chamber VI, Decision on Victims' Participation in Trial Proceedings, ICC-01/04-02/06-449, 6 February 2015, para 46.

[128] ICC, *Prosecutor v. Jean-Pierre Bemba Gombo*, Trial Chamber III, Decision on 270 applications by victims to participate in the proceedings, ICC-01/05-01/08-1862, 25 October 2011, para 28.

[129] ICC, *Prosecutor v. Germain Katanga and Mathieu Ngudjolo Chui*, Trial Chamber II, Public Redacted Version of Grounds for the Decision on the 345 Applications for Participation in the Pro ceedings Submitted by Victims, ICC-01/04-01/07-1491-Red-tENG, 23 September 2009, para 32.

[130] STL, *Prosecutor v. Ayyash* et al., Pre-Trial Judge, Decision on Victims' Participation in the Proceedings, STL-11-01/PT/PTJ, 8 May 2012, para 33(i).

the Pre-Trial Judge also accepted alternatives to identification documents such as documents relating to medical treatment, work identification documents, letters from the local authorities and membership cards.[131] Where a person acts on behalf of an applicant, he or she can prove kinship to the applicant using "family record books, identity cards (indicating the name of the spouse and of the parents), guardianship decisions of courts, and statements of credible witnesses."[132]

At the ECCC, the Trial Chamber in *Case 001* decided that the identity of a person seeking to participate in the proceedings as a civil party must be unequivocal.[133] Nonetheless, the Trial Chamber stated that it would adopt a flexible approach and determine on a case-by-case basis when proving identity is problematic. It then went on to accept, *inter alia*, copies of electoral cards and a voter registration form.[134] The Pre-Trial Chamber in *Case 002* acknowledged that 'the nature of the birth and death registration procedures in Cambodia made it difficult and sometimes impossible for some applicants to provide satisfactory proof of identity', and decided that a flexible approach is to be applied in relation to the requirement of Internal Rule 23*bis*(1)(a). Referring to the practice in Cambodian courts, it accepted as proof of identity statements issued by the village elder or the communal chiefs.[135] The Co-Investigating Judges have acknowledged and accepted some discrepancies in the spelling in victims' applications, particularly due to the fact that it is not uncommon that Khmer names can be spelled in different ways.[136]

3.3.2.2 Harm

ICC practice requires applicants to provide a general description of the harm suffered.[137] Corroborative documentary evidence of the harm suffered has so far not been required, nor is a detailed description from the applicant. For example, in the *Bemba* case, where pillage was a crime charged, applicants did not a need to

[131] Ibid., para 33 (ii).

[132] Ibid., para 34.

[133] ECCC, *Case 001*, Decision of the Trial Chamber Concerning Proof of Identity for Civil Party Applicants, Trial Chamber, Case No. 001/18-07-2007/ECCC/TC, 26 February 2009, para 6.

[134] ECCC, *Case 001*, Trial Chamber, Decision on the Civil Party Status of Applicants E2/36, E2/51 and E2/69, Case No. 001/18-07-2007/ECCC/TC, 4 March 2009, p. 2.

[135] ECCC, *Case 002*, Pre-Trial Chamber, Decision on Appeals Against Orders of the Co-Investigating Judges on the Admissibility of Civil Party Applications, Case No. 002/19-09-2007/ECCC/OCIJ, 24 June 2011, para 95.

[136] Written correspondence with Eleonor Fernandez, Senior legal consultant, Civil Party Lead Co-Lawyers Section, ECCC, 23 and 29 March 2015 (records on file with the author).

[137] ICC, *Prosecutor v. Francis Kirimi Muthaura, Uhuru Muigai Kenyatta and Mohammed Hussein Ali,* Pre-Trial Chamber II, Decision on Victims' Participation at the Confirmation of Charges Hearing and in the Related Proceedings, ICC-01/09-02/11-267, 26 August 2011, para 63; ICC, *Prosecutor v. Jean-Pierre Bemba Gombo*, Pre-Trial Chamber III, Fourth Decision on Victims' Participation, ICC-01/05-01/08-320, 12 December 2008, para 72.

provide a precise description of the items stolen.[138] More precise information detailing the harm suffered by victims may become relevant for the purposes of reparation proceedings before a trial chamber.[139]

Despite this, where an organisation or institution applies to participate as a victim, some decisions have required the person acting on its behalf to submit, in addition to the evidence mentioned in Sect. 3.2.1.1, any credible document establishing that the organisation has sustained 'direct harm to any of [its] property which is dedicated to religion, education, art or science or charitable purposes, and to their historic monuments, hospitals and other places and objects for humanitarian purposes' pursuant to Rule 85(b).[140] It is however not clear whether this requirement would be satisfied by the statement of the person acting on behalf of the organisation (for example in the application form), describing the harm suffered.

The Pre-Trial Judge of the STL has required as a general rule that victim applicants produce documentary evidence of the harm sustained to substantiate their applications. Although in his decision setting forth the principles for the admission of victims in the *Ayyash* et al. case, he seemed open to admit a certain degree of flexibility in exceptional cases,[141] or where the production of official documents was not possible,[142] the Pre-Trial Judge has in practice applied a very high threshold with regard to the evidence required to support an applicant's claim.[143]

---

[138] ICC, *Prosecutor v. Jean-Pierre Bemba Gombo*, Trial Chamber III, Decision on 653 Applications by Victims to Participate in the Proceeding, ICC-01/05-01/08-1091, 23 December 2010, para 31.

[139] ICC, *Prosecutor v. Bosco Ntaganda*, Pre-Trial Chamber II, Decision on Victims' Participation at the Confirmation of Charges Hearing and in the Related Proceedings, ICC-01/04-02/06-211, 15 January 2014, para 62.

[140] ICC, *Prosecutor v. Thomas Lubanga Dyilo,* Trial Chamber I, Decision on Victims' Participation, ICC-01/04-01/06-1119, 18 January 2008, para 89; ICC, *Prosecutor v. Francis Kirimi Muthaura, Uhuru Muigai Kenyatta and Mohammed Hussein Ali,* Pre-Trial Chamber II, First Decision on Victims' Participation in the Case, ICC-01/09-02/11-23, 30 March 2011, para 10; ICC, *Prosecutor v. William Samoei Ruto, Henry Kiprono Kosgey and Joshua Arap Sang*, Pre-Trial Chamber II, First Decision on Victims' Participation in the Case, ICC-01/09-01/11-17, 30 March 2011, para 10.

[141] STL, *Prosecutor v. Ayyash* et al., Pre-Trial Judge, Decision on Victims' Participation in the Proceedings, STL-11-01/PT/PTJ, 8 May 2012, para 74.

[142] Ibid., para 67. See also para 52, in which the Pre-Trial Judge held the following in relation to the proof requirements of direct result: 'What evidence (be it documentary or otherwise) is sufficient to satisfy this requirement should be assessed on a case by case basis and taking into account all relevant circumstances. [...] If all reasonable steps to provide official documents or a written statement to that effect have been taken, but yielded no results, applicants must notify the Pre-Trial Judge of the impossibility of producing the required documents and the reasons therefor.'

[143] Written correspondence with Megan Hirst, former legal officer, Victims' Participation Unit, STL, 7 March 2015 (records on file with the author).

The Pre-Trial Judge gave examples of the types of documents that he would accept to prove harm. They included, for physical harm: medical records of the harm sustained, such as medical reports from a doctor, hospital or health centre, X-rays and scan results and prescriptions for medication;[144] for material harm: the Pre-Trial Judge suggested documents such as "title deeds, registration papers or equivalent documents establishing ownership in Lebanon, as well as invoices, insurance certificates and similar materials" to prove title over property. The material harm suffered could also be shown by "insurance claim documents and other documentary evidence (for example, photographs or audio-visual footage of the damaged property)". In exceptional cases, the Pre-Trial Judge said that he may consider "other documents as proof of material harm, such as witness statements attesting to the material damage suffered by an applicant." In the case of loss of income, proof of prior income should be provided, in the form of, *inter alia*, "employment contracts, payslips and tax returns, as well as of the victim's inability to work either temporarily or permanently." To prove the latter, the applicant could submit documentary evidence of, "*inter alia*: (i) a destroyed workplace; (ii) a disability; or (iii) receipt of unemployment benefits."[145] For mental harm, evidence of the harm suffered should be provided, "in the form of an attestation by a qualified medical practitioner, psychologist, psychiatrist or counsellor."[146]

Applicants claiming to have suffered physical or mental harm as direct victims need to show at a minimum that they were present at the scene of the attack at the relevant time. If all reasonable steps to provide official documents or a written statement to that effect have been taken, but yielded no results, applicants must notify the Pre-Trial Judge of the impossibility of producing the required documents, as well as the reasons therefor.[147] The same requirements apply *mutatis mutandis* to applicants claiming to have suffered material harm as a direct result of the attack, as they must show at a minimum that the asset(s) that have been damaged or destroyed were located in the proximity of the scene of the crime.[148]

At the ECCC, the victim application form asks civil party applicants to provide information about the harm suffered, such as records regarding any medical or psychological treatment, and to provide a copy, if available. The same applies to physical records of any property loss. In practice, victims have been accepted without having provided such documents.[149]

---

[144] STL, *Prosecutor v. Ayyash* et al., Pre-Trial Judge, Decision on Victims' Participation in the Proceedings, STL-11-01/PT/PTJ, 8 May 2012, paras 62 and 67.

[145] STL, *Prosecutor v. Ayyash* et al., Pre-Trial Judge, Decision on Victims' Participation in the Proceedings, STL-11-01/PT/PTJ, 8 May 2012, paras 74–75.

[146] Ibid., para 79.

[147] Ibid., para 52.

[148] Ibid., para 54.

[149] Written correspondence with Eleonor Fernandez, Senior legal Consultant, Civil Party Lead Co-Lawyers Section, ECCC, 23 and 29 March 2015 (records on file with the author).

As explained above, the ICC Appeals Chamber has held that close personal relationships are a precondition of participation by indirect victims for the personal harm they suffered as a result of a crime committed against another,[150] and chambers have recognised immediate family members, such as parents, children, siblings and spouses as indirect victims. In order to authorise an indirect victim to participate based on the presumption that they suffered as a result of the harm inflicted on their loved one, the Appeals Chamber has ruled in the *Kony* et al. case, that the applicant must provide proof of the identity of the direct victim and of his or her kinship with the applicant.[151] The type of document that should be provided is usually assessed on a case-by-case basis. Relevant circumstances, including the context in which the Court operates, are taken into account. For instance, in the *Katanga and Ngudjolo Chui* case, Trial Chamber II took into consideration the difficulties encountered by applicants living in the Ituri region (in the DRC) in providing documents proving the death of a family member or their family relationship with that person. The Chamber accepted the submission of a certificate signed by two credible witnesses to establish the death of a person or that individual's family relationship with the applicant. It further recalled that 'in order to assess the credibility of witnesses who signed these declarations, it [would] take into consideration, non-cumulatively, factors such as the nature and length of the relationship of those witnesses with the applicant, or their standing in the community.'[152]

In the case of non-immediate family members or persons outside the family, the applicant was required to provide information or evidence of a sufficient proximity. In the *Banda and Jerbo* case, the Trial Chamber granted participant status to members of the extended family of a victim (nephew, niece, uncles, aunts, sister-in-law and cousin), who had provided statements on the roles extended family members play in their culture as well as information describing their family relationship to the direct victim, along with personal recollections of the emotional harm suffered or the loss of economic support arising from the death. The Trial Chamber did not grant such status to some other members of the extended family when it found that it had not been provided with adequate individualised personal recollections of the emotional harm suffered. It also rejected an application from a

[150] ICC, *Prosecutor v. Thomas Lubanga Dyilo*, Appeals Chamber, Judgment on the Appeals of the Prosecutor and the Defence against Trial Chamber I's Decision on Victims' Participation of 18 January 2008, ICC-01/04-01/06-1432, 11 July 2008, para 32.

[151] ICC, *Prosecutor v. Kony* et al., Appeals Chamber, Judgment on the Appeals of the Defence Against the Decisions Entitled "Decision on victims' applications for participation a/0010/06, a/0064/06 to a/0070/06, a/0081/06, a/0082/06, a/0084/06 to a/0089/06, a/0091/06 to a/0097/06, a/0099/06, a/0100/06, a/0102/06 to a/0104/06, a/0111/06, a/0113/06 to a/0117/06, a/0120/06, a/0121/06 and a/0123/06 to a/0127/06" of Pre-Trial Chamber II, ICC-02/04-01/05-371, 23 February 2009, para 1.

[152] ICC, *Prosecutor v. Germain Katanga and Mathieu Ngudjolo Chui*, Trial Chamber II, Public Redacted Version of Grounds for the Decision on the 345 Applications for Participation in the Proceedings Submitted by Victims, ICC-01/04-01/07-1491-Red, 23 September 2009, para 38.

close friend of the same victim, finding that there was no information establishing that the relationship could be assimilated to that of a close family bond.[153] The Chamber further found that the information provided by a relative and by the close friend of the direct victim did not demonstrate financial dependency, in the form of financial support provided by the direct victim, such that the death of the direct victim could be understood to have reasonably resulted in economic loss for the applicants.[154]

At the STL, indirect victims have to show (i) the mental harm they have suffered; as well as provide evidence of (ii) the harm suffered by the direct victim; and (iii) their kinship or otherwise close personal relationship with the direct victim.[155] There is however one exception to this requirement. In case of death of the direct victim, the harm suffered by immediate family members is presumed and the applicant only has to show proof of harm suffered by the direct victim (for example a death certificate) and proof of the relationship with the direct victim, for instance, through a family record book or the statements of credible witnesses.[156] However, there is an assumption that if the direct victim sustained only minor injuries, the indirect victim would not have suffered emotional distress reaching the level of harm required for the granting of VPP status, unless shown otherwise.[157]

At the ECCC, the Trial Chamber in *Case 001* considered that immediate family members could be presumed to have suffered harm and therefore be indirect victims. The indirect victim needed however to prove that their relative or loved one had been detained in one of the detention centres with which the case was concerned (i.e. S-21 or S-24). The Trial Chamber and Supreme Court Chamber accepted documents such as registers, detainee lists, photographs, recorded confessions, and biographies in the preliminary part where they recorded the detainee's identity and could not reasonably be presumed to have been obtained under torture. When the name of the direct victim was not found in registers and no other documentary evidence could prove the direct victim's detention, civil party status was denied to the applicant. The status was also denied when the information provided was deemed unreliable, such as when it was based on hearsay from a source qualified by the Chamber as 'highly dubious'.[158]

[153]ICC, *Prosecutor v. Abdallah Banda Abakaer Nourain*, Trial Chamber IV, Decision on 19 Applications to Participate in the Proceedings, ICC-02/05-03/09-528, 12 December 2013, paras 34–35.

[154]Ibid., para 36.

[155]STL, *Prosecutor v. Ayyash* et al., Pre-Trial Judge, Decision on Victims' Participation in the Proceedings, STL-11-01/PT/PTJ, 8 May 2012, paras 50 and 82.

[156]Ibid., para 84.

[157]Written correspondence with Megan Hirst, former legal officer, Victims' Participation Unit, STL, 14 May 2015 (records on file with the author).

[158]ECCC, *Case 001*, Supreme Court Chamber, Appeal Judgment, Case No. 001/18-07-/2007/ECCC/SC, 3 February 2012, paras 547 and 551.

In order to establish kinship, the Trial Chamber accepted birth certificates and identity cards, attestations from commune chiefs, election cards and voter registration forms, and photographs accompanied by statements from third parties.[159] In *Case 002*, when assessing the appeals of rejected civil party applications, the Pre-Trial Chamber applied a presumption of collective injury based on the nature of victimisation in the context of mass atrocities underlying crimes against humanity and genocide.[160] This presumption entails that a civil party applicant who is not part of the family of the direct victim can still submit that he/she was a member of the same targeted group and that the psychological harm the applicant suffered arises from the harm suffered by the direct victim.[161]

3.4 Key Points

- When it comes to assessing victims' applications, the three courts (ICC, ECCC and STL) have had to deal with the logistics of allowing victims to participate on a potentially massive scale without overwhelming the proceedings. This has required striking a balance between being satisfied overall with the reliability of victims' applications, while ensuring that such requirements are not so demanding that participation would become inaccessible.
- Flexibility regarding certain requirements has helped to deal with the contextual difficulties faced by the victims in proving the required elements for participation.
- This chapter has revealed important similarities in the practice of the three courts, as regards the requirements and the type of documents that are recognised to substantiate an application.

Substantive requirements for participation: identity, harm, and causal link

- The first requirement verified by all three courts is that the victim is a natural person whose identity appears to be duly established. All three courts have asked that applicants provide documentary means of identification.
- The three courts have allowed for the possibility that a person applies on behalf of a victim, when the latter cannot legally give consent either because this person is disabled or underage. In those cases, the person applying on his or her behalf needs to provide proof of identity and proof of the relationship to the victim.

[159] Ibid., para 526.

[160] See ECCC, *Case 002,* Pre-Trial Chamber, Decision on Appeals Against Orders of the Co-Investigating Judges on the Admissibility of Civil Party Applications, Case No. 002/19-09-2007/ECCC/OCIJ, 24 June 2011, para 86.

[161] See ECCC, *Case 002*, Pre-Trial Chamber, Decision on Appeals Against Orders of the Co-Investigating Judges on the Admissibility of Civil Party Applications, Case No. 002/19-09-2007/ECCC/OCIJ, 24 June 2011, para 93.

- At the ICC, the jurisprudence has been inconsistent on the question of whether a deceased victim can participate via a person acting on his or her behalf. At the ECCC, successors can resume participation on behalf of civil parties who die during the proceedings. At the STL no application has been made to date for any form of participation by a deceased victim.
- The harm recognised by the three courts can be categorised into three types: physical, psychological and material.
- Certain ICC chambers have also recognised as harm the substantial impairment of a fundamental right, based on the Declaration of Basic Principles of Justice for Victims of Crime and Abuse of Power.
- At the STL, the definition of victim set out in Rule 2 of the STL RPE refers to physical, material or mental harm in a way which appears to suggest that these categories are exhaustive rather than inclusive as it the case at the ICC.
- Harm is defined in Rule 23*bis*(1)(b) of the ECCC Internal Rules as 'physical, material or psychological injury.'
- All three courts allow, in one way or another, the participation of indirect victims.
- In all three courts participation in the proceedings is limited to those victims who have suffered from the specific crimes which are the subject of the proceedings.

Evidentiary matters

- The legal texts and jurisprudence of the three courts have set out a relatively similar standard of review to grant participating victim or civil party status.
- The main difference between the practices of the three courts when it comes to victims' applications relates to the type of documents required to support an application to participate. Whereas all three courts require applicants to provide documentary proof of identification, it is only the STL that requires, as a general rule, documentary proof of the harm suffered.
- At the ICC, corroborative documentary evidence of the harm suffered has not been required.
- At the ECCC, the victim application form asks civil party applicants to provide information on the harm suffered. In practice, victims have been accepted without having provided documentary evidence of harm.
- At the ICC, indirect victim applicants are required to submit proof of the identity of the direct victim and his or her kinship with the applicant.
- At the STL, indirect victims must show the mental harm they have suffered and provide evidence of the harm suffered by the direct victim, together with proof of their kinship or otherwise close personal relationship with the direct victim. The mental harm suffered by immediate family members of a deceased direct victim is presumed so long as the death and the kinship with the deceased is proved.
- At the ECCC, immediate family members of direct victims are presumed to have suffered harm.

References

Pham PN, Vinck P, Balthazard M, Strasser J, Om C (2011) Victim participation and the trial of Duch at the Extraordinary Chambers in the Courts of Cambodia. J Hum Rights Pract 3:264–287

United Nations General Assembly (1985) Declaration of Basic Principles of Justice for Victims of Crime and Abuse of Power, UN Doc. A/RES/40/34 (1985)

United Nations General Assembly (2006) Basic Principles and Guidelines on the Right to a Remedy and Reparation for Victims of Gross Violations of International Human Rights Law and Serious Violations of International Humanitarian Law, UN Doc. A/RES/60/147 (2006)

Chapter 4
The Role of Intermediaries and Third Parties in Victim Participation

Mariana Pena

Abstract This chapter seeks to draw practitioners' attention to the extent and importance of the role played by intermediaries and other parties in support for victims to exercise their rights before international criminal courts. The chapter explains the reasons that have led to reliance on third parties and describes the different tasks in which third parties have been involved. It offers practical considerations on both advantages and opportunities, and challenges involved when cooperating with third parties. The chapter also describes the legal and administrative framework applicable to intermediaries collaborating with the International Criminal Court (ICC) and provides critical analysis in relation to the ICC Guidelines on intermediaries. Practical advice is included for practitioners who may consider using, or have to rely on, third parties.

Keywords Intermediaries · Third parties · Civil society · Non-governmental organisations/NGOs · Guidelines

---

Mariana Pena is a legal officer with the Open Society Justice Initiative. This chapter draws extensively on the author's prior experience working with participating victims, legal representatives and other civil society organisations. The author would like to acknowledge the International Refugee Rights Initiative for allowing her to draw on research she conducted on their behalf on the question of intermediaries. The views expressed herein are those of the author and do not necessarily reflect the views of the Open Society Foundations. This chapter was written in 2014 and updated in September 2016.

M. Pena (✉)
The Hague, The Netherlands
e-mail: marianacpena@gmail.com

K. Tibori-Szabó and M. Hirst (eds.), *Victim Participation in International Criminal Justice*, International Criminal Justice Series 11,
DOI 10.1007/978-94-6265-177-7_4

Contents

4.1 Introduction

The introduction of victims as actors in judicial proceedings before international criminal courts has led in practice to the informal intervention of other parties which inform, introduce and support victims in these processes. These actors have received a great deal of attention in proceedings before the International Criminal Court (ICC). However, and although they have not attracted the level of controversy and visibility in proceedings as their peers at the ICC, third parties have also played a very significant role before the Extraordinary Chambers in the Court of Cambodia (ECCC). Specific traits of the Special Tribunal for Lebanon (STL), including the nature of the crimes and the number of victim participants, have limited the need for such intervention before that court.

These actors, commonly referred to as 'intermediaries' at the ICC, have been defined as follows:

> An intermediary is someone who comes between one person and another; who facilitates contact or provides a link between one of the organs or units of the Court or Counsel on the one hand, and victims, witnesses, beneficiaries of reparations and/or affected communities more broadly on the other.[1]

Intermediaries became well known—and actually rather infamous—as a result of their involvement, on behalf of the ICC Office of the Prosecutor (OTP), in investigations in the *Lubanga* case.[2] However, intermediaries play a role not only in supporting the OTP in investigations, but also in respect of many other ICC functions, as reflected in the definition reproduced in the previous paragraph.

---

[1] ICC, Guidelines Governing the Relations between the Court and Intermediaries (2014b) (The 'ICC Guidelines'), https://www.icc-cpi.int/iccdocs/lt/GRCI-Eng.pdf. Accessed 20 July 2016, p. 6.

[2] De Vos 2013, pp. 1021–1024.

They have been relied upon somewhat extensively when it comes to support to victim participation. Intermediaries supporting victims may be organisations or individuals. While not necessarily always the case, it has been observed that a relevant number of intermediaries involved in victim participation are human rights activists or have links with civil society.

Independent civil society and individuals have also played a relevant role in supporting civil parties before the ECCC. The underlying reasons and the extent of their involvement differ from those of intermediaries who have collaborated with the ICC. There are, however, many similarities, and interventions before both courts highlight the need for victims to receive support from external parties to access and exercise their rights before international courts.

This chapter is divided in three parts. It will first look at who the independent parties that support victims in accessing the courts are and how they interact with the courts. Second, it will briefly summarise some of the advantages and disadvantages of those parties' involvement. Finally, it will discuss their legal status, and the rights and duties that have been recognised to them. The conclusion also offers practical advice for practitioners.

The use of the term 'third parties' in this chapter should be understood as referring to those organisations and individuals that assist victims in accessing the courts for the purpose of exercising their rights. The terms 'non-governmental organisations (NGOs)' or 'civil society' will be used to refer to those third parties when applicable (especially in the context of the ECCC). 'Intermediaries' will be used primarily when referring to third parties in the context of the ICC.

As indicated above, intermediaries and third parties may collaborate with different organs of the courts, as well as counsel, and perform different functions. This chapter will focus solely on their role and involvement in relation to support to victim participants, civil parties and beneficiaries of reparations.

4.2 Who Are These Third Parties and How Do They Interact with International Courts When It Comes to Victim Participation?

It is relevant to note at the outset that the intervention of third parties came about as a spontaneous phenomenon. As such, it was not specifically planned nor defined in advance. Nor was such intervention foreseen in the courts' core legal texts.[3] The

[3] There is no reference to third parties or intermediaries in either the Rome Statute of the International Criminal Court (ICC Statute) or the ICC Rules of Procedure and Evidence (the 'ICC RPE'). The term 'intermediaries' was, however, introduced into the Regulations of the Court (Regulation 97 of the Regulations of the Court, ICC-BD/01-03-11 (2012)) and the Regulations of the Trust Fund for Victims (Regulations 67 and 71 of the Regulations of the Trust Fund for Victims, ICC-ASP/4/Res.3 (2005)) (ICC Regulations of the Trust Fund for Victims). While the initial version of the ECCC Internal Rules had some references to non-governmental organisations, those did not concern the intermediary role played in relation to assistance to civil parties.

assistance in particular of civil society organisations could be expected as an extension of such organisations' intense involvement in the creation of the courts, and some specifically in advocacy for the recognition of victims' rights.[4] As a phenomenon that was not specifically or carefully planned, the involvement of third parties in victim participation is the result of practice and evolution of both the role and needs of victims, as well as developments in judicial proceedings and in the relevant countries.

As will be described below in more detail, third parties assist victims who wish to become participants or civil parties in international criminal proceedings and/or request reparations to exercise their rights, and they do so through a variety of tasks. As indicated above, a large number of those assisting victims are civil society organisations, whether international NGOs or local grass-roots associations. Individuals including local activists, community leaders, religious leaders, lawyers and victims themselves may also fulfil that role. It is important to highlight that intervention of third parties has worked both at third parties' initiatives as well as in response to requests from the courts.

The following sub-sections will provide more details as to the specific conditions that led to the involvement of third parties in the context of each of the courts. It will also describe the manner in which they have assisted in different activities to support victims' involvement and their claims.

4.2.1 ICC

Intermediaries have emerged as a result of the limitations of the ICC. The reasons why the Court has sought to collaborate with local partners include their understanding of local context; knowledge of local languages; cultural and physical proximity to the victim communities; trust of members of those communities and ability to operate in a covert manner.[5] These traits are essential for the ICC to reach out to victims. Another factor that needs to be taken into account is the high numbers of victims likely to be in a position to exercise their rights given the very nature of the crimes that the ICC is called to try.[6] In addition, the crimes that the Court investigates have often been committed over a vast geographical area. Therefore, intermediaries have filled the gaps created by the ICC's financial, physical and ideological limitations to reach out to numerous victims in distant and remote locations.

---

[4] For an overview of the role of civil society in the lead-up to the adoption of the ICC Statute, see generally Glasius 2002.

[5] ICC Guidelines, p. 2.

[6] The number of participating victims has gone from a few hundred in the first two ICC cases to several thousands in more recent cases.

4.2.1.1 Outreach to Victims and Form Collection

According to the ICC legal texts, the Registry is in charge of administering victim participation.[7] Responsibilities in relation to administration of victim participation include assisting victims and groups of victims,[8] including by providing information on the right to participate in proceedings and allowing victims to make an informed decision about their participation, and by disseminating standard application forms and assisting in completion of such forms.[9]

When the ICC Registry started undertaking this task, it soon became apparent that the help of other actors with a presence on the ground would be necessary in order for the application forms to be disseminated widely and 'most efficiently reach wide-spread and often hard to access victims.'[10] The Regulations of the Court, adopted in 2004, established that '[the] standard application forms shall, to the extent possible, be made available to victims, groups of victims, or intergovernmental and non-governmental organisations, which may assist in their dissemination, as widely as possible.'[11] The Regulations of the Registry, adopted in 2006, have further established that

> In order to ensure that the application forms […] are completed as efficiently as possible, the Registry may establish contact and maintain regular relations with the groups mentioned in Regulation 86, sub-regulation 1, of the Regulations of the Court, and may, *inter alia*, prepare guidance booklets and other materials, or provide education and training, in order to guide those assisting victims in completing the standard application forms.[12]

In practice, the Registry has made a very extensive use of intermediaries to reach out to victims and to assist them in completing the application forms. The Registry has indeed acknowledged that it has found it 'exceedingly difficult to communicate effectively with victims in remote and/or hard to reach locations [or due to] security or lack of [human or financial] resources.'[13] The ICC reported in 2012 that '[f]or the most part, local intermediaries (rather than Court staff or a lawyer) assist victims in completing their applications for participation.'[14]

In short, the practice of the ICC Registry has been to make standard application forms available to local intermediaries and to train those intermediaries to

---

[7] ICC RPE, Rule 16.

[8] ICC Regulations of the Court, Regulation 86(9).

[9] See e.g. Proposed Programme Budget for 2014 of the International Criminal Court, ICC-ASP/12/10 (2013), paras 531–532.

[10] ICC, Report of the Court on the Revised Strategy in relation to Victims, ICC-ASP/11/40 (2012), para 39.

[11] ICC Regulations of the Court, Regulation 86(1).

[12] Regulation 105 of the ICC Regulations of the Registry, ICC-BD/03-01-06 (2013).

[13] ICC, Report of the Court on the Revised Strategy in relation to Victims, ICC-ASP/11/40 (2012), para 17.

[14] Ibid., para 39.

enable them to assist victims filling in the forms.[15] As we shall see below, the ICC chambers and Registry have revisited this practice in recent cases with the aim of enhancing efficiency in collection and administration of application forms through increased engagement of Registry staff. The revised practice also involves 'provision of target support to a smaller number of intermediaries who go through an enhanced selection process.'[16] However, as we shall also see, despite some adjustment in practice, the ICC Registry has continued to resort extensively to intermediaries for the purpose of outreach to victims and assistance in form completion.

4.2.1.2 Support to Legal Representation

Victims' lawyers are under an obligation to keep their clients informed about developments in the proceedings and to receive instructions from them. Regular communication between the victims and their lawyers is essential for victims to exercise their right to participate in a meaningful manner. Given the distance between the Court and the countries where the ICC is undertaking investigations at present and the high numbers of participating victims, reaching out to victims can generally only be done with the help of intermediaries. The ICC has put in place different models for legal representation of victims.[17] Some of those models have included the set-up of a support structure in the field to assist the legal representatives in communicating with their clients.[18] In some cases, the chambers have ordered that the legal representatives themselves be based in the country where the victims reside.[19] Finally, in other cases, the Court has set up a structure that combines participation of counsel from the Office of Public Counsel for Victims (OPCV) and locally-based team members.[20]

---

[15] ICC, *Prosecutor v. Bosco Ntaganda*, Registry, Registry Observations in compliance with the Decision ICC-01/04-02/06-54-Conf, ICC-01/04-02/06-57, 6 May 2013, para 3.

[16] ICC, Report of the Court on the Revised Strategy in relation to Victims, ICC-ASP/11/40 (2012), para 44. In addition, while the Registry initially worked primarily with national human rights organisations, it later shifted towards grassroots organisations or individuals with a prominent role in the communities. See Avocats sans frontières (ASF) 2013, pp. 19–20.

[17] The ICC's approach to the legal representation of victims is further discussed in Chap. 5.

[18] E.g. ICC, *Prosecutor v. Germain Katanga and Matthieu Ngudjolo Chui*, Trial Chamber II, Order on the organisation of common legal representation of victims, ICC-01/04-01/07-1328, 22 July 2009, para 17.

[19] ICC, *Prosecutor v. William Samoei Ruto & Joshua Arap Sang*, Trial Chamber V, Decision on victims' representation and participation, ICC-01/09-01/11-460, 3 October 2012, para 60; *Prosecutor v. Uhuru Muigiai Kenyatta*, Trial Chamber V, Decision on victims' participation and representation, ICC-01/09-02/11-498, 3 October 2012, para 59.

[20] E.g. ICC, *Prosecutor v. Laurent Gbagbo*, Pre-Trial Chamber I, Decision on Victims' Participation and Victims' Common Legal Representation at the Confirmation of Charges Hearing and in the Related Proceedings, ICC-02/11-01/11-138, 4 June 2012, para 44.

The creation of support structures, appointment of field personnel and orders for the legal representative to be based in the country concerned acknowledge the importance of direct and regular communication with the victims and reduce in principle the need to resort to intermediaries. However, while teams who have a base in the relevant countries have been able to establish direct contact with the victims and victim communities, they continue to use intermediaries to different degrees.[21] The extent to which intermediaries are used depends on factors such as the number of participating victims and the geographical area over which they are spread. For example, in cases that feature crimes committed in different and distant locations or where victims were displaced over a large area as a result of the crimes,[22] the presence of field-based personnel proves insufficient to reach out to all clients in a significant manner. It is also relevant to note that in some cases, where field personnel, a legal representative or external counsel assisting the OPCV are based in the field, they may be based in the capital cities of the countries concerned, which are not always (close to) the areas where the victims live.[23]

Assistance offered to support legal representation is different from that provided to reach out to victims and help fill application or registration forms. Again, the exact role will be shaped by the presence of legal representation team members in the field or lack thereof, the number and location of victims and the tasks at hand. Some legal representatives have used intermediaries, for example, to notify decisions to clients, to mobilise large numbers of victims to attend meetings with the legal representative, and/or to monitor victims' security.

Intermediaries who assist victims' lawyers may be the same as those who assisted the victims initially to apply for participation in the proceedings. Those intermediaries have often an established relationship of trust with the members of the communities. Their assistance can be crucial to help create a relationship of trust between victims and their lawyer when the latter is appointed by the Court and not the victims themselves.

4.2.1.3 Implementation of Assistance Projects and Reparations

The word 'intermediary' is included in the Regulations of the Trust Fund for Victims. According to Regulation 67:

> The Trust Fund may decide to use intermediaries to facilitate the disbursement of reparations awards, as necessary, where to do so would provide greater access to the beneficiary group and would not create a conflict of interest. Intermediaries may include interested

[21] ICC, ASF 2013, p. 21.

[22] For example, victims in *Prosecutor v. William Samoei Ruto & Joshua Arap Sang*.

[23] For example, Nairobi in *Prosecutor v. William Samoei Ruto & Joshua Arap Sang* (most victims are in the Rift Valley); Kinshasa for *Prosecutor v. Bosco Ntaganda* case (victims are in the Ituri district, Eastern Democratic Republic of Congo).

> States, intergovernmental organisations, as well as national or international nongovernmental organisations working in close proximity with the beneficiary groups.[24]

The ICC Trust Fund has a dual mandate. It implements Court-ordered reparations following conviction of an accused for specific crimes, and it provides assistance (physical and psychosocial rehabilitation and material support) to victims of crimes within the jurisdiction of the Court and their families.[25]

The Trust Fund has worked with intermediaries to implement assistance projects. Those include 'local grassroots organisations, victims' survivor groups, women's associations, faith-based organisations, village savings and loans associations, and international non-governmental organisations.'[26] Practitioners should be aware that intermediaries collaborating with the Trust Fund are normally called 'implementing partners'. Other names commonly used are 'partners' and 'grantees'. In some cases implementing partners deliver assistance through grants to other (smaller) organisations (called 'sub-grantees' or 'sub-partners').[27]

Implementing partners cooperating with the Trust Fund appear to have a more established relationship than other intermediaries assisting victims to exercise their rights before the ICC. Firstly, the Trust Fund would not be able to operate (or at least would not be able to do so at a relevant scale given the size of its Secretariat) without such collaboration.[28] Secondly, the selection process is more formal, including the launching of an open tender and the involvement of procurement proceedings.[29] Finally, the Trust Fund appears to provide closer monitoring through field visits to oversee programme development, and capacity-building activities including monitoring and evaluation training.[30]

---

[24] Intermediaries are also mentioned in Regulation 71 of the Regulations of the Trust Fund: 'The Trust Fund may identify intermediaries or partners, or invite proposals for the implementation of the award.'

[25] See also Chap. 13.

[26] ICC, Report to the Assembly of States Parties on the Projects and the Activities of the Board of Directors of the Trust Fund for Victims for the Period 1 July 2013 to 30 June 2014, ICC-ASP/13/14 (2014f), para 20.

[27] See e.g. McCleary-Sills and Mukasa 2013, pp. 44 and 46.

[28] An evaluation report from 2013 considers that the use of international and local NGOs as intermediaries to provide assistance to beneficiaries is a relevant cost-effective measure in the implementation of assistance by the Trust Fund. See McCleary-Sills and Mukasa 2013, p. 43.

[29] See e.g. ICC, Press Release, ICC's Trust Fund for Victims Launches Expression of Interest Supporting Victim Survivors of Sexual and Gender-Based Violence in the Central African Republic (6 May 2011), http://www.icc-cpi.int/en_menus/icc/press%20and%20media/press%20releases/press%20releases%20(2011)/Pages/pr660.aspx. Accessed 19 October 2014.

[30] See e.g. ICC, Report to the Assembly of States Parties on the Projects and the Activities of the Board of Directors of the Trust Fund for Victims for the Period 1 July 2013 to 30 June 2014, ICC-ASP/13/14 (2014f), para 20; ICC Trust Fund for Victims, TFV Strategic Plan for 2014–2017 (2014), http://www.trustfundforvictims.org/sites/default/files/media_library/documents/pdf/TFV_Strategic_Plan_2014_2017__approved.pdf. Accessed 2 November 2014; ICC Trust Fund for Victims, Programme Progress Report Summer 2013 (2013), http://www.trustfundforvictims.org/sites/default/files/media_library/documents/pdf/TFVSummer2013PPR_FINAL_VERSION___rev_060913.pdf. Accessed 2 November 2014.

At the time of writing the ICC does not yet have experience in the implementation of reparations awards.[31] It is likely that a process akin to the one used for delivery of assistance will be used to implement reparations, in particular with regard to collaboration with implementing partners.[32]

The reparations proceedings in the *Lubanga* case are ongoing at the time of writing. Following the Appeals Chamber's decision on the principles and procedure applicable to reparations[33] the Trust Fund for Victims submitted its filing on reparations and draft implementation plan.[34] Part of this plan referring to symbolic reparations was approved by Trial Chamber II on 21 October 2016.[35] The implementation plan proposed to rely heavily on intermediaries, which it refers to as implementing partners. The plan pledged that, once it was approved by the Chamber, the Trust Fund would consider the availability of intermediaries, and their respective skill sets and presence in Ituri province at that time, and assess them against the technical programmatic qualities of the approved implementation plan to determine whether or not it was appropriate to sole source some or all of the reparations projects to implementing partners, or rather to use an open tender procurement process.[36] The plan also noted that implementing partners must pose no conflict of interest with either the Trust Fund or the ICC by way of their (other) activities or associated staff members. To avoid conflicts of interest, the plan

[31] Convictions have been handed down in the *Lubanga* Case and in the *Katanga* case respectively. In the *Lubanga* case, a decision on reparations was issued on 7 August 2012 (ICC-01/04-01/06-2904), and it was appealed. The Appeals Chamber handed down its decision on 3 March 2015 (ICC-01/04-01/06-3129). On 3 November 2015, the Trust Fund submitted to Trial Chamber II its 'Filing on Reparations and Draft Implementation Plan' (ICC-01/04-01/06-3177-Red). No reparations decision has yet been adopted in the *Katanga* case.

[32] ICC, Report of the Court and the Trust Fund for Victims on the rules to be observed for the payment of reparations, ICC-ASP/13/7 (2014e), paras 4–7. See also ICC, *Prosecutor v. Thomas Lubanga Dyilo*, Trust Fund for Victims, Observations on Reparations in Response to the Scheduling Order of 14 March 2012, ICC-01/04-01/06-2872, 25 April 2012, paras 204, 214, 227; ICC, *Prosecutor v. Thomas Lubanga Dyilo*, Trial Chamber I, Decision establishing the principles and procedures to be applied to reparations, ICC-01/04-01/06-2904, 7 August 2012, para 197 (N.B. The role of the Trust Fund in reparations proceedings was one of the issues litigated in the appeals of the decision on reparations in *Lubanga* Case. See paras 181–184 of ICC-01/04-01/06-3129).

[33] ICC, *Prosecutor v. Thomas Lubanga Dyilo*, Appeals Chamber, Judgment on the appeals against the "Decision establishing the principles and procedures to be applied to reparations" of 7 August 2012 with amended order for reparations (Annex A) and public annexes 1 and 2, ICC-01/04-01/06-3129, 3 March 2015.

[34] ICC, *Prosecutor v. Thomas Lubanga Dyilo,* Trust Fund for Victims, Filing on Reparations and Draft Implementation Plan, ICC-01/04-01/06-3177-Red, 3 November 2015.

[35] ICC, *Prosecutor v. Thomas Lubanga Dyilo*, Trial Chamber II, Order approving the proposed plan of the Trust Fund for victims in relation to symbolic collective reparations, ICC-01/04-01/06-3251, 21 October 2016.

[36] ICC, *Prosecutor v. Thomas Lubanga Dyilo*, Trust Fund for Victims, Draft Implementation Plan for collective reparations to victims, Trust Fund for Victims. ICC-01/04-01/06-3177-AnxA, 3 November 2015, para 181.

recommended that Trust Fund implementing partners should not be engaged as intermediaries with the ICC's organs or sections.[37] Moreover, the Trust Fund would only consider proposals from non-governmental organisations and technical service providers that:

(a) Have been legally registered in the DRC for at least 2 years, and are in compliance with all required laws, regulations and other requirements of the Government of the DRC (as demonstrated by a registration certificate);
(b) Have in place appropriate and functional management and governance structures with decision-making authority positioned in the DRC;
(c) Are DRC entities in accordance with the requirements and spirit of the national NGO policy;
(d) Have a demonstrable record of sound financial management and successful implementation of comparable grant-funded projects;
(e) Meet any additional technical competencies referenced in the collective reparation proposal template.[38]

While these criteria at first glance appear to be justifiable efforts to protect the integrity of the reparations process, it remains to be seen whether the Trust Fund will find it possible to identify intermediaries meeting such requirements. Given the length of time for which the OTP and the Registry have been active in Ituri and particularly in dealing with victim communities, it is equally unclear whether appropriate intermediaries exist which have not already had longstanding dealings with those other parts of the Court.

4.2.2 ECCC

While the emergence of third parties' assistance to victims in the context of ECCC proceedings bears some similarities with the reasons that led the ICC to resort to intermediaries, there are differences. In contrast to the ICC, which from the outset had the budget and capability—even if limited—to reach out to victims and pay for legal representation, the ECCC initially lacked the capacity, infrastructure and funding to undertake such tasks. Those tasks were also not prioritised in the beginning due to many other competing concerns in the set-up of the ECCC.[39] This gap

[37] Ibid., para 184. The Trust Fund has already implemented a policy of not working with intermediaries who have assisted other ICC organs/sections when implementing its assistance mandate.

[38] Ibid., para 185. The same details were reiterated in a subsequent, supplementing filing (ICC, *Prosecutor v. Thomas Lubanga Dyilo*, Trust Fund for Victims, Additional Programme Information Filing, ICC-01/04-01/06-3209, 7 June 2016, paras 45–48).

[39] Sperfeldt 2012, pp. 152 and 158.

was filled in by civil society organisations, which in practice took over roles and functions that belonged to the Court.[40]

4.2.2.1 Outreach to Victims and Form Collection

The ECCC started operating in 2006. However, it was not until 2009 that the ECCC's unit in charge of civil parties, the Victims Support Section (VSS), received the level of funding necessary to fulfil its mandate at a reasonable level. Prior to that, the Court relied heavily on the support of civil society organisations.[41] From 2007 onwards, a relevant number of Cambodian NGOs started to include information related to the intervention of civil parties in their ECCC outreach programmes.[42] By 2008, the level of involvement and organisation of NGOs in outreach to victims and support to fill out victim information forms and submission of those forms to the Court was quite impressive.[43] Some NGOs established programmes to support this process.[44] Outreach programmes included the organisation of workshops in different provinces and districts, use of regional offices to disseminate information about the ECCC and victims' rights, radio programmes and distribution of monthly magazines.[45]

Even though the capacity of the VSS increased in 2009, the role of NGOs continued to be crucial in support for victims to access the Court. In 2011, the ECCC reported that about 84% of all victim forms received had been submitted through intermediary NGOs.[46] In contrast to the ICC, there appears to be more of a recognition at the ECCC of the role played by civil society/intermediary organisations. At the ICC, the extent to which core functions of the Court have been delegated to intermediaries is often not acknowledged. In contrast, the ECCC appears to have been more open, especially given the financial constraints that left it with no option but to rely largely on the work of NGOs for victim participation purposes.[47]

[40] Ibid., p. 152.

[41] Ibid., p. 156.

[42] Ibid., p. 151.

[43] Notes from author's mission to Phnom Penh in February 2008 on behalf of Fédération internationale des ligues des droits de l'Homme (FIDH) (records on file with the author).

[44] Sperfeldt 2012, p. 152.

[45] Notes from author's mission to Phnom Penh in February 2008 on behalf of FIDH (records on file with the author).

[46] Sperfeldt 2012, p. 151.

[47] For example, names and contact details of intermediary organisations are listed on the ECCC website. https://www.eccc.gov.kh/en/victims-support/intermediary-organizations-ios-0. Accessed 18 January 2017.

4.2.2.2 Support to Legal Representation

Initially, the ECCC did not offer legal aid to civil parties who could not afford to pay for legal representation. This function was therefore also assumed by NGOs, through agreements with Cambodian legal aid organisations and cooperation with international lawyers.[48] NGO outreach programmes thus developed into 'comprehensive victim support projects involving notifying survivors about the status of their applications, facilitating their legal representation and regularly informing and supporting civil parties to attend the trials and meet with their lawyers.'[49] NGO programmes have also covered eventual investigative activities by lawyers representing civil parties and most of the costs associated with civil parties' testimony in court. However, in a number of cases international lawyers who are members of the legal representation team backed by NGOs have acted on a *pro bono* basis.[50]

Grouping of civil parties for the purpose of legal representation has been done around the NGOs that supported them, and sometimes in relation to a common theme (for example, genocide against a specific group, forced marriage, diaspora victims, etc.).[51] Although an ECCC legal aid scheme was put in place in 2010, it was only meant to support the Civil Party Lead Co-Lawyers, who were put in place to play an umbrella function and represent all civil party legal teams before the Court.[52] Civil society organisations have continued to provide support to some civil party lawyers through external funding. Some of the NGOs involved have provided invaluable assistance to lawyers especially to ensure communication with their clients.[53] Cooperation with NGOs has also made it possible for civil parties to receive psychological assistance in some cases.[54] Some groups of lawyers who had an interest in assisting civil parties created their own NGOs, so that they could raise funds for that purpose.[55] Dependence on external funding and a certain degree of donor fatigue in relation to funding around the ECCC has resulted in

---

[48] Sperfeldt 2012, p. 151.

[49] Ibid., p. 156.

[50] FIDH 2012, p. 32.

[51] Ibid., p. 34. See also the lists of legal representation teams per case on the ECCC website, for *Case 001* (http://www.eccc.gov.kh/sites/default/files/List_of_Legal_Teams_001.pdf. Accessed 22 July 2016) and for *Case 002* (http://www.eccc.gov.kh/sites/default/files/List_of_Legal_Teams_case_file_002.pdf. Accessed 22 July 2016). Note that these lists may not be updated.

[52] FIDH 2012, p. 33. See Chap. 5.

[53] Interview with Silke Studzinsky, former civil party lawyer, ECCC, 22 October 2014 (records on file with the author). The NGOs that provided such support were those that had a specific ECCC programme and therefore sufficient funds to that end.

[54] This happened as a result of a memorandum of understanding between the ECCC and the Transcultural Psychological Organisation (Sperfeldt 2012, p. 156). FIDH also facilitated psychological assistance to the civil parties it supported through an agreement with the association TRACES.

[55] For example *Justice pour le Cambodge*.

significantly lower levels of support from civil society organisations to civil parties in the latest ECCC case, *Case No.002/02*, which covers a significant number of crimes committed under the Khmer Rouge regime.

4.2.2.3 Design, Fundraising and Implementation of Reparation Projects

According to the ECCC Internal Rules, victims can only receive collective and moral reparations.[56] The interpretation of that provision and the award of only a few very symbolic reparation measures in the first ECCC judgment was the object of criticisms and led to victims' disappointment.[57] Following the first judgment, which highlighted limitations in the Court's power to award reparations, the ECCC amended its Internal Rules. The amendment introduced the possibility for the Court to order implementation of reparation projects when such projects have already been designed and have secured external funding, in cases where the accused is indigent.[58] Although the awards are sought by the civil parties' lawyers and projects must be identified in cooperation with the VSS, in practice NGOs have also contributed greatly towards reparation projects' design and fundraising, and have been involved in implementation.[59] Following submissions by the Civil Parties Lead Co-Lawyers, the ECCC awarded 11 reparations projects in its second judgment, which was delivered after the entry into force of the said amendment.[60]

4.2.3 STL

The specific circumstances at the STL have made it possible for the Tribunal to work without resorting to intermediaries or third parties. The different nature of the crimes and increased accessibility of the victim groups enabled the Tribunal to establish direct contact with victims who wished to participate in the proceedings through the local liaison office. In addition, the fact that there are only 72 participating victims[61] makes it possible for the Legal Representative of Victims (and his co-counsel) to interact with victims individually through telephone or face-to-face

---

[56] Ibid., Rule 23(1)(b). See also Chap. 13.

[57] See ECCC, *Case 001*, Trial Chamber, Judgment, Case No. 001/18-07-2007/ECCC/TC, 26 July 2010, paras 660–675.

[58] Rule 23*quinquies* of the ECCC Internal Rules, Rev. 9 (2015).

[59] Interview with Alice Banens, lawyer, former member of *Justice pour le Cambodge*, 13 August 2014 (records on file with the author). See also Rule 42*bis*(2) of the ECCC Internal Rules.

[60] ECCC, *Case 002*, Trial Chamber, *Case 002/01* Judgement, Case No. 002/19-09-2007/ECCC/TC, 7 August 2014, paras 1109–1164. See also Chap. 13.

[61] As at 30 August 2016.

contact. Finally, given the victims' social and educational status and considering their relatively easier access to technology (in comparison to victims who participate in the proceedings before the ICC or the ECCC), they can also be kept informed of the proceedings through electronic communication and information posted online.

4.3 Advantages and Challenges of Using Intermediaries and Collaborating with Third Parties

Interaction with victims through third parties presents both advantages and disadvantages, for the courts and for the third parties involved. Practitioners who may need to decide whether using third parties would be appropriate in a given situation, and those who are compelled to do so in light of the circumstances, should be mindful of both the advantages and opportunities, and the challenges involved.

4.3.1 Advantages and Opportunities

The emergence of international courts has provided third parties, and in particular local civil society organisations, with an opportunity to contribute to justice for past atrocities and, through that, to the reinforcement of the rule of law in their countries or communities. In some cases, the expectations put on the courts have been immense, which has boosted local organisations' will to assist in the process. This has created concrete opportunities, including funding opportunities, for both international and local civil society organisations. Some have (partially) adapted their programmes to assist the courts in the implementation of their mandate to facilitate the participation of victims.[62] Working with the courts also provides local actors with an opportunity for capacity-building and, in some cases, to raise their profile.[63]

For international courts, one of the advantages provided by the use of intermediaries and third parties is that they have access to areas of the countries concerned where court staff would not go, either because they are difficult to access or because strict security directives apply. Local activists and organisations, instead, have an established local presence, are used to working in the areas and can easily operate with a low profile, as their presence in principle does not raise the type of suspicions that the presence of international court staff would. Local organisations can also reach out to other communities through their existing networks. In short,

62 Sperfeldt 2012, p. 158.

63 United Nations Office of the High Commissioner for Human Rights (OHCHR) 2008, p. 21.

the courts benefit from increased opportunities to reach out to a greater number of victims, including in remote locations.

Local NGOs, which often operate as third parties, had been working in the affected communities before the courts were established and will continue to do so once the latter close down or leave the country concerned. The same goes for community and other local leaders. These actors have gained the trust of members of the communities. Trust is not easy to obtain in the aftermath of atrocities and among those who were victimised. The use of third parties allows the courts to gain victims' trust through work with those whom victims already know and trust. Local third parties speak the local languages and understand the local culture. They may be able to translate complex legal concepts in ways that are accessible to persons who often do not have any prior experience with the judicial system. Their knowledge of the field puts them in a position to provide expert advice on meeting locations and safest routes to access the communities, and come up with credible alibis to ensure greater safety for the victims. These skills can greatly assist the courts in a conflict or post-conflict setting. In essence, third parties help bridge the gap between the courts and the local communities, not only physically but also linguistically and culturally.

Finally, the use of third parties presents a relevant financial advantage for the courts.[64] It allows them to multiply the effect of their work at a very reduced cost, as the courts are only responsible for training and—in some cases—reimbursement while other costs, including local organisations' staff time, are borne by third parties. When it comes to victim participation in countries with large numbers of victims, savings in terms of travel costs and expensive international courts' staff time are very significant. This advantage is, however, contestable especially in cases where local actors end up undertaking tasks that are part of the courts' core mandates.

4.3.2 Challenges for the Courts and for Third Parties

Collaboration with the courts to contribute towards implementation of their victim-related mandate can pose significant challenges for third parties. Firstly, the financial implications of such engagement may be daunting and third parties may fail to anticipate the extent of those implications from the beginning. Those implications can take the form of an unexpected amount of time, for example for repeated contacts for lack of or missing information or documents in victim applications. External funding may not always be readily available and it is generally difficult to obtain for local organisations with a limited capacity. Moreover, donors' interest may decline over time. It appears as though the financial burden that involvement of third parties represents for the latter is not always fully

[64] Sperfeldt 2012, p. 159.

grasped or recognised by the courts. There seems to be an assumption on the part of international courts that assistance to the courts comes under local organisations' mandate. While this may be true in certain cases, such assistance brings about inevitable financial consequences which local organisations may not be ready to face. Other parties such as community leaders or victims acting as intermediaries also do not often have the necessary financial capability. On the other hand, providing support to third parties also poses challenges for the courts given their limited financial capacity. In addition, an ethical question arises: Should the courts pay for victims to be helped to apply? It is a delicate question. It should be noted that the courts have a mandate to reach out to and assist victims and, in some cases, make a positive decision to outsource those tasks to third parties.

Secondly, third parties who link victims to the courts may face considerable security threats. Those threats may or may not exist prior to their engagement with the courts. Where they exist, they could be exacerbated by such engagement. Security conditions may have financial consequences, for example if the organisation does not have the means to store documentation securely or to encrypt electronic information.

Thirdly, third parties may find themselves in a difficult position when they need to pass on messages on behalf of the courts or counsel. There are indeed certain messages which victims should hear directly from the courts, for example in relation to the courts' limitations, the constraints of participation and the fact that some victims may not be able to participate while others will.[65] Court staff (or counsel) may be better placed than intermediaries to manage expectations.[66] In addition, intermediaries may have a hard time explaining decisions that reject participation either initially or at a later stage of the proceedings. Because victims have an established relationship with third parties and may not interact at all with staff from the courts, they may hold the intermediary responsible for unsuccessful applications or proceedings.

Another question that presents challenges to both third parties and the courts is what could be considered an "overreliance" on intermediary organisations and individuals. The question is to what extent should international courts delegate core aspects of their mandate to third parties. At the ICC, for example, it has been highlighted that 'intermediaries should not be called upon to undertake core functions of the Court.'[67] In practice, however, the courts' limited field presence leads inevitably to the use of third parties, including to undertake tasks that should in principle only be carried out by court staff. Overreliance on third parties can pose problems, especially considering that intermediaries are often not compensated for

---

[65] This is because of the conditions established for participation and the need to prove a link with the facts underlying the case.

[66] Sperfeldt 2012, pp. 152–153.

[67] ICC Guidelines, p. 3.

their work.[68] It should also be pointed out that the use of third parties does not always lead to savings in court staff's time and workload. For example, incomplete or inaccurate application forms demand more work from both court staff and third parties. So does collection of forms for crimes that are outside the scope of the cases (as they need to be processed). It is also fair to acknowledge that local activists acting as intermediaries may not have the legal knowledge or may not understand the legal implications of statements made by victims in application or registration forms, even after having received training on victims' rights and form completion. Questions such as the exact date and location of the crime have crucial implications for the victims' admission to participate in proceedings and, later on, to receive reparations. Some of these difficulties have been acknowledged in some ICC decisions, whereby chambers mandated the Registry to undertake a more direct role in filling out of application forms and in supervision of intermediaries.[69] Practitioners who become involved at later stages of the proceedings should be aware that application or reparation forms filled out with the assistance of an intermediary may present inconsistencies or lack information.

Finally, the courts need to be careful when mapping third parties possibly willing to assist the court and seek to uncover their motivations. Because of the opportunities created by collaboration with the courts, many local organisations may be ready to help and new NGOs may be created. However, mapping local actors prior to initiating an engagement can help understand civil society dynamics[70] and find out the reasons why some organisations may decide to engage with the court. Some will have a reasonable motivation such as the will to make a genuine contribution, for example by strengthening the courts' legitimacy through assistance to victims to participate in proceedings.[71] Others, however, may have less legitimate reasons and be seeking financial gains including to the detriment or in disregard of the victims whom they purport to assist.[72]

---

[68] Unless they have a programme within their organisation that supports their work, which has been the case in Cambodia, and could be the case of international NGOs acting as intermediaries for the ICC.

[69] ICC, *Prosecutor v. Laurent Gbagbo*, Pre-Trial Chamber I, Second decision on issues related to the victims' application process, ICC-02/11-01/11-86, 5 April 2012, paras 25–29; ICC, *Prosecutor v. Bosco Ntaganda*, Pre-Trial Chamber II, Decision establishing principles on the Victims' Application Process, ICC-01/04-02/06-67, 28 May 2013, para 28; ICC, *Prosecutor v. Dominic Ongwen*, Pre Trial Chamber II, Decision Establishing Principles on the Victims' Application Process, ICC-02/04-01/15-205, 4 March 2015, paras 10 and 24.

[70] OHCHR 2008, p. 21.

[71] Sperfeldt 2012, p. 156.

[72] For example, the ICC Registry has alerted the Court to the practice of some lawyers in certain countries of 'fishing' for victim clients. See ICC, *Prosecutor v. William Samoei Ruto and Joshua Arap Sang*, Registry, Proposal for the common legal representation of victims, Annex I: Legal framework and experience to date on common legal representation, 1 August 2008, ICC-01/09-01/11-243-Anx-1, paras 8–9.

4.4 What Is the Intermediary's Legal Status? What Are Their Rights and Duties?

The degree of third parties' involvement has posed questions as to their legal status and the rights and duties that they should be recognised as having. The extent to which this matter has been regulated, through case-law or administrative frameworks, varies significantly from one court to another.

4.4.1 Absence of Regulation at ECCC and STL

There is no regulation regarding third parties or intermediaries at the STL because, as explained above, they do not play a role in relation to that court's proceedings.

When it comes to the ECCC, despite the very extensive role that they have played, there is no specific regulation about NGOs (for example in terms of support, compensation for their work, limitations or ethical standards). NGOs are only mentioned twice in the Internal Rules in relation to the possibility for the VSS to cooperate with such organisations in the identification, design and implementation of reparations projects,[73] and 'development and implementation of non-judicial programs and measures addressing the broader interests of victims.'[74] It is worth highlighting that at the ECCC victims can also participate through an association,[75] but this provision has rarely been used.[76]

4.4.2 Regulation of Intermediaries at ICC

In contrast, at the ICC intermediaries have been the object of judicial rulings. Cooperation between intermediaries and the Court has also raised questions as to the administrative rules that should apply to that relationship. This led to the adoption of the Guidelines Governing the Relations between the Court and Intermediaries (Guidelines).

4.4.2.1 Intermediaries in the ICC Case-Law

The ICC case-law has dealt with intermediaries assisting different organs of the Court and performing diverse tasks. When it comes to intermediaries who support

[73] ECCC Internal Rules, Rule 12*bis*(2).

[74] Ibid., Rule 12*bis*(3).

[75] Ibid., Rule 23*quater*.

[76] FIDH 2012, p. 33.

victims to participate in proceedings, decisions have focused exclusively on their role in relation to collection of the application forms.

A question that has arisen is whether the name of an intermediary should be disclosed to the Defence. This is relevant because the name of the intermediary is normally written in the standard victim application forms when those are used.[77] An intermediary could have security problems as a result of their name being revealed publicly or to certain parties in the proceedings, especially the Defence (application forms are usually shared with the OTP and the Defence).[78] The ICC chambers have authorised redaction of different types of information to the application forms. Redactions to the names and contact details of intermediaries have generally been authorised,[79] with the following exceptions:

(a) 'When the intermediary is a person known to the parties, when he or she works for the Court or he or she is a participant involved in the [...] proceedings.'[80]
(b) When 'there are substantive reasons for suspecting that the individuals who assisted the applicants to fill in the application forms to participate as victims attempted to persuade one or more of them to give false evidence, or otherwise misused their position.'[81]

In relation to the second exception, it is relevant to note that the judgment in the *Lubanga* case unveiled that intermediaries had coached victim witnesses. The court considered the victims' accounts to be unreliable and decided to withdraw their right to participation because they no longer met the criteria to be considered victims in the case. Their testimonies were also disregarded.[82]

Another matter on which the ICC chambers have made rulings is the role of the Registry staff in form collection and intermediary supervision. As explained above, intermediaries normally do not have a legal background or may not always fully understand the legal implications of statements made in the forms. It is not unusual for the ICC Registry to receive incomplete forms or forms that may lack the necessary enclosed documentation such as identity cards. In addition, it is

[77] The ICC Standard form for applications to participate includes the following questions: '23. Is somebody assisting this victim to fill in this form?' and '24. If yes, what is that person's name and organisations (if any)?'. For more information on the application process, see Chap. 2.

[78] In accordance with Rule 89 of the ICC Rules. See also Chap. 2.

[79] See e.g. ICC, *Prosecutor v. Bosco Ntaganda*, Pre-Trial Chamber II, Decision on victims' participation at the confirmation of charges hearing and in related proceedings, ICC-01/04-02/06-211, 15 January 2014, paras 42–46.

[80] ICC, *Prosecutor v. Jean-Pierre Bemba Gombo*, Trial Chamber III, Public redacted version of the 'Decision on the tenth and seventeenth transmissions of applications by victims to participate in proceedings', ICC-01/05-01/08-2247-Red, 19 July 2012, para 25.

[81] ICC, *Prosecutor v. Thomas Lubanga Dyilo,* Trial Chamber I, Redacted version of the Corrigendum of Decision on the applications by 15 victims to participate in the proceedings, ICC-01/04-01/06-2659-Corr-Red, 8 February 2011, para 30.

[82] ICC, *Prosecutor v. Thomas Lubanga Dyilo*, Trial Chamber I, Judgment pursuant to Article 74 of the Statute, ICC-01/04-01/06-2842, 14 March 2012, paras 478–484. See further Chap. 14.

uncertain to what extent intermediaries have always been able to convey in a clear manner what participation means to the victims they reach out to. In decisions issued in different cases since 2012, the Court has ordered that the Registry staff play a more active and prominent role in form collection, either by doing it themselves instead of delegating that task to intermediaries,[83] or by supervising them.[84] These decisions highlight the need for the Registry to be more significantly involved in outreach and form collection, including by not delegating or not delegating fully its core responsibilities. They also emphasise the need to oversee and direct the work of third parties to avoid mistakes, unclear or untrue statements, or a lack of information. Nevertheless, the practice of different cases has shown that the Registry continues to use third parties quite extensively, including for new tasks. For example, in the cases arising from the situation in Kenya, the chambers decided to maintain the application forms only for a limited number of situations and allowed that all other victims wanting to participate could, if they so wished, 'register with the Registry'.[85] Mapping of victim communities was necessary for the purpose of reaching out to victims and registering those interested. In practice, the Registry trained intermediaries to undertake such mapping.[86] And it delegated registration to the victims' legal representatives.[87]

4.4.2.2 Need for an Administrative Framework: The Intermediaries' Guidelines

The ICC organs' extensive use of intermediaries created a variety of situations in which intermediaries were subject to very diverse policies according to the ICC unit they worked with. The reliance—and in some cases overreliance—on intermediaries led to unethical situations where intermediaries would be relied upon and have a number of duties, but be acknowledged no rights.[88] In the meantime, the *Lubanga* case highlighted difficulties arising from the lack of sufficient oversight and illegal behaviour on the part of intermediaries, which could have caused

[83] ICC, *Prosecutor v. Laurent Gbagbo*, Pre-Trial Chamber I, Second decision on issues related to the victims' application process, ICC-02/11-01/11-86, 5 April 2012, para 27.

[84] ICC, *Prosecutor v. Bosco Ntaganda*, Pre-Trial Chamber II, Decision establishing principles on the Victims' Application Process, ICC-01/04-02/06-67, 28 May 2013, para 28.

[85] ICC, *Prosecutor v. William Samoei Ruto & Joshua Arap Sang*, Trial Chamber V, Decision on victims' participation and representation, ICC-01/09-01/11-460, 3 October 2012, para 49; ICC, *Prosecutor v. Uhuru Muigai Kenyatta*, Trial Chamber V, Decision on victims' participation and representation, ICC-01/09-02/11-498, 3 October 2012, para 48.

[86] ICC, *Prosecutor v. William Samoei Ruto & Joshua Arap Sang*, Registry, First periodic report on the general situation of victims in Kenya, Annex, ICC-01/09-01/11-566-Anx, 23 January 2013, para 6; ICC, *Prosecutor v. Uhuru Muigai Kenyatta*, Registry, First periodic report on the general situation of victims in Kenya, Annex, ICC-01/09-02/11-606-Anx, 21 January 2013, para 6.

[87] Sehmi 2013, p. 6.

[88] See e.g. Victims' Rights Working Group (VRWG) 2009, p. 3.

the collapse of the first ICC case. All of this raised the need for an administrative framework that regulated the intervention of intermediaries and provided guidance to the Court as to the rules applicable to interaction with third parties.

In 2008, the Court initiated a lengthy process of internal and external consultations[89] that led to the adoption—in March 2014—of the ICC Guidelines, as well as a Model Contract for Intermediaries and a Code of Conduct for Intermediaries.[90] It is important to take into consideration that the Guidelines are a Court-wide document and, therefore, they are meant to cater for a set of very diverse situations as intermediaries' tasks and relationships may vary greatly from one unit or organ of the Court to another. They apply not only to organs and units of the Court but also to counsel who represent individuals before the ICC. Significantly, the Guidelines are not binding.[91] They simply offer guidance to units and organs of the Court on matters including selection of intermediaries, formalising the relationship, different forms of support, security considerations, and intermediaries' accountability and confidentiality obligations. Specific decisions are left to the unit or organ concerned. Those decisions appear to be based either on a specific unit/organ policy or to be made on a case-by-case basis and in accordance with the nature of the intermediaries' function and the relevant section/organ's needs, capability and available resources, among other considerations. The Guidelines do not provide a solution to the intermediaries' lack of legal status (while some may qualify as contractors or service providers, others may not).

Some of the main provisions of the Guidelines include (references to the Court's units or organs should be understood to include also counsel acting before the ICC):

(a) *Selection of intermediaries*: There is a recognition that intermediaries may be selected by the Court, chosen by a victim or another individual to assist them in contacts with the ICC, or be self-appointed.[92] The Guidelines list a series of criteria that are to be taken into consideration by units of the Court when they decide to work with an intermediary. Those criteria regard the intermediary's capacity (including concerning adherence to confidentiality), reliability and risks faced. When the Court does not select the intermediary, the criteria can be used to assess whether the intermediary can continue to carry out tasks for the relevant section/organ.[93]

89 FIDH 2010, p. 11.

90 All three documents are available on the ICC website. Guidelines: https://www.icc-cpi.int/iccdocs/lt/GRCI-Eng.pdf. Model Contract for Intermediaries: https://www.icc-cpi.int/iccdocs/LT/MCI-Eng.pdf. Code of Conduct for Intermediaries: https://www.icc-cpi.int/iccdocs/lt/CCI-Eng.pdf Accessed 19 September 2016.

91 In particular 'it is recognized that the Guidelines do not in any way bind or limit the Chambers' exercise of their powers' (ICC Guidelines, p. 3).

92 ICC Guidelines, p. 5.

93 Ibid., pp. 7–9.

(b) *Formalising a relationship*: Intermediaries may cooperate with the Court either within or outside the framework of a contract.[94] The Guidelines do not determine which cases warrant conclusion of a contract. The Court has drafted a standard template agreement (Model Contract for Intermediaries), which is to be used when entering a contractual relationship.[95] The Guidelines apply mainly to intermediaries who have a contractual relationship with the Court and others that have been approved by the Court.[96]

(c) *Intermediaries' duties*: Intermediaries must be instructed about the different levels of confidentiality of information and ensure that their communications respect confidentiality and security.[97] Intermediaries are bound by the Code of Conduct for Intermediaries, which sets out a series of duties in relation to personal and professional conduct, confidentiality, security and other duties towards the Court. Intermediaries are supervised.[98] In principle, the Court will not disclose the intermediaries' identity. However, the intermediary must accept that the Court may disclose their identity if requested to do so by a judicial authority.[99] Intermediaries could also be called to testify in proceedings and be cross-examined by opposing parties.[100]

(d) *Support to intermediaries*: a series of soft rules are established in relation to reimbursement of expenses and compensation. Expenses are generally reimbursed when the task carried out by the intermediary has been requested by the Court and reimbursement has been agreed upon in advance.[101] Compensation is exceptional, as intermediaries are expected to provide support on a voluntary basis.[102] However, intermediaries acting within the framework of a contract as 'individual contractors' or 'service providers' may receive compensation as per the terms of conditions of that contract.[103] Other support offered to intermediaries can include provision of materials (for example equipment or materials such to ensure confidentiality of information or prevent risks), capacity-building and referrals to other organisations for psychological support.[104]

---

94 Ibid., p. 10.

95 Ibid., p. 11.

96 Ibid., pp. 6 and 10. Determination as to whether the Guidelines apply to unapproved intermediaries (self-appointed intermediaries, one-off intermediaries) will be made on a case-by-case basis.

97 Ibid., pp. 10–11, 17.

98 Ibid., p. 11.

99 Ibid., p. 17. See also ICC, Model Contract for Intermediaries, Article 10.

100 ICC Guidelines, p. 10.

101 Ibid., pp. 12–13.

102 Ibid., p. 5.

103 Ibid., p. 12.

104 Ibid., pp. 13–14.

(e) *Security and protection*: Importantly, the Guidelines acknowledge that the Court 'has a duty to prevent or manage security risks to intermediaries when those risks result from the intermediaries' interaction with the Court and fulfilment of the intermediaries' functions on behalf of the Court.'[105] Before the Court engages or contacts an intermediary, an individual risk assessment must be conducted by a specialised security unit.[106] Prevention is the general rule: Court staff should apply good practices to prevent or minimise risks to intermediaries. Intermediaries should also be instructed about how to best protect themselves.[107] Exceptionally, protective measures can be provided when a risk is caused as a result of the intermediaries' work for the Court.[108]

While the Guidelines represent a significant development and are meant to be updated following further practice,[109] some of the provisions are inconsistent, unclear or incompatible with other ICC policies. As stated above, the Guidelines apply equally to the Court's units and organs and to counsel. Practitioners may want to be aware of the following:

(a) While the Guidelines are the result of extensive internal and external consultations, the consultation process failed to adequately involve counsel. The Guidelines place counsel in an equal position to units and organs of the Court, without consideration for their different standing and capabilities. There appears to be a certain degree of incompatibility or lack of harmonisation between the Guidelines and legal aid policies.[110]

---

105 Ibid., p. 14.

106 Ibid., pp. 15–16.

107 Ibid., pp. 14–17.

108 Ibid., p. 17.

109 The Guidelines establish a monitoring process and schedule a review (18 months after adoption of the Guidelines) that will result in an update. See ICC Guidelines, p. 18. However, no review has been conducted to date, over 32 months after their adoption.

110 For example, compensation to intermediaries is not contemplated in the legal aid budget. According to the Guidelines (p. 12), 'intermediaries who are tasked upon the request of Counsel may receive compensation if they are contracted as a 'resource person' per regulation 139 of the Regulations of the Registry.' In cases where fees for a resource person are not foreseen by the legal aid budget (generally the position of resource person is only available to support Defence counsel at certain stages of the proceedings), counsel will in principle not be able to provide compensation to intermediaries. When it comes to the reimbursement of expenses, the ICC Registry has acknowledged that intermediaries' expenses were not taken into consideration when establishing the legal aid budget but can be accepted on an '*ad hoc* case-by-case basis, when they are 'reasonably necessary for an effective and efficient' legal representation' (ICC, Second Report of the Court on the financial implications of the draft Guidelines governing the relations between the Court and Intermediaries, ICC-ASP/12/53 (2013b), paras 11–12). As a result, counsel may agree with an intermediary as to a task that needs to be carried out and undertake to provide reimbursement of expenses, but such expenses may subsequently not be reimbursed by the Registry (who is in charge of managing legal aid and approving all of counsel's expenses). Counsel and the Registry may not share the same opinion as to what is 'reasonably necessary for an effective and efficient' legal representation (this being a subjective notion).

(b) As far as selection and selection criteria are concerned, it is noted that some intermediaries assisting victims (for example, individuals who have been victims themselves or community leaders) may not fulfil relevant criteria, especially in terms of capacity and experience. In the case of legal representatives who often work with the same intermediaries that assisted victims to fill out the application forms, it is unclear whether they need to reassess the selection criteria and request an individual risk assessment for intermediaries that have already been screened for collaboration with the Registry.
(c) The Guidelines state that intermediaries provide services in principle on a voluntary basis, unless they are contracted intermediaries. However, other provisions of the Guidelines appear to indicate that not all contracted intermediaries shall receive compensation.[111]
(d) It is unclear whether the Guidelines apply to international NGOs. It is certain that they do not apply when such organisations have cooperation agreements with the Court.[112] It is unclear whether they can apply in other cases.
(e) The Guidelines refer to other documents that should be shared with intermediaries (Good Practices on Risk Prevention and Management)[113] or be public and transparent (reimbursement rates).[114] However, those documents have not been made public nor do they appear to have been shared with counsel.
(f) The Guidelines refer to 'intermediaries approved by affidavit'.[115] It is unclear when intermediaries could be approved in such a way and what the process would be.
(g) While the Guidelines establish rights and duties for both the Court and intermediaries, the Model Contract only refers to the intermediaries' obligations. In this regard, it is relevant to recall that external actors had observed in relation to a previous draft version of Guidelines that it was important to recognise 'the reciprocal nature of the relationship between the ICC and intermediaries.'[116] While the Guidelines evolved into a more balanced text, the Model Contract—which was drafted later and not submitted to consultations—does not match such evolution. It is unclear whether an intermediary can request that the contract be amended so that their rights can also be reflected.[117]

111 ICC Guidelines, p. 12.

112 Ibid., p. 6.

113 Ibid., pp. 10 and 16.

114 Ibid., p. 13.

115 Ibid., pp. 10 and 12.

116 IRRI and Open Society Justice Initiative (OSJI) 2011, p. 2.

117 ICC Guidelines, p. 11: 'The organs and units of the Court and Counsel *will* use the standard template agreement…' (emphasis added).

(h) The Guidelines do not resolve the question of avoiding that intermediaries undertake core tasks of the Court. It is stated that intermediaries 'should not be called upon to undertake core functions of the Court'[118] and that 'there is a need to ensure that intermediaries are not a substitute for staff for the implementation of the mandate of the Court.'[119] However, no guidance is offered as to how that should be determined. This is concerning because, as we have seen, the ICC has actually delegated core aspects of its mandate to intermediaries.

(i) The Guidelines do not resolve potential problems and conflicts of interests that may arise when intermediaries work for different organs of the Court.[120] The Guidelines state that an intermediary 'may work with only one organ or unit of the Court or Counsel, or it may have contact with multiple organs and units of the Court or individual Counsel.'[121] During the consultations that led to the adoption of the Guidelines, the Court sought to establish whether the organs of the Court should share information about the intermediaries they work with.[122] No solution was apparently found to this matter and the responsibility has been put on the intermediaries' shoulders: 'The Intermediary undertakes to inform the Court (or the counsel) of any previous and/or ongoing contact established between the Intermediary and any other organ, division, section or unit of the Court (or counsel).'[123] Resolving this issue could have ensured better coordination among ICC units and prevent duplication of support.[124]

(j) Depending on the context and the relevant intermediary's capabilities, fulfilling some of the duties may be too onerous for the intermediary. For example, unless specific support is provided by the Court, the intermediary may not have safe office space or access to safe internet connection to guarantee confidentiality and security of information in their possession.[125] In some cases, intermediaries may also lack the necessary technological knowledge. While capacity-building can be offered, the ICC operates in a complex legal and institutional framework that may not be easy for intermediaries to understand.

---

118 ICC Guidelines, p. 2.

119 Ibid., p. 3.

120 There is only one general provision in the Code of Conduct for Intermediaries, by which intermediaries undertake to inform the Court of any existing or impending conflict of interests affecting their work (Code of Conduct, Article 7.7).

121 ICC Guidelines, p. 5.

122 This is revealed by comments provided by external actors. See e.g. VRWG 2011, pp. 3–4.

123 ICC, Model Contract for Intermediaries, Article 8.3.

124 VRWG 2011, pp. 3–4.

125 The ICC Registry has indicated that it has been providing 'passive protection capacity, e.g. encrypted USB sticks and lockable safes, to certain selected intermediaries in order to equip them to secure information and conduct their activities safely if they do not already have the means to do so.' See ICC, Report of the Court on the Revised strategy in relation to victims, ICC-ASP/11/40 (2012), para 17.

(k) Finally, as a result of the Guidelines and in accordance with the Model Contract, intermediaries are expected to follow instructions from the organ or unit that has contracted them.[126] While this cannot be questioned in principle, it may pose problems in practice. It is not unusual for intermediaries to be (or be part of) independent civil society organisations, which may have their own policies and position on the conflict and post-conflict developments. While such situations could be resolved through the provision on conflict of interests,[127] it is important that practitioners are alert to this fact. Lastly, it has been observed that adoption of the Guidelines may lead to the "professionalization" of intermediaries and a semi-institutionalised status for intermediaries. That could affect broader participation of civil society and could lead to silencing critical voices.[128]

Even if the Guidelines were only formally adopted and published in 2014, the units and organs of the Court had reportedly already started implementing them. However, implementation has been limited in certain cases due to resource constraints. In 2013, the Registry's Victims' Participation and Reparations Section (VPRS) reported:

> The VPRS have also been implementing the Guidelines to the extent possible, including applying the criteria for the selection of intermediaries and providing support to intermediaries (including reimbursing expenses when necessary). The VPRS has also provided training to intermediaries including on interacting with victims and ethical behaviour with victims. Due to resource limitations, VPRS have not been able to implement contractual relations with intermediaries of the type envisaged in the Guidelines (i.e. the Model Contract).[129]

Local NGOs have reported that they have not been informed about or received the Guidelines or related documents.[130]

4.5 Key Points

The role of third parties at the ICC and the ECCC

- Assistance by third parties has proven crucial to allow victims to access the ICC and the ECCC. Third parties have been involved at all relevant stages of the

[126] ICC, Model Contract for Intermediaries, Article 5.

[127] ICC, Code of Conduct for Intermediaries, Article 7.7.

[128] See generally Haslam and Edmunds 2013.

[129] ICC, Report of the Court on the implementation in 2013 of the revised strategy in relation to victims, ICC-ASP/12/41 (2013a), para 45.

[130] Personal experience and notes of the author. Inquiries were conducted by the author in the framework of her work with the Open Society Justice Initiative (notes on file with the author).

process, from collection of application forms, through participation and legal representation, to assistance and reparations.

- Third parties' intervention has come about as a result of a combination of different factors. Intermediaries and other third parties fill in gaps left by the courts' capacity and financial limitations. Their specific role has been shaped both by the courts' needs, and considerations related to the nature of the crimes and specific traits of the victim communities.
- Support offered by third parties has both advantages and disadvantages, which practitioners may want to take into consideration.
- The extent to which each court has regulated participation of third parties varies greatly. While NGOs are simply mentioned in a few provisions of the ECCC Internal Rules, the ICC has issued both case-law and a specific administrative framework on intermediaries.

Using third parties to maintain contact with victims

- In devising strategies to enter into or maintain contact with victims, practitioners may want to consider networks that are established in the community. Relying on existing networks avoids creation of new structures and allows for information on participation in proceedings to be channelled through trusted actors within the communities.[131]
- When interacting in particular with individuals and organisations from the affected countries, it is important for practitioners who come from abroad to value and show respect for the locals' knowledge and culture.[132] It is advised to seek to understand and learn from them, have them feel involved in the justice process, consider using interaction and communications as opportunities for capacity building, and establishing a cooperative relationship of equals.[133]
- There will be occasions when practitioners cannot share information with third parties for confidentiality reasons. When such is the case, it is advisable to explain so. Secrecy can raise suspicions and lead to mistrust. Being trusted by local third parties is essential to gain or maintain victims' trust. In other words, because of the strong ties that exist between third parties and members of the communities, problems in the relationship with third parties may affect relationships with clients or stakeholders.
- When third parties are NGOs it is important to consider that there may be tension among different organisations. Competition could arise as a result of legitimate funding needs. Other forms of tension could result from diverse views on political or legal issues and may, in some cases, date back to several years back. This may make it be challenging for practitioners to manage relationships with

131 Interview with member of ICC legal representation team, 22 October 2014 (records on file with the author, interviewee preferred to remain unnamed).

132 Interview with Silke Studzinsky, former civil party lawyer at the ECCC, 22 October 2014 (records on file with the author).

133 Ibid.

multiple third parties. In such cases, it is important to seek to understand the politics and personalities involved.
- The more practitioners understand the local context, the better they will be equipped to navigate relationships with third parties.

References

Avocats sans frontières (2013) Modes of participation and legal representation. http://www.asf.be/wp-content/uploads/2013/11/ASF_IJ_Modes-of-participation-and-legal-representation.pdf. Accessed 2 Nov 2014

De Vos C (2013) Investigating from afar: The ICC's evidence problem. Leiden J Int Law 26:1009–1024

Glasius M (2002) Expertise in the cause of justice: global civil society influence on the statute for an international criminal court. In: Glasius M et al (eds) Global Civil Society Yearbook 2002, pp 137–168

Fédération internationale des ligues de droits de l'Homme (FIDH) (2010) ICC Review Conference: Renewing commitment to accountability. http://www.fidh.org/IMG/pdf/KampalaCPI543a-2.pdf. Accessed 2 Nov 2014

FIDH (2012) Victims' rights before the Extraordinary Chambers in the Courts of Cambodia: A mixed record for civil parties. http://www.fidh.org/IMG/pdf/eccc_victrights_rep_nov2012_en_web.pdf. Accessed 2 Nov 2014

Haslam E, Edmunds R (2013) Managing a new 'partnership': 'Professionalisation', intermediaries and the International Criminal Court. Crim Law Forum 24:49–85

ICC Trust Fund for Victims (2011) Press Release 'ICC's Trust Fund for Victims launches Expression of Interest supporting victim survivors of sexual and gender-based violence in the Central African Republic.' http://www.icc-cpi.int/en_menus/icc/press%20and%20media/press%20releases/press%20releases%20(2011)/Pages/pr660.aspx. Accessed 19 Oct 2014

ICC Trust Fund for Victims (2013) Programme Progress Report. http://www.trustfundforvictims.org/sites/default/files/media_library/documents/pdf/TFVSummer2013PPR_FINAL_VERSION___rev_060913.pdf. Accessed 2 Nov 2014

ICC Trust Fund for Victims (2014) TFV Strategic Plan for 2014–2017. http://www.trustfundforvictims.org/sites/default/files/media_library/documents/pdf/TFV_Strategic_Plan_2014_2017__approved.pdf. Accessed 2 Nov 2014

International Criminal Court (2012) Report of the Court on the revised strategy in relation to victims: Past, present and future. http://www.icc-cpi.int/iccdocs/asp_docs/ASP11/ICC-ASP-11-40-ENG.pdf. Accessed 2 Nov 2014

International Criminal Court (2013a) Report of the Court on the implementation in 2013 of the revised strategy in relation to victims. http://www.icc-cpi.int/iccdocs/asp_docs/ASP12/ICC-ASP-12-41-ENG.pdf. Accessed 2 Nov 2014

International Criminal Court (2013b) Second report of the Court on the financial implications of the draft guidelines governing the relations between the Court and intermediaries. http://www.icc-cpi.int/iccdocs/asp_docs/ASP12/ICC-ASP-12-53-ENG.pdf. Accessed 2 Nov 2014

International Criminal Court (2014a) Proposed Programme Budget for 2014 of the International Criminal Court. http://www.icc-cpi.int/iccdocs/asp_docs/ASP12/ICC-ASP-12-10-ENG.pdf. Accessed 2 Nov 2014

International Criminal Court (2014b) Guidelines governing the relations between the Court and intermediaries. https://www.icc-cpi.int/iccdocs/lt/GRCI-Eng.pdf. Accessed 19 Sept 2016

International Criminal Court (2014c) Code of conduct for intermediaries. https://www.icc-cpi.int/iccdocs/lt/CCI-Eng.pdf. Accessed 19 Sept 2016

International Criminal Court (2014d) Model contract for intermediaries. https://www.icc-cpi.int/iccdocs/LT/MCI-Eng.pdf. Accessed 19 Sept 2016

International Criminal Court (2014e) Report of the Court and the Trust Fund for Victims on the rules to be observed for the payment of reparations. http://www.icc-cpi.int/iccdocs/asp_docs/ASP13/ICC-ASP-13-7-ENG.pdf. Accessed 2 Nov 2014

International Criminal Court (2014f) Report to the Assembly of States Parties on the projects and the activities of the Board of Directors of the Trust Fund for Victims for the period 1 July 2013 to 30 June 2014. http://www.icc-cpi.int/iccdocs/asp_docs/ASP13/ICC-ASP-13-14-ENG.pdf. Accessed 2 Nov 2014

International Refugee Rights Initiative (IRRI) and Open Society Justice Initiative (OSJI) (2011) Commentary on the ICC draft guidelines on intermediaries. http://www.opensocietyfoundations.org/sites/default/files/icc-intermediaries-commentary-20110818.pdf. Accessed 29 Oct 2014

McCleary-Sills J, Mukasa S (2013) External evaluation of the Trust Fund for Victims programmes in Northern Uganda and the Democratic Republic of Congo: Towards a perspective for upcoming interventions, International Center for Research on Women (ICRW). http://www.trustfundforvictims.org/sites/default/files/media_library/documents/pdf/ICRWTFVExternalProgEvaluation2013Final.pdf. Accessed 2 Nov 2014

Sehmi A (2013) 'New victim participation regime in Kenya', ACCESS—Victims' Rights Working Group Bulletin, Issue 22:6. http://www.vrwg.org/downloads/130617EnglishVersionFinal.pdf. Accessed 29 Oct 2014

Sperfeldt C (2012) Cambodian civil society and the Khmer Rouge Tribunal. Int J Transit Justice 6:149–160

United Nations Office of the High Commissioner for Human Rights (OHCHR) (2008) Rule-of-law tools for post-conflict States: Maximising the legacy of hybrid courts. http://www.ohchr.org/documents/publications/hybridcourts.pdf. Accessed 2 Nov 2014

Victims' Rights Working Group (VRWG) (2009) Comments on the role and relationship of 'intermediaries' with the International Criminal Court. http://www.vrwg.org/VRWG_DOC/2009_Feb_VRWG_intermediaries.pdf. Accessed 29 Oct 2014

VRWG (2011) Intermediaries guidelines: Outstanding issues. http://www.vrwg.org/VRWG_DOC/2011_VRWG_Intermediaries.pdf. Accessed 29 Oct 2014

Chapter 5
Legal Representation of Participating Victims

Megan Hirst

Abstract Victims who participate in international criminal proceedings are required, whether by law or in practice, to be represented by a qualified lawyer. This chapter provides an overview of the legal framework relating to victims' legal representation. It considers the systems in place for court-arranged collective legal representation, as well as the resourcing of victims' lawyers, counsel's obligations and the duration of victims' representation.

Keywords Self-representation · Common legal representation · Duty counsel · Legal aid · Effective representation · Termination of representation

Contents

Megan Hirst is a barrister at Doughty Street Chambers in London and a member of an LRV team in *Prosecutor v. Dominic Ongwen*. She has previously worked on victims' participation in the Registries of the ICC and the STL.

M. Hirst (✉)
London, UK
e-mail: m.hirst@doughtystreet.co.uk

K. Tibori-Szabó and M. Hirst (eds.), *Victim Participation in International Criminal Justice*, International Criminal Justice Series 11,
DOI 10.1007/978-94-6265-177-7_5

5.1 Background: Historical Development and Institutional Arrangements

Long before the introduction of victims' participation in international criminal tribunals, the International Criminal Tribunal for the former Yugoslavia (ICTY) and the International Criminal Tribunal for Rwanda (ICTR) had established legal frameworks in relation to the roles of counsel in their proceedings. These provided the historical and conceptual backdrops against which victims' legal representation has since developed.

One key development at the *ad hoc* tribunals was the different status of the Prosecution and Defence lawyers. In both of those institutions, the Prosecution was established as an organ of the tribunal while representatives of the Defence were entirely external.[1] Within limits accused persons were entitled to choose a private counsel. Few requirements or regulations of counsel were contained in the original Rules of Procedure and Evidence (RPE) of the *ad hoc* Tribunals, but over time these developed and were complemented by codes of conduct and policies on the payment of legal aid.

Significant aspects of these systems have been adopted by the International Criminal Court (ICC), the Special Tribunal for Lebanon (STL) and the Extraordinary Chambers in the Courts of Cambodia (ECCC). However, some particular considerations arise where the persons represented are participating victims. This chapter will focus on those aspects of legal representation at the ICC, STL and ECCC which are particular to the representation of participating victims.

[1] ICTY Statute, Article 11; ICTR Statute, Article 10.

5.2 Institutional Frameworks for the Representation of Victims

Before turning to the specific rules and jurisprudence governing the legal representation of victims, some background is necessary regarding the institutional context in which such representation exists. Information relating to the institutional units involved in assisting victims to apply for participation is contained in Chap. 2. Many of the same units play a role in relation to the legal representation of victims.

At the STL, one victims' office within the Registry, the Victims' Participation Unit (VPU), plays a number of roles relating to victims' legal representation. The Unit maintains a list of qualified counsel,[2] consults with victims on their preferences regarding legal representation,[3] advises the Pre-Trial Judge on the grouping of victims for legal representation,[4] and advises the Registrar on the selection and designation of legal representatives of victims (LRVs).[5] Once LRVs are appointed, the VPU administers legal aid,[6] monitors the work of LRVs,[7] and provides some forms of support to them as required, including legal research assistance and logistical assistance.[8] The VPU is not empowered to represent participating victims itself. That role is exclusively played by external counsel.

At the ECCC, the Office of Administration includes a Victims Support Section (VSS) and a Civil Party Lead Co-Lawyer's Section.[9] The VSS maintains a list of registered lawyers,[10] assists civil parties in arranging legal representation,[11] and provides support to civil party lawyers. The Civil Party Lead Co-Lawyers coordinate and lead the representation of all civil parties (through civil party lawyers) in ECCC proceedings at trial.

---

[2] STL RPE, Rule 51(C)(i); STL Directive on Victims' Legal Representation, Articles 10–15.

[3] STL Directive on Victims' Legal Representation, Article 20(A).

[4] STL, *Prosecutor v. Salim Jamil Ayyash, Mustafa Amine Badreddine, Hussein Hassan Oneissi and Assad Hassan Sabra (Ayyash* et al.*)*, Pre-Trial Judge, Decision on Victims' Participation in the Proceedings, STL-11-01/PT/PTJ, 8 May 2012, para 11.

[5] STL RPE, Rule 51(G)(i); STL Directive on Victims' Legal Representation, Article 20(B).

[6] STL RPE, Rule 51(B)(ii); STL Directive on Victims' Legal Representation, Articles 33–34; STL Legal Aid Policy for Victims' Participation.

[7] STL RPE, Rule 51(C)(v); Code of Professional Conduct for Defence Counsel and Legal Representatives of Victims appearing before the Special Tribunal for Lebanon, Articles 32–34.

[8] STL RPE, Rule 51(B)(vi), Rule 51(C)(iii); STL Directive on Victims' Legal Representation, Articles 32, 36–38.

[9] ECCC Internal Rules, Rule 12.

[10] ECCC Internal Rules, Rule 12*bis*(1)(c)–(d).

[11] ECCC Internal Rules, Rule 12*bis*(1)(g).

At the ICC, three key units of the Court play a role in victims' legal representation. The Victims Participation and Reparations Section (VPRS), within the Registry, consults with victims and assists them to arrange their legal representation. It also advises the chambers on the grouping of victims for the purposes of legal representation, and selects or recommends common legal representatives. Another section within the Registry, the Counsel Support Section, administers legal aid for participating victims.[12] Finally, an autonomous office, the Office of Public Counsel for Victims (OPCV) plays the dual role of providing legal research and advice to external counsel representing victims,[13] while also itself providing counsel who may be appointed by chambers to directly represent participating victims.[14]

It bears noting that this structure at the ICC has been the subject of considerable debate, particularly concerning the role of the OPCV and that of external counsel. Some chambers, and especially during earlier cases, took the view that the primary role of OPCV should be to assist external counsel and that its counsel should only exceptionally represent victims themselves.[15] Civil society organisations and others commenting on the Court's victims' mandate have frequently voiced a strong preference for external victims' counsel over the OPCV.[16] However, in recent cases, Pre-Trial Chambers have demonstrated a readiness to appoint counsel from the OPCV as common legal representatives[17] or as lawyers for otherwise unrepresented victims under regulation 80 of the Regulations of the Court.[18] During the course of the Registrar's "ReVision"

[12] These two units—the VPRS and CSS—together undertake the Registry's responsibilities in relation to victims' legal representation as set out in ICC RPE, Rule 16(1)(b).

[13] ICC Regulations of the Court, Regulation 81(4).

[14] ICC Regulations of the Court, Regulation 80(2).

[15] ICC, *Prosecutor v. Jean-Pierre Bemba Gombo,* Trial Chamber III, Decision on common legal representation of victims for the purpose of trial, ICC-01/05-01/08-1005, 10 November 2010, paras 28–30.

[16] See for example: Supplementary report of the Registry on four aspects of the Court's legal aid system, ICC-ASP/11/43 (2012), para 50; Redress, Comments to the Registrar in relation to the ReVision project as it relates to victims' rights before the ICC, February 2015, http://www.redress.org/downloads/publications/2015-feb-redress-comments-on-revision.pdf. Accessed 22 August 2016, pp. 4–5; FIDH, Five Myths about Victim Participation in ICC Proceedings, https://www.fidh.org/IMG/pdf/cpi649a.pdf. Accessed 22 August 2016, pp. 35–40.

[17] ICC, *Prosecutor v. Laurent Gbagbo*, Pre-Trial Chamber I, Decision on Victims' Participation and Victims' Common Legal Representation at the Confirmation of Charges Hearing and in the Related Proceedings, ICC-02/11-01/11-138, 4 June 2012, paras 42–45; ICC, *Prosecutor v. Charles Blé Goude*, Pre-Trial Chamber I, Decision on victims' participation in the pre-trial proceedings and related issues, ICC-02/11-02/11-83, 11 June 2014, para 25; ICC, *Prosecutor v. Bosco Ntaganda*, Pre-Trial Chamber I, Decision Concerning the Organisation of Common Legal Representation of Victims, ICC-01/04-02/06-160, 2 December 2013, para 25.

[18] ICC, *Prosecutor v. Dominic Ongwen*, Pre-Trial Chamber II, Decision on contested victims' applications for participation, legal representation of victims and their procedural rights, ICC-02/04-01/15-350, para 21.

process proposals were made to modify existing systems for victims' legal representation so as to provide a more significant default role to the OPCV, however such changes have not been approved and it is not clear whether they will proceed.[19]

5.2.1 Legal Representation as a Requirement for Participating Victims

In practice, legal representation is a requirement before the ICC, the STL and the ECCC for victims who have been granted formal status to participate.[20]

Before the ECCC, civil parties must be represented by a lawyer at all times after the issue of an indictment.[21]

The ICC RPE does not state explicitly, but implies, that victims must be legally represented before the Court.[22] Despite an early decision opining that legal representation was not required for participating victims,[23] in practice victims do not participate unrepresented in any cases before the ICC today. A 2011 request for self-representation in the *Ruto and Sang* case[24] was rejected.[25] In instances

[19] ICC, Comprehensive Report on the Reorganisation of the Registry of the International Criminal Court, August 2016. https://www.icc-cpi.int/itemsDocuments/ICC-Registry-CR.pdf. Accessed 4 Nov 2016, p. 12.

[20] Both the ICC and the ECCC provide some other means by which victims may engage in proceedings—for example by filing complaints, or making representations on whether the ICC Prosecutor should be permitted to open an investigation *proprio motu*. These *ad hoc* forms of participation do not require legal representation.

[21] ECCC Internal Rules, Rule 23 *ter*(1) and (2).

[22] ICC RPE, Rule 90.

[23] ICC, *Prosecutor v. Joseph Kony, Vincent Otti, Okot Odhiambo, Raska Lukwiya, Dominic Ongwen*, Pre-Trial Chamber II, Decision on legal representation, appointment of counsel for the defence, protective measures and time-limit for submission of observations on applications for participation a/0010/06, a/0064/06 to a/0070/06, a/0081/06 to a/0104/06 and a/0111/06 to a/0127/06, ICC-02/04-01/05-134, 1 February 2007, paras 3–11.

[24] ICC, *Prosecutor v. William Samoei Ruto, Henry Kiprono Kosgey and Joshua Arap Sang*, Victims, Motion from Victims a/0041/10, a/0045/10, a/0051/10 and a/0056/10 requesting the Pre-Trial Chamber to Reconsider the Appointment of Common Legal Representative Sureta CHANA for All Victims, ICC-01/09-01/11-314, 31 August 2011, paras 26–27.

[25] ICC, *Prosecutor v. William Samoei Ruto, Henry Kiprono Kosgey and Joshua Arap Sang*, Pre-Trial Chamber II, Decision on the "Motion from Victims a/0041/10, a/0045/10, a/0051/10 and a/0056/10 requesting the Pre-Trial Chamber to Reconsider the Appointment of Common Legal Representative Sureta Chana for All Victims", ICC-01/09-01/11-330, 9 September 2011, para 18. The Single Judge did not provide detailed reasons, referring only to the fact that Article 68(3) of the statute provides that victims' views and concerns 'may be presented by the legal representatives of the victims.'

where victims are unrepresented when their application to participate is accepted, chambers have appointed counsel to represent the victims,[26] suggesting that legal representation is considered necessary.

At the ECCC the introduction of Rule 23*ter* into the Internal Rules in February 2010 made it compulsory for all civil parties to be represented by a civil party lawyer from the issuance of the Closing Order onwards. In addition, all civil parties are represented by the Civil Party Lead Co-Lawyers. It is therefore not permitted at the ECCC for civil parties to participate without legal representation.

Only at the STL is self-representation for participating victims expressly contemplated. There, a victim must participate through a lawyer 'unless the Pre-Trial Judge authorises otherwise.'[27] To date no participating victims have sought to self-represent. The Pre-Trial Judge has noted that the legal representation of participating victims is an important means of ensuring that victims' participation does not impede an expeditious trial or the rights of the accused.[28] It remains unclear in which, if any, circumstances the self-representation of victims would be permitted.

5.3 Identification, Selection and Formal Recognition of LRVs

5.3.1 Minimum Qualification Requirements

The ICC, STL and ECCC use similar systems to regulate the qualifications of private lawyers who represent victims. Minimum requirements are set out in relation to professional experience, language skills, and the absence of criminal or disciplinary offences.[29] Lawyers may apply and if they meet the requirements are

[26] For example: ICC, *Prosecutor v. Bahar Idriss Abu Garda*, Pre-Trial Chamber I, Decision on Applications a/0655/09, a/0656/09, a/0736/09 to a/0747/09, and a/0750/09 to a/0755/09 for Participation in the Proceedings at the Pre-Trial Stage of the Case, ICC-02/05-02/09-255, 19 March 2010, para 33; ICC, *Prosecutor v. Abdallah Banda Abakaer Nourain and Saleh Mohammad Jerbo Jamus*, Pre-Trial Chamber I, Decision on Victims' Participation at the Hearing on the Confirmation of Charges, ICC-02/05-03/09-89, 29 October 2010, para 57; ICC, *Prosecutor v. Dominic Ongwen*, Pre-Trial Chamber II, Decision on contested victims' applications for participation, legal representation of victims and their procedural rights, ICC-02/04-01/15-350, para 21.

[27] STL RPE, Rule 86(C)(ii).

[28] STL, *Prosecutor v. Ayyash* et al., Pre-Trial Judge, Decision on Victims' Participation in the Proceedings, STL11-01/PT/PTJ, 8 May 2012, para 111.

[29] ICC RPE, Rule 22(1), ICC Regulations of the Court, Regulation 67; STL RPE, Rule 51(C)(i) and Rule 59(B); ECCC Internal Rules, Rule 12*bis*(2).

included on a list of qualified counsel.[30] At the STL and ECCC, separate lists are maintained for victims' and Defence counsel, although the minimum qualification requirements are the same. The ICC maintains one list of qualified counsel from which victims' or Defence counsel can be drawn.

5.3.2 A Right to Choose or to Be Consulted on Legal Representation?

Before the ICTY and ICTR, defendants able to afford their own legal representation were entitled to select their own counsel (subject to the minimum qualification requirements).[31] Even an indigent accused person, although not accorded an absolute right to his or her choice of counsel, was presumptively allowed to choose the counsel to be assigned by the tribunal's Registrar.[32]

However, the situation is more complex for participating victims. This is principally because of the large number of participating victims in any given case, as a result of which an unfettered right to select counsel would almost inevitably result in the involvement of numerous counsel. For this reason, participating victims' ability to choose their legal representation is restricted before all three tribunals.

At the STL, no legal provision purports to give victims a right to choose their own legal representation before the Tribunal. This is in clear contrast with the situation of accused persons and suspects before the STL (other than those tried *in absentia*) who are able to choose their counsel.[33] Only the Registrar is empowered to designate counsel to represent victims in the Tribunal's proceedings.[34] At most, victims can expect to be consulted regarding their preferences in relation to legal representation.[35] While victims are free to use the services of privately retained

---

[30] ICC RPE, Rule 21(2); STL RPE, Rule 51(c)(i) and Rule 59(B); ECCC Internal Rules, Rule 11(2)(c) and Rule 12*bis*(1)(c). Regarding procedures related to the lists of counsel see also for the ICC Regulations of the Court, Regulations 69–70, and for the STL the Directive on Victims' Legal Representation, Articles 11–15.

[31] ICTY Statute, Article 21(4); ICTR Statute, Article 20(4).

[32] ICTY, *Prosecutor v. Delalić* et al., Trial Chamber, Decision on Request by Accused Mucić for Assignment of New Counsel, Case No. IT-96-21-T 24 June 1996, para 2; ICTY, *Prosecutor v. Martić*, Trial Chamber, Decision on Appeal Against Decision of Registry, Case No. IT-95-11-PT, 2 August 2002; ICTR, *Prosecutor v. Gérard Ntakirutimana*, Trial Chamber I, Decision on the Motions of the Accused for Replacement of Assigned Counsel, Case No. ICTR-96-10-T, ICTR-96-17-T, 11 June 1997.

[33] STL RPE, Rules 57(D)(iv), 57(D)(vi), 57(D)(vii), 58; STL Directive the Appointment and Assignment of Defence Counsel, on Articles 6(A), 18*bis*, 19(C), 20(A), 21.

[34] STL RPE, Rule 51(G)(i); STL Directive on Victims' Legal Representation, Articles 16–18.

[35] STL Directive on Victims' Legal Representation, Article 20(A).

lawyers to assist in their applications for participation, such lawyers have no status or standing before the STL.

At the ECCC, a civil party may choose his or her own "civil party lawyer" for representation before the Court in pre-trial proceedings.[36] However, as the result of a 2010 amendment to the Internal Rules, from the commencement of proceedings before the Trial Chamber all civil parties are represented collectively by two "Civil Party Lead Co-Lawyers".[37] The Civil Party Lead Co-Lawyers—one Cambodian and one international—are selected by the ECCC.[38] Civil party lawyers selected by civil parties during pre-trial continue to be involved by providing support to the Civil Party Lead Co-Lawyers and serving as intermediaries between the latter and the civil parties they represent, but no longer have standing before the Court in their own right.

The ICC Rules of Procedure and Evidence include Rule 90(1), stating that 'a victim shall be free to choose a legal representative'.[39] However, ICC chambers have consistently held that a victim's right under Rule 90(1) is not absolute, but is subject to the Court's ability to impose common legal representation, as set out in paragraphs (2)–(4) of Rule 90.[40] The practical result is that victims are able to select their own external lawyers,[41] subject to the minimum qualification requirements,

---

[36] ECCC Internal Rules, Rule 22(1)(a) and (b); see also ECCC Practice Direction on Victim Participation, Practice Direction 02/2007/Rev.1, Article 4.

[37] ECCC Internal Rules, Rule 12*ter*.

[38] ECCC Internal Rules, Rule 12*ter*(4).

[39] ICC RPE, Rule 90(1).

[40] ICC, *Prosecutor v. Germain Katanga and Mathieu Ngudjolo Chui*, Trial Chamber II, Trial Chamber III, Order on the organisation of common legal representation of victims, ICC-01/04-01/07-1328, 22 July 2009, para 11; ICC, *Prosecutor v. Jean-Pierre Bemba Gombo,* Trial Chamber III, Decision on common legal representation of victims for the purpose of trial, ICC-01/05-01/08-1005, 10 November 2010, paras 15–16; ICC, *Prosecutor v. Abdallah Banda Abakaer Nourain and Saleh Mohammed Jerbo Jamus*, Trial Chamber IV, Decision on common legal representation, ICC-02/05-03/09-337, 25 May 2012, paras 12–14; *ICC, Prosecutor v. Laurent Gbagbo*, Pre-Trial Chamber I, Decision on Victims' Participation and Victims' Common Legal Representation at the Confirmation of Charges Hearing and in the Related Proceedings, ICC-02/11-01/11-138, 4 June 2012, para 35; ICC, *Prosecutor v. Ahmad Al Faqi Al Mahdi*, Trial Chamber VIII, Public redacted version of 'Decision on Victim Participation at Trial and on Common Legal representation of Victims", ICC01/12-01/15-97-Red, 8 June 2016, para 36.

[41] Victims may not appoint counsel from the OPCV to represent them: only a Chamber may do this: see ICC, *Prosecutor v. Thomas Lubanga Dyilo*, Trial Chamber I, Decision on the role of the Office of Public Counsel for Victims and its request for access to documents, ICC-01/04-01-06-1211, 6 March 2008, para 30; ICC, *Prosecutor v. Jean-Pierre Bemba Gombo*, Trial Chamber III, Decision on the Observations on legal representation of unrepresented applicants, ICC-01/05-01/08-651, 9 December 2009, paras 8–9; ICC, *Prosecutor v. Jean-Pierre Bemba Gombo,* Trial Chamber III, Decision on common legal representation of victims for the purpose of trial, ICC-01/05-01/08-1005, 10 November 2010, para 29.

and can do so in practice by providing a power of attorney.[42] However, this representation will only be recognised by the Court until such time as common legal representation is ordered. As further explained below, once common legal representation is arranged, lawyers are chosen by the Registrar or the chamber, with victims only entitled to be consulted.[43] As common legal representation has been arranged at increasingly earlier stages in ICC proceedings, the practical value of a victim's "right" to select their own lawyer has become extremely limited.

Indeed, in practice victims can at best usually expect to be *consulted* in the choice of their LRV rather than to claim a right to *choose* that person. The extent to which victims are consulted, and their views are taken into account in the selection of a common legal representative is discussed further below.

5.3.3 Legal Representation During the Application Process

As detailed in Chap. 2, all three courts require victims to submit an application and then await a formal grant of status in order to participate in proceedings on an ongoing manner. In practice, lawyers may assist victims during this process in different ways. They may assist victims to complete an application for participation. Good quality legal representation at this point in the application process can ensure that applications are completed clearly and consistently with all the information necessary for demonstrating that the legal requirements for participation are met. It can also serve to protect the victim from the inclusion of unnecessary information which might later prove identifying or otherwise harmful if the applications are disclosed to parties during the proceedings. Having applications well-completed from a legal point of view may be beneficial not only to the victims, but may also increase the efficiency of the applications' processing by the courts.

Unfortunately, none of the three courts provides systems or resources to assist victims in obtaining legal assistance in the completion of their applications. In some instances, non-government organisations working with victims link them to a lawyer for the purpose, or private lawyers offer their services pro-bono. In many other cases, however, victims submit an application for participation without

[42] See for example: ICC, *Prosecutor v Dominic Ongwen*, Pre-Trial Chamber II, Order to the Registrar in relation to the legal representation of victims participating in the proceedings, ICC-02/04-01/15-331, 28 October 2015, para 4. In *Ongwen* the Single Judge during pre-trial proceedings also required that the Registry verify all powers of attorney received before formally recognising the counsel concerned. See ibid., at paras 5–7, and ICC, *Prosecutor v Dominic Ongwen*, Pre-Trial Chamber II, Decision on contested victims' applications for participation, legal representation of victims and their procedural rights, ICC-02/04-01/15-350, 27 November 2015, para 16.

[43] See for example the decision in *Bemba*, by which Trial Chamber III rejected a Registry proposal to provide victims with a form so that they could provide a power of attorney choosing their common legal representative. The Chamber emphasised that a common legal representative is chosen by the court, not by the victims: ICC, *Prosecutor v. Jean-Pierre Bemba Gombo*, Trial Chamber III, Decision on common legal representation, ICC-01/05-01/08-1005, 10 November 2010, paras 15–17.

legal assistance. In some instances, they may then appoint or be provided with a lawyer to represent them until such time as their application is accepted. None of the tribunals recognise a *right* of victims to be legally represented prior to the acceptance of their application for participation, however at least at the ICC and the ECCC such representation is possible.

At the STL, victims' legal representation is recognised once they have been granted the status of victim participating in the proceedings.[44] Since victims are unable to arrange their own legal representation before the STL and must await the designation of LRVs by the Registrar after being granted participation status, the Tribunal does not formally recognise any legal representation which may be privately arranged by victims during the application stage. However, in the event that a victim's application for participation is rejected, the Registrar may exercise his discretion to designate a duty LRV to assist the victim in an appeal.[45]

At the ECCC, victims who apply for civil party status may appoint a civil party lawyer to represent them by providing a power of attorney, and that lawyer is then recognised by the Court.[46] The role of that lawyer is somewhat limited until a decision is taken granting formal status to the victim. During the application process the civil party lawyer may assist the victim to complete an application form and collect any necessary supplementary information. However, victims may also apply for civil party status without legal representation, in which case they are later assisted by the VSS to select civil party lawyers once they obtain civil party status.

ICC practice does not demonstrate an entitlement for victims to benefit from legal representation during the application process. Nonetheless, where applicants provide powers of attorney for private lawyers their representation is recognised by the Registry, which in practice will then deal with the appointed lawyer where any issues arise during the application process. Additionally, some chambers have opted to appoint the OPCV to represent otherwise unrepresented applicants from the time their application is received by the Registry.[47] In other cases no represen-

---

[44] STL Directive on Victims' Legal Representation, Article 6.

[45] STL Directive on Victims' Legal Representation, Article 18(A)(i).

[46] Interview with Eleonor Fernandez, Senior legal consultant, Civil Party Lead Co-Lawyers Section, ECCC, 8 June 2015 (records on file with the author).

[47] ICC, *Situation in the Democratic Republic of Congo*, Pre-Trial Chamber I, Decision on the Requests of the Legal Representative of Applicants on application process for victims' participation and legal representation, ICC-01/04-374, 17 August 2007, paras 43–44, 50; ICC, *Prosecutor v. Jean-Pierre Bemba Gombo*, Pre-Trial Chamber III, Decision on Victim Participation, ICC-01/05-01/08-103-tENG, 12 September 2008, para 10; ICC, *Prosecutor v. Jean-Pierre Bemba Gombo*, Trial Chamber III, Decision on the Observations on legal representation of unrepresented applicants, ICC-01/05-01/08-651, 9 December 2009; ICC, *Prosecutor v. Jean-Pierre Bemba Gombo*, Trial Chamber III, Decision on the legal representation of victim applicants at trial, ICC-01/-05-01/08-1020, 19 November 2010; ICC, *Prosecutor v. Willliam Samoei Ruto, Henry Kiprono Kosgey and Joshua Arap Sang*, Registry, Proposal for the common legal representation of victims, ICC-01/09-01/11-243, 1 August 2011, para 23; ICC, *Prosecutor v. Francis Kirimi Muthaura, Uhuru Muigai Kenyatta and Mohammad Hussein Ali*, Registry, Proposal for the common legal representation of victims, ICC-01/09-02/11-214, 5 August 2011, para 23.

tation was provided for such applicants. At least one chamber expressly stated that no legal representation is required prior to victim status being granted, and that the support of the VPRS is sufficient to protect applicants' rights.[48]

Indeed, the usefulness of legal representation for applicants at the ICC is limited by the very restricted standing of such applicants: they are unable in any event to respond to observations on their applications, or to appeal if their applications for participation are rejected (see Chap. 2). Despite this, legal representation at this stage is not entirely without value. Where applications are incomplete or faulty, an LRV can assist the victim in submitting supplementary information. Legal representation for applicants may even become necessary in specific rare instances in which applicants not yet granted formal status may be heard before the Court. This has occurred for example in relation to an Article 19 challenge to jurisdiction or admissibility, in which OPCV has been appointed to represent applicants in relation to the challenge.[49] In at least one instance applications were permitted to be heard at opening statements where time had been insufficient to process their applications, with OPCV representing them for this purpose.[50]

---

[48] ICC, *Prosecutor v. Bosco Ntaganda*, Pre-Trial Chamber I, Decision Establishing Principles on the victims' Application Process, ICC-01/04-02/06-67, 28 May 2013, para 45.

[49] ICC, *Prosecutor v. Laurent Gbagbo*, Pre-Trial Chamber I, Decision on the conduct of the proceedings following the defence challenge to the jurisdiction of the court pursuant to Article 19 of the Rome Statute, ICC-02/11-01/11-153, 15 June 2012, para 7; ICC, *Prosecutor v. Saif Al-Islam Gaddafi and Abddullah Al-Senussi*, Pre-Trial Chamber I, Decision on the Conduct of the Proceedings Following the "Application on behalf of the Government of Libya pursuant to Article 19 of the Statute", ICC-01/11-01/11-134, 4 May 2012, para 13; ICC, *Prosecutor v. Simone Gbagbo*, Pre-Trial Chamber I, Decision on the conduct of the proceedings following Côte d'Ivoire's challenge to the admissibility of the case against Simone Gbagbo, ICC-02/11-01/12-15, 15 November 2013, para 10. See also the *Kony* case, in which the OPCV was appointed to represent applicants for participation: ICC, *Prosecutor v. Joseph Kony, Vincent Otti, Okot Odhiambo, Raska Lukwiya, Dominic Ongwen*, Pre-Trial Chamber II, Decision on legal representation, appointment of counsel for the defence, protective measures and time-limit for submission of observations on applications for participation a/0010/06, a/0064/06, to a/0070/06, a/0081/06 to a/0104/06 and a/0111/06 to a/0127/06, ICC-02/04-01/05-134, 1 February 2007, para 13; ICC, *Prosecutor v. Joseph Kony, Vincent Otti, Okot Odhiambo, Dominic Ongwen*, Pre-Trial Chamber II, Decision on legal representation, appointment of counsel for the defence, criteria for redactions of applications for participation, and submission of observations on applications for participation a/0014/07 to a/0020/07 and a/0076/07 to a/0125/07, ICC-02/04-01/05-312, 17 September 2008, p. 7. Such applicants were subsequently permitted to participate in the Article 19 process: ICC, *Prosecutor v. Joseph Kony, Vincent Otti, Okot Odhiambo, Dominic Ongwen*, Pre-Trial Chamber II, Decision initiating proceedings under Article 19, requesting observations and appointing counsel for the Defence, 21 October 2008, ICC-02/04-01/05-320, p. 7.

[50] ICC, *Prosecutor v. Jean-Pierre Bemba Gombo*, Trial Chamber III, Decision on the legal representation of victim applicants at trial, ICC-01/05-01/08-1020, 19 November 2010. But note that a similar approach was rejected in: ICC, *Prosecutor v. Callixte Mbarushimana*, Pre-Trial Chamber I, Decision on the "Proposal for victim participation in the confirmation hearing", 10 June 2011.

In the instances where OPCV has represented applicants, and where common legal representation has not yet been arranged, OPCV has sometimes been permitted to continue the representation of those persons once they have been granted victim status.[51] Nonetheless, where external common legal representation has been arranged, applicants represented by OPCV will have their representation taken over by the common legal representative once they are granted status to participate.[52] The resulting discontinuity in legal representation has led the Registry to propose that once common legal representation has been arranged, applicants should also be represented by the common legal representative, rather than by OPCV.[53] To date this has not been done.

5.3.4 Common Legal Representation/Court-Arranged Collective Legal Representation

As explained above, all three tribunals limit a participating victim's right to select his or her own legal representative. In all three instances, this is because the tribunals themselves intervene to arrange collective representation.

Each tribunal uses its own approach for arranging collective legal representation, and variation among ICC chambers is also notable. It is, however, possible, in general terms, to identify some common features of the system of collective legal representation used at the tribunals:

---

[51] Trial Chambers I and III required Registrar to designate an alternative counsel, but was prepared to consider any objection to this made by OPCV if a reason was given why representation by the alternative counsel 'may be detrimental' to the victims: ICC, *Prosecutor v. Thomas Lubanga Dyilo*, Trial Chamber I, Decision on the role of the Office of Public Counsel for Victims and its request for access to documents, ICC-01/04-01-06-1211, 6 March 2008, para 34; ICC, *Prosecutor v. Jean-Pierre Bemba Gombo*, Trial Chamber III, Decision on the Observations on legal representation of unrepresented applicants, ICC-01/05-01/08-651, 9 December 2009, *dispositif.*

[52] ICC, *Prosecutor v. Jean-Pierre Bemba Gombo*, Trial Chamber III, Decision on the legal representation of victim applicants at trial, ICC-01/-05-01/08-1020, 19 November 2010, para 25; ICC, *Prosecutor v. Willliam Samoei Ruto, Henry Kiprono Kosgey and Joshua Arap Sang*, Registry, Proposal for the common legal representation of victims, ICC-01/09-01/11-243, 1 August 2011, para 23; ICC, *Prosecutor v. Francis Kirimi Muthaura, Uhuru Muigai Kenyatta and Mohammad Hussein Ali*, Registry, Proposal for the common legal representation of victims, ICC-01/09-02/11-214, 5 August 2011, para 23.

[53] ICC, *Prosecutor v. Willliam Samoei Ruto, Henry Kiprono Kosgey and Joshua Arap Sang*, Registry, Proposal for the common legal representation of victims, ICC-01/09-01/11-243, 1 August 2011, para 38; ICC, *Prosecutor v. Francis Kirimi Muthaura, Uhuru Muigai Kenyatta and Mohammad Hussein Ali*, Registry, Proposal for the common legal representation of victims, ICC-01/09-02/11-214, 5 August 2011, para 38.

- The court determines that victims will be represented in one or more groups.
- Where victims are divided into more than one group, the court determines the criteria which form the basis for their division.
- The court selects at least one LRV for each group.

The following considers the approach taken by each tribunal on various essential features of collective representation: when collective representation is initiated, how victims are grouped for collective representation, how LRVs are selected, and how they are formally designated. First, however, it is useful to consider the justifications given for the arrangement of collective legal representation by the courts.

(i) Rationale for Court-arranged Collective Legal Representation

At the ICC and the ECCC early experience with victims' legal representation was characterised by multiple groups of participating victims, arranged by intermediaries and/or the lawyers themselves. In *Case 001* at the ECCC, four groups of civil parties were represented at trial.[54] In *Lubanga* at the ICC, three groups of victims participated at trial.[55] Subsequent cases at each court seemed likely to involve significantly larger numbers of victims, and therefore perhaps more separately represented groups.

Referring to the 'need to streamline and consolidate civil party participation' in light of large victim numbers in *Case 002*, in 2010 the ECCC plenary amended the Internal Rules to create a system of court-arranged collective representation which would operate at the trial stage.[56] At the ICC, while the power to impose "common legal representation" already existed in the original RPE, it was applied with increased vigour after the *Lubanga* case. Common legal representation is intended to ensure 'the effectiveness of the proceedings'.[57] Chambers have pointed out that, in addition to ensuring proceedings are able to be conducted fairly expeditiously, common legal representation contributes to effective and meaningful participation

---

[54] ECCC, *Case 001,* Trial Chamber, Judgement, Case No. 001/18-07-2007/ECCC/TC, 26 July 2010, para 9.

[55] ICC, *Prosecutor v. Thomas Lubanga Dyilo*, Transcript 22 January 2009, ICC-01/04-01/06-T-105-ENG, p. 13.

[56] ECCC Press release: 7th Plenary Session of the ECCC commences Tuesday 2 February, 28 January 2010; ECCC Internal Rules, Rule 12*ter* and Rule 23(5).

[57] ICC RPE, Rule 90(2); ICC, *Prosecutor v. Thomas Lubanga Dyilo*, Trial Chamber I, Decision on Victims' Participation, ICC-01/04-01/06-1119, 18 January 2008, para 123; ICC, *Prosecutor v. Jean-Pierre Bemba Gombo*, Pre-Trial Chamber III, Fifth Decision on Victims' Issues Concerning Common Legal Representation, ICC-01/05-01/08-322, 16 December 2008, para 7; ICC, *Prosecutor v. Abdallah Banda Abakaer Nourain and Saleh Mohammed Jerbo Jamus*, Trial Chamber IV, Decision on common legal representation, ICC-02/05-03/09-337, 25 May 2012, para 38.

by victims.[58] Indeed, when conducted effectively, a system of collective representation should ensure that victims can be represented more coherently and concisely, by removing the risk of duplication or unexplained inconsistency among the submissions of multiple representatives.

By virtue of amendments to its RPE in February 2012, and a Directive on Victims' Legal Representation (the 'Directive') adopted in May 2012, the STL followed the ECCC and ICC in adopting a system of tribunal-arranged collective representation. In arranging legal representation for the first time the Pre-Trial Judge endorsed the rationales for common legal representation given by ICC chambers.[59]

(ii) When Is the Arrangement of Collective Legal Representation Initiated?

At both the ECCC and the STL the question of when victims' collective representation begins is clearly fixed by the relevant texts.

Under the ECCC Internal Rules, the role of the Civil Party Lead Co-Lawyers begins in a given case once the Trial Chamber is seized of the case.[60]

At the STL the process is triggered as soon as victims are granted the status to participate by the Pre-Trial Judge: he is required to decide at the same time on their grouping for the purposes of legal representation,[61] following which the Registrar must designate a lead LRV for each group of victims.[62] In practice in the *Ayyash* et al. case, this occurred during pre-trial proceedings, more than a year and a half before the eventual start of trial.[63]

At the ICC, the RPE creates a more flexible situation, allowing the chamber seized of a case (whether a Pre-Trial Chamber or a Trial Chamber) to determine if and when common legal representation is necessary.[64] The chamber will do so

---

[58] ICC, *Prosecutor v. Abdallah Banda Abakaer Nourain and Saleh Mohammed Jerbo Jamus*, Trial Chamber IV, Order instructing the Registry to start Consultations on the Organisation of Common Legal Representation, ICC-02/05-03/09-138, 21 April 2011, para 4; ICC, *Prosecutor v. William Samoei Ruto, Henry Kiprono Kosgey and Joshua Arap Sang*, Pre-Trial Chamber II, Decision on Victims' Participation at the confirmation of Charges Hearing and In the Related Proceedings, ICC-01/09-01/11-249, 5 August 2011, para 65; ICC, *Prosecutor v. Francis Kirimi Muthaura, Uhuru Muigai Kenyatta and Mohammad Hussein Ali*, Pre-Trial Chamber II, Decision on Victims' Participation at the Confirmation of Charges Hearing and in the Related Proceedings, ICC-01/09-02/11-267, 26 August 2011, para 79.

[59] STL, *Prosecutor v. Ayyash* et al., Pre-Trial Judge, Decision on Victims' Participation in the Proceedings, STL11-01/T/PTJ, 8 May 2012, paras 110–111.

[60] ECCC Internal Rules, Rule 12*ter*(4).

[61] STL RPE, Rule 86(D).

[62] STL Directive on Victims' Legal Representation, Article 16(A).

[63] STL, *Prosecutor v. Ayyash* et al., Pre-Trial Judge, Decision on Victims' Participation in the Proceedings, STL11-01/T/PTJ, 8 May 2012; STL, *Prosecutor v. Ayyash* et al., Pre-Trial Judge, Designation of Victims' Legal Representatives, 16 May 2012. The trial in *Prosecutor v. Ayyash* et al. commenced on 16 January 2014.

[64] ICC RPE, Rule 90(2) and (3). See also ICC, *Prosecutor v. Thomas Lubanga Dyilo*, Trial Chamber I, Decision on Victims' Participation, ICC-01/04-01/06-1119, 18 January 2008, para 123.

when it considers it 'necessary in order to ensure the effectiveness of the proceedings'[65] or 'to safeguard the expeditiousness of the proceedings and the effectiveness of victim participation'[66] or 'with the view to ensuring meaningful victims' participation as well as fairness and expeditiousness of the proceedings'.[67]

In the early cases—*Lubanga* as well as *Katanga and Ngudjolo Chui*—the process was not initiated until after the confirmation of charges and the transfer of the case to a trial chamber. In subsequent cases efforts have sometimes been made to arrange common legal representation as early as possible. In most of the cases following *Katanga and Ngudjolo Chui*, Pre-Trial Chambers have ordered common legal representation to be arranged before the confirmation of charges hearing.[68] In *Ntaganda*, Pre-Trial Chamber I took its first steps towards arranging common legal representation only two months after the suspect was surrendered to the Court.[69] The Chamber explained that it was appropriate to arrange common legal representation early, even before victims had been accepted to participate in the proceedings, as there was otherwise a danger of doing so too soon before the

[65] ICC, *Prosecutor v. Thomas Lubanga Dyilo*, Trial Chamber I, Decision on Victims' Participation, ICC-01/04-01/06-1119, 18 January 2008, para 123; ICC, *Prosecutor v. Jean-Pierre Bemba Gombo*, Pre-Trial Chamber III, Fifth Decision on Victims' Issues Concerning Common Legal Representation, ICC-01/05-01/08-322, 16 December 2008, para 7.

[66] ICC, *Prosecutor v. Abdallah Banda Abakaer Nourain and Saleh Mohammed Jerbo Jamus*, Trial Chamber IV, Order instructing the Registry to start Consultations on the Organisation of Common Legal Representation, ICC-02/05-03/09-138, 21 April 2011, para 4.

[67] ICC, *Prosecutor v. William Samoei Ruto, Henry Kiprono Kosgey and Joshua Arap Sang*, Pre-Trial Chamber II, Decision on Victims' Participation at the confirmation of Charges Hearing and In the Related Proceedings, ICC-01/09-01/11-249, 5 August 2011, para 65; ICC, *Prosecutor v. Francis Kirimi Muthaura, Uhuru Muigai Kenyatta and Mohammad Hussein Ali*, Pre Trial Chamber II, Decision on Victims' Participation at the Confirmation of Charges Hearing and in the Related Proceedings, ICC-01/09-02/11-267, 26 August 2011, para 79.

[68] ICC, *Prosecutor v. Jean-Pierre Bemba Gombo*, Pre-Trial Chamber III, Fifth Decision on Victims' Issues Concerning Common Legal Representation, ICC-01/05-01/08-322, 16 December 2008, para 7; ICC, *Prosecutor v. William Samoei Ruto, Henry Kiprono Kosgey and Joshua Arap Sang*, Pre-Trial Chamber II, First Decision on Victims' Participation in the Case, ICC-01/09-01/11-17, 30 March 2011, para 24; ICC, *Prosecutor v. Francis Kirimi Muthaura, Uhuru Muigai Kenyatta and Mohammad Hussein Ali*, Pre-Trial Chamber II, First Decision on Victims' Participation in the Case, ICC-01/09-02/11-23, 30 March 2011, para 24; ICC, *Prosecutor v. Callixte Mbarushimana*, Pre-Trial Chamber I, Decision on the 138 applications for victims' participation in the proceedings, 11 August 2011, paras 46–48; ICC, *Prosecutor v. Laurent Gbagbo*, Pre-Trial Chamber I, Second decision on issues related to the victims' application process, ICC-02/11-01/11-86, 5 April 2012, para 44. ICC, *Prosecutor v. Charles Blé Goudé*, Pre-Trial Chamber I, Decision on victims' participation in the pre-trial proceedings and related issues, ICC-02/11-02/11-83, 11 June 2014, paras 22–25. Exceptions to this practice occurred in the *Abu Garda* and *Banda and Jerbo* cases, in which common legal representation was not arranged during pre-trial proceedings, and various lawyers selected by the victims appeared in the confirmation of charges hearings.

[69] ICC, *Prosecutor v. Bosco Ntaganda*, Pre-Trial I, Decision Establishing Principles on the Victims' Application Process, ICC-01/04-02/06-67, 28 May 2013, para 46.

confirmation of charges hearing, leaving inadequate time for the appointed lawyers to prepare.[70]

Indeed, since the experience in *Lubanga*, the ICC Registry has often urged chambers to begin early with the initiation of common legal representation.[71] Despite this, recent experience is not uniform in this respect. For example, in the *Ongwen* case, common legal representation had not been initiated by the Pre-Trial Chamber by the time of the confirmation of charges hearing, and despite a request from LRVs the Trial Chamber later declined to initiate common legal representation.[72]

Additionally, while an ICC chamber has the power to determine when it is necessary to begin the process of arranging common legal representation, an additional step is required (at least according to the legal texts) before the Court can itself impose its arrangement of legal representation on participating victims. According to Rule 90(2), where a chamber determines that common legal representation is to be arranged, it should first provide victims with an opportunity to *themselves* 'choose a common legal representative or representatives'. Assistance to enable this may be provided by the Registry.[73]

In practice, however, this requirement has become nugatory. In some early cases, chambers required the Registry to assist victims to arrange their own legal representation,[74] leaving the Registry faced with enormous logistical challenges

---

[70] ICC, *Prosecutor v. Bosco Ntaganda*, Pre-Trial Chamber I, Decision Concerning the Organisation of Common Legal Representation of Victims, ICC-01/04-02/06-160, 2 December 2013, paras 20–21.

[71] ICC, *Prosecutor v. Germain Katanga and Mathieu Ngudjolo Chui*, Registrar, Response to the questions raised by the Trial Chamber II on 13 November 2008 and additional observations, ICC-01/04-01/07-765, 24 November 2008, p. 10; ICC, *Prosecutor v. Abdallah Banda Abakaer Nourain and Saleh Mohammed Jerbo Jamus*, Registry, Report recommending a decision concerning the common legal representation of victims participating in the case, ICC-02/05-03/09-134, 15 April 2011, para 8; ICC, *Prosecutor v. Willliam Samoei Ruto, Henry Kiprono Kosgey and Joshua Arap Sang*, Registry, Proposal for the common legal representation of victims, ICC-01/09-01/11-243, 1 August 2011, para 3; ICC, *Prosecutor v. Francis Kirimi Muthaura, Uhuru Muigai Kenyatta and Mohammad Hussein Ali*, Registry, Proposal for the common legal representation of victims, ICC-01/09-02/11-214, 5 August 2011, para 3.

[72] ICC, *Prosecutor v. Dominic Ongwen*, Trial Chamber IX, Decision on Requests Concerning Organisation of Victim Representation, ICC-02/04-01/15-476, 17 June 2016.

[73] ICC RPE, Rule 90(2).

[74] For example: ICC, *Prosecutor v. Jean-Pierre Bemba Gombo*, Pre-Trial Chamber III, ICC-01/05-01/08-322, 16 December 2008, para 10; ICC, *Prosecutor v. Abdallah Banda Abakaer Nourain and Saleh Mohammed Jerbo Jamus*, Trial Chamber IV, Order instructing the Registry to start consultations on the organisation of common legal representation, ICC-02/05-03/09-138, 21 April 2011, para 5; and the order of Trial Chamber IV quoted in: ICC, *Prosecutor v. Abdallah Banda Abakaer Nourain and Saleh Mohammed Jerbo Jamus*, Registry, Report on the organization of common legal representation, ICC-02/05-03/09-187, 5 August 2011, para 1.

and often a short timeframe.[75] In some cases the Registry sought to rely on proposals for arranging legal representation made by existing LRVs rather than speaking directly with victims,[76] but later abandoned this practice as problematic.[77] Indeed, some chambers have apparently refused to accept an arrangement reached upon existing LRVs as constituting a choice by victims under Rule 90(2).[78] In other instances the Registry simply reported that it had insufficient time or resources to assist victims to choose their own LRV(s) or was unable to do so because victims had not yet been accepted to participate in the proceedings.[79] Attempts to challenge the appointment of common legal represen-

[75] ICC, *Prosecutor v. Willliam Samoei Ruto, Henry Kiprono Kosgey and Joshua Arap Sang*, Registry, Proposal for the common legal representation of victims, ICC-01/09-01/11-243, 1 August 2011, paras 4–5; ICC, *Prosecutor v. Francis Kirimi Muthaura, Uhuru Muigai Kenyatta and Mohammad Hussein Ali*, Registry, Proposal for the common legal representation of victims, ICC-01/09-02/11-214, 5 August 2011, paras 4–5.

[76] ICC, *Prosecutor v. Thomas Lubanga Dyilo*, Trial Chamber I, Decision on the applications by victims to participate in the proceedings, ICC-01/04-01/06-1556-Corr-Anx 3, 15 December 2008, para 137(e); ICC, *Prosecutor v. Germain Katanga and Mathieu Ngudjolo Chui*, Registry, Response to the questions raised by the Trial Chamber II on 13 November 2008 and additional observations, ICC-01/04-01/07-765, 24 November 2008, pp. 10–11.

[77] ICC, *Prosecutor v. Abdallah Banda Abakaer Nourain and Saleh Mohammed Jerbo Jamus*, Registry, Report on the organization of common legal representation, ICC-02/05-03/09-187, 5 August 2011, para 5; ICC, *Prosecutor v. Willliam Samoei Ruto, Henry Kiprono Kosgey and Joshua Arap Sang*, Registry, Proposal for the common legal representation of victims, ICC-01/09-01/11-243, 1 August 2011, para 7; ICC, *Prosecutor v. Francis Kirimi Muthaura, Uhuru Muigai Kenyatta and Mohammad Hussein Ali*, Registry, Proposal for the common legal representation of victims, ICC-01/09-02/11-214, 5 August 2011, para 7.

[78] See for example in *Katanga and Ngudjolo Chui*, where a proposal was made jointly by existing legal representatives but not accepted by the Chamber: ICC, *Prosecutor v. Germain Katanga and Mathieu Ngudjolo Chui*, Legal Representatives of Victims, Corrigendum à la Soumission relative à la representation légale commune, ICC-01/04-01/07-876-Corr, 6 February 2009; ICC, *Prosecutor v. Germain Katanga and Mathieu Ngudjolo Chui*, Trial Chamber II, Order on the organisation of common legal representation of victims, ICC-01/04-01/07-1328, 22 July 2009, *dispositif*.

[79] ICC, *Prosecutor v. Abdallah Banda Abakaer Nourain and Saleh Mohammed Jerbo Jamus*, Registry, Report on the organization of common legal representation, ICC-02/05-03/09-187, 5 August 2011, paras 2–4; ICC, *Prosecutor v. William Samoei Ruto, Henry Kipromo Kosget and Joshuua Arap Sang*, Registry, Proposal for the common legal representation of victims, ICC-01/09-01/11-243, 1 August 2011, paras 5–8; *Prosecutor v. Francis Kirimi Muthaura, Uhuru Muigai Kenyatta and Mohammed Hussein Ali*, Registry, Proposal for the common legal representation of victims, ICC-01/09-02/11-214, 1 August 2011, paras 5–8.

tation for a failure to implement Rule 90(2) have not succeeded.[80] And in more recent cases, chambers appear to dispense entirely with the step required by Rule 90(2), instead proceeding directly to the grouping of victims and the selection of lawyers.[81]

(iii) Grouping of Victims for the Purpose of Court-arranged Collective Legal Representation

While the ICC and STL undertake discretionary processes for the determination of victim groupings, at the ECCC the position is fixed by the Internal Rules: in any given case all civil parties will be represented in one "consolidated group" by the Civil Party Lead Co-Lawyers.[82] This represents a kind of umbrella grouping, within which any number of smaller groups of victims can be represented by civil party lawyers. Ultimately, however, it is the Civil Party Lead Co-Lawyers who are responsible for the representation in court of all civil parties. This situation has been criticised as failing to account for possible conflicts of interest among civil parties in a case.[83] In practice, such conflicts have only very rarely been brought to the attention of the Court: in one instance in which a civil party was said to have suffered harm during the Khmer Rouge period as a result of crimes committed by another civil party, the Court ordered for them to be

[80] See e.g. objections raised in ICC, *Prosecutor v. Abdallah Banda Abakaer Nourain and Saleh Mohammed Jerbo Jamus*, Victims' Legal Representatives, Joint Observations of Victims' Legal Representatives on Common Legal Representation, ICC-02/05-03/09-182, 18 July 2011 and ICC, *Prosecutor v. Abdallah Banda Abakaer Nourain and Saleh Mohammed Jerbo Jamus*, Victims' Legal Representatives, Joint Victims' Observations on the Registry "Report on the organisation of common legal representation" and Request for the Joint Agreement on Common Legal Representation to the adopted pursuant to the Trial Chamber's Order, ICC-02/05-03/09-200, 22 August 2011, which were not accepted by the Chamber: ICC, *Prosecutor v. Abdallah Banda Abakaer Nourain and Saleh Mohammed Jerbo Jamus*, Trial Chamber IV, Order inviting the Registrar to appoint a common legal representative, ICC-02/05-03/09-209, 6 September 2011. See also ICC, *Prosecutor v. William Samoei Ruto, Henry Kiprono Kosgey and Joshua Arap Sang*, Victims' Legal Representatives, Motion from Victims a/0041/10, a/0045/10, a/0051/10 and a/0056/10 requesting the Pre-Trial Chamber to Reconsider the Appointment of Common Legal Representative Sureta CHANA for All Victims, ICC-01/09-01/11-314, 31 August 2011; which was rejected by the Chamber in: ICC, *Prosecutor v. William Samoei Ruto, Henry Kiprono Kosgey and Joshua Arap Sang*, Pre-Trial Chamber II, Decision on the "Motion from Victims a/0041/10, a/0045/10, a/0051/10 and a/0056/10 requesting the Pre-Trial Chamber to Reconsider the Appointment of Common Legal Representative Sureta Chana for All Victims", ICC-01/09-01/11-330, 9 September 2011.

[81] For example: ICC, *Prosecutor v. Bosco Ntaganda*, Pre-Trial Chamber II, Decision Concerning the Organisation of Common Legal Representation of Victims, ICC-01/04-02/06-160, 2 December 2013.

[82] ECCC Internal Rules, Rule 23(3). See also Rule 12*ter*(5)(a).

[83] A Werner and D Rudy, "Civil Party Representation at the ECCC: Sounding the Retreat in International Criminal Law, *Northwestern Journal of International Human Rights*, vol. 8, issue 3, Summer 2010.

represented by different civil party lawyers, although both remaining as participants within the single consolidated group.[84]

In contrast, at both the ICC and the STL, judges determine the number of victim groups in a case, and the constitution of those groups where they are more than one. At the STL this is done by the Pre-Trial Judge.[85] The VPU may make submissions on the issue, but these are not determinative.[86] At the ICC although no Rule expressly provides as such,[87] in practice the chamber seized of the case will decide on the grouping of victims,[88] though usually based on a Registry proposal including an analysis of the victim population.

The approaches of the ICC and STL are also very similar regarding the criteria to be used by the chamber in taking a decision on victim grouping. At the ICC the RPE require reasonable steps to ensure that the 'distinct interests of the victims [...] are represented, and that any conflict of interest is avoided'.[89] At the STL, the Pre-Trial Judge shall consider 'any conflicting interests that may hinder common representation; [...] any shared or similar interests that may facilitate common representation; and [...] the rights of the accused and the interests of a fair and expeditious trial.'[90]

Despite some early deviations at the ICC,[91] the jurisprudence at both courts now appears to demonstrate a presumption in favour of victims being represented

---

84 Interview with Eleonor Fernandez, Senior legal consultant, Civil Party Lead Co-Lawyers Section, ECCC, 8 June 2015 (records on file with the authors). Further details are not available as the matter was considered in confidential filings.

85 STL RPE, Rule 86(D).

86 For example, in the *Ayyash* et al. case, the VPU's recommendations were rejected by the Pre-Trial Judge: STL, *Prosecutor v. Ayyash* et al., Pre-Trial Judge, Decision on Victims' Participation in the Proceedings, STL-11-01/T/PTJ, 8 May 2012, paras 121–127.

87 Although this may arguably be inferred from Rule 90(3) which says that the Chamber may request the Registrar to 'choose one or more common legal representative': ICC RPE, Rule 90(3).

88 For example: ICC, *Prosecutor v. Laurent Gbagbo*, Pre-Trial Chamber I, Decision on Victims' Participation and Victims' Common Legal Representation at the Confirmation of Charges Hearing and in the Related Proceedings, ICC-02/11-01/11-138, 4 June 2012, para 40; ICC, *Prosecutor v. Bosco Ntaganda*, Pre-Trial Chamber II, Decision Concerning the Organisation of Common Legal Representation of Victims, ICC-01/04-02/06-160, 2 December 2013, para 23.

89 ICC RPE, Rule 90(4).

90 STL RPE, Rule 86(D).

91 In both the *Lubanga* case and at the trial stage in *Bemba*, decisions were taken to create more than one group, but with no explanation provided as to why victims could not be represented in one group: ICC, *Prosecutor v. Thomas Lubanga Dyilo*, Transcript 22 January 2009, ICC-01/04-01/06-T-105-ENG, p. 13; ICC, *Prosecutor v. Jean-Pierre Bemba Gombo*, Trial Chamber III, Decision on common legal representation of victims for the purpose of trial, ICC-01/05-01/08-1005, 10 November 2010, paras 18–21.

through a single group. This has been stated expressly at the STL,[92] and can be inferred from several ICC decisions.[93] As the ICC Registry has pointed out, minimising the number of groups has various benefits: it increases the expeditiousness of the proceedings (fewer representatives making submissions), maximises the prospects of coherent strategy from victims, and is more financially efficient, being cheaper than constituting multiple teams of a smaller size.[94] Some of these reasons have also been given by chambers.[95]

Nonetheless, the presumption in favour of a single group may be displaced where it is shown that there is a conflict of interest, or possibly where there is a significant division of interests, among the participating victims in a case.

Defining in abstract terms what constitutes a conflict of interest requiring separate representation remains difficult. Trial Chamber IV at the ICC indicated that 'conflict of interest may arise when the situation or the specificity of the victims is so different that their interests are irreconcilable.'[96] In two cases to date—*Katanga and Ngudjolo Chui* and *Ntaganda*—ICC chambers have specifically divided victims into two separate groups because of an identified conflict of interest among them. Both cases involved some participating victims who had been child soldiers and were said to have participated in the attacks

---

92 STL, *Prosecutor v. Ayyash* et al., Pre-Trial Judge, Decision on Victims' Participation in the Proceedings, STL11-01/T/PTJ, 8 May 2012, paras 119–120.

93 ICC, *Prosecutor v. William Samoei Ruto, Henry Kiprono Kosgey and Joshua Arap Sang*, Pre-Trial Chamber II, Decision on Victims' Participation at the confirmation of Charges Hearing and In the Related Proceedings, ICC-01/09-01/11-249, 5 August 2011, para 65; ICC, *Prosecutor v. Francis Kirimi Muthaura, Uhuru Muigai Kenyatta and Mohammad Hussein Ali*, Pre-Trial Chamber II, Decision on Victims' Participation at the Confirmation of Charges Hearing and in the Related Proceedings, ICC-01/09-02/11-267, 26 August 2011, para 79; see also ICC, *Prosecutor v. Laurent Gbagbo*, Pre-Trial Chamber I, Decision on Victims' Participation and Victims' Common Legal Representation at the Confirmation of Charges Hearing and in the Related Proceedings, ICC-02/11-01/11-138, 4 June 2012, para 40 which endorsed the reasons of the Registry for a single grouping given in ICC, *Prosecutor v. Laurent Gbagbo*, Pre-Trial Chamber I, Legal framework and Registry's approach on common legal representation, ICC-02/11-01/11-120-Anx1, 16 May 2012, paras 9–10.

94 ICC, *Prosecutor v. Willliam Samoei Ruto, Henry Kiprono Kosgey and Joshua Arap Sang*, Registry, Proposal for the common legal representation of victims, ICC-01/09-01/11-243, 1 August 2011, para 9; ICC, *Prosecutor v. Francis Kirimi Muthaura, Uhuru Muigai Kenyatta and Mohammad Hussein Ali*, Registry, Proposal for the common legal representation of victims, ICC-01/09-02/11-214, 5 August 2011, para 9; ICC, *Prosecutor v. Laurent Gbagbo*, Pre-Trial Chamber I, Proposal for the common legal representation of victims, ICC-02/11-01/11-120, 16 May 2012, para 9.

95 ICC, *Prosecutor v. Germain Katanga and Mathieu Ngudjolo Chui*, Trial Chamber II, Order on the organisation of common legal representation of victims, ICC-01/04-01/07-1328, 22 July 2009, para 10; STL, *Prosecutor v. Ayyash* et al., Pre-Trial Judge, Decision on Victims' Participation in the Proceedings, STL11-01/T/PTJ, 8 May 2012, para 120.

96 ICC, *Prosecutor v. Abdallah Banda Abakaer Nourain and Saleh Mohammed Jerbo Jamus*, Trial Chamber IV, Decision on common legal representation, ICC-02/05-03/09-337, 25 May 2012, para 42.

which were the cause of the other victims' harm.[97] In both cases the two groups were also ethnically distinct from each other, although it is not clear from the decisions that this would have in itself been a basis for separate representation.[98]

At the ICC, Rule 90(4) also provides that victims may be grouped separately to accommodate the 'distinct interests of the victims', however it is unclear in which circumstances this would occur. That the threshold is high may be suggested by the fact that this ground has not been invoked by any ICC chamber, despite numerous potential differences of interests considered in Registry reports (on which, see further below) and some attempts by victims' lawyers to argue for separate representation of victim sub-groups.[99] Indeed the Registry has taken the position in its proposals on common legal representation that it is 'inevitable' that a variety of interests will exist among participating victims.[100] Therefore while considering that 'distinct interests of the victims' is intended to have a meaning which is broader than conflicts of interests in a strictly legal sense,[101] the Registry

---

[97] ICC, *Prosecutor v. Germain Katanga and Mathieu Ngudjolo Chui*, Trial Chamber II, Order on the organisation of common legal representation of victims, ICC-01/04-01/07-1328, 22 July 2009, para 12(c); ICC, *Prosecutor v. Bosco Ntaganda*, Pre-Trial Chamber I, Decision Requesting the VPRS and the OPCV to take steps with regard to the legal representation of victims in the confirmation of charges hearing and in the related proceedings, ICC-01/04-02/06-150, para 8; ICC, *Prosecutor v. Bosco Ntaganda*, Pre-Trial Chamber I, Decision Concerning the Organisation of Common Legal Representation of Victims, ICC-01/04-02/06-160, 2 December 2013, para 10.

[98] ICC, *Prosecutor v. Germain Katanga and Mathieu Ngudjolo Chui*, Trial Chamber II, Order on the organisation of common legal representation of victims, ICC-01/04-01/07-1328, 22 July 2009, para 12(c); ICC, *Prosecutor v. Bosco Ntaganda*, Pre-Trial Chamber I, Decision Requesting the VPRS and the OPCV to take steps with regard to the legal representation of victims in the confirmation of charges hearing and in the related proceedings, ICC-01/04-02/06-150, para 8; ICC, *Prosecutor v. Bosco Ntaganda*, Pre-Trial Chamber I, Decision Concerning the Organisation of Common Legal Representation of Victims, ICC-01/04-02/06-160, 2 December 2013, para 10.

[99] For example: ICC, *Prosecutor v. Abdallah Banda Abakaer Nourain and Saleh Mohammed Jerbo Jamus*, Victims' Legal Representatives, Joint Observations of Victims' Legal Representatives on Common Legal Representation, ICC-02/05-03/09-182, 18 July 2011, para 14; ICC, *Prosecutor v. Abdallah Banda Abakaer Nourain and Saleh Mohammed Jerbo Jamus*, Participating Victims, Request of Victims a/1646/10 and a/1647/10 for the Trial Chamber to review the Registry's "Notification of appointment of common legal representatives of victims" in accordance with Regulation 79(3), ICC-02/05-03/09-228, 30 September 2011.

[100] ICC, *Prosecutor v. Abdallah Banda Abakaer Nourain and Saleh Mohammed Jerbo Jamus*, Registry, Summary of information relevant to the grouping of victims, ICC-02/05-03/09-203-Anx2-Red, 25 August 2011, paras 2, 5; ICC, *Prosecutor v. William Samoei Ruto, Henry Kiprono Kosgey and Joshua Arap Sang*, Registry, Summary of information relevant to the grouping of victims, ICC-01/09-01/11-243-Anx2, 1 August 2011, para 2; ICC, *Prosecutor v. Francis Kirimi Muthaura, Uhuru Muigai Kenyatta and Mohammad Hussein Ali*, Registry, Summary of information relevant to the grouping of victims, ICC-01/09-02/11-214-Anx2, 5 August 2011, para 2; ICC, *Prosecutor v. Laurent Gbagbo*, Pre-Trial Chamber I, Proposal for the common legal representation of victims, ICC-02/11-01/11-120, 16 May 2012, footnote 12.

[101] ICC, *Prosecutor v. Abdallah Banda Abakaer Nourain and Saleh Mohammed Jerbo Jamus*, Registry, Summary of information relevant to the grouping of victims, ICC-02/05-03/09-203-Anx2-Red, 25 August 2011, para 5.

has interpreted this phrase as requiring a difference of interests which is 'so substantial as to justify separate representation',[102] taking into account nature and extent of differences, number of victims in each potential group, and existence of other bases for separating the victims into groups for representation.[103] Based on this approach, the Registry has recommended *against* divided representation where:

- some victims have an additional interest or view, which is not shared but not disputed by other victims;[104]
- victims suffered different forms of harm;[105]
- victims suffered harm as a result of different crimes;[106]

---

[102] ICC, *Prosecutor v. Abdallah Banda Abakaer Nourain and Saleh Mohammed Jerbo Jamus*, Registry, Summary of information relevant to the grouping of victims, ICC-02/05-03/09-203-Anx2-Red, 25 August 2011, paras 2, 5; ICC, *Prosecutor v. Henry Kiprono Kosgey and Joshua Arap Sang*, Registry, Summary of information relevant to the grouping of victims, ICC-01/09-01/11-243-Anx2, 1 August 2011, para 2; ICC, *Prosecutor v. Francis Kirimi Muthaura, Uhuru Muigai Kenyatta and Mohammad Hussein Ali*, Registry, Summary of information relevant to the grouping of victims, ICC-01/09-02/11-214-Anx2, 5 August 2011, para 2; ICC, *Prosecutor v. Laurent Gbagbo*, Pre-Trial Chamber I, Proposal for the common legal representation of victims, ICC-02/11-01/11-120, 16 May 2012, footnote 12.

[103] ICC, *Prosecutor v. Abdallah Banda Abakaer Nourain and Saleh Mohammed Jerbo Jamus*, Registry, Summary of information relevant to the grouping of victims, ICC-02/05-03/09-203-Anx2-Red, 25 August 2011, para 2; ICC, *Prosecutor v. Henry Kiprono Kosgey and Joshua Arap Sang*, Registry, Summary of information relevant to the grouping of victims, ICC-01/09-01/11-243-Anx2, 1 August 2011, para 2; ICC, *Prosecutor v. Francis Kirimi Muthaura, Uhuru Muigai Kenyatta and Mohammad Hussein Ali*, Registry, Summary of information relevant to the grouping of victims, ICC-01/09-02/11-214-Anx2, 5 August 2011, para 2; ICC, *Prosecutor v. Prosecutor v. Laurent Gbagbo*, Pre-Trial Chamber I, Proposal for the common legal representation of victims, ICC-02/11-01/11-120, 16 May 2012, footnote 12.

[104] ICC, *Prosecutor v. Abdallah Banda Abakaer Nourain and Saleh Mohammed Jerbo Jamus*, Registry, Summary of information relevant to the grouping of victims, ICC-02/05-03/09-203-Anx2-Red, 25 August 2011, para 5.

[105] ICC, *Prosecutor v. Henry Kiprono Kosgey and Joshua Arap Sang*, Registry, Summary of information relevant to the grouping of victims, ICC-01/09-01/11-243-Anx2, 1 August 2011, para 3; ICC, *Prosecutor v. Francis Kirimi Muthaura, Uhuru Muigai Kenyatta and Mohammad Hussein Ali*, Registry, Summary of information relevant to the grouping of victims, ICC-01/09-02/11-214-Anx2, 5 August 2011, para 3; ICC, *Prosecutor v. Abdallah Banda Abakaer Nourain and Saleh Mohammed Jerbo Jamus*, Registry, Summary of information relevant to the grouping of victims, ICC-02/05-03/09-203-Anx2-Red, 25 August 2011, para 7.

[106] ICC, *Prosecutor v. Henry Kiprono Kosgey and Joshua Arap Sang*, Registry, Summary of information relevant to the grouping of victims, ICC-01/09-01/11-243-Anx2, 1 August 2011, para 3; ICC, *Prosecutor v. Francis Kirimi Muthaura, Uhuru Muigai Kenyatta and Mohammad Hussein Ali*, Registry, Summary of information relevant to the grouping of victims, ICC-01/09-02/11-214-Anx2, 5 August 2011, para 3.

- victims reside in different areas;[107]
- victims have different ethnicities or tribal allegiances.[108]

Echoing the Registry recommendations, Trial Chamber IV held in *Banda and Jerbo* that the fact that victims came from different countries and spoke different languages, was not enough to justify separate representation.[109] Trial Chamber IV pointed out that '[s]uch an approach would be incompatible with the system of common legal representation provided for in Rule 90(2) of the Rules and the necessary grouping of victims according to their common interest.'[110]

The STL's Pre-Trial Judge has taken a similar approach. He held that political division among victims, or an aversion on the part of some victims to be associated with others for political reasons, was not a sufficient basis for separate representation.[111] Nor did he consider it appropriate to take into consideration the 'weight and influence' of some victims,[112] or the preferences of existing LRVs regarding the grouping.[113]

---

[107] ICC, *Prosecutor v. Henry Kiprono Kosgey and Joshua Arap Sang*, Registry, Summary of information relevant to the grouping of victims, ICC-01/09-01/11-243-Anx2, 1 August 2011, para 2; ICC, *Prosecutor v. Francis Kirimi Muthaura, Uhuru Muigai Kenyatta and Mohammad Hussein Ali*, Registry, Summary of information relevant to the grouping of victims, ICC-01/09-02/11-214-Anx2, 5 August 2011, para 2.

[108] In the Kenya cases, in which ethnicity was such a significant factor in the social factor the Registry considered at length whether this was a basis for separately representing victims. Ultimately it considered that in each case the various ethnic groups among the victims did not have 'clear and significant distinct interests'. Indeed, the Registry noted that intermediaries, lawyers and others working with victims had warned *against* separating victim groupings along ethnic lines, for fear that this would only serve to reinforce ethnic divisions. ICC, *Prosecutor v. Henry Kiprono Kosgey and Joshua Arap Sang*, Registry, Summary of information relevant to the grouping of victims, ICC-01/09-01/11-243-Anx2, 1 August 2011, paras 7–11; ICC, *Prosecutor v. Francis Kirimi Muthaura, Uhuru Muigai Kenyatta and Mohammad Hussein Ali*, Registry, Summary of information relevant to the grouping of victims, ICC-01/09-02/11-214-Anx2, 5 August 2011, paras 8–12.

[109] ICC, *Prosecutor v. Abdallah Banda Abakaer Nourain and Saleh Mohammed Jerbo Jamus*, Registry, Summary of Information Relevant to the Grouping of Victims, ICC-02/05-03/09-203-Anx2-Red, 25 August 2011, para 8; ICC, *Prosecutor v. Abdallah Banda Abakaer Nourain and Saleh Mohammed Jerbo Jamus*, Trial Chamber IV, Decision on common legal representation, ICC-02/05-03/09-337, 25 May 2012, para 34.

[110] ICC, *Prosecutor v. Prosecutor v. Abdallah Banda Abakaer Nourain and Saleh Mohammed Jerbo Jamus*, Trial Chamber IV, Decision on common legal representation, ICC-02/05-03/09-337, 25 May 2012, para 34.

[111] STL, *Prosecutor v. Ayyash* et al., Pre-Trial Judge, Decision on Victims' Participation in the Proceedings, STL11-01/T/PTJ, 8 May 2012, para 124.

[112] Ibid., para 123.

[113] Ibid., paras 125–126.

(iv) Selection and Formal Designation of Legal Representatives

Once grouping of victims is determined, at least one lawyer must be selected to represent each group. The process by which this is carried out is of some procedural importance in that it may have a bearing (at least at the ICC or STL) on the ability of victims to challenge the court's choice of lawyer.

At the ECCC, Civil Party Lead Co-Lawyers (one Cambodian and one international) are hired as consultants through open United Nations recruitment procedures the same as those used for other positions in the Court. The selection panel is composed of senior ECCC officials such as judges, the chief prosecutor, and senior administrators. No consultation process involving civil parties or civil party lawyers is undertaken.[114]

LRVs at the STL are chosen by the Registrar,[115] although he or she is required to consult with the VPU and to comply with the requirements of the Directive.[116] The Directive does not set out a particular process for the selection of LRVs, however it sets out mandatory and discretionary criteria to be considered by the Registrar[117] as well as steps which the VPU may undertake in order to facilitate the Registrar's assessment of a candidate's suitability for the role of LRV.[118] The latter include requesting information, holding interviews and setting written examinations. In addition, the VPU must 'to the extent reasonably possible' consult with victim applicants regarding their preferences on legal representation,[119] and these preferences may be taken into account by the Registrar in selecting a LRV.[120]

To date, practice at the STL is limited. In the *Ayyash* et al. case, no formal procedure was used for the identification of LRVs. Information was gathered through interviews undertaken for the purpose of including lawyers on the list of counsel or, where these were not held, through *ad hoc* informal interviews. A training session attended by many counsel on the list provided further opportunities for assessing candidates.[121] No formal structured consultation with victims was undertaken either (the Directive on Victims' Legal Representation, which mandated such a process, was adopted after the initial submission of victims' applications to the Pre-Trial Judge). However, the Pre-Trial Judge held that the requirement to consult with victims accords the Registrar a 'margin of

[114] Interview with Eleonor Fernandez, Senior legal consultant, Civil Party Lead Co-Lawyers Section, ECCC, 8 June 2015 (records on file with the authors).

[115] STL RPE, Rule 51(G)(i); STL Directive on Victims' Legal Representation, Article 16.

[116] STL RPE, Rule 51(G)(i).

[117] STL Directive on Victims' Legal Representation, Article 19.

[118] Ibid., Article 20(B).

[119] Ibid., Article 20(A).

[120] Ibid., Article 19(C)(i).

[121] Personal notes and experience of the author as former legal officer for the STL Victims' Participation Unit.

appreciation as to the nature and extent of this consultation process.'[122] He considered that where victims had retained a private counsel to assist them in the application process, consultations by the VPU in good faith with such counsel were sufficient to meet the obligation to seek victims' views.[123]

Once the choice of LRV has been made, a formal designation is filed by the Registrar in the record of the case.[124]

At the ICC, procedures for the selection and appointment of common legal representatives of victims have varied.

Under Rule 90(3) of the RPE, where victims have been "unable" to arrange their own common legal representation, the chamber may request the Registrar to choose one or more common legal representatives. Thus in a number of cases, chambers have relied on the Registrar to choose legal representatives, although in some of these cases the chamber provided limiting criteria for the choice of lawyer. For example, in *Bemba*, Pre-Trial Chamber III considered that unless victims objected, they should be represented by a lawyer from their own country.[125] In the two Kenya cases, Trial Chamber V required that the Registry choose a lawyer who was willing to be based in Kenya.[126]

Having requested the Registrar to undertake a selection, chambers have in some cases simply had the Registry appoint its chosen lawyer.[127] In other cases, the chamber has made an appointment itself, usually adopting the Registry's recommendation, particularly where it considers that a private lawyer should be

---

[122] STL, *Prosecutor v. Ayyash* et al., Pre-Trial Judge, Decision on the Duty Legal Representative's Motion for Review of the Registrar's Designation of the Lead Legal Representative for Victims, Case No. STL-11-01/PT/PTJ, 27 September 2012, para 37.

[123] Ibid., para 39.

[124] STL, *Prosecutor v. Ayyash* et al., Registrar, Designation of Victims' Legal Representatives, Case No. STL-11-01/PT/PTJ, 16 May 2012.

[125] ICC, *Prosecutor v. Jean-Pierre Bemba Gombo*, Pre-Trial Chamber III, Fifth Decision on Victims' Issues Concerning Common Legal Representation, ICC-01/05-01/08-322, 16 December 2008, para 14.

[126] ICC, *Prosecutor v. William Samoei Ruto and Joshua Arap Sang*, Trial Chamber V, Decision on victims' representation and participation, ICC-01/09-01/11-460, 3 October 2012, paras 60–61; ICC, *Prosecutor v. Uhuru Muigai Kenyatta*, Trial Chamber V, Decision on victims' representation and participation, ICC-01/09-02/11-498, 3 October 2012, paras 59–60; ICC, *Prosecutor v. William Samoei Ruto and Joshua Sang*, Trial Chamber V, Decision appointing a common legal representative of victims, ICC-01/09-01/11-479, 23 November 2012, para 5.

[127] ICC, *Prosecutor v. Abdallah Banda Abakaer Nourain and Saleh Mohammed Jerbo Jamus*, Trial Chamber IV, Order inviting the Registrar to appoint a common legal representative, ICC-02/05-03/09-209, 6 September 2011.

appointed.[128] In some cases, however, chambers have simply appointed counsel from the OPCV,[129] in one case even despite the Registry having identified a suitable private lawyer.[130]

Where the selection of common legal representative is undertaken by the ICC Registry, no particular procedure is mandated by the Court's texts. However, having identified problems which arose in its early practice,[131] in 2011 the Registry established an 'open, transparent and objective' process for choosing common legal representatives.[132] This process involves making an open call for

---

[128] ICC, *Prosecutor v. William Samoei Ruto, Henry Kiprono Kosgey and Joshua Arap Sang*, Pre-Trial Chamber II, Decision on Victims' Participation at the Confirmation of Charges Hearing and in the Related Proceedings, ICC-01/09-01/11-249, 5 August 2011, p. 48; ICC, *Prosecutor v. Francis Kirimi Muthaura, Uhuru Muigai Kenyatta and Mohammed Hussein Ali*, Pre-Trial Chamber II, Decision on Victims' Participation at the Confirmation of Charges Hearing and in the Related Proceedings, ICC-01/09-02/11-267, 26 August 2011, p. 46; ICC, *Prosecutor v. William Samoei Ruto and Joshua Arap Sang*, Trial Chamber V, Decision appointing a common legal representative of victims, ICC-01/09-01/11-479, 23 November 2012, p. 7; ICC, *Prosecutor v. Francis Kirimi Muthaura and Uhuru Muigai Kenyatta*, Trial Chamber V, Decision appointing a common legal representative of victims, ICC-01/09-02/11-537, 20 November 2012, p. 6.

[129] ICC, *Prosecutor v. Bosco Ntaganda*, Pre-Trial Chamber, Decision Concerning the Organisation of Common Legal Representation of Victims, ICC-01/04-02/06-160, 2 December 2013, para 25. Note that the Chamber appointed counsel from the OPCV pursuant to regulation 80 of the Regulations of the Court, rather than through the RPE's rule 90 procedure for common legal representation.

[130] ICC, *Prosecutor v. Laurent Gbagbo*, Pre-Trial Chamber I, Decision on Victims' Participation and Victims' Common Legal Representation at the Confirmation of Charges Hearing and in the Related Proceedings, ICC-02/11-01/11-138, 4 June 2012, paras 42–45.

[131] ICC, *Prosecutor v. Abdallah Banda Abakaer Nourain and Saleh Mohammed Jerbo Jamus*, Registry, Legal framework and Registry's approach on common legal representation, ICC-02/05-03/09-203-Anx1, 25 August 2011, para 8; ICC, *Prosecutor v. William Samoei Ruto, Henry Kiprono Kosgey and Joshua Arap Sang*, Registry, Legal framework and experience to date on common legal representation, ICC-01/09-01/11-243-Anx1, 1 August 2011, paras 8–9; ICC, *Prosecutor v. Francis Kirimi Muthaura, Uhuru Muigai Kenyatta and Mohammad Hussein Ali*, Registry, Legal framework and experience to date on common legal representation, ICC-01/09-02/11-214-Anx1, 5 August 2011, paras 8–9.

[132] ICC, *Prosecutor v. Abdallah Banda Abakaer Nourain and Saleh Mohammed Jerbo Jamus*, Registry, Proposal for the common legal representation of victims, ICC-02/05-03/09-203, 25 August 2011, paras 3, 10; see also ICC, *Prosecutor v. Abdallah Banda Abakaer Nourain and Saleh Mohammed Jerbo Jamus*, Registry, Legal framework and Registry's approach on common legal representation, ICC-02/05-03/09-203-Anx1, 25 August 2011, para 13; ICC, *Prosecutor v. Willliam Samoei Ruto, Henry Kiprono Kosgey and Joshua Arap Sang*, Registry, Proposal for the common legal representation of victims, ICC-01/09-01/11-243, 1 August 2011, para 16; ICC, *Prosecutor v. Francis Kirimi Muthaura, Uhuru Muigai Kenyatta and Mohammad Hussein Ali*, Registry, Proposal for the common legal representation of victims, ICC-01/09-02/11-214, 5 August 2011, para 16; ICC, *Prosecutor v. William Samoei Ruto and Joshua Arap Sang*, Registry, Recommendation for the position of Common Legal Representative of victims, ICC-01/09-01/11-467, 5 November 2012, para 5; ICC, *Prosecutor v. Francis Kirimi Muthaura and Uhuru Muigai Kenyatta*, Registry, Recommendation for the Position of Common Legal Representative of Victims, ICC-01/09-02/11-517, 5 November 2012, para 5; ICC, *Prosecutor v. Laurent Gbagbo*, Registry, Proposal for the common legal representation of victims, ICC-02/11-01/11-120, 16 May 2012, paras 3 and 9.

expressions of interest from any qualified counsel,[133] and conducting what is in effect a competitive recruitment.[134] This approach appears to have received judicial endorsement.[135]

---

[133] ICC, *Prosecutor v. Abdallah Banda Abakaer Nourain and Saleh Mohammed Jerbo Jamus*, Registry, Information document distributed to counsel on 11 July 2011, ICC-02/05-03/09-203-Anx3, 25 August 2011; ICC, *Prosecutor v. Willliam Samoei Ruto, Henry Kiprono Kosgey and Joshua Arap Sang*, Registry, Proposal for the common legal representation of victims, ICC-01/09-01/11-243, 1 August 2011, paras 4 and 24; ICC, *Prosecutor v. Henry Kiprono Kosgey and Joshua Arap Sang*, Registry, Information document distributed to counsel on 17 June 2011, ICC-01/09-01/11-243-Anx3, 1 August 2011; ICC, *Prosecutor v. Francis Kirimi Muthaura, Uhuru Muigai Kenyatta and Mohammad Hussein Ali*, Registry, Proposal for the common legal representation of victims, ICC-01/09-02/11-214, 5 August 2011, paras 4 and 24; ICC, *Prosecutor v. Francis Kirimi Muthaura, Uhuru Muigai Kenyatta and Mohammad Hussein Ali*, Registry, Information document distributed to counsel on 17 June 2011, ICC-01/09-02/11-214-Anx3, 5 August 2011; ICC, *Prosecutor v. William Samoei Ruto and Joshua Arap Sang*, Registry, Recommendation for the position of Common Legal Representative of victims, ICC-01/09-01/11-467, 5 November 2012, para 11; ICC, *Prosecutor v. William Samoei Ruto and Joshua Arap Sang*, Registry, Annex 1, ICC-01/09-01/11-467-Anx1, 5 November 2012; ICC, *Prosecutor v. Francis Kirimi Muthaura and Uhuru Muigai Kenyatta*, Registry, Recommendation for the position of Common Legal Representative of victims, ICC-01/09-02/11-517, 5 November 2012, para 11; ICC, *Prosecutor v. Francis Kirimi Muthaura and Uhuru Muigai Kenyatta*, Registry, Annex 1, ICC-01/09-02/11-517-Anx1, 5 November 2012; ICC, *Prosecutor v. Laurent Gbagbo*, Registry, Proposal for the common legal representation of victims, ICC-02/11-01/11-120, 16 May 2012, para 11; ICC, *Prosecutor v. Laurent Gbagbo*, Registry, Registry's Call for Counsel, ICC-02/11-01/11-120-Anx2, 16 May 2012.

[134] ICC, *Prosecutor v. Abdallah Banda Abakaer Nourain and Saleh Mohammed Jerbo Jamus*, Registrar, Report on the organization of common legal representation, ICC-02/05-03/09-187, 5 August 2011, para 7; ICC, *Prosecutor v. Abdallah Banda Abakaer Nourain and Saleh Mohammed Jerbo Jamus*, Registrar, Proposal for the common legal representation of victims, ICC-02/05-03/09-203, 25 August 2011, paras 16–21; ICC, *Prosecutor v. Willliam Samoei Ruto, Henry Kiprono Kosgey and Joshua Arap Sang*, Registrar, Proposal for the common legal representation of victims, ICC-01/09-01/11-243, 1 August 2011, paras 24–26; ICC, *Prosecutor v. Francis Kirimi Muthaura, Uhuru Muigai Kenyatta and Mohammad Hussein Ali*, Registrar, Proposal for the common legal representation of victims, ICC-01/09-02/11-214, 5 August 2011, paras 24-29; ICC, *Prosecutor v. William Samoei Ruto and Joshua Arap Sang*, Registrar, Recommendation for the position of Common Legal Representative of victims, ICC-01/09-01/11-467, 5 November 2012, paras 10–17; ICC, *Prosecutor v. Francis Kirimi Muthaura and Uhuru Muigai Kenyatta*, Registrar, Recommendation for the position of Common Legal Representative of victims, ICC-01/09-02/11-517, 5 November 2012, paras 10–17; ICC, *Prosecutor v. Laurent Gbagbo*, Registrar, Proposal for the common legal representation of victims, ICC-02/11-01/11-120, 16 May 2012, paras 11–16.

[135] ICC, *Prosecutor v. Abdallah Banda Abakaer Nourain and Saleh Mohammed Jerbo Jamus*, Trial Chamber IV, Decision on common legal representation, ICC-02/05-03/09-337, 25 May 2012, especially at para 2. ICC, *Prosecutor v. William Samoei Ruto, Henry Kiprono Kosgey and Joshua Arap Sang*, Pre-Trial Chamber II, Decision on Victims' Participation at the confirmation of Charges Hearing and In the Related Proceedings, ICC-01/09-01/11-249, 5 August 2011, para 76; ICC, *Prosecutor v. Francis Kirimi Muthaura, Uhuru Muigai Kenyatta and Mohammad Hussein Ali*, Pre-Trial Chamber II, Decision on Victims' Participation at the Confirmation of Charges Hearing and in the Related Proceedings, ICC-01/09-02/11-267, 26 August 2011, para 90.

Unlike the STL, the ICC's texts provide little guidance on the criteria to be used in the selection of LRVs, whether by the Registrar or the chamber. Regulation 79(2) of the Regulations of the Court only provides that when choosing a lawyer under Rule 90(3), 'consideration should be given to the views of the victims, and the need to respect local traditions and to assist specific groups of victims.' Ascertaining the views of victims can pose logistical challenges similar to those involved in having the victims arrange their own common legal representation. In the light of these obstacles, the Registry has often relied on the general preferences about representation expressed by victims or applicants during their interactions with the Registry to date.[136] Where the process of arranging common legal representation is undertaken before victims have been granted status, the Registry has consulted with applicants for their views.[137]

The "victims' views" collected as a result of these processes are of a general nature, rather than identifying a particular lawyer. For example in *Banda and Jerbo*, the Registry cited victims' preference for a lawyer with significant relevant experience; for a multilingual lawyer or a lawyer who spoke the victims' languages; or for a lawyer who lived nearby and could visit the victims easily.[138] In *Ntaganda,* the Pre-Trial Chamber relied on the victims' views gathered by the Registry, including that the selected common legal representative should be 'competent and available, regardless of his or her nationality, and that he or she be capable of understanding the victims, the background of the conflict and of the case and the context in which [the victims] live.'[139]

---

[136] ICC, *Prosecutor v. Abdallah Banda Abakaer Nourain and Saleh Mohammed Jerbo Jamus*, Registry, Report on the Implementation of the Chamber's Order instructing the Registry to start consultations on the organisation of common legal representation, ICC-02/05-03/09-164-Red, 21 June 2011, paras 13–14; ICC, *Prosecutor v. Abdallah Banda Abakaer Nourain and Saleh Mohammed Jerbo Jamus*, Registry, Proposal for the common legal representation of victims, ICC-02/05-03/09-203, 25 August 2011, para 11; ICC, *Prosecutor v. Willliam Samoei Ruto, Henry Kiprono Kosgey and Joshua Arap Sang*, Registry, Proposal for the common legal representation of victims, ICC-01/09-01/11-243, 1 August 2011, para 6; ICC, *Prosecutor v. Francis Kirimi Muthaura, Uhuru Muigai Kenyatta and Mohammad Hussein Ali*, Registry, Proposal for the common legal representation of victims, ICC-01/09-02/11-214, 5 August 2011, para 6; ICC, *Prosecutor v. Laurent Gbagbo*, Registry, Proposal for the common legal representation of victims, ICC-02/11-01/11-120, 16 May 2012, paras 4–5; ICC, *Prosecutor v. William Samoei Ruto and Joshua Arap Sang*, Registry, Recommendation for the position of Common Legal Representative of victims, ICC-01/09-01/11-467, 5 November 2012, para 8; ICC, *Prosecutor v. Francis Kirimi Muthaura and Uhuru Muigai Kenyatta*, Registry, Recommendation for the position of Common Legal Representative of victims, ICC-01/09-02/11-517, 5 November 2012, para 8.

[137] ICC, *Prosecutor v. Bosco Ntaganda*, Pre-Trial Chamber I, Decision Concerning the Organisation of Common Legal Representation of Victims, ICC-01/04-02/06-160, 2 December 2013, para 8.

[138] ICC, *Prosecutor v. Abdallah Banda Abakaer Nourain and Saleh Mohammed Jerbo Jamus*, Registry, Proposal for the common legal representation of victims, ICC-02/05-03/09-203, 25 August 2011, para 11.

[139] ICC, *Prosecutor v. Bosco Ntaganda*, Pre-Trial Chamber I, Decision Concerning the Organisation of Common Legal Representation of Victims, ICC-01/04-02/06-160, 2 December 2013, para 24.

While Regulation 79(2) apparently mandates the Registry to take such views into account when selecting a LRV, this does not mean that the Registry is bound to follow the victims' preferences.[140] Furthermore, in light of the challenges involved in ascertaining victims' views, one chamber has held that 'the views of each victim on such issue can only be taken into account to the extent possible.'[141]

Beyond the requirements of Regulation 79(2), many other criteria have been posited, including the following:

- sufficient availability throughout the likely course of the proceedings;[142]
- familiarity with, or connection to, the situation country;[143]

---

[140] ICC, *Prosecutor v. Abdallah Banda Abakaer Nourain and Saleh Mohammed Jerbo Jamus*, Trial Chamber IV, Decision on common legal representation, ICC-02/05-03/09-337, 25 May 2012, para 49.

[141] ICC, *Prosecutor v. Jean-Pierre Bemba Gombo,* Trial Chamber III, Decision on common legal representation of victims for the purpose of trial, ICC-01/05-01/08-1005, 10 November 2010, para 14.

[142] ICC, *Prosecutor v. Germain Katanga and Mathieu Ngudjolo Chui*, Trial Chamber II, Order on the organisation of common legal representation of victims, ICC-01/04-01/07-1328, 22 July 2009, para 14; ICC, *Prosecutor v. Jean-Pierre Bemba Gombo*, Trial Chamber III, Decision on common legal representation of victims for the purpose of trial, ICC-01/05-01/08-1005, 10 November 2010, paras 10 and 12; ICC, *Prosecutor v. Abdallah Banda Abakaer Nourain and Saleh Mohammed Jerbo Jamus*, Registry, Registry's proposed general criteria for selection of common legal representatives under rule 90(3) of the rules of Procedure and Evidence, ICC-02/05-03/09-164-Anx, 21 June 2011, paras 10–11; ICC, *Prosecutor v. William Samoei Ruto, Henry Kiprono Kosgey and Joshua Arap Sang*, Pre-Trial Chamber II, Decision on Victims' Participation at the confirmation of Charges Hearing and In the Related Proceedings, ICC-01/09-01/11-249, 5 August 2011, para 73; ICC, *Prosecutor v. Francis Kirimi Muthaura, Uhuru Muigai Kenyatta and Mohammad Hussein Ali*, Pre-Trial Chamber II, Decision on Victims' Participation at the Confirmation of Charges Hearing and in the Related Proceedings, ICC-01/09-02/11-267, 26 August 2011, para 87; ICC, *Prosecutor v. William Samoei Ruto and Joshua Arap Sang*, Trial Chamber V, Decision on victims' representation and participation, ICC-01/09-01/11-460, 3 October 2012, para 61; ICC, *Prosecutor v. Uhuru Muigai Kenyatta*, Trial Chamber V, Decision on victims' representation and participation, ICC-01/09-01/11-498, 3 October 2012, para 60.

[143] ICC, *Prosecutor v. Germain Katanga and Mathieu Ngudjolo Chui*, Trial Chamber II, Order on the organisation of common legal representation of victims, ICC-01/04-01/07-1328, 22 July 2009, para 15; ICC, *Prosecutor v. Jean-Pierre Bemba Gombo,* Trial Chamber III, Decision on common legal representation of victims for the purpose of trial, ICC-01/05-01/08-1005, 10 November 2010, para 11; ICC, *Prosecutor v. Abdallah Banda Abakaer Nourain and Saleh Mohammed Jerbo Jamus*, Registry, Registry's proposed general criteria for selection of common legal representatives under rule 90(3) of the rules of Procedure and Evidence, ICC-02/05-03/09-164-Anx, 21 June 2011, para 7; ICC, *Prosecutor v. William Samoei Ruto, Henry Kiprono Kosgey and Joshua Arap Sang*, Pre-Trial Chamber II, Decision on Victims' Participation at the confirmation of Charges Hearing and In the Related Proceedings, ICC-01/09-01/11-249, 5 August 2011, para 71; ICC, *Prosecutor v. Francis Kirimi Muthaura, Uhuru Muigai Kenyatta and Mohammad Hussein Ali*, Pre-Trial Chamber II, Decision on Victims' Participation at the Confirmation of Charges Hearing and in the Related Proceedings, ICC-01/09-02/11-267, 26 August 2011, para 85; ICC, *Prosecutor v. William Samoei Ruto and Joshua Arap Sang*, Trial Chamber V, Decision on victims' representation and participation, ICC-01/09-01/11-460, 3 October 2012, para 61; ICC, *Prosecutor v. Uhuru Muigai Kenyatta*, Trial Chamber V, Decision on victims' representation and participation, ICC-01/09-01/11-498, 3 October 2012, para 60.

- relevant education and/or relevant academic or litigation experience;[144]
- commitment to victim-centred approach;[145]
- familiarity with the case;[146]
- common language with the represented victims;[147]

---

[144] ICC, *Prosecutor v. Abdallah Banda Abakaer Nourain and Saleh Mohammed Jerbo Jamus*, Registry, Registry's proposed general criteria for selection of common legal representatives under rule 90(3) of the rules of Procedure and Evidence, ICC-02/05-03/09-164-Anx, 21 June 2011, paras 8–9; ICC, *Prosecutor v. William Samoei Ruto, Henry Kiprono Kosgey and Joshua Arap Sang*, Pre-Trial Chamber II, Decision on Victims' Participation at the confirmation of Charges Hearing and In the Related Proceedings, ICC-01/09-01/11-249, 5 August 2011, para 72; ICC, *Prosecutor v. Francis Kirimi Muthaura, Uhuru Muigai Kenyatta and Mohammad Hussein Ali*, Pre-Trial Chamber II, Decision on Victims' Participation at the Confirmation of Charges Hearing and in the Related Proceedings, ICC-01/09-02/11-267, 26 August 2011, para 86; ICC, *Prosecutor v. William Samoei Ruto and Joshua Arap Sang*, Trial Chamber V, Decision on victims' representation and participation, ICC-01/09-01/11-460, 3 October 2012, para 61; ICC, *Prosecutor v. Uhuru Muigai Kenyatta*, Trial Chamber V, Decision on victims' representation and participation, ICC-01/09-01/11-498, 3 October 2012, para 60.

[145] ICC, *Prosecutor v. Abdallah Banda Abakaer Nourain and Saleh Mohammed Jerbo Jamus*, Registry's proposed general criteria for selection of common legal representatives under rule 90(3) of the Rules of Procedure and Evidence, ICC-02/05-03/09-164-Anx, 21 June 2011, para 6; ICC, *Prosecutor v. William Samoei Ruto, Henry Kiprono Kosgey and Joshua Arap Sang*, Decision on Victims' Participation at the confirmation of Charges Hearing and In the Related Proceedings, ICC-01/09-01/11-249, 5 August 2011, para 70; ICC, *Prosecutor v. Francis Kirimi Muthaura, Uhuru Muigai Kenyatta and Mohammad Hussein Ali*, Pre-Trial Chamber II, Decision on Victims' Participation at the Confirmation of Charges Hearing and in the Related Proceedings, ICC-01/09-02/11-267, 26 August 2011, para 84; ICC, *Prosecutor v. William Samoei Ruto and Joshua Arap Sang*, Trial Chamber V, Decision on victims' representation and participation, ICC-01/09-01/11-460, 3 October 2012, para 61; ICC, *Prosecutor v. Uhuru Muigai Kenyatta*, Trial Chamber V, Decision on victims' representation and participation, ICC-01/09-01/11-498, 3 October 2012, para 60.

[146] ICC, *Prosecutor v. Jean-Pierre Bemba Gombo,* Trial Chamber II, *Decision* on common legal representation of victims for the purpose of trial, ICC-01/05-01/08-1005, 10 November 2010, para 12; ICC, *Prosecutor v. William Samoei Ruto and Joshua Arap Sang*, Trial Chamber V, Decision on victims' representation and participation, ICC-01/09-01/11-460, 3 October 2012, para 61; ICC, *Prosecutor v. Uhuru Muigai Kenyatta*, Trial Chamber V, Decision on victims' representation and participation, ICC-01/09-01/11-498, 3 October 2012, para 60.

[147] ICC, *Prosecutor v. Thomas Lubanga Dyilo*, Trial Chamber I, Decision on Victims' Participation, ICC-01/04-01/06-1119, 18 January 2008, para 124; ICC, *Prosecutor v. Jean-Pierre Bemba Gombo,* Trial Chamber III, Decision on common legal representation of victims for the purpose of trial, ICC-01/05-01/08-1005, 10 November 2010, para 11.

- sufficient information technology skills;[148] and
- absence of any conflict of interests between counsel and victims.[149]

In some cases, the Registry has proposed reliance on a standard set of criteria, based on its experience and the Court's jurisprudence, but noting that the weight accorded to respective criteria should vary according to the particularities of a case and the preferences of victims.[150] Several chambers have approved the use of these criteria.[151] It remains doubtful, however, whether any criteria other than those contained in Regulation 79(2) are mandatory, leaving the Registry and the chamber with a significant margin of discretion.

---

[148] ICC, *Prosecutor v. Abdallah Banda Abakaer Nourain and Saleh Mohammed Jerbo Jamus*, Registry, Annex: Registry's proposed general criteria for selection of common legal representatives under rule 90(3) of the rules of Procedure and Evidence, ICC-02/05-03/09-164-Anx, 21 June 2011, para 12; ICC, *Prosecutor v. William Samoei Ruto, Henry Kiprono Kosgey and Joshua Arap Sang*, Pre-Trial Chamber II, Decision on Victims' Participation at the confirmation of Charges Hearing and In the Related Proceedings, ICC-01/09-01/11-249, 5 August 2011, para 74; ICC, *Prosecutor v. Francis Kirimi Muthaura, Uhuru Muigai Kenyatta and Mohammad Hussein Ali*, Pre-Trial Chamber II, Decision on Victims' Participation at the Confirmation of Charges Hearing and in the Related Proceedings, ICC-01/09-02/11-267, 26 August 2011, para 88; ICC, *Prosecutor v. William Samoei Ruto and Joshua Arap Sang*, Trial Chamber V, Decision on victims' representation and participation, ICC 01/09 01/11-460, 3 October 2012, para 61; ICC, *Prosecutor v. Uhuru Muigai Kenyatta*, Trial Chamber V, Decision on victims' representation and participation, ICC-01/09-01/11-498, 3 October 2012, para 60.

[149] ICC, *Prosecutor v. Abdallah Banda Abakaer Nourain and Saleh Mohammed Jerbo Jamus*, Registry, Report on the implementation of the Chamber's Order instructing the Registry to start consultations on the organisation of common legal representation, ICC-02/05-03/09-164-Red, 21 June 2011, paras 23–24.

[150] ICC, *Prosecutor v. Abdallah Banda Abakaer Nourain and Saleh Mohammed Jerbo Jamus*, Registry, Report on the implementation of the Chamber's Order instructing the Registry to start consultations on the organisation of common legal representation, ICC-02/05-03/09-164-Red, 21 June 2011, para 21; ICC, *Prosecutor v. Willliam Samoei Ruto, Henry Kiprono Kosgey and Joshua Arap Sang*, Registry, Proposal for the common legal representation of victims, ICC-01/09-01/11-243, 1 August 2011, para 17; ICC, *Prosecutor v. Francis Kirimi Muthaura, Uhuru Muigai Kenyatta and Mohammad Hussein Ali*, Registry, Proposal for the common legal representation of victims, ICC-01/09-02/11-214, 5 August 2011, para 17.

[151] ICC, *Prosecutor v. Abdallah Banda Abakaer Nourain and Saleh Mohammed Jerbo Jamus*, Trial Chamber IV, Decision on common legal representation, ICC-02/05-03/09-337, 25 May 2012, paras 2 and 24; ICC, *Prosecutor v. William Samoei Ruto, Henry Kiprono Kosgey and Joshua Arap Sang*, Pre-Trial Chamber II, Decision on Victims' Participation at the confirmation of Charges Hearing and In the Related Proceedings, ICC-01/09-01/11-249, 5 August 2011, paras 68–75; ICC, *Prosecutor v. Francis Kirimi Muthaura, Uhuru Muigai Kenyatta and Mohammad Hussein Ali*, Pre-Trial Chamber II, Decision on Victims' Participation at the Confirmation of Charges Hearing and in the Related Proceedings, ICC-01/09-02/11-267, 26 August 2011, paras 82–89; ICC, *Prosecutor v. William Samoei Ruto and Joshua Arap Sang*, Trial Chamber V, Decision on victims' representation and participation, ICC-01/09-01/11-460, 3 October 2012, para 61; ICC, *Prosecutor v. Uhuru Muigai Kenyatta*, Trial Chamber V, Decision on victims' representation and participation, ICC-01/09-01/11-498, 3 October 2012, para 60.

One particular criterion has proved contentious in the practice of the ICC, namely the weight to be given to any existing legal representation of the participating victims. In early cases, common legal representatives were exclusively chosen from among the existing LRVs who had been appointed by individual victims in the application process. In later cases, privately retained counsel who were replaced through the process of common legal representation sought to challenge the relevant decisions. While various grounds were argued, these motions in practice sought the continuation of existing legal representation.[152]

Indeed, by 2011, the Registry appeared to have moved away from an approach wherein it was presumed that an existing LRV should be appointed as common legal representative, stating that such an approach 'may tend to reward and encourage the practice among counsel of "fishing" for victim clients since solicitation enables a lawyer to enter the group of current counsel to be considered as common legal representative.'[153] Instead, in an approach explicitly endorsed at least by one chamber,[154] the Registry said that the established role of current LRVs would be taken into account in an open and transparent selection process,

[152] ICC, *Prosecutor v. William Samoei Ruto, Henry Kiprono Kosgey and Joshua Arap Sang*, Victims, Motion from Victims a/0041/10, a/0045/10, a/0051/10 and a/0056/10 requesting the Pre-Trial Chamber to Reconsider the Appointment of Common Legal Representative Sureta CHANA for All Victims, ICC-01/09-01/11-314, 31 August 2011; ICC, *Prosecutor v. Abdallah Banda Abakaer Nourain and Saleh Mohammed Jerbo Jamus*, Victims' Legal Representatives, Request of Victims a/1646/10 and a/1647/10 for the Trial Chamber to review the Registry's "Notification of appointment of common legal representatives of victims" in accordance with Regulation 79(3), ICC-02/05-03/09-288, 30 September 2011.

[153] The Registry went on to note that: 'As most victims do not know of a lawyer who might represent them at the ICC, they will usually appoint a lawyer who makes him or herself known proactively to the victims (either directly or through the intermediary who assists the victim to apply for participation). Questions may be asked about whether the victims have had a real, informed choice about their representation. Furthermore, they are likely not aware of other options for legal representation and can be ill-equipped to assess the relative skill and professionalism of the lawyer contacting them as compared with others. While lawyers involved in this practice might sometimes have qualities which are desirable in a victims' legal representative, this is not necessarily the case.' ICC, *Prosecutor v. Abdallah Banda Abakaer Nourain and Saleh Mohammed Jerbo Jamus*, Registry, Legal framework and Registry's approach on common legal representation, ICC-02/05-03/09-203-Anx1, 25 August 2011, para 8; ICC, *Prosecutor v. William Samoei Ruto, Henry Kiprono Kosgey and Joshua Arap Sang*, Registry, Legal framework and experience to date on common legal representation, ICC-01/09-01/11-243-Anx1, 1 August 2011, paras 8–9; ICC, *Prosecutor v. Francis Kirimi Muthaura, Uhuru Muigai Kenyatta and Mohammad Hussein Ali*, Registry, Legal framework and experience to date on common legal representation, ICC-01/09-02/11-214-Anx1, 5 August 2011, paras 8–9.

[154] ICC, *Prosecutor v. William Samoei Ruto, Henry Kiprono Kosgey and Joshua Arap Sang*, Pre-Trial Chamber II, Decision on Victims' Participation at the confirmation of Charges Hearing and In the Related Proceedings, ICC-01/09-01/11-249, 5 August 2011, para 67; ICC, *Prosecutor v. Francis Kirimi Muthaura, Uhuru Muigai Kenyatta and Mohammad Hussein Ali*, Pre-Trial Chamber II, Decision on Victims' Participation at the Confirmation of Charges Hearing and in the Related Proceedings, ICC-01/09-02/11-267, 26 August 2011, para 81.

but that this role would not be considered determinative in itself.[155] Existing counsel would thus be assessed on the same criteria as other counsel, with due recognition given to an established relationship of trust, but consideration also given to their work to date (including any performance problems).[156] Counsel would be informed of any such performance problems and be given a chance to respond.[157]

5.3.5 Temporary or "Duty" Legal Representation for Specific Procedural Steps

Only the STL explicitly provides for the possibility of a temporary LRV, appointed by the Tribunal to represent victims in specific instances. Such "duty" LRVs may be appointed at the discretion of the Registrar in any of four situations:

- where a victim has had his or her application to participate in the proceedings rejected and seeks to appeal;
- where a victim has been determined to be non-indigent and therefore required to contribute to the Tribunal's legal aid budget and seeks review of that decision;
- where a victim seeks to review the Registrar's decision on the designation of lead LRV for the group of victims of which he or she is a part; or
- where, if permitted to do so, an applicant for victim status wishes to respond to observations made by the Prosecution or Defence.[158]

Where a duty LRV is designated at the STL, the same procedure and criteria apply as in relation to the appointment of a permanent LRV,[159] with one exception:

---

155 ICC, *Prosecutor v. Abdallah Banda Abakaer Nourain and Saleh Mohammed Jerbo Jamus*, Registry, Proposal for the common legal representation of victims, ICC-02/05-03/09-203, 25 August 2011, paras 3 and 13; ICC, *Prosecutor v. Willliam Samoei Ruto, Henry Kiprono Kosgey and Joshua Arap Sang*, Registry, Proposal for the common legal representation of victims, ICC-01/09-01/11-243, 1 August 2011, paras 21–23; ICC, *Prosecutor v. Francis Kirimi Muthaura, Uhuru Muigai Kenyatta and Mohammad Hussein Ali*, Registry, Proposal for the common legal representation of victims, ICC-01/09-02/11-214, 5 August 2011, paras 21–23.

156 ICC, *Prosecutor v. Abdallah Banda Abakaer Nourain and Saleh Mohammed Jerbo Jamus*, Registry, Legal framework and Registry's approach on common legal representation, ICC-02/05-03/09-203-Anx1, 25 August 2011, paras 14–17; ICC, *Prosecutor v. Willliam Samoei Ruto, Henry Kiprono Kosgey and Joshua Arap Sang*, Registry, Proposal for the common legal representation of victims, ICC-01/09-01/11-243, 1 August 2011, paras 4 and 21; ICC, *Prosecutor v. Francis Kirimi Muthaura, Uhuru Muigai Kenyatta and Mohammad Hussein Ali*, Registry, Proposal for the common legal representation of victims, ICC-01/09-02/11-214, 5 August 2011, paras 4 and 21.

157 ICC, *Prosecutor v. Abdallah Banda Abakaer Nourain and Saleh Mohammed Jerbo Jamus*, Registry, Proposal for the common legal representation of victims, ICC-02/05-03/09-203, 25 August 2011, para 15.

158 STL Directive on Victims' Legal Representation, Article 18(A).

159 Ibid., Articles 19–20.

where the duty representative is to represent victims in a review of the Registrar's designation of lead LRV, the Registrar may not select "any legal representative who has previously represented or expressed an interest in representing the victims participating in the proceedings who are seeking the review."[160]

Duty LRVs designated at the STL are paid under the Tribunal's legal aid scheme for participating victims.[161] To date the scheme has only been used once, for the purpose of reviewing the designation of the lead LRV of victims in the *Ayyash* et al. case at the request of two victims participating in that case.[162]

At the ICC no specific scheme exists for the provision of "duty counsel." Indeed, most of the procedural steps for which duty counsel can be designated at the STL are not available to victims at the ICC. While victims may seek review of the Registrar's choice of a common legal representative the Court does not arrange legal representation for this purpose. Victims may use privately retained counsel for undertaking such a review,[163] although the practical consequence of some ICC jurisprudence appears to be that they must have permission from the designated common legal representative in order to do so.[164]

While no express mention of duty counsel for victims exists in the ICC's texts, the chamber retains the power to appoint a LRV wherever the interests of justice so require, including counsel from the OPCV.[165] In *Katanga and Ngudjolo Chui,* the Trial Chamber indicated that this power might be used to arrange temporary representation in the event of a conflict of interest on a particular issue among victims within a collectively represented group. In such an event, the Chamber contemplated that it might appoint the OPCV to represent part of the group 'with regard to the specific issue which gives rise to the conflict of interest.'[166]

---

[160] Ibid., Article 19(B).

[161] STL Legal Aid Policy for Victims' Participation, Section 13.3.

[162] STL, *Prosecutor v. Ayyash* et al., Registrar, Designation of Duty Legal Representative for Victim V027, Case No. STL-11-01/PT/PTJ, 19 July 2012; STL, *Prosecutor v. Ayyash* et al., Registrar, Designation of Duty Legal Representative for Victim V028, Case No. STL-11-01/PT/PTJ, 25 July 2012.

[163] See for example: ICC, *Prosecutor v. Abdallah Banda Abakaer Nourain and Saleh Mohammed Jerbo Jamus*, Participating Victims, Request of Victims a/1646/10 and a/1647/10 for the Trial Chamber to review the Registry's "Notification of appointment of common legal representatives of victims" in accordance with Regulation 79(3), ICC-02/05-03/09-228, 30 September 2011; ICC, *Prosecutor v. William Samoei Ruto, Henry Kiprono Kosgey and Joshua Arap Sang*, Victims' Legal Representative, Motion from Victims a/0041/10, a/0045/10, a/0051/10 and a/0056/10 requesting the Pre-Trial Chamber to Reconsider the Appointment of Common Legal Representative Sureta CHANA for All Victims, ICC-01/09-01/11-314, 31 August 2011.

[164] ICC, *Prosecutor v. William Samoei Ruto, Henry Kiprono Kosgey and Joshua Arap Sang*, Pre-Trial Chamber II, Decision on the "Motion from Victims a/0041/10, a/0045/10, a/0051/10 and a/0056/10 requesting the Pre-Trial Chamber to Reconsider the Appointment of Common Legal Representative Sureta Chana for All Victims", ICC-01/09-01/11-330, 9 September 2011, para 17.

[165] ICC Regulations of the Court, Regulation 80.

[166] ICC, *Prosecutor v. Germain Katanga and Mathieu Ngudjolo Chui*, Trial Chamber II, Order on the organisation of common legal representation of victims, ICC-01/04-01/07-1328, 22 July 2009, para 16.

At the ECCC no provision or experience exists to date concerning the *ad hoc* appointment of lawyers to represent civil parties for specific procedural steps.

5.3.6 Challenges to Legal Representation Decisions

5.3.6.1 Availability of Review

Both the ICC and the STL offer some avenues for victims to challenge court-arranged collective legal representation. At the ECCC, where the selection of Civil Party Lead Co-Lawyers is effectively run as an institutional recruitment process, no avenue exists for challenging the selection of the latter.

At the STL, victims have the possibility to challenge the Registrar's choice of lead LRV. A request by a victim for review must be filed with the Pre-Trial Judge within 15 days of the date that the victim was notified of the designation of the LRV.[167] In contrast, participating victims may not request a review of the Registrar's designation of a co-LRV of victims; such a review can only be initiated by the lead LRV.[168]

At the ICC, Regulation 79(3) of the Regulations of the Court allows victims to request a chamber to review the Registrar's choice of a common legal representative under Rule 90(3).[169] Any such request must be made within 30 days of notification of the Registrar's decision.[170] It is not clear whether the date of notification is deemed to be the date that the decision is distributed through the court record systems or when it is notified *in fact* to the victim in question, bearing in mind that the latter will often be done in person and could occur quite some time after the former.

In practice, a significant limitation on reviews under Regulation 79(3) is that they pertain only where a common legal representative has been chosen and appointed by the Registrar. Where a chamber has opted to itself appoint a legal representative, relying on Regulation 80 of the Regulations of the Court, review under Regulation 79(3) is unavailable.[171] This is the case even where the chamber has effectively endorsed the outcome of a Registry-run selection process. Thus, in the *Ruto and Sang* case, a challenge to the Chamber's power to circumvent Rule 90, on the basis that it defeats victims' rights of appeal under

[167] STL Directive on Victims' Legal Representation, Article 22(A).

[168] Ibid., Article 23(B).

[169] ICC Regulations of the Court, Regulation 79(3).

[170] Ibid.

[171] ICC, *Prosecutor v. William Samoei Ruto, Henry Kiprono Kosgey and Joshua Arap Sang*, Pre-Trial Chamber II, Decision on the "Motion from Victims a/0041/10, a/0045/10, a/0051/10 and a/0056/10 requesting the Pre-Trial Chamber to Reconsider the Appointment of Common Legal Representative Sureta Chana for All Victims", ICC-01/09-01/11-330, 9 September 2011, para 15.

regulation 79(3), proved unsuccessful.[172] Likewise an attempt to request *reconsideration* of the Chamber's decision on the designation of a common legal representative failed: the Chamber relied on the fact that its decision was 'taken on the basis, *inter alia*, of information provided by the Registry as the relevant neutral body of the Court' in order to conclude that there was no reason to reconsider.[173] The increasing tendency of ICC chambers to themselves appoint common legal representatives (rather than asking the Registry to do so) therefore has the consequence of significantly eroding victims' rights to challenge the choice of their legal representative.

5.3.6.2 Scope and Grounds of Review

The STL's Directive on Victims' Legal Representation does not detail the possible grounds on which the Pre-Trial Judge may quash the designation of a legal representative. However, the Pre-Trial Judge has ruled that the review 'concerns the propriety of a certain procedure followed when reaching a decision, as well as the outcome of that decision', and that as a result

> A successful motion for review should thus demonstrate either that the decision is tainted by a procedural error, in view of the fact that the Registrar: (i) failed to comply with the legal requirements; (ii) acted in a disproportionate manner; (iii) acted without procedural fairness; (iv) did not take into account relevant factors; or demonstrate that the Registrar reached a conclusion that no sensible person who has properly applied his mind to the issue could have reached.[174]

At the ICC two challenges have been brought to date (one under Regulation 79(3) and one framed as a reconsideration request). Both proved unsuccessful, but in neither instance did the chambers give generally applicable direction regarding the standard of review or the circumstances in which a challenge might succeed. Nonetheless, some guidance may be gleaned from the decision of Trial Chamber IV in *Banda and Jerbo*. Regarding the scope of available review, the wording of

---

[172] ICC, *Prosecutor v. William Samoei Ruto, Henry Kiprono Kosgey and Joshua Arap Sang*, Victims' Legal Representative, Motion from Victims a/0041/10, a/0045/10, a/0051/10 and a/0056/10 requesting the Pre-Trial Chamber to Reconsider the Appointment of Common Legal Representative Sureta CHANA for All Victims, ICC-01/09-01/11-314, 31 August 2011; ICC, *Prosecutor v. William Samoei Ruto, Henry Kiprono Kosgey and Joshua Arap Sang*, Pre-Trial Chamber II, Decision on the "Motion from Victims a/0041/10, a/0045/10, a/0051/10 and a/0056/10 requesting the Pre-Trial Chamber to Reconsider the Appointment of Common Legal Representative Sureta Chana for All Victims", ICC-01/09-01/11-330, 9 September 2011.

[173] ICC, *Prosecutor v. William Samoei Ruto, Henry Kiprono Kosgey and Joshua Arap Sang*, Pre-Trial Chamber II, Decision on the "Motion from Victims a/0041/10, a/0045/10, a/0051/10 and a/0056/10 requesting the Pre-Trial Chamber to Reconsider the Appointment of Common Legal Representative Sureta Chana for All Victims", ICC-01/09-01/11-330, 9 September 2011, para 11.

[174] STL, *Prosecutor v. Ayyash* et al, Pre-Trial Judge, Decision on the Duty Legal Representative's Motion for Review of the Registrar's Designation of the Lead Legal Representative for Victims, Case No. STL-011-01/PT/PTJ, 27 September 2012, para 32.

Regulation 79(3) may appear to suggest that it is only the selection of counsel which may be reviewed, as opposed to the grouping of victims (victims may seek review of 'the Registrar's choice of a common legal representative'). However, the Chamber considered arguments relating to grouping and did not dismiss them as being outside the scope of Regulation 79(3).[175]

In rejecting an argument of the applicants, the Chamber said that it was not satisfied that 'the ability of [the applicant victims] to present their views and concerns will be affected negatively and that they will suffer prejudice in being represented by the Appointed Legal Representatives.'[176] The Chamber went on to consider that the distinct interests of the applicant victims could be represented, that there was no conflict of interest between them and the other victims, and that the Registry's consultation with victims was appropriate.[177] While it cannot necessarily be inferred from these comments that a contrary finding by the Chamber on any of these points would have resulted in the setting aside of the Registrar's decision designating LRVs, these comments may provide some guidance. They appear to suggest that at the ICC a review under Regulation 79(3) is not limited to the procedural propriety of the selection process, but can involve a consideration of the merits of the decision.

5.3.6.3 Procedure on Motion of Review

Neither the texts of the STL nor those of the ICC detail the procedure to be followed where a challenge is brought to court-arranged legal representation.

At the STL the Directive only stipulates that the Pre-Trial Judge may solicit the views of other members of the represented group of victims.[178] In the one case brought to date the Pre-Trial Judge did not exercise this power, but did invite the Registrar to respond to the motion for review.[179]

At the ICC, the Registrar has not been expressly invited to submit a response, although it is his or her decision which is under review. However, where the

[175] The Chamber indicated that it would consider 'whether the interests of the [victims seeking review] are significantly distinct from the ones [of the other victims] to the extent that this would warrant a separate legal representation.' ICC, *Prosecutor v. Abdallah Banda Abakaer Nourain and Saleh Mohammed Jerbo Jamus*, Trial Chamber IV, Decision on common legal representation, ICC-02/05-03/09-337, 25 May 2012, para 26.

[176] ICC, *Prosecutor v. Abdallah Banda Abakaer Nourain and Saleh Mohammed Jerbo Jamus*, Trial Chamber IV, Decision on common legal representation, ICC-02/05-03/09-337, 25 May 2012, para 33.

[177] ICC, *Prosecutor v. Abdallah Banda Abakaer Nourain and Saleh Mohammed Jerbo Jamus*, Trial Chamber IV, Decision on common legal representation, ICC-02/05-03/09-337, 25 May 2012, paras 40, 46, 49.

[178] STL Directive on Victim' Legal Representation, Article 22(B).

[179] STL, *Prosecutor v. Ayyash* et al., Pre-Trial Judge, Order Inviting the Registrar to Respond to the Duty Legal Representative's Motion for Review of Designation, Case No. STL-11-01/PT/PTJ, 15 August 2012.

Registry does have information or views to submit in response there is nothing preventing a submission.[180] In *Banda and Jerbo*, the Chamber considered observations filed by the designated common legal representatives in response to the application for review.[181]

A further procedural point arose in the *Ruto and Sang* case. There Pre-Trial Chamber II censured the lawyers who brought the motion for review for having apparently acted in contravention of Article 28 of the Code of Professional Conduct for counsel. It prohibits counsel from 'address[ing] directly the client of another counsel except through or with the permission of that counsel'.[182] The Chamber therefore considered that any concerns should have been addressed to the newly appointed LRV.[183] It is unclear whether this approach would be followed by other chambers. The request for review in *Banda and Jerbo*, brought around the same time and decided subsequently to that in *Ruto and Sang*, included statements signed by the applicant victims and resulting from discussions after the appointment of a common legal representative.[184] In that case, however, the Trial Chamber made no condemnation of the lawyers for having continued to speak with their former clients after the appointment of a common legal representative and without permission from the latter.[185]

---

[180] For example: ICC, *Prosecutor v. William Samoei Ruto, Henry Kiprono Kosgey and Joshua Arap Sang*, Registry, Submission of information relating to the former Legal Representatives' Motion, ICC-01/09-01/11-320, 2 September 2011.

[181] ICC, *Prosecutor v. Abdallah Banda Abakaer Nourain and Saleh Mohammed Jerbo Jamus*, Common legal representatives, Observations in response to the request for review of the proposed appointment of common legal representatives, ICC-02/05-03/09-230, 12 October 2011 (reclassified as public on 25 May 2012); ICC, *Prosecutor v. Abdallah Banda Abakaer Nourain and Saleh Mohammed Jerbo Jamus*, Trial Chamber IV, Decision on common legal representation, ICC-02/05-03/09-337, 25 May 2012, paras 20–22.

[182] ICC, *Prosecutor v. William Samoei Ruto, Henry Kiprono Kosgey and Joshua Arap Sang*, Pre-Trial Chamber II, Decision on the "Motion from Victims a/0041/10, a/0045/10, a/0051/10 and a/0056/10 requesting the Pre-Trial Chamber to Reconsider the Appointment of Common Legal Representative Sureta CHANA for All Victims", ICC-01/09-01/11-330, 9 September 2011, para 17.

[183] ICC, *Prosecutor v. William Samoei Ruto, Henry Kiprono Kosgey and Joshua Arap Sang*, Pre-Trial Chamber II, Decision on the "Motion from Victims a/0041/10, a/0045/10, a/0051/10 and a/0056/10 requesting the Pre-Trial Chamber to Reconsider the Appointment of Common Legal Representative Sureta CHANA for All Victims", ICC-01/09-01/11-330, 9 September 2011, para 17.

[184] ICC, *Prosecutor v. Abdallah Banda Abakaer Nourain and Saleh Mohammed Jerbo Jamus*, Participating Victims, Request of Victims a/1646/10 and a/1647/10 for the Trial Chamber to review the Registry's "Notification of appointment of common legal representatives of victims" in accordance with Regulation 79(3), ICC-02/05-03/09-228, 30 September 2011, para 2 and Annex 1 (ICC- ICC-02/05-03/09-228-Anx1-Red).

[185] See ICC, *Prosecutor v. Abdallah Banda Abakaer Nourain and Saleh Mohammed Jerbo Jamus*, Victim's Legal Representatives, Request of Victims a/1646/10 and a/1647/10 for the Trial Chamber to review the Registry's "Notification of appointment of common legal representatives of victims" in accordance with Regulation 79(3), ICC-02/05-03/09-288, 30 September 2011; ICC, *Prosecutor v. Abdallah Banda Abakaer Nourain and Saleh Mohammed Jerbo Jamus*, Trial Chamber IV, Decision on common legal representation, ICC-02/05-03/09-337, 25 May 2012.

Indeed, it is difficult to conceive of how Pre-Trial Chamber II's approach would not fatally undermine the effectiveness of Regulation 79(3). Given that the ICC does not, like the STL, provide funded duty counsel to undertake challenges against legal representation, most victims will be unable to bring a challenge without assistance from a privately retained lawyer. Yet the practical effect of Pre-Trial Chamber II's approach is that such a lawyer cannot receive instructions from the applicant victims without the consent of the common legal representative whose designation is sought to be challenged. Such a result could be avoided by a practical interpretation of the ethical obligation, which might treat as an exceptional circumstance a meeting undertaken for the purpose of challenging the appointment of a common legal representation. Given the timeframe for making such a challenge this would remain a narrow exception and would not undermine the benefit of Article 28 of the ICC Code of Professional Conduct for Counsel.

5.3.6.4 Subsequent Complaints or Challenges Regarding Legal Representation

While the procedures described above offer some options for victims at the STL or ICC who are immediately dissatisfied with a Registrar's arrangement of collective legal representation, none of the tribunals provides a clear procedure for complaints or challenges for victims who have grown dissatisfied over time by the quality of court-arranged representation.

The closest thing to such a system is the "effective representation" regime at the STL (see further below). It would enable a victim dissatisfied with the quality of his or her legal representation to provide information to that effect to the VPU. If the information disclosed a "serious concern" about the effectiveness of the representation, the VPU could then initiate formal monitoring procedures intended to either rectify the problem or trigger disciplinary procedures which could in theory lead to a change in legal representation. It is yet to be seen whether this system will provide practical assistance to victims who are dissatisfied with their representation. One obvious deficiency is that there is no requirement for the VPU to inform victims of the possibility to contact the VPU with concerns about their representation or to establish accessible mechanisms for doing so.

In contrast, at the ICC, the Registry has no express mandate to scrutinise the work of LRVs. On request from a chamber, the VPRS may consult with victims regarding their views on their legal representation to date and whether it should be continued, but to date this has occurred rarely.[186] In other instances, where the Registry has sought to consult with victims regarding their legal representation, the attempt has been hampered by a requirement that the discussion be held in the

[186] ICC, *Prosecutor v. Bosco Ntaganda*, Trial Chamber VI, Decision on victims' participation in trial proceedings, ICC-01/04-02/06-449, 6 February 2015, para 54.

presence of the LRV.[187] One chamber has noted that victims as a group may petition the Registry in the case of 'significant problems' with the representative function of the common legal representative, and if the problem is not able to be resolved by the Registry it shall inform the chamber.[188] There are, however, clear logistical challenges to victims achieving such a step pro-actively. It is also not clear whether the Registry is expected to (and whether it does) pass on every complaint received about legal representation to the relevant chamber, or whether some scrutiny is to be exercised, regarding for example the number of victims in support of the complaint and the reasons for it.

An example of the frustration felt by victims because of the lack of an appropriate complaints mechanism occurred in the *Ongwen* case. There a non-governmental organisation working with victims requested to file *amicus curiae* submissions regarding victims' dissatisfaction with the existing arrangements for legal representation (by the OPCV) in the *Kony* case, and stating that 'victims currently have no alternative avenues to seize the Chamber' of this matter.[189] Despite this plea, it does not appear that any formal steps were taken to inquire into the effectiveness of the existing representation and counsel from OPCV were again appointed in the *Ongwen* case.

5.4 Resourcing of Legal Representatives

5.4.1 In-House Representation Versus Private Counsel

Systems for resourcing victims' legal representation vary principally depending on whether the lawyers involved are "in-house" or external.

Typically in-house lawyers are salaried as staff or long-term consultants of the court in question and treated as part of that institution. Their resourcing will therefore be determined in accordance with the normal budgeting procedures of the organisation. Decisions on resources in these instances are largely at the discretion of institutional management and any donor-controlled structures for budget oversight. Other than contractual entitlements (whether as staff or

---

[187] ICC, *Prosecutor v. Abdallah Banda Abakaer Nourain and Saleh Mohammed Jerbo Jamus*, Trial Chamber IV, Order instructing the Registry to start consultations on the organisation of common legal representation, ICC-02/05-03/09-138, 21 April 2011, para 7.

[188] ICC, *Prosecutor v. Germain Katanga and Mathieu Ngudjolo Chui*, Trial Chamber II, Decision on the organisation of common legal representation of victims, ICC-01/04-01/07-1328, 22 July 2009, para 13.

[189] The substance of the victims' concerns was reported as being a lack of contact from the OPCV during the preceding years, during which the OPCV counsel were on record as representing victims but proceedings in the case remained dormant pending the surrender of an accused person: ICC, *Prosecutor v. Dominic Ongwen*, Application by the Uganda Victims Foundation to Submit *Amicus Curiae* Observations pursuant to Rule 103 of the Rules of Procedure and Evidence, ICC-02/04/01/15-211, 19 March 2015, pp. 5–6.

consultants) there is therefore little or no prospect of legal challenges by victims or lawyers to the level of resourcing provided.

In contrast, where various external counsel are engaged to represent victims in a given case, they will usually be resourced (if at all) according to a structured "legal aid" system. Such a system is in principle driven by a standard set of regulations, applied to given lawyers or teams by an administrative decision-maker in the tribunal.

Different combinations of these systems exist at the three tribunals. The STL to date uses only a system of external counsel funded by legal aid. At the ECCC, Civil Party Lead Co-Lawyers effectively serve as in-house lawyers. Most civil party lawyers are external counsel who are not funded by the court, many doing their work *pro bono*. However, following the introduction of compulsory legal representation under Rule 23*ter*(1) in February 2010, the ECCC began to fund a small number of Cambodian civil party lawyers to represent otherwise unrepresented civil parties. These lawyers are funded and provided with facilities by the ECCC.[190]

At the ICC, the OPCV may represent victims and when doing so function as in-house lawyers whose resourcing is controlled through the centralised budget processes of the Court. All other counsel—whether appointed as common legal representative by the Court or privately retained by victims before court-arranged legal representation is implemented in a given case—are external and may be funded by the Court's legal aid program. In some cases mixed representation has been arranged: either with a lead counsel from OPCV supported by specifically recruited external team members funded by legal aid,[191] or by the arrangement of an external team which includes an embedded OPCV lawyer.[192] In earlier cases

[190] Written correspondence with Christoph Sperfeldt, PhD Scholar, Australian National University, 2 October 2016 (notes on file with the editors).

[191] ICC, *Prosecutor v. Laurent Gbagbo*, Pre-Trial Chamber I, Decision on Victims' Participation and Victims' Common Legal Representation at the Confirmation of Charges Hearing and in the Related Proceedings, ICC-02/11-01/11-138, 4 June 2012, para 44; ICC, *Prosecutor v. Charles Blé Goude*, Pre-Trial Chamber I, Decision on victims' participation in the pre-trial proceedings and related issues, ICC-02/11-02/11-83, 11 June 2014, paras 24–25; ICC, *Prosecutor v. Bosco Ntaganda*, Pre-Trial Chamber I, Decision Concerning the Organisation of Common Legal Representation of Victims, ICC-01/04-02/06-160, 2 December 2013, para 26; ICC, *Prosecutor v. Dominic Ongwen*, Pre-Trial Chamber II, Decision on contested victims' applications for participation, legal representation of victims and their procedural rights, ICC-02/04-01/15-350, 27 November 2015, paras 23–24.

[192] ICC, *Prosecutor v. William Samoei Ruto and Joshua Arap Sang*, Trial Chamber V, Decision on victims' representation and participation, ICC-01/09-01/11-460, 3 October 2012, paras 41–45, 60; ICC, *Prosecutor v. Uhuru Muigai Kenyatta*, Trial Chamber V, Decision on victims' representation and participation, ICC-01/09-01/11-498, 3 October 2012, paras 40–44, 59; ICC, *Prosecutor v. William Samoei Ruto and Joshua Arap Sang*, Trial Chamber V, Decision appointing a common legal representative of victims, ICC-01/09-01/11-479, 23 November 2012, para 8; ICC, *Prosecutor v. Francis Kirimi Muthaura and Uhuru Muigai Kenyatta*, Trial Chamber V, Decision appointing a common legal representative of victims, ICC-01/09-02/11-537, 20 November 2012, para 7.

chambers also indicated that external LRVs may be able to make use of Registry facilities and/or support staff, including the secondment of Registry staff to operate under the supervision of external lawyers.[193] This suggestion does not appear to have been implemented in practice and has likely been overtaken by the use of members of the OPCV for this purpose.

A debate continues at the ICC over the relative merits (and cost implications) of representation by the OPCV versus external legal representation of victims. Although the Registry has previously opposed the idea of adopting an exclusive system of in-house legal representation for victims,[194] a more recent proposal as part of the Registry "ReVision" project appeared to move in this direction.[195] However adopting this proposal would require an amendment to the Regulations of the Court which establish the current OPCV and its role.[196] To date it has not proved possible to agree such an amendment and it is unclear whether this will change.[197]

The remainder of this section will consider the rules and principles applicable where a legal aid system is used to regulate the resourcing of external counsel.

5.4.2 The Regulation of Legal Aid

The ICC and STL both operate systems of legal aid for external counsel representing victims.

At the STL, a specific Legal Aid Policy for Victims' Participation has been adopted by the Registrar, pursuant to the RPE,[198] and following the approval of the Tribunal's Management Committee.[199] The document is a detailed legal text intending to regulate all aspects of the management of legal aid funds. It is broadly based on and similar to the STL's Legal Aid Policy for the Defence.

---

193 ICC, *Prosecutor v. Germain Katanga and Mathieu Ngudjolo Chui*, Trial Chamber II, Order on the organisation of common legal representation of victims, ICC-01/04-01/07-1328, 22 July 2009, para 18; ICC, *Prosecutor v. Jean-Pierre Bemba Gombo,* Trial Chamber III, Decision on common legal representation of victims for the purpose of trial, ICC-01/05-01/08-1005, 10 November 2010, para 27.

194 Supplementary report of the Registry on four aspects of the Court's legal aid system, ICC-ASP/11/43 (2012), para 54.

195 ICC Registry, ReVision Project: Basic Outline of Proposals to Establish Defence and Victims Offices, http://www.uianet.org/sites/default/files/Registry_ReVision_BasicOutline_Defence_Victims_Offices_0.pdf. Accessed 6 Sept 2016, p. 5.

196 Regulations of the Court, Regulation 81.

197 ICC, Comprehensive Report on the Reorganisation of the Registry of the International Criminal Court, August 2016. https://www.icc-cpi.int/itemsDocuments/ICC-Registry-CR.pdf. Accessed 4 Nov 2016, p. 12.

198 STL RPE, Rule 51(C)(ii).

199 STL Legal Aid Policy for Victims' Participation, preamble.

In contrast, the ICC does not possess a specific regulatory document in relation to legal aid (also referred to as "legal assistance" in many of the Court's texts). The RPE require that legal aid 'criteria and procedures' shall be established by the Regulations of the Court 'based on a proposal by the Registrar.'[200] However, the Regulations of the Court contain only three provisions relating to legal aid, setting out broad general principles.[201] In practice, legal aid policy is ostensibly determined through a series of exchanges between the Registry and the Assembly of State Parties (ASP), including reports by the former and some decisions by the latter. In 2013, in response to a request from the ASP, the Court submitted a document that it referred to as a "single policy document" on legal aid.[202] Further recommendations for changes to this policy have been submitted since,[203] and no updated consolidated document has been produced. The legal status of these documents received and created by the ASP is also not entirely clear. None of the legal texts of the Court gives the ASP power to regulate the details of legal aid (in contrast to a number of other specific legislative powers granted to the ASP[204]). Indeed, the RPE appear to require that the plenary (responsible for the Regulations of the Court) should legislate on legal aid, based on a proposal from the Registrar who is required only to consult with any independent representative body of counsel or legal associations.[205] When deciding on legal aid matters for the Defence chambers have indicated that the Registrar's role in elaborating and managing legal aid, and any reports to the ASP prepared in that capacity, remain subject to the statutory framework of the Court.[206] More specifically, the Trial Chamber in *Katanga and Ngudjolo Chui* considered reports on legal aid from the ASP to have the status of 'useful indicators for the Court, which the Court will take into account to the extent possible.'[207]

---

200 ICC RPE, Rule 21(1). See also Rule 20(3) and the definition of "Regulations" in Rule 1.

201 ICC Regulations of the Court, Regulations 83–85.

202 Registry's single policy document on the Court's legal aid system, ICC-ASP/12/3, 4 June 2013.

203 See for example Registry report on ways to improve the legal aid procedures, ICC-ASP/13/6, 22 May 2014.

204 See for example: ICC Statute, Articles 9(1) and (2); 49; and 51(1) and (2).

205 ICC RPE, Rules 20(3) and 21(1).

206 ICC, *Prosecutor v. Callixte Mbarushimana*, Pre-Trial Chamber I, Decision on the "Defence Request for the Review of the Scope of Legal Assistance", ICC-01/04-01/10-142, 11 May 2011, para 11; ICC, *Prosecutor v. Thomas Lubanga Dyilo*, Trial Chamber I, Decision reviewing the Registry's decision on legal assistance for Mr. Thomas Lubanga Dyilo pursuant to Regulation 135 of the Regulations of the Registry, ICC-01/04-01/-06-2800, 30 August 2011, paras 53–54; ICC, *Prosecutor v. Germain Katanga and Mathieu Ngudjolo Chui*, Transcript of oral order, ICC-01/04-01/07-T-341-ENG, 18 June 2012, p. 9.

207 ICC, *Prosecutor v. Germain Katanga and Mathieu Ngudjolo Chui*, Transcript of oral order, ICC-01/04-01/07-T-341-ENG, 18 June 2012, p. 9.

5.4.3 Legal Aid Entitlements and the Relevance of Indigence

At both the ICC and STL the question of victims' indigence plays some role in legal aid, at least on paper.

At the ICC, Regulation 84 requires that '[w]here a person applies for legal assistance to be paid by the Court, the Registrar shall determine the applicant's means and whether he or she shall be provided with full or partial payment of legal assistance'.[208] Further details are provided in the Regulations of the Registry.[209] The Registry has interpreted these provisions as requiring an individual determination of indigence for each participating victim, although the Registry has required that less financial information be provided by victims than by accused persons.[210]

When an LRV from the Democratic Republic of the Congo proposed that the Registry adopt a presumption of indigence, given the difficulties faced in providing detailed financial information, the Registry resisted this approach, indicating that it required from each victim information concerning the victim's financial situation, as well as a signed statement certifying the correctness of the information provided, authorising the Registrar to investigate, and undertaking to inform the Registrar of any changes in the victim's financial situation.[211] The Presidency held that the Registry's requirements were permissible.[212] However, it

[208] ICC Regulations of the Court, Regulation 84(1).

[209] ICC Regulations of the Registry, Regulation 132.

[210] Report of the Court on legal aid: Legal and financial aspects of funding of victims' legal representation before the Court, ICC-ASP/8/25, 5 October 2009, paras 17–19; ICC, *Situation in the Democratic Republic of the Congo*, Registrar, Registrar's Observations under regulation 24*bis* and 34(b) of the Regulations of the Court in respect of the Request for Review of the Registrar's *Decision on the Application for Legal Assistance Paid by the Court Filed by Mr. Keta in behalf of Victims a/0016/06, a/0018/06, a/0021/06, a/0025/06, a/0028/06, a/0031/06, a/0032/06, a/0034/06, a/0042/06, a/0044/06, a/0045/06, a/0142/06, a/0148/06, a/0150/06, a/0188/06, a/0199/06, a/0228/06*, dated 28 March 2008, ICC-01/04-497-tENG, 6 May 2008, paras 9–15.

[211] ICC, *Situation in the Democratic Republic of the Congo*, Registrar, Registrar's Observations under regulation 24*bis* and 34(b) of the Regulations of the Court in respect of the Request for Review of the Registrar's *Decision on the Application for Legal Assistance Paid by the Court Filed by Mr. Keta in behalf of Victims a/0016/06, a/0018/06, a/0021/06, a/0025/06, a/0028/06, a/0031/06, a/0032/06, a/0034/06, a/0042/06, a/0044/06, a/0045/06, a/0142/06, a/0148/06, a/0150/06, a/0188/06, a/0199/06, a/0228/06*, dated 28 March 2008, ICC-01/04-497-tENG, 6 May 2008.

[212] ICC, *Situation in the Democratic Republic of the Congo*, Presidency, Reasons for the Decision on the "Request for Review of the Registrar's Decision of 28 March 2008 on the Application for Legal Assistance Paid by the Court Filed by Mr. Keta on behalf of Victims *a*/0016/06, a/0018/06, a/0021/06, a/0025/06, a/0028/06, a/0031/06, a/0032/06, a/0034/06, a/0042/06, a/0044/06, a/0045/06, a/0142/06, a/0148/06, a/0150/06, a/0188/06, a/0199/06, a/0228/06 under Regulation 85(3) of the Regulations of the Court", ICC-01/04-559, 18 February 2009, paras 21–24.

also noted that the legal assistance scheme established by the Court's texts 'does not prevent the application of a rebuttable presumption of indigence'[213] and requested the Registry to address the viability of a scheme utilising a presumption of indigence.[214] In reporting to the Assembly of States Parties, the Registry has taken the position that it must undertake at least a *prima facie* assessment of each participating victims' financial means based on a declaration submitted by the victim.[215]

Despite this, the Registry has been open to using presumptions in certain instances: notably where the victim in question is a child.[216] It is unclear why, if this approach is compatible with the legal texts, it could not be broadened to involve the use of other appropriate presumptions based, for example, on the region in which a victim lives or a victim's stated occupation. So long as such presumptions remained rebuttable it is difficult to see how they would interfere with the Registrar's financial oversight responsibilities.

During the earlier years of the Court's operation, some formal decisions on the indigence of victims were taken. In these, victims were determined to be *provisionally* indigent if they had provided information on their assets to the Court and had authorised the Court to investigate their indigence, pending the outcome

[213] ICC, *Situation in the Democratic Republic of the Congo*, Presidency, Reasons for the Decision on the "Request for Review of the Registrar's Decision of 28 March 2008 on the Application for Legal Assistance Paid by the Court Filed by Mr. Keta on behalf of Victims *a*/0016/06, a/0018/06, a/0021/06, a/0025/06, a/0028/06, a/0031/06, a/0032/06, a/0034/06, a/0042/06, a/0044/06, a/0045/06, a/0142/06, a/0148/06, a/0150/06, a/0188/06, a/0199/06, a/0228/06 under Regulation 85(3) of the Regulations of the Court", ICC-01/04-559, 18 February 2009, para 25.

[214] ICC, *Situation in the Democratic Republic of the Congo*, Presidency, Reasons for the Decision on the "Request for Review of the Registrar's Decision of 28 March 2008 on the Application for Legal Assistance Paid by the Court Filed by Mr. Keta on behalf of Victims *a*/0016/06, a/0018/06, a/0021/06, a/0025/06, a/0028/06, a/0031/06, a/0032/06, a/0034/06, a/0042/06, a/0044/06, a/0045/06, a/0142/06, a/0148/06, a/0150/06, a/0188/06, a/0199/06, a/0228/06 under Regulation 85(3) of the Regulations of the Court", ICC-01/04-559, 18 February 2009, para 27.

[215] Report of the Court on legal aid: Legal and financial aspects of funding of victims' legal representation before the Court, ICC-ASP/8/25, 5 October 2009, paras 17–19.

[216] ICC, *Situation in the Democratic Republic of the Congo*, Registrar, Registrar's Observations under regulation 24*bis* and 34(b) of the Regulations of the Court in respect of the Request for Review of the Registrar's *Decision on the Application for Legal Assistance Paid by the Court Filed by Mr. Keta in behalf of Victims a/0016/06, a/0018/06, a/0021/06, a/0025/06, a/0028/06, a/0031/06, a/0032/06, a/0034/06, a/0042/06, a/0044/06, a/0045/06, a/0142/06, a/0148/06, a/0150/06, a/0188/06, a/0199/06, a/0228/06*, dated 28 March 2008, ICC-01/04-497-tENG, 6 May 2008, para 15.

of a full financial investigation.[217] It does not appear, however, that final decisions were subsequently made based on a complete financial investigation.

An added complexity is generated by the fact that victims participating in ICC proceedings are almost always represented collectively (whether as a result of court-imposed collective representation or as a result of having privately appointed a lawyer who is also representing other victims). A question therefore arises as to the situation in which only some of the victims represented by a given counsel are determined to be indigent by the Registry. The Court's texts and decisions are silent on this issue. The Registry has indicated that in the process of determining indigence, collective representation is taken into account, with the result that victims are assessed on their 'ability to meet a relevant proportion of the costs rather than the entire cost.'[218] Nonetheless, it is not clear how payments by non-indigent victims would be made: Would they be made directly to the LRV or to the Court? Would the amount be determined by the LRV or by the Court? On what basis would such an amount be determined? In fact where, in one early decision, the Registrar refused to recognise some collectively represented victims as indigent (due to a failure to supply sufficient information), no requirement for payments were imposed and it appeared that the victims would continue to be represented together with victims determined to be indigent without any distinction being made between the two groups in practice.[219] This approach means that in order to be remunerated under the Court's legal aid scheme, in practice, a lawyer only has to demonstrate that at least one of his or her clients is indigent. Given that the resourcing of LRVs under the legal aid scheme does not vary significantly with the number of (indigent) victims represented, it is

[217] ICC, *Prosecutor v. Thomas Lubanga Dyilo*, Registrar, Décision du Greffier sur la demande d'aide judiciaire aux frais de la Cour déposée par la victim a/0105/06, ICC-01/04-01/06-650, 3 November 2006; ICC, *Situation in the Democratic Republic of Congo*, Registrar's Decision on the Indigence of Victims a/0016/06, a/0018/06, a/0021/06, a/0025/06, a/0028/06, a/0031/06, a/0032/06, a/0034/06, a/0042/06, a/0044/06, a/0045/06, a/0142/06, a/0148/06, a/0150/06, a/0188/06, a/0199/06, a/0228/06, ICC-01/04-490-tENG, 26 March 2008; ICC, *Situation in Darfur, Sudan*, Decision on the Indigence of Victims a/0015/06, a/0029/07, a/0036/07, a/0037/07 and a/0038/07, ICC-02/05-156-tENG, 8 September 2008; ICC, *Prosecutor v. Jean-Pierre Bemba Gombo*, Registrar, Registrar's Decision on the Indigence of Victims a/0271/08, a/0272/08, a/0273/08, a/0275/08, a/0277/08, a/0283/08, a/0284/08, a/0285/08, a/0286/08, a/0287/08, a/0288/08, a/0289/08, a/0290/08, a/0294/08, a/0390/08, a/0391/08, a/0393/08, a/0394/08, a/0395/08, a/0396/08, a/0468/08, a/0469/08, a/0470/08, a/0471/08, a/0472/08, a/0473/08, a/0474/08, a/0475/08, a/0476/08, a/0477/08, a/0478/08, a/0479/08, a/0480/08 and a/0481/08, ICC-01/05-01/08-348-tENG, 7 January 2009.

[218] Report of the Court on legal aid: Legal and financial aspects of funding of victims' legal representation before the Court, ICC-ASP/8/25, 5 October 2009, para 20.

[219] ICC, *Prosecutor v. Jean-Pierre Bemba Gombo*, Registrar, Registrar's Decision on the Indigence of Victims a/0271/08, a/0272/08, a/0273/08, a/0275/08, a/0277/08, a/0283/08, a/0284/08, a/0285/08, a/0286/08, a/0287/08, a/0288/08, a/0289/08, a/0290/08, a/0294/08, a/0390/08, a/0391/08, a/0393/08, a/0394/08, a/0395/08, a/0396/08, a/0468/08, a/0469/08, a/0470/08, a/0471/08, a/0472/08, a/0473/08, a/0474/08, a/0475/08, a/0476/08, a/0477/08, a/0478/08, a/0479/08, a/0480/08 and a/0481/08, ICC-01/05-01/08-348-tENG, 7 January 2009.

questionable whether there is any value in undertaking individual assessments of indigence for large numbers of victims, since it appears that their outcome is of little or no consequence.

Indeed, it appears that the Court is moving away from such individual assessments in practice, at least where common legal representation has been organised. In recent years no formal decisions on indigence have been published, notwithstanding the grant of victim status to thousands of victims in various cases, and the fact that their legal representation has been paid for by legal aid. It therefore appears that a *de facto* presumption of indigence is now operating, at least to the extent that common legal representation will be paid for by legal aid regardless of whether the victims have been determined indigent. Indeed, when arranging common legal representation, the Pre-Trial Chamber in *Ntaganda* was willing to assume that victims would benefit from legal aid where they had 'not indicated that they themselves would pay' for legal representation.[220] The relevance of indigence determinations may in practice have been reduced to the period before common legal representation is arranged. However, this period itself is increasingly short and may in many cases not include any pre-trial activities that would be covered by legal aid.

In contrast to this situation at the ICC, the STL has established a clearly defined approach to the indigence of participating victims, as set out in its Legal Aid Policy for Victims' Participation.[221] According to this scheme participating victims are presumed to be indigent,[222] unless 'there are any grounds for believing that a victim is not indigent'[223] in which case the Registrar may make a determination of non-indigence,[224] where appropriate following an independent financial inquiry.[225] A victim is considered to be non-indigent when his or her household earns at least €3000 per month more than its reasonable expenses,[226] or where the victim owns sufficient disposable assets according to a specific formula.[227] Determinations on non-indigence may be made confidentially at the Registrar's discretion,[228] and to date none has been published.

The Tribunal's Legal Aid Policy for Victims' Participation also stipulates how indigence or non-indigence impacts on legal aid arrangements, including in the usual scenario of collective representation. Where a lawyer is designated to

---

220 ICC, *Prosecutor v. Bosco Ntaganda*, Pre-Trial Chamber I, Decision Concerning the Organisation of Common Legal Representation of Victims, ICC-01/04-02/06-160, 2 December 2013, para 23.

221 STL Legal Aid Policy for Victims' Participation, Sections 2, 3 and 6.1–6.3.

222 Ibid., Section 2.2.

223 Ibid., Section 3.1.

224 Ibid., Section 3.1.

225 Ibid., Section 3.4.

226 Ibid., Sections 3.6–3.9.

227 Ibid., Sections 3.10–3.14.

228 Ibid., Section 3.2.

represent victims all of whom are determined to be non-indigent, the lawyer is not entitled to legal aid from the Tribunal,[229] but may be paid directly by the clients.[230] Where a lawyer is designated to represent at least one victim who has not been declared non-indigent, he or she will be paid and resourced under the Tribunal's legal aid scheme.[231] Any non-indigent victims in the represented group must make a fixed contribution to the Tribunal's legal aid budget of €2500 per month.[232]

5.4.4 Availability of Legal Aid Prior to Common Legal Representation

As explained above, no legal representation is recognised at the STL prior to the arrangement of legal representation by the Tribunal.

In contrast, at the ICC private lawyers may be appointed by participating victims (or applicants) prior to the arrangement of common legal representation. This raises the question of legal aid entitlements for these lawyers.

Until late 2015, ICC practice had been consistent in providing legal aid to privately retained lawyers prior to the arrangement of common legal representation (subject to the questions of indigence, discussed above).[233] Notwithstanding this practice, for the first time[234] in the *Ongwen* case a different approach was taken by Pre-Trial Chamber II. There the Single Judge referred to Rule 90(5) of the RPE, which provides that: '[a] victim or group of victims who lack the necessary means to pay for a common legal representative chosen by the Court may receive assistance from the Registry, including, as appropriate, financial assistance'. The Single Judge went on to hold that *only* common legal

[229] Ibid., Section 6.2.

[230] STL Code of Professional Conduct for Defence Counsel and Legal Representatives of Victims appearing before the Special Tribunal for Lebanon, Article 16(A).

[231] STL Legal Aid Policy for Victims' Participation, Sections 6.1 and 6.3.

[232] Ibid., Sections 4.1–4.9, 6.3.

[233] See for example: ICC, *Prosecutor v. Abdallah Banda Abakaer Nourain and Saleh Mohammed Jerbo Jamus*, Registry, Report recommending a decision concerning the common legal representation of victims participating in the case, ICC-02/05-03/09-134, 15 April 2011, para 7; Report on the operation of the Court's legal aid system and proposals for its amendment, ICC-ASP/6/4, 31 May 2007, para 7 (regarding the *Lubanga* case); Interim report of the Court on legal aid: legal and financial aspects for funding victims' legal representation before the Court, ICC-ASP-8/3, 6 May 2009, para 21 (regarding the *Lubanga* and *Katanga* cases).

[234] Although note earlier comments in a similar vein by Trial Chamber III: ICC, *Prosecutor v. Jean-Pierre Bemba Gombo*, Trial Chamber III, Decision on common legal representation of victims for the purpose of trial, ICC-01/05-01/08-1005, 10 November 2010, para 16.

representatives chosen by the Court, and *not* counsel appointed directly by victims under Rule 90(1), are able to receive legal aid.[235]

It is not yet clear whether this approach will be followed in other cases. It has been the subject of criticism from civil society,[236] and there are a number of reasons why it does not appear consistent with Registry and ASP documents or the intention behind Rule 90. No distinction between common legal representatives and other victims' counsel is made in the provisions of the Regulations of the Court which deal with legal aid,[237] as mandated by the RPE,[238] which instead leave a broad discretion to the Registry. The ASP and Registry documents which guide the exercise of that discretion appear to reject the approach taken by the Single Judge in Ongwen. One ASP document explicitly states that victims' legal representation should be broader than the "permissive language" of Rule 90.[239] Meanwhile, the Registry's Single Policy Document provides for standard legal aid to be provided to victims' counsel at pre-trial,[240] and later addresses separately the question of legal aid where common legal representation has been arranged.[241] More importantly still, restricting legal aid to common legal representatives would likely render meaningless Rule 90(1). It would effectively mean that victims could only freely choose their own lawyers to the extent that such lawyers are able to undertake the substantial work involved without remuneration from the court, and to expend their own money on costs such as travel.

5.4.5 Resourcing of Legally Aided Victims' Legal Representatives

5.4.5.1 Legal Principles and Regulations

As set out above, at the STL, the extent and nature of legal aid provided to counsel is regulated by a detailed Legal Aid Policy for Victims' Participation. It covers

[235] ICC, *Prosecutor v. Dominic Ongwen*, Pre-Trial Chamber II, Decision on contested victims' applications for participation, legal representation of victims and their procedural rights, ICC-02/04-01/15-350, 27 November 2015, para 18.

[236] See for example, Mariana Pena, International Justice Monitor, Giving Victims their Voice: Ongwen Case Highlights the ICC's Policy Challenge (5 January 2016), http://www.ijmonitor.org/2016/01/giving-victims-their-voice-ongwen-case-highlights-the-iccs-policy-challenge/. Accessed 27 July 2016.

[237] ICC Regulations of the Court, Regulations 83–85.

[238] ICC RPE, Rule 21(1).

[239] Hague Working Group of the ASP Bureau, Report of the Bureau on legal aid for victims' legal representation, ICC-ASP/8/38, 28 October 2009, para 12.

[240] Registry's single policy document on the Court's legal aid system, ICC-ASP/12/3, 4 June 2013, para 55.

[241] Ibid., para 59 *et seq.*

levels of remuneration for counsel, as well as other entitlements including travel and staffing.

At the ICC the situation is much less clear, although some guidance is provided by the Single Policy Document on legal aid. Beyond this, minimal guidance has been provided by some chambers on the guiding principles applicable to legal aid determinations. For example, Trial Chamber II indicated that the common legal representative's team's resources should be sufficient to ensure he was able to comply with his key obligations.[242] Pre-Trial Chamber II similarly stated that sufficient support should be provided in order for LRVs to be able to perform their duties in an efficient and expeditious manner.[243] Factors relevant to the Registrar's decisions on legal aid are set out in Regulation 113(2) of the Regulations of the Registry.

5.4.5.2 Scope of Legal Aid in Practice

As between the two courts providing legal aid to external counsel, it is clear that the STL's system provides more comprehensive resources. In the *Ayyash* et al. case victims are represented by a team composed of one lead counsel, two co-counsel, a legal officer, a case manager and an evidence reviewer and assisted by a victimology expert as well as interns. The team receives a sufficient travel budget to enable Lebanon-based co-counsel to participate in hearings in The Hague and for Hague-based team members to travel several times a year to Lebanon.

At the ICC resources have generally been significantly more limited, even despite the arguably larger burden of communicating with large numbers of victims spread across large and insecure regions. For example:

- In *Bemba* Trial Chamber III indicated that the minimum number of persons necessary to represent victims was two per team (including counsel)—one in the field and one in The Hague.[244] In practice each team included one counsel,

[242] ICC, *Prosecutor v. Germain Katanga and Mathieu Ngudjolo Chui*, Trial Chamber II, Order on the organisation of common legal representation of victims, ICC-01/04-01/07-1328, 22 July 2009, para 17.

[243] ICC, *Prosecutor v. William Samoei Ruto, Henry Kiprono Kosgey and Joshua Arap Sang*, Pre-Trial Chamber II, Decision on Victims' Participation at the confirmation of Charges Hearing and In the Related Proceedings, ICC-01/09-01/11-249, 5 August 2011, para 78; ICC, *Prosecutor v. Francis Kirimi Muthaura, Uhuru Muigai Kenyatta and Mohammad Hussein Ali*, Pre-Trial Chamber II, Decision on Victims' Participation at the Confirmation of Charges Hearing and in the Related Proceedings, ICC-01/09-02/11-267, 26 August 2011, para 92.

[244] ICC, *Prosecutor v. Jean-Pierre Bemba Gombo,* Trial Chamber III, Decision on common legal representation of victims for the purpose of trial, ICC-01/05-01/08-1005, 10 November 2010, para 26.

one legal officer/case manager and one assistant in the field, until the death of one of the victims' counsel caused the two teams to be amalgamated into one.[245]

- In each of the two Kenya cases victims' were represented by a team composed of one counsel, one case manager, two field assistants and a legal assistant provided by OPCV.[246]
- In *Gbagbo,* the Registry recommended a team composed of counsel, a team member based in the field and a case manager,[247] and this was endorsed by Chamber[248] which also appointed an OPCV lawyer as lead counsel.[249] The Chamber required that there be an appropriate team member paid for by legal aid funds, based in the field.[250] This model was later followed in *Goude*[251] and *Ntaganda*.[252]

As these examples demonstrate, although the Registry states that its approach to legal aid is contingent on the specifics of a particular case,[253] in practice there is minimal variation in team size and structure.

This raises the question of how well the ICC's legal aid systems respond to the specific nature of victim participation in a given case. For example, the staffing needs of a particular team may vary significantly depending on victim numbers

245 ICC, *Prosecutor v. Jean-Pierre Bemba Gombo,* Trial Chamber III, Order on the legal representation of victims previously represented by Me Assingambi Zarambaud, ICC-01/05-01/08-2964, 7 February 2014, para 7.

246 ICC, *Prosecutor v. William Samoei Ruto, Henry Kiprono Kosgey and Joshua Arap Sang*, Pre-Trial Chamber II, Decision on Victims' Participation at the confirmation of Charges Hearing and In the Related Proceedings, ICC-01/09-01/11-249, 5 August 2011, paras 79–80; *Prosecutor v. Francis Kirimi Muthaura, Uhuru Muigai Kenyatta and Mohammad Hussein Ali*, Pre-Trial Chamber II, Decision on Victims' Participation at the Confirmation of Charges Hearing and in the Related Proceedings, Pre-Trial Chamber II, ICC 01/09 02/11 267, 26 August 2011, paras 93–94.

247 ICC, *Prosecutor v. Laurent Gbagbo*, Registry, Proposal for the common legal representation of victims, ICC-02/11-01/11-120, 16 May 2012, para 21.

248 ICC, *Prosecutor v. Laurent Gbagbo*, Pre-Trial Chamber I, Decision on Victims' Participation and Victims' Common Legal Representation at the Confirmation of Charges Hearing and in the Related Proceedings, ICC-02/11-01/11-138, 4 June 2012, para 40.

249 Ibid., paras 42–44.

250 Ibid., para 44.

251 ICC, *Prosecutor v. Charles Blé Goude*, Pre-Trial Chamber I, Decision on victims' participation in the pre-trial proceedings and related issues, ICC-02/11-02/11-83, 11 June 2014, para 15.

252 ICC, *Prosecutor v. Bosco Ntaganda*, Pre-Trial Chamber I, Decision Concerning the Organisation of Common Legal Representation of Victims, ICC-01/04-02/06-160, 2 December 2013, para 26.

253 See for example ICC, *Prosecutor v. Willliam Samoei Ruto, Henry Kiprono Kosgey and Joshua Arap Sang*, Registry, Proposal for the common legal representation of victims, ICC-01/09-01/11-243, 1 August 2011, paras 32–33; ICC, *Prosecutor v. Francis Kirimi Muthaura, Uhuru Muigai Kenyatta and Mohammad Hussein Ali*, Registry, Proposal for the common legal representation of victims, ICC-01/09-02/11-214, 5 August 2011; paras 32–33.

and field conditions as well as the activity levels in the proceedings and the modalities of participation granted to victims. For example: where victims' lawyers are permitted access to the entire confidential case file and disclosed material in a particular case, such access may be rendered meaningless if sufficient resources are not provided to ensure that the team is able to review and make use of such material.

5.4.5.3 Appeals on Legal Aid Matters

At the STL, the Legal Aid Policy for Victims' Participation sets out applicable procedures for the review of decisions on legal aid entitlements. Where the amount in dispute is greater than €1000 a review by the Registrar may be requested.[254] For amounts of over €10,000 the Registrar's decision may be further subject to administrative review by the President.[255]

At the ICC, Regulation 83(4) of the Regulations of the Court provides that the Registrar's decisions on the scope of legal assistance paid by the Court may be reviewed by the relevant chamber. However, chambers appear to have been in general reluctant to interfere with the Registrar's positions on legal aid.[256]

At both the STL and the ICC separate procedures for appeal lie to the President where the question is not the extent but the availability of legal aid or a determination concerning indigence.[257]

5.5 Obligations on Legal Representatives

5.5.1 Contents of the Obligations on Victims' Legal Representatives

At all three tribunals victims' legal representatives are bound by codes of conduct which also regulate Defence counsel: at the STL and ICC codes specific to those

254 STL Legal Aid Policy for Victims' Participation, Section 5.4.

255 Ibid., Section 5.5.

256 See for example, ICC, *Prosecutor v. William Samoei Ruto and Joshua Arap Sang*, Pre-Trial Chamber II, Decision on the "Urgent Request by the Victims' Representative for an order from the Chamber requiring the Registrar to provide appropriate resources for the current mission in Kenya", ICC-01/09-01/11-398, 9 March 2012; ICC, *Prosecutor v. William Samoei Ruto and Joshua Arap Sang*, Appeals Chamber, Decision on the "Application of the Victims' Representative pursuant to Article 83 of the Regulations", ICC-01/09-01/11-409, 23 April 2012.

257 STL Legal Aid Policy for Victims' Participation, Section 3.16; ICC Regulations of the Court, Regulation 85(3).

institutions exist,[258] while at the ECCC lawyers are bound by the code regulating Cambodian lawyers.[259]

Most of these obligations are of the same nature as lawyers would owe in a domestic context or when representing defendants. However, some specific ethical challenges might be expected to arise from the particular nature of victims' representation.

Limited case-law on these issues exists to date, and only at the STL does the Code of Professional Conduct for Defence Counsel and LRV attempt to grapple in detail with these issues. It sets out criteria concerning the effectiveness of victims' legal representation.[260] Many of these criteria are the same as those applied in respect of the Defence.[261] Two key exceptions relate to:

- the need for LRVs to maintain "scrutiny" of prosecution activity, including by continuously reviewing the extent to which it upholds the interests of the victims and responding as necessary.[262]
- particular obligations relating to communication with clients which reflect the collective nature of the representation.[263]

Regarding the latter question, while limited standards exist in the ICC texts, some judicial comments were made in the *Katanga and Ngudjolo Chui case*. There, Trial Chamber II stated that legal representatives must communicate with victims in a language they understand,[264] keep the victims informed, and respond to a reasonable number of specific legal inquiries from individual victims.[265] The chamber appeared to consider that the legal representative should follow "instructions" from clients.[266] In the event that conflicting instructions are received, the chamber considered that the legal representative must 'endeavour to represent both positions fairly and equally before the Chamber.'[267] The Chamber appeared to consider that

[258] ICC Code of Professional Conduct for counsel, ICC-ASP/4/Res.1; STL Code of Professional Conduct for Counsel Appearing before the Tribunal, and STL, Code of Professional conduct for Defence Counsel and Legal Representatives of Victims appearing before the Special Tribunal for Lebanon.

[259] Code of Ethics for Lawyers Licensed with the Bar Association of the Kingdom of Cambodia; See also the Cambodian Law on the Bar.

[260] STL Code of Professional Conduct for Defence Counsel and Legal Representatives of Victims appearing before the Special Tribunal for Lebanon, Article 33(B).

[261] Ibid., Article 33(A).

[262] Ibid., Article 33(B)(vi).

[263] Ibid., Article 33(B)(xi).

[264] ICC, *Prosecutor v. Germain Katanga and Mathieu Ngudjolo Chui*, Trial Chamber II, Order on the organisation of common legal representation of victims, ICC-01/04-01/07-1328, 22 July 2009, para 17(f).

[265] Ibid.

[266] Ibid., para 17(b).

[267] Ibid., para 16.

only where "irreconcilable" instructions are received that a conflict of interest would arise.[268] Article 16 of the ICC's Code of Professional Conduct for Counsel addresses such conflicts. It requires counsel to advise clients from the outset of the nature of representation and the potential for conflicting interests and to 'exercise all care to ensure a fair representation of the different yet consistent positions' of the victims.[269] However where a conflict does arise, counsel must immediately inform all potentially affected clients and either withdraw from the representation of one or more clients, with the consent of the chamber, or seek full and informed consent in writing of all potentially affected clients for continued representation. In the former case the chamber may appoint separate representation for some victims on the specific issue in question.[270] This has not yet occurred in practice and it is therefore unclear what would be the impact on ongoing legal representation.

5.5.2 Monitoring and Disciplinary Regimes

Disciplinary regimes exist in respect of all three courts for counsel who violate ethical obligations. However, mechanisms for ensuring that represented victims have access to grievance procedures are lacking. At the STL an effort to compensate for these challenges exists in the form of a monitoring regime whereby the Tribunal's Registry can institute monitoring if information comes to light suggesting that legal representation is ineffective.[271] Discussions around creating a system of this kind at the ICC have been initiated but have proved controversial and so far no equivalent mechanism exists.[272]

5.6 Duration and Termination of Victims' Legal Representation

5.6.1 Continuity of Representation and the Means by Which Representation May Be Ended

At all three courts legal representation is generally continuous throughout the proceedings unless some express step is taken to end the relationship of legal representation.

---

[268] Ibid., para 16.

[269] ICC Code of Professional Conduct for Counsel, Article 16(2).

[270] ICC, *Prosecutor v. Germain Katanga and Mathieu Ngudjolo Chui*, Trial Chamber II, Order on the organisation of common legal representation of victims, ICC-01/04-01/07-1328, 22 July 2009, para 13.

[271] STL, Code of Professional Conduct for Defence Counsel and Legal Representatives of Victims appearing before the Special Tribunal for Lebanon, Article 32.

[272] For a discussion of these issues see: Redress, Representing Victims before the IC: Recommendations on the Legal Representation System, April 2015, http://www.redress.org/downloads/publications/1504reprentingvictims.pdf. Accessed 29 August 2016, pp. 19–27.

At the STL this is made clear in the Code of Professional Conduct for Defence Counsel and Legal Representatives of Victims appearing before the Special Tribunal for Lebanon,[273] and the Directive on Victims' Legal Representation.[274] Under those texts, a legal representative's mandate continues until one of the following occurs:

(i) All the LRV's clients have ceased to participate in the proceedings;[275]
(ii) Proceedings in the case have been concluded against all accused persons;[276]
(iii) The LRVs' designation is withdrawn at his or her own request: either because the LRV's physical or mental condition requires it,[277] or at the discretion of a Judge or chamber for any other reason given by the LRV;
(iv) The LRV's mandate is ended against his or her will by a Judge or chamber in certain specified instances.[278]

The STL's legal texts also permit a legal representative's mandate to be *suspended* rather than terminated in certain circumstances, either at the LRV's own request or for other reasons.[279]

No equivalent text on the termination of a legal representative's mandate exists at the ICC. It is clear that where counsel has been appointed by victims pursuant to Rule 90(1), the resulting mandate can be terminated by a decision to arrange common legal representation under Rule 90(2), and this has occurred in a number of cases.

The duration of an appointment as common legal representative was less clear until this matter was determined by the Appeals Chamber in the *Ruto and Sang* case. The Chamber held that common legal representatives appointed during pre-trial do not lose their mandate with the end of pre-trial proceedings. They continue to represent their clients until the case is concluded, the LRV withdraws, or is withdrawn by a chamber (in accordance with Code of Professional Conduct for Counsel Article 17(1)).[280] The Chamber considered that this interpretation is supported by the importance of continuity of representation.[281]

---

[273] See especially Article 7(E).

[274] See especially Article 29.

[275] STL, Directive on Victims' Legal Representation, Article 29(A)(ii); STL, Code of Professional Conduct for Defence Counsel and Legal Representatives of Victims appearing before the Special Tribunal for Lebanon, Article 7(E)(ii).

[276] STL, Directive on Victims' Legal Representation, Article 29(A)(iii).

[277] STL, Code of Professional Conduct for Defence Counsel and Legal Representatives of Victims appearing before the Special Tribunal for Lebanon, Article 7(E)(iii) and 7(G).

[278] STL, Directive on Victims' Legal Representation, Article 40.

[279] Ibid., Article 39.

[280] ICC, *Prosecutor v. William Samoei Ruto and Joshua Arap Sang*, Appeals Chamber, Decision on the "Application of the Victims' Representative pursuant to Article 83 of the Regulations", ICC-01/09-01/11-409, 23 April 2012, paras 19–20.

[281] Ibid., para 20.

The Appeals Chamber clarified that a chamber could limit representation to a phase of proceedings but this could only be done by using express language to that effect.[282] Despite this, in *Ntaganda* Pre-Trial Chamber I appears to have intended to establish common legal representation limited to the confirmation phase, although it did not say so explicitly.[283] And indeed when the case reached Trial Chamber VI it ordered the Registry to review legal representation before trial,[284] although ultimately the existing legal representation by the OPCV was maintained.[285]

Indeed, in the absence of legal texts, the range of circumstances in which a chamber may decide to terminate or limit a common legal representative's mandate appear to be significantly wider at the ICC than they are before the STL. Indeed in the *Kenya* cases Trial Chamber V ordered the Registry to *re-initiate* a process for common legal representation at the trial stage, although this had already occurred during pre-trial proceedings.[286] By introducing a specific requirement that the common legal representatives must reside in Kenya during trial proceedings[287] the Trial Chamber effectively brought about the termination of the existing legal representatives' mandates, neither of whom were available to live in Kenya.[288]

---

[282] Ibid., para 21.

[283] See for example the Chamber's comment that a relevant consideration in the design of the scheme was the 'limited scope of the confirmation of charges hearing': ICC, *Prosecutor v. Bosco Ntaganda*, Pre-Trial Chamber I, Decision Concerning the Organisation of Common Legal Representation of Victims, ICC-01/04-02/06-160, 2 December 2013, para 24.

[284] ICC, *Prosecutor v. Bosco Ntaganda*, Trial Chamber VI, Decision on victims' participation in trial proceedings, ICC-01/04-02/06-449, 6 February 2015, para 54.

[285] ICC, *Prosecutor v. Bosco Ntaganda*, Trial Chamber VI, Second decision on victims' participation in trial proceedings, ICC-01/04-02/06-650, 16 June 2015, paras 28–32.

[286] ICC, *Prosecutor v. William Samoei Ruto and Joshua Arap Sang*, Trial Chamber V, Decision on victims' representation and participation, ICC-01/09-01/11-460, 3 October 2012, para 61; ICC, *Prosecutor v. Uhuru Muigai Kenyatta*, Trial Chamber V, Decision on victims' representation and participation, ICC-01/09-01/11-498, 3 October 2012, para 60.

[287] ICC, *Prosecutor v. William Samoei Ruto and Joshua Arap Sang*, Trial Chamber V, Decision on victims' representation and participation, ICC-01/09-01/11-460, 3 October 2012, para 60; ICC, *Prosecutor v. Uhuru Muigai Kenyatta*, Trial Chamber V, Decision on victims' representation and participation, ICC-01/09-01/11-498, 3 October 2012, para 59.

[288] ICC, *Prosecutor v. William Samoei Ruto and Joshua Arap Sang*, Trial Chamber V, Decision appointing a common legal representative of victims, ICC-01/09-01/11-479, 23 November 2012; ICC, *Prosecutor v. Francis Kirimi Muthaura and Uhuru Muigai Kenyatta*, Trial Chamber V, Decision appointing a common legal representative of victims, ICC-01/09-02/11-537, 20 November 2012.

5.6.2 Timing of End of Representation

Where representation is ended, a question arises as to whether this occurs immediately following the event which ends the mandate.

At least as concerns the conclusion of proceedings in a case, representation may continue for a short time after this occurs. In the *Kenyatta* case at the ICC the proceedings were terminated but the Trial Chamber recognised that the LRV's mandate would continue 'for such limited period as may be necessary to enable him to properly inform and advise the victims regarding the impact of the withdrawal of charges in this case and of the present decision, as well as, if applicable to participate in the outstanding proceedings before the Appeals Chamber.'[289] It may be arguable that even after the conclusion of appellate proceedings, that legal representation must continue for long enough to enable counsel to inform clients about the conclusion of proceedings.

By analogy it could be argued that the same approach could apply to at least some other circumstances in which a counsel's mandate to represent victims is ended.

5.7 Key Points

Requirement for legal representation

- At the ICC, requests by victims to self-represent have not been successful and it is assumed in practice that all victims will have legal representation before the Court.
- The ECCC requires that all civil parties are represented by a lawyer following the issue of an indictment.
- Although the STL's RPE theoretically permits the Pre-Trial Judge to authorise self-representation of participating victims this has not occurred in practice.
- However, at all three courts legal representation is required and facilitated only once a victim's application for participation has been granted. While in some cases victims who have lodged applications have been granted legal representation, legal assistance is not routinely provided to assist victims with completing and lodging their applications for participation.

Choice of counsel and court-arranged representation

- All three courts constrict victims' freedom to choose their own counsel by allowing for the possibility (or requirement) that victims' will be collectively represented as determined by the court.

---

[289] ICC, *Prosecutor v. Uhuru Muigai Kenyatta*, Trial Chamber V(B), Decision on the Withdrawal of Charges against Mr. Kenyatta, ICC-01/09-02/11-1005, 13 March 2015, para 12.

- At the STL victims are not provided with any entitlement to choose a lawyer. The Pre-Trial Judge decides on the grouping of victims for the purpose of their legal representation and the Registrar thereafter assigns one or more lawyers to each group. Victims are only entitled to be consulted in this process.
- At the ECCC victims may choose their own "civil party lawyer", however these lawyers do not have standing before the court and are in effect an intermediary between the civil party and the Civil Party Lead Co-Lawyers who represent all civil parties in a case.
- At the ICC Rule 90(1) permits victims in theory to choose their own legal representation. However, the Court has repeatedly held that this "right" is subject to the Court's power to arrange common legal representation. In practice this involves the chamber determining the number of groups through which victims will be represented, and either the Chamber or the Registrar identifying a legal representative for each group.

In-house and external representation

- In the legal texts of the STL no provision is made for in-house legal representation. The Registry selects external counsel to represent victims.
- At the ECCC the "civil party lawyers" who directly represent victims are external, independent lawyers. However, the Civil Party Lead Co-Lawyers are hired by the ECCC.
- At the ICC victims may be represented either by in-house lawyers from the OPCV, or by external counsel, or in some cases by a team composed of both components. Discussions about modifying the current system, possibly towards an in-house representation model, have been taking place for several years but so far without resolution.

Legal aid for external representation

- At the ECCC, civil party lawyers generally do not receive legal aid from the Court, although a small number of Cambodian civil party lawyers are salaried by the ECCC to represent otherwise unrepresented civil parties. Civil Party Lead Co-Lawyers are paid salaries rather than according to legal aid.
- At the STL and ICC external counsel have their remuneration and team resourcing regulated by the tribunals' respective legal aid systems as they apply to participating victims.
- At the STL it is presumed that participating victims are indigent and entitled to legal aid, unless the contrary is demonstrated. In any event non-indigent victims share their legal representation with indigent victims and are required only to make a fixed contribution to the cost of legal aid.
- The ICC's legal texts make the availability of legal aid to participating victims contingent on their indigence. In theory the Registry assesses the indigence of all participating victims and has declined to formally apply a presumption of indigence. However, in practice it is doubtful that meaningful assessments are able to be made of thousands of victims, most of whom are not in a position

to provide meaningful financial information. Therefore, in practice if not in law victims are effectively presumed to be indigent for the purpose of legal aid decisions.

Termination of legal representation

- At all three courts victims' legal representation can be ended or changed in specified circumstances, however there is a presumption that once court-arranged representation is undertaken it will continue throughout the course of the proceedings.

References

FIDH (2014) Five myths about victim participation in ICC Proceedings. https://www.fidh.org/IMG/pdf/cpi649a.pdf. Accessed 22 Aug 2016

Hague Working Group of the ASP Bureau (2009) Report of the Bureau on legal aid for victims' legal representation, ICC-ASP/8/38

International Criminal Court (2007) Report on the operation of the Court's legal aid system and proposals for its amendment, ICC-ASP/6/4

International Criminal Court (2009) Interim report of the Court on legal aid: legal and financial aspects for funding victims' legal representation before the Court, ICC-ASP-8/3

International Criminal Court (2012) Supplementary report of the Registry on four aspects of the Court's legal aid system, ICC-ASP/11/43

International Criminal Court (2013) Registry's single policy document on the Court's legal aid system, ICC-ASP/12/3

International Criminal Court (2016) Comprehensive report on the reorganisation of the Registry of the International Criminal Court, August 2016. https://www.icc-cpi.int/itemsDocuments/ICC-Registry-CR.pdf. Accessed 4 Nov 2016

Redress (2015) Comments to the Registrar in relation to the ReVision project as it relates to victims' rights before the ICC. http://www.redress.org/downloads/publications/2015-feb-redress-comments-on-revision.pdf. Accessed 22 Aug 2016

Redress (2015) Representing victims before the ICC: Recommendations on the Legal Representation System. http://www.redress.org/downloads/publications/1504reprentingvictims.pdf. Accessed 29 Aug 2016

Chapter 6
The Protection of Victims Participating in International Criminal Justice

Yaiza Alvarez Reyes

Abstract The protection scheme available to victims participating in international criminal proceedings is mostly based on the systems available for the protection of witnesses testifying before the *ad hoc* Tribunals. The special role and involvement of participating victims in the case, coupled with the psychosocial circumstances they may have, however calls for an interpretation of those legal tools in light of their specific needs. This chapter analyses the law and practice of the International Criminal Court, the Special Tribunal for Lebanon and the Extraordinary Chambers in the Courts of Cambodia regarding protective measures available to victims participating in the proceedings.

Keywords VWU · VWS · WESU · Protective measures · Security risk · Confidentiality · Anonymity · Risk assessment · Closed session · Pseudonym · Public · Operational protective measures · Initial response system · Protection programme · Relocation · Psychosocial measures

Contents

Yaiza Alvarez Reyes, Legal Officer, Victims and Witnesses Unit, Special Tribunal for Lebanon. The views expressed herein do not necessarily represent the views of the STL.

Y. Alvarez Reyes (✉)
Leidschendam, The Netherlands
e-mail: yaiza.alvarez@gmail.com

K. Tibori-Szabó and M. Hirst (eds.), *Victim Participation in International Criminal Justice*, International Criminal Justice Series 11,
DOI 10.1007/978-94-6265-177-7_6

6.1 Introduction: Protective Measures for Participating Victims as a Procedural Right

As set out in the United Nations Declaration of Basic Principles of Justice for Victims of Crime and Abuse of Power,[1] the promotion of victims' access to justice must be accompanied by the provision of the necessary legal and procedural tools to allow the exercise of such right. That includes providing participating victims with proper assistance throughout the legal process with measures to minimise inconvenience, protect their privacy, when necessary, and ensure their safety, as well as that of their families and witnesses on their behalf, from intimidation and retaliation.[2]

The laws and jurisprudence of the International Criminal Court (ICC), the Special Tribunal for Lebanon (STL) and the Extraordinary Chambers in the Courts of Cambodia (ECCC), have taken on board these recommendations, and have considered the obstacles that victims encounter when seeking to effectively participate in proceedings. Each of these courts has consequently included protective mechanisms which aim to ensure an efficient and effective implementation of victims' participatory role.

The three courts have designed schemes of protective measures with the following four main goals: (i) to minimise the serious risk to the security of the victims and that of their families, especially in cases where they live in societies characterised by ongoing conflicts, (ii) to reduce the secondary victimisation associated with giving testimony or expressing their views and concerns in the context of criminal proceedings, (iii) to prevent serious incursions into their privacy and dignity by the media or the public in general, and finally (iv) to encourage victims to step forward and participate in the proceedings and/or give testimony.[3]

Already in its first decision on victims' participation, the ICC echoed the goals identified above. Accepting the suggestion of the Legal Representatives of Victims (LRVs) in the *Lubanga* case, Trial Chamber I stated that 'protective and special measures for victims are often the legal means by which the Court can secure the participation of victims in the proceedings.'[4] The Trial Chamber further held that 'protective measures are not favours but are instead the rights of the victims, enshrined in Article 68(1) of the Statute. The participation of victims and their

[1] A/RES/40/34, 29 November 1985 (the 'UN Declaration').

[2] UN Declaration, Article 6.

[3] These four goals are discussed by de Brouwer and Groenhuijsen 2009; also recognised in *inter alia*, Article 6(d) of the UN Declaration and the Council of Europe Recommendation on the Position of Victims in the Framework of Criminal Law and Procedure, R(85)11, 28 June 1985. See also: Perez Leon Acevedo 2014, pp. 228–229.

[4] ICC, *Prosecutor v. Thomas Lubanga Dyilo,* Trial Chamber I, Decision on Victims' Participation, ICC-01/04-01/06-1119, 18 January 2008, para 128.

protection are included in the same statutory provision, namely Article 68 in its paragraphs 1 and 3, and to a real extent they complement each other.'[5]

This chapter will focus on the challenge of protecting participating victims, and the scheme of measures developed by the international criminal courts to address these victims' safety and security. The chapter will concentrate on the legal provisions and jurisprudence related to the protection of victims participating in the proceedings in their own right, as opposed to the protection provided for victims appearing to give testimony in a case.

6.2 Institutional Players

Before discussing the different types of protection available to victims during the different stages of trial, it is important to identify the institutional players involved in the request and implementation of protective measures for victims, and the role they play at each stage of the criminal proceedings. Despite the structural differences between the ECCC, the ICC and the STL, the nature of the players involved in the requests of protective measures and their implementation coincide in great part. The following will explore the differences in the scope of the mandate of each player.

It is possible to differentiate four levels in the implementation of the courts' mandates to provide for the safety and security of victims: (i) the overall responsibility to protect victims, setting in place specific units to provide for such services,[6] (ii) the authority to order protective measures *proprio motu* or on request,[7] (iii) the power to exercise control over questioning of the parties, in order to avoid any harassment or intimidation when victims appear before the court,[8] and (iv) the

[5] Ibid., para 129.

[6] Note that among the three courts analysed in this chapter, only the texts of the ICC and the ECCC recognise specifically the chambers' overall responsibility to conduct trials with due regard of the protection of victims. See Articles 64(2) and (6) of the Rome Statute of the International Criminal Court, A/CONF.183/9 (2010) (the 'ICC Statute') and Rule 29 of the ECCC Internal Rules, Rev. 9 (2015) (the 'ECCC Internal Rules'). The texts governing the STL however place responsibility on the Tribunal as a whole, and more specifically on the Registrar (See Article 12 (4) of the Statute of the Special Tribunal for Lebanon, S/RES/1757 (2007) (the 'STL Statute') and Rule 50 of the STL Rules of Procedure and Evidence, STL-BD-2009-01-Rev.7-Corr. 1 (2015) (the 'STL RPE'). The STL's judges are however invested with powers or order specific measures to protect victims (STL RPE, Rule 133) or hold in contempt those who violate such orders (Rule 60*bis* of the STL RPE).

[7] STL RPE, Rule 133(A); Rule 87(1) of the ICC Rules of Procedure and Evidence, ICC-ASP/1/3 Corr.1 (Part.II-A) (2002) (the 'ICC RPE'); Rule 29(3) of the ECCC Internal Rules, Rev. 9 (2015) (the 'ECCC Internal Rules') and Article 1 of the ECCC Practice Direction on Protective Measures 03/2007/Rev.1 (2008) (the 'ECCC Practice Direction on Protective Measures').

[8] ICC RPE, Rule 88(5); STL RPE, Rule 133(E).

power to impose criminal sanctions against those who knowingly and wilfully threaten, intimidate or cause any injury to witnesses or potential witnesses, or disclose confidential information relating to proceedings such as the identity of protected victims and witnesses.[9]

The courts analysed in this chapter have set up in their administrative organs, independent and specialised units mandated to cater for the protection of witnesses and victims participating in the proceedings. These are the Victims and Witnesses Section (VWS) (formerly Victims and Witnesses Unit) of the ICC, the Victims and Witnesses Unit (VWU) of the STL, and the Witness/Experts Support Unit (WESU) of the ECCC. As established in the legal texts governing the protective mandates of these courts, these specialised units, shall (i) provide the protective measures and security arrangements necessary for the safety and security of victims participating in the proceedings, (ii) provide such advice to chambers, parties, victims and their lawyers as is necessary to implement adequate measures, and (iii) in the case of the STL,[10] and to some extent the ECCC,[11] request protective measures in their own right or on behalf of the victims. These units work closely with the Prosecution, the Defence and the victims' lawyers and are to operate with the highest levels of integrity, impartiality and confidentiality.

The VWS of the ICC has implemented its mandate of advisor on protection matters, *inter alia*, by providing Prosecution investigators with a code of conduct covering the best practices regarding the security, confidentiality and psychological well-being of victims and witnesses.[12] The VWS also provides support and *ad hoc* protection advice to the Victims Participation and Reparations Section of the Court aimed to minimise the risk that victims may encounter when applying for or benefitting from status as a participating victim.[13] Similarly, the VWU of the STL has issued guidelines on good practices to the parties and the legal representatives of victims (LRVs).[14]

Pursuant to the respective texts and jurisprudence of these three courts, the level of involvement of the units in requests for and determinations of protective measures varies from one court to the other. In that respect, while only the VWU of the STL, and to some extent the WESU of the ECCC have standing to request protective measures, all three units hold an advisory role on the determination of protective measures sought.[15] In the case of the VWU of the STL, the advisory

---

9 STL RPE, Rule 60*bis*; ICC Statute, Article 70; ECCC Internal Rules, Rule 35(d).

10 STL RPE, Rule 133(A).

11 ECCC Practice Direction on Protective Measures, Article 2(5).

12 ICC RPE, Rule 17(2)(v).

13 Information provided by the Head of Protection of the (then) VWU, ICC, (records on file with the author). December 2014.

14 The Guidelines on good practices for the parties and LRVs are STL internal documents.

15 ECCC Internal Rules, Rule 29(3); ECCC Practice Direction on Protective Measures, Article 2(3); ICC RPE, Rule 87(1).

role finds its legal basis in jurisprudence rather than in the Rules of Procedure and Evidence. The Pre-Trial Judge in the *Ayyash* et al. case established the specific involvement of the VWU in the determination of protective measures to participating victims when ordering that the LRVs, assisted by the VWU, shall conduct a risk assessment prior to submitting any request for protective measures.[16]

The temporal scope of the VWS's mandate on victims' protection has been the subject of judicial dispute at the ICC. Contrary to the early position of the Registry that the VWS's mandate towards victims only starts when a chamber grants them leave to participate in the proceedings,[17] Trial Chamber I in the *Lubanga* case found that the process of 'appearing before the Court' is not dependent on either an application to participate having been accepted or not, or whether the victim physically attends a hearing. The critical moment that prompts the VWS's mandate is the point at which the application form requesting participating status is submitted to the Court, regardless of the outcome of the request.[18] The Chamber went on to say that 'whilst the Chamber readily understands that considerable demands are made on the [VWS] and there are undoubted limitations on the extent of the protective measures that can be provided, nonetheless to the extent that protection can realistically be provided by the Court during the application process, the responsibility for this rests with the [VWS], pursuant to Article 43(6).'[19] While the protection of victims at this early stage is doubtlessly important, it creates significant challenges in practice, particularly given that the VWS is already over-burdened relative to its responsibilities.[20] This in part because the number of persons subject to the VWS's protection mandate are significantly increased by this approach, but also because of other factors specific to applicants: applicants' first contact is often with intermediaries or other persons unfamiliar with good practices for minimising risks, the VWS has minimal information about the applicants (who are usually not legally represented, increasing the burden on the VWS to gather relevant information); and the VWS must consider in its work the possibility that an applicant will not be granted victim status. These factors, as well as the substantial other responsibilities carried by the VWS, make it extremely complicated for the VWS to transform this legal obligation towards victim applicants into practical measures.

[16] STL, *Prosecutor v. Ayyash* et al., Pre-Trial Judge, Decision on Victims' Participation in the Proceedings, STL-11-01/PT/PTJ, 8 May 2012, para 131.

[17] ICC, *Prosecutor v. Thomas Lubanga Dyilo,* Registrar, Protection of Victims and Mandate of the Victims and Witnesses Unit, ICC-1/04-01/06-1078, 12 December 2007, para 18.

[18] ICC, *Prosecutor v. Thomas Lubanga Dyilo,* Trial Chamber I, Decision on Victims' Participation, ICC-01/04-01/06-1119, 18 January 2008, para 137.

[19] Ibid., para 137.

[20] Mahony 2010, p. 48.

Also within their administrative organs, all three courts have set up specialised units to provide other forms of support to victims participating in the proceedings. These are the Victims Support Section (VSS)—originally called the Victims' Unit—of the ECCC,[21] the Victims Participation and Reparations Section (VPRS) of the ICC[22] and the Victims' Participation Unit (VPU) of the STL.[23] The role played by these units when it comes to matters related to the application or implementation of protective measures is relatively limited given the lack of protection expertise of these units. It has been suggested that during the application process—which is carried out by or under the auspices of these units—victims should be candidly informed of the general security risks associated with their role as participating victims, and about the limited ability of the court to provide protection.[24] This should be coupled with a detailed explanation of the protective measures available and the importance of the self-protective measures they can implement themselves. At the ICC, where intermediaries are relied on by the Registry to assist in the completion of application forms, training and information should be provided to them on issues of security and best practices in this regard.[25] At all three courts these units may also refer a specific security concern to the relevant victims and witnesses sections or units (particularly where the victim in question is not yet legally represented). Exceptionally, the VPU of the STL,[26] and to some extent the Victims' Unit of the ECCC may play a formal legal role before a chamber on issues concerning victims' participation, including requesting protective measures.[27]

The victims' lawyers play a crucial role in requests for protective measures and, perhaps more importantly still, in guaranteeing that the security and privacy of their clients is not affected as result of their contact with them when preparing the case. Victims' lawyers, like the organs of the courts, must conduct their contact with clients, whether directly or through intermediaries, with the highest levels of confidentiality. In order to improve the victims' lawyers' communications, the VWU of STL[28] and ICC have created good practices guides aimed at assisting

[21] ECCC Internal Rules, Rule 29(3); Article 3(4) of the ECCC Practice Direction on Victim Participation 02/2007/Rev.1 (2008) (the 'ECCC Practice Direction on Victim Participation').

[22] Regulation 86(9) of the ICC Regulation of the Court, ICC-BD/01-03-11 (2011).

[23] STL RPE, Rule 51.

[24] See *supra* footnote 20.

[25] ICC, Guidelines Governing the Relations between the Court and Intermediaries (2014), http://www.icc-cpi.int/en_menus/icc/legal%20texts%20and%20tools/strategies-and-guidelines/Documents/GRCI-Eng.pdf. Accessed 26 November 2015 (the 'ICC Guidelines on Intermediaries'), pp. 12, 15, 16.

[26] Pursuant to Rule 133(A) of the STL RPE, the VPU may request protective for victims. In practice such a role would usually be exercised before LRVs are designated to represent the participating victims.

[27] Article 3(9) and Article 2(5) of the ECCC Practice Directions on Victim Participation and Protective Measures respectively.

[28] See *supra* footnote 14.

them to identify, or assess security concerns reported by their clients. These tools also contain information as to how to manage contact with victims and witnesses in a secure and confidential manner, and how to integrate victims' and witnesses' security considerations into daily working practices.[29]

Additionally, the responsibility to represent the interests of victims (whether borne by their lawyers or a relevant unit of the court, such as the STL's VPU) certainly includes the burden to request the implementation of the necessary measures to protect their privacy and security.[30]

Finally, victims themselves bear an important responsibility when it comes to their protection. In behaving in an appropriate way, maintaining the required degree of confidentiality and avoiding placing themselves at unnecessary risk, victims can complement the efforts of the courts, and work constructively towards the prevention or mitigation of potential security risks.

The legal texts of each court afford participating victims the right to seek protective measures directly from a chamber.[31] Similarly, in cases where a chamber acts *proprio motu* to order measures for the protection of a victim, the victims affected, or their lawyers, must be notified and given the opportunity to respond.[32]

6.3 Types of Protection

As prescribed by the texts and jurisprudence of the courts analysed here, applications for protective measures ought to request the measures available that, while protecting the safety and security of victims, also honour the rights of the accused. The balance exercised by the judges between the rights of the accused and the obligation to protect victims and witnesses in the adjudication of protective measures may vary substantially throughout the course of the judicial proceedings. In that vein for instance, whilst an ICC chamber may consider that the anonymity of victims is consistent with the rights of the accused, subsequent developments, in particular confirmation that a victim will testify as a witness in the proceedings, may lead the same chamber to order that the identity of the victim is disclosed to the accused in order to guarantee a proper defence. Similarly, while risks

[29] Information provided by the Head of Protection of the (then) VWU, ICC, December 2014 (records on file with the author).

[30] STL RPE, Rule 133; ICC RPE, Rule 87(1); ECCC Practice Direction on Protective Measures, Article 1(1).

[31] ECCC Practice Direction on Protective Measures, Article 1; STL RPE, Rule 133(A); ICC RPE, Rule 87(1).

[32] Although only specifically mentioned in the ICC's texts (see ICC RPE, Rule 87(2)(d)), given the spirit of the general provision on protective measures of the STL and the ECCC, the same principle may be presumed to apply to them (see STL RPE, Rule 133(B) and (H) and ECCC Practice Direction on Protective Measures, Article 2(3)).

associated with a victim's participation during an early stage of the case may be limited, this could substantially change if he or she subsequently decides to give testimony. In both cases, the protective measures initially granted, would need to be adjusted in accordance with the specific circumstances, i.e. the different modalities of victim participation or type and level of risk faced by the victim at a given time.

The types of protection available to victims when appearing before the court in person are essentially the same regardless of whether they do it in order to convey their views and concerns or to testify as a witness. For the purpose of a better presentation, these measures are clustered here below in three categories: judicial protection, operational protective measures and special measures.

6.3.1 Judicial Protection

6.3.1.1 Legal Requirements

Although the approaches taken by the ICC, STL and ECCC to the judicial protection of victims are in practice very similar, the lack of consistency in the language used in their texts may lead to differing interpretations of similar provisions. This has special relevance when the lack of clarity affects essential elements of the protection such as the identification of the subject eligible for protection, or the demarcation of its scope.

In that regard, for instance, the language used in the provisions governing the protection of victims by the ICC or the STL has a different meaning to that used by the International Criminal Tribunal for the former Yugoslavia (ICTY) and the International Criminal Tribunal for Rwanda (ICTR),[33] even though it appears to be similar. As such, the protection scheme created at the *ad hoc* tribunals provides protection to victims only when they appear as "victim-witnesses", as opposed to the applicable rules of the STL and ICC that include the protection of victims participating in the proceedings.

Despite the lack of consistency in the terminology used by different courts, the judges of the STL and the ICC have found no trouble when interpreting the relevant rules in the context of victims' protection and as such they have done so in accordance with the extended role afforded to victims by these courts. Both the STL and the ICC have found that the provisions catering for the protection of victims apply not only to "victim-witnesses", but equally apply to the protection of

[33] See Article 22 of the Statute of the International Criminal Tribunal for the former Yugoslavia, S/RES/827 (1993); and Article 21 of the Statute of the International Criminal Tribunal for Rwanda, S/RES/955 (1994): 'The International Tribunal shall provide in its Rules of Procedure and Evidence for the protection of **victims and witnesses.** Such protection measures shall include, but shall not be limited to, the conduct of *in camera* proceedings and the protection of the victim's identity.' (Emphasis added).

victims participating in their own right. At the STL, the Pre-Trial Judge explicitly included in his first decision on protective measures for victims that the STL RPE provides for the protection of victims participating in the proceedings.[34] The ICC similarly interpreted the term "victims" in the context of protective measures as encompassing victims participating in the proceedings.[35]

The legal texts of the ECCC are the only ones that explicitly provide that the protection of "victims" extends more broadly, namely to ensuring 'the protection of Victims who participate in the proceedings, whether as complainants, or Civil Parties [···]'.[36]

The confines of the protection set out for victims are clearly described in the statutory documents of the ICC and the STL. As such, it is outlined that the obligation to protect shall encompass the physical and psychological safety of the victim, as well as the protection of their dignity and privacy.[37] On the other hand, the foundational law of the ECCC refers to the scope of the Court's responsibility toward victims in a rather undefined manner, '[t]he Court shall provide for the protection of victims and witnesses.'[38]

The legal standard required by the laws and jurisprudence for the adjudication of protective measures to victims, is the same in all three courts, and in turn, coincides with the legal requirements prescribed for the protection of witnesses.[39] Pursuant to the statutes and RPEs of the ICC, STL and ECCC, an application for protective measures shall demonstrate that the protective measures requested are *appropriate* and that they are *consistent with the rights of the accused*.[40]

---

[34] STL, *Prosecutor v. Ayyash* et al., PTJ, Decision on the Legal Representative of Victims' First, Second and Third Motions for Protective Measures for Victims Participating in the Proceedings, STL-11-01/PT/PTJ, 19 December 2012, para 15.

[35] ICC, *Prosecutor v. Jean-Pierre Bemba Gombo*, Trial Chamber III, Decision Defining the Status of 54 Victims who Participated at the Pre-Trial stage, and Inviting the Parties' observations on Applications for Participation by 86 Applicants, ICC-01/05-01/08-699, 22 February 2010, para 24.

[36] ECCC Internal Rules, Rule 29(1).

[37] ICC Statute, Article 68(1); STL Statute, Article 12(4).

[38] Article 33 new of the Law on the Establishment of the Extraordinary Chambers in the Courts of Cambodia for the Prosecution of Crimes Committed during the period of Democratic Kampuchea, NS/RKM/1004/006 (2004).

[39] ECCC, *Case 001*, Trial Chamber, Decision on Protective Measures for Civil Parties, Case No. 001/18-07-2007/ECCC/TC, 2 June 2009, para 7; STL, *Prosecutor v. Ayyash* et al, PTJ, Decision on the Legal Representative of Victims' First, Second and Third Motions for Protective Measures for Victims Participating in the Proceedings, STL-11-01/PT/PTJ, 19 December 2012, para 15.

[40] STL RPE, Rule 133(A); ICC RPE, Rule 87(1); ECCC Practice Direction on Protective Measures, Articles 1(3) and 1(4).

The ICC chambers have interpreted this standard as requiring the protective measures requested to be *necessary* and *proportional*.[41] The STL case-law specified the notion of "necessity" in the context of victims' protection by determining, in light of the ICC jurisprudence, that for a protective measure to be granted, the fear for the safety of the victim must be real and objective and the measure requested strictly necessary to override or mitigate such risk.[42] The jurisprudence of the ECCC points in the same direction when stating that '[t]he subjective perceptions of the applicant alone are insufficient for the grant of protective measures and it is necessary to demonstrate a genuine risk of harm to the applicant or his or her family.'[43] Following the ICC interpretation of "proportionality", applicants requesting protective measures for victims must demonstrate that the measures requested are the least restrictive to the rights of the accused, and that they are the only sufficient and feasible measures available for the individual case.[44]

Similar reference to the appropriateness of the protective measures is included in the Internal Rules of the ECCC and the Practice Direction on Protective Measures,[45] as well as in its jurisprudence.[46]

Finally, and although not identified in the jurisprudence of the courts as one of the legal requirements, the consent of the victims should be considered when

---

[41] ICC, *Prosecutor v. Thomas Lubanga Dyilo,* Trial Chamber I, Decision inviting the parties' observations on applications for participation of a/0001/06 to a/0004/06, a/00047/06 to a/0052/06, a/0077/06, a/0078/06, a/0105/06, a/0221/06, a/0224/06 to a/0233/06, a/0236/06, a/237/06 to a/0250/06, a/0001/07 to a/0005/07, a/0054/07 to a/0062/07, a/0064/07, a/0065/07, a/0149/07, a/155/07, a/0156/07, a/162/07, a/168/07 to a/0185/07, a/0187/07 to a/07 to a/0191/07, a/0251/07 to a/0253/07, a/0255/07 to a/0257/07, a/0270/07 to a/0285/07, and a/0007/08, ICC-01/04/01/06-1308, 6 May 2008, para 25; ICC, *Prosecutor v. Jean-Pierre Bemba Gombo*, Trial Chamber III, Decision Defining the Status of 54 Victims who Participated at the Pre-Trial stage, and Inviting the Parties' observations on Applications for Participation by 86 Applicants, ICC-01/05-01/08-699, 22 February 2010, paras 25–26.

[42] STL, *Prosecutor v. Ayyash* et al, PTJ, Decision on the Legal Representative of Victims' First, Second and Third Motions for Protective Measures for Victims Participating in the Proceedings, STL-11-01/PT/PTJ, 19 December 2012, para 19.

[43] ECCC, *Case 002*, Trial Chamber, Trial Chamber's Disposition of all Requests for Protective Measures sought in *Case 002/01* and response to Co-Prosecutors' Request for the Recall of Civil Party SAR Sarin and on Order for a Formal Assessment of the Need for Protective Measures (E286), Case No. 002/19-09-2007-ECCC/TC, 28 June 2013, para 7.

[44] ICC, *Prosecutor v. Jean-Pierre Bemba Gombo*, Trial Chamber III, Decision Defining the Status of 54 Victims who Participated at the Pre-Trial stage, and Inviting the Parties' observations on Applications for Participation by 86 Applicants, ICC-01/05-01/08-699, 22 February 2010, para 25.

[45] See Rule 29(3) of the ECCC Internal Rules and Article 1(3) and 1(4) of the ECCC Practice Direction of Protective Measures.

[46] ECCC, *Case 002*, Trial Chamber, Trial Chamber's Disposition of all Requests for Protective Measures sought in *Case 002/01* and response to Co-Prosecutors' Request for the Recall of Civil Party SAR Sarin and on Order for a Formal Assessment of the Need for Protective Measures (E286), Case No. 002/19-09-2007-ECCC/TC, 28 June 2013.

requesting protective measures. As such, the ICC[47] and the STL RPE[48] establish that the party requesting protective measures shall seek to obtain the consent of the person in respect of whom the measures are sought.[49] Article 1(5) of the Practice Direction on Protective Measures of the ECCC, relates this requirement to the appropriateness of the measures sought stating that '[i]n determining the appropriateness of the protective measures sought, the Co-Investigating Judge or Chamber shall seek to obtain the consent of the persons in respect of whom protective measures are sought.'

6.3.1.2 Protection for Victims Who Engage with the Court Before (or Without) Submitting an Application for Participation

Although not always phrased as protection for victims participating in the proceedings, each of the ICC, STL and ECCC recognises the obligation to protect victims in general, including before they have applied for participation, where these victims come into contact with one of the courts or are at risk because of its activities. This may occur for example during the period when the Office of the Prosecutor, or the Co-Investigating Judges are conducting their inquiries prior to the issue of an arrest warrant or indictment against an accused. It may also occur where a case has been opened but particular victims are yet to apply, although they have had contact with a section of the court conducting outreach or working on victims' issues.

In the case of the ICC, the Statute establishes that it is the responsibility of the Prosecution to take the necessary measures to ensure the effective investigation and prosecution of crimes. In doing so, it shall respect the interest and personal circumstances of victims, and take, or request measures to be taken, to ensure the protection of any person.[50] This idea is strengthened in Article 68(1) which establishes that the Court is responsible for the safety, physical and psychological well-being, dignity and privacy of victims and that among its organs, the Prosecutor shall take the appropriate measures to protect them particularly during the investigation of the crimes under the jurisdiction of the Court.

---

[47] Rule 87(1) of the ICC RPE states that '[...] The Chamber shall seek to obtain, **whenever possible**, the consent of the person in respect of whom the protective measure is sought prior to ordering the protective measures.' (Emphasis added).

[48] Rule 133(B) of the STL RPE states that '[a] Party requesting the Trial Chamber to order protective measures shall seek to obtain the consent of the person in respect of whom the protective measures are sought.'

[49] In cases where the application for protective measures does not include the explicit consent of the victim, it could be argued that a chamber could order the protected measures anyway since the protection could be granted 'in the interest of justice' and following the court´s obligation to protect the security of victims.

[50] ICC Statute, Article 54(1)(b) and (3)(f).

The jurisprudence of the ICC has echoed the notion of the Prosecution's obligation regarding the protection of victims during its investigations when finding that the Prosecutor is bound to take protective measures for the safety and well-being of victims, even if victims are not able to participate formally in the investigations.[51] The Prosecutor is equally under an obligation to take measures or request measures to be taken for the protection of any person including victims.[52]

Furthermore, Rule 84(1) of the ICC RPE states that the Court is responsible for 'the persons at risk on account of their contact with the Court.' As interpreted by the Appeals Chamber in *Katanga and Ngudjolo Chui*,[53] this reflects the intention of the States Parties to protect a wider group of people, which may include victim applicants in contact with the Court for that very purpose.[54]

In the case of the STL, the Statute includes in Article 12 that the VWU shall provide measures to protect the safety, physical and psychological well-being, dignity and privacy of victims. This provision does not impose any limitation in terms of the stage of the proceedings at which the protection is applicable or a specific requirement that it applies only where an application for participation has been submitted. Moreover, when describing in detail the functions of the VWU, Rule 50 of the STL RPE states that the unit is responsible for the protection of witnesses, victims participating in the proceedings and, where appropriate, others at risk on account of their interaction with the Tribunal. Although at the time of drafting of this chapter there was no jurisprudence on the matter, one could argue that 'others at risk on account of their interaction with the Tribunal' may as well include victims who do not or have not yet applied for participation in the proceedings. This would include individuals in contact with the Registry for the purpose of applying to be participants in the proceedings, as well as victims who are contacted by the Prosecution during its investigation and before the issue of an indictment enables victims' participation to occur.

---

[51] Note that the ICC's Appeals Chamber has made clear that the participation of victims during the investigation of a situation does not allow them to be involved in the investigation *per se* but rather only in any judicial proceeding arisen during the investigation or while the investigation is ongoing. See ICC, *Situation in the Republic Democratic of The Congo*, Appeals Chamber, Judgment on Victim Participation in the Investigation Stage of the Proceedings in the Appeal of the OPCD against the Decision of Pre-Trial Chamber I of 7 December 2007 and in the Appeals of the OPCD and the Prosecutor against the Decision of Pre-Trial Chamber I of 24 December 2007, ICC-01/04-556, 19 December 2008, para 59.

[52] Ibid., para 54.

[53] ICC, *Prosecutor v. Germain Katanga and Mathieu Ngudjolo Chui*, Appeals Chamber, Judgment on the appeal of the Prosecutor against the decision of Pre-Trial Chamber I entitled 'First Decision on the Prosecution Request for Authorization to Redact Witness Statements', ICC-01/04-01/07-475, 13 May 2008.

[54] Note the ICC Guidelines on Intermediaries. The VWU (now VWS) provides security advice to the VPRS and applicants during first contacts, even before formal investigations have been authorised.

The STL provisions governing the Prosecution's investigations also establish in Rule 62 that in case of urgency, the Prosecutor may request that a State take all the appropriate measures to prevent injury to or intimidation of a victim. Also, Rule 115 states that in exceptional circumstances, the Prosecutor may apply for the interim non-disclosure of the identity of victims who may be in danger or at risk until appropriate protective measures have been implemented. These provisions are not worded so as to be limited in their application to victims already participating in the proceedings or who have submitted an application for participation.

The Internal Rules and Practice Directions of the ECCC also incorporate the protection of victims during the investigation phase of a case regardless of whether or not they have already applied for or been granted the status of civil parties or complainants. As such, victims will receive protection from the relevant authority in charge of conducting the investigations. In that vein, and although the Internal Rules do not recognise the protection of victims or witnesses as a responsibility of the Prosecutor while conducting investigations, it is established that, when filing the submissions before the Co-Investigating Judges, due regard shall be given to the interest of victims and witnesses and any other persons mentioned therein.[55] Furthermore, Rule 25(4) states that when interviewing persons other than the suspects or charged persons, the Co-Prosecutors or Co-Investigating Judges may choose to apply measures to assist in reducing any subsequent traumatisation of a victim of sexual violence or gender violence, a child, an elderly person or person with disabilities. Finally, as included in Article 2(9) of the Practice Direction on Victim Participation, the Victims Unit and the Co-Prosecutors will ensure the confidentiality of all complaints and consequently all victims choosing to participate in the proceedings by reporting to the Co-Prosecutors information about the crimes falling under the jurisdiction of the Court.

In the conduct of the judicial investigation, the Co-Investigating Judges may take any appropriate measure to provide for the safety and support of potential witnesses or other source such as complainants and civil parties.[56] It is important to bear in mind that pursuant to Rule 56 of the Internal Rules, all judicial investigations undertaken by the Co-Investigating Judges shall be confidential in order to preserve the rights and interest of all parties.

6.3.1.3 Protection and the Disclosure of Victim Identities at the Application Stage

As mentioned above, before the ECCC, victims may participate in the proceedings as complainants by providing information to the Prosecutor, or as civil parties, with the latter implying a much more significant role during the trial. The Internal

[55] ECCC Internal Rules, Rule 54.

[56] Ibid., Rule 55(5)(b); ECCC Practice Direction on Protective Measures, Rule 1(2).

Rules and the Practice Direction on Victim Participation regulate the procedure to be followed in order to apply for protection during the application process. Where complaints are filed, as explained in the previous section, both the Co-Prosecutors and the Victims Unit are responsible for maintaining the complaints' confidentiality. On the other hand, victims' applications to be admitted as civil parties shall be submitted in writing to the Co-Investigating Judges and, unless protective measures are granted, the Co-Investigating Judges must notify the Co-Prosecutors and the charged person.

Pursuant to the Practice Direction on Victim Participation, victims applying as complainants or civil parties have to complete the Victim Information Form annexed to the Practice Direction. Victims requesting protective measures must complete the section of the form whereby they are asked about the negative consequences that the victims or their families may fear as a result of the filing of the application. The little jurisprudence available on protective measures during the application process is mute regarding whether protective measures were ever granted, and consequently whether the identity of civil parties has ever been withheld from the charged persons and/or the Prosecution. The available jurisprudence shows however the Trial Chamber's predisposition to avoid the public dissemination of victims' identities, on an interim basis and up until the decision was rendered, even when the application for protective measures *a priori* did not particularise the type of protective measures sought or the reasons why they were requested.[57]

As at the ECCC, the ICC has a general provision within its Rules stating that the applications filed by victims seeking participating status shall be provided to the Prosecutor and the Defence, who are entitled to reply within the time limit set by the chamber. However the transmission of victims' applications is subject to the measures granted in order to protect the safety, physical and psychological well-being, dignity and privacy of victims and witnesses.[58] The Regulations of the Registry go a step further by contemplating the possibility of a chamber preventing the disclosure of victims' identities to the Prosecutor, the Defence and/or other participant when this may jeopardise the safety and security of the applicants.[59] The Regulations of the Registry set up a procedure, whereby the Registry shall assess each application, taking into account, *inter alia*, the level of security in the area where the victim lives, and the feasibility of implementing local measures for their protection. The Registrar shall inform the chamber of the results of the assessment.

---

[57] ECCC, *Case 001*, Trial Chamber, Decision on Protective Measures for Civil Parties, Case No. 001/18-07-2007/ECCC/TC, 2 June 2009, para 4 and ECCC, *Case 002*, Trial Chamber, Trial Chamber's Disposition of all Requests for Protective Measures sought in *Case 002/01* and response to Co-Prosecutors' Request for the Recall of Civil Party SAR Sarin and on Order for a Formal Assessment of the Need for Protective Measures, Case No. 002/19-09-2007-ECCC/TC, 28 June 2013, para 2.

[58] ICC RPE, Rule 89.

[59] Regulation 99 of the ICC Regulations of the Registry, ICC-BD/03-03-13 (2013).

The different trial chambers of the ICC have interpreted and applied the above mentioned provision in different manners. In the *Lubanga* case for instance, Trial Chamber I found that conducting individual risk assessments of each applicant was not necessary to make an informed decision on individual protective measures. In its decision, the Trial Chamber considered the elevated cost and time associated with the individual assessment of each application, and the fact that the redaction of victim identities in the applications sent to the parties was the only sufficient and feasible measure available, and that this measure restricted the rights of the accused only as far as necessary.[60] The Trial Chamber held however that the protective measures granted (i.e., redaction of the victims' identifying information from the application) should be further 're-evaluated' by the Trial Chamber for those applicants granted victims status when considering the types of participation in the proceedings.[61]

When assessing whether identifying information in victims' application is to be redacted from applications sent to both the Prosecution and the Defence, or only from those sent to the Defence, the different chambers have ruled differently. The Pre-Trial Chamber in the *Lubanga* case found that granting the Prosecutor access to the full applications for participation while providing the Defence with a redacted version does not raise an issue of the fairness of the proceedings in view of the obligations and powers of the Prosecutor in respect of investigations and within the meaning of Article 54 of the ICC Statute and in particular the fact that '[he] respects the interests and personal circumstances of victims and witnesses.'[62] On the other hand, in *Kony* et al., the Single Judge of Pre-Trial Chamber II found that redacted applications are to be transmitted to both parties alike in light of the 'fundamental considerations of fairness (namely, the need to preserve the equality of arms), which require that both parties be placed on an equal footing in respect of the exercise of a right which is bestowed on them both by the statutory texts.'[63]

[60] See ICC, *Prosecutor v. Thomas Lubanga Dyilo,* Trial Chamber I, Decision inviting the parties' observations on applications for participation of a/0001/06 to a/0004/06, a/00047/06 to a/0052/06, a/0077/06, a/0078/06, a/0105/06, a/0221/06, a/0224/06 to a/0233/06, a/0236/06, a/237/06 to a/0250/06, a/0001/07 to a/0005/07, a/0054/07 to a/0062/07, a/0064/07, a/0065/07, a/0149/07, a/155/07, a/0156/07, a/162/07, a/168/07 to a/0185/07, a/0187/07 to a/07 to a/0191/07, a/0251/07 to a/0253/07, a/0255/07 to a/0257/07, a/0270/07 to a/0285/07, and a/0007/08, ICC-01/04/01/06-1308, 6 May 2008, paras 19–25.

[61] Ibid, para 29.

[62] ICC, *Prosecutor v. Thomas Lubanga Dyilo*, Trial Chamber I, Decision on the Defence request for leave to appeal regarding the transmission of applications for victim participation, ICC-01/04/01/06-672, 6 November 2006, para 7.

[63] ICC, *Prosecutor v. Joseph Kony, Vincent Otti, Okot Odhiambo, Raska Lukwiya and Dominic Ongwen*, (ICC-02/04-01/05-134), Pre-Trial Chamber II, Decision on legal representation, appointment of counsel for the defence, protective measures and time-limit for submission of observations on applications for participation a/0010/06, a/0064/06 to a/0070/06, a/0081/06 to a/0104/06 and a/0111/06 to a/0127/06, ICC-02/04-01/05-134, 1 February 2007, para 25.

The STL system in relation to victims' application to participate in the proceedings generally follows the ICC's model. One of the differences, however, is the regime governing the transmission of victims' applications before and after the participating status of victims is granted by the Pre-Trial Judge. Unlike the system adopted by the ICC, the STL RPE only require that victims' applications shall be transmitted to the Pre-Trial Judge who, after seeking submission from the parties and the VPU on relevant legal issues, shall rule on the matter.[64] No requirement exists for providing the application forms to the parties.

In the same vein, the Pre-Trial Judge in the *Ayyash* et al. case found that 'pending the Pre-Trial Judge's decision on the applications, there are no [victims participating in the proceedings] yet, only victims in the sense of Rule 2 of the Rules. (...) Where applicants are denied the status of VPP, a degree of anonymity is required in order to ensure that their personal information is protected and not disclosed to the Parties, since they would not be participating in the proceedings at any stage. (...) The Pre-Trial Judge therefore consider[ed] that all the [a]pplications should remain confidential and *ex parte* for the time being.'[65] Equally, even after participation is granted and the identities of VPPs have been disclosed to the public and/or the parties, the Pre-Trial Judge found that the application documents themselves should not be reclassified and therefore the confidential and *ex-parte* classification established initially shall continue.[66]

In his first decision granting victims the status of participating victims, the Pre-Trial Judge further reminded parties that, the withholding of the identities of the applicants, and their applications, is justified in order to protect their interests at that stage of the proceedings. He qualified such statement however by saying that subject to the authorisation of a chamber, the parties may either be provided with the identities of some or all of the VPPs, or be granted access to some or all of their applications.[67]

6.3.1.4 General and Ongoing Measures of Protection for Victims Admitted to Participate in the Proceedings

There are two types of judicial protective measures available to victims once they have been granted status to participate in the proceedings, whether as participating

[64] STL RPE, Rule 86(C)(i).

[65] STL, *Prosecutor v. Ayyash* et al., Pre-Trial Judge, Decision on Defence Motion of 17 February 2012 for an Order to the Victims' Participation Unit to Refile its Submission *INTER PARTES* and Inviting Submissions on Legal Issues Related to Applications for the Status of Victims Participating in the Proceedings, STL11-01-PT/PTJ, 5 April 2012, paras 42–44.

[66] STL, *Prosecutor v. Ayyash* et al., Pre-Trial Judge, Decision on Prosecution's Request for the Reclassification as Confidential of the Identities and Application of Victims seeking to Participate in the Proceedings, STL11-01-PT/PTJ, 31 May 2013, para 44.

[67] STL, *Prosecutor v. Ayyash et al*, Pre-Trial Judge, Decision on Victims' Participation in the Proceedings, STL-11-01/PT/PTJ, 8 May 2012, para 130.

victims before the ICC or the STL, or as civil party before the ECCC. The first is aimed at concealing the identity of a participating victim or civil party from the public, and the second is aimed at withholding his or her identity both from the public and from one or more parties in the case. This second type of protection is commonly referred to as anonymity.

The non-disclosure of victims' identities *vis-à-vis* the public is implemented in different manners, and these will depend on the mode of participation of the victims in the proceedings (i.e. victims participating through their lawyers with no physical appearance before the court, victims appearing in court expressing their views and concerns, or victims appearing in court as witnesses for other parties), and the specific protection required given the particular circumstances of each victim. In this regard, and as it is commonly regulated by the courts,[68] the confidentiality of victims is implemented by removing all identifying information from public documents, referring to each individual by a pseudonym[69] or the number of their application,[70] and when necessary, by the implementation of a series of measures aimed at allowing the appearance of the victim before the chamber whilst avoiding his or her identification by the public.[71]

At the STL the Pre-Trial Judge has held that if participating victims wish to have their identities remain confidential, requests to that end should be submitted to the Pre-Trial Judge as soon as possible after they have been notified of the decision granting them the status of victims participating in the proceedings, pursuant to Rule 133 (A) of the STL RPE. In order to expedite that process, and in keeping with the Tribunal's jurisprudence, the Pre-Trial Judge invited the VPU or the LRVs, as appropriate, to submit any such requests to the Pre-Trial Judge after having conducted a risk assessment for the relevant applicant(s) with the assistance of the VWU of the Tribunal.[72]

The legal requirements to be met for protective measures of this kind are those explained above in Sect. 6.3.1.1.

Anonymity, or non-disclosure of the identity of the victims participating in the proceedings to the accused, has been proven problematic in some jurisdictions

[68] STL RPE, Rule 133(A); ICC RPE, Rule 87; ECCC Internal Rules, Rule 29(4); ECCC Practice Direction on Protective Measures, Article 3.

[69] ICC, *Prosecutor v. Bahar Idriss Abu Garda,* Pre-Trial Chamber I, Decision on victims' modalities of participation at the Pre-trial Stage of the Case, ICC-02/05-02/09-136, 6 October 2009, p. 12.

[70] ECCC, *Case 001*, Trial Chamber, Decision on Protective Measures for Civil Parties, Case No. 001/18-07-2007/ECCC/TC, 2 June 2009, para 4.

[71] In these cases, and as it will be explained below in Sect. 6.3.1.5, depending on their participation in the proceedings, victims can be granted a series of in-court protective measures which may include *inter alia*: the assignment of pseudonyms, expunging their names and identifying information from public documents, using image and voice distortion when broadcasting trial proceedings, or the use of closed sessions.

[72] STL, *Prosecutor v. Ayyash* et al., Pre-Trial Judge, Decision on Victims' Participation in the Proceedings, STL11-01-PT/PTJ, 8 May 2012, paras 130–131.

where this measure has been considered contrary to the right of the accused to a fair trial and a public hearing. This issue is not clearly regulated by the legal texts of the courts, and consequently it is their jurisprudence, including at times the different interpretations and applications by multiple chambers within the same court, which has defined the implications and limitations that anonymity may have on its beneficiaries.

Before the ICC, anonymity has become the default position for participating victims as opposed to a situation whereby victims are obliged to disclose their identity to the parties, whether at the application stage or once participating status has been granted. Consequently, they are not required to submit individually justified requests for anonymity.[73] In the first case before the ICC, Trial Chamber I rejected the submissions of the Defence and the Prosecution suggesting that anonymous victims should never be permitted to participate in the proceedings. Although the Trial Chamber recognised that it is preferable that the identities of victims are disclosed to the parties, it noted the particularly vulnerable position of many victims living in an area of on-going conflict where it is difficult to ensure their safety. The Trial Chamber further stated that:

> However, the Trial Chamber is of the view that extreme care must be exercised before permitting the participation of anonymous victims, particularly in relation to the rights of the accused. While the safety and security of victims is a central responsibility of the Court, their participation in the proceedings cannot be allowed to undermine the fundamental guarantee of a fair trial. The greater the extent and the significance of the proposed participation, the more likely it will be that the Chamber will require the victim to identify himself or herself. Accordingly, when resolving a request for anonymity by a victim who has applied to participate, the Chamber will scrutinise carefully the precise circumstances and the potential prejudice to the parties and other participants. Given the Chamber will always know the victim's true identity, it will be well placed to assess the extent and the impact of the prejudice whenever this arises, and to determine whether steps that fall short of revealing the victim's identity.[74]

Other trial chambers have followed in permitting victims to remain anonymous before the ICC[75] and the permissibility of anonymity has been endorsed by

---

[73] See STL, *Prosecutor v. Ayyash* et al., Victims' Participation Unit, Public Redacted Version of the Submission from the Victims' Participation Unit on Protective Measures for Victims Participating in the Proceedings, STL11-01-PT/PTJ, 1 March 2013, paras 12 and 21.

[74] See ICC, *Prosecutor v. Jean-Pierre Bemba Gombo*, Trial Chamber III, Decision Defining the Status of 54 Victims who Participated at the Pre-Trial stage, and Inviting the Parties' observations on Applications for Participation by 86 Applicants, ICC-01/05-01/08-699, 22 February 2010, paras 130–131.

[75] ICC, *Prosecutor v. Germain Katanga and Mathieu Ngudjolo Chui,* Trial Chamber II, Decision on the Modalities of Victim Participation at Trial, ICC-1/04-01/07-1788, 22 January 2010, paras 92–93; ICC, *Prosecutor v. Jean-Pierre Bemba Gombo,* Trial Chamber III, Second Order regarding the applications of the legal representatives of victims to present evidence and the views and concerns of victims, ICC-1/05-01/08-2027, 21 December 2011, para 19; ICC, *Prosecutor v. Francis Kirimi Muthaura, Uhuru Muigai Kenyatta and Mohammed Hussein Ali.*, Pre-Trial Chamber II, Decision on the Defence Requests in Relation to the Victims' Applications for Participation in the Present Case, ICC-1/09-02/11-164, 8 July 2011.

the Appeals Chamber in regards to the participation of anonymous victims in the appeal of a case.[76]

Although participating victims have been allowed to preserve their anonymity, this has frequently led the ICC chambers to limit or qualify their modalities of participation during trial. In the *Katanga and Ngudjolo Chui* case, for instance, anonymous victims were not allowed during the pre-trial stage to access confidential documents and to participate in closed session hearings.[77] Similarly, during trial, anonymous victims were not allowed to present evidence on their own behalf.[78] In the *Bemba* case, those victims who were permitted to present their views and concerns would need to relinquish their anonymity *vis-à-vis* the parties once permission to be heard before the chamber was granted.[79] Limitations on the modalities of participation were also imposed during the appeal stage in *Ngudjolo*. In that case the Appeal Chamber found that 'the protective measure of anonymity does not violate Mr. Ngudjolo's right to a fair trial. However, should the anonymous victims wish to participate as individuals at a hearing or to make individual observations they would have to disclose their identities to the parties.'[80]

The texts governing the participation of victims before the ECCC do not refer to the specific type of protective measures applicable to them. As mentioned in the previous section, there is little jurisprudence available on decisions regarding protective measures requested or granted to civil parties. We can only note that according to the judgment of *Case 001*, among the 90 civil parties participating during the trial, none was anonymous.[81]

Finally, the Appeals Chamber of the STL found in its first and so far only decision regarding victims' anonymity that, although they have considered the jurisprudence of the ICC, they do not find it persuasive as in their view it does not take fully into account the potential prejudice to the accused if the identities of the

[76] ICC, *Prosecutor v. Mathieu Ngudjolo Chui,* Appeals Chamber, Decision on the participation of anonymous victims in the appeal and on the maintenance of deceased victims on the list of participating victims, ICC-1/04-02/12-140, 23 September 2013.

[77] ICC, *Prosecutor v. Germain Katanga and Mathieu Ngudjolo Chui,* Pre-Trial Chamber I, Decision on the Set of Procedural Rights Attached to Procedural Status of Victim at the Pre-Trial Stage of the Case, ICC-1/04-01/07-474, 13 May 2008, para 182. See Chap. 7.

[78] ICC, *Prosecutor v. Germain Katanga and Mathieu Ngudjolo Chui,* Trial Chamber II, Decision on Modalities of Victim Participation at Trial, ICC-1/04-01/07-1788, 22 January 2010, para 92.

[79] ICC, *Prosecutor v. Jean-Pierre Bemba Gombo,* Trial Chamber III, Second Order regarding the applications of the legal representatives of victims to present evidence and the views and concerns of victims, ICC-1/05-01/08-2027, 21 December 2011, para 19.

[80] ICC, *Prosecutor v. Mathieu Ngudjolo Chui,* Case No.ICC-1/04-02/12-140, Appeals Chamber, Decision on the participation of anonymous victims in the appeal and on the maintenance of deceased victims on the list of participating victims, ICC-1/04-02/12-140, 23 September 2013, para 19.

[81] ECCC, *Case 001*, Trial Chamber, Judgment, 26 July 2010, Annex III.

participating victims were to be withheld from them.[82] The Appeals Chamber further found 'unnecessary to address the prejudice arising from specific forms of participation. This is because totally anonymous participation by victims is inherently prejudicial to the accused, regardless of how active or passive their desired method of participation and even for victims who do not seek to give or tender evidence.'[83] Accordingly no victim has been permitted to remain anonymous during participation at the STL.

6.3.1.5 Protection of Participating Victims Who Appear Before the Court During a Hearing

Ordinarily victims participating in the proceedings do so through a lawyer. Typically, victims' lawyers will present the views and concerns of the participating victims when allowed by a judge or a chamber.[84]

However, participating victims may request permission to exercise their right by being physically present at court hearings in different capacities.[85] As such, participating victims have been present during opening statements and attended trial during the presentation of evidence,[86] have participated in the presentation of their views and concerns, and have provided their testimony to the courts, either in their own case or another party's case.[87] Regardless of the purpose of such appearances, these forms of participation may result in the undesired disclosure of victims' identity, and consequently an increase in the risk against them. In order to avoid that from happening, the ECCC, ICC and STL have listed in their legal texts a series of measures aimed at restricting to some extent, public access to the proceedings. These lists of measures, far from being exhaustive, are examples of the tools available to shield victims from potential physical or mental harm.

Regulation 94 of the ICC Regulations of the Registry, Rule 133 of the STL RPE and Rule 29 of the Internal Rules and the Practice Direction on Protective Measures of the ECCC set an exception to the principle of publicity of proceedings that is common to all international courts, and certainly to those referred to in

---

82 STL, *Prosecutor v. Ayyash* et al., Appeals Chamber Decision on Appeal by Legal Representative of Victims Against Pre-Trial Judge's Decision on Protective Measures, STL-11-01/PT/AC, 10 April 2013, para 26.

83 Ibid., para 27.

84 STL Statute, Article 17; STL RPE, Rule 86(C)(ii); ICC Statute, Article 68(3); ECCC Internal Rules, Rule 23(3), ECCC Practice Direction on Victim Participation, Article 4.

85 See for instance, STL, *Prosecutor v. Ayyash* et al., Legal Representative of Victims, Request of the Legal Representative of Victims to Allow Two Participating Victims to Attend Proceedings in the Courtroom, STL-11-01/T/TC, 9 January 2015.

86 For the attendance of victims participating in the proceedings at the opening statements of the case against *Ayyash* et al. at the STL on 17 January 2014, see STL, *Prosecutor v. Ayyash* et al., Transcript 14 October 2014, STL-11-01/T/TC, pp. 8-9. See Chap. 11.

87 See Chaps. 8 and 9.

this chapter.[88] Those provisions cover a spectrum of measures that range from less restrictive ones, like the assignment of pseudonyms or the redaction of victims' identities from public documents, to more restrictive measures whereby full hearings may be conducted in closed session. It is for the party requesting the protective measures to advance arguments on which one is the most appropriate, bearing in mind that 'the more extreme the protection sought, the more onerous will be the obligation [...] to establish the risk asserted.'[89]

Before discussing the different measures available to conceal victims' information from the public, and the specific procedures to request them, it is important to examine the definitions of the terms 'public' in order to define the scope of these measures. Although both the ICTY and the ICTR have extensive jurisprudence regarding the definition of 'public' and 'media',[90] among the three courts under scrutiny here, the ICC is perhaps the only one that has developed a more detailed definition of the term 'public'. Trial Chamber I found in the *Lubanga* case that the term includes 'all persons, governments, organisations, entities, associations and groups. It does not include the judges of the Court, members of the Registry, the Prosecutor and his representatives, the Accused, the Defence team, victims granted the right to participate in the proceedings and their lawyers.'[91] This definition, or very similar formulations, have since been adopted in other cases.[92]

The case-law of the STL has been less specific in this respect. During the pre-trial phase of the *Ayyash* et al. case, for instance, the Pre-Trial Judge found that it was not necessary to define the terms "public" and "media" and that it was appropriate 'to refer to their commonly accepted sense.'[93] More recently however, the Contempt Judge in the case against *Akhbar Beirut S.A.L and Ibrahim Mohamed Ali Al Amin* has chosen to develop the definition of 'public' by finding that 'public is everyone

[88] ECCC Agreement, Article 12(2); STL Statute, Article 20(4); STL RPE, Rule 96; ICC Statute, Article 67.

[89] ICTY, *Prosecutor v. Slobodan Milosević*, Case No. IT-02-54-T, Trial Chamber, Decision on Prosecution Motion for Trial Related Protective Measures for Witnesses, Case No. IT-02-54-T, 30 July 2002, para 5.

[90] Acquaviva and Heikkilä 2013, p. 821.

[91] ICC, *Prosecutor v. Thomas Lubanga and Dyilo*, Case No ICC-01/04-01/06-1372, Trial Chamber I, Decision on the prosecution's application for an order governing disclosure of non-public information to members of the public and an order regulating contact with witnesses, ICC-01/04-01/06-1372, 3 June 2008, para 12.

[92] E.g. ICC, *Prosecutor v. William Samoeiruto and Joshua Arap Sang*, Trial Chamber V, Decision on the protocol concerning the handling of confidential information and contacts of a party with witnesses whom the opposing party intends to call, ICC-01/09-01/11-449, 24 August 2012, Annex.

[93] STL, *Prosecutor v. Ayyash* et al., Pre-Trial Judge, Decision Relating to the Prosecution Request Seeking Measures for the Non-dissemination of Material of 2 May 2012, STL-11-01/PT-PTJ, 25 May 2012, para 20.

except the Tribunal's Judge, the staff of Chambers, and the Registry, the Prosecutor and the Defence. The "public" includes families, friends and the media.'[94]

The types of protective measures available to victims appearing before the court as witnesses or to express their views and concerns, are the same as those afforded to witnesses testifying in the case, and, in turn, they are also similar in all three courts.[95] Decisions on protective measures may include the expunction of the name and identifying information of the victim from the trial records; the assignment of a pseudonym; ordering that the record of specific parts of the proceedings be placed under seal; forbidding public access to specific material from the case file or access to the classified register which identifies the protected person; the use of image or voice altering devices during the testimony of the victim-witness; the use of only audio modes of communication; testifying from a remote location through a closed circuit television or video-conference link; and testifying in closed session. It is worth noting a type of protective measure specifically addressed for the protection of victims before the ECCC, namely, the possibility of declaring the contact address of the victim to be that of their lawyers of their Victims' Association or of the ECCC itself.[96]

The legal texts of the three courts differ, however, on the procedures in place to request such measures. For instance, in the case of the ECCC, pursuant to the Practice Direction on Protective Measures, the requests shall be in writing and once filed, shall be served on the person for whom the measures are sought or his or her lawyers or the WESU or the Victims Unit.[97] Regarding the filing of the requests, the ICC, as the ECCC, requires motions to be in writing, but specifically excludes their *ex parte* submission. As at the ECCC, a copy of the motions filed before the ICC shall be served on the victim or witness for whom protective measures are requested, who in turn, should be given the opportunity to be heard.[98] The STL RPE remains silent in relation to these points. The practice shows however that motions for protective measures are filed and are distributed to all parties in the proceedings.

It is however common to all three courts that once applications are lodged, and following the process of consultation required by the law of each court,[99] the

---

[94] STL, *In the case against Akhbar Beirut S.A.L and Ibrahim Mohamed Ali Al Amin*, Decision on the Amicus Curiae Prosecutor's Application for Protective Measures and Non-Disclosure, STL-14-06/PT/CJ, 3 July 2014.

[95] ECCC, *Case 001*, Trial Chamber, Decision on Protective Measures for Civil Parties, Case No. 001/18-07-2007/ECCC/TC, 2 June 2009, para 7: 'Although referring to the protection of witnesses appearing at trial, The Chamber finds that this caselaw may provide guidance in respect also to the protection of civil parties before the ECCC.'

[96] ECCC Internal Rules, Rule 29(4)(a).

[97] ECCC Practice Direction on Protective Measures, Article 2.

[98] ICC RPE, Rule 87(2).

[99] According to Rule 29(3) of the ECCC Internal Rules of the ECCC and Article 2(3) of the ECCC Practice Direction on Protective Measures of the ECCC, the judges, before making an order regarding protective measures, shall consult with the WESU and they shall seek to obtain the consent of the person in respect of whom protective measures are sought. A similar principle applies before the STL and ICC. See STL RPE, Rule 133(B) and ICC RPE, Rule 87(2)(c).

judge or chamber seized of the request decides on protective measure appropriate for the specific case. Finally, and in order to determine whether the measures requested are more suitable to prevent the release of the identity or identifying information pertaining to a victim to the public, the judge or chamber may hold *in camera* hearings.[100]

One might think that the attendance of victims at court hearings as observers does not entail any risk to their safety and security, and therefore victims should not be granted protective measures when exercising that form of participation. Before making such assumption however, it is important to analyse the different modalities of victims' participation among the courts.

In the case of the ICC and the ECCC, the numbers of victims granted the status of victims participating in the proceedings have surpassed the thousands. At the ICC at least, such extended recognition has not been followed however by the implementation of financial and logistical measures aimed at facilitating a systematic and sustainable attendance of victims to court proceedings. This is not the case at the ECCC and the STL where the courts have facilitated the attendance of participating victims to observe court proceedings.[101] At the STL the VWU is actively involved in reviewing each instance of such victim attendance and, where necessary, advises on or provides appropriate protective measures. One such measure includes the use of a private victim viewing room where victims with confidential status can view the proceedings without being seen.

6.3.1.6 Variation of Protective Measures

Regardless of whether the protective measures are granted during trial or pre-trial, their variation, augmentation or rescission must follow the specific procedure foreseen by the relevant legal texts of the ICC, STL and ECCC.

The procedural principle common to the three courts establishes that protective measures, once ordered, shall apply *mutatis mutandis* throughout the entire proceedings in the case concerned, and in relation to other proceedings before the court, unless and until they are rescinded, varied or augmented in accordance with the relevant provisions.[102]

The system in place for the variation, rescission or augmentation of protective measures requires that the applicant apply to the chamber currently seized of the proceedings,[103] after having sought the consent of the victim(s) in respect of

[100] ICC RPE, Rule 87(3); STL RPE, Rule 133(C).

[101] See Chap.11.

[102] STL RPE, Rule 133(G) and (H); ECCC Practice Direction on Protective Measures of the ECCC, Article 4; ICC Regulations of the Court, Regulation 42.

[103] Pursuant to Regulation 42(3) of the ICC Regulations of the Court, an application for the variation of protective measures must be filed before the Chamber which originally granted the measures. Only if that Chamber is no longer seized of the proceedings in which the protective measure was ordered may application be made to the Chamber now seized.

whom the application is made. The chamber seized of the request shall obtain all relevant information from the first proceedings and consult with the judge or judges who originally ordered the protective measures if he, she or they remain a judge or judges of the court.[104]

According to ICC jurisprudence, an application to vary protective measures under the Regulations of the Court necessarily implies 'a claim from the applicant that a change occurred in the factual circumstances under which those measures were taken, and, correspondently, in the level of risk for the security of the person (or persons) concerned.'[105] Requests for variation of protective measures therefore should not be utilised as an alternative to, or as a second attempt at, appealing decisions which granted protective measures in the first place.[106]

6.3.2 Operational Protective Measures

Aside from the judicial protective measures explained above, each of the three courts analysed in this chapter includes in its legal texts reference to sets of operational protective measures intended to provide for the physical protection of victims.[107] These measures are formulated and generally implemented by dedicated units of the Registry or the administration of the courts, upon the request of the victims' lawyers, the relevant parties, or the victims themselves.

At the ICC, the VWS strives to find appropriate protective measures that are the least intrusive or disruptive to victims or witnesses. In order to achieve such a goal, the VWS is present in countries which are the subject of cases before the Court. Additionally, and given the fact that its mandate begins at the initial phases of the investigations of the situations, the VWS has extended its operational presence to countries where the Prosecution is conducting investigations. As submitted by the Registrar in the *Katanga and Ngudjolo Chui* case, the system of protection

[104] STL RPE, Rule 133(H); ECCC Practice Direction on Protective Measures, Article 4(3); ICC Regulations of the Court, Regulation 42(3).

[105] ICC, *Prosecutor v. Joseph Kony, Vincent Otti, Okot Odhiambo, Raska Lukwiya, Dominic Ongwen*, (ICC-02/04-01/05-239), Pre-Trial Chamber II, Decision on the Prosecutor's Application dated 22 March 2007 and on the OPCV's Request dated 29 March 2007, 4 April 2007, ICC-02/04-01/05-239, p. 5; ICC, *Prosecutor v. Abdallah Banda Abakaer Nourain and Saleh Mohammed Jerbo Jamus*, (ICC-02/05-03/09-368), Decision on the Prosecutor's Application for Variation of Protective Measures Pursuant to Regulation 42 of the Regulations of the Court by Lifting Certain Redactions Authorised Pursuant to Rule 81(4) of the Rules of Procedure and Evidence, ICC-02/05-03/09-368, 13 July 2012, p. 6.

[106] ICC, *Prosecutor v. Joseph Kony, Vincent Otti, Okot Odhiambo, Raska Lukwiya, Dominic Ongwen*, Pre-Trial Chamber II, Decision on the Prosecutor's Application dated 22 March 2007 and on the OPCV's Request dated 29 March 2007, 4 April 2007, ICC-02/04-01/05-239, p. 6.

[107] ECCC Internal Rules, Rule 29.7; ICC Regulations of the Registry, Regulations 92-93; STL RPE, Rule 50(B) (i).

envisaged by the Registry 'is based on limiting the exposure of the witnesses to the threats, providing an adequate response if required and as last resort hiding them from the threats.'[108] In doing so, the VWS has developed a sustainable system of protective measures, which includes an Initial Response System (IRS) providing participants with around-the-clock telephone contact, enabling the Court to be immediately informed of any threat against a victim or witness.[109] The IRS further enables the VWS to immediately extract victims or witnesses who are afraid of being immediately targeted, or who have been targeted, to a safe location in the field.

To enable the implementation of this protection system, the VWS has established cooperation agreements with local security forces and international organisations such as the UNHCR.[110] These organisations, private or international, are provided with limited information about the identity of the persons requiring protection, and/or about the reasons motivating their extraction.[111] The assistance of national or international institutions is requested, when appropriate, and on a case-by-case basis such requests may include *inter alia* the strengthening of the physical security of the residences of witnesses and victims. Any protective measure implemented by the VWS must adhere in any case to the basic principle of neutrality.[112]

Finally, as measure of last resort, and considered as the most extreme measure of protection, victims may be included in the ICC protection programme (ICCPP), and be relocated together with their family if necessary. As established in the ICC Regulations of the Registry, the Prosecutor, Defence counsel or victims' lawyers may file applications for the inclusion in the protection programme of persons at risk.[113] As found by the Trial Chamber in the *Lubanga* case,[114] the criteria to be met for the admission of witnesses in the ICCPP is that following a careful

---

[108] ICC, *Prosecutor v. Germain Katanga and Matthieu Ngudjolo Chui*, Registrar, Victims and Witnesses Unit's Considerations on the System of witness Protection and the practice of 'preventive relocation', ICC-01/-04-01/07-585, 12 June 2008 (ICC VWU's Submission 12 June 2008), para 10.

[109] ICC, Behind the scene: the Registry of the International Criminal Tribunal (2010), http://www.icc-cpi.int/iccdocs/PIDS/docs/behindTheSce.pdf Accessed 26 November 2015, p. 13.

[110] ICC, Summary Report on the Seminar on Protection of Victims and Witnesses Appearing before the International Criminal Court (2010), http://www.icc-cpi.int/NR/rdonlyres/08767415-4F1D-46BA-B408-5B447B3AFC8D/0/ProtectionseminarSUMMARY.pdf. Accessed 26 November 2015, para 35.

[111] Mahony 2010, p. 48.

[112] ICC, *Prosecutor v. Germain Katanga and Matthieu Ngudjolo Chui*, Registrar, Victims and Witnesses Unit's Considerations on the System of witness Protection and the practice of 'preventive relocation', ICC-01/-04-01/07-585, 12 June 2008.

[113] See ICC Regulations of the Registry, Regulation 96.

[114] ICC, *Prosecutor v. Thomas Lubanga Dyilo*, Trial Chamber I, Decision on the prosecution and defence applications for leave to appeal the Trial Chamber's 'Decision on Disclosure Issues, Responsibilities for Protective Measures and other Procedural Matters', 16 December 2008, para 27.

investigation, the witness (or victim) is considered to be exposed to an evidence-based danger of harm or death. The harm referred to by the Trial Chamber might include 'physical as well as psychological harm and that evidence of intimidation, depending on the circumstances—may be powerful evidence of the existence of a danger of harm.'[115] The decision on the application of such intrusive measures falls with the Registrar, following the independent assessment and recommendation of the VWS. It is therefore the responsibility of the Registrar to maintain a protection programme and as such, to negotiate agreements on behalf of the Court with States parties for the relocation of traumatised and threatened victims and witnesses and others at risk on account of the testimony given by such witnesses.[116] Given the nature of their subject, the content of the agreements and the States cooperating with the ICC in the matter remain confidential.

Similar to the system in place at the ICC, the VWU of the STL provides specialised protection and security advice to victims and witnesses who are assessed as being at heightened risk as a result of their interaction with the Tribunal. Pursuant to Rule 50(B)(i) of the STL RPE, the VWU formulates strategies and provides measures for victims and witnesses in conjunction with the relevant parties, States and intergovernmental or non-governmental organisations where appropriate. In order to provide this service, the Unit employs expert staff in charge of evaluating and identifying the measures necessary to address the risk encountered by each victim or witness. These measures are confidential and specific to the individual concerned.

Additionally, the Registrar has established a protection program within the VWU for the purpose of protecting individuals at risk of imminent serious harm or death as a result of their interaction with the Tribunal, through relocation to third states.[117] As at the ICC, participation in the STL's protection programme is the highest and most intrusive level of protection for an individual, and is therefore only implemented when no other measures are sufficient to mitigate the identified risk. The admission of victims or witnesses into the STL's protection programme is triggered by the referral of the case by the LRVs or relevant party, and it is subject to the assessment of the VWU and the approval of the Registrar. All procedures and administrative functions related to the protection programme are confidential.

Finally, the WESU of the ECCC has a similar institutional structure for the assessment and recommendation of operational protective measures. Following the independent assessment of each security claim received, WESU articulates

---

[115] Ibid., para 29. Although there is no jurisprudence available on the criteria for the admission to the ICCCPP for participating victims, it should be recalled that the determining factor for admission into these programs is the level of risk faced by the person as a result of their cooperation with justice, more so than the role played in the proceedings. With that in mind one could argue that the same requirements established in the *Lubanga* case, i.e. evidence-based danger of harm of death, equally apply when requesting the admission of participating victims into the ICCPP.

[116] ICC RPE, Rule 16(4); ICC Regulation for the Registry, Regulation 96.

[117] STL RPE, Rule 166.

individualised protection schemes as necessary, tailored to the circumstances of the individual at risk. Contrary to the practice of other courts where the decision on operational measures rests with the registrars of the courts, the Practice Direction on Protective Measures of the ECCC establishes that the Co-Investigating Judges or the chamber is competent to order measures aimed to physically protect the person at risk.[118] These measures may include security services provided by Cambodian police, operational measures implemented directly and independently by WESU, and/or the relocation of the person at risk within Cambodia or internationally.[119]

Regardless of the protective systems designed by each court, the effective implementation of the operational protective measures explained above, and therefore the success of the protective measures applied beyond the walls of the courtroom, depends to some degree on the cooperation of states. While the cooperation offered by host states is often included in the agreements establishing the courts in their territories;[120] the cooperation of third states on relocation matters requires from each court the negotiations of *ad hoc* agreements. These agreements, relatively few in numbers, are only the first step in a long process for the inclusion of individuals into national protection programs, since each request for relocation must be subject to a thorough assessment by the national authorities of the receiving state.

6.3.3 Special Measures (Psychosocial Measures)

Aside from the psychosocial and support services offered by the specialised victims and witnesses units in order to facilitate the testimony (or the participation) of victims and witnesses, especially in the case of vulnerable ones, the ICC, STL and ECCC have included in their internal rules provisions intended to allow the continuation of such support when inside the courtroom.[121]

Labelled as 'Special Measures' in Rule 88 of the ICC RPE, this set of measures is envisaged to facilitate the testimony of vulnerable victims and witnesses, and to

---

[118] See ECCC Practice Direction on Protective Measures, Article 1.1 and Article 3.1.

[119] ECCC, Protective Measures in the ECCC Proceedings (2013), http://www.eccc.gov.kh/en/node/26274. Accessed 26 November 2015.

[120] Article 38 of the Agreement between the United Nations and the Kingdom of the Netherlands Concerning the Headquarters of the Special Tribunal for Lebanon of 21 December 2007; Article 24 of the Agreement between the United Nations and The Royal Government of Cambodia Concerning the Prosecution under Cambodian Law of Crimes Committed during the Period of Democratic Kampuchea of 6 June 2003; Article 43 of the Headquarters Agreement between the International Criminal Court and the Host State of 1 March 2008.

[121] See Chapter 3 of the ICC Regulations of the Registry; STL Registry Regulation on Assistance and Allowance for Victims and Witnesses Testifying before the Special Tribunal for Lebanon, STL/RR/2013/01 (2013).

prevent further traumatisation. Similarly to what is the case for measures available to protect the privacy and security of victims and witnesses when testifying before the court, the legal texts do not refer to victims participating in the proceedings as specific beneficiaries of these measures. The legal basis for the request or provision of these measures shall be found however in a broader interpretation of the term victim, including therefore those victims participating in the proceedings in a capacity other than as witnesses.

Although not referred to as special measures, methods intended to protect the well-being of vulnerable victims and witnesses are also included in the legal texts of the STL or the ECCC.[122] The examples included in the texts, similarly to the protective measures granted in court, are an illustration of the possibilities at the disposal of the courts. They include: allowing a family member or a psychologist to attend the testimony of the victim or witness; conducting the testimony of the victim or witness through a closed-circuit television; conducting *in camera* proceedings.[123]

In addition to these forms of measures, the ICC has taken steps to establish a system whereby vulnerable witnesses are promptly identified, referred to and assessed by the VWS so that the specific needs of each individual are addressed appropriately. The VWS's Protocol on the vulnerability assessment and support procedure, which is used to facilitate the testimony of vulnerable witnesses, is one of the measures offered by the VWS to protect the psychological well-being, dignity and privacy of witnesses, in particular those who are at increased risk of psychological harm through the process of testimony. Pursuant to the Protocol, the special measures recommended by the unit may include measures to adapt the setup of the courtroom to the needs of the witness, in-court assistance and other in-court support, or measures to adapt the questioning of the parties to the needs and capacities of the witnesses. This protocol has been adopted by different trial chambers and implemented in different cases.[124] In the *Bemba* case, the Trial Chamber found that the Protocol should only apply to witnesses and victims appearing before the Court for the purpose of giving oral testimony.[125]

---

[122] See STL RPE, Rule 133(C)(iii); ECCC Practice Direction on Protective Measures, Article 3.3(b).

[123] Although not included in any of the STL public documents, the VPU, in cooperation with the VWU, may provide psychosocial support to victims participating in the proceedings when they attend court hearings.

[124] See ICC, *Prosecutor v. Jean Pierre Bemba Gombo,* Trial Chamber III, Decision on the Unified Protocol on the practices used to prepare and familiarise witnesses for giving testimony at trial, ICC-01/05-01/08-1016, 18 November 2010; ICC, *Prosecutor v. Laurent Gbagbo*, Pre-Trial Chamber I, Victims and Witnesses Unit's Unified Protocol on the practices used to prepare and familiarise witnesses for giving testimony and Protocol on the vulnerability assessment and support procedure used to facilitate the testimony of vulnerable witnesses, ICC-02/11-01/11-93, 16 April 2012.

[125] ICC, *Prosecutor v. Jean Pierre Bemba Gombo,* Trial Chamber III, Decision on the Unified Protocol on the practices used to prepare and familiarise witnesses for giving testimony at trial, ICC-01/05-01/08-1016, 18 November 2010, para 8.

Although unregulated by the courts, special measures intended to cater for the psychological wellbeing of participating victims are provided in some cases, even when they do not participate in the case as witnesses. Such is the case at the STL where, further to the case-by-case analysis of the circumstances and needs of the participating victim, specific measures can be granted. These might include, for example, funding a support person to accompany a participating victim when travelling to the seat of the Tribunal to observe the proceedings, referring a victim to psychosocial or medical institutions for the follow-up of identified needs connected to their participation in proceedings, or providing psychosocial or medical assistance *in loco*. Before the ICC, the provision of psychosocial support to participating victims appearing in their own right is provided following a very strict criterion and hence involves a very low number of beneficiaries. The ICC's VWS intervenes if and when there is a link between the harm suffered by the participating victim and the fact that he or she is participating in the proceedings. This support, if granted, can comprise both psychosocial and medical support. Finally, and in cases where the participating victim is under a protection scheme, the VWS would also provide for the support services needed.[126]

6.4 Key Points

Institutional Players

- *Mandate of the courts*: All three courts have (i) the mandate and overall responsibility to provide for the protection and security of victims against risks incurred as a result of their participation/cooperation with the courts, (ii) the authority to order measures to protect their participation in the proceedings, (iii) the power to control questioning by the parties when victims appear as witnesses or to express views and concerns and (iv) the power to hold criminal proceedings in respect of persons who knowingly and wilfully have threatened or intimidated victims.
- *Specialised protection units*: VWS, VWU and WESU provide the measures and security arrangements necessary to protect victims against risks incurred as a result of their contact with the Tribunal or Court; provide security advice to the court participants and to victims and their lawyers; and in some cases can request judicial protective measures to be ordered by the competent judge(s).
- *Specialised victims units*: The protection role of the VPU, the VSS and the VPRS is limited to an informative/advisory/requesting one.
- *Victims' lawyers*: Lawyers representing victims play an important role in requesting judicial and operational protective measures.

[126] Information provided by the Psychologist/Trauma Expert of the (then) VWU, ICC (records on file with the author). 11 February 2015.

Judicial protection

(1) *Legal requirements*: the legal provisions envisaged for the protection of witnesses are equally applicable for the protection of participating victims. As such, protection encompasses the physical and psychological safety of victims as well as the protection of their dignity and privacy.

- The legal standard required is similar at all three courts: the protective measures shall be *appropriate* and *consistent with the rights of the accused.*
- Protective measures shall be *necessary* to mitigate a real and objective fear for the safety of the victim, and *proportional* to the restriction of rights imposed to the accused.

(2) *Before an application for participation is submitted*: All three courts provide for protection to victims who have not (or not yet) submitted an application for participation, including persons contacted during investigations:

- *ICC*: The Court as a whole and the Prosecution in particular are to ensure that all activities respect the personal interests of victims, and to request measures when necessary.
- *STL*: The VWU is responsible for the protection of victims and others at risk on account of their interaction with the Tribunal, including victims who are not participating but are in contact with the Tribunal, regardless of the stage at which the proceedings are, provided the risk against them is due to their interaction with the Tribunal.
- *ECCC*: Victims engaging with the Court shall receive protection from the authorities in charge of conducting investigations, regardless of whether they have applied for civil party status.

(3) *At the application stage*:

- *ICC*: Applications filed by victims seeking participation are provided to the Prosecution and the Defence who are entitled to submit observations. The applications are subject to protective measures whereby information identifying the victim and third parties is redacted. The specific redaction regime, and whether it is applied to applications provided to both parties or only to the Defence, is governed by jurisprudence which differs between chambers.
- *STL*: Victims' applications are only transmitted to the Pre-Trial Judge. Application documents are never disclosed to the Prosecutor or the Defence.
- *ECCC*: Victims' complaints before the Co-Prosecutors and the Victims Unit remain confidential. In contrast, victims' applications to participate as civil parties are filed and, unless protective measures are granted, shall be notified to the Co-Prosecutors and the charged persons.

(4) *Protection for participating victims and civil parties*: two types of judicial protective measures are available to participating victims:

- *Confidentiality:* Aimed at concealing the identity of participating victims by withholding identifying information from the public.
- *Anonymity:* Non-disclosure of the identity of the participating victim to the accused.
- *ICC*: Anonymity has become the default position for participating victims and therefore specific request for such protection is not required. The protection however implies some degree of limitation in the extent or form of victims' participation.
- *STL*: Anonymity is not permitted for participating victims.
- *ECCC*: The governing texts do not refer to the possibility of anonymity as protective measure for civil parties.

(5) *Protection of participating victims appearing before the court or observing proceedings in person*:

- Measures to protect participating victims who choose to be physically present in court (*i.e.* attendance to trial hearings, presentation of views and concerns, giving testimony in their own case) may have a restrictive effect on public access to the proceedings.
- *'Public'* is generally understood as all persons, government, organisations, entities, associations and groups. The term does not include the judges of the court, members of the Registry, the Prosecution, the Accused, Defence teams, and the participating victims' lawyers.
- The *types* of measures available are similar to those for witnesses testifying in the case (*i.e.* pseudonym, expunction of names from public records, forbidding access of public to hearings, using image and voice distortion, participating from remote location, participating in closed session).
- The *procedures* to request the measures differ from one court to another.

(6) *Variation of protective measures*

- Protective measures apply *mutatis mutandis* through the entire proceedings in the case and in relation to other proceedings before the court unless they are rescinded, varied, or augmented in accordance with the relevant provisions.
- An application for variation implies a claim from the applicant that a *change in the circumstances* has reduced or increased the level of risk faced by the participating victim.

Operational protective measures

- These are measures intended to provide for the physical protection of participating victims, formulated and implemented by the Registry or the administration of the court.
- *ICC*: The VWS is present in countries which are the subject of cases or investigations before the court, with two systems in place: IRS, with around the clock phone contact for protected victims, and ICCPP for the relocation of victims and their families who have been assessed as facing evidence-based danger of harm or death.
- *STL*: Specialised protection and security advice is formulated and offered by the VWU on a case-by-case basis. The VWU also has a Protection Programme for individuals who are determined to be at risk of imminent serious harm or death as a result of their interaction with the Tribunal.
- *ECCC*: A similar structure is in place to that of the other international courts. However, as opposed to those above, the decisions on operational measures are reserved to the Co-Investigating Judges or the chamber.

Special measures

- Measures aimed to facilitate the participation of victims in the proceedings and to *prevent further traumatisation.*
- These measures may include *inter alia* the presence of a family member or a psychologist within the courtroom or the participation of the victim from a remote room.
- At the ICC a protocol on vulnerability assessment is used by the VWS.
- At the STL a case-by-case assessment is made, followed by the allocation of special measures where necessary for participating victims who do not participate as witnesses.

References

Acquaviva G, Heikkilä M (2013) Protective and special measures for witnesses. In: Sluiter G et al (eds) International Criminal Procedure: Principles and rules. Oxford University Press, Oxford, pp 818–859

Baumgartner E (2008) Aspects of victim participation in the proceedings of the International Criminal Court. Int Rev Red Cross 90(870):409–440

Boyle D (2006) The rights of victims, participation, representation, protection, reparation. J Int Crim Justice 4(2):307–313

De Brouwer AM, Groenhuijsen M (2009) The role of victims in international criminal proceedings. In: Sluiter G, Vasiliev S (eds) International Criminal Procedure: Towards a coherent body of law. Cameron May, London, pp 149–204

De Hemptinne J, Rindi F (2006) ICC Pre-Trial Chamber allows victims to participate in the investigation phase of proceedings. J Int Crim Justice 4(2):342–350

ICC (2010) Behind the scene: the Registry of the International Criminal Tribunal. http://www.icc-cpi.int/iccdocs/PIDS/docs/behindTheSce.pdf. Accessed 26 November 2015

ICC (2010) Summary Report on the Seminar on Protection of Victims and Witnesses Appearing before the International Criminal Court. http://www.icc-cpi.int/NR/rdonlyres/08767415-4F1D-46BA-B408-5B447B3AFC8D/0/ProtectionseminarSUMMARY.pdf. Accessed 26 November 2015

Mahony C (2010) The justice sector afterthought: Witness protection in Africa. Institute for Security Studies, Pretoria

McKay F (2008) Victims participation in proceedings before the International Criminal Court. Hum Rights Brief 15(3):2–5

Morrison H, Pountney E (2014) Victim participation at the Special Tribunal for Lebanon. In: Alamuddin A et al (eds) The Special Tribunal for Lebanon: Law and practice. Oxford University Press, Oxford, pp 153–176

Office of Public Counsel for Victims of the International Criminal Court (OPCV) (2013) Representing victims before the International Criminal Court, a manual for legal representatives. https://www.icc-cpi.int/iccdocs/pids/tmp/representing%20victims%20before%20icc.pdf. Accessed 26 November 2015

Perez Leon Acevedo JP (2014) Victims' status at international and hybrid criminal courts. Åbo Akademi University Press, Åbo

Stahn C et al (2006) Participation of victims in pre-trial proceedings of the ICC. J Int Crim Justice 4(2):219–238

Studzinsky S (2011a) Participation and protection of victims of sexual violence before the ECCC. Presentation for the Second Hague Colloquium on Systematic Sexual Violence and Victims' Rights organized by the Center on Law and Globalization. Session VII: Participation and protection of victims of sexual violence in international criminal law, The Hague, April 2011

Studzinsky S (2011b) Victims' participation before the Extraordinary Chambers in the Courts of Cambodia. Zeitschrift für Internationale Strafrechtsdogmatik 10:887–891

Taylor D (2014) Victim participation in transitional justice mechanisms: Real power or empty ritual? http://www.impunitywatch.org/docs/IW_Discussion_Paper_Victim_Participation1.pdf. Accessed 26 November 2015

United Nations Office for Drug Control and Crime Prevention (UNODC) (1999) Handbook on justice for victims. UNODC, New York, p 1999

Chapter 7
Victims' Rights and Obligations as Regards the Case File: Access, Disclosure and Filing Submissions

Caroline Walter

Abstract Representing victims before the ICC or the STL, and civil parties before the ECCC translates in practice in modalities of participation developed differently by each of the courts concerned. Knowing them and understanding them is crucial for practitioners in order to efficiently and effectively represent their clients. This chapter introduces the main rules and practices so far developed by each court with regard to access to documents and material, disclosure issues and filings of submissions. The goal is to share insights aimed at equipping practitioners with an understanding on which to base their current or coming practice. Knowing how and what set of documents and material can be accessed and submitted before these three courts constitutes the key to all other modalities of participation.

Keywords Notification · Disclosure (obligations) · Access rights · Filing of submissions · Case file · Case record · Confidential documents · Public documents

Contents

Ms. Caroline Walter is Legal Officer at the Office of Public Counsel for Victims (at the ICC) where she has been working since 2007. The views expressed herein are those of the author and do not necessarily reflect the views of the International Criminal Court.

C. Walter (✉)
International Criminal Court, The Hague, The Netherlands
e-mail: caroline.walter@icc-cpi.int

K. Tibori-Szabó and M. Hirst (eds.), *Victim Participation in International Criminal Justice*, International Criminal Justice Series 11,
DOI 10.1007/978-94-6265-177-7_7

7.1 Access to Material in the Case File[1]

Access to material in the case record or case file mainly refers to access to two types of material: procedural documents (submissions of the parties or participants, and decisions of the chambers) and evidentiary material (material disclosed by parties or participants in relation to their case). Before discussing these two types of access relevant to participating victims, it is important to emphasise that at all three courts analysed herein (the Extraordinary Chambers at the Courts of Cambodia (ECCC), the International Criminal Court (ICC) and the Special Tribunal for Lebanon (STL)) differentiation is made between the access rights of individual victims and those of the lawyers representing the victims.

The general rule is that individual participating victims can have access to public, but not to confidential information. Requests for access to confidential information by an individual victim, if allowed at all, must be specifically justified. At the ICC, the legal representatives of victims (LRVs) must provide detailed information about the requesting victim, why the disclosure of the confidential information is necessary and how it would guarantee that the information would not be circulated beyond the specifically authorised victim(s).[2] At the STL, if the LRV considers it necessary to disclose confidential information to the victims in order to represent their interests, he or she may seek the consent of the party which provided the material. If this process yields no results, the LRV may apply before the relevant chamber, which will decide on a case-by-case basis, after having heard

[1] Often the term 'record of the case' is used at the ICC, whereas the expression 'case file' is used at the STL and at the ECCC. In this chapter the term 'case file' is used broadly to encompass documents pertaining to a specific case at any of the three courts.

[2] See ICC, *Prosecutor v. Germain Katanga and Mathieu Ngudjolo* Chui, Trial Chamber II, Decision on the Modalities of Victim Participation at Trial, ICC-01/04-01/07-1788-tENG, 22 January 2010, para 123; ICC, *Prosecutor v. Jean-Pierre Bemba*, Trial Chamber III, Corrigendum to Decision on the participation of victims in the trial and on 86 applications by victims to participate in the proceedings, ICC-01/05-01/08-807-Corr, 12 July 2010, para 47; ICC, *Prosecutor v. William Samoei Rutio and Joshua Arap Sang*, Trial Chamber V, Decision on victims' representation and participation, ICC-01/09-01/11-460, 3 October 2012, paras 68–69; ICC, *Prosecutor v. Uhuru Muigai Kenyatta*, Trial Chamber V, Decision on victims' representation and participation, ICC-01/09-02/11-498, 3 October 2012, paras 67–68.

the party which provided the material.[3] ECCC practice gives civil parties access to public information and allows their lawyers to access or inspect documents containing confidential information.

As regards the lawyers representing victims, STL case-law grants them access to confidential information. Recalling that the LRVs are professional counsel with ethical obligations pursuant to the Code of Professional Conduct for Counsel Appearing before the Tribunal, the Pre-Trial Judge decided to grant access to confidential documents to the LRV. Although Rule 87 of the STL Rules of Procedure and Evidence (RPE), which establishes victims' modalities of participation including regarding access rights, expressly refers to participating victims rather than their lawyers, it is understood as referring to the latter.

The ICC's initial approach was to deny access to confidential information to victims' lawyers, although recent decisions have shown a tendency to depart from that approach (see Sect. 7.1.1.3 below).

In the practice of the ECCC, lawyers representing civil parties are permitted access to confidential documents of the case file.[4]

This chapter will mostly discuss the access rights of lawyers representing victims and where necessary, the rules relevant to individual victims.

The possibility for victims' lawyers to access documents[5] filed and material disclosed in the case record constitutes the key to all other modalities of victim participation granted at the ICC, STL and ECCC. Without such access, the lawyers cannot adequately follow the proceedings they are involved in and cannot fulfil their role and mandate of ensuring the effective participation of the represented victims.

Written submissions filed by the parties or participants and written decisions issued by the chambers are the main procedural documents to which access should be provided: if victims' lawyers are not notified of, or granted access to, submissions made by the (other) parties or participants on various issues, the participation of the victims will not be in accordance with the principle of fair proceedings and may as a result run counter their effectiveness and expeditiousness. The same applies even more so to decisions of the chambers.

---

[3] STL, *Prosecutor v. Ayyash* et al., Pre-Trial Judge, Decision on the VPU's Access to Materials and the Modalities of Victims' Participation in Proceedings before the Pre Trial Judge, STL-11-01/PT/PTJ, 18 May 2012, paras 55–57. The Trial Chamber in the *Ayyash* et al. case confirmed the applicability of the same rules during the trial phase (STL, *Prosecutor v. Ayyash* et al., Trial Chamber, Direction on the Conduct of the Proceedings, STL-11-01/T/TC, 16 January 2014, para 19).

[4] See Article 2(d)(ii) of the ECCC Practice Direction on Classification and Management of Case-Related Information, which implies that only 'lawyers for the civil parties' have access to confidential documents.

[5] See *inter alia*, ICC, Regulations of the Court Regulation 22: 'The term "document" shall include any motion, application, request, response, reply, observation, representation and any other submission in a form capable of delivering a written record to the Court'.

Transcripts of hearings, which include oral submissions by parties and participants and oral decisions by the chambers also form part of the record of the case and are equally important procedural documents, to which victims' lawyers should have access.

Finally, evidentiary material disclosed by the Prosecution and the Defence (and/or by another team of victims' lawyers) is in turn the basis on which the case is ultimately decided by the judges—if victims' lawyers do not have access to this material, they will be unable to effectively represent their clients.

If victims' lawyers are not aware of a subject being dealt with between the parties and the chamber (whether it concerns written or oral submissions or evidentiary material), they cannot inform their clients on the content of the proceedings and will not know to seek their clients' views on the matter—as a result, effective and meaningful victims' participation cannot be achieved. The chamber and parties may also lose the benefit of a potential alternative perspective or source of information. In addition, victims' lawyers may make submissions which are moot or off point, thus wasting the court's time, because they are not fully apprised of the matters discussed in the proceedings.

Given the fundamental importance of access to securing meaningful and effective participation of victims, regardless of the particular court involved, access should not be considered as an (optional) luxury or a favour, whether by victims' lawyers or any other actor involved in the proceedings. Victims' lawyers carry a vital responsibility in securing this right to the widest extent possible, from the very start of their involvement in a case, and as commanded by the best interests of their clients.

7.1.1 Access to Filings and Decisions in the Case File

In order to appreciate the levels of access granted to participating victims and their lawyers it is necessary to understand the different levels of document classification applied before each of the tribunals.

At the ICC, Regulation 14 of the Regulations of the Registry establishes four distinct levels of classification for judicial records and material: Public (available to the public); Confidential (not to be disclosed to the public); Under Seal (confidential and accessible and known only to a limited number of persons); and Secret (accessible and known to a very limited number of persons, with restricted circulation rules). In addition, Regulation 24(4) of the Registry also refers to judicial records marked as *Ex Parte*, only available to specific participants in a case (and the chamber).

The Practice Direction on Filings at the STL also sets out four different levels of classification of documents filed before the Tribunal: 'Public', 'Confidential',

'Confidential and *Ex Parte'*, and 'Under Seal and *Ex Parte* with Limited Distribution'.[6]

At the ECCC, three levels of classification have been established: Public (open to the public without restriction), Confidential (open only to judges, the Co-Prosecutors, lawyers for the civil parties, Defence counsel, authorised court staff and any other person expressly given access by the Court), and Strictly Confidential (open only to the judges and such other persons, including court staff who require access in the discharge of their duties, expressly given access by the Court).[7] Such access, obviously, is covered by a duty of confidentiality.[8]

7.1.1.1 Notification as an Intrinsic Part of Access

The right to access certain documents also intrinsically includes the right to be notified of them, because this ensures that lawyers are aware of the documents' existence. Notifications also ensure that lawyers can follow the proceedings in real-time, and are consequently able to react and respect applicable time-limits.

At the ICC, Rule 92 of the RPE establishes that 'victims or their legal representatives participating in proceedings shall, in respect of those proceedings, be notified by the Registrar in a timely manner of: (a) Proceedings before the Court, including the date of hearings and any postponements thereof, and the date of delivery of the decision; (b) Requests, submissions, motions and other documents relating to such requests, submissions or motions.' The jurisprudence mirrors this principle by confirming that LRVs must be notified of all public requests, submissions, motions, responses and other procedural documents, as well as of the decisions of the chamber (including all public proceedings).[9]

Rule 51(B)(iv) and (v) of the STL RPE also appears to establish that there is an entitlement on the part of the victims and their lawyers to be notified of the documents to which they have access. In practice, victims' lawyers are notified through the same court management system as other participants in the proceedings.[10]

[6] STL, Practice Direction on Filing of Documents before the Special Tribunal for Lebanon, STL/PD/2010/01/Rev.2, 14 June 2013.

[7] ECCC, Practice Direction ECCC/004/2009/Rev.2, Practice Direction on Classification and Management of Case-Related Information, Amended on 7 March 2012 and 24 April 2014, Article 2(d).

[8] Ibid., Article 8.

[9] See for instance, ICC, *Prosecutor v. Charles Blé Goudé*, Pre-Trial Chamber I, Second Decision on victims' participation in the pre-trial proceedings and related issues, ICC-02/11-02/11, 1 August 2014, paras 16–28. See also in particular ICC RPE, Rule 92(1), (5) and (6).

[10] The Victims' Participation Unit at the STL also plays an active role in relation to notification and access but principally before LRVs are assigned or before the judges rule on the modalities of victims' rights in the proceedings.

According to ECCC practice, lawyers representing civil parties are notified of documents placed on the case file.[11]

Notification of documents to victims is effected by electronic communication to their lawyers, through the court management systems put in place by the three tribunals.[12] Despite variation in the detail of the courts' legal texts, the principle of notification is essentially the same before all three institutions: victims and their lawyers must be notified of all documents in the proceedings which they are or may be permitted to access.[13]

Documents filed *ex parte* or under seal at the ICC and at the STL or 'strictly confidential' at the ECCC are notified, and further accessible, only to the party or participant concerned with their content.

The following sections will address the law and the practice of each of the three courts concerning access to submissions filed and decisions issued in the record of a case.

---

[11] Rule 21 of the ECCC Internal Rules makes clear that the 'ECCC shall ensure that victims are kept informed'. In accordance with Rule 46, especially paragraphs (1) and (4), the civil parties shall be notified of all orders of the co-investigating judges or the chambers, and at the trial stage and beyond, of orders. Rule 66 covers the parties' notification of the Conclusion of a Judicial Investigation. Rule 67(5) prescribes the immediate notification of a Closing Order issued by the Co-Investigating Judges. Further, Rule 80 prescribes the notification in writing to the parties of the trial date, as soon as possible. Finally, Rule 106 sets the immediate notification of all other parties and their lawyers in the case of the filing of an appeal or an immediate appeal. In practice, the chambers generally acknowledge that 'the recognized lawyers will receive electronic notification of documents placed on the case file'. See for instance, ECCC, *Case 004*, Office of the Co-Investigating Judges, Lawyer's recognition decision concerning all civil party applications on Case File No. 004, Case No. 004/07-09-2009-ECCC-OCIJ, 1 April 2013, para 12.

[12] Even the ECCC, which began otherwise, now integrates all components of an electronic system. Article 6 of the Practice Direction 02/2007/Rev.1 sets the notification system with the *greffier* of the Office of the Co-Investigating Judges or the chambers through the Case File Officer. At the ICC, Regulations 26, 29 and 32 of the Regulations of the Court deal respectively with the establishment of an electronic management system and with notifications. Regulations 10, 20 to 23–35*bis* of the ICC Regulations of the Registry refer to the e-court system, the content of situation and case records, and the filing of documents and notifications.

[13] ICC, *Prosecutor v. Germain Katanga and Mathieu Ngudjolo Chui*, Pre-Trial Chamber I, Decision on the Set of Procedural Rights Attached to Procedural Status of Victim at the Pre-Trial Stage of the Case, ICC-01/04-01/07-474, 13 May 2008, paras 127–133, 141–144. Documents filed confidentially in the record of the case are notified to the LRV—at the pre-trial stage, as a consequence of their access granted to the index of the case and in order to put them in a position to request access to specific confidential documents. ICC, *Prosecutor v. Bosco Ntaganda*, Pre-Trial Chamber II, Decision on the "Joint request of the Common Legal Representatives to access documents in the Bosco Ntaganda case record", ICC-01/04-02/06-237, 29 January 2014, paras 13–16: 'The Single Judge is of the view that a full index of the case record to be generated by the Court Management Section (the 'CMS') could represent a useful instrument for the common legal representatives to conduct a review of the case file, without providing them indiscriminately with access to confidential information contained therein absent prior authorization by the Single Judge.' At the trial stage, Rule 131(2) of the ICC RPE gives access to the LRV to the index of the situation and case records, subject to any restrictions concerning confidentiality and the protection of national security information.

7.1.1.2 The Basic Principle of Access to Public Documents

As a matter of principle, victims' lawyers enjoy broad access to public documents. Where a filing is classified public it will be notified and accessible to victims' lawyers even if the filing party does not expressly list them for notification on the notification page.[14] This constitutes an important starting point for enabling the participation of victims in the proceedings. Public filings and decisions are equally available to the public at large through the websites of the three tribunals. For lawyers involved in a proceeding, there is a marked difference between following the proceedings through systematic notifications of documents accessible through the internal document management system of a tribunal, and following the proceedings through websites which may not always be promptly updated. This is a key difference between being an active participant/party in the proceedings of the case and passively following proceedings as an outsider.

7.1.1.3 Towards a Uniform Rule of Access to Both Public and Confidential Documents

Despite the principle of public proceedings applicable in each of the three courts,[15] many submissions and decisions are filed confidentially. When a party or a participant opts for this level of classification, it must justify why restricting access to the information contained in its document is necessary. The use of public redacted versions of confidential documents assists but may not be sufficient to ensure meaningful involvement of victims' lawyers in the proceedings. The same applies where documents classified as confidential are later reclassified as public. If lawyers are excluded from accessing confidential documents when they are first filed and while they maintain a confidential classification, they are accordingly deprived of effectively following the proceedings they are involved in.

As explained above, the ability of victims' lawyers to access public and confidential documents has been recognised at the ECCC and the STL, and has recently also been upheld by some trial chambers at the ICC. However, the practice of the ICC to date remains inconsistent (see Sect. 7.1.1.3 below).

As previously mentioned, at the ECCC, victims' lawyers enjoy nearly unrestricted access to the case file from the moment of the admission of their clients as civil parties in a case, and throughout the case (including at the investigation

[14] Typically, every procedural document has a notification page that includes the name of the court and the chamber before which the document is filed, the name(s) of the judge(s), the date, the classification and the filing party of the document as well as the parties and participants who are to be granted access to the document.

[15] ICC RPE, Rules 96, 136, 137; ICC Statute, Articles 64(7) and 67(1); ICC Regulations of the Court, Regulations 20, 21, 23*bis*; ECCC Internal Rules (Rev. 9), Rule 79(6).

phase, and at any time during the proceedings of the trial).[16] Indeed, enjoying the status of *party* in the proceedings puts them on an equal footing with the other parties and no justification can be advanced for blanket restrictions of their access to information in the proceedings. Since the lawyers representing civil parties enjoy broad access to confidential documents, through their access to the inventory of the confidential section of the case file, they have access to generic titles of strictly confidential documents.[17] This enables them to understand the nature of such documents to some extent, without their strictly confidential contents being disclosed. In principle, the lawyers of civil parties are informed of the existence and content of documents classified strictly confidential where this is necessary for the implementation of their mandate, but they nonetheless must specifically request such access if they wish to consult them.[18]

In accordance with the jurisprudence of the STL, at both the pre-trial[19] and trial[20] stages, Rule 87(A) of the RPE is to be understood as granting access for the LRV to all documents filed confidentially, with no need for such access to be justified on a case-by-case basis. This includes access to confidential filings, decisions and orders forming part of the record of the case file.[21] Applications for participation submitted by applicant victims, which are classified as confidential and *ex parte*, are made accessible to the LRV once the applicants are granted the status of victims participating in the proceedings, in order to enable the LRV to 'perform his duties as well as meaningfully exercise his entitlements'.[22]

---

[16] ECCC, Practice Direction ECCC 02/2007/Rev.1, Practice Direction on Victim Participation, Rev.1, Article 6. See also Internal Rules, Rule 69(3) and Rule 77(4).

[17] ECCC, Practice Direction ECCC/004/2009/Rev.2, Practice Direction on Classification and Management of Case-Related Information, Amended on 7 March 2012 and 24 April 2014, Article 10.

[18] Ibid., Article 2(d).

[19] STL, *Prosecutor v. Ayyash* et al., Pre-Trial Judge, Decision on the VPU's Access to Materials and the Modalities of Victims' Participation in Proceedings before the Pre Trial Judge, STL-11-01/PT/PTJ, 18 May 2012, paras 49–51.

[20] STL, *Prosecutor v. Ayyash* et al., Trial Chamber, Directions on the conduct of the Proceedings, STL-11-01/T/TC, 16 January 2014, para 19.

[21] Ibid., and STL, *Prosecutor v. Ayyash* et al., Pre-Trial Judge, Decision on the VPU's Access to Materials and the Modalities of Victims' Participation in Proceedings before the Pre Trial Judge, STL-11-01/PT/PTJ, 18 May 2012, paras 51–52.

[22] Ibid., para 53. Following observations filed by the LRV on the modalities of participation of victims, the Prosecution supported such access by the LRV to confidential filings as the Trial Chamber deems appropriate. See STL, *Prosecutor v. Ayyash* et al., Observations of the Legal Representative of Victims on the Modalities of Victim Participation at Trial, STL-11-01/PT/TC, 1 November 2013; STL, *Prosecutor v. Ayyash* et al., Prosecution Response to LRV Observations on the Modalities of Victim Participation at Trial, STL-11-01/PT/TC, 18 November 2013, para 3. The Defence did not challenge this proposition at the time. See STL, *Prosecutor v. Ayyash* et al., Defence Submissions on the Observations of the Legal Representative for Victims on the Modalities of Victim Participation at Trial, STL-11-01/PT/TC, 18 November 2013. See also STL RPE, STL-BD-2009-01-Rev.7, amended on 12 February 2015, Rule 51(B)(iv) and (v).

Throughout the ICC's jurisprudence to date, different approaches have been taken by different chambers as regards access to public and confidential documents at the pre-trial stage and at the trial stage.

The ICC's pre-trial chambers have mostly been consistent in allowing LRVs access to public documents only. Accordingly, the following are usually granted:[23] access, prior to and during the confirmation of charges hearing, to the *public* record of the case kept by the Registry, to all public filings and decisions contained therein and to the transcripts of the public hearings.

Nonetheless, Pre-Trial Chamber I in the *Katanga and Ngudjolo Chui* case departed from this approach.[24] The LRV in that case was granted access to all public and confidential filings and decisions and to the transcripts of both public and closed session hearings contained in the record of the case. This case was the second one opened before the Court and this jurisprudence represented an encouraging start for the right of victims.

Notwithstanding this promising start, Pre-Trial Chamber III in the *Bemba* case allowed the LRV access only to the public documents contained in the record

[23] ICC, *Prosecutor v. Charles Blé Goudé*, Pre-Trial Chamber I, Decision on victims' participation in the pre-trial proceedings and related issues, ICC-02/11-02/11, 13 June 2014, paras 32–36; ICC, *Prosecutor v. Bosco Ntaganda*, Pre-Trial Chamber II, Decision on the "Joint request of the Common Legal Representatives to access documents in the Bosco Ntaganda case record", ICC-01/04-02/06, 29 January 2014, paras 14–25; ICC, *Prosecutor v. Laurent Gbagbo*, Pre-Trial Chamber I, Decision on Victims' Participation and Victims' Common Legal Representation at the Confirmation of Charges Hearing and in the Related Proceedings, ICC-02/11-01/11-138, 4 June 2012, paras 53–58 and Corrigendum to the Second decision on victims' participation at the confirmation of charges hearing and in the related proceedings, ICC-02/11-01/11-384-Corr, 6 February 2013, paras 53–57; ICC, *Prosecutor v. Uhuru Muigai Kenyatta*, Pre-Trial Chamber II, Decision on Victims' Participation at the Confirmation of Charges Hearing and in the Related Proceedings, ICC-01/09-02/11-267, 26 August 2011, paras 107–113; ICC, *Prosecutor v. Callixte Mbarushimana*, Pre-Trial Chamber I, Decision on the 138 applications for victims' participation in the proceedings, ICC-01/04-01/10-351, 11 August 2011, paras 42–43, about the notification of public proceedings and documents; ICC, *Prosecutor v. William Samoei Ruto and Joshua Arap Sang*, Pre-Trial Chamber II, Decision on Victims' Participation at the Confirmation of Charges Hearing and in the Related Proceedings, ICC-01/09-01/11-249, 7 August 2011, paras 90–95; ICC, *Prosecutor v. Abdallah Banda Abakaer Nourain and Saleh Mohammed Jerbo Jamus*, Pre-Trial Chamber I, Decision on Victims' Participation at the Hearing on the Confirmation of the Charges, ICC-02/05-03/09-89, 29 October 2010, paras 60–62; ICC, *Prosecutor v. Bahar Idriss Abu Garda*, Pre-Trial Chamber I, Decision on victims' modalities of participation at the Pre-Trial Stage of the Case, ICC-02/05-02/09-136, 6 October 2009, paras 11–15 and Oral decision, ICC-02/05-02/09-T-12-Red-ENG WT, 19 October 2009, p. 12; ICC, *Prosecutor v. Thomas Lubanga Dyilo*, Pre-Trial Chamber I, Decision on the Arrangements for Participation of Victims a/0001/06, a/0002/06 and a/0003/06 at the Confirmation Hearing, ICC-01/04-01/06-462-tEN, 22 September 2006, pp. 7–8.

[24] ICC, *Prosecutor v. Germain Katanga and Mathieu Ngudjolo Chui*, Pre-Trial Chamber I, Decision on the Set of Procedural Rights Attached to Procedural Status of Victim at the Pre-Trial Stage of the Case, ICC-01/04-01/07-474, 13 May 2008, paras 127–133, 141–144.

of the case[25] and since then, pre-trial chambers have mostly not departed substantially from that restrictive approach.[26] Pre-Trial Chamber I, in each of the *Mbarushimana* and *Banda and Jerbo* cases, granted LRVs access to one document then classified as confidential which was deemed necessary for the LRV to participate on behalf of victims: the document containing the charges.[27] In the *Abu Garda* case too, Pre-Trial Chamber I granted the LRV access to confidential documents related to a witness called by the Prosecution in order to allow the LRV to put their questions to the latter, but denied the same access to documents introduced by the Defence.[28] However, more recently, in *Ongwen*, LRVs were granted full access to the confidential case file from the pre-trial stage, potentially signalling a positive change in this area.[29]

At the trial stage, the chambers in the *Lubanga*, *Bemba*, *Banda* and in the *Kenyan* cases[30] all required LRVs to file specific motivated requests demonstrating

---

[25] ICC, *Prosecutor v. Jean-Pierre Bemba*, Pre-Trial Chamber III, Fourth Decision on Victims' Participation, ICC-01/05-01/08-320, 12 December 2008, paras 103–107. Pre-Trial Chamber III also refused to grant the LRV access to witness statements classified confidential of the dual status victim witnesses they then represented. See Pre-Trial Chamber III, Sixth Decision on Victims' Participation Relating to Certain Questions Raised by the Office of Public Counsel for Victims, ICC-01/05-01/08-349, 8 January 2009, paras 10–11.

[26] However, it could be noted that pre-trial chambers started to adopt more flexibility in their approaches, instructing parties and participants that if they so wish, they can notify their own filings classified confidential to the LRV, while, additionally, restating that the chambers retain the option to decide on a case-by-case basis, either *proprio motu* or upon specific request, whether to grant the LRVs such access too. See for instance ICC, *Prosecutor v. Charles Blé Goudé*, Pre-Trial Chamber I, Second Decision on victims' participation in the pre-trial proceedings and related issues, ICC-02/11-02/11, 1 August 2014, paras 22–25.

[27] ICC, *Prosecutor v. Callixte Mbarushimana*, Pre-Trial Chamber I, Decision on the 138 applications for victims' participation in the proceedings, ICC-01/04-01/10-351, 11 August 2011, para 44; ICC, *Prosecutor v. Abdallah Banda Abakaer Nourain and Saleh Mohammed Jerbo Jamus*, Pre-Trial Chamber I, Decision on Victims' Participation at the Hearing on the Confirmation of the Charges, ICC-02/05-03/09-89, 29 October 2010, para 68.

[28] ICC, *Prosecutor v. Bahar Idriss Abu Garda*, Pre-Trial Chamber I, Oral decision, ICC-02/05-02/09-T-13-ENG CT WT, 20 October 2009, p. 13.

[29] ICC, *Prosecutor v. Dominic Ongwen*, Pre-Trial Chamber II, ICC-02/04-01/15-350, Decision on contested victims' applications for participation, legal representation of victims and their procedural rights, 27 November 2015, para 29.

[30] In the *Lubanga* case, Trial Chamber I only permitted the LRV access to public filings and decisions. However, access to some specific confidential documents was permitted on a case-by-case basis, including access to the confidential version of the Prosecution's Summary of the Presentation of Evidence and all witnesses' statements: ICC, *Prosecutor v. Thomas Lubanga Dyilo*, Trial Chamber I, Decision on victims' participation, ICC-01/04-01/06-1119, 18 January 2008, paras 97–100, and Oral Decision, ICC-01/04-01/06-T-105-ENG-Et WT, 22 January 2009, pp. 43–44. See also ICC, *Prosecutor v. William Samoei Ruto and Joshua Arap Sang* and ICC, *Prosecutor v. Uhuru Muigai Kenyatta*, Trial Chamber V, Decision on victims' representation and participation, ICC-01/09-01/11-460 and ICC-01/09-02/11-498, 3 October 2012, respectively paras 64–69 and paras 63–68. See also ICC, *Prosecutor v. Jean-Pierre Bemba*, Trial Chamber III, Corrigendum to Decision on the participation of victims in the trial and on 86 applications by victims to participate in the proceedings, ICC-01/05-01/08-807-Corr, 12 July 2010, paras 47–49.

how the personal interests of victims were affected in order to be granted access to particular confidential documents filed in the record of the case—and otherwise leaving to the filing party the responsibility to opt for granting access to the LRV or not. Conversely, in the *Katanga and Ngudjolo Chui* case, the Trial Chamber granted the LRV a continuation of the general access to confidential documents which had been granted at pre-trial in that case, pursuant to Rules 131(2) and 92(5) of the ICC RPE.[31]

Further progress has since been made toward a practice of general access to the confidential case file for LRVs. In the *Gbagbo* case,[32] the Prosecution, the Defence and the LRV were directed always to notify all other participants of their confidential filings. 'Where the party or participant filing the document has a good reason not to [notify], it should indicate pursuant to Regulation 23*bis* of the Regulations of the Court the status of the filings as 'confidential and *ex parte*' and the reason for the said classification in the filing itself to enable the Chamber to make its ultimate decision'.[33] This constitutes a step further in as much as the Chamber considers that access to confidential documents at the trial stage is the rule, which implies that the LRVs no longer have to file a specific request to access each and every document filed confidentially.[34] Trial Chamber I in the *Gbagbo*

Footnote 30 (continued)

Trial Chamber III even more restrictively decided to grant access to some specific confidential documents only whenever it resolved that the victims' interests were engaged. Finally, see ICC, *Prosecutor v. Abdallah Banda Abakaer Nourain*, Trial Chamber IV, Decision on the participation of victims in the trial proceedings, ICC-02/05-03/09, 20 March 2014, paras 35–36.

[31] ICC, *Prosecutor v. Germain Katanga and Mathieu Ngudjolo Chui*, Trial Chamber II, Decision on the Modalities of Victim Participation at Trial, ICC-01/04-01/07-1788-tENG, 22 January 2010, paras 121–122.

[32] While this decision was taken prior to the joinder of the *Gbagbo* and the *Blé Goudé* cases, this decision appears to be maintained to date in the new joined case. On 2 and 13 April 2015, Trial Chamber I instructed the parties and participants to indicate any objection, and the reasons therefore, to any party or participant (including the LRV) being granted access to any 'confidential', 'confidential, *ex parte*' or 'under seal' material on the *Gbagbo* and *Blé Goudé* pre-trial and trial case records. ICC, *Prosecutor v. Laurent Gbagbo and Charles Blé Goudé*, Trial Chamber I, Decision on requests for clarification concerning review of the case record and extension of time, ICC-02/11-01/15-30. The Defence (ICC-02/11-01/15-45-Conf), the Prosecution (ICC-02/11-01/15-46) and the Registry (ICC-02/11-01/15-48) submitted their respective observations on 28 and 29 April 2015. On 24 June 2015, Trial Chamber I decided withholding access from any party or participant to any other document or material classified as 'confidential' on the *Gbagbo and Blé Goudé* case records was not justified. ICC, *Prosecutor v. Laurent Gbagbo and Charles Blé Goudé*, Trial Chamber I, Decision on objections concerning access to confidential material on the case record, 24 June 2015, ICC-02/11-01/15-101, para 19.

[33] ICC, *Prosecutor v. Laurent Gbagbo*, Trial Chamber I, Order on the notification of confidential filings to the Legal Representative of victims, ICC-02/11-01/11-724, 20 November 2014, para 1 (referring to the Transcript of hearing on 4 November 2014, ICC-02/11-01/11-T-25-CONF-ENG CT, pp. 4–5).

[34] This decision was upheld by the Trial Chamber following an appeal filed by the Defence. In its 11 March 2015 Decision, the Single Judge of Trial Chamber I confirmed that 'victims' personal interests have been duly taken into consideration in reaching the decision that the LRV

case also dismissed as misconceived a defence argument that materials available to the LRVs be limited on grounds that they are 'third parties'. Rather, the Chamber emphasised the need to ensure that victims' participation is effective. The Chamber underlined that victims 'are participants who are expressly entitled to be notified by the Registrar in a timely manner of, among other things, requests, submissions, motions and documents that form part of the proceedings.'[35] This practice was confirmed by Trial Chamber VI in the *Ntaganda* case a few months later,[36] and by Trial Chamber VIII in the *Al Mahdi* case.[37]

For practitioners, it is important to note that, as illustrated above, ICC Defence teams have generally opposed LRVs' access to confidential filings. Defence teams have argued that at a minimum, the LRV should file a specific motivated request in this regard.[38] The Prosecution, while generally less resistant to such access, nonetheless provides varying levels of access in practice. For example, notification of confidential filings to the LRV is sometimes omitted, without apparent reason.[39] Such instances are likely a combination of oversight and resource limitations (notification appears to improve where Prosecution teams are less busy) although remaining resistance to the role of victims may occasionally still play a role. In some cases, it appears to take trial participants some time to adjust to the notion of having three players rather than two in court proceedings, and hence some time

Footnote 34 (continued)

shall have access to the confidential record of the case, as well as to documents disclosed pursuant to Rule 77 of the Rules and Article 67(2) of the Statute.' The legal basis for granting the LRV access to the confidential record of the case is Rules 92(5) and 131(2) of the RPE (para 22), including to documents disclosed pursuant to Rule 77 of the RPE (paras 24–25) but 'the disclosing party retains the option to not disclose specific documents to the LRV, should there be a justification for it.' See ICC, *Prosecutor v. Laurent Gbagbo*, Trial Chamber I, Decision on Defence's requests seeking leave to appeal the 'Decision on the Legal Representative of Victims' access to certain confidential filings and to the case record' and seeking suspensive effect of it, ICC-02/11-01/11-809, 11 March 2015, paras 22–25, 28, 31, 33, 39.

[35] ICC, *Prosecutor v. Laurent Gbagbo*, Trial Chamber I, Decision on the Legal Representative of Victims' access to certain confidential filings and to the case record, ICC-02/11-01/11-749, 19 January 2015, paras 15 and 20. In so doing, Trial Chamber I also decided that access must be retroactive.

[36] ICC, *Prosecutor v. Bosco Ntaganda*, Trial Chamber VI, Decision on victims' participation in trial proceedings, ICC-01/04-02/06-449, 6 February 2015, paras 55–56.

[37] ICC, *Prosecutor v. Ahmad Al Faqi Al Mahdi*, Trial Chamber VIII, Public redacted version of 'Decision on Victim Participation at Trial and on Common Legal Representation of Victims', ICC-01/12-01/15-97-Red, 8 June 2016, paras 42–43. See also, for restrictions specifically relevant to the case (i.e. notably justified by the accused person's expressed intention to plead guilty and the limited scope of the trial): Public redacted version of 'Decision on Legal Representative of Victims' access to the case record', ICC-01/12-01/15-138-Red, 22 July 2016.

[38] ICC, *Prosecutor v. Laurent Gbagbo*, Trial Chamber I, Single Judge, Decision on the Legal Representative of Victims' access to certain confidential filings and to the case record, ICC-02/11-01/11-749, 19 January 2015.

[39] Personal notes and experience of the author.

is needed for victims to secure their space in those proceedings. In such a context, LRVs ought not to take the implementation of their access rights for granted. However, they should equally view access entitlements (in law and in practice) as something capable of expansion with the right efforts. Should confidential filings be discussed or referred to which the LRV has not had access to, he or she should react promptly and systematically. Ensuring that access rights are achieved in practice will also turn on the development of effective relationships with the parties.

7.1.1.4 Specific Issues Regarding LRV Access to Confidential Documents at the ICC

Although it granted the LRV access to all public and confidential filings, the Pre-trial Chamber in the *Katanga and Ngudjolo Chui* case drew a distinction between access granted to the legal representatives of non-anonymous victims and that granted to legal representatives of anonymous victims.[40] However, given the discriminatory effect of this distinction towards anonymous victims and its impracticability in the context of a collective representation system, this jurisprudence has been progressively abandoned.

As regards the cases where LRVs do not have access to confidential documents, LRVs are also barred from accessing documents that are intrinsically related to their clients: the parties' observations on victims' applications under Rule 89 of the ICC RPE when these observations or their annexes containing the party's analysis *per* victims are classified as confidential.[41] Parties have usually refused to share these observations with LRVs, taking the view that access to this material is not necessary for LRVs to fulfil their mandates.

Despite the generally restrictive approach taken in these cases, some positive developments in the jurisprudence have occurred over time. For example, although chambers have routinely required that the Registry provide LRVs with the application forms of their clients,[42] LRVs were initially provided with only the unredacted versions of their clients' application forms, and were not granted access

---

[40] ICC, *Prosecutor v. Germain Katanga and Mathieu Ngudjolo Chui*, Pre-Trial Chamber I, Decision on Limitations of Set of Procedural Rights for Non-Anonymous Victims, ICC-01/04-01/07-537, 30 May 2008, p. 12.

[41] ICC, *Situation in the Democratic Republic of the Congo*, Pre-Trial Chamber I, Decision on the Requests of the OPCV, ICC-01/04-418, 10 December 2007, paras 16–17; Decision on the Application for Leave to Appeal the Decision on the Requests of the OPCV, ICC-01/04-437, 18 January 2008, p. 3. For different reasoning see: ICC, *Prosecutor v. Thomas Lubanga Dyilo*, Trial Chamber I, Decision on the role of the Office of Public Counsel for Victims and its request for access to documents, ICC-01/04-01/06-1211, 6 March 2008, paras 36–39. See also Chap. 2.

[42] See *inter alia*, ICC, *Prosecutor v. Jean-Pierre Bemba*, Trial Chamber III, Corrigendum to Decision on the participation of victims in the trial and on 86 applications by victims to participate in the proceedings, ICC-01/05-01/08-807-Corr, 12 July 2010, para 102-d-i.

to the redacted versions of these forms which had been provided to the parties for their observations. After several requests introduced by LRVs to gain access to the redacted versions of the application forms of the victims admitted to participate,[43] chambers finally started to include in their decisions an order for the Registry to transmit both the redacted and the unredacted versions of these forms to the LRV.[44] This enables a LRV to know the extent of information to which the Defence and the Prosecution are privy in relation to their clients, 'in order for the [LRV] to discharge [their] duties'.[45]

In addition, ICC jurisprudence has also seen some constructive developments in relation to specific documents which have been recognised as accessible to the LRV. In particular, chambers have recognised that victims' interests are affected by whether the case against the accused is admissible or not, and consequently, LRVs have been given access to the material relevant to admissibility challenges, even where that material is classified as confidential.[46] The same applies to confidential information relating to victims' safety and security, as well as to the overall assessment of the general security situation in the relevant situation—but only upon specific motivated request from the LRV demonstrating how such information may

[43] See *inter alia*, ICC, *Prosecutor v. Jean-Pierre Bemba*, Legal Representatives of Victims, Joint Submissions by the Legal Representatives of Victims on matters which require determination prior to trial, ICC-01/05-01/08-791, 10 June 2010. Progressively since then, chambers have started to provide the LRV access *proprio motu*.

[44] ICC, *Prosecutor v. Charles Blé Goudé*, Pre-Trial Chamber I, Decision on victims' participation in the pre-trial proceedings and related issues, ICC-02/11-02/11-83, 13 June 2014, para 36; ICC, *Prosecutor v. Laurent Gbagbo*, Pre-Trial Chamber I, Corrigendum to the Second decision on victims' participation at the confirmation of charges hearing and in the related proceedings, ICC-02/11-01/11-384-Corr, 6 February 2013, para 57 and Decision on Victims' Participation and Victims' Common Legal Representation at the Confirmation of Charges Hearing and in the Related Proceedings, ICC-02/11-01/11-138, 4 June 2012, para 58; ICC, *Prosecutor v. Uhuru Muigai Kenyatta*, Pre-Trial Chamber II, Decision on Victims' Participation at the Confirmation of Charges Hearing and in the Related Proceedings, ICC-01/09-02/11-267, 26 August 2011, para 109; ICC, *Prosecutor v. William Samoei Ruto and Joshua Arap Sang*, Pre-Trial Chamber II, Decision on Victims' Participation at the Confirmation of Charges Hearing and in the Related Proceedings, ICC-01/09-01/11-249, 7 August 2011, para 94.

[45] ICC, *Prosecutor v. Charles Blé Goudé*, Pre-Trial Chamber I, Second Decision on victims' participation in the pre-trial proceedings and related issues, ICC-02/11-02/11-111, 1 August 2014, paras 18–26, and Decision on victims' participation in the pre-trial proceedings and related issues, ICC-02/11-02/11-83, 11 June 2014, paras 26–38.

[46] ICC, *Prosecutor v. Laurent Gbagbo*, Pre-Trial Chamber I, Decision on the OPCV's "Request to access documents related to the 'Requête relative à la recevabilité de l'affaire en vertu des Articles 19 et 17 du Statut' filed by the Defence on 15 February 2013", ICC-02/11-01/11-406, 18 February 2013, paras 8 and 10. However, earlier in the *Mbarushimana* case, the Pre-Trial Chamber rejected the request of the OPCV (as LRV), to have access to all confidential material related to the Defence's Challenge of the jurisdiction of the Court. See Pre-Trial Chamber I, Decision on the Office of the Public Counsel for Victims' "Request to access documents in the case record in relation to the Defence Challenge to the Jurisdiction of the Court", ICC-01/04-01/10-382, 18 August 2011.

be necessary and/or appropriate for the purposes of the proper discharge of his/her mandate.[47]

Further, individual participating victims 'are to enjoy equal access to any information relating to their right to reparations and to assistance from the Court, as part of their entitlement to fair and equal treatment throughout the proceedings.'[48]

Finally, LRVs should take all necessary steps to seek access to key filings outlining the evidence relied on in the case. Should the pre-trial brief or any similar document be filed confidentially by the Prosecution and not provided to the LRV, the latter should seek access to it in an unredacted form since they have access to all the evidence disclosed in the record of the case, in order to properly prepare for trial and, once again, ensure their effective and efficient participation. The same applies for any document at the heart of the case, such as the decision confirming the charges or the updated document containing the charges.

7.1.2 Access to Evidentiary Material Disclosed by the Parties

Like the questions of access to filings discussed above, the ability of victims' lawyers to access evidence and disclosed material has a fundamental impact on their capacity to carry out their roles in the proceedings.

Practitioners should note that whichever access right is concerned, it is always recommended to request its implementation at the earliest stage possible. This clearly allows a LRV to become familiar with the case at the earliest possible time and be in the best position to follow the proceedings, respect time-limits set, and efficiently participate on any issue touching on the victims' interests, while at the same time minimising the risk of interference with the rights of the other participants, notably the right of the Defence to expeditious proceedings.

7.1.2.1 The Development of This Right in ICC Proceedings

Before the ICC, victims and their legal representatives are recognised as "participants".[49] Whether at the pre-trial or trial stage, disclosure is understood as a process occurring between the Prosecution and the Defence, which are considered the only two "parties" in the proceedings. From the start though, the chambers

---

47 ICC, *Prosecutor v. Joseph Kony, Vincent Otti, Okot Odhiambo and Dominic Ongwen*, Pre-Trial Chamber II, Decision on the OPCV's 'Request to access documents and material', ICC-02/04-01/05-222, 16 March 2007.

48 ICC, *Prosecutor v. Thomas Lubanga Dyilo*, Trial Chamber I, Decision establishing the principles and procedures to be applied to reparations, ICC-01/04-01/06-2904, 7 August 2012, paras 187–188, 198–199, 202–206, 259, 267–268, 284.

49 Except at the reparations stage, where they are recognised as a party, next to the Defence.

recognised the need for LRVs to have access to certain material. Although initially slow-paced, access by LRVs to disclosed material is growing in scope thanks to the frequent and repeated requests made by the LRVs themselves.

At the pre-trial stage, the extent of victims' access to evidentiary material is fundamentally interlinked to the particular approach to disclosure used in ICC pre-trial proceedings. Under the ICC's RPE, evidence which is disclosed between the parties for the purpose of the confirmation hearing shall be communicated to the relevant pre-trial chamber and included in the record of the case.[50] Pre-trial chambers have varied in their views on whether this involves the filing of *all* disclosed material, or only such material as is *relied on* by the parties for the purpose of the confirmation hearing.[51] For victims' lawyers, the consequence of this approach is that their ability to access evidentiary material is closely linked to the extent of their access to the case file (discussed above) and the classification given to the filed evidentiary material.

In most cases at pre-trial before the ICC, LRVs have only been granted access to evidence disclosed by the Prosecution or the Defence where it is classified as public.[52] Consequently, LRVs have usually not been granted access to disclosed evidentiary material filed with a confidential classification. However, some pre-trial chambers have granted LRVs access to the lists of evidence filed by both the parties.[53] The basis of these decisions was that the lists of evidence could be of assistance to the LRV in following the discussions during the hearings and that the *inter partes* nature of the disclosure process was, as such, an insufficient reason to deny access to said material for the LRV.[54] These lists may also be used by LRVs

---

[50] ICC RPE, Rule 121(2)(c) and (10).

[51] See ICC, *Prosecutor v. Thomas Lubanga Dyilo*, Pre-Trial Chamber I, Decision on the final system of disclosure and the establishment of a timetable, ICC-01/04-01/06-102, 16 May 2006; *Prosecutor v. Jean-Pierre Bemba*, Pre-Trial Chamber III, Decision on the Evidence Disclosure System and Setting a Timetable for Disclosure between the Parties, ICC-01/05-01/08-55, 31 July 2008.

[52] When the parties and participants disclose evidentiary material, each item bears the classification public or confidential. Access to any evidence is not automatic for the LRV and it depends on the access rights given by the relevant chamber.

[53] In the *Ruto* case (ICC), following a request submitted by the LRV, the Pre-Trial Chamber also granted the latter access to the lists of evidence which were classified as confidential. See ICC, *Prosecutor v. William Samoei Ruto and Joshua Arap* Sang, Pre-Trial Chamber II, Second Decision on the "Request by the Victims' Representative for access to confidential materials", ICC-01/09-01/11-340, 23 September 2011, para 15.

[54] ICC, *Prosecutor v. Charles Blé Goudé*, Pre-Trial Chamber I, Decision on OPCV requests in relation to the Defence disclosure and list of evidence, ICC-02/11-02/11-167, 24 September 2014, para 11. Actually Rule 121(10) of the RPE foresees that '*the record* [including all documents transmitted pursuant to rule 121, i.e. especially the lists of evidence] *may be consulted by the prosecutor, the person and victims or their legal representatives participating* [...]'—subject to any restrictions concerning confidentiality.

to identify specific documents they consider necessary to access in order to represent the best interest of their clients.[55]

Again, the first exception at pre-trial in the jurisprudence of the Court to date was during the confirmation of charges hearing in the *Katanga and Ngudjolo Chui* case.[56] In that case, the Pre-Trial Chamber gave the LRV access to *all* evidence which had been filed in the record of the case, insisting that if the LRVs cannot access evidence classified confidential, they would be prevented from participating in the evidentiary debates of the hearing.[57] The Pre-Trial Chamber highlighted however some situations in which access to confidential materials would go against the protection of another competing interest and where such access may be limited by a decision of the Chamber.[58] This includes for example where a limitation on access is necessary for the protection of national security, the well-being of victims or witnesses or to safeguard the Prosecution's ongoing investigations.[59] However, any such limitations should be exceptional and must be kept proportional to the interest protected.[60] As previously mentioned, the chamber also drew an additional distinction regarding access, based on the anonymity of participating victims: access to confidential material was granted to legal representatives of any non-anonymous victims, while access to public material only was granted to the legal representatives representing solely anonymous victims. Although this distinction based on anonymity of participating victims has been overcome in subsequent cases, access to confidential evidentiary material in those later cases has mostly been permitted on a case-by-case basis, upon a specifically justified LRV request.[61] However, more recently, the Pre-Trial Chamber in the *Blé Goudé* case

[55] ICC, *Prosecutor v. Laurent Gbagbo*, Pre-Trial Chamber I, Decision on the OPCV's "Requests to receive information and access documents for the effective participation of victims at the confirmation of charges hearing", ICC-02/11-01/11-400, 13 February 2013, paras 15 and 19; ICC, *Prosecutor v. Charles Blé Goudé*, Pre-Trial Chamber I, Second decision on OPCV requests in relation to the Defence disclosure and list of evidence, ICC-02/11-02/11-170, 25 September 2014, p. 5.

[56] ICC, *Prosecutor v. Germain Katanga and Mathieu Ngudjolo Chui*, Pre-Trial Chamber I, Decision on the Set of Procedural Rights Attached to Procedural Status of Victim at the Pre-Trial Stage of the Case, ICC-01/04-01/07-474, 13 May 2008, paras 127 and 132.

[57] Ibid., para 151.

[58] Ibid., paras 146–150.

[59] Ibid., para 147.

[60] Ibid., paras 148 and 150.

[61] ICC, *Prosecutor v. Bosco Ntaganda*, Pre-Trial Chamber II, Decision on the "Joint Request of the Common Legal Representatives to access documents in the Bosco Ntaganda case record", ICC-01/04-02/06-237, 29 January 2014; ICC, *Prosecutor v. Laurent Gbagbo*, Pre-Trial Chamber I, Decision on the OPCV's "Requests to receive information and access documents for the effective participation of victims at the confirmation of charges hearing", ICC-02/11-01/11-400, 13 February 2013. Despite the fact that the following decisions rejected the LRV's requests, they nonetheless reaffirmed the principle of access to confidential documents upon specific motivated request: ICC, *Prosecutor v. William Samoei Ruto and Joshua Arap Sang*, Pre-Trial Chamber II, Decision on the "Request by the Victims' Representative for access to confidential materials" and Requesting Observations from the Prosecutor, ICC-01/09-01/11-337, 21 September 2011 and

requested the Defence and the Prosecution to consider, when disclosing confidential evidence, whether the concerned items/material could be immediately disclosed to the LRV or not.[62] More significantly still, access to all disclosed material was provided to LRVs at the pre-trial stage in *Ongwen*.[63]

Several pre-trial chambers have also required that in preparation for the confirmation of charges hearing, the parties produce an 'in-depth analysis chart' to complement the disclosure of evidence. The chart is 'an auxiliary document next to the document containing the charges and the list of evidence'.[64] This chart is to be filed by the Prosecution,[65] and if the Defence intends to present evidence, by the Defence too, no later than 30 days prior to the commencement of the confirmation of charges hearing pursuant to Rule 121(3) of the ICC RPE.[66] Wherever used it is imperative for the legal representatives of victims to secure access to this document—or at the very minimum a redacted version of it, in order to be in the best

Footnote 61 (continued)

Second Decision on the "Request by the Victims' Representative for access to confidential materials", ICC-01/09-01/11-340, 23 September 2011; ICC, *Prosecutor v. Uhuru Muigai Kenyatta*, Pre-Trial Chamber II, Decision on the Request for Access to Confidential *Inter Partes* Material, ICC-01/09-02/11-326, 14 September 2011.

[62] ICC, *Prosecutor v. Charles Blé Goudé*, Pre-Trial Chamber I, Decision on OPCV requests in relation to the Defence disclosure and list of evidence, ICC-02/11-02/11-167, 24 September 2014. See also Pre-Trial Chamber I, Second decision on OPCV requests in relation to the Defence disclosure and list of evidence, ICC-02/11-02/11-170, 25 September 2014, p. 5.

[63] ICC, *Prosecutor v. Dominic Ongwen*, Pre-Trial Chamber II, ICC-02/04-01/15-350, Decision on contested victims' applications for participation, legal representation of victims and their procedural rights, 27 November 2015, para 29.

[64] ICC, *Prosecutor v. Dominic Ongwen*, Pre-Trial Chamber II, Decision Setting the Regime for Evidence Disclosure and Other Related Matters, ICC-02/04-01/15-203, 27 February 2015, para 39; ICC, *Prosecutor v. Bosco Ntaganda*, Pre-Trial Chamber II, Decision on the "Joint request of the Common Legal Representatives to access documents in the Bosco Ntaganda case record", ICC-01/04-02/06-237, 29 January 2014, paras 20–22.

[65] In-Depth Analysis Charts ('IDAC') have been prepared by the ICC Prosecution as ordered by the pre-trial chambers on a case-specific basis. To date, IDAC have been submitted by the Prosecution in the *Ntaganda* case (ICC-01/04-02/06-217), in the Kenyan cases (ICC-01/09-01/11-241 and ICC-01/09-02/11-257), in the *Bemba* case (ICC-01/05-01/08-781) and in the *Katanga and Ngudjolo Chui case* (ICC-01/04-01/07-1643-Conf). In *Prosecutor v. Jean-Pierre Bemba Gombo* et al., the Prosecution opposed the Defence's request for the production of an IDAC and the Chamber rejected the Defence request (ICC-01/05-01/13-134). In the *Gbagbo* case, an alternative to an IDAC was found more appropriate (ICC-02/11-01/11-432 and 592).

[66] ICC, *Prosecutor v. Dominic Ongwen*, Pre-Trial Chamber II, Decision Setting the Regime for Evidence Disclosure and Other Related Matters, ICC-02/04-01/15-203, 27 February 2015, paras 40–42. See also the Public redacted version of "Notice of intended charges against Dominic Ongwen", 18 September 2015, ICC-02/04-01/15-305-Red2, 24 September 2015; and the Order of Pre-Trial Chamber II, ICC-02/04-01/15-T-6-ENG ET WT, 19 May 2015.

possible position to prepare for the confirmation of charges hearing and to effectively and efficiently participate in it.[67]

It is however important to note that despite the positive development in the *Blé Goudé* and *Ongwen* cases and access to evidence lists and analysis charts, actual access to evidentiary material does not always follow in practice. Consequently, orders following up on the initial, access-granting decisions sometimes become necessary and the legal representatives of victims must follow this process closely in order to ensure timely access.[68]

A different situation applies during the trial phase. In part this arises because material disclosed during the trial phase is not automatically included in the case file, but is disclosed through a separate electronic mechanism. This might be seen as making it easier for chambers to treat the question of access to evidentiary material as distinct from that of access to material in the case file (usually submissions and decisions).

In contrast to that of the pre-trial chambers, the jurisprudence of the Court's trial chambers now requires at a minimum that the Prosecution and Defence provide access to the LRV—via the software used for managing evidentiary material at the trial phase—to all documents relevant to victims' personal interests.[69] The difficulty of course is *how* the parties can identify victims' personal interests. However, this gives a firmer basis for the LRV to request access to such material disclosed between the parties[70]—in the form they have been disclosed to the other party. In addition, the legal representative of dual status victims should enjoy a broader access to material pertaining directly to such individuals he or she represents, in an unredacted form.

[67] ICC, *Prosecutor v. Bosco Ntaganda*, Pre-Trial Chamber II, Decision on the "Joint request of the Common Legal Representatives to access documents in the Bosco Ntaganda case record", ICC-01/04-02/06-237, 29 January 2014, paras 21–22.

[68] ICC, *Prosecutor v. Charles Blé Goudé,* Pre-Trial Chamber I, Decision on OPCV requests in relation to the Defence disclosure and list of evidence, ICC-02/11-02/11-167, 24 September 2014: 'Finally, as concerns the access of the OPCV to the evidence on the Defence list of evidence, it appears that, despite a previous order to this effect [Pre-Trial Chamber I, Decision on victims' participation in the pre-trial proceedings and related issues, ICC-02/11-02/11-83, p. 21; Pre-Trial Chamber I, Second Decision on victims' participation in the pre-trial proceedings and related issues, ICC-02/11-02/11-111, p. 15], the OPCV currently does not have access to the public evidence on the Defence list of evidence. As a result, a specific order to the Registrar is warranted.'

[69] In this regard, the ICC chambers have ordered the parties to review the confidential evidence disclosed with a view to determine whether some items can be disclosed to the LRV. See *inter alia*, ICC, *Prosecutor v. Abdallah Banda Abakaer Nourain*, Trial Chamber IV, Decision on the participation of victims in the trial proceedings, ICC-02/05-03/09-545, 20 March 2014, para 39.

[70] The quoted case-law specified that this access to documents encompasses material disclosed under Article 67(2) of the ICC Statute (exonerating or potentially exonerating evidence) and Rule 77 of the ICC RPE (items in possession or control of the Prosecution which are material to the preparation of the Defence), for which access had not been granted so far.

More recently it appears that the chambers are taking a simpler approach which provides LRVs with blanket access to disclosed material in the case. This approach has been taken in the *Gbagbo/Blé Goudé* and in the *Ntaganda* cases.[71] Similarly, more recently, it has been reaffirmed in the *Al Mahdi* case.[72] In *Ongwen*, general access to confidential disclosed materials has been continued from pre-trial to trial.

Accordingly, practice has developed significantly since the early approach in *Lubanga* which granted access to confidential material only upon a specific and reasoned request.[73] LRVs now enjoy access to both public and, to varying degrees, confidential evidence, in order to ensure effective participation at trial.[74] This access is limited to the legal representatives who are bound by the Code of Professional Conduct for counsel, and cannot be extended to the represented victims themselves.[75]

Documents similar to the in-depth analysis chart submitted at the pre-trial stage are produced at trial, although not provided for expressly in the Court's statutory framework. In the *Kenyan* cases, Trial Chamber V ordered the Prosecution to file a Pre-Trial Brief ('PTB') approximately three months before

---

[71] ICC, *Prosecutor v. Laurent Gbagbo*, Trial Chamber I, Decision on the Legal Representative of Victims' access to certain confidential filings and to the case record, ICC-02/11-01/11-749, 19 January 2015, para 15; see also ICC, *Prosecutor v. Bosco Ntaganda*, Trial Chamber VI, Decision on victims' participation in trial proceedings, ICC-01/04-02/06-449, 6 February 2015, paras 55–56.

[72] ICC, *Prosecutor v. Ahmad Al Faqi Al Mahdi*, Trial Chamber VIII, Public redacted version of 'Decision on Victim Participation at Trial and on Common Legal Representation of Victims', ICC-01/12-01/15-97-Red, 8 June 2016, paras 42–43, and Public redacted version of 'Decision on Legal Representative of Victims' access to the case record', ICC-01/12-01/15-138-Red, 22 July 2016, para 21: in this case though, the Single Judge considered that 'the particular nature of the present case does not make it strictly necessary for the LRV to have access to the confidential 'evidence' disclosed unless the parties intend to rely on them at trial.'

[73] However, in the *Lubanga* case (ICC), the LRVs were systematically notified by the Prosecution of potentially exonerating material and Rule 77 material at trial.

[74] ICC, *Prosecutor v. Uhuru Muigai Kenyatta*, Trial Chamber V, Decision on victims' representation and participation, ICC-01/09-02/11-498, 3 October 2012, para 68; ICC, *Prosecutor v. William Samoei Ruto and Joshua Arap Sang*, Decision on victims' representation and participation, ICC-01/09-01/11-460, 3 October 2012, para 69. This is consistent with the past practice of the Court in the *Lubanga* and *Bemba* cases, where the Prosecution made available to the Legal Representatives of Victims potentially exonerating material disclosed to the Defence pursuant to Article 67(2) of the ICC Statute and Prosecution evidence allowed for inspection by the Defence pursuant to Rule 77 of the ICC RPE. Finally, see ICC, *Prosecutor v. Germain Katanga and Mathieu Ngudjolo Chui*, Trial Chamber II, Decision on the Modalities of Victim Participation at Trial, ICC-01/04-01/07-1788-tENG, 22 January 2010.

[75] See *inter alia*, ICC, *Prosecutor v. Abdallah Banda Abakaer Nourain*, Trial Chamber IV, Decision on the participation of victims in the trial proceedings, ICC-02/05-03/09-545, 20 March 2014, para 38. It is also to be noted that Trial Chamber IV in the *Banda* case made a distinction between access to confidential evidence granted to anonymous and non-anonymous victims. Ibid., paras 18–19.

the trial commencement date.[76] In the *Lubanga* case, Trial Chamber I ordered the Prosecution to prepare a 'Summary of presentation of evidence'.[77] Such documents in essence are deemed to specify, in relation to each count, a summary of the evidence the Prosecution intends to rely upon and clearly explain how the relevant evidence relates to the charges.[78] As discussed above, LRVs should actively seek access to these key documents if such access is not otherwise provided.

Finally, it is important for victims' lawyers to ensure their prompt access to the material disclosed by the Prosecution and by the Defence in preparation of examination/cross-examination of witnesses called at trial. Indeed, because of the way electronic disclosure systems are set up, disclosure between the parties does not automatically correspond to disclosure to the LRV, and consequently, material can be disclosed through the e-discovery software (Ringtail) of the Prosecution and the Defence, but yet not through the Ringtail accounts of the LRV. In this regard, it is important that LRVs follow the process of disclosure very closely and react immediately if, despite orders from the relevant chamber, material is not disclosed to them simultaneously.

7.1.2.2 The Law and Practice at the STL

According to the jurisprudence of the STL to date, Rule 87(A) of the STL RPE entitles victims' legal representatives to receive (and not only inspect) disclosed materials, at both the pre-trial and trial stages.[79] Regarding the scope of the material concerned, the Pre-Trial Judge differentiated between the material disclosed as supporting the Indictment,[80] and materials disclosed on other bases.[81] With regard to the former, he held that, in order for the legal representatives to duly

---

[76] ICC, *Prosecutor v. William Samoei Ruto and Joshua Arap Sang*, Trial Chamber V, Decision on the schedule leading up to trial, ICC-01/09-01/11-440, 9 July 2012, para 16; ICC, *Prosecutor v. Uhuru Kenyatta*, Trial Chamber V, Decision on the schedule leading up to trial, ICC-01/09-02/11-451, 9 July 2012, para 20. The production of such a document was also ordered in the *Ntaganda* case, but this has not been a systematic practice before all trial chambers: ICC, *Prosecutor v. Bosco Ntaganda,* Trial Chamber VI, Decision on the updated document containing the charges, ICC-01/04-02/06-450, 6 February 2015, paras 88–89.

[77] ICC, *Prosecutor v. Thomas Lubanga Dyilo*, Trial Chamber I, Decision Regarding the Timing and Manner of Disclosure and the Date of Trial, 9 November 2007, ICC-01/04-01/06-1019, para 26.

[78] ICC, *Prosecutor v. Bosco Ntaganda*, Trial Chamber VI, Decision on the updated document containing the charges, ICC-01/04-02/06-450, 6 February 2015, paras 88–89.

[79] STL, *Prosecutor v. Ayyash* et al., Pre-Trial Judge, Decision on the VPU's Access to Materials and the Modalities of Victims' Participation in Proceedings before the Pre Trial Judge, Case STL-11-01/PTJ, 18 May 2012, paras 43–46, 54. See also STL, *Prosecutor v. Ayyash* et al., Trial Chamber, Directions on the conduct of the Proceedings, Case STL-11-01/PTJ, 16 January 2014.

[80] Ibid., paras 71–78. Subject to any restriction that the Pre-Trial Judge or the Trial Chamber may determine in the interests of justice, at such time as they are transmitted to the Trial Chamber pursuant to Rule 95(A)(ii) of the STL Rules.

[81] Ibid., para 79.

perform their duties, they should be granted access to the material as soon as possible after their designation. Regarding the latter, the Judge considered that despite the absence of an explicit provision in the Rules granting access to it, in order for 'victims' participation in the proceedings to be effective, the [Legal Representative of Victims] needs to have access to such materials in the same format in which they are made available to the Party to which they were disclosed', and with the same restrictions.[82] These access rights have also been recognised by the Trial Chamber.[83] In practice, the distinction between material disclosed in support of the Indictment and material disclosed on other bases has produced no effect on the LRV's entitlement.

It is further interesting to underline the position of the Pre-Trial Judge in light of a Prosecution request that the Legal Representatives acting on behalf of anonymous victims not be granted access to any Rule 87(A) material: noting that victims are represented in a group by a common legal representative and recalling the professional obligations binding the latter (and the related interdiction to provide such materials to the participating victims themselves), the Pre-Trial Judge decided not to restrict the LRV's right of access.[84]

Finally, in addition, Rule 161 refers to the disclosure of the full statement of any expert witnesses to the opposing party and to the victims participating in the proceedings.

Consequently, access granted to evidence at the STL is quite broad and generally seems to follow a less intricate approach than at the ICC.

7.1.2.3 The General Access to the Case File at the ECCC

At the ECCC, the case file contains all court records and evidence.[85] Rule 86 of the Internal Rules sets the general principle of access to case files: at all times, the lawyers for all parties shall have the right to examine and obtain copies of it.[86] In accordance with the jurisprudence, as a result of being designated as a civil party lawyer, specific rights and obligations apply, among which is access to the case

[82] Ibid., paras 58, 64, 79.

[83] STL, *Prosecutor v. Ayyash* et al., Direction on the Conduct of the Proceedings, STL-11-01/T/TC, 16 January 2014, para 19.

[84] STL, *Prosecutor v. Ayyash* et al., Decision on the VPU's Access to Materials and the Modalities of Victims' Participation in Proceedings Before the Pre-Trial Judge, STL-11-01/PT/PTJ, 18 May 2012, para 80.

[85] As defined in the ECCC Internal Rules, the 'Case file refers to all the written records (*procés verbaux*) of investigative action undertaken in the course of a Preliminary Investigation or a Judicial Investigation, together with all applications by parties, written decisions and any attachments thereto at all stages of the proceedings, including the record of proceedings before the Chambers.' See Internal Rules, Glossary, p. 82.

[86] This is true but for the strictly confidential part of the case file, for which the lawyers of the civil parties at the ECCC have to submit a specific request to access specific documents and files.

file of the judicial investigation to which their client is a party, in paper and electronically.[87] Where confidential information is accessed, civil party lawyers are bound to maintain the confidentiality of that information.

In addition, in accordance with Rule 69(3) of the Internal Rules, if an appeal is filed against a Closing Order, the Civil Party Lead Co-Lawyers will continue having access to the case file 'for the purposes of advance preparation for trial.'

Such general access directly flows from the status of the victims as civil parties in the proceedings, and the lawyers representing civil parties consequently enjoy the same rights and obligations as the other parties before the ECCC. Moreover, this is directly linked to the purpose set for the civil party action before the ECCC, which is to participate in the proceedings by supporting the Prosecution and to seek collective and moral reparations.

7.1.2.4 Challenges Arising from Access to Evidentiary Material

While access to evidentiary material is vital in enabling LRVs at all three tribunals to effectively participate in proceedings, it nonetheless comes with its own challenges.

Typically, cases before international criminal jurisdictions will involve voluminous evidence, and may also include expert evidence of a highly technical nature. Properly engaging with the full body of evidence accessed may present challenges, particularly where LRVs face resource limitations.[88] LRVs should consider at the earliest opportunity what additional resources may be required to facilitate sufficient review of the evidence disclosed to them. This may include importantly: access to document management and case-mapping software, language assistance, additional junior staffing support to review evidence and the involvement of expert witnesses. However, LRVs must also be realistic about their prospects of obtaining significant additional resources, and should not expect to achieve parity with the Prosecution or even the Defence in this respect. As a result, LRVs will almost inevitably need to take strategic decisions about areas of focus and priority, linked also to broader case strategy, in order to maximise the benefits of their evidentiary access without becoming overwhelmed by evidence review.

7.2 Existence of Disclosure Obligations for LRV

The notion of disclosure is closely linked to the role granted to the LRV in proceedings.

---

[87] See for instance, ECCC, *Case 004*, Office of the Co-Investigating Judges, Lawyer's recognition decision concerning all civil party applications on Case File No. 004, Case No. 004/07-09-2009-ECCC-OCIJ, 1 April 2013, para 12.

[88] On the respective arrangements for resourcing victims' legal teams before the three tribunals, see further Chap. 5.

7.2.1 Disclosure Seen as an Inter Partes Process at the ICC

Before the ICC, no general obligations of disclosure fall on the legal representatives of victims. The Appeals Chamber has stated the following on this issue:

> As recalled by the Trial Chamber and conceded by the accused neither the Statute nor the Rules of Procedure and Evidence expressly oblige the Victims to disclose exculpatory evidence to the accused. Rather, article 67(2) of the Statute provides that the Prosecutor is responsible for disclosure of exculpatory evidence. In addition, rule 77 of the Rules of Procedure and Evidence provides that the Prosecutor shall disclose evidence which is material for the preparation of the defence, and evidence which will be used at trial.
>
> The Appeals Chamber also recalls that the drafting history of the Statute supports the notion that the Prosecutor's disclosure obligations to the accused are linked to the Prosecutor's role in conducting the investigation, and stem from the Prosecutor's obligation to investigate incriminating and exonerating circumstance equally under article 54(1)(a) of the Statute. In contrast, as explained in greater detail in the preceding section relating to the first ground of appeal, pursuant to article 68(3) of the Statute, the victims' role in the proceedings is significantly more limited. The Appeals Chamber considers that imposing a general disclosure obligation on the victims to disclose evidence to the accused would disregard the limited role of the victims of presenting their views and concerns where their personal interests are affected. Bearing in mind the differing roles of the victims vis-à-vis the parties, the Appeals Chamber finds that it is inappropriate simply to extend the Prosecutor's statutory obligations to victims participating in the proceedings.[89]

The reason behind the absence of any general disclosure obligation is expressed in the Appeals Chamber's judgment: disclosure at the ICC is conceived as an *inter partes* process.[90] Legal representatives of victims are participants in the proceedings and thus not involved in that process. More specifically, in contrast to the Prosecution, the nature of victims' role in the proceedings means that they *need* not lead evidence.[91]

Despite this, Trial Chamber IV in *Banda*, held that 'there may be specific instances in which a Trial Chamber may require victims to disclose exculpatory evidence in their possession to the accused, such as when a party or participant brings to the attention of the Trial Chamber that such information is available and the Trial Chamber finds that such information is necessary for the determination of

[89] ICC, *Prosecutor v. Germain Katanga and Mathieu Ngudjolo Chui*, Appeals Chamber, Judgment on the Appeal of Mr Katanga Against the Decision of Trial Chamber II of 22 January 2010 Entitled "Decision on the Modalities of Victim Participation at Trial", ICC-01/04-01/07-2288 OA11, 16 July 2010, paras 72 and 75 (emphasis added).

[90] *Idem*, paras 74–75. See also ICC, *Prosecutor v. Dominic Ongwen*, Pre-Trial Chamber II, Decision Setting the Regime for Evidence Disclosure and Other Related Matters, ICC-02/04-01/15-203, 27 February 2015, para 10.

[91] Interestingly, in the *Ongwen* case recently and for the first time, the Trial Chamber invited the LRVs to submit, should they so wish, a "Pre-Trial Brief", like the Prosecution and the Defence. The Trial Chamber did not define or explain what its expectations were with regard to such a document, and it was consequently not understood for the moment as binding the LRVs in relation to any specific possible future disclosure. See ICC, *Prosecutor v. Dominic Ongwen*, Trial Chamber IX, Decision Setting the Commencement Date of the Trial, ICC-02/04-01/15-449, 30 May 2016, para 8.

the truth.'[92] However Trial Chamber IV finally did not issue such an order in that case and it does not appear that this has yet occurred in any other case.

Notwithstanding the absence of a general disclosure obligation, the scenario changes if and when an LRV is granted the possibility to present evidence or have his or her clients appear in person to present their views and concerns. Where an LRV makes an application for one of these purposes, the Trial Chambers have required the submission of a signed statement summarising the proposed testimony or views and concerns. The Trial Chambers specified that such statements will be treated as disclosure in accordance with Regulation 54(f) of the Regulations of the Court—if the Chamber grants the application.[93] In other words, in such circumstances the LRV need not disclose full statements of witnesses comparable to those produced for witnesses called by the Prosecution.

The scenario described above is the usual form of disclosure obligation which can arise for LRVs before the ICC. Disclosure will additionally be required where a legal representative of victims is authorised to meet a witness for a preparation session. In such a case, the chambers will require the LRV to disclose to the Prosecution and the Defence, before the commencement of the evidence of the witness, any new information obtained during the meeting with the witness.[94]

Finally, note that despite Defence requests,[95] ICC chambers have held that there is no general obligation for legal representatives of victims to disclose unredacted versions of their clients' application forms to the parties.[96] A narrow but

---

[92] ICC, *Prosecutor v. Abdallah Banda Abakaer Nourain*, Trial Chamber IV, Decision on the participation of victims in the trial proceedings, ICC-02/05-03/09-545, 20 March 2014, para 40 (referring to ICC, *Prosecutor v. Germain Katanga and Mathieu Ngudjolo Chui*, Appeals Chamber, Judgment on the Appeal of Mr Katanga Against the Decision of Trial Chamber II of 22 January 2010 Entitled "Decision on the Modalities of Victim Participation at Trial", ICC-01/04-01/07-2288 OA11, 16 July 2010, para 71).

[93] ICC, *Prosecutor v. Germain Katanga and Mathieu Ngudjolo Chui*, Trial Chamber II, Directions for the conduct of the proceedings and testimony in accordance with rule 140, ICC-01/04-01/07-1665, 20 November 2009, paras 19–30; ICC, *Prosecutor v. Jean-Pierre Bemba*, Trial Chamber III, ICC-01/05-01/08-2138, Decision on the supplemented applications by the legal representatives of victims to present evidence and the views and concerns of victims, 22 February 2012, paras 23–25. See also Regulations of the Court, ICC-BD/01-03-11, as amended on 2 November 2011.

[94] ICC, *Prosecutor v. William Samoei Ruto and Joshua Arap Sang*, Trial Chamber V(a), Order on the Common Legal Representative's Contact with Witness 536, ICC-01/09-01/11-938, 13 September 2013.

[95] The Defence relied on Rule 81(2) and (5) of the ICC RPE which concern information not disclosed between the parties and that cannot be later introduced into evidence without adequate prior disclosure.

[96] However, if victims' applications for participation which are in the possession of the Prosecution indicate that victims may possess potentially exculpatory information, the Prosecutor's investigation should extend to discovering any such information in the victims' possession. Such information would then be disclosed to the accused pursuant to Article 67(2) of the ICC Statute and Rule 77 of the ICC RPE: ICC, *Prosecutor v. Germain Katanga and Mathieu Ngudjolo Chui*, Appeals Chamber, Judgment on the Appeal of Mr Katanga Against the Decision of Trial Chamber II of 22 January 2010 Entitled "Decision on the Modalities of Victim Participation at Trial", ICC-01/04-01/07-2288 OA11, 16 July 2010, para 81.

important exception in respect of the disclosure of application forms applies where a participating victim has or obtains dual status, or appears to present views and concerns in person (these issues are considered in Chap. 9). If there is a need to maintain redactions of any kind on those application forms (for example to protect third parties), nonetheless the Defence should receive lesser redacted versions than those already provided during the course of the victim application process.[97]

7.2.2 Disclosure Obligations Formalised at the STL

At the STL, disclosure obligations falling on the legal representatives of victims are expressly foreseen in the RPE. Rule 112*bis* provides that when the participating victims are permitted to call evidence at trial, the chamber shall decide on the corresponding disclosure obligations that will be imposed on them.[98] Further, Rule 113(B) also anticipates cases where the LRVs would have in their possession or actual knowledge any information which may reasonably suggest the innocence or mitigate the guilt of the accused. If such a situation arises, the LRVs are bound by the same obligations as the Prosecution, but before disclosing any such information to the Defence, they shall first disclose the material to the Prosecutor. These obligations are subject to Rule 116, which covers applications and grounds for non-disclosure and is applicable *mutatis mutandis* to the LRV.[99]

Rule 114 prescribes that sanctions can equally be imposed by the relevant chamber on LRVs who fail to perform their disclosure obligations pursuant to the Rules.

It follows that at the STL, LRVs are an integral part of the disclosure process. At the time of writing, the Prosecution case in the *Ayyash* et al. trial is still ongoing and decisions have not been rendered yet on the disclosure obligations of the legal representative of victims.

7.2.3 Procedures for the Sharing of Evidence Before the ECCC

Being based on an inquisitorial model, the ECCC legal framework does not involve a system of *inter partes* "disclosure" of the kind which exists at the ICC and STL. In practice, the parties submit documents and materials in the case file

[97] ICC, *Prosecutor v. Thomas Lubanga Dyilo*, Trial Chamber I, Redacted Decision on the disclosure of information from victims' application forms (a/0225/06, a/0229/06 and a/0270/07), ICC-01/04-01/06-2586-Red, 4 February 2011, paras 4–5.

[98] STL RPE, STL-BD-2009-01-Rev.7, amended on 12 February 2015.

[99] STL RPE, STL-BD-2009-01-Rev.7, amended on 12 February 2015, Rule 116(E).

and that action constitutes the equivalent of what at the ICC or the STL is referred to as "disclosure", a term which is not used at the ECCC.

Given the role of the lawyers representing civil parties in the proceedings and the purpose of their participation,[100] typical obligations to provide evidence to the case file apply to them, as much as to the other parties to the case. However, despite the fact that in the ECCC system victims' participation is envisaged as involving the full role of a party, obligations to share evidentiary material are not set out in the same level of detail as is seen in the legal texts of the STL or the jurisprudence of the ICC.

One circumstance in which civil parties' legal representatives are clearly required to provide material to the case file is where they call a witness. Rule 80(2) deals with situations in which a Civil Party Lead Co-Lawyer summonses a witness who is not on the list provided by the Co-Prosecutors, and the documents they must submit into the case file in such circumstances. In practice the Trial Chamber may order the Civil Party Lead Co-Lawyers to file a summary of the facts on which a certain witness is to be heard, including for example the impact on the alleged crimes and the points of the indictment on which said witness is to be heard.[101] In the case where a civil party is interviewed as foreseen in Rule 23(4), similar modalities may attach.

7.3 Submissions by Victims' Lawyers

Before all three courts, the right of victims' lawyers to submit filings is largely uncontested. However the modalities and conditions for such submissions vary from one forum to another.[102]

At the ICC, Article 68(3) of the ICC Statute is the key provision in this regard, and its content is also mirrored by Article 17 of the STL Statute: where the personal interests of the victims are affected, the relevant chamber shall permit their views and concerns to be presented and considered at stages of the proceedings determined to be appropriate and in a manner that is not prejudicial to or inconsistent with the rights of the accused and a fair and impartial trial. At the ICC, Rules 89 to 91 and Rule 93 of the ICC RPE further refer to the possibilities for LRVs to file written submissions or have their views sought by a chamber on specific issues.

---

[100] ECCC Internal Rules, Rule 23(1).

[101] See the reference in ECCC, *Case 002/02*, Trial Chamber, Addendum to Civil Party Lead Co-Lawyers' Rule 80 Witness, Expert and Civil Party Lists for *Case 002/02* with Confidential Annex, Case No. 002/19-09-2007/ECCC/TC, 22 July 2014, para 3.

[102] See for instance, Practice Direction on Filing Documents before the ECCC (Revision 8), ECCC/01/2007/Rev.8, 10 May 2012, Article 2.5.

Indeed, ICC jurisprudence consistently shows that LRVs can submit written submissions, observations or requests if they demonstrate that the criteria of Article 68(3) of the ICC Statute are met. This requires them to show that the personal interests of their clients are affected by the issue at stake, and that their participation will not be prejudicial to or inconsistent with the rights of the accused. As explained in an early decision of Trial Chamber I:

> [I]n relation to the request of the victims legal representatives to be granted the right to initiate procedures (for instance by filing applications and requests), the Trial Chamber considers that there is nothing in the Court's statutory and regulatory provisions which prevents victims from filing requests or applications to the Chamber whenever an issue arises that affects their interests (individually or collectively), in accordance with Article 68(3) of the Statute. The Trial Chamber will decide on any application or request of this kind, having consulted with the parties and other participants to the extent that is appropriate, and bearing in mind the right of the accused to a fair and expeditious trial.[103]

The subject matters on which victims' participation is authorised are not listed in the legal texts of the Court[104] and, rather, it is up to the LRV to follow the proceedings and assess whether and when victims should be heard on a specific issue. It is hence very important for practitioners in general to be continuously informed of the views and concerns of their clients. It is equally important to follow the proceedings consistently in order to be in a position to identify issues concerning their clients and to react in a timely manner. According to some case-law, the legal representatives of victims must present a reasoned application to be allowed to file written submissions on specific issues of law and/or fact.[105] In practice this can take the form of an oral request when the relevant issues arise, advancing the relevant justifications. Alternatively, the written submission for which leave is requested can incorporate the justification for the filing. However, observers of ICC practice may notice that this requirement is not always consistently complied with by victims' representatives, and in some cases chambers do not appear to require it.

In only one case to date this requirement for a specific justification has been expressly dispensed with. Trial Chamber II in the *Katanga and Ngudjolo Chui* case importantly underlined that 'once the Chamber has established that an individual victim may participate in the proceedings under rule 89 of the Rules, this

[103] ICC, *Prosecutor v. Thomas Lubanga Dyilo*, Trial Chamber I, Decision on victims' participation, ICC-01/04-01/06-1119, 18 January 2008, para 118.

[104] ICC, *Prosecutor v. Germain Katanga and Mathieu Ngudjolo Chui*, Pre-Trial Chamber I, Decision on the Set of Procedural Rights Attached to Procedural Status of Victim at the Pre-Trial Stage of the Case, ICC-01/04-01/07-474, 13 May 2008, para 56.

[105] ICC, *Prosecutor v. William Samoei Ruto and Joshua Arap Sang*, Pre-Trial Chamber II, Decision on Victims' Participation at the Confirmation of Charges Hearing and in the Related Proceedings, ICC-01/09-01/11-249, Pre-Trial Chamber II, 5 August 2011, para 101; ICC, *Prosecutor v. Uhuru Muigai Kenyatta*, Pre-Trial Chamber II, Decision on Victims' Participation at the Confirmation of Charges Hearing and in the Related Proceedings, ICC-01/09-02/11-267, 26 August 2011, para 118.

means that the Chamber has thereby recognised that this individual has a personal interest in the trial proceedings' and the 'Chamber considers that the personal interests of each of the victims individually have therefore been demonstrated and that their Legal Representatives need not demonstrate these again at trial.'[106] The Partly Dissenting Opinion of Judge Steiner in the *Bemba* case reaffirms this position: 'Pursuant to article 68(3) of the Statute, victims enjoy an unequivocal statutory right to present their views and concerns whenever their personal interests are affected. Limitations to such an autonomous statutory right shall be interpreted in a strict manner and in compliance with the statutory framework.'[107]

However, where a justification is required for the presentation of victims' views and concerns through written submissions, there is significant support to draw on in the form of statements from various chambers commenting on the importance of making victims' participation meaningful and effective.[108] Such jurisprudence clarifies that the role of victims' participation goes far beyond an interest in reparations and goes to the heart of the proceedings: the search for and the determination of the truth, and the determination of the guilt or innocence of the accused. Trial Chamber II in the *Katanga and Ngudjolo Chui* case recalled that 'the participation of victims in the fact-finding process of the Court is conditional upon their making a real contribution to the search for the truth'.[109] In the *Lubanga* case, Trial Chamber I insisted on the fact that 'the participation by victims should encompass their personal interests in an appropriately broad sense, and [...] whenever necessary they should be entitled to express their views and concerns through statements, examination of witnesses or by filing written submissions.'[110] The Trial Chamber specified also that victims' participation 'may be an important factor

---

[106] ICC, *Prosecutor v. Germain Katanga and Mathieu Ngudjolo Chui*, Trial Chamber II, Decision on the Modalities of Victim Participation at Trial, ICC-01/04-01/07-1788-tENG, 22 January 2010, paras 61–64.

[107] ICC, *Prosecutor v. Jean-Pierre Bemba*, Partly Dissenting Opinion of Judge Sylvia Steiner on the Decision on the supplemented applications by the Legal Representatives of victims to present evidence and the views and concerns of victims, Trial Chamber III, ICC-01/05-01/08-2140, 22 February 2012, para 18.

[108] ICC, *Situation in The Democratic Republic of the Congo*, Pre-Trial Chamber I, Decision on the Applications for participation in the proceedings of VPRS 1, VPRS 2, VPRS 3, VPRS 4, VPRS 5 and VPRS 6 (Public Redacted Version), ICC-01/04-101-tEN-Corr, 17 January 2006, para 71: At the outset, '[t]he use of the present tense in the French version of the text ('la Cour permet') of article 68(3) of the ICC Statute makes it clear that the victims' guaranteed rights of access to the Court entails a positive obligation for the Court to enable them to exercise that right concretely and effectively'.

[109] ICC, *Prosecutor v. Germain Katanga and Mathieu Ngudjolo Chui*, Trial Chamber II, Decision on the Modalities of Victim Participation at Trial, ICC-01/04-01/07-1788-tENG, 22 January 2010, paras 86–93.

[110] ICC, *Prosecutor v. Thomas Lubanga Dyilo*, Trial Chamber I, Decision on victims' participation, ICC-01/04-01/06-1119, 18 January 2008, paras 97–100. See also ICC, *Prosecutor v. Germain Katanga and Mathieu Ngudjolo Chui*, Trial Chamber II, Decision on the Modalities of Victim Participation at Trial, ICC-01/04-01/07-1788-tENG, 22 January 2010, paras 53–57.

in helping the Chamber to better understand the contentious issues of the case in light of their local knowledge and socio-cultural background'.[111]

In requesting leave to file submissions on certain issues, victims' lawyers are likely to be assisted by precedents demonstrating that particular types of issues affect the interests of victims. Thus for example, previous decisions have permitted victims to make submissions on issues relating to the admissibility and probative value of the evidence on which the Prosecution and the Defence intend to rely.[112] Likewise, victims have been permitted to file written submissions with the pre-trial and trial chambers on legal issues to be discussed at the confirmation hearing and at trial[113] and to raise objections or make observations concerning issues related to the proper conduct of the proceedings.[114] In practice, however,

[111] ICC, *Prosecutor v. Germain Katanga and Mathieu Ngudjolo Chui*, Trial Chamber II, Directions for the conduct of the proceedings and testimony in accordance with rule 140, ICC-01/04-01/07-1665, 20 November 2009, paras 82–91. Although the Chamber's comment was made in the context of questions put by the LRV to a witness, it illustrates the value which the Judges attribute to victims' participation in the proceedings, something which may also be relevant in respect of written submissions. In the *Lubanga* case for instance, Trial Chamber I expressed appreciation for local and national knowledge brought to the proceedings by the written filings of the LRVs: See ICC, *Prosecutor v. Thomas Lubanga Dyilo*, Trial Chamber I, Decision on victims' participation, ICC-01/04-01/06-1119, 18 January 2008, paras 108-111; ICC, *Prosecutor v. Jean-Pierre Bemba*, Trial Chamber III, Corrigendum to Decision on the participation of victims in the trial and on 86 applications by victims to participate in the proceedings, ICC-01/05-01/08-807-Corr, 30 June 2010, paras 30–40.

[112] See for instance submissions authorised on Article 61(7)(c)(ii) of the ICC Statute, ICC, *Prosecutor v. William Samoei Ruto and Joshua Arap* Sang, Pre-Trial Chamber II, Decision on the "Renewed Request by the Victims' Representative for authorisation by the Chamber to make submissions on specific issues of law and/or fact", ICC-01/09-01/11-338, 22 September 2011, paras 5–12.

[113] See ICC, *Prosecutor v. Thomas Lubanga Dyilo*, Pre-Trial Chamber I, Decision on the Arrangements for Participation of Victims a/0001/06, a/0002/06 and a/0003/06 at the Confirmation Hearing, ICC-01/04-01/06-462-tEN, 22 September 2006, para 5; ICC, *Prosecutor v. Bahar Idriss Abu Garda*, Pre-Trial Chamber I, Decision on victims' modalities of participation at the Pre-Trial Stage of the Case, ICC-02/05-02/09-136, 6 October 2009, paras 16–20. See also submissions authorised in the context of review proceedings based on Article 53(3)(a) of the ICC Statute: ICC, *Situation on Registered Vessels of the Union of the Comoros, the Hellenic Republic and the Kingdom of Cambodia*, Pre-Trial Chamber I, Decision on the Victims' Participation, ICC-01/13-18, 24 April 2015 (victims participation in the context of the review proceedings regarding the Prosecutor's decision not to open an investigation pursuant to Article 53(3)(a) of the ICC Statute). See finally submissions in the context of judicial proceedings affecting investigations: ICC, *Situation in the Republic of Kenya*, Pre-Trial Chamber II, Decision on the "Victims' request for review of Prosecution's decision to cease active investigation", ICC-01/09-159, 5 November 2015. As previously mentioned (*supra* footnote 93), note also the recent novelty introduced in the *Ongwen* case, in which the Chamber invited the LRVs to file, if they so wished, a "Pre-Trial Brief" too, next to the ones to be filed by the Prosecution and eventually the Defence, See ICC, *Prosecutor v. Dominic Ongwen*, Trial Chamber IX, Decision Setting the Commencement Date of the Trial, ICC-02/04-01/15-449, 30 May 2016, para 8.

[114] This is despite the fact that some provisions in the Court's legal texts appear to suggest that such submissions may only be received from the parties: see for example Rules 121(9) and 122(3) of the ICC RPE.

the LRV will still be required by some chambers to explain why the personal interests of victims are concerned by the issues discussed.

One important exception from the need to request and specifically justify submissions concerns the filing of responses. Once granted the right to participate in the proceedings, Regulation 24(2) of the Regulations of the Court permits the LRV to file responses to any submissions. According to the practice of the Court, this possibility is always available, and does not require victims' lawyers to specifically demonstrate how their clients' interests are affected by the issue in question. In this regard, the Single Judge of Pre-Trial Chamber I in the *Katanga and Ngudjolo Chui* case underlined that the systematic approach adopted 'aims to ensure that the rule attributed to those granted the procedural status of victim at the pre-trial stage of a case before the Court is: [...] (iv) meaningful—and not purely symbolic—as would be the case if victims were required to ask for the leave of the competent Chamber to perform the most simple procedural activity, such as responding to the submissions of a party'.[115] However, just like other participants, victims wishing leave to reply to a response from another party must request leave of a chamber, as specified in Regulation 24(5) of the Regulations of the Court.[116]

In contrast, it is clear that on certain other matters victims are not permitted to file submissions. For example, victims have not been permitted to file submissions aimed at *extending* the *factual* basis of the charges, since this is a matter remaining under the sole responsibility of the Prosecution.[117]

A final point concerns the classifications which are available to victims' representatives when filing submissions. Initially a restrictive approach was taken.

[115] ICC, *Prosecutor v. Germain Katanga and Mathieu Ngudjolo Chui*, Pre-Trial Chamber I, Decision on the Set of Procedural Rights Attached to Procedural Status of Victim at the Pre-Trial Stage of the Case, ICC-01/04-01/07-474, 13 May 2008, para 51.

[116] In some cases chambers may anticipate and grant leave to reply in advance of any request being made. For example, ICC, *Prosecutor v. Jean-Pierre Bemba*, Trial Chamber III, Decision (i) ruling on legal representatives' applications to question Witness 33 and (ii) setting a schedule for the filing of submissions in relation to future applications to question witnesses, ICC-01/05-01/08-1729, 9 September 2011, paras 13–14.

[117] ICC, *Prosecutor v. Germain Katanga and Mathieu Ngudjolo Chui*, Pre-Trial Chamber I, Decision on the Set of Procedural Rules Attached to Procedural Status of Victim at the Pre-Trial Stage of the Case, ICC-01/04-01/07-474, 13 May 2008, paras 141–144; Trial Chamber II, Directions for the conduct of the proceedings and testimony in accordance with rule 140, ICC-01/04-01/07-1665, 20 November 2009; Trial Chamber II, Decision on the "Prosecution's Application Concerning Disclosure by the Defence Pursuant to Rules 78 and 79(4)", ICC-01/04-01/07-2388-Corr, 14 September 2010. The right to make challenges to, or raise issues relating to, the jurisdiction of the Court or the admissibility of a case pursuant to Article 19(2) and (3) of the ICC Statute and Rule 122(2) of the ICC RPE is also not granted to the LRVs. See ICC, *Prosecutor v. Germain Katanga and Mathieu Ngudjolo Chui*, Pre-Trial Chamber I, Decision on the Set of Procedural Rules Attached to Procedural Status of Victim at the Pre-Trial Stage of the Case, ICC-01/04-01/07-474, 13 May 2008, paras 122–123.

In the *Lubanga* case, Trial Chamber I considered that the Legal Representatives of Victims would only be permitted to make written submissions classified confidential or *ex parte* on a very exceptional basis. This, despite the fact that the criteria applying to such submissions are clearly set and regulated by the Regulations of the Court for all parties and participants.[118] However, chambers no longer question the possibility for LRVs to file submissions on a confidential or *ex parte* basis when those classifications are properly justified (for instance for protective issues related to some of their clients). Like other participants, LRVs must justify the restricted status of a filing and are requested to file redacted confidential or public versions of their applications when it is possible to do so without defeating the purpose of the submission or its original restricted classification.

At the STL, the LRV can submit filings at both pre-trial and trial stages. Although Rule 87(B) of the STL RPE only refers to the trial stage when stating the right of the LRV to file motions and briefs, this same approach has been applied at pre-trial as well.[119] Moreover, in the *Ayyash* et al. case, the LRV does not need to request leave to submit filings, although submissions are typically filed pursuant to Article 17 and thc rclevance of the personal interests of victims is also explained. Rule 87(C) also permits the filing of written submissions relating to the personal impact of the crimes on the victims at the sentencing stage. As for the appeal stage, Rule 87(D) simply says that participating victims may participate in the proceedings in a manner deemed appropriate by the Appeals Chamber. The LRV have certain limited rights to file interlocutory appeals, an aspect which is elaborated in Chap. 12.

At the ECCC, Rules 55(10) (investigative requests)[120] and 92 (written submissions)[121] set out the legal grounds on which lawyers representing civil parties may make written submissions as provided in the Practice Direction on Filing of Documents,[122] up until closing statements.[123] Civil parties have a broad right to

[118] ICC, *Prosecutor v. Thomas Lubanga Dyilo*, Trial Chamber I, Decision on victims' participation, ICC-01/04-01/06-1119, 18 January 2008, paras 113–114.

[119] STL, *Prosecutor v. Ayyash* et al., Pre-Trial Judge, Decision on the VPU's Access to Materials and the Modalities of Victims' Participation in Proceedings before the Pre Trial Judge, Case STL-11-01/PTJ, 18 May 2012, para 31. See also STL, *Prosecutor v. Ayyash* et al., Trial Chamber, Directions on the conduct of the Proceedings, Case STL-11-01/TC, 16 January 2014.

[120] ECCC, Internal Rules, Rule 55(10): 'At any time during an investigation, the Co-Prosecutors, a Charged Person or a Civil Party may request the Co-Investigating Judges to make such orders or undertake such investigative action as they consider useful for the conduct of the investigation.'

[121] ECCC, Internal Rules, Rule 92: 'The parties may, up until the closing statements, make written submissions as provided in the Practice Direction on filing of documents.

[122] ECCC, Practice Direction on Filing Documents (Revision 8), ECCC/01/2007/Rev.8, 10 May 2012.

[123] ECCC, Internal Rules, Rule 39. On Time Limits and Conditions for Filing Documents.

file submissions.[124] In this regard, the Civil Party Lead Co-Lawyers can submit observations and requests on any area identified as of interest to their clients, without having to provide any justification. In concrete terms, such an opportunity can help achieve specific steps in the proceedings for the benefit of victims, leaving more space for the victims' lawyers to present the views of victims in the proceedings and to translate throughout the proceedings their stories and the consequences of the harms they have suffered.[125]

In the same vein, civil parties benefit from an automatic right to file responses to any submissions introduced in the case file, but, as is also the case before the ICC and the STL, must request leave to file a reply.[126] Submissions filed on behalf of civil parties must be signed by the Civil Party Lead Co-Lawyers, as opposed to civil party lawyers engaged by only part of the civil party group.[127]

Finally, while at the ICC participating victims have not yet been granted the right to react to decisions assessing victims' applications, the Internal Rules of the ECCC and the RPE of the STL enable victims to do so, albeit through appeal proceedings.[128]

7.4 Key Points

General

- Access to material in the case mainly refers to access to two types of material: procedural documents (submissions of the parties or participants, and decisions of the chambers) and evidentiary material (material disclosed by parties or participants in relation to their case).
- The possibility for victims' lawyers to access documents filed and material disclosed in the case constitutes the key to all other modalities of victim participation granted at the ICC, STL and ECCC. Without such access, the lawyers

---

[124] See for instance: ECCC, *Case 002*, Requests for Further Investigation: Civil Party Lawyers' Request for Supplementary Investigations regarding Genocide of the Khmer Krom and the Vietnamese, Case No. 002/19-09-2007/ECCC/OCIJ, 10 August 2012; Request for financial investigation into the assets of the accused in Case 2; Case No. 002/19-09-2007/ECCC/OCIJ, Civil Party Lawyers' Request For Supplementary Investigations regarding Genocide Of The Khmer Krom and The Vietnamese, 3 December 2009.

[125] ECCC, *Case 002*, Civil Parties' Co-lawyers' 4th Request for investigative actions concerning Forced Marriages and Sexually Related Crimes, Case No. 002/19-09-2007/ECCC/OCIJ, 4 December 2009.

[126] Practice Direction on Filing Documents before the ECCC (Revision 8), ECCC/01/2007/Rev.8, 10 May 2012.

[127] See Chap. 5.

[128] ECCC, Internal Rules, Rule 74.4. This type of decision is not appealable by the LRV at the ICC for instance. See also STL RPE, Rule 86(C). See also Chap. 12.

cannot follow adequately the proceedings they are involved in and cannot fulfil their role and mandate of ensuring the effective participation of the represented victims.

Access rights of participating victims

- The general rule at the ICC and the STL is that individual participating victims (as opposed to their lawyers) can access public, but not confidential, information. Requests for access to confidential information by an individual victim, if allowed at all, must be specifically justified. ECCC practice gives civil parties access to public information and allows their lawyers to access or inspect documents containing confidential information.

Access rights of victims' lawyers

(a) *Access to filings*

- STL case-law grants legal representatives access to confidential information. The ICC initially denied access to confidential information to victims' lawyers, although recent decisions have shown a neat tendency to depart from that approach. At the ECCC, the lawyers representing civil parties are permitted to examine and copy the original case file of the judicial investigation to which their clients are party.
- As a matter of principle, victims' lawyers at all three courts enjoy broad access to public documents.
- ICC pre-trial chambers have mostly limited LRVs' access to public documents. Conversely, Pre-Trial Chamber I in the *Katanga and Ngudjolo Chui* case granted access to all public and confidential filings and decisions and to the transcripts of both public and closed session hearings contained in the record of the case. More recently pre-trial access to the confidential case file was also provided in *Ongwen*.
- At the trial stage, the chambers in the *Lubanga*, *Bemba*, *Banda* and in the *Kenyan* cases all required LRVs to file specific motivated requests demonstrating how the personal interests of victims were affected in order to be granted access to particular confidential documents filed in the record of the case. Conversely, in the *Katanga and Ngudjolo Chui* case and in *Gbagbo and Blé Goudé*, *Bosco* and *Ongwen*, trial chambers granted the LRV a general access to confidential documents.
- Despite the often restrictive approach at the ICC, legal representatives of victims have been given access to the material relevant to admissibility challenges, even where that material is classified as confidential, to confidential information relating to victims' safety and security, as well as to the overall assessment of the general security situation in the relevant situation. However, before some chambers such access has been provided only upon a specific motivated request from the LRV demonstrating how such information relates to the proper discharge of his or her mandate.

- Where access to confidential material has been restricted by a chamber, LRVs should nonetheless take all necessary steps to seek access to key filings outlining the evidence relied on in the case. Should the Pre-Trial Brief or any similar documents be filed confidentially by the Prosecution and not provided to the LRV, the latter should seek access to it, in order to prepare properly for trial and ensure the effective participation of victims. The same applies for any document at the heart of the case, such as the decision confirming the charges or the updated document containing the charges.

(b) *Access to evidentiary material*

- The ability of victims' lawyers to access evidence and material disclosed has a fundamental impact on their capacity to carry out their roles in the proceedings.
- In most cases at pre-trial before the ICC, LRVs have only been granted access to evidence disclosed by the Prosecution or the Defence where it is classified as public. However, some pre-trial chambers have granted LRVs access to the lists of evidence filed by both the parties. Broader access during the pre-trial stage was granted in the *Katanga and Ngudjolo Chui* case, where the Pre-Trial Chamber gave the LRVs access to *all* evidence which had been filed in the record of the case. The same approach has since been taken in *Gbagbo and Blé Goudé*, *Bosco* and *Ongwen*.
- Several ICC pre-trial chambers have also required that in preparation for the confirmation of charges hearing, the parties produce an 'in-depth analysis chart' to complement the disclosure of evidence. Wherever used it is imperative for the legal representatives of victims to secure access to this document—or at the very minimum a redacted version of it, in order to be in the best possible position to prepare for the confirmation of charges hearing and to effectively participate in it.
- The jurisprudence of most ICC trial chambers now requires the Prosecution and Defence to provide access to LRVs—via the software used for managing evidentiary material at the trial phase—to all documents relevant to victims' personal interests. The difficulty of course is *how* the parties can identify victims' personal interests. However, this gives a firmer basis for the legal representatives to request access to such material disclosed between the parties. More recently some chambers have granted full access to all disclosed material—this has occurred for example in *Ongwen*.
- STL Rule 87(A) entitles LRV to receive (and not only inspect) disclosed materials, at both the pre-trial and trial stages.
- At the ECCC, as a result of being designated as a civil party lawyer, specific rights and obligations apply, among which access to the case file

of the judicial investigation to which their client is a party, in paper and electronically.

Disclosure obligations of victims' lawyers

- Before the ICC, no general obligations of disclosure fall on the legal representatives of victims. Specific obligations will arise if LRVs are granted the possibility to present evidence or have their clients appear in person to present their views and concerns, or if an LRV is authorised to meet a witness for a preparation session.
- STL Rule 112*bis* provides that when the participating victims are permitted to call evidence at trial, the Chamber shall decide on the corresponding disclosure obligations that will be imposed on them. Rule 113(B) provides that, as regards exculpatory information, the LRVs have the same disclosure obligation as the Prosecution.
- The ECCC legal framework does not involve a system of *inter partes* "disclosure" of the kind which exists at the ICC and STL. In practice, the parties submit documents and materials in the case file and that action constitutes the equivalent of what at the ICC or the STL is referred to as "disclosure". Given the role of the lawyers representing civil parties in the proceedings and the purpose of their participation, typical obligations to provide evidence to the case file apply to them, as much as to the other parties to the case.

Rights to submit filings

- Before all three courts, the right of victims' lawyers to submit filings is largely uncontested. However, the modalities and conditions for such submissions vary from one forum to another.
- ICC jurisprudence consistently shows that legal representatives of victims can submit written submissions, observations or requests. However, they may be required to demonstrate that the criteria of Article 68(3) of the ICC Statute are met: namely that the personal interests of their clients are affected by the issue at stake and that their participation will not be prejudicial to or inconsistent with the rights of the accused. Some chambers have taken, however, a generally permissive approach. Trial Chamber II in the *Katanga and Ngudjolo Chui* case held that 'once the Chamber has established that an individual victim may participate in the proceedings', the 'Chamber considers that the personal interests of each of the victims individually have therefore been demonstrated and that their Legal Representatives need not demonstrate these again at trial'.
- At the STL, the LRV can submit filings at both pre-trial and trial stages. Although Rule 87(B) only refers to the trial stage when stating the right of the LRV to file motions and briefs, this right was interpreted to apply at pre-trial stage as well. Moreover, in the *Ayyash* et al. case, the LRV does not need to request leave to submit filings, although submissions are typically filed pursuant to Article 17 and the relevance of the personal interests of victims is also explained.

- At the ECCC, Civil Party Lead Co-Lawyers can submit observations and requests on any area identified as of interests for their clients, without having to provide any justification.

References

Code of Professional Conduct for Counsel, Resolution ICC-ASP/4/Res.1, adopted at the 3rd Plenary Meeting on 2 December 2005, by consensus

Code of Professional Conduct for Defence Counsel and Legal Representatives of Victims appearing before the Special Tribunal for Lebanon, STL/CC/2012/03, adopted 14 December 2012

Chapter 8
Victims' Lawyers in the Courtroom: Opening and Closing Statements, Questioning Witnesses, Challenging and Presenting Evidence

Peter Haynes

Abstract The role victims' lawyers fulfil in the courtroom is one of the most significant expressions of victims' rights in international criminal justice. The three courts analysed in this book—the International Criminal Court, the Extraordinary Chambers in the Courts of Cambodia, and the Special Tribunal for Lebanon—all permit, albeit to varying degrees, the presence and active participation of lawyers representing victims in their proceedings. This chapter will look at the main content of that participation: making opening and closing statements, questioning the witnesses of the (other) parties, calling evidence and making submissions on sentencing. The chapter will highlight the existing practice on these issues and make brief recommendations, where necessary. The main conclusion to be drawn is, however, that the rights and duties of victims' lawyers in the courtroom are still under development and case-law at all three courts is still evolving. The key points at the end of the chapter will summarise the main findings.

Keywords Opening statements · Questioning witnesses · List of questions · Scope of questioning · Mode of questioning · Length of questioning · Challenging evidence · Calling evidence · Personal interests of victims · Rights of the accused · Determination of the truth · Closing arguments · Sentencing submissions

---

Peter Haynes is Lead Legal Representative of Victims in the *Ayyash* et al. case at the Special Tribunal for Lebanon. He is also Lead Counsel for Defence in *Prosecutor v. Jean Pierre Bemba Gombo* at the International Criminal Court. The views expressed herein are those of the author and do not necessarily reflect the views of the employing organisations.

P. Haynes (✉)
Special Tribunal for Lebanon, The Hague, The Netherlands
e-mail: haynes@stl-tsl.org

K. Tibori-Szabó and M. Hirst (eds.), *Victim Participation in International Criminal Justice*, International Criminal Justice Series 11,
DOI 10.1007/978-94-6265-177-7_8

Contents

8.1 Introduction

This chapter focuses on the role played by victims' lawyers in the courtroom. Among the many modalities of participation, those related to court proceedings are arguably the most significant for ensuring effective victim representation. The next chapter looks at the forms in which victims can participate in person in the proceedings. The two chapters should therefore be read together.

This chapter will briefly review the rules and the practice regarding the extent to which victims' lawyers may make opening statements, question the parties' witnesses, challenge their evidence, call evidence in the victims' case, submit closing arguments and statements on sentencing at the International Criminal Court (ICC), the Extraordinary Chambers for the Courts of Cambodia (ECCC) and the Special Tribunal for Lebanon (STL). The chapter will only focus on these modalities during trial proceedings.

There is scant consistency, not just between these three institutions as to extent to which those representing victims are permitted to participate in the trial, but even as between the various trial chambers which have set the limits of participation within one court.

In practical terms, there has been significant difference between the most restrictive practices, which have placed rigid temporal and contextual limits upon the ability of lawyers representing victims to call or challenge evidence at trial, and the most permissive, which have allowed them broad rights of examination.

8.2 The Right to Make Opening Statements

At the ECCC, the right to make an opening statement under Internal Rule 89*bis* is limited to the Defence and the Prosecution. However, at the ICC and the STL, also victims' lawyers are able to make opening statements. The courts' texts do not provide clarity regarding the purpose and permissible content of these statements. It is therefore useful to consider the practice to date in this area.

Rule 89(1) of the ICC RPE states that appropriate modalities of victim participation may include making opening statements, if the Chamber so specifies. Thus far, Chambers have allowed the legal representative of victims to make opening statements immediately after that of the Prosecution.[1] In the *Ongwen* case Trial Chamber IX permitted the legal representatives to opt instead for an opening statement presented immediately before the commencement of the victims' case, following the end of evidence led by the Prosecution.[2]

In the *Lubanga* case, the OPCV representative and each of the six legal representatives present at the opening hearing was allowed to submit remarks for 15–20 min.[3] The Trial Chamber warned victims' lawyers that, '[i]n order to ensure that what happens during opening statements remains proportional and appropriate', the judges will act as 'astute policemen and policewomen of the length of time that speeches take.'[4] In their opening statements, the legal representatives touched upon various topics, such as the importance of and reasons for victim participation,[5] its cathartic and restorative virtues,[6] the practice of (forced) recruitment of child soldiers and the often ensuing rape, forced marriage and sexual slavery, the resulting physical and psychological harm suffered by victims, as well as the risks involved in participation before the ICC.[7] One legal representative was cautioned by the Chamber to focus on the case at hand rather than make allegations regarding an accused in another case of the Court.[8] Another representative was cautioned against addressing directly the accused Lubanga.[9]

In the *Katanga and Ngudjolo Chui* case, opening statements by the legal representatives were made on 24 November 2009.[10] The Chamber granted a total of

---

[1] ICC, *Prosecutor v. Thomas Lubanga Dyilo*, Trial Chamber I, Decision on Victims' Participation, ICC-01/04-01/06-1119, 18 January 2008, para 117; ICC, *Prosecutor v. Germain Katanga and Mathieu Ngudjolo Chui*, Trial Chamber II, Decision on the Modalities of Victim Participation at Trial, ICC-01/04-01/07-1788-tENG, 22 January 2010, para 68.

[2] ICC, *Prosecutor v. Dominic Ongwen*, Trial Chamber IX, Initial Directions on the Conduct of the Proceedings, ICC-02/04-01/15-497, 13 July 2016, para 7.

[3] ICC, *Prosecutor v. Thomas Lubanga Dyilo*, Trial Chamber I, Official Public Transcript, ICC-01/04-01/06-T-101-ENG, 12 January 2009, pp. 9–10.

[4] ICC, *Prosecutor v. Thomas Lubanga Dyilo*, Trial Chamber I, Official Public Transcript, ICC-01/04-01/06-T-104-ENG, 16 January 2009, p. 58.

[5] ICC, *Prosecutor v. Thomas Lubanga Dyilo*, Trial Chamber I, Official Public Transcript, ICC-01/04-01/06-T-107-ENG, 26 January 2009, pp. 39–42 (Remarks by Ms. P. Massida).

[6] Ibid., p. 41 (Remarks by Ms. P. Massida).

[7] Ibid., pp. 50–57 (Remarks by Ms. C. Bapita).

[8] Ibid., p. 47 (Remarks by Mr. H. Diakiese) and 70.

[9] Ibid., pp. 69 (Remarks by Mr. L. Walleyn) and 70–71.

[10] ICC, *Prosecutor v. Germain Katanga and Mathieu Ngudjolo Chui*, Trial Chamber II, Official Public Transcript, ICC-01/04-01/07-T-80-ENG, 24 November 2009, pp. 39–48.

40 min for their submissions.[11] In his opening remarks, the lawyer representing the group of participating victims consisting of child soldiers talked about the plight of his clients, the physical and psychological harm they suffered as well as the concerns of the victims as regards the many other crimes left unprosecuted by the Court.[12] The legal representative for the other group of victims highlighted his clients' regret as regards the geographic remoteness of the Court, but emphasised that the trial would also have several beneficial effects, such as help victims mourn their loss, establish the truth, end impunity and the cycle of violence as well as provide reparation.[13]

In the *Bemba* case, victims' representatives were allowed a total of 1 h to make their opening statements.[14] Both legal representatives focused mainly on the crimes purportedly committed by troops allegedly under command of the accused as well as his alleged acts.[15] One of the representatives greatly emphasised the role rape played as a weapon of war.[16]

The prosecutorial tenor is palpable in virtually all opening statements in the cases mentioned above.[17] Nonetheless, compared to the opening statements in the *Lubanga* and *Katanga and Ngudjolo Chui* cases, the remarks of the legal representatives in *Bemba* struck a significantly more prosecutorial tone.

Victims participating at the STL are authorised to make opening statements under Rule 143. The *Ayyash* et al. trial began on 16 January 2014. After the Prosecution's opening statement, on 17 January 2014, each of the three legal representatives (assigned to represent the same group of participating victims) took the floor, for a total of approximately 90 min. The first representative to speak focused on the importance of the STL in the fight to end impunity in Lebanon and compared the Tribunal to a 'lever of justice'.[18] The second representative spoke about the 14 February 2005 attack (forming the basis of the indictment) and its impact on Lebanese society.[19] The third counsel to take the floor stressed the importance of victim participation and outlined the rights and the case theory of the participating victims. He also introduced the nine (9) victims attending the courtroom that day.[20]

---

[11] Ibid., p. 38.

[12] Ibid., pp. 39–45 (Remarks by Mr. J.L. Gilissen).

[13] Ibid., pp. 45–48 (Remarks by Mr. F.N. Luvengika).

[14] ICC, *Prosecutor v. Jean Pierre Bemba Gombo*, Trial Chamber III, Official Public Transcript, ICC-01/05-01/08-T-30-ENG, 21 October 2010, p. 6.

[15] ICC, *Prosecutor v. Jean Pierre Bemba Gombo*, Trial Chamber III, Official Public Transcript, ICC-01/05-01/08-T-32-ENG, 22 November 2010, pp. 36–39 (Remarks by Mr. A. Zarambaud), pp. 40–43 (Remarks by Ms. M.E. Douzima-Lawson).

[16] Ibid., p. 41 (Remarks by Ms. M.E. Douzima-Lawson).

[17] Panel of Independent Experts Report 2014, p. 178, note 8.

[18] STL, *Prosecutor v. Ayyash* et al., STL-11-01, Official Public Transcript, 17 January 2014, pp. 53–60.

[19] Ibid., pp. 60–75.

[20] Ibid., pp. 76–87.

The practice of the ICC and STL shows that legal representatives are given considerable leeway as regards the topics covered in their opening statements. Most of the times, these remarks cover the plight of and harm suffered by the victims as well as the rights and expectations of participating victims. Legal practitioners are encouraged to use the opening statements to outline their case theory next to highlighting the views and concerns of their clients. When speaking of alleged crimes, victims' lawyers should limit themselves to events stated in the indictment and should at all times show respect towards the accused. Strong prosecutorial style on behalf of the legal representative has been criticised in the past and may deflect attention from the victims' views and concerns, which should at all times be the crucial point to address.

8.3 Examining Witnesses of the (Other) Parties on Behalf of the Participating Victims

All three courts analysed herein allow victims' lawyers to examine witnesses called by the other parties or the Chamber. The limits of this right vary, however, from court to court, and in some cases, from chamber to chamber.

8.3.1 Examining Witnesses: General Rules, Order and Notice of Questioning

At the ICC, Rule 91(2) of the ICC RPE provides that a legal representative will be entitled to participate in hearings unless, in the circumstances of the case, the Chamber concerned is of the view that the representative's intervention should be confined to written observations or submissions. Rule 91(3)(a) states that when a legal representative wishes to question a witness, an expert or the accused, he or she must apply to the Chamber for permission. Paragraph (b) of Rule 91(3) provides that the Chamber then may require the legal representative to provide a written note of the questions and in that case the questions shall be communicated to the Prosecutor and, if appropriate, the Defence, who shall be allowed to make observations within the set time limit. The Chamber then decides on the request, taking into account the stage of the proceedings, the rights of the accused, the interests of witnesses, the need for a fair, impartial and expeditious trial and in order to give effect to Article 68(3) of the ICC Statute.

Accordingly, it has routinely been the practice of chambers at the ICC to require victims' legal representatives to apply for leave to question the witnesses of the parties. In early cases, when the legal representative wished to examine a witness, he or she was directed, as a general practice, to apply to the relevant chamber, by means of a filing, notified to the parties, seven days in advance,[21] or, later, in *Ntaganda*, four days before the beginning of the witness' examination-in-chief.[22] Some chambers also set deadlines for parties to file submissions on the request of the legal representatives.[23] In the event of unexpected changes to the witness schedule or unanticipated topics raised during the testimony of the witness, these deadlines could be altered as necessary.[24] Chambers required legal representatives to explain in the application how the questioning serves the personal interests of the victims and include a list of questions or areas for examination.[25] Likewise, chambers have required legal representatives to submit the documents proposed to be used during the examination.[26]

More recent practice shows a relaxation of these requirements. In *Gbagbo and Blé Goudé* Trial Chamber I directed that an oral application would suffice, unless the LRV wishes to rely in his or her questioning on items of evidence which had

---

[21] ICC, *Prosecutor v. Thomas Lubanga Dyilo*, Trial Chamber I, Decision on victims' participation, ICC-01/04-01/06-1119, 18 January 2008, para 103; ICC, *Prosecutor v. Germain Katanga and Mathieu Ngudjolo Chui*, Trial Chamber II, Corrigendum to Directions for the conduct of the proceedings and testimony in accordance with Rule 140, ICC-01/04-01/07-1665-Corr, 1 December 2009, paras 87–88, 102(h); ICC, *Prosecutor v. Jean Pierre Bemba Gombo*, Trial Chamber III, Corrigendum to Decision on the participation of victims in the trial and on 86 applications by victims to participate in the proceedings, ICC-01/05-01/08-807-Corr, 12 July 2010, paras 37, 40; ICC, *Prosecutor v. William Samoei Ruto and Joshua Arap Sang*, Trial Chamber V(A), Decision on the Conduct of Trial Proceedings (General Directions), ICC-01/09-01/11-847, 9 August 2013, para 19; ICC, *Prosecutor v. Uhuru Muigai Kenyatta*, Trial Chamber V(B), Decision on the conduct of the trial proceedings, ICC-01/09-02/11-867, 2 December 2013, para 24.

[22] ICC, *Prosecutor v. Bosco Ntaganda*, Trial Chamber VI, Decision on the conduct of the proceedings, ICC-01/04-02/06-619, 2 June 2015, para 64.

[23] ICC, *Prosecutor v. Jean Pierre Bemba Gombo*, Trial Chamber III, Decision (i) ruling on legal representatives' applications to question Witness 33 and (ii) setting a schedule for the filing of submissions in relation to future applications to question witnesses, ICC-01/05-01/08-1729, 9 September 2011, para 14 (four days before the relevant witness is scheduled to testify): *Prosecutor v. Uhuru Muigai Kenyatta*, Trial Chamber V(B), Decision on the conduct of the trial proceedings, ICC-01/09-02/11-867, 2 December 2013, para 24 (within two working days of the notification of the application).

[24] ICC, *Prosecutor v. William Samoei Ruto and Joshua Arap Sang*, Trial Chamber V(A), Decision on the Conduct of Trial Proceedings (General Directions), ICC-01/09-01/11-847, 9 August 2013, para 19; ICC, Prosecutor v. Uhuru Muigai Kenyatta, Trial Chamber V(B), Decision on the conduct of the trial proceedings, ICC-01/09-02/11-867, 2 December 2013, para 24.

[25] ICC, *Prosecutor v. Germain Katanga and Mathieu Ngudjolo Chui*, Trial Chamber II, Corrigendum to Directions for the conduct of the proceedings and testimony in accordance with Rule 140, ICC-01/04-01/07-1665-Corr, 1 December 2009, paras 87–88; ICC, *Prosecutor v. William Samoei Ruto and Joshua Arap Sang*, Trial Chamber V(A), Decision on the Conduct of Trial Proceedings (General Directions), ICC-01/09-01/11-847, 9 August 2013, para 19.

[26] ICC, *Prosecutor v. William Samoei Ruto and Joshua Arap Sang*, Trial Chamber V(A), Decision on the Conduct of Trial Proceedings (General Directions), ICC-01/09-01/11-847, 9 August 2013, para 19; ICC, *Prosecutor v. Uhuru Muigai Kenyatta*, Trial Chamber V(B), Decision on the conduct of the trial proceedings, ICC-01/09-02/11-867, 2 December 2013, para 24.

not already been relied on in respect of the specific witness by a party. In that case a written application should be made at least 48 h before the calling party is expected to finish questioning the witness.[27] In the *Ongwen* case Trial Chamber IX went further still, directing that the LRVs need not provide advance written notice of questions they intend to ask to the parties' witnesses, and that application may always be presented orally immediately before questioning.[28]

Rule 91(3)(b) of the ICC RPE also states that the Chamber, after ruling on the request of the legal representative to question a witness, an expert or the accused, may provide directions on the manner and order of the questions and the production of documents in accordance with the functions and powers of the chamber. Trial chambers have usually allowed the legal representatives to ask their questions after the Prosecution and before the Defence:

> To the extent that questioning is permitted, the CLR shall ask her questions only after the completion of the prosecution's questioning, save for the situation where the evidence has been brought to the Chamber by the participating victims and its submission has been requested by the Chamber pursuant to Article 69(3) of the Statute. In this case, the CLR may ask her questions prior to those of the prosecution.[29]

Rule 91(3)(b) also provides that the Chamber may, if it considers it appropriate, put the question to the witness, expert or accused on behalf of the victim's legal representative.

The regulatory framework of the ECCC permits civil parties and their lawyers the freedom to ask questions subject only to it being conducive to ascertaining the truth. Rule 91*bis* of the Internal Rules affords trial chambers a broad discretion to establish their own modalities for the questioning of witnesses, providing that the President of the Trial Chamber determines the order in which the judges, the Co-Prosecutors and all the other parties and their lawyers can question the Accused, the witnesses, experts and civil parties. Lawyers representing civil parties need not submit any request or notice prior to questioning the witness of another Party, although time estimates are elicited by judges in advance of testimony (see Sect. 8.3.4 below).

At the STL, Rule 87(B) of the RPE expressly provides that '[a]t the trial stage, a victim participating in the proceedings may, subject to the authorisation by, and under the control of, the Trial Chamber after hearing the Parties, examine or cross-examine

[27] ICC, *Prosecutor v. Laurent Gbagbo and Charles Blé Goudé*, Annex to Decision adopting amended and supplemented directions on the conduct of the proceedings, ICC-02/11-01/15-498-AnxA, 4 May 2016, para 16.

[28] ICC, *Prosecutor v. Dominic Ongwen*, Trial Chamber IX, Initial Directions on the Conduct of the Proceedings, ICC-02/04-01/15-497, 13 July 2016, para 10.

[29] ICC, *Prosecutor v. Abdallah Banda Abakaer Nourain*, Trial Chamber IV, Decision on the participation of victims in the trial proceedings, ICC-02/05-03/09-545, 20 March 2014, para 33. See also: ICC, *Prosecutor v. William Samoei Ruto and Joshua Arap Sang*, Trial Chamber V(A), Decision on the Conduct of Trial Proceedings (General Directions), ICC-01/09-01/11-847, 9 August 2013, para 16.

witnesses'. Rule 145 sets out the sequence in which questions will be asked of witnesses and Rule 146 describes the sequence in which evidence is to be called. Collectively they confirm the right of the participating victims to examine witnesses after the Prosecution and before the Defence.

In the *Ayyash* et al. case, the Trial Chamber gave Rule 87(B) an implicitly liberal interpretation by not requiring the LRV to request, in advance of testimony, for leave to question witnesses. Likewise, the Trial Chamber has placed no requirement upon the LRV to provide lists of questions, or even the lines of proposed questioning. Notice of the LRV's intention to question a witness is given in the same manner as with the parties, via email or *ad hoc* oral request.

Rule 144(B) also specifically provides that the Trial Chamber may put questions to the accused at any stage of the proceedings, including at the requests of an LRV or a party. However, in practice this possibility has not been available to the participating victims in the *Ayyash* et al. case since the accused remain *in absentia*.

8.3.2 Examining Witnesses: Scope of Questioning

The three courts have set varying limits to the scope of questioning witnesses by victims' lawyers.

In the first two trials before the ICC, the Trial Chambers were meticulous in their delineation of the scope of victims' participation. In *Lubanga*, Trial Chamber I was interventionist in limiting the scope of questioning by legal representatives, allowing only those questions which were in the interests of victims. A 'general interest in the outcome of the case or in the issues or evidence the Chamber will be considering at that stage' was 'likely to be insufficient' to justify questioning of witnesses by legal representatives.[30] The Trial Chamber required a showing of 'involvement in or presence at a particular incident which the Chamber is considering, or if the victim has suffered identifiable harm from that incident'.[31] The Legal Representatives of Victims were required to demonstrate a concrete link between their proposed questions and the views and concerns the particular victims they represented.[32] As such, the LRV questioned only 25 of the 67 witnesses heard in that case.[33]

---

[30] ICC, *Prosecutor v. Thomas Lubanga Dyilo*, Trial Chamber I, Decision on Victims' Participation, ICC-01/04-01/06-1119, 18 January 2008, para 96.

[31] Ibid.

[32] ICC, *Prosecutor v. Thomas Lubanga Dyilo*, Trial Chamber I, Official Public Redacted Transcript, ICC-01/04-01/06-T-200-Red2-ENG, 26 June 2009, pp. 52–54. See also, ICC, *Prosecutor v. Thomas Lubanga Dyilo*, Trial Chamber I, Official Public Redacted Transcript, ICC-01/04-01/06-T-124-Red3-ENG, 11 February 2009, pp. 53–54.

[33] ICC, *Prosecutor v. Thomas Lubanga Dyilo*, Trial Chamber I, Judgment pursuant to Article 74 of the Statute, ICC-01/04-01/06-2842, 14 March 2012, para 21, footnote 62.

The same approach was adopted in *Katanga and Ngudjolo Chui*, with Trial Chamber II reminding the Legal Representatives of Victims that it was not their role to 'reinforce the Prosecution team'[34] or play 'part two of the Prosecution',[35] and they were warned against putting questions to witnesses which would end up providing some form of direct or indirect assistance to the Prosecution team.[36] The Chamber strictly regulated questioning in order to prevent legal representatives from asking questions which had not received authorisation or which were too general.[37]

In contrast, in the *Bemba* case, Trial Chamber III held that

> [t]he interests of victims are not limited to the physical commission of the alleged crimes under consideration. Rather, their interests extend to the question of the person or persons who should be held liable for those crimes, whether physical perpetrators or others. In this respect, victims have a general interest in the proceedings and in their outcome. As such, they have an interest in making sure that all pertinent questions are put to witnesses.[38]

The Chamber initially acknowledged the constraints of Rule 91(3) by requiring that follow-up questions be supported by a justification detailing 'both the nature and the details of the proposed questioning as well as specify in what way the personal interests of the victims are affected'.[39] Later on, however, the Trial Chamber adopted a more permissive approach and generally allowed the legal representatives to ask "follow-up" questions with authorisation granted orally on the spot, or by simply allowing the question *de facto*, without interruption.[40] The practice was contested by the Defence and numerous objections in that regard were raised in court.[41]

The Chamber explained its practice as follows:

---

[34] ICC, *Prosecutor v. Germain Katanga and Mathieu Ngudjolo Chui*, Trial Chamber II, Official Public Redacted Transcript, ICC-01/04-01/07-T-87-Red-ENG, 30 November 2009, p. 26.

[35] Ibid., p. 33.

[36] ICC, *Prosecutor v. Germain Katanga and Mathieu Ngudjolo Chui*, Trial Chamber II, Official Public Redacted Transcript, ICC-01/04-01/07-T-160-Red-ENG, 23 June 2010, p. 20.

[37] ICC, *Prosecutor v. Germain Katanga and Mathieu Ngudjolo Chui*, Trial Chamber II, Official Public Redacted Transcript, ICC-01/04-01/07-T-252-ENG, 21 April 2011, pp. 42–43.

[38] ICC, *Prosecutor v. Jean Pierre Bemba Gombo*, Trial Chamber III, Decision (i) ruling on legal representatives' applications to question Witness 33 and (ii) setting a schedule for the filing of submissions in relation to future applications to question witnesses, ICC-01/05-01/08-1729, 9 September 2011, para 15.

[39] ICC, *Prosecutor v. Jean Pierre Bemba Gombo*, Trial Chamber III, Decision on Directions for the Conduct of the Proceedings, ICC-01/05-01/08-1023, 19 November 2010, para 19.

[40] See, for instance: ICC, *Prosecutor v. Jean Pierre Bemba Gombo*, Trial Chamber III, Official Public Redacted Transcript, ICC-01/05-01/08-T-42-Red2-ENG, 2 December 2010, p. 18; ICC, *Prosecutor v. Jean Pierre Bemba Gombo*, Trial Chamber III, Official Public Redacted Transcript, ICC-01/05-01/08-T-329-Red-ENG, 24 June 2013, pp. 34–35.

[41] See, for instance: ICC, *Prosecutor v. Jean Pierre Bemba Gombo*, Trial Chamber III, Official Public Redacted Transcript, ICC-01/05-01/08-T-329-Red-ENG, 24 June 2013, pp. 34–35.

> [...] the Chamber has always been mindful of the need to restrict the legal representatives to only those questions which are relevant to the interests of the victims they represent. Far from allowing "virtually unrestrained" questioning, as alleged by the defence, the Chamber has carefully considered the legal representatives' applications to question each defence witness, and has issued oral and written decisions authorising some questions and not others, on the basis of, *inter alia*, whether the questions were sufficiently linked to the personal interests of the victims. Although it is true that, in order to expedite the proceedings, the Chamber has not requested a new application each time the legal representatives wish to ask follow-up questions, the Chamber has loosely monitored the nature of the follow-up questions and has requested clarification when the relationship of the questions to the personal interests of victims was not clear.

The Chamber held that it continued to exercise control over the form and manner of the legal representatives' questioning in order to ensure that the questions were not repetitive, irrelevant or otherwise inappropriate.[42]

In *Ruto and Sang* and in *Kenyatta*, the modalities for victims' participation were again delineated narrowly, reflecting the practice of the *Lubanga* and *Katanga and Ngudjolo Chui* trials. Legal representatives were only authorised to ask questions relevant to the victim's interests, and on the basis that they were not repetitive of questions asked by the calling party.[43] The same approach has since been reiterated by Trial Chamber I in *Gbagbo and Blé Goudé*.[44]

The regulatory framework of the ECCC permits civil parties and their lawyers the freedom to ask questions which tangibly inculpate the accused. Internal Rule 91(3) permits objections to the continued hearing of the testimony of any witnesses, only if such testimony is not conducive to ascertaining the truth. Despite the silence of Internal Rule 91 as regards the rights of the accused, Internal Rule 21 directs that applicable provisions must be interpreted so as to always safeguard the interests of suspects, charged persons, accused and victims and so as to ensure legal certainty and transparency of proceedings. That being said, Internal Rule 23(1)(a) explicitly provides that one of the purposes of civil party participation is to support the Prosecution, thus the licence for questioning is broad. However, questions have been restrained if they are repetitious, long-winded or outside the confines of the topic.[45] The Trial Chamber in *Case 001* later went on to restrain the civil parties' questioning of the accused or other witnesses on matters which went to the accused's character,[46] on the basis that character was directly relevant

---

[42] ICC, *Prosecutor v. Jean Pierre Bemba Gombo*, Trial Chamber III, Decision on the Defence Motion on the Questioning of Defence Witnesses by the Legal Representatives of Victims, ICC-01/05-01/08-2751, 21 August 2013, paras 10–11.

[43] ICC, *Prosecutor v. William Samoei Ruto and Joshua Arap Sang*, Trial Chamber V, Decision on victims' representation and participation, ICC-01/09-01/11-460, 3 October 2012, para 75; ICC, *Prosecutor v. Francis Kirimi Muthaura and Uhuru Muigai Kenyatta*, Decision on victims' representation and participation, ICC-01/09-02/11-498, 3 October 2012, para 74.

[44] ICC, *Prosecutor v. Laurent Gbagbo and Charles Blé Goudé*, Annex to Decision adopting amended and supplemented directions on the conduct of the proceedings, ICC-02/11-01/15-498-AnxA, 4 May 2016, para 17.

[45] ECCC, *Case 001*, Official Public Transcript, 22 June 2009, p. 98.

[46] ECCC, *Case 001*, Official Public Transcript, 27 August 2009, p. 74.

to sentencing, and unrelated to the guilt of the accused or appropriate reparations,[47] although one of the two international judges dissented from this ruling.[48] That being said, questions eliciting a description of the mental state of the accused at a particular time were allowed.[49] 'Personal' or 'hypothetical' questions as well as questions not related to facts not before the Chamber were also curtailed.[50]

At the STL, the Trial Chamber in the *Ayyash* et al. case has not expressly set out any limits to the scope of questioning by the LRV. However, the Chamber has at times limited lines of questioning which it deemed not to be borne of the victims' interests. For instance, while the Trial Chamber did not reject the contention that questions regarding the diplomatic efforts undertaken to establish the STL were in the victims' general interest, the LRV was directed to 'condense' his examination on that particular topic.[51]

8.3.3 Examining Witnesses: Mode of Questioning

It might be expected that at the ICC and STL, there is a basic presumption, borne of the nature of the victims' role in the proceedings, that questions put to witnesses by victims, whether called by them, the chamber, or some other party, will be in a neutral and non-leading form. However, there is no absolute prohibition on cross-examination in its truer form, if challenging a witness is within the personal interest of the victims, and it is approved by the Chamber.

ICC chambers have consistently affirmed that '[i]n general, questioning by the CLR shall be conducted in a neutral manner, without the use of leading or closed questions, unless otherwise authorised by the Chamber.'[52]

---

47 ECCC, *Case 001*, Trial Chamber, Decision on Civil Party Co-Lawyers' Joint request for a ruling on the standing of Civil Party Lawyers to make submissions on sentencing and directions concerning the questioning of the accused, experts, and witnesses testifying on character, 9 October 2009, para 48.

48 ECCC, *Case 001*, Trial Chamber, Dissenting Opinion of Judge Jean-Marc Lavergne to the Decision on Civil Party Co-Lawyers' Joint request for a ruling on the standing of Civil Party Lawyers to make submissions on sentencing and directions concerning the questioning of the accused, experts, and witnesses testifying on character, 9 Oct. 2009, para 32.

49 ECCC, *Case 001*, Official Public Transcript, 12 August 2009, pp. 39–40.

50 ECCC, *Case 001*, Official Public Transcript, 12 August 2009, p. 41; ECCC, *Case 001*, Official Public Transcript, 13 July 2009, pp. 47–48.

51 STL, *Prosecutor v. Ayyash* et al., STL-11-01, Official Public Transcript, 24 March 2015, p. 39.

52 ICC, *Prosecutor v. Abdallah Banda Abakaer Nourain*, Trial Chamber IV, Decision on the participation of victims in the trial proceedings, ICC-02/05-03/09-545, 20 March 2014, para 33. See also: ICC, *Prosecutor v. Thomas Lubanga Dyilo*, Trial Chamber I, Decision on the Manner of Questioning Witnesses by the Legal Representatives of Victims, ICC-01/04-01/06-2127, 16 September 2009, para 28; ICC, *Prosecutor v. Jean Pierre Bemba Gombo*, Trial Chamber III, Corrigendum to Decision on the participation of victims in the trial and on 86 applications by victims to participate in the proceedings, ICC-01/05-01/08-807-Corr, 12 July 2010, para 38.

Trial Chamber I in *Lubanga,* however, added a more explicit caveat:

> In certain circumstances, however, it may be fully consistent with the role of the victims' legal representatives to seek to press, challenge or discredit a witness, for example when the views and concerns of a victim conflicts with the evidence given by that witness, or when material evidence has not been forthcoming. Under such circumstances, it may be appropriate for the victims' legal representatives to use closed, leading or challenging questions, if approved by the Chamber.[53]

In this respect, the Trial Chamber in *Lubanga* also held that if a representative of victims wishes to depart from a neutral style of questioning, an oral request should be made to the bench at the stage in the examination when this possibility arises.[54]

No systematic limitations as to the mode of questioning have been imposed on lawyers representing civil parties at the ECCC.

To date, in the *Ayyash* et al. case at the STL, the LRV has generally followed a neutral style of questioning. There is, however, no express limitation against a more leading mode of examination.

8.3.4 Examining Witnesses: Length of Questioning

The three courts vary greatly when it comes to temporal limits imposed to questioning of witnesses by victims' lawyers.

At the ICC, chambers have generally refrained from allocating standard time-limits for questioning witnesses. Trial Chamber I in *Lubanga* decided that ensuring that the manner and the timing of the questioning was not prejudicial to, or inconsistent with, the rights of the accused and a fair and impartial trial was a quintessentially fact-based issue, which could not be determined in advance, absent a detailed examination of the proposed manner of questioning of all the participating victims who have applied to examine the witness in question.[55] Nonetheless, in the *Bemba* case, the Trial Chamber revised its initial policy of not imposing limits to the length of questioning by legal representatives to one where

[53] ICC, *Prosecutor v. Thomas Lubanga Dyilo*, Trial Chamber I, Decision on the Manner of Questioning Witnesses by the Legal Representatives of Victims, ICC-01/04-01/06-2127, 16 September 2009, para 28. See also ICC, *Prosecutor v. Jean Pierre Bemba Gombo*, Trial Chamber III, Corrigendum to Decision on the participation of victims in the trial and on 86 applications by victims to participate in the proceedings, ICC-01/05-01/08-807-Corr, 12 July 2010, para 38.

[54] ICC, *Prosecutor v. Thomas Lubanga Dyilo*, Trial Chamber I, ICC-01/04-01/06-2127, Decision on the Manner of Questioning Witnesses by the Legal Representatives of Victims, 16 September 2009, para 30.

[55] ICC, *Prosecutor v. Thomas Lubanga Dyilo*, Trial Chamber I, Decision on the defence observations regarding the right of the legal representatives of victims to question defence witnesses and on the notion of personal interest, ICC-01/04-01/06-2340, 11 March 2010, paras 34–35.

the two representatives had to share an allotment of 2 h per witness between them.[56]

In *Ongwen* the Trial Chamber directed that parties would be allocated the same amount of time for the questioning of witnesses, but that given 'the LRVs' more limited role in the trial proceedings, they are collectively expected to take substantially less time' than a party.[57]

At the ECCC, the initial approach in *Case 001* was to allow all parties to examine witnesses without any temporal limitations. This led, however, to an increasingly slow pace of the trial. To remedy this shortcoming, the Trial Chamber introduced a system of standard time allotments. On the 28th day of the trial, the Trial Chamber announced:

> The Chamber cannot yet announce an end date for the presentation of evidence, but it wishes to announce that it will adopt the practice of assigning speaking times to the parties. So far in the trial, the Chamber has permitted the parties to give their own estimates of time but this has not been altogether successful.
>
> The Chamber will assess the time it thinks appropriate for the hearing of each witness on a case-by-case basis, but it wishes now to give an indication of the time it considers generally appropriate for the questioning of witnesses and for the presentation of submissions so that the parties can prepare. First the questioning of witnesses; generally, this will be 30 minutes for the prosecutors, 40 minutes for all civil parties combined, and 40 minutes for the defence. Secondly, submissions; the Chamber will permit between five and 10 minutes for the raising of questions and objections, and five minutes for responses. The Trial Chamber will not permit lengthy dispute by the parties to these time estimates. The distribution of the 40-minutes speaking time among the civil parties lawyers is for them to decide; however, the Chamber suggests, as a possible method, that the four civil party groups assign one Cambodian and one international lawyer with the responsibility for the questioning of each witness on behalf of all civil parties. The Chamber emphasizes, however, that this is a suggestion only for the efficient use of the 40-minutes time allocation.[58]

On the length of questioning of the Accused, the Chamber noted the following day that it

> [had] determined times for each party to put questions regarding the above-mentioned facts to the accused; three hours for the prosecutors, three hours for the civil parties, four hours for the defence counsel.[59]

---

[56] ICC, *Prosecutor v. Jean Pierre Bemba Gombo*, Trial Chamber III, Oral Decision, Official Public Redacted Transcript, 15 October 2012, pp. 66–67; ICC, *Prosecutor v. Jean Pierre Bemba Gombo*, Trial Chamber III, Decision on the Defence Motion on the Questioning of Defence Witnesses by the Legal Representatives of Victims, ICC-01/05-01/08-2751, 21 August 2013, para 11; ICC, *Prosecutor v. Jean Pierre Bemba Gombo*, Trial Chamber III, Decision on Defence Request for Leave to Appeal the Decision on the Defence Motion on the Questioning of Defence Witnesses by the Legal Representatives of Victims, 11 September 2013, paras 19–20.

[57] ICC, *Prosecutor v. Dominic Ongwen*, Trial Chamber IX, Initial Directions on the Conduct of the Proceedings, ICC-02/04-01/15-497, 13 July 2016, para 14.

[58] ECCC, *Case 001*, Trial Chamber, Official Public Transcript, 15 June 2009, pp. 4–5.

[59] ECCC, *Case 001*, Trial Chamber, Official Public Transcript, 16 June 2009, pp. 2–3.

The Defence objected to the latter time allotment, pointing out that the Prosecution and civil parties had in total six, whereas the Defence only 4 hours to question the accused, and averred that it should be given a time limit equal to that of its opponents.[60] Although the Chamber maintained its time allotment, it noted on a subsequent day of trial that

> Bearing in mind that the civil parties are allowed to put their questions with a view to supporting the prosecution, the Chamber is aware that in order to preserve the rights of the defence particularly the right to a fair trial that guarantees equality of arms, it may become necessary to accord more time to the defence than is set aside for it in the scheduling of the hearing. (…) Accordingly, the Chamber is of the opinion that in order to allow for realistic scheduling consistent with expeditious trial requirements, it is appropriate to maintain the time allocated for each party to take the floor; it being clear that should the Chamber consider it necessary, in light of the questions already put, the defence may apply to the Chamber for a further period of time to enable it to put all the questions it may consider necessary to ensure that its rights are preserved.[61]

The time allotments were strictly observed and questioning stopped if the allocated time was exceeded.[62] The reaction of the Trial Chamber in *Case 001* has to be regarded as somewhat extreme, reducing as it did the right of victims' lawyers to question witnesses to often impracticable brevity. In *Case 002/01*, no standard time limits were imposed; the Chamber usually assigned a particular portion of each hearing to the different parties and retained discretion in the allocation.[63]

At the STL, to date no standard temporal limits have been imposed in the *Ayyash* et al. case. All parties and participants are, however, invited to provide estimates of (cross-)examination (via email or in court), but the Chamber has so far been lenient about enforcing those estimates.

8.4 The Right to Challenge Evidence Called by the Parties

All three courts permit victims' lawyers to challenge the relevance or admissibility of evidence tendered by the (other) parties.

At the ICC the position seems settled following the Appeals Chamber decision in the *Lubanga* case. The Trial Chamber had originally determined that:

> As regards the request of the victims' legal representatives to have the opportunity to challenge the admissibility or relevance of evidence when their interests are engaged, the right to make submissions on matters of evidence is not reserved to the parties, and there is no provision within the Rome Statute framework which prohibits the Trial Chamber from ruling on the admissibility.[64]

---

60 Ibid., p. 8.

61 ECCC, *Case 001*, Trial Chamber, Official Public Transcript, 27 July 2009, pp. 29–30.

62 See, for example, ECCC, *Case 001*, Trial Chamber, Official Public Transcript, 22 July 2009, p. 45.

63 ECCC, *Case 002/01*, Trial Chamber, Official Public Transcript, 4 October 2012, p. 52.

64 ICC, *Prosecutor v. Thomas Lubanga Dyilo*, Trial Chamber I, Decision on victims' participation, ICC-01/04-01/06-1119, 18 January 2008, para 109.

In determining the appeals by both the Prosecution and the Defence against this ruling, the Appeals Chamber concluded:

> In relation to the right afforded to victims to challenge the admissibility or relevance of evidence, the Trial Chamber relied on its general powers under article 69 (4) to declare any evidence admissible or relevant. The provision is silent as to who may challenge such evidence. Under article 64 (9) of the Statute, the Trial Chamber has the power to rule on the admissibility or relevance of evidence on its own motion. These provisions must be seen in light of the provisions on victims' participation, in particular article 68 (3) of the Statute and rules 89 and 91 of the Rules. In light of these provisions, nothing in articles 69 (4) and 64 (9) excludes the possibility of a Trial Chamber ruling on the admissibility or relevance of evidence after having received submissions by the victims on said evidence. The approach of the Trial Chamber in interpreting its powers, once again does not result in an unfettered right for victims but is subject to the application of article 68 (3), which is the founding provision governing victim participation in the proceedings.[65]

The right is not unfettered and must be based on the victims' personal interests. Other trial chambers have been less clear about the extent to which victims can challenge evidence. In *Katanga and Ngudjolo Chui*, Trial Chamber II held that victims could challenge evidence as such:

> As regards a potential challenge to the admissibility and relevance of evidence pursuant to article 69(4) of the Statute, the Chamber again considers that this is a means for the victims to express their views and concerns within the meaning of article 68(3) of the Statute. It is of the view that such a possibility cannot be completely ruled out. Thus it must permit a victim who has information clearly indicating the admissibility of disputed evidence, or, on the contrary, establishing that such evidence cannot be admitted or is irrelevant, to transmit that information to the Chamber. Such information may prevent the Chamber from being misled by relying on inadmissible or irrelevant evidence – or dismissing evidence that is in fact admissible and relevant – in order to establish the facts.[66]

In *Banda*, however, the Trial Chamber appeared to suggest that victims can only make observations upon issues of relevance and admissibility litigated by the parties:

> [t]he Chamber may permit the views and concerns of victims to be presented and considered whenever the Chamber is called to determine the relevance or admissibility of evidence under Article 69(4) or Article 64(9) of the Statute, provided that all the requirements of Article 68(3) of the Statute are met. The Chamber will request, as appropriate, the CLR to make submissions on the admissibility of evidence only if the victims' personal interests are affected.[67]

---

[65] ICC, *Prosecutor v. Thomas Lubanga Dyilo*, Appeals Chamber, Judgement on the Appeals of the Prosecution and the Defence against Trial Chamber I's Decision on Victim's Participation of 18 January 2008, ICC-01/04-01/06-1432, Appeals Chamber, 11 July 2008, para 101.

[66] ICC, *Prosecutor v. Germain Katanga and Mathieu Ngudjolo Chui*, Trial Chamber II, Decision on Modalities of Victim Participation at Trial, ICC-01/04-01/07-1788-tENG, 22 January 2010, para 104.

[67] ICC, *Prosecutor v. Abdallah Banda Abakaer Nourain*, Trial Chamber IV, Decision on the participation of victims in the trial proceedings, ICC-02/05-03/09-545, 20 March 2014, para 30.

At the ECCC, by virtue of Internal Rule 91(3), the right to object to the continued hearing of testimony plainly extends to lawyers representing civil parties. The basis of any objection, namely, that it is not conducive to the truth, is sufficiently wide to countenance any objection based on relevance, admissibility or even provenance.

At the STL, no rule prevents the LRV from challenging the evidence presented by the Parties. In the *Ayyash* et al. case, the LRV was allowed to submit observations challenging the probative value of evidence presented by the Prosecution and Defence as regards the death of one of the accused tried *in absentia*. The LRV challenged that evidence both in oral submissions before the Trial Chamber and in a written submission before the Appeals Chamber.[68] In its request for leave to file observations before the Appeals Chamber, the LRV maintained that it was in the personal interest of the victims to determine the death of an accused through conclusive evidence:

> Article 25 of the STL Statute permits victims or persons claiming through the victim to bring an action in a national court or other competent body to obtain compensation based on the decision of the Tribunal and pursuant to the relevant national legislation. The death of an accused, if acknowledged by the court, terminates the criminal proceedings against that person and precludes a criminal conviction. Even if the final judgment records some of the actions and/or omissions of the formerly accused person in his or her capacity as a co-perpetrator or co-conspirator, the prospects of obtaining compensation for harm caused by those acts might be adversely affected. Such an outcome significantly affects the right of victims to obtain reparations for the harm they suffered. For this reason, it is plainly in the personal interests of the victims that the death of an accused is properly determined on the basis of conclusive evidence.[69]

The Appeals Chamber confirmed that the matter clearly affected the personal interests of the victims, including their potential ability to claim compensation.[70]

None of the three courts specifically disqualifies victims' lawyers from making in-court interventions or objections to evidence. Indeed, often they will be best placed either through their instructions or their local knowledge to advise the trier of fact of inadvertent factual inaccuracies, local customs or inaccuracies of translation in questions put by the parties.[71] In any case, the objection would have to be

---

[68] STL, *Prosecutor v. Ayyash* et al., STL-11-01, Official Public Transcript, 30 May 2016, pp. 86–95 and Official Public Transcript, 1 June 2016, pp. 2–3, 34–36; *Prosecutor v. Ayyash* et al., STL-11-01, Legal Representative of Victims, Submissions of the Legal Representative of Victims on the Interlocutory Appeal of the "Interim Decision on the Death of Mr. Mustafa Amine Badreddine and Possible Termination of Proceedings", 27 June 2016.

[69] STL, *Prosecutor v. Ayyash* et al., STL-11-01, Legal Representative of Victims, Request of the Legal Representative of Victims for Leave to Respond to the Badreddine Interlocutory Appeal of the "Interim Decision on the Death of Mr. Mustafa Amine Badreddine and Possible Termination of Proceedings", 15 June 2016, para 5 (footnotes omitted).

[70] STL, *Prosecutor v. Ayyash* et al., STL-11-01, Appeals Chamber, Decision on the Request of the Legal Representative of Victims Seeking Leave to Respond to the Badreddine Defence Interlocutory Appeal, 17 June 2016, para 5.

[71] See, for example, an intervention by the Co-Legal Representative of Victims in *Ayyash* et al., advising the Chamber on the correct Arabic transliteration of a particular name. STL, *Prosecutor v. Ayyash* et al., STL-11-01, Official Public Transcript, 23 January 2015, p. 33.

framed in terms either that it was an aid to the search for the truth or that it was borne of the victims' interest or an expression of their views and concerns.

8.5 The Right to Call Evidence

All three courts analysed herein allow, although to varying extents, the presentation of evidence by victims' lawyers. This section will focus mainly on the ICC practice on presentation of evidence by participating victims, as its chambers have produced complex case-law on this issue. The ECCC and STL practice will also be described.

8.5.1 Victims Calling Evidence at the ICC

The possibility for victims to tender evidence at the ICC was established early, and approved by the Appeals Chamber in both the *Lubanga* and the *Katanga and Ngudjolo Chui* cases. Although the leading of evidence relating to the guilt or innocence of the accused is primarily the role of the parties (Prosecutor and Defence),[72] this does not preclude entirely the possibility for victims to lead evidence.[73] This includes evidence which is not related to reparations.[74] The Trial

[72] ICC, *Prosecutor v. Thomas Lubanga Dyilo*, Appeals Chamber, Judgment on the appeals of the Prosecutor and the Defence against Trial Chamber I's Decision on Victims' Participation of 18 January 2008, ICC-01/04-01/06-1432, 11 July 2008, para 93. See also ICC, *Prosecutor v. Jean Pierre Bemba Gombo*, Trial Chamber III, Decision on the supplemented applications by the legal representatives of victims to present evidence and the views and concerns of victims, ICC-01/05-01/08-2138, 22 February 2012, para 13.

[73] ICC, *Prosecutor v. Thomas Lubanga Dyilo*, Appeals Chamber, Judgment on the appeals of the Prosecutor and the Defence against Trial Chamber I's Decision on Victims' Participation of 18 January 2008, ICC-01/04-01/06-1432, 11 July 2008, para 94; ICC, *Prosecutor v. Germain Katanga and Mathieu Ngudjolo Chui*, Appeals Chamber, Judgment on the Appeal of Mr. Katanga Against the Decision of Trial Chamber II of 22 January 2010 Entitled "Decision on the Modalities of Victim Participation at Trial", ICC-01/04-01/07-2288, 16 July 2010, paras 37, 110–115; ICC, *Prosecutor v. Germain Katanga and Mathieu Ngudjolo Chui*, Trial Chamber II, Decision authorising the appearance of Victims a/0381/09, a/0018/09, a/0191/08, and pan/0363/09 acting on behalf of a/0363/09, ICC-01/04-01/07-2517-tENG, 9 November 2010, para 32; ICC, *Prosecutor v. Jean Pierre Bemba Gombo*, Trial Chamber III, Decision on the supplemented applications by the legal representatives of victims to present evidence and the views and concerns of victims, ICC-01/05-01/08-2138, 22 February 2012, para 18.

[74] ICC, *Prosecutor v. Thomas Lubanga Dyilo*, Trial Chamber I, Decision on victims' participation, ICC-01/04-01/06-1119, 18 January 2008, para 108. See also ICC, *Prosecutor v. Jean Pierre Bemba Gombo*, Trial Chamber III, Decision on the supplemented applications by the legal representatives of victims to present evidence and the views and concerns of victims, ICC-01/05-01/08-2138, 22 February 2012, para 18.

and Appeals Chambers relied principally on Article 69(3) of the ICC Statute which permits the court to request the submission of all evidence considered necessary for the determination of the truth.[75] According to this approach victims do not have an entitlement to lead evidence, but rather must request permission from the Chamber to do so case-by-case.[76]

Witnesses called by an LRV can include the participating victims whom the LRV represents, in which case these victims acquire "dual status" (see Chap. 9). Such cases include where evidence is given by an adult who does not participate in his or her own right, but acts on behalf of a child victim participant.[77] However it is also clear that LRVs may tender evidence from sources other than their own clients. At the ICC this has been recognised,[78] although to date it has not occurred in practice.

ICC case law is not entirely clear on the question of who it is that technically "calls" these witnesses. Some decisions appear to suggest that the LRV simply calls any witness for whom he or she is given permission.[79] Others apparently take

---

[75] ICC, *Prosecutor v. Thomas Lubanga Dyilo*, Trial Chamber I, Decision on victims' participation, 18 January 2008, ICC-01/04-01/06-1119, para 108; ICC, *Prosecutor v. Thomas Lubanga Dyilo*, Appeals Chamber, Judgment on the appeals of the Prosecutor and the Defence against Trial Chamber I's Decision on Victims' Participation of 18 January 2008, ICC-01/04-01/06-1432, 11 July 2008, paras 95 and 98.

[76] ICC, *Prosecutor v. Thomas Lubanga Dyilo*, Appeals Chamber, Judgment on the appeals of the Prosecutor and the Defence against Trial Chamber I's Decision on Victims' Participation of 18 January 2008, ICC-01/04-01/06-1432, 11 July 2008, para 99; ICC, *Prosecutor v. Germain Katanga and Mathieu Ngudjolo Chui*, Trial Chamber II, Directions for the conduct of the proceedings and testimony in accordance with rule 140, ICC-01/04-01/07-1665-Corr, 1 December 2009, para 19; ICC, *Prosecutor v. Germain Katanga and Mathieu Ngudjolo Chui*, Trial Chamber II, Decision on the Modalities of Victim Participation at Trial, ICC-01/04-01/07-1788-tENG, 22 January 2010, para 84.

[77] ICC, *Prosecutor v. Germain Katanga and Mathieu Ngudjolo Chui*, Trial Chamber II, Decision authorising the appearance of Victims a/0381/09, a/0018/09, a/0191/08, and pan/0363/09 acting on behalf of a/0363/09, ICC-01/04-01/07-2517-tENG, 9 November 2010, para 18. Trial Chamber II held that were called in this capacity by an LRV, the person's statement must be limited to issues which are affected by the personal interests of the child who is represented. In order to be questioned on a broader range of issues the person must be called by the Chamber, as occurred in the instance considered by Trial Chamber II in *Katanga* (paras 18–19).

[78] ICC, *Prosecutor v. Germain Katanga and Mathieu Ngudjolo Chui*, Trial Chamber II, Decision on the Modalities of Victim Participation at Trial, ICC-01/04-01/07-1788-tENG, 22 January 2010, paras 94–96. Although contrast the earlier statement appearing to suggest otherwise at ICC, *Prosecutor v. Germain Katanga and Mathieu Ngudjolo Chui*, Trial Chamber II, Directions for the conduct of the proceedings and testimony in accordance with rule 140, ICC-01/04-01/07-1665-Corr, 1 December 2009, paras 24 and 45.

[79] ICC, *Prosecutor v. Thomas Lubanga Dyilo*, Appeals Chamber, Judgment on the appeals of the Prosecutor and the Defence against Trial Chamber I's Decision on Victims' Participation of 18 January 2008, ICC-01/04-01/06-1432, 11 July 2008, paras 94, 98–99; ICC, *Prosecutor v. Jean Pierre Bemba Gombo*, Trial Chamber III, Order regarding applications by victims to present their views and concerns or to present evidence ICC-01/05-01/08-1935, 21 November 2011, para 2.

the position that LRVs are not able to call witnesses at all, but may only request that a trial chamber exercise its power to do so.[80] In the *Katanga and Ngudjolo Chui* case, Trial Chamber II considered that, subject to authorisation, a legal representative may call as witnesses the victims whom he or she represents; whereas any other witnesses whom the LRV wished to hear could only be called by the Chamber, including at LRV's suggestion.[81] Ultimately, however, it is not clear that this distinction has very much practical impact. For example, in *Katanga and Ngudjolo Chui*, the requirements set out by Trial Chamber II for an LRV to call his or her own clients as witnesses do not appear to differ in substance from those which should be met where an LRV requests a Chamber to call another witness.[82] This suggests that the distinction has little meaning in practice: on both approaches the substantive requirements are the same, and the Chamber retains the ultimate discretion to permit or refuse the appearance. To the extent that any impact arises, it is likely to relate to the order in which the witness is questioned, and possibly when in the proceedings the testimony is heard.

ICC jurisprudence in this area has been shaped in the context of LRV practice to date. Thus far, no LRV at the ICC has called a witness other than his or her own clients.[83] This has meant that it is difficult to distinguish in the ICC jurisprudence between principles which relate specifically to the situation in which an LRV calls his or her own clients as witnesses and those principles which would be applicable even if the person called was not a client. This chapter largely assumes that most of those principles which have been set down are equally applicable to other LRV

---

[80] ICC, *Prosecutor v. Abdallah Banda Abakaer Nourain*, Trial Chamber IV, Decision on the participation of victims in the trial proceedings, ICC-02/05-03/09-545, 20 March 2014, paras 22, 27–28.

[81] ICC, *Prosecutor v. Germain Katanga and Mathieu Ngudjolo Chui*, Trial Chamber II, Directions for the conduct of the proceedings and testimony in accordance with rule 140, ICC-01/04-01/07-1665-Corr, 1 December 2009, paras 7 and 45.

[82] Compare paras 20 and 47 of ICC, *Prosecutor v. Germain Katanga and Mathieu Ngudjolo Chui*, Trial Chamber II, Directions for the conduct of the proceedings and testimony in accordance with rule 140, ICC-01/04-01/07-1665-Corr, 1 December 2009. Although the Chamber appeared to elaborate additional requirements in respect of victims called by the LRV (paras 21–23), these all relate to the rights of the accused, which apply throughout the trial in general, and are therefore equally applicable where an LRV suggests that a chamber call a witness *proprio motu*.

[83] In *Lubanga*, two participating victims were allowed to give evidence. See ICC, *Prosecutor v. Thomas Lubanga Dyilo*, Trial Chamber I, Decision on the request by victims a/0225/06, a/0229/06 and a/0270/07 to express their views and concerns in person and to present evidence during the trial, ICC-01/04-01/06-2032, 26 June 2009. In the *Katanga and Ngudjolo* case, four victims were allowed to testify: ICC, *Prosecutor v. Germain Katanga and Mathieu Ngudjolo Chui*, Trial Chamber II, Décision aux fins de comparution des victimes a/0381/09, a/0018/09, a/0191/08 et pan/0363/09 agissant au nom de a/0363/09, ICC-01/04-01/07-2517, 9 November 2010. In Bemba, two victims were authorised to give evidence. See ICC, *Prosecutor v. Jean Pierre Bemba Gombo*, Trial Chamber III, Decision on the supplemented applications by the legal representatives of victims to present evidence and the views and concerns of victims, Trial Chamber III, ICC-01/05-01/08-2138, 22 February 2012.

witnesses, unless something about them suggests that they relate specifically to victim witnesses. The issues specifically arising where a victim gives evidence in person (whether called by the Chamber, the LRV or a party) are covered in Chap. 9.

8.5.1.1 Procedural Requirements for the LRV Request to Call Evidence

ICC chambers require that an LRV wishing to call witnesses must make a written application.[84] The required timing of such an application has varied between Chambers, but will usually be soon before or after the end of the Prosecution's presentation of evidence.[85] These applications are notified to the parties who are permitted to respond.[86]

Some chambers have set out detailed requirements for what must be included in an application by an LRV to call witnesses. Others have provided less detail.

---

[84] ICC, *Prosecutor v. Thomas Lubanga Dyilo*, Appeals Chamber, Judgment on the appeals of the Prosecutor and the Defence against Trial Chamber I's Decision on Victims' Participation of 18 January 2008, ICC-01/04-01/06-1432, 11 July 2008, para 104; ICC, *Prosecutor v. Germain Katanga and Mathieu Ngudjolo Chui*, Trial Chamber II, Directions for the conduct of the proceedings and testimony in accordance with rule 140, ICC-01/04-01/07-1665-Corr, 1 December 2009, para 25; ICC, *Prosecutor v. Germain Katanga and Mathieu Ngudjolo Chui*, Trial Chamber II, Decision authorising the appearance of Victims a/0381/09, a/0018/09, a/0191/08, and pan/0363/09 acting on behalf of a/0363/09, ICC-01/04-01/07-2517-tENG, 9 November 2010, paras 5–6; ICC, *Prosecutor v. Jean Pierre Bemba Gombo*, Trial Chamber III, Order regarding applications by victims to present their views and concerns or to present evidence ICC-01/05-01/08-1935, 21 November 2011, para 3; ICC, *Prosecutor v. Laurent Gbagbo and Charles Blé Goudé*, Trial Chamber I, Directions on the conduct of the proceedings, ICC-02/11-01/15-205, 3 September 2015, para 31; ICC, *Prosecutor v. Bosko Ntaganda*, Trial Chamber VI, Decision on the conduct of the proceedings, ICC-01/04-02/06-619, 2 June 2015, para 69; ICC, *Prosecutor v. William Samoei Ruto and Joshua Arap Sang*, Trial Chamber V, Decision on victims' representation and participation, ICC-01/09-01/11-460, 3 October 2012, para 77; ICC, *Prosecutor v. Francis Kirimi Muthaura and Uhuru Muigai Kenyatta*, Trial Chamber V, Decision on victims' representation and participation, ICC-01/09-02/11-498, 3 October 2012, para 76.

[85] ICC, *Prosecutor v. Germain Katanga and Mathieu Ngudjolo Chui*, Trial Chamber II, Directions for the conduct of the proceedings and testimony in accordance with rule 140, ICC-01/04-01/07-1665-Corr, 1 December 2009, para 25; ICC, *Prosecutor v. Germain Katanga and Mathieu Ngudjolo Chui*, Trial Chamber II, Decision authorising the appearance of Victims a/0381/09, a/0018/09, a/0191/08, and pan/0363/09 acting on behalf of a/0363/09, ICC-01/04-01/07-2517-tENG, 9 November 2010, paras 5–6; ICC, *Prosecutor v. Laurent Gbagbo and Charles Blé Goudé*, Trial Chamber I, Directions on the conduct of the proceedings, ICC-02/11-01/15-205, 3 September 2015, para 31; ICC, *Prosecutor v. Bosko Ntaganda*, Trial Chamber VI, Decision on the conduct of the proceedings, ICC-01/04-02/06-619, 2 June 2015, para 69.

[86] ICC, *Prosecutor v. Thomas Lubanga Dyilo*, Appeals Chamber, Judgment on the appeals of the Prosecutor and the Defence against Trial Chamber I's Decision on Victims' Participation of 18 January 2008, ICC-01/04-01/06-1432, 11 July 2008, para 104; ICC, *Prosecutor v. Germain Katanga and Mathieu Ngudjolo Chui*, Trial Chamber II, Directions for the conduct of the proceedings and testimony in accordance with rule 140, ICC-01/04-01/07-1665-Corr, 1 December 2009, para 28.

Practitioners should clearly be guided by the requirements of the Chamber before which they appear. However the core requirements are usually the following, which should be provided individually in respect of each proposed witness: (i) identification of the proposed witness; (ii) summary of the evidence which is expected from the witness; (iii) time estimates; (iv) submissions on the substantive requirements; and (v) protective measures.[87]

(i) Identification of the Proposed Witness

Identifying information about the proposed witness must be included in the application.[88] To date, no clear practice has arisen as to how this issue will be dealt with where a victim seeking to give evidence is currently anonymous. Victims who give evidence may not maintain their anonymity.[89] However, a cautious LRV may wish to maintain the anonymity of a client until the request to give evidence has been determined in the affirmative. This was permitted in the *Bemba* case.[90]

(ii) Summary of the Evidence Expected from the Witness

Applications should always include a summary of the expected evidence.[91] Some chambers have required or suggested that this summary be provided by way of a signed statement.[92] In *Katanga and Ngudjolo Chui* a signed statement was required and was treated by Trial Chamber II as meeting the LRV's disclosure requirements

---

[87] ICC, *Prosecutor v. Jean Pierre Bemba Gombo*, Trial Chamber III, Decision on the supplemented applications by the legal representatives of victims to present evidence and the views and concerns of victims, ICC-01/05-01/08-2138, 22 February 2012, para 30.

[88] ICC, *Prosecutor v. Laurent Gbagbo and Charles Blé Goudé*, Trial Chamber I, Directions on the conduct of the proceedings, ICC-02/11-01/15-205, 3 September 2015, para 31.

[89] ICC, *Prosecutor v. Germain Katanga and Mathieu Ngudjolo Chui*, Trial Chamber II, Corrigendum to Directions for the conduct of the proceedings and testimony in accordance with Rule 140, ICC-01/04-01/07-1665-Corr, 1 December 2009, para 22; ICC, *Prosecutor v. Germain Katanga and Mathieu Ngudjolo Chui*, Trial Chamber II, Decision on the Modalities of Victim Participation at Trial, ICC-01/04-01/07-1788-tENG, 22 January 2010, para 92.

[90] ICC, *Prosecutor v. Jean Pierre Bemba Gombo*, Trial Chamber III, Second order regarding the applications of the legal representatives of victims to present evidence and the views and concerns of victims, ICC-01/05-01/08-2027, 21 December 2011, para 19.

[91] ICC, *Prosecutor v. Jean Pierre Bemba Gombo*, Trial Chamber III, Order regarding applications by victims to present their views and concerns or to present evidence ICC-01/05-01/08-1935, 21 November 2011, para 3; ICC, *Prosecutor v. Laurent Gbagbo and Charles Blé Goudé*, Trial Chamber I, Directions on the conduct of the proceedings, ICC-02/11-01/15-205, 3 September 2015, para 31; ICC, *Prosecutor v. Bosko Ntaganda*, Trial Chamber VI, Decision on the conduct of the proceedings, ICC-01/04-02/06-619, 2 June 2015, para 69.

[92] ICC, *Prosecutor v. Germain Katanga and Mathieu Ngudjolo Chui*, Trial Chamber II, Directions for the conduct of the proceedings and testimony in accordance with rule 140, ICC-01/04-01/07-1665-Corr, 1 December 2009, para 26; ICC, *Prosecutor v. Germain Katanga and Mathieu Ngudjolo Chui*, Trial Chamber II, Decision authorising the appearance of Victims a/0381/09, a/0018/09, a/0191/08, and pan/0363/09 acting on behalf of a/0363/09, ICC-01/04-01/07-2517-tENG, 9 November 2010, para 6; ICC, *Prosecutor v. Laurent Gbagbo and Charles Blé Goudé*, Trial Chamber I, Directions on the conduct of the proceedings, ICC-02/11-01/15-205, 3 September 2015, para 31.

under Regulation 54(f) of the Regulations of the Court.[93] Redactions in this statement should be kept to a minimum but can be authorised by the Chamber on request.[94]

(iii) Time Estimates

LRVs should provide an estimate of the time required for each witness.[95]

(iv) Protective Measures

If any protective measures are sought for the witness (on these see further Chap. 6), this should also be indicated in the application, along with a justification for those measures.[96] This can include in-court measures during testimony, or the redaction of statements and transcripts.

(v) Submissions on the Substantive Requirements

Lastly, the LRV must make submissions addressing the substantive requirements which are set out in the following section of this chapter.

8.5.1.2 Substantive Requirements for the LRV Request to Call Evidence

It is not necessary for an LRV to demonstrate 'exceptional circumstances' in order for LRVs to call evidence.[97] Such a requirement would 'artificially and unfairly limit the opportunity for victims to participate.'[98]

---

[93] ICC, *Prosecutor v. Germain Katanga and Mathieu Ngudjolo Chui*, Trial Chamber II, Directions for the conduct of the proceedings and testimony in accordance with rule 140, ICC-01/04-01/07-1665-Corr, 1 December 2009, para 26.

[94] Ibid., para 27; see also ICC, *Prosecutor v. Germain Katanga and Mathieu Ngudjolo Chui*, Trial Chamber II, Decision authorising the appearance of Victims a/0381/09, a/0018/09, a/0191/08, and pan/0363/09 acting on behalf of a/0363/09, ICC-01/04-01/07-2517-tENG, 9 November 2010, para 6.

[95] ICC, *Prosecutor v. Jean Pierre Bemba Gombo*, Trial Chamber III, Order regarding applications by victims to present their views and concerns or to present evidence ICC-01/05-01/08-1935, 21 November 2011, para 3; ICC, *Prosecutor v. Abdallah Banda Abakaer Nourain*, Trial Chamber IV, Decision on the participation of victims in the trial proceedings, ICC-02/05-03/09-545, 20 March 2014, para 26; ICC, *Prosecutor v. Laurent Gbagbo and Charles Blé Goudé*, Trial Chamber I, Directions on the conduct of the proceedings, ICC-02/11-01/15-205, 3 September 2015, para 31; ICC, *Prosecutor v. Bosko Ntaganda*, Trial Chamber VI, Decision on the conduct of the proceedings, ICC-01/04-02/06-619, 2 June 2015, para 69.

[96] ICC, *Prosecutor v. Jean Pierre Bemba Gombo*, Trial Chamber III, Order regarding applications by victims to present their views and concerns or to present evidence ICC-01/05-01/08-1935, 21 November 2011, para 3; ICC, *Prosecutor v. Laurent Gbagbo and Charles Blé Goudé*, Trial Chamber I, Directions on the conduct of the proceedings, ICC-02/11-01/15-205, 3 September 2015, para 31.

[97] ICC, *Prosecutor v. Thomas Lubanga Dyilo*, Trial Chamber I, Annex to: Order issuing public redacted version of the 'Decision on the request by victims a/ 0225/06, a/0229/06 and a/0270/07 to express their views and concerns in person and to present evidence during the trial', ICC-01/04-01/06-2032-Anx, 9 July 2009, para 21; ICC, *Prosecutor v. Jean Pierre Bemba Gombo*, Trial Chamber III, Corrigendum to Decision on the participation of victims in the trial and on 86 applications by victims to participate in the proceedings, ICC-01/05-01/08-807-Corr, 12 July 2010, para 36.

[98] ICC, *Prosecutor v. Jean Pierre Bemba Gombo*, Trial Chamber III, Corrigendum to Decision on the participation of victims in the trial and on 86 applications by victims to participate in the proceedings, ICC-01/05-01/08-807-Corr, 12 July 2010, para 36.

The combined jurisprudence of the ICC indicates that at a minimum the following must be demonstrated for a chamber to approve an LRV request to call a witness:

(i) The personal interests of the victims are affected;[99]
(ii) The presentation of the proposed evidence would not be adverse to the rights of the accused or the fairness of the proceedings;[100]
(iii) The evidence would assist the chamber in its determination of the truth.[101]

---

[99] ICC, *Prosecutor v. Thomas Lubanga Dyilo*, Appeals Chamber, Judgment on the appeals of the Prosecutor and the Defence against Trial Chamber I's Decision on Victims' Participation of 18 January 2008, ICC-01/04-01/06-1432, 11 July 2008, para 104; ICC, *Prosecutor v. Germain Katanga and Mathieu Ngudjolo Chui*, Appeals Chamber, Judgment on the Appeal of Mr. Katanga Against the Decision of Trial Chamber II of 22 January 2010 Entitled 'Decision on the Modalities of Victim Participation at Trial', ICC-01/04-01/07-2288, 16 July 2010, paras 3, 40, 44; ICC, *Prosecutor v. Abdallah Banda Abakaer Nourain*, Trial Chamber IV, Decision on the participation of victims in the trial proceedings, ICC-02/05-03/09-545, 20 March 2014, para 25; ICC, *Prosecutor v. William Samoei Ruto and Joshua Arap Sang*, Trial Chamber V, Decision on victims' representation and participation, ICC-01/09-01/11-460, 3 October 2012, para 77; ICC, *Prosecutor v. Francis Kirimi Muthaura and Uhuru Muigai Kenyatta*, Trial Chamber V, Decision on victims' representation and participation, ICC-01/09-02/11-498, 3 October 2012, para 66.

[100] ICC, *Prosecutor v. Thomas Lubanga Dyilo*, Appeals Chamber, Judgment on the appeals of the Prosecutor and the Defence against Trial Chamber I's Decision on Victims' Participation of 18 January 2008, ICC-01/04-01/06-1432, 11 July 2008, para 104; ICC, *Prosecutor v. Germain Katanga and Mathieu Ngudjolo Chui*, Trial Chamber II, Directions for the conduct of the proceedings and testimony in accordance with rule 140, ICC-01/04-01/07-1665-Corr, 1 December 2009, para 21; ICC, *Prosecutor v. Germain Katanga and Mathieu Ngudjolo Chui*, Trial Chamber II, Decision authorising the appearance of Victims a/0381/09, a/0018/09, a/0191/08, and pan/0363/09 acting on behalf of a/0363/09, ICC-01/04-01/07-2517-tENG, 9 November 2010, paras 5 and 21; ICC, *Prosecutor v. Jean Pierre Bemba Gombo*, Trial Chamber III, Decision on the supplemented applications by the legal representatives of victims to present evidence and the views and concerns of victims, ICC-01/05-01/08-2138, 22 February 2012, para 23(i); ICC, *Prosecutor v. Abdallah Banda Abakaer Nourain*, Trial Chamber IV, Decision on the participation of victims in the trial proceedings, ICC-02/05-03/09-545, 20 March 2014, para 25.

[101] ICC, *Prosecutor v. Thomas Lubanga Dyilo*, Trial Chamber I, Decision on Victims' Participation, ICC-01/04-01/06-1119, 18 January 2008, para 108; See also ICC, *Prosecutor v. Germain Katanga and Mathieu Ngudjolo Chui*, Trial Chamber II, Decision on the Modalities of Victim Participation at Trial, ICC-01/04-01/07-1788-tENG, 22 January 2010, paras 91, 96; ICC, *Prosecutor v. Germain Katanga and Mathieu Ngudjolo Chui*, Appeals Chamber, Judgment on the Appeal of Mr. Katanga Against the Decision of Trial Chamber II of 22 January 2010 Entitled "Decision on the Modalities of Victim Participation at Trial", ICC-01/04-01/07-2288, 16 July 2010, para 3; ICC, *Prosecutor v. Germain Katanga and Mathieu Ngudjolo Chui*, Trial Chamber II, Directions for the conduct of the proceedings and testimony in accordance with rule 140, ICC-01/04-01/07-1665-Corr, 1 December 2009, para 20; ICC, *Prosecutor v. Jean Pierre Bemba Gombo*, Trial Chamber III, Decision on the supplemented applications by the legal representatives of victims to present evidence and the views and concerns of victims, ICC-01/05-01/08-2138, 22 February 2012, para 23(ii); ICC, *Prosecutor v. Abdallah Banda Abakaer Nourain*, Trial Chamber IV, Decision on the participation of victims in the trial proceedings, ICC-02/05-03/09-545, 20 March 2014, para 25; ICC, *Prosecutor v. William Samoei Ruto and Joshua Arap Sang*, Trial Chamber V, Decision on victims' representation and participation, ICC-01/09-01/11-460, 3 October 2012, para 77; ICC, *Prosecutor v. Francis Kirimi Muthaura and Uhuru Muigai Kenyatta*, Trial Chamber V, Decision on victims' representation and participation, ICC-01/09-02/11-498, 3 October 2012, para 66.

The first two of these requirements are sourced from Article 68(3) of the ICC Statute, while the last arises from Article 69(3). The Appeals Chamber has also referred to the requirement of 'appropriateness' under Article 68(3),[102] however, it seems that, in practice, this requirement is generally subsumed within the others rather than being considered independently from them. In at least two cases, chambers appear to have imported an additional requirement where the witness to be called is a participating victim: namely that 'the proposed testimony is typical of a larger group of participating victims, who have had similar experiences as the victim who wishes to testify.'[103] Indeed, in *Bemba*, Trial Chamber III appears to have rejected some of the LRVs' applications at least partly on this basis.[104] However, the chambers' jurisprudence does not clarify what the source or rationale or this requirement is. The following paragraphs will only elaborate on the three core requirements enunciated above.

(i) Personal Interests

Chambers have given little guidance in this context of the ways in which the victims' interests must be engaged. However it is clear from the Appeals Chamber's decision in *Lubanga*, that victims' interests in presenting evidence go beyond evidence which might support a claim to reparations.[105] The minimal discussion of this requirement in the relevant decisions suggests that the chambers take a relatively flexible approach on this requirement.

(ii) Impact on the Rights of the Accused and the Fairness of the Trial

Several defence rights have been specifically referred to by chambers in this context. The first is the right of an accused 'to adequate time and facilities to

[102] ICC, *Prosecutor v. Thomas Lubanga Dyilo*, Appeals Chamber, Judgment on the appeals of the Prosecutor and the Defence against Trial Chamber I's Decision on Victims' Participation of 18 January 2008, ICC-01/04-01/06-1432, 11 July 2008, para 104.

[103] ICC, *Prosecutor v. Germain Katanga and Mathieu Ngudjolo Chui*, Trial Chamber II, Directions for the conduct of the proceedings and testimony in accordance with rule 140, ICC-01/04-01/07-1665-Corr, 1 December 2009, para 30; ICC, *Prosecutor v. Jean Pierre Bemba Gombo*, Trial Chamber III, Decision on the supplemented applications by the legal representatives of victims to present evidence and the views and concerns of victims, ICC-01/05-01/08-2138, 22 February 2012, para 24.

[104] ICC, *Prosecutor v. Jean Pierre Bemba Gombo*, Trial Chamber III, Decision on the supplemented applications by the legal representatives of victims to present evidence and the views and concerns of victims, ICC-01/05-01/08-2138, 22 February 2012, paras 36 and 49.

[105] ICC, *Prosecutor v. Thomas Lubanga Dyilo*, Trial Chamber I, Decision on Victims' Participation, ICC-01/04-01/06-1119, 18 January 2008, para 108; see also ICC, *Prosecutor v. Jean Pierre Bemba Gombo*, Trial Chamber III, Decision on the supplemented applications by the legal representatives of victims to present evidence and the views and concerns of victims, ICC-01/05-01/08-2138, 22 February 2012, para 18.

prepare a defence.'[106] Whether this right is respected in the context of an LRV's request to lead evidence, will depend largely on questions of disclosure (see Chap. 7). The other concern which has been raised relates to the right of the accused to an expeditious trial.[107] In order to protect this right, chambers may regulate the amount of evidence led by an LRV or the number of witnesses called. Thus in *Bemba*, requests by LRVs to call (between them) 17 witnesses were rejected as excessive, and the Chamber ordered the LRVs to reduce their request to no more than 8 persons.[108]

The prohibition on victims giving testimony as witnesses anonymously can also be seen as an implementation of this rule.[109]

Finally, in *Katanga and Ngudjolo Chui*, Trial Chamber II ruled that the Chamber would only allow an LRV to call witnesses 'to the extent that this does not in effect transform them into auxiliary prosecutors.'[110] However it remains unclear what the practical implications of this ruling are. To date this principle has not been used to exclude witnesses sought to be called by an LRV.

(iii) Contribution to the Determination of the Truth

The key substantive test regarding this requirement is whether or not the chamber is convinced that the evidence in question will assist it in (or make a

---

[106] ICC, *Prosecutor v. Abdallah Banda Abakaer Nourain*, Trial Chamber IV, Decision on the participation of victims in the trial proceedings, ICC-02/05-03/09-545, 20 March 2014, para 25.

[107] ICC, *Prosecutor v. Germain Katanga and Mathieu Ngudjolo Chui*, Trial Chamber II, Directions for the conduct of the proceedings and testimony in accordance with rule 140, ICC-01/04-01/07-1665-Corr, 1 December 2009, paras 21–22; ICC, *Prosecutor v. Germain Katanga and Mathieu Ngudjolo Chui*, Trial Chamber II, Decision authorising the appearance of Victims a/0381/09, a/0018/09, a/0191/08, and pan/0363/09 acting on behalf of a/0363/09, ICC-01/04-01/07-2517-tENG, 9 November 2010, paras 5 and 21; also ICC, *Prosecutor v. Jean Pierre Bemba Gombo*, Trial Chamber III, Decision on the supplemented applications by the legal representatives of victims to present evidence and the views and concerns of victims, ICC-01/05-01/08-2138, 22 February 2012, para 23(i).

[108] ICC, *Prosecutor v. Jean Pierre Bemba Gombo*, Trial Chamber III, Second order regarding the applications of the legal representatives of victims to present evidence and the views and concerns of victims, ICC-01/05-01/08-2027, 21 December 2011, pp. 9–13.

[109] ICC, *Prosecutor v. Germain Katanga and Mathieu Ngudjolo Chui*, Trial Chamber II, Directions for the conduct of the proceedings and testimony in accordance with rule 140, ICC-01/04-01/07-1665-Corr, 1 December 2009, para 22.

[110] ICC, *Prosecutor v. Germain Katanga and Mathieu Ngudjolo Chui*, Trial Chamber II, Directions for the conduct of the proceedings and testimony in accordance with rule 140, ICC-01/04-01/07-1665-Corr, 1 December 2009, para 22.

genuine contribution to) the determination of the truth,[111] as required for the admission of evidence through Article 69(3) of the ICC Statute. This decision is made at the discretion of the chamber.[112] The most fundamental aspect of this requirement appears to be that the evidence is relevant to the charges.[113] Some chambers have formulated this as a separate substantive requirement,[114] however it may alternatively be seen as a factor going to whether or not the evidence will assist the chamber in determining the truth.

Even where the proposed evidence is apparently relevant to the charges, a chamber may nonetheless reject it as unhelpful for the determination of the truth.

[111] ICC, *Prosecutor v. Thomas Lubanga Dyilo*, Trial Chamber I, Decision on Victims' Participation, ICC-01/04-01/06-1119, 18 January 2008, para 108; See also ICC, *Prosecutor v. Germain Katanga and Mathieu Ngudjolo Chui*, Trial Chamber II, Decision on the Modalities of Victim Participation at Trial, ICC-01/04-01/07-1788-tENG, 22 January 2010, paras 91 and 96; ICC, *Prosecutor v. Germain Katanga and Mathieu Ngudjolo Chui*, Appeals Chamber, Judgment on the Appeal of Mr. Katanga Against the Decision of Trial Chamber II of 22 January 2010 Entitled "Decision on the Modalities of Victim Participation at Trial", ICC-01/04-01/07-2288, 16 July 2010, para 3; ICC, *Prosecutor v. Germain Katanga and Mathieu Ngudjolo Chui*, Trial Chamber II, Directions for the conduct of the proceedings and testimony in accordance with rule 140, ICC-01/04-01/07-1665-Corr, 1 December 2009, para 20; ICC, *Prosecutor v. Jean Pierre Bemba Gombo*, Trial Chamber III, Decision on the supplemented applications by the legal representatives of victims to present evidence and the views and concerns of victims, ICC-01/05-01/08-2138, 22 February 2012, para 23(ii); ICC, *Prosecutor v. Abdallah Banda Abakaer Nourain*, Trial Chamber IV, Decision on the participation of victims in the trial proceedings, ICC-02/05-03/09-545, 20 March 2014, para 25; ICC, *Prosecutor v. William Samoei Ruto and Joshua Arap Sang*, Trial Chamber V, Decision on victims' representation and participation, ICC-01/09-01/11-460, 3 October 2012, para 77; ICC, *Prosecutor v. Francis Kirimi Muthaura and Uhuru Muigai Kenyatta*, Trial Chamber V, Decision on victims' representation and participation, ICC-01/09-02/11-498, 3 October 2012, para 66.

[112] ICC, *Prosecutor v. Germain Katanga and Mathieu Ngudjolo Chui*, Appeals Chamber, Judgment on the Appeal of Mr. Katanga Against the Decision of Trial Chamber II of 22 January 2010 Entitled "Decision on the Modalities of Victim Participation at Trial", ICC-01/04-01/07-2288, 16 July 2010, para 40.

[113] ICC, *Prosecutor v. Germain Katanga and Mathieu Ngudjolo Chui*, Trial Chamber II, Decision authorising the appearance of Victims a/0381/09, a/0018/09, a/0191/08, and pan/0363/09 acting on behalf of a/0363/09, ICC-01/04-01/07-2517-tENG, 9 November 2010, para 14. ICC, *Prosecutor v. Germain Katanga and Mathieu Ngudjolo Chui*, Trial Chamber II, Directions for the conduct of the proceedings and testimony in accordance with rule 140, ICC-01/04-01/07-1665-Corr, 1 December 2009, para 30; ICC, *Prosecutor v. Jean Pierre Bemba Gombo*, Trial Chamber III, Decision on the supplemented applications by the legal representatives of victims to present evidence and the views and concerns of victims, ICC-01/05-01/08-2138, 22 February 2012, para 24; ICC, *Prosecutor v. Abdallah Banda Abakaer Nourain*, Trial Chamber IV, Decision on the participation of victims in the trial proceedings, ICC-02/05-03/09-545, 20 March 2014, para 25.

[114] ICC, *Prosecutor v. Abdallah Banda Abakaer Nourain*, Trial Chamber IV, Decision on the participation of victims in the trial proceedings, ICC-02/05-03/09-545, 20 March 2014, para 25.

This may happen, for example, if there are doubts about a witness' reliability.[115] It may also happen where the evidence is duplicative of evidence already heard or likely to be called by another party.[116] However, whether or not evidence is duplicative will involve a very fact specific determination. In *Lubanga*, the Prosecution argued against the presentation of evidence by the LRVs, saying that it would be duplicative of that already heard.[117] Trial Chamber I rejected this argument, noting in particular that the evidence concerned a geographical region which had not yet been the subject of prosecution evidence.[118]

Despite the consistency with which this requirement has been referred to in the ICC jurisprudence, at least one judge has rejected it. In *Bemba*, Judge Steiner considered that the requirement to show that evidence would assist the chamber in its determination of the truth 'unduly and unfairly' limited victims' ability to present evidence and is without legal basis in the court's texts. She considered them to reflect a 'utilitarian approach' to victims' participation.[119] Instead, she considered that it should be sufficient for victims to lead evidence where they have demonstrated that personal interests are affected, that the participation is appropriate and that it is consistent with the rights of the accused and a fair trial.[120] To date this appears to remain a minority view.

---

[115] ICC, *Prosecutor v. Germain Katanga and Mathieu Ngudjolo Chui*, Trial Chamber II, Decision on the Modalities of Victim Participation at Trial, ICC-01/04-01/07-1788-tENG, 22 January 2010, para 91.

[116] ICC, *Prosecutor v. Germain Katanga and Mathieu Ngudjolo Chui*, Trial Chamber II, Directions for the conduct of the proceedings and testimony in accordance with rule 140, ICC-01/04-01/07-1665-Corr, 1 December 2009, para 30; ICC, *Prosecutor v. Jean Pierre Bemba Gombo*, Trial Chamber III, Decision on the supplemented applications by the legal representatives of victims to present evidence and the views and concerns of victims, ICC-01/05-01/08-2138, 22 February 2012, para 24; ICC, *Prosecutor v. Germain Katanga and Mathieu Ngudjolo Chui*, Trial Chamber II, Decision authorising the appearance of Victims a/0381/09, a/0018/09, a/0191/08, and pan/0363/09 acting on behalf of a/0363/09, ICC-01/04-01/07-2517-tENG, 9 November 2010, para 14; ICC, *Prosecutor v. Thomas Lubanga Dyilo*, Trial Chamber I, Annex to: Order issuing public redacted version of the 'Decision on the request by victims a/ 0225/06, a/0229/06 and a/0270/07 to express their views and concerns in person and to present evidence during the trial', ICC-01/04-01/06-2032-Anx, 9 July 2009, para 26.

[117] ICC, *Prosecutor v. Thomas Lubanga Dyilo*, Trial Chamber I, Annex to: Order issuing public redacted version of the 'Decision on the request by victims a/ 0225/06, a/0229/06 and a/0270/07 to express their views and concerns in person and to present evidence during the trial', ICC-01/04-01/06-2032-Anx, 9 July 2009, para 37.

[118] Ibid.

[119] ICC, *Prosecutor. Jean Pierre Bemba Gombo*, Trial Chamber III, Partly Dissenting Opinion of Judge Sylvia Steiner on the Decision on the supplemented applications by the legal representatives of victims to present evidence and the views and concerns of victims, ICC-01/05-01/08-2138, ICC-01/05-01/08-2140, 23 February 2012, para 14.

[120] Ibid.

8.5.1.3 Questioning of Witnesses Called by the LRV

Witnesses called by the LRV are to be treated in an equivalent way to those called by parties. For example, other parties may interview them before their testimony but the calling party is entitled to have a representative present unless the chamber gives permission otherwise or the witness voluntarily consents.[121] This practice applies equally to the LRV when he or she calls a witness.[122]

In the *Katanga and Ngudjolo Chui case*, the Trial Chamber held that where an LRV requests to present evidence, its timing will depend on its content. Where participating victims themselves appear at the LRV's request to give evidence, this will occur after the close of the Prosecution case and before the Defence case.[123] However, if an LRV is given permission to lead evidence from other witnesses, this would occur after all Defence teams have concluded their cases.[124]

The Trial Chamber also explained that the reason for requiring victims called by the LRV to be heard between the Prosecution and Defence case was for the protection of the rights of the Defence: i.e., to enable the Defence to hear all the evidence against it before bringing its own case, and to effectively have 'the last word'.[125] In light of this valid consideration, it is difficult to see why non-victim witnesses called by or at the request of an LRV should not also be heard before the Defence case, given that their evidence must be expected to further the interests of the victims. Indeed other chambers have held that LRV evidence should be heard after the Prosecution case and before the Defence case.[126]

Where a witness is called either by or at the request of an LRV, it will be usual for the LRV to question the witness first, followed by the Prosecution and the

---

[121] ICC, *Prosecutor v. Germain Katanga and Mathieu Ngudjolo Chui*, Trial Chamber II, Decision on a number of procedural issues raised by the Registry, ICC-01/04-01/07-1134, 14 May 2009, para 28.

[122] ICC, *Prosecutor v. Germain Katanga and Mathieu Ngudjolo Chui*, Trial Chamber II, Decision authorising the appearance of Victims a/0381/09, a/0018/09, a/0191/08, and pan/0363/09 acting on behalf of a/0363/09, ICC-01/04-01/07-2517-tENG, 9 November 2010, para 38.

[123] ICC, *Prosecutor v. Germain Katanga and Mathieu Ngudjolo Chui*, Trial Chamber II, Decision on the Modalities of Victim Participation at Trial, ICC-01/04-01/07-1788-tENG, 22 January 2010, para 86.

[124] Ibid., paras 94–96.

[125] ICC, *Prosecutor v. Germain Katanga and Mathieu Ngudjolo Chui*, Trial Chamber II, Decision authorising the appearance of Victims a/0381/09, a/0018/09, a/0191/08, and pan/0363/09 acting on behalf of a/0363/09, ICC-01/04-01/07-2517-tENG, 9 November 2010, para 25; see also ICC, *Prosecutor v. Germain Katanga and Mathieu Ngudjolo Chui*, Trial Chamber II, Decision on the Modalities of Victim Participation at Trial, ICC-01/04-01/07-1788-tENG, 22 January 2010, para 86.

[126] ICC, *Prosecutor v. Laurent Gbagbo and Charles Blé Goudé*, Trial Chamber I, Directions on the conduct of the proceedings, ICC-02/11-01/15-205, 3 September 2015, para 12.

Defence.[127] Where a chamber calls a witness at the request of an LRV, it may decide to question the witness itself first.[128]

In principle, questioning of LRV witnesses should be neutral (not leading), but the chamber can determine otherwise on a case-by-case basis.[129]

Where witnesses are authorised to appear for an LRV, the LRV should liaise directly with Victims and Witnesses Section to make arrangements and discuss security concerns.[130]

8.5.2 Civil Parties and the Presentation of Evidence at the ECCC

At the ECCC, because they are parties to the proceedings, civil parties are not considered 'witnesses'. Notwithstanding that, civil parties may give evidence before the court (without taking an oath) and its weight and probative value is assessed on a case-by-case basis.[131] Additionally, ECCC provisions permit civil parties to request and propose witnesses both during the pre-trial and trial phases of the proceedings.[132]

For instance, in the pre-trial stage, Rule 31(10) of the Internal Rules permits civil parties or their lawyers to request the Co-Investigating Judges or the Chambers, as appropriate, to appoint additional experts to conduct new examinations or to re-examine a matter already the subject of an expert report.

---

[127] ICC, *Prosecutor v. Laurent Gbagbo and Charles Blé Goudé*, Trial Chamber I, Directions on the conduct of the proceedings, ICC-02/11-01/15-205, 3 September 2015, para 32; ICC, *Prosecutor v. Germain Katanga and Mathieu Ngudjolo Chui,* Trial Chamber II, Directions for the conduct of the proceedings and testimony in accordance with rule 140, ICC-01/04-01/07-1665-Corr, 1 December 2009, para 32.

[128] ICC, *Prosecutor v. Germain Katanga and Mathieu Ngudjolo Chui*, Trial Chamber II, Decision on the Modalities of Victim Participation at Trial, ICC-01/04-01/07-1788-tENG, 22 January 2010, para 97.

[129] ICC, *Prosecutor v. Germain Katanga and Mathieu Ngudjolo Chui*, Trial Chamber II, Directions for the conduct of the proceedings and testimony in accordance with rule 140, ICC-01/04-01/07-1665-Corr, 1 December 2009, para 32; ICC, *Prosecutor v. Germain Katanga and Mathieu Ngudjolo Chui*, Trial Chamber II, Decision authorising the appearance of Victims a/0381/09, a/0018/09, a/0191/08, and pan/0363/09 acting on behalf of a/0363/09, ICC-01/04-01/07-2517-tENG, 9 November 2010, para 35.

[130] ICC, *Prosecutor v. Germain Katanga and Mathieu Ngudjolo Chui*, Trial Chamber II, Directions for the conduct of the proceedings and testimony in accordance with rule 140, ICC-01/04-01/07-1665-Corr, 1 December 2009, para 29. See also Chap. 6.

[131] See ECCC Rules, Rule 23(4). See also Practice Direction 004/2009, Classification and Management of Case-Related Information, Article 2(e), which defines a witness as a 'person, other than a civil party'.

[132] ECCC Internal Rules, Rules 31(10), 74(e), 80, 80*bis*.

Prior to the start of the trial, the Co-Prosecutors are required to provide the Trial Chamber with a list of witnesses and experts they would like to call.[133] The civil parties then have 15 days within which to submit a list of any additional witnesses who do not feature on the Co-Prosecutor's list.[134] According to Rule 80(3) of the Internal Rules, the Trial Chamber may then order the parties, within a prescribed time limit prior to the initial hearing, to file documents additional to the submitted lists, including: (i) a summary of the facts on which each witness is expected to testify; (ii) the points of the Indictment to which each witness is expected to testify; (iii) the estimated length of testimony; (iv) a list of exhibits they intend to offer in the case; (v) an indication of the legal issues, if any, they intend to raise at the initial hearing; (vi) a list of new documents which they intend to put before the Chamber; and (vii) a list of uncontested facts, together with a reference to the relevant evidence.

In *Case 001*, several civil parties testified before the court and provided statements on their suffering.[135] The Chamber was, however, reluctant to allow *witnesses* (i.e. individuals other than civil parties) proposed by the four civil party groups. The Chamber eventually agreed to call two witnesses, out of whom only one, an expert on psychological trauma, ultimately testified.[136]

In Case *002/01*, several civil parties proposed by the Civil Party Lead Co-Lawyers testified on facts before the Chamber (in particular, movement of population) and 15 civil parties were also permitted to speak about their suffering ('impact statements').[137] No *witness* was ultimately proposed by the lawyers representing civil parties.

8.5.3 Victims Calling Evidence at the STL

At the STL, the right to call evidence is enshrined in the Rule 87(B) of the RPE, according to which 'at the trial stage, a victim participating in the proceedings may request the Trial Chamber, after hearing the Parties, to call witnesses and to authorise him to tender other evidence'. Rule 91(H) of the RPE further provides that, in preparation for trial, victims participating in the proceedings are required

[133] Ibid., Rule 80(1).

[134] Ibid., Rule 80(2).

[135] The KRT Trial Monitor, Report Issue No. 18, Week Ending August 23, 2009, https://krttrialmonitor.files.wordpress.com/2012/07/aiji_eccc_case1_no18_23aug09_en.pdf. Accessed 30 September 2016. Written correspondence with Christoph Sperfeldt, PhD Scholar, Australian National University, 2 October 2016 (notes on file with the editors).

[136] ECCC, *Case 001*, Official Public Transcript, 25 August 2009; McGonigle Leyh 2011, pp. 207–208.

[137] ECCC, *Case 002/01*, Factsheet (2014), pp. 13–14; ECCC, *Case 002/01*, Trial Chamber, Annex I (Individuals heard in *Case 002/01*) to Final decision on witness, experts and civil parties to be heard in *Case 002/01*, 7 August 2014.

to submit a list of witnesses they would like the Trial Chamber to call as well as a list of exhibits to be admitted into evidence. In practice, as with other provisions of the RPE, it is expected that this rule will be interpreted to LRVs rather than the individual victims.

In the *Ayyash* et al. case, the LRV submitted its initial lists of witnesses and exhibits on 13 December 2013.[138] The lists have since been updated and amended on two occasions.[139]

At the time of writing, the Prosecution case is still ongoing in *Ayyash* et al. It remains to be seen how the relevant rules will be interpreted in relation to the LRVs' right to present evidence.

8.6 The Right to Make Closing Submissions

Victims' lawyers have the right to make closing statements in all three of the courts analysed. At the ICC, participating victims' closing statements are routinely made immediately after the Prosecution's statements, whereas at the ECCC civil parties submit their closing statements before all others. The STL RPE suggests that legal representatives may make closing arguments after the Prosecution and before the Defence, as at the ICC.

As with opening statements, closing arguments are listed by Rule 89(1) of the ICC RPE as appropriate modalities of victim participation, if the relevant Chamber so decides.

In *Lubanga*, the OPCV lawyer and the other legal representatives were given a total of 2 h for the presentation of their closing arguments.[140] The representative of the OPCV highlighted the historical nature of the trial and the "tremendous expectations" the victims had in relation to it.[141] She stated that such expectations were fully satisfied by the trial, because the Chamber did not only recognise their statutory rights, but also granted additional prerogatives to victims.[142] Moreover, the victims' initiatives often went "over and beyond" what the Prosecution had

[138] STL, *Prosecutor v. Ayyash* et al., STL-11-01, Legal Representative of Victims, List of Witnesses and Exhibits Filed on Behalf of the Participating Victims with Confidential Annexes, 13 December 2012.

[139] STL, *Prosecutor v. Ayyash* et al., STL-11-01, Legal Representative of Victims, Amended and Updated Lists of Witnesses and Exhibits of the Legal Representative of Victims with Confidential Annexes, 26 February 2014; STL, *Prosecutor v. Ayyash* et al., Legal Representative of Victims, Amended and Updated Lists of Witnesses and Exhibits of the Legal Representative of Victims with Confidential Annexes, 1 October 2014.

[140] ICC, *Prosecutor v. Thomas Lubanga Dyilo*, Closing Statements, Official Public Transcript, ICC-01/04-01/06-T-356-ENG, 25 August 2011, p. 3.

[141] Ibid., pp. 56–57 (Remarks by Ms. P. Massida).

[142] Ibid., p. 57 (Remarks by Ms. P. Massida).

requested.[143] Nonetheless, the OPCV representative stressed that this did not mean that the victims became secondary prosecutors.[144] She further rejected the idea that child soldiers had to be viewed as criminals rather than victims and focused on the harm they had suffered.[145] The OPCV representative also underscored the higher significance of the ritual of the trial and public recognition as opposed to the sanction to be received by the accused.[146] She highlighted the difficulties faced by victims for deciding to participate and, in some cases, testify in the trial.[147] The next victims' representative to speak discussed three main points in her statement: the historical context of the armed conflict seen by the victims, the training camps, the ill-treatment undergone by children under the age of 15 and the harm they consequently suffered, as well as the specific situation of girls and the crimes committed against them in training camps.[148] The next legal representative described child soldiers participating in combat as "cannon fodder",[149] eluding this way to their precarious treatment and situation. The representative then went on to quote from NGO reports describing the methods of recruiting child soldiers in Ituri.[150] He was interrupted by the Presiding Judge and warned that referring to material not in evidence was not the most helpful line to take.[151] The legal representative then continued with quoting victims describing the crimes committed against them and finished his statement emphasising that participation in combat covered more than mere active participation in hostilities.[152] The next victims' lawyer to take the floor evoked the process through which his clients became participating victims before the ICC and stressed that their only concern when they sought participatory rights was the right to justice and truth.[153] He then defended the reliability of his clients' statements and rejected the argument of the Defence that his client had falsified their identities.[154]

In *Katanga*, closing arguments on behalf of the participating victims were presented on 16 May 2012.[155] The first legal representative to take the floor described the criteria of armed groups and stressed the importance of the characterisation of

143 Ibid., p. 58 (Remarks by Ms. P. Massida).

144 Ibid., p. 59 (Remarks by Ms. P. Massida).

145 Ibid., pp. 60–61 (Remarks by Ms. P. Massida).

146 Ibid., p. 62 (Remarks by Ms. P. Massida).

147 Ibid., pp. 63–64 (Remarks by Ms. P. Massida).

148 Ibid., pp. 66–71 (Remarks by Ms. C. Bapita).

149 Ibid., pp. 72–77 (Remarks by Mr. P. Kabongo).

150 Ibid., pp. 74–75 (Remarks by Mr. P. Kabongo).

151 Ibid., p. 75.

152 Ibid., pp. 75–76 (Remarks by Mr. P. Kabongo).

153 Ibid., pp. 77–78 (Remarks by Mr. J. Keta).

154 Ibid., 25 August 2011, pp. 79–81 (Remarks by Mr. J. Keta).

155 ICC, *Prosecutor v. Germain Katanga,* Trial Chamber II, Closing Statements, Official Public Transcript, ICC-01/04-01/07-T-337-Red-ENG, 16 May 2012.

the conflict for the status of the victims.[156] He evoked the testimony of child soldiers to emphasise their young age and vulnerability.[157] The same representative criticised the Defence for purportedly oversimplifying the facts before the Chamber.[158] The other legal representative to take the floor echoed the discomfort of his clients in the face of the perpetrators' denial that the crimes indeed took place.[159]

The closing arguments of the participating victims in the *Bemba* case were heard on 12 and 13 November 2014.[160] The first speaker from the LRV team referred to the ongoing harm and suffering that his clients still experienced.[161] In particular, he emphasised the mental and physical harm as well as the social stigma that rape caused among the victims. He also averred that the ICC Trust Fund's programme for assisting rape victims was inadequate and wrongfully executed, because the suffering and the need for assistance of the victims was not being addressed.[162] The lead legal representative for the victims then addressed the Court and outlined the historical and geographical context of the conflict in the Central African Republic as well as the facts before the Trial Chamber.[163] After welcoming the high number of participating victims and examining the most important decisions in the case,[164] the legal representative went on to highlight parts of the evidence she considered crucial in proving the guilt of the accused.[165]

At the ECCC, Internal Rule 94 permits the making of closing statements by civil parties, as well as a further statement in rebuttal of any Defence closing address. In *Case 001*, closing statements of the lawyers representing the four civil party groups were heard on 23 November 2009.[166] Those who took the floor highlighted the role, expectations and suffering of victims in the first trial of the ECCC.[167] While one lawyer emphasised that beyond any defects, there was 'a

[156] Ibid., p. 38 (Remarks by Mr. J.L. Gilissen).

[157] Ibid., p. 46 (Remarks by Mr. J.L. Gilissen).

[158] Ibid., pp. 49–51 (Remarks by Mr. J.L. Gilissen).

[159] Ibid., p. 54 (Remarks by Mr. F.N. Luvengika).

[160] ICC, *Prosecutor v. Jean-Pierre Bemba Gombo*, Trial Chamber III, Closing Statements, Official Public Transcript, ICC-01/05-01/08-T-364-Red-ENG, 12 November 2014 and Official Public Transcript, ICC-01/05-01/08-T-365-Red2-ENG, 13 November 2014.

[161] Ibid., pp. 83–85 (Remarks by Mr. C. Nzala).

[162] Ibid., pp. 85–86 (Remarks by Mr. C. Nzala).

[163] Ibid., pp. 88–90, 92–95 (Remarks by Ms. M.E. Douzima Lawson).

[164] Ibid., pp. 91–92 (Remarks by Ms. M.E. Douzima Lawson).

[165] Ibid., pp. 95–97 (Remarks by Ms. M.E. Douzima Lawson); ICC, *Prosecutor v. Jean-Pierre Bemba Gombo*, Trial Chamber III, Official Public Transcript, ICC-01/05-01/08-T-365-Red2-ENG, 13 November 2014, pp. 3–15 (Remarks by Ms. M.E. Douzima Lawson).

[166] ECCC, *Case 001*, Written Record of Proceedings, 23 November 2009, Public, p. 2.

[167] ECCC, *Case 001*, Official Public Redacted Transcript, 23 November 2009, pp. 11–22 (first group), 36–58 (second group), 74–95 (third group), 103–123 (fourth group).

sincere attempt to make the system work',[168] another highlighted the re-victimisation some of her clients suffered during their testimony.[169] The lawyers spoke at length about the evidence showing the guilt of the accused.[170] Proposed reparations projects were also outlined during the closing statements.[171]

In *Case 002/01*, lawyers representing civil parties submitted their closing statements on 16 October 2013, the first day of the final statements.[172] They highlighted parts of the evidence that illustrated the criminal design of the regime and the suffering of the civil parties throughout the relevant period.[173] They also stressed the importance of victims' participation and their desire to seek justice.[174] The lawyers further outlined thirteen proposed reparation projects to be awarded if the accused were found guilty. Projects were divided under three main categories: remembrance and memorisation; rehabilitation; and documentation and education.[175]

Victims participating at the STL are authorised to submit closing arguments under Rule 147. The hearing of the evidence in *Ayyash* et al. is still ongoing.

In general, it is clear that closing arguments at both the ICC and the ECCC have highlighted the suffering of participating victims. Submissions on the various types of harm suffered by victims are indeed important, as they summarise the pertinent evidence as well as the views and concerns of victims, where relevant. Submissions on the guilt of the accused should be made, where permitted, to complement and strengthen statements regarding the harm suffered. Evidence presented at trial linking the harm suffered to the commission of the crimes by the accused should be emphasised. Where relevant, the topic of reparations should also be addressed. Lawyers representing victims should be mindful to focus on facts before the Chamber and evidence presented at trial, both showing the harm suffered by their clients. Information outside these parameters should be sparingly used.

---

168 ECCC, *Case 001*, Official Public Redacted Transcript, 23 November 2009, pp. 4 (Remarks by Mr. K.A.A. Khan).

169 ECCC, *Case 001*, Official Public Redacted Transcript, 23 November 2009, pp. 50–53 (Remarks by Ms. S. Studzinsky).

170 ECCC, *Case 001*, Official Public Redacted Transcript, 23 November 2009, pp. 22–35 (first group), 58–71 (second group).

171 ECCC, *Case 001*, Official Public Redacted Transcript, 23 November 2009, pp. 71 (second group), 96–102 (third group), 103–123 (fourth group).

172 ECCC, *Case 002/01*, Written Record of Proceedings, 16 October 2013, Public, p. 2.

173 ECCC, *Case 002/01*, Official Public Transcript, 16 October 2013, p. 15 et seq.

174 ECCC, *Case 002/01*, Official Public Transcript, 16 October 2013, pp. 97–102.

175 ECCC, *Case 002/01*, Official Public Transcript, 16 October 2013, pp. 143–161; ECCC, *Case 002/01*, Factsheet (2014), p. 19.

8.7 The Right to Make Observations on Sentence

Only the ICC and the STL affords a role to participating victims at the sentencing stage.

At the ICC, a separate sentencing stage is permitted by Article 76(3) of the ICC Statute, and to date this approach has been favoured, resulting in sentence being imposed separately some time after the conviction.

These sentencing hearings have involved oral submissions, and the calling of additional witnesses. Legal representatives of victims were authorised to file written submissions in advance of the hearing, and make oral submissions during the hearing itself.[176] In the *Lubanga* case, both groups of victims made submissions, speaking to the gravity of the crimes, the number of victims affected, the harm suffered, the impact of the crimes on these victims, and other aggravating circumstances which they submitted the Chamber should take into account.[177] In the *Katanga* case, since the trial judgment acquitted the accused of all charges relating to the use of child soldiers,[178] and the Prosecution did not appeal this acquittal, the legal representative representing child soldiers was not given standing to participate in the sentencing phase, given the lack of a link between his clients and the sentence to be rendered. The remaining legal representative spoke about the continuing suffering of the victims, the trauma experienced as a result of the crimes, and the gravity of the crimes.[179] In *Bemba*, Trial Chamber III heard the legal representative's submissions on sentencing on 18 May 2016. The legal representative criticised the Defence for reportedly understating the seriousness of the accused's crimes, and highlighted the suffering of the victims as well as the gravity of the crimes committed.[180]

In ECCC cases to date, sentences have been handed down concurrently with the verdict. However, at the ECCC, sentencing falls within the exclusive mandate of the Co-Prosecutors. The Trial Chamber in *Case 001* expressly directed the civil parties not to make any submissions on the sentence to be imposed or submissions

---

[176] For legal representatives' written submissions, see, for example: ICC, *Prosecutor v. Germain Katanga*, Trial Chamber II, Observations relatives à la procédure et aux principes relatifs à la fixation de la peine (Ordonnance ICC-01/04-01/07-3437), ICC-01/04-01/07-3441, 17 March 2014.

[177] ICC, *Prosecutor v. Thomas Lubanga Dyilo*, Trial Chamber I, Official Public Redacted Transcript, ICC-01/04-01/06-T-360-Red-ENG, 13 June 2012, pp. 36–43.

[178] ICC, *Prosecutor v. Germain Katanga*, Trial Chamber II, Jugement rendu en application de l'article 74 du Statut, ICC-01/04-01/07-3436, 7 March 2014.

[179] ICC, *Prosecutor v. Germain Katanga*, Trial Chamber II, Official Public Redacted Transcript, ICC-01/04-01/07-T-345-Red-ENG, 6 May 2014, pp. 3–10.

[180] ICC, *Prosecutor v. Jean Pierre Bemba Gombo*, Trial Chamber III, Official Public Redacted Transcript, ICC-01/05-01/08-T-370-ENG, 18 May 2016, pp. 30–37.

relevant to sentencing, reiterating that the civil parties did not enjoy the same right of equal participation as the Co-Prosecutors.[181]

The Trial Chamber in *Case 002/01*, again by majority, confirmed that the civil parties may not intervene on questions of sentencing.[182]

Rule 87(C) of the STL Rules permits victims to voice their views and concerns at the sentencing stage. It is yet to be seen how this provision will be implemented.

8.8 Key Points

Opening statements

- Victims' lawyers have the right to make opening statements at the ICC and STL.
- Rule 89(1) of the ICC RPE states that appropriate modalities of victim participation may include making opening statements, if the Chamber so specifies. Thus far, Chambers have allowed the legal representative of victims to make opening statements immediately after that of the Prosecution.
- Victims participating at the STL are authorised to make opening statements under Rule 143. In the *Ayyash* et al. case, the LRV made an opening statement after the Prosecution.
- At the ECCC, the right to make an opening statement under Rule 89*bis* is limited to the Defence and the Prosecution.
- The practice of the ICC and STL shows that legal representatives are given considerable leeway as regards the topics covered in their opening statements. Most of the times, these remarks cover the plight of and harm suffered by the victims as well as the rights and expectations of participating victims.
- Legal practitioners are encouraged to use the opening statements to outline their case theory next to highlighting the views and concerns of their clients. When speaking of alleged crimes, victims' lawyers should limit themselves to events stated in the indictment and should at all times show respect towards the accused.

Questioning witnesses

- All three of the courts analysed allow victims' lawyers to examine witnesses called by the (other) parties or the Chamber. The limits of this right vary, however, from court to court, and in some cases, from chamber to chamber.
- At the ICC, Rule 91(2) of the RPE provides that a legal representative will be entitled to participate in hearings unless, in the circumstances of the case, the

---

[181] ECCC, *Case 001*, Trial Chamber, Decision on Civil Party Co-Lawyers' Joint request for a ruling on the standing of Civil Party Lawyers to make submissions on sentencing and directions concerning the questioning of the accused, experts, and witnesses testifying on character, 9 October 2009, para 40.

[182] ECCC, *Case 002/01*, Trial Chamber, *Case 002/01* Judgment, 7 August 2014, para 1064.

chamber concerned is of the view that the representative's intervention should be confined to written observations or submissions.

- Each trial chamber determines its own requirements to be met by legal representatives wishing to question parties' witnesses. In some cases a written filing in advance has been required. More recently oral requests immediately before the questioning have been permitted.
- The regulatory framework of the ECCC permits civil parties and their lawyers the freedom to ask questions subject only to its being conducive to ascertaining the truth. Lawyers representing civil parties need not submit any request or notice prior to questioning the witness of another Party, although time estimates are elicited by judges in advance of testimony.
- At the STL, Rule 87(B) provides that at the trial stage, a victim participating in the proceedings may, subject to the authorisation by, and under the control of, the Trial Chamber after hearing the Parties, examine or cross-examine witnesses. In the *Ayyash* et al. case, the Trial Chamber gave Rule 87(B) of the RPE an implicitly liberal interpretation by not requiring the LRV to request, in advance of testimony, leave to question witnesses. Likewise, the Trial Chamber has placed no requirement upon the LRV to provide lists of questions, or even the lines of proposed questioning. Notice of the LRV's intention to question a witness is given in the same manner as with the parties, via email or *ad hoc* oral request.
- *Scope of questioning*: The three courts have set varying limits to the scope of questioning witnesses by victims' lawyers. Generally, the personal interests of the victims have been invoked as parameters, but the interpretations given vary.
- *Mode of questioning*: There is a basic presumption that questions put to witnesses by victims, whether called by them, the chamber, or some other party, will be in a neutral and non-leading form. However, there is no absolute prohibition on cross-examination in its truer form, if challenging a witness is within the personal interest of the victims, and it is approved by the chamber.
- *Length of questioning*: The three courts vary greatly when it comes to temporal limits imposed to questioning of witnesses by victims' lawyers. At the ICC, chambers have generally refrained from allocating standard time-limits for questioning witnesses. At the ECCC, the initial approach in *Case 001* was to allow all parties to examine witnesses without any temporal limitations. This led, however, to an increasingly slow pace of the trial. To remedy this shortcoming, the Trial Chamber introduced a system of standard time allotments. At the STL, to date no standard temporal limits have been imposed in the *Ayyash* et al. case. All parties and participants are, however, invited to provide estimates of (cross-)examination (via email or in court), but the Chamber has so far been lenient about enforcing those estimates.

Challenging evidence

- All three courts permit victims' lawyers to challenge the relevance or admissibility of evidence tendered by the parties.

- At the ICC, the right of legal representatives to challenge evidence is confirmed by the Appeals Chamber. Nonetheless, the right is not unfettered and must be based on the victims' personal interests.
- At the ECCC, by virtue of Internal Rule 91(3), the right to object to the continued hearing of testimony extends to lawyers representing civil parties. The basis of any objection, namely, that it is not conducive to the truth, is sufficiently wide to countenance any objection based on relevance, admissibility or even provenance.
- At the STL, no rule prevents the LRV from challenging the evidence presented by the Parties. In the *Ayyash* et al. case, the LRV was allowed to submit observations challenging the probative value of evidence presented by the Prosecution and Defence as regards the death of one of the accused tried *in absentia*. The LRV challenged that evidence both in oral submissions before the Trial Chamber and in a written submission before the Appeals Chamber.

Calling evidence

- All three courts allow the presentation of evidence by victims' lawyers, although to varying extents.
- The possibility for victims to tender evidence at the ICC was established early, and approved by the Appeals Chamber in both the *Lubanga* and *Katanga and Ngudjolo Chui* cases. Although leading evidence relating to the guilt or innocence of the accused is primarily a right of the parties (Prosecutor and Defence), this does not preclude entirely the possibility for victims to lead evidence. This includes evidence which is not related to the issue of reparations.
- ICC chambers require that an LRV wishing to call witnesses must make a written application, which includes: (i) the identification of the proposed witness; (ii) summary the evidence which is expected from the witness; (iii) time estimates; (iv) protective measures, if relevant; and (v) submissions on the substantive requirements.
- The combined jurisprudence of the Court indicates that at a minimum the following substantive requirements must be demonstrated for a Chamber to approve an LRV request to call a witness: (i) the personal interests of the victims are affected; (ii) the presentation of the proposed evidence would not be adverse to the rights of the accused or the fairness of the proceedings; and (iii) the evidence would assist the chamber in its determination of the truth.
- In principle, civil parties at the ECCC may request and propose witnesses both during the pre-trial and trial phases of the proceedings. Prior to the start of the trial, the Co-Prosecutors are required to provide the Trial Chamber with a list of witnesses and experts they would like to call. The civil parties then have 15 days within which to submit a list of any additional witnesses who do not feature on the Co-Prosecutor's list.
- At the STL, the right to call evidence is enshrined in the Rule 87(B) of the RPE. During the trial stage, an LRV may request the Trial Chamber, after hearing the Parties, to call witnesses and to authorise the tendering of other evidence.

Rule 91(H) of the RPE requires an LRV to submit a list of witnesses which it is requested that the Trial Chamber call, as well as a list of exhibits to be admitted into evidence.

Closing statements

- Victims' lawyers have the right to make closing statements in all the courts analysed herein. At the ICC these are routinely made immediately after the Prosecution's statements, whereas at the ECCC civil parties submit their closing statements before all others. The STL RPE suggests that legal representatives may make closing arguments after the Prosecution and before the Defence.

Submissions on sentencing

- At the ICC and the STL, the legal representatives of victims are permitted to make submissions on sentencing. At the ICC, legal representatives were authorised to file written submissions in advance of the hearing, and make oral submissions during the hearing itself. Rule 87(C) of the STL Rules permits victims to voice their views and concerns at the sentencing stage. It is yet to be seen how this provision will be implemented. At the ECCC, civil parties have so far not been permitted to make submissions on sentencing.

References

Extraordinary Chambers in the Courts of Cambodia (2014) Case 002/01, Factsheet. https://www.eccc.gov.kh/sites/default/files/Guide%20to%20the%20First%20Trial%20in%20Case%20002%20-%20April2014_FINAL.pdf

McGonigle Leyh B (2011) Procedural justice? Victim participation in international criminal proceedings. Intersentia, Cambridge

Panel of Independent Experts (2014) Expert Initiative on Promoting Effectiveness at the International Criminal Court. http://ilawyerblog.com/wp-content/uploads/2014/12/Expert-Initiative-on-Promoting-Effectiveness-at-the-International-Criminal-Court-December-2014.pdf

Chapter 9
Victims Appearing in Person Before a Chamber

Daniella Rudy and Megan Hirst

Abstract This chapter analyses the approaches taken by the ICC, the STL, and the ECCC in regard to victims who appear in person to provide material to a chamber. This encompasses the situation in which a victim provides views and concerns in person, as well as the provision of testimony by a participating victim or civil party. The rules and practice of the ICC, STL and ECCC vary regarding whether these forms of participation are available to victims, and if so how they can be exercised. Notwithstanding the different approaches, all three courts recognise the value in allowing victim participants to provide information regarding the crimes charged in the indictment, and all take the position that a victim's participating status does not automatically render his or her evidence less credible. The different approaches taken by these courts can be explained in part by the fact that while victim participants may possess relevant information about a crime, they are also assumed to have an inherent interest in the outcome of the proceedings, whether in the form of a conviction, a particular sentence or being granted reparations for the damages they suffered as a result of the crimes committed. Accordingly, the courts have found various ways to minimise any prejudice caused to the rights of the accused by having participating victims providing evidence or presenting views in person.

Daniella Rudy is a legal officer at the Mechanism for International Criminal Tribunals, The Hague, The Netherlands. The views expressed herein are those of the author alone and do not necessarily reflect the views of the Mechanism for International Criminal Tribunals or the United Nations in general. Megan Hirst is a barrister at Doughty Street Chambers in London and a member of an LRV team in *Prosecutor v. Dominic Ongwen*. She has previously worked on victims' participation in the Registries of the ICC and the STL.

D. Rudy (✉)
Mechanism for International Criminal Tribunals, The Hague, The Netherlands
e-mail: daniellarudy@gmail.com

M. Hirst
London, UK
e-mail: m.hirst@doughtystreet.co.uk

K. Tibori-Szabó and M. Hirst (eds.), *Victim Participation in International Criminal Justice*, International Criminal Justice Series 11,
DOI 10.1007/978-94-6265-177-7_9

Keywords Dual status · Protective measures · Confidentiality · Disclosure obligations · Providing evidence

Contents

9.1 Introduction

Victims of the crimes outlined in the relevant Statutes are granted *in-person* participatory rights to varying degrees at the International Criminal Court (ICC), the Special Tribunal for Lebanon (STL) and the Extraordinary Chambers of the Courts of Cambodia (ECCC). Differences exist at the ICC (and might exist at the STL) with respect to the approaches depending on whether the victim seeks to appear in order to express views and concerns or to provide evidence. Among the latter category, further differences may exist depending on whether the victim is called by a party (the Prosecution or the Defence) or at the behest of the legal representatives of victims (LRVs). This chapter will deal with participating victims who either provide views and concerns in person, or who appear in person to provide information that is treated as evidence. Specifically, it will first provide an overview of different forms of in-person participation by victims at the tribunals, followed by a more detailed discussion of the appearance of victims in person to present views and concerns and the appearance of participating victims or civil parties to give evidence. Thereafter, the chapter will analyse the procedural requirements at the three courts for victims who give evidence and the practical implications of giving evidence as a participating victim or civil party. The chapter will briefly touch on the risks associated with calling a participating victim to give evidence. Lastly, the chapter will discuss matters associated with witness familiarisation and preparation, concluding with the key points to take away from in-person participation of victims at the different tribunals.

This chapter should be read together with the previous one, which looks at the various modalities through which victims' lawyers can represent their clients' interests in the courtroom.

9.2 Overview: Forms of In-Person Participation by Victims

As mentioned above, victims may be granted permission to appear in person before a tribunal in different capacities. The most fundamental distinction in theory is between an appearance to provide views and concerns in person, and an appearance in person to provide evidence. To date, the possibility for the former type of participation has only been identified at the ICC, and at the time of writing had only occurred in the *Bemba* case. Overall, the majority of victim appearances at the ICC are of victims called to provide evidence as witnesses.

Where victims appear in person to provide evidence, further categories can be discerned. At the ICC and the STL, these victims are usually referred to as 'dual status' victims.[1] Different rules and procedures may apply to dual status victims depending on whether the victim is called by a party (Prosecution or Defence) or appears at the request of the LRV (see Chap. 8).

At the ECCC, civil parties can be called by the Civil Party Lead Co-Lawyers, by the Prosecution, or by the Defence to provide evidence before the court. They can also provide statements of suffering after their testimony or at a so-called impact hearing. Contrary to the situation before the ICC and the STL, and as explained in further detail below, civil parties are parties to the proceedings, do not testify under oath, and are not considered witnesses.[2]

9.3 Appearance of Victims in Person to Present Views and Concerns

The ICC is the first, and to date only, court that has allowed victims to appear in person before a chamber to provide their *views and concerns*, as opposed to giving evidence. Participation of victims at the ICC is based on Article 68(3) of

[1] While Trial Chamber I appears to refer to dual status victims only when victims are called by the Prosecution to testify (See, e.g., ICC, *Prosecutor v. Thomas Lubanga Dyilo*, Trial Chamber I, Judgment pursuant to Article 74 of the Statute, ICC-01/04-01/06-2842, 14 March 2012, para 19), other trial chambers appear to refer to dual status victims more broadly, including to those victims called by their LRV to testify. See ICC, *Prosecutor v. Abdallah Banda Abakaer Nourain*, Trial Chamber IV, Decision on the participation of victims in the trial proceedings, ICC-02/05-03/09-545, 20 March 2014, paras 21–22.

[2] See Sect. 9.4.2.

the ICC Statute, which provides that: '[w]here the personal interests of the victims are affected, the Court shall permit their views and concerns to be presented and considered at stages of the proceedings determined to be appropriate by the Court and in a manner which is not prejudicial to or inconsistent with the rights of the accused and a fair and impartial trial.' While 'views and concerns' are usually presented on behalf of victims by their legal representatives, ICC jurisprudence indicates that in some instances they may be presented by victims themselves in person.

Only three victims who participated in the *Bemba* case have appeared in person for the sole purpose to present views and concerns before the ICC. However, some other ICC chambers have discussed this possibility.

The system of victim participation established at the STL follows that of the ICC in that it is centred around the concept of victims being able to express their views and concerns in the proceedings in various forms.[3] To date, requests for participating victims to present their views and concerns in person have not yet been raised at the STL. In any case, at the time of writing, proceedings in the *Ayyash* et al. case have not yet reached the end of the Prosecution case. It is therefore unclear whether this issue will be raised by the LRVs and, if so, how it will be resolved by that Tribunal.

In contrast, the role of civil parties at the ECCC is different. It does not involve a focus on the expression of views and concerns. To date victims have only appeared in person before the ECCC for the purpose of giving evidence, either about the crimes alleged or the harm suffered by the civil parties. No request has been made for a civil party to appear in person before a chamber for the purpose of providing submissions or views.

As it is only the ICC which has developed this concept to date, the following section of this chapter will review the principles developed to date at the ICC regarding the in-person presentation of views and concerns by participating victims.

9.3.1 The Nature and Content of Views and Concerns Presented in Person

Trial Chamber I in the *Lubanga* case was the first to deal with this issue. It explained that the presentation of views and concerns by victims are essentially considered submissions, rather than evidence.[4] The Chamber clarified that while the views and concerns of the participating victims may assist the Chamber in its approach to the evidence in the case, these views and concerns (whether made personally or submitted through the legal representatives) will not form part of the trial evidence.[5]

[3] See STL Statute, Article 17. See also STL RPE, Rules 86–87.

[4] ICC, *Prosecutor v. Thomas Lubanga Dyilo*, Trial Chamber, Decision on the request by victims a/0225/06, a/0229/06 and a/0270/07 to express their views and concerns in person and to present evidence during the trial, ICC-01/04-01/06-2032-Anx, 26 June 2009, para 25.

[5] Ibid.

Trial Chamber I's approach in the *Lubanga* case was, at least initially and in principle, endorsed by Trial Chamber III in the *Bemba* case. Trial Chamber III also noted the difference between giving evidence and expressing views and concerns.[6] It insisted that 'views and concerns' given by victims in person would not be treated as part of the evidence in the case.[7]

Trial Chamber III requested that the victims focus their 'views and concerns' on the harm suffered and on the impact of the alleged crimes on their lives.[8] There appear to be two problems with this approach. The first is that it unduly restricts the material on which victims might have been interested in addressing the court. The wording of Article 68(3) of the ICC Statute implies no such limitation on the subject matter of the views and concerns which victims might express, requiring only that the victims' 'personal interests' must be affected by the matter at hand. No explanation or justification was given by the Chamber as to why victims should only be permitted to provide views and concerns on the specific question of the harm suffered and its impact.

In addition, Trial Chamber III's approach in this regard appears to be at odds with the recognition (by both Trial Chambers I and III) that views and concerns essentially amount to *submissions*. They may therefore conceivably relate to a variety of matters, not only concerning the evidence about events which are the subject of the case, but also concerning the conduct of the proceedings or its possible outcomes. It is also not clear how the 'views and concerns' envisaged by Trial Chamber III, which concern the specific harm suffered by victims, differ from evidence concerning such harm. Indeed, as further discussed below, the consequence of Trial Chamber III's approach was that the material which was eventually presented as 'views and concerns' by victims in the *Bemba* case was not easily distinguishable from that which might have been presented as evidence.

9.3.2 Exceptionality of Victims Presenting Views and Concerns in Person

In *Lubanga*, Trial Chamber I explained that victims' appearance in person to present views and concerns would be an exception rather than the norm, explaining that: 'It needs to be remembered that this is a court of law and, in particular, this is the criminal trial of an accused, and the presumption is that those

6 ICC, *Prosecutor v. Jean-Pierre Bemba Gombo*, Trial Chamber III, Decision on the supplemental applications by the legal representatives of victims to present evidence and the views and concerns of victims, ICC-01/05-01/08-2138, 22 February 2012, paras 19–20.

7 Ibid.

8 ICC, *Prosecutor v. Jean-Pierre Bemba Gombo*, Trial Chamber, Transcript 25 June 2010, ICC-01/05-01/08-T-227-Red, pp. 21–22; ICC, *Prosecutor v. Jean-Pierre Bemba Gombo*, Trial Chamber, Transcript 26 June 2010, ICC-01/05-01/08-T-228-Red, p. 10.

who participate in the proceedings will be lawyers …'.[9] The Chamber therefore indicated that for a victim to present views or concerns in person, 'cogent, indeed powerful reasons' would need to be demonstrated.[10] This approach appears to have been endorsed by Trial Chamber IV in the *Banda* case.[11]

Although Trial Chamber III in the *Bemba* case did not expressly approve or follow this principle, its approach to requests for victims to present views and concerns also appears to reflect the idea that such requests should be granted exceptionally. The LRVs initially requested 17 victims to appear in person either to present evidence or views or concerns, but this was considered excessive by the Chamber and the LRVs were asked to present a new request limited to no more than eight victims.[12] From the eight victims then requested to present views and concerns, three were authorised to do so by the majority of the Chamber.[13] They remain the only three victims to have been granted such authorisation at the ICC to date. While Judge Steiner dissented regarding some of the victims not permitted to express their views and concerns in person, she nonetheless agreed with the majority that 'strict limitations' are required on numbers of victims who may express their views and concerns in person, in order to ensure expeditious proceedings.[14]

9.3.3 Requirements for Victims to Present Views and Concerns in Person

Requests to present views and concerns in person must be made in writing.[15] However, the specific information required to be included in such requests has

9 ICC, *Prosecutor v. Thomas Lubanga Dyilo*, Trial Chamber, Transcript 12 January 2009, ICC-01/04-01/06-T-101-ENG, p. 43.

10 Ibid.

11 *Prosecutor v. Abdallah Banda Abakaer Nourain*, Trial Chamber IV, Decision on the participation of victims in the trial proceedings, ICC-02/05-03/09-545, 20 March 2014, para 20.

12 ICC, *Prosecutor v. Jean-Pierre Bemba Gombo*, Trial Chamber III, Second order regarding the applications of the legal representatives of victims to present evidence and the views and concerns of victims, ICC-01/05-01/08-2027, 21 December 2011, paras 11–12.

13 ICC, *Prosecutor v. Jean-Pierre Bemba Gombo*, Trial Chamber III, Decision on the supplemental applications by the legal representatives of victims to present evidence and the views and concerns of victims, ICC-01/05-01/08-2138, 22 February 2012, para 55.

14 ICC, *Prosecutor v. Jean-Pierre Bemba Gombo*, Trial Chamber III, Partly Dissenting Opinion of Judge Sylvia Steiner on the Decision on the supplemented applications by the legal representatives of victims to present evidence and the views and concerns of victims, ICC-01/05-01/08-2138, ICC-01/05-01/08-2140, 23 February 2012, paras 18–20.

15 ICC, *Prosecutor v. Thomas Lubanga Dyilo*, Trial Chamber I, Decision on Victims' Participation, ICC-01/04-01/06-1119, 18 January 2008, paras 103–104; ICC, *Prosecutor v. Ruto and Sang*, Trial Chamber, Decision on victim's participation, ICC-01/09-01/11-460, 3 October 2012, para 56–57; ICC, *Prosecutor v Uhuru Muigai Kenyatta*, Trial Chamber V, Decision on victims' representation and participation, ICC-01/09-02/11-498, 3 October 2012, paras 55–56.

varied among chambers. Trial Chambers I and III also took different views regarding the substantive criteria which would be used to determine whether a victim may present his or her views and concerns in person.

In the *Lubanga* case an initial application for three participating victims to appear in person following the end of the Prosecution case was deemed insufficiently informative by the Chamber, including because it did not make clear whether the victims wished to appear in person to give evidence or to present views and concerns. Trial Chamber I set out a number of matters that the LRV must address when re-filing the application:

(i) a detailed account as to the areas that each of the three victims wish to address when expressing their views and concerns (if this is to be the suggested approach);
(ii) is it intended that their participation should be within the context of and limited to their entitlement to express their views and concerns as opposed to giving evidence under oath tested by questioning;
(iii) why is it considered more appropriate for this material to be presented by the witnesses themselves rather than by counsel on their behalf;
(iv) the rationale underlying the suggestion that their intervention should be at the end of the evidence called by the Prosecution rather than as a part of the general submissions at the close of the case;
(v) whether it is proposed that any of the victims participating in this way are to remain anonymous vis-a-vis the Defence and, if so, the suggested justification for this approach; and
(vi) if any victims are intending to give evidence, what proposals are made as regards disclosure to the parties and other interested participants (particularly if the issues potentially relate to the alleged guilt of the accused).[16]

Trial Chamber I indicated that it would need to consider case-by-case any application for in-person presentation of views and concerns,[17] but anticipated some factors that it would consider. These included whether granting the application would result in issues and facts being 'unnecessarily repeated (e.g. first in a victims' personal presentation of his or her views and concerns, then repeated by them in evidence and finally addressed on a third occasion by the LRVs in submissions).' The Chamber explained that '[a]lthough evidence can be commented upon in submissions or during the process of presenting views and concerns, overall this exercise must be proportionate and consistent with a fair trial.'[18]

[16] ICC, *Prosecutor v. Thomas Lubanga Dyilo*, Trial Chamber, Transcript 8 May 2009, ICC-01/04-01/06-T-171-ENG, pp. 37–38.

[17] ICC, *Prosecutor v. Thomas Lubanga Dyilo*, Trial Chamber, Decision on the request by victims a/0225/06, a/0229/06 and a/0270/07 to express their views and concerns in person and to present evidence during the trial, ICC-01/04-01/06-2032-Anx, 26 June 2009, para 27.

[18] Ibid.

The Chamber also reiterated that it would consider whether it was appropriate for the victims' views and concerns to be presented in person or whether their LRV was better placed to make submissions for them.[19] The Chamber granted the victims' requests to give evidence in person, but instructed that having done so they reconsider on advice from their LRV whether they still wished to present views and concerns in person, or whether this would better be done by counsel on their behalf.[20] Ultimately the request to present views and concerns in person was not renewed following the giving of evidence by the participating victims, and so no further decision on this matter was required from the Trial Chamber.

In the *Bemba* case, Trial Chamber III specified slightly different requirements to be met by an LRV seeking permission for victims to present their views and concerns in person. The Chamber indicated that the LRV must address the following issues in a written application:

(i.) The manner in which the victims' views and concerns are to be presented, e.g., in-person pursuant to Rule 89 of the Rules or in writing;
(ii.) The estimated time needed for the victims to present their views and concerns;
(iii.) How the personal interests of the participating victims would be affected by the presentation of their views and concerns to the Chamber;
(iv.) Whether the victims wish their views and concerns to be presented publicly, or whether they need to be afforded in-court protective measures;
(v.) Whether the victims are persons authorised to participate in the trial, and if so, the application numbers under which those persons are registered.[21]

The last of these requirements curiously appears to suggest the possibility that victims not authorised formally to participate in the trial proceedings might nonetheless be granted the possibility to present their views and concerns in person. However, the Chamber provided no further elaboration on the rationale for this or the circumstances in which it may be appropriate.

In establishing the substantive requirements for the in-person presentation of views and concerns Trial Chamber III appears to have created its own principles, somewhat divergent from the approach suggested by Trial Chamber I, although with little explanation or reference to legal texts or jurisprudence. First, the Chamber considered that 'the threshold to grant applications by victims to give evidence is significantly higher than the threshold applicable to applications by victims to

[19] Ibid.

[20] ICC, *Prosecutor v. Thomas Lubanga Dyilo*, Trial Chamber, Decision on the request by victims a/0225/06, a/0229/06 and a/0270/07 to express their views and concerns in person and to present evidence during the trial, ICC-01/04-01/06-2032-Anx, 26 June 2009, para 40.

[21] ICC, *Prosecutor v. Jean-Pierre Bemba Gombo*, Trial Chamber, Order regarding applications by victims to present their views and concerns or to present evidence, ICC-01/05-01/08-1935, 21 November 2011, para 3(c).

express their views and concerns in person'.[22] This appears to suggest a departure from the approach of Trial Chamber I, which highlighted that the presentation of views and concerns (in contrast to the presentation of evidence) is squarely within the normal work of an LRV, and required that some special reason should therefore exist before victims be permitted to do this themselves.

Secondly, although the Chamber endorsed the statement of Trial Chamber I from *Lubanga* that deciding on requests to present views and concerns in person involves 'fact-specific decisions [...] taking into account the circumstances of the trial as a whole'[23] it appears to have adopted a different approach in practice. The Chamber stated that it would 'consider whether the personal interests of the individual victims are affected and whether the accounts expected to be provided are representative of a larger number of victims'.[24] However rather than analysing the content of the 'views and concerns' to be presented by each victim, the Chamber focused exclusively on the nature of the harm suffered by the victim in question.[25]

Trial Chamber III in *Bemba* ultimately allowed three victims to present their views and concerns in person.[26] Other victims were refused the opportunity to do so purely because of the type of harm they suffered, which apparently indicated that the 'account that could be provided' was not 'representative of a larger number of victims'.[27] As mentioned above, the Trial Chamber requested that the victims focus their accounts on the harm suffered and on the impact of the alleged crimes on their lives.[28] Although Presiding Judge Steiner issued a partially dissenting opinion on the requests, and preferred an approach whereby permission to present views and concerns should more readily be granted to victims, she nonetheless appeared to endorse the link made by the majority between the harm suffered by a victim and the views and concerns the victim would present.[29]

[22] ICC, *Prosecutor v. Jean-Pierre Bemba Gombo*, Trial Chamber, Decision on the supplemental applications by the legal representatives of victims to present evidence and the views and concerns of victims, ICC-01/05-01/08-2138, 22 February 2012, para 20. See also ICC, *Prosecutor v. Jean-Pierre Bemba Gombo*, Trial Chamber, Transcript 25 June 2012, ICC-01/05-01/08-T-Red-ENG WT, pp. 20–21.

[23] ICC, *Prosecutor v. Jean-Pierre Bemba Gombo*, Trial Chamber, Decision on the supplemental applications by the legal representatives of victims to present evidence and the views and concerns of victims, ICC-01/05-01/08-2138, 22 February 2012, para 22.

[24] Ibid.

[25] Ibid., paras 22, 36, 39, 42, 54.

[26] Ibid., para 55(b).

[27] Ibid., para 36; see also para 49.

[28] ICC, *Prosecutor v. Jean-Pierre Bemba Gombo*, Trial Chamber, Transcript 25 June 2010, ICC-01/05-01/08-T-227-Red, pp. 21–22; ICC, *Prosecutor v. Jean-Pierre Bemba Gombo*, Trial Chamber, Transcript 26 June 2010, ICC-01/05-01/08-T-228-Red, p. 10.

[29] ICC, *Prosecutor v. Jean-Pierre Bemba Gombo*, Trial Chamber III, Partly Dissenting Opinion of Judge Sylvia Steiner on the Decision on the supplemented applications by the legal representatives of victims to present evidence and the views and concerns of victims, ICC-01/05-01/08-2138, ICC-01/05-01/08-2140, 23 February 2012, para 31.

In the Kenya cases, Trial Chamber V required that where an LRV wished to request for victims to present views and concerns in person, the LRV was to submit a request on the victims' behalf 'explaining why they are considered best placed to reflect the interests of the victims, together with a detailed summary of the aspects that will be addressed by each victim if authorised to present his or her views and concerns'.[30] These victims would also be required to undergo the detailed application process set out in Rule 89(1) of the Rules of Procedure and Evidence (ICC RPE) and Regulation 86 of the Regulations of the Court, whereas other victims were not required to do so in these cases.[31] Trial Chamber V did not elaborate in detail on what basis it would determine the requests for presenting views and concerns in person, saying only that it would make a 'preliminary assessment as to whether the suggested form of participation is appropriate and identify a limited number of victims who may be authorised [to appear in person]'.[32] A final decision would then be taken following the receipt of observations from the parties.[33]

Finally, Trial Chamber VI in the *Ntaganda* case has allowed for the possibility that victims may be permitted to 'participate directly', meaning to present their views and concerns in person to the court, but indicated that the relevant procedure would be decided upon if and when the Chamber decided to allow for this kind of participation.[34] To date the Chamber has not further pronounced itself on this matter.

---

30 ICC, *Prosecutor v. Ruto and Sang*, Trial Chamber, Decision on victim's participation, ICC-01/09-01/11-460, 3 October 2012, para 56–57; ICC, *Prosecutor v. Uhuru Muigai Kenyatta*, Trial Chamber V, Decision on victims' representation and participation, ICC-01/09-02/11-498, 3 October 2012, paras 55–56.

31 ICC, *Prosecutor v. Ruto and Sang*, Trial Chamber, Decision on victim's participation, ICC-01/09-01/11-460, 3 October 2012, paras 25; ICC, *Prosecutor v. Uhuru Muigai Kenyatta*, Trial Chamber V, Decision on victims' representation and participation, ICC-01/09-02/11-498, 3 October 2012, paras 24.

32 ICC, *Prosecutor v. Ruto and Sang*, Trial Chamber, Decision on victim's participation, ICC-01/09-01/11-460, 3 October 2012, para 57; ICC, *Prosecutor v. Uhuru Muigai Kenyatta*, Trial Chamber V, Decision on victims' representation and participation, ICC-01/09-02/11-498, 3 October 2012, para 56.

33 ICC, *Prosecutor v. Ruto and Sang*, Trial Chamber, Decision on victim's participation, ICC-01/09-01/11-460, 3 October 2012, para 58; ICC, *Prosecutor v. Uhuru Muigai Kenyatta*, Trial Chamber V, Decision on victims' representation and participation, ICC-01/09-02/11-498, 3 October 2012, para 57. Charges against Kenyatta were withdrawn in December 2014. Proceedings against Ruto and Sang were terminated in April 2016.

34 ICC, *Prosecutor v. Bosco Ntaganda,* Trial Chamber VI, Decision on Victim Participation, ICC-01/04-02/06-449, 6 February 2015, para 38. See also ICC, *Prosecutor v. Jean-Pierre Bemba Gombo*, Second order regarding the applications of the legal representatives of victims to present evidence and the views and concerns of victims, ICC-01/05-01/08-2027, 21 December 2011, para 13.

9.3.4 Timing of the Presentation of Views and Concerns

In the *Bemba* case, the three victims who presented their views and concerns in person did so between the Prosecution and Defence cases, and after the Court had heard from two participating victims who gave evidence. Trial Chamber III had previously determined that this is when such views and concerns, presented in person, would be heard.[35]

In contrast, Trial Chamber I in the *Lubanga* case appeared to have in mind the possibility that such views and concerns might be more appropriately heard after the conclusion of evidence in the case. Although ultimately no victims appeared in person in the *Lubanga* case for the purpose of expressing views and concerns, the Chamber responded to the LRV's initial request by requesting, *inter alia*, clarification as to 'the rationale underlying the suggestion that [the victims'] intervention should be at the end of the evidence called by the Prosecution rather than as a part of the general submissions at the close of the case.'[36]

The approach suggested by Trial Chamber I in *Lubanga* reflects the Chamber's view that the in-person presentation of views and concerns needs to be distinguished from evidence, and that it in effect constitutes a form of submission. From this perspective it is not clear why Trial Chamber III considered that this material should be heard together with victims' evidence in the *Bemba* case, except by reference to the interpretation that the Chamber's approach in effect conflated these 'views and concerns' with evidence (see 9.3.1 above). However, if the presentation of 'views and concerns' by a victim is equivalent to the in-person making of submissions, then neither is it clear that they should be restricted to being heard at the close of the case. Rather the timing of the 'views and concerns', like the timing of any other submissions, should arguably depend on their content. As apparently contemplated by Trial Chamber I's request for clarification, 'views and concerns' touching on the substance of the case may be best heard at the close of the case. However, those relating to procedural issues should be dealt with when those issues arise in the proceedings. Indeed, this appears to have been the approach proposed by Trial Chamber V in the Kenya cases (although no victims ultimately presented views and concerns in person in either of those cases). The Chamber indicated that victims wishing to present their views and concerns in person 'may be allowed to do so at various stages of the trial' although it specifically highlighted opening and closing statements as moments when this could occur.[37]

---

[35] ICC, *Prosecutor v. Jean-Pierre Bemba Gombo*, Trial Chamber, Order regarding applications by victims to present their views and concerns or to present evidence, ICC-01/05-01/08-1935, 21 November 2011, para 3(f).

[36] ICC, *Prosecutor v. Thomas Lubanga Dyilo*, Trial Chamber, Transcript 8 May 2009, ICC-01/04-01/06-T-171-ENG, p. 37.

[37] ICC, *Prosecutor v. William Samoei Ruto and Joshua Arap Sang*, Trial Chamber V, Decision on victims' representation and participation, ICC-01/09-01/11-460, 3 October 2012, paras 56 and 73; ICC, *Prosecutor v. Uhuru Muigai Kenyatta*, Trial Chamber V, Decision on victims' representation and participation, ICC-01/09-02/11-498, 3 October 2012, paras 55 and 72.

9.3.5 Procedure for the Presentation of Views and Concerns

In the *Bemba* case, all three victims who appeared to present their 'views and concerns' did so via video-link.[38] The Chamber did not accept a proposal from the Prosecution that victims' views and concerns be provided in writing.[39] Similarly, in discussing the possibility for victims to present views and concerns, the Chambers in the two Kenya cases considered that this could be done either in person or via video-link.[40]

In the *Bemba* case, Trial Chamber III held that the LRV would be responsible for 'guiding the victim through his or her presentation of views and concerns but shall limit the intervention to questions that would facilitate this presentation'.[41] In addition, the Chamber noted that it may also address the victims at any time considered appropriate.[42] In practice, victims' 'views and concerns' were presented in person through a procedure very similar to examination in chief: the victims' legal representative asked questions and responses were given by the victim.[43] However in light of the principle that the 'views and concerns' do not constitute evidence, Trial Chamber III held that the victims would not take an oath or be subjected to questioning by the parties or other participants.[44]

Similarly, because they were not providing evidence, victims who appeared to provide views and concerns in person did not undergo the kind of formal familiarisation provided to witnesses. However, Trial Chamber III required that the Victims and Witnesses Unit (VWU) provide the victims with 'certain minimal guidance and explanation relating to the process of providing their view and concerns.'[45]

---

[38] ICC, *Prosecutor v. Jean-Pierre Bemba Gombo*, Trial Chamber III, Decision on the presentation of views and concerns by victims a/0542/08, a/0394/08 and a/0511/08, ICC-01/05-01/08-2220, 24 May 2012, para 7. See also ICC, *Prosecutor v. Jean-Pierre Bemba Gombo*, Transcript 25 June 2010, ICC-01/05-01/08-T-227-Red, p. 2.

[39] ICC, *Prosecutor v. Jean-Pierre Bemba Gombo*, Trial Chamber III, Decision on the presentation of views and concerns by victims a/0542/08, a/0394/08 and a/0511/08, ICC-01/05-01/08-2220, 24 May 2012, para 2.

[40] ICC, *Prosecutor v. William Samoei Ruto and Joshua Arap Sang*, Trial Chamber V, Decision on victims' representation and participation, ICC-01/09-01/11-460, 3 October 2012, paras 25, 56, 58; ICC, *Prosecutor v. Uhuru Muigai Kenyatta*, Trial Chamber V, Decision on victims' representation and participation, ICC-01/09-02/11-498, 3 October 2012, paras 24, 55, 57.

[41] ICC, *Prosecutor v. Jean-Pierre Bemba Gombo*, Trial Chamber III, Decision on the presentation of views and concerns by victims a/0542/08, a/0394/08 and a/0511/08, ICC-01/05-01/08-2220, 24 May 2012, para 8.

[42] Ibid.

[43] ICC, *Prosecutor v. Jean-Pierre Bemba Gombo*, Transcript 25 June 2010, ICC-01/05-01/08-T-227-Red, pp. 6–15, 22–29, 37–46; *Prosecutor v. Jean-Pierre Bemba Gombo*, Transcript 26 June 2010, ICC-01/05-01/08-T-228-Red, pp. 3–8, 13–27.

[44] ICC, *Prosecutor v. Jean-Pierre Bemba Gombo*, Trial Chamber III, Decision on the presentation of views and concerns by victims a/0542/08, a/0394/08 and a/0511/08, ICC-01/05-01/08-2220, 24 May 2012, para 7.

[45] Ibid., para 10.

9.3.6 Disclosure Obligations for Victims Expressing Views and Concerns in Person

In *Bemba*, the only case to date where victims have presented their views and concerns in person, Trial Chamber III found that the disclosure obligations incumbent on the victims presenting their views and concerns were the same as for those giving evidence:

> In line with the procedure applied in the context of victims that had been authorised to give evidence, the Chamber needs to ensure that the parties are provided, for their information, with the relevant portions of the *ex parte* annexes to the Chamber's decisions on victims' applications [...], less redacted versions of the victims' application forms, and less redacted versions of the victims' written statements.[46]

Accordingly, the Chamber ordered that less redacted versions of the three application forms should be provided to the parties before the victims' appearance.[47] Likewise, Trial Chamber III ordered that lesser redacted versions of their witness statements should be filed confidentially.[48] When providing lesser redacted versions of the statements, the Chamber instructed the legal representatives to ensure that any redactions to information pertaining to the victims' identities were lifted while any redactions to the identities of third parties and the victims' exact addresses were maintained.[49]

Trial Chamber III's approach on these issues is consistent with its tendency, discussed above, to treat the presentation of views and concerns as something very much akin to the provision of testimony. It is unclear what, if any, disclosure obligations may arise if victims were ever permitted to present views or concerns in person which did not concern *factual* matters.

9.3.7 Protective Measures for Victims Expressing Views and Concerns in Person

The general principles relating to protective measures for participating victims are found in Chap. 6 of this book. This section will therefore consider only the specific approach applied to date at the ICC where victims appear in person to express their views and concerns. Two questions arise in this regard: To what extent such victims may maintain procedural protective measures such as anonymity (permitted at the ICC)? And what forms of in-court protective measures may be made available to them?

46 Ibid., para 12.

47 Ibid., para 13(f).

48 Ibid., para 13(g).

49 Ibid., para 12.

Regarding the maintenance of procedural protective measures, Trial Chamber I in *Lubanga* did not take a clear position. The Chamber requested submissions from the LRV on 'whether it is proposed that any of the victims participating in this way are to remain anonymous *vis-a-vis* the Defence and, if so, the suggested justification for this approach.'[50] However, since the LRV ultimately did not pursue the application for victims to present views in person, this matter was not decided by the Trial Chamber.

In the *Bemba* case, Trial Chamber III held that victims granted authorisation to appear in person to present views and concerns must first relinquish their anonymity and have their identities disclosed to the parties.[51] The Chamber did not explain its reasoning for this approach, citing only previous jurisprudence from the *Katanga and Ngudjolo Chui* case which related not to victims presenting views and concerns in person but to the presentation of *evidence* by participating victims.[52] The Chamber did not explain why it considered that a principle applicable to witnesses, and intending to protect the accused from anonymous accusations, should be applicable to victims simply because their views and concerns (i.e. submissions) were being expressed in person rather than through their LRV, and apparently regardless of the content of those submissions.

In the Kenya cases, Trial Chamber V went even further, and determined that victims *seeking* to appear in person before the court to express their views and concerns would have their identities disclosed to the parties in order that observations could be made.[53] These victims would therefore lose their anonymity regardless of whether they were ultimately permitted to appear in person or not. Again, the Chamber did not offer an explanation as to why anonymity was impermissible in these circumstances.

---

[50] ICC, *Prosecutor v. Thomas Lubanga Dyilo*, Trial Chamber, Transcript 8 May 2009, ICC-01/04-01/06-T-171-ENG, p. 37.

[51] ICC, *Prosecutor v. Jean Pierre Bemba Gombo*, Trial Chamber III, Second order regarding the applications of the legal representative of victims to present evidence and the views and concerns of victims, ICC-01/05-01/08-2027, 21 December 2011, para 19. See also ICC, *Prosecutor v. Jean-Pierre Bemba Gombo*, Trial Chamber III, Decision on the presentation of views and concerns by victims a/0542/08, a/0394/08 and a/0511/08, ICC-01/05-01/08-2220, 24 May 2012, para 12.

[52] ICC, *Prosecutor v. Jean Pierre Bemba Gombo*, Trial Chamber III, Second order regarding the applications of the legal representative of victims to present evidence and the views and concerns of victims, ICC-01/05-01/08-2027, 21 December 2011, para 19, referring to ICC, *Prosecutor v. Germain Katanga and Mathieu Ngudjolo Chui*, Trial Chamber II, Directions for the conduct of the proceedings and testimony in accordance with rule 140, ICC-01/04-01/07-1665, 20 November 2009, para 22 and ICC, *Prosecutor v. Germain Katanga and Mathieu Ngudjolo Chui*, Trial Chamber II, Decision on the Modalities of Victim Participation at Trial, ICC-01/04-01/07-1788-tENG, 22 January 2010, para 92.

[53] ICC, *Prosecutor v. William Samoei Ruto and Joshua Arap Sang*, Trial Chamber V, Decision on victims' representation and participation, ICC-01/09-01/11-460, 3 October 2012, para 58; ICC, *Prosecutor v. Uhuru Muigai Kenyatta*, Trial Chamber V, Decision on victims' representation and participation, ICC-01/09-02/11-498, 3 October 2012, para 57.

Regarding the use of in-court protective measures for victims who appear in person to present views and concerns, case-law to date is limited to the *Bemba* case, in which such appearances occurred for the first time. There, Trial Chamber III received assessments from the VWU[54] and on its recommendation implemented measures to protect and support the victims as appropriate for each individual victim, including the use of a pseudonym, image and voice distortion and the use of private or closed sessions.[55] For all three victims who presented their views and concerns the Chamber ordered (on VWU's recommendation) the presence of a support assistant outside the video-link room to provide support during breaks and the presence of a VWU (now Victims and Witnesses Section) psychologist in the courtroom to monitor the victim via video-link.[56] While Trial Chamber III did not elaborate on this issue, it appears that the approach to in-court protective measures may be the same for victims presenting views and concerns in person as it is for those who appear to present evidence.

9.3.8 Presentation of Views and Concerns in Practice

As stated above, to date 'views and concerns' have only been presented in person by three victims, in the *Bemba* case. However, as explained above, Trial Chamber III required those victims to focus their presentations on the harm they had suffered and its impact on their lives. The result was that the 'views and concerns' presented by these three participating victims were ultimately very much in the nature of evidence concerning alleged crimes committed, and indeed covered a number of topics dealt with by witnesses in the case, including the details of the alleged crimes, and the apparent affiliation of their perpetrators.[57] This information was presented without an oath, and without any possibility for questioning by the parties.[58] Objections to this approach were made by the parties, who pointed out that the 'views and concerns' should merely be submissions, but were in fact consisting of incriminating factual matters in the nature of evidence

---

[54] ICC, *Prosecutor v. Jean-Pierre Bemba Gombo*, Transcript 25 June 2010, ICC-01/05-01/08-T-227-Red, pp. 2–3, 31; ICC, *Prosecutor v. Jean-Pierre Bemba Gombo*, Transcript 26 June 2010, ICC-01/05-01/08-T-228-Red, p. 10..

[55] ICC, *Prosecutor v. Jean-Pierre Bemba Gombo*, Transcript 25 June 2010, ICC-01/05-01/08-T-227-Red, p. 31.

[56] ICC, *Prosecutor v. Jean-Pierre Bemba Gombo*, Transcript 25 June 2010, ICC-01/05-01/08-T-227-Red, pp. 3, 31–32; ICC, *Prosecutor v. Jean-Pierre Bemba Gombo*, Transcript 26 June 2010, ICC-01/05-01/08-T-228-Red, pp. 10–11.

[57] ICC, *Prosecutor v. Jean-Pierre Bemba Gombo*, Transcript 25 June 2010, ICC-01/05-01/08-T-227-Red, pp. 6–15, 22–29, 37–46; ICC, *Prosecutor v. Jean-Pierre Bemba Gombo*, Transcript 26 June 2010, ICC-01/05-01/08-T-228-Red, pp. 3–8, 13–27.

[58] Ibid.

but without the necessary safeguards to protect the rights of the Defence.[59] However, the Chamber dismissed such concerns, reiterating that it did not consider the information being provided to constitute evidence.[60]

In its judgment, Trial Chamber III reiterated that the three victims did not appear as witnesses, their submissions were not presented under oath, they were not questioned by the parties, and their views and concerns did not form part of the evidence of the case.[61] As a result, the approach followed by Trial Chamber III did not provide a clear understanding of what a victim's in-person presentation of views and concerns could involve, or in what circumstances it should be used, as distinct from the presentation of evidence by a participating victim. Despite purporting to endorse the distinction between these concepts explained by Trial Chamber I, Trial Chamber III instead conflated them.

9.4 Appearance of Participating Victims in Person to Give Evidence

The ICC, the ECCC and the STL, all allow for victims to give evidence, whether they are called by the Prosecution or the Defence, by their own representative, or by the relevant chamber.

The following section of this chapter deals with the specific rules that apply where a victim is called (or sought to be called) to give evidence. It aims to cover broadly all circumstances in which victims give evidence, regardless of who calls them. A separate discussion, set out in Chap. 8 of this book, deals with the specific rules applicable where an LRV seeks to call evidence, whether from a victim or another source. Since LRVs have most frequently in practice called their own clients to give evidence, there is significant overlap in practice between the application of these two chapters. They should be read together.

9.4.1 Special Pre-conditions to Calling a Victim to Give Evidence

At the ICC, where an LRV wishes to call evidence from a participating victim, in principle the procedural and substantive requirements appear to be the same as those pertaining to any other witnesses called by an LRV (on which see Chap. 8).

---

[59] ICC, *Prosecutor v. Jean-Pierre Bemba Gombo*, Transcript 25 June 2010, ICC-01/05-01/08-T-227-Red, pp. 16–18.

[60] Ibid., pp. 21–22.

[61] ICC, *Prosecutor v. Jean-Pierre Bemba Gombo,* Trial Chamber III, Judgment pursuant to Article 74 of the Statute, ICC-01/05-01/08-3343, 21 March 2016, para 28.

However, this is difficult to gauge because to date participating victims are the only persons who have been called as witnesses by LRVs. In particular, three participating victims gave evidence for the LRV in *Lubanga*, four in *Katanga and Ngudjolo Chui* and two in *Bemba*.[62]

Two possible exceptions to this approach have arisen to date. First, in two cases, chambers appear to have imposed a special requirement which could have application only to participating victims. In both the *Katanga and Ngudjolo Chui* and the *Bemba* cases, the trial chambers required that to be called to give evidence a participating victim must have an account which is broadly representative of the wider group of participating victims.[63] In the *Bemba* case, some proposed victim-witnesses appear to have been rejected on this basis.[64] However, the legal or policy basis for such a requirement has not been made clear, and it is not yet known whether other chambers will follow this approach, which was not used in the *Lubanga* case.

Secondly, in the particular circumstances of the Kenya cases, where Trial Chamber V did not require that all victims submit an individual written application for the Chamber's determination, such a process was in principle required from victims wishing to give evidence.[65]

At the STL, Rule 150(D) of the Rules of Procedure and Evidence (STL RPE) provides that a participating victim 'may be permitted to give evidence if a Chamber decides that the interests of justice so require.'[66] This wording is the

---

[62] ICC, *Prosecutor v. Thomas Lubanga Dyilo*, Trial Chamber I, Decision on the request by victims a/0225/06, a/0229/06 and a/0270/07 to express their views and concerns in person and to present evidence during the trial, ICC-01/04-01/06-2032, 26 June 2009; ICC, *Prosecutor v. Germain Katanga & Mathieu Ngudjolo Chui*, Trial Chamber II, Décision aux fins de comparution des victimes a/0381/09, a/0018/09, a/0191/08 et pan/0363/09 agissant au nom de a/0363/09, ICC-01/04-01/07-2517, 9 November 2010; ICC, *Prosecutor v. Jean Pierre Bemba Gombo*, Trial Chamber III, Decision on the supplemented applications by the legal representatives of victims to present evidence and the views and concerns of victims, Trial Chamber III, ICC-01/05-01/08-2138, 22 February 2012.

[63] ICC, *Prosecutor v. Germain Katanga and Mathieu Ngudjolo Chui,* Office of the Prosecutor, Prosecution's Communication of Update to eCourt Compatible Witness List Provided to the Defence on 19 November 2009, ICC-01/04-01/07-1655, 20 November 2009, para 30; ICC, *Prosecutor v. Jean-Pierre Bemba Gombo*, Trial Chamber III, Decision on the supplemental applications by the legal representatives of victims to present evidence and the views and concerns of victims, ICC-01/05-01/08-2138, 22 February 2012, para 24.

[64] ICC, *Prosecutor v. Jean-Pierre Bemba Gombo*, Trial Chamber III, Decision on the supplemental applications by the legal representatives of victims to present evidence and the views and concerns of victims, ICC-01/05-01/08-2138, 22 February 2012, paras 36 and 49.

[65] ICC, *Prosecutor v. Ruto and Sang*, Trial Chamber, Decision on victim's participation, ICC-01/09-01/11-460, 3 October 2012, para 25; ICC, *Prosecutor v Uhuru Muigai Kenyatta*, Trial Chamber V, Decision on victims' representation and participation, ICC-01/09-02/11-498, 3 October 2012, para 24.

[66] STL RPE, Rule 150(D).

result of an amendment in February 2012, prior to which it was provided that a participating victim '*shall not* be permitted to give evidence *unless* a Chamber decides that the interests of justice so require.'[67] [Emphasis added] The explanatory memorandum issued by the Tribunal in respect of the February 2012 amendments indicates that the original wording was considered by the judges to be 'too restrictive' and that the amendment was therefore adopted in order to reverse the presumption so that it now operates in favour of allowing participating victims to testify.[68] The judges indicated that they considered this change to bring the relevant rule into harmony with Article 17, the STL Statute's operative provision enabling victims to express their views and concerns through an LRV.[69]

Following this amendment the Pre-Trial Judge determined that a victim can be called to testify as a witness, provided that the rights of the accused to a fair and expeditious trial are guaranteed, as well as the interests of the Prosecution and the victims themselves.[70] The Pre-Trial Judge stated that should the situation of dual status victims arise, the applicable modalities shall be determined by the appropriate chamber.[71]

The approach taken by the STL Trial Chamber to date in the *Ayyash* et al. case appears to reflect the motivation behind this amendment. Indeed, the Chamber's approach appears to be more permissive than the plain wording of Rule 150(D) of the STL RPE, which allows victim testimony 'if a Chamber decides …'. Despite this, and despite a suggestion from the LRVs that specific requests should be made under Rule 150(D) where the Prosecution intends to call a participating victim which could then be judicially determined,[72] the Trial Chamber has neither required requests nor taken decisions under Rule 150(D). While no jurisprudence has explained this approach explicitly, it appears to suggest that the Chamber interprets the presumption in Rule 150 as operating so as to automatically allow participating victims to testify unless an objection is taken. So far no such objection has been made to the use of any dual status victims by the Prosecution.

There is no reason to believe that a less permissive approach would be taken when the LRV seeks to call participating victims as witnesses, given that Rule 150(D) does not draw a distinction based on who calls the victim.

---

[67] STL RPE, Rule 150(D).

[68] STL, Summary of Accepted Rule Amendments and Some Key Rejected Rule Amendment Proposals pursuant to Rule 5(1) of the Special Tribunal for Lebanon's Rules of Procedure and Evidence (Fourth Plenary of Judges, February 2012), p. 19.

[69] Ibid.

[70] STL, *Prosecutor v. Ayyash* et al., Pre-Trial Judge, Decision on the VPU's Access to Materials and the Modalities of Victim' Participation in the Proceedings before the Pre-Trial Judge, STL-11-01/PT/PTJ, para 61.

[71] Ibid.

[72] STL, *Prosecutor v. Ayyash* et al., LRV, Amended Public Redacted Version of the Response of the Legal Representative of Victims to the "Prosecution's Submission for an Order on Re-Classification of Victims' Identities and Applications for Victim Participation Status, As Confidential", STL-11-01/PT/PTJ, 24 October 2012, para 65.

At the ECCC, parties (including the civil parties themselves) do not need to meet any special requirements in order to call a civil party to give evidence, other than the ordinary requirements (such as relevance) applicable to witnesses. It is at the Trial Chamber's discretion who would ultimately be allowed to take the stand.

9.4.2 Evidential Value Accorded to Participating Victims' Testimony

While all three tribunals allow participating victims to give evidence, the ECCC gives a slightly different characterisation and legal effect to this situation than do the ICC and STL.

At the ICC and STL, participating victims who give evidence are referred to as witnesses and treated in the same way as other witnesses.

At the ICC, Trial Chamber II in the *Katanga and Ngudjolo Chui* case confirmed that there was nothing in the ICC Statute or the Rules that *per se* limited the probative value to be given to a witness's evidence who is also a victim in that case, and that evidence from victims should not be excluded on this basis.[73] Indeed, the Trial Chamber recognised that participating victims in the proceedings provide evidence under oath, whether they are called to testify as a witness by the Prosecution, the Defence, or the legal representative.[74] Trial Chamber II reasoned that it would be contrary to its obligation of establishing the truth if it were to exclude highly relevant and probative testimony of a victim-witness for the sole reason that he or she has also been authorised to participate as a victim in the proceedings.[75] The Chamber further reasoned that the very fact that the victim gives evidence under oath, which in itself gives him or her the status of a witness, allows the Defence to cross-examine the victim-witness, which in turn acts as a safeguard and makes the victim liable to prosecution under Article 70(1)(a) of the ICC Statute if he or she gives false testimony.[76] Indeed, lying under oath not only exposes a victim-witness to the risk of prosecution for perjury pursuant to Rule 66 of the ICC Rules, but can also result in the Chamber disregarding their evidence

[73] ICC, *Prosecutor v. Germain Katanga and Mathieu Ngudjolo Chui,* Trial Chamber II, Decision on Modalities of Victim Participation at Trial, ICC-01/04-01/07-1788-tENG, 3 March 2010, para 24.

[74] Ibid., para 88.

[75] Ibid.

[76] Ibid.

and stripping individuals of their victim status.[77] However Trial Chamber II indicated that it was open to hearing submissions on whether the dual status of a particular victim compromised the probative value of his or her testimony in a given case.[78]

While the STL has not rendered a judgment in a case involving participating victims or indicated exactly the manner in which it intends to rely on the evidence provided by victim-witnesses, it seems likely that the STL Trial Chamber will do so in a manner consistent with that of the ICC. In other words, there is no reason to doubt that the Chamber will consider victim-witnesses' evidence any different from that of other witnesses. An explanatory document on the STL RPE appears to indicate that the judges consider participating victims who testify to have the same status as other witnesses. It explains that since the Rules require that 'every witness' must give a solemn declaration,[79] the judges saw no need to specify that victims participating in the proceedings should give evidence 'under oath'.[80] However, it is also stated that the Trial Chamber 'will decide on the most appropriate ways for witnesses who also have the status of victims participating in the proceedings to give evidence.'[81] To date, all participating victims who have given evidence for the Prosecution in the *Ayyash* et al. case have done so under oath and there is nothing to suggest that a different procedure would be used for victims called to testify at the request of their legal representative.

In contrast, the ECCC's rules and regulations preclude a victim who has been admitted as a civil party to the proceedings from also testifying under oath as a witness in that case.[82] However, the ECCC's internal rules and regulations do not preclude civil parties from providing unsworn testimony in court. While the information provided by the civil parties is not given under oath, it is nonetheless treated and referred to as evidence. In practice then, although civil parties are not characterised as witnesses, it is difficult to discern any real consequence arising from this legal distinction.

---

[77] ICC, *Prosecutor v. Thomas Lubanga Dyilo,* Trial Chamber I, Judgment pursuant to Article 74 of the Statute, ICC-01/04-01/06-2842, 14 March 2012, paras 484, 502. The Trial Chamber determined that it would be unsustainable to allow victims to continue participating if a more detailed understanding of the evidence demonstrated that they no longer meet the relevant criteria. ICC, *Prosecutor v. Thomas Lubanga Dyilo,* Trial Chamber I, Judgment pursuant to Article 74 of the Statute, ICC-01/04-01/06-2842, 14 March 2012, para 484.

[78] ICC, *Prosecutor v. Germain Katanga and Mathieu Ngudjolo Chui*, Trial Chamber II, Decision on the Modalities of Victim Participation at Trial, ICC-01/04-01/07-1788-tENG, 23 January 2010, para 90.

[79] STL RPE, Rule 150(A).

[80] STL, Summary of Accepted Rule Amendments and Some Key Rejected Rule Amendment Proposals pursuant to Rule 5(1) of the Special Tribunal for Lebanon's Rules of Procedure and Evidence (Fourth Plenary of Judges, February 2012), p. 19.

[81] Ibid.

[82] See ECCC Rules, Rule 23(4). See also Practice Direction 004/2009, Classification and Management of Case-Related Information, Article 2(e), which defines a witness as a 'person, other than a civil party'.

In Cases *001* and *002/01*, the Trial Chamber relied heavily on civil party testimony to support factual findings and their evidence was evaluated similarly to that of witnesses who testified under oath.[83] The Trial Chamber in *Case 002/01* determined that 'the weight to be accorded to civil party testimony will be assessed on a case-by-case basis in light of the credibility of that testimony',[84] adopting a similar approach to that taken in *Case 001*.[85]

Accordingly, while the ECCC Rules do not provide for the dual status of civil parties, in practice, they are not treated very differently from victim-witnesses at the ICC and STL. Similarly, the statements on suffering provided by the civil parties in *Case 001* and Case *002/01* have to date been relied upon as a source of evidence by the Trial Chamber.[86]

9.4.3 Practical Implications Arising Where Participating Victims Give Evidence

9.4.3.1 Identifying Dual Status Victims

Particular problems of identifying victims with dual status have arisen in some ICC proceedings. This is principally due to the fact that anonymity is the general rule for participating victims in ICC proceedings.[87] Where the Prosecution interviews a victim after he or she has applied for participation, the victim would usually be asked about and disclose this information to the Prosecution. However, in some cases the victim meets the Prosecution and gives a statement first and only subsequently submits an application for participation in the proceedings. In such a

[83] ECCC, *Case 001*, Trial Chamber, Judgment, 26 July 2010, paras (e.g.) 53, 266–267, 323, 598; ECCC, *Case 002/01*, Trial Chamber, Annex I (Individuals heard in *Case 002/01*) to Final decision on witness, experts and civil parties to be heard in *Case 002/01*, 7 August 2014.

[84] ECCC, *Case 002/01*, Trial Chamber, Decision on request to recall Civil Party TCCP-187, for review of procedure concerning Civil Parties' statements on suffering and related motions and responses (E240, E240/1, E250, E250/1, E267, E267/1 and E267/2), 2 May 2013, para 22.

[85] ECCC, *Case 001*, Trial Chamber, Judgment, 26 July 2010, paras 42, 52–55.

[86] The KRT Trial Monitor, Report Issue No. 18, Week Ending August 23, 2009, https://krttrial-monitor.files.wordpress.com/2012/07/aiji_eccc_case1_no18_23aug09_en.pdf. Accessed 30 September 2016; Written correspondence with Christoph Sperfeldt, PhD Scholar, Australian National University, 2 October 2016 (notes on file with the editors). ECCC, *Case 002/01*, Trial Chamber, Judgment, 7 August 2015, paras 30–31; ECCC, *Case 002/01*, Trial Chamber, Annex I (Individuals heard in *Case 002/01*) to Final decision on witness, experts and civil parties to be heard in *Case 002/01*, 7 August 2014. The reliance of the Trial Chamber on victim impact statements was appealed by the Defence for Nuon Chea as an error of law. ECCC, *Case 002/01*, Nuon Chea Defence, Nuon Chea's Appeal against the Judgment in *Case 002/01*, 002/19-09-2007-ECCC-SC, 29 December 2014, paras 187–193. Judgment on appeal in *Case 002/01* was pronounced on 23 November 2016. The Supreme Court Chamber dismissed these arguments. ECCC, *Case 002/01*, Supreme Court Chamber, Appeal Judgment, 002/19-09-2007-ECCC-SC, 23 November 2016, paras 305–324.

[87] See Chap. 6.

scenario the Prosecution may not become aware that its witness (or potential witness) has also acquired the status of participating victim, except in those cases where unredacted victim applications have been provided to the Prosecution. This was a particular problem in some early ICC cases in which LRVs have not had access to confidential information, including Prosecution witness lists, and therefore were not able to identify independently which Prosecution witnesses were also among their participating victim clients.

In the *Lubanga* case, the Trial Chamber grappled with this difficulty and put in place certain procedures intended to address it. The Chamber held that when the LRV became aware that a client may have dual status, he or she could provide the Prosecution with the client's identifying information, to the extent possible and provided the client had given consent thereto.[88] The Prosecution would thereafter check whether the individual had dual status and, if so, communicate this in writing to the LRV, whether or not the individual was in the ICC protection program.[89] Where the name of the individual was already known to the Defence, the LRV was required to communicate the name of his or her client to the Defence, who was thereafter required to inform the LRV of whether the individual was on its list as a potential witness.[90] If the Defence was unaware of the client's name, the LRV was to make an application to the Chamber.[91] Where an LRV suspected that a client had dual status and was unable to obtain information about this from the relevant party (including because the victim may be in the ICC protection program) an application was to be made to the Chamber to resolve the question. The Chamber would then seek input from the Registry, and could require the Registry to communicate with the individual to seek consent for the disclosure of specific information to the LRV.[92]

It is clear that this solution could not resolve the problem entirely, since the procedure established is only able to operate where the LRV (or potentially a party) becomes aware that there is some reason to believe a particular person has dual status. At least in the early cases it was very possible, given the restrictions on access to information explained above, that this would not occur. An alternative solution in such cases could be for the Registry to play the role of identifying dual status victims, since the VWS has access to the parties' witness lists once they are filed, and the VPRS has access to the identities of all participating victims. In the absence of appropriately tailored software however, playing such a role is likely to be labour intensive for an already under-resourced Registry. The difficulty may be solved if chambers continue to move towards providing LRVs with appropriate access to confidential documents in the case file.[93]

---

[88] ICC, *Prosecutor v. Thomas Lubanga Dyilo*, Trial Chamber I, Decision on certain practicalities regarding individuals who have the dual status of witness and victim, ICC-01/04-01/06-1379, 5 June 2008, para 55(a) (d).

[89] Ibid., para 55(b).

[90] Ibid., para 57.

[91] Ibid., para 58.

[92] Ibid., para 56.

[93] See Chap. 7.

Ultimately however, the problem which arose in the *Lubanga* case is occurring less frequently. This is reflected in more recent developments in ICC jurisprudence, which demonstrates that LRVs have been provided with access to the confidential case files which contain the parties' witness lists.[94] Similarly, in a number of cases, chambers have provided the Prosecution with access to the identities of all participating victims.[95] This means that both the Prosecution and the LRVs are in a position to identify dual status victims. To date, no decision indicates clearly which participant is principally responsible for carrying out this task. Protocols developed in the *Ntaganda* and *Gbagbo and Blé Goudé* cases, and subsequently also applied in the *Ongwen* case,[96] place obligations on all participants to inform each other, as well as the Registry, as soon as they become aware that a victim or witness has dual status.[97]

This issue does not arise at the ECCC or STL where victims are not able to participate anonymously and therefore have their identities known to the parties.

9.4.3.2 Communication with Dual Status Victims

In view of the potential communication complications with respect to dual status victims, Trial Chamber I in the *Lubanga* case at the ICC put in place a regime that was to be followed once the dual status nature of a participating victim was known. This regime has largely been followed through the subsequent use of 'dual status protocols' in some cases. These have also in some respects contributed further nuances to the system applied in the *Lubanga* case. The key features of this regime are presented below.

---

[94] Some early case law of the ICC trial chambers required that the Prosecution and Defence provide access to the LRV only to documents relevant to victims' personal interests (*Lubanga*, *Bemba*), and in practice witness lists were not provided. However, since then some chambers have provided the legal representatives with blanket access to disclosed material in the case (*Katanga and Ngudjolo Chui*, *Gbagbo/Blé Goudé*, *Ntaganda*, *Al-Mahdi*, *Ongwen*). For details see Chap. 7.

[95] See Chaps. 2 and 6.

[96] ICC, *Prosecutor v. Dominic Ongwen*, Trial Chamber IX, Decision on Protocols to be Adopted at Trial, ICC-02/04-01/15-504, 22 July 2016, para 31.

[97] ICC, *Prosecutor v. Bosco Ntaganda*, Trial Chamber VI, Decision adopting the Protocol on dual status witnesses and the Protocol on vulnerable witnesses, ICC-01/04-02/06-464, 18 February 2015, p. 4; ICC, *Prosecutor v. Bosco Ntaganda*, Trial Chamber VI, Proposed Mechanisms for exchange of information on individuals enjoying dual status, ICC-01/04-02/06-430-Anx1, 23 January 2015, pp. 2–3; ICC, *Prosecutor v. Laurent Gbagbo and Charles Blé Goudé*, Trial Chamber I, Decision adopting mechanisms for exchange of information in individuals enjoying dual status, ICC-02/11-01/15-199, 31 August 2015, p. 11; ICC, *Prosecutor v. Laurent Gbagbo and Charles Blé Goudé*, Trial Chamber I, Mechanisms for exchange of information on individuals enjoying dual status ("Protocol"), ICC-02/11-01/15-199-Anx, 1 September 2015, pp. 2–3.

In the *Lubanga* case, the Trial Chamber held that as a general rule, the LRV was permitted contact with his or her client if that client was a dual status victim.[98] This approach has been followed in subsequent cases.[99]

The LRV has also been allowed to be present at parties' interviews with the dual status victim, provided the client consented thereto.[100] This approach has been followed in later cases, although in *Ntaganda* the Trial Chamber endorsed a caveat: in some circumstances, interviews may take place without the LRV's presence if this is considered appropriate, but that unless a delay cannot be justified, permission from the Chamber must first be sought.[101] No such caveat was included by the Trial Chamber in the protocol adopted in *Gbagbo and Blé Goudé* and subsequently also applied in *Ongwen*.[102] Legal representatives of victims have also been permitted to attend medical examinations of their dual status clients, so long as the client consents.[103] Legal representatives are entitled to receive copies of statements and other materials created during interviews between a calling party and a client participating victim, unless the Chamber authorises an exception to this.[104]

---

[98] ICC, *Prosecutor v. Thomas Lubanga Dyilo*, Trial Chamber I, Decision on certain practicalities regarding individuals who have the dual status of witness and victim, ICC-01/04-01/06-1379, 5 June 2008, para 61.

[99] ICC, *Prosecutor v. Bosco Ntaganda*, Trial Chamber VI, Proposed Mechanisms for exchange of information on individuals enjoying dual status, ICC-01/04-02/06-430-Anx1, 23 January 2015, p. 3; ICC, *Prosecutor v. Laurent Gbagbo and Charles Blé Goudé*, Trial Chamber I, Mechanisms for exchange of information on individuals enjoying dual status ("Protocol"), ICC-02/11-01/15-199-Anx, 1 September 2015, p. 3; ICC, *Prosecutor v. Dominic Ongwen*, Trial Chamber IX, Decision on Protocols to be Adopted at Trial, ICC-02/04-01/15-504, 22 July 2016, para 31.

[100] ICC, *Prosecutor v. Thomas Lubanga Dyilo*, Trial Chamber I, Decision on certain practicalities regarding individuals who have the dual status of witness and victim, ICC-01/04-01/06-1379, 5 June 2008, para 67.

[101] ICC, *Prosecutor v. Bosco Ntaganda*, Trial Chamber VI, Proposed Mechanisms for exchange of information on individuals enjoying dual status, ICC-01/04-02/06-430-Anx1, 23 January 2015, p. 4.

[102] ICC, *Prosecutor v. v. Laurent Gbagbo and Charles Blé Goudé*, Trial Chamber I, Mechanisms for exchange of information on individuals enjoying dual status ("Protocol"), ICC-02/11-01/15-199-Anx, 1 September 2015, p. 4; ICC, *Prosecutor v. Dominic Ongwen*, Trial Chamber IX, Decision on Protocols to be Adopted at Trial, ICC-02/04-01/15-504, 22 July 2016, para 31.

[103] ICC, *Prosecutor v. Bosco Ntaganda*, Trial Chamber VI, Proposed Mechanisms for exchange of information on individuals enjoying dual status, ICC-01/04-02/06-430-Anx1, 23 January 2015, p. 4; ICC, *Prosecutor v. Laurent Gbagbo and Charles Blé Goudé*, Trial Chamber I, Mechanisms for exchange of information on individuals enjoying dual status ("Protocol"), ICC-02/11-01/15-199-Anx, 1 September 2015, pp. 3–4; ICC, *Prosecutor v. Dominic Ongwen*, Trial Chamber IX, Decision on Protocols to be Adopted at Trial, ICC-02/04-01/15-504, 22 July 2016, para 31.

[104] ICC, *Prosecutor v. Bosco Ntaganda*, Trial Chamber VI, Proposed Mechanisms for exchange of information on individuals enjoying dual status, ICC-01/04-02/06-430-Anx1, 23 January 2015, pp. 3–4; ICC, *Prosecutor v. Laurent Gbagbo and Charles Blé Goudé*, Trial Chamber I, Mechanisms for exchange of information on individuals enjoying dual status ("Protocol"), ICC-02/11-01/15-199-Anx, 1 September 2015, p. 3; ICC, *Prosecutor v. Dominic Ongwen*, Trial Chamber IX, Decision on Protocols to be Adopted at Trial, ICC-02/04-01/15-504, 22 July 2016, para 31.

When a party wished to contact a dual status victim, it was required to provide notice thereof to the victim's LRV, in the event the party was aware of the legal representation.[105] In the event a party did not contact the LRV prior to reaching out to the dual status victim in cases of urgency to preserve or collect evidence, the party was required as soon as possible thereafter to inform the LRV thereof and disclose any relevant material obtained through this contact.[106]

Given that 'witness proofing' (in the sense of substantive preparation of a witness before trial) was prohibited in *Lubanga*, neither the parties nor the legal representatives were allowed to communicate with witnesses (including dual status ones) once the process of 'familiarisation' of the witness (conducted by the VWU – now VWS) had commenced.[107] The same approach was adopted in *Bemba* as well as in the *Gbagbo and Blé Goudé* and *Ongwen* cases.[108] However, Trial Chamber V in *Ruto and Sang* and Trial Chamber VI in *Ntaganda* allowed witness preparation.[109] In all cases, however, the legal representatives were allowed to communicate with their clients even if they were not the calling party,

[105] ICC, *Prosecutor v. Thomas Lubanga Dyilo*, Trial Chamber I, Decision on certain practicalities regarding individuals who have the dual status of witness and victim, ICC-01/04-01/06-1379, 5 June 2008, para 59(a).

[106] Ibid., para 60. The approach of Trial Chamber I was followed in the *Bemba* case: ICC, *Prosecutor v. Jean Pierre Bemba Gombo*, Trial Chamber III, Corrigendum to Decision on the participation of victims in the trial and on 86 applications by victims to participate in the proceedings, ICC-01/05-01/08-807-Corr, 12 July 2010, paras 53–54; ICC, *Prosecutor v. Bosco Ntaganda*, Trial Chamber VI, Proposed Mechanisms for exchange of information on individuals enjoying dual status, ICC-01/04-02/06-430-Anx1, 23 January 2015, p. 3; ICC, *Prosecutor v. Laurent Gbagbo and Charles Blé Goudé*, Trial Chamber I, Mechanisms for exchange of information on individuals enjoying dual status ("Protocol"), ICC-02/11-01/15-199-Anx, 1 September 2015, p. 3; ICC, *Prosecutor v. Dominic Ongwen*, Trial Chamber IX, Decision on Protocols to be Adopted at Trial, ICC-02/04-01/15-504, 22 July 2016, para 31.

[107] ICC, *Prosecutor v. Thomas Lubanga Dyilo*, Pre-Trial Chamber I, Decision on the Practices of Witness Familiarisation and Witness Proofing, ICC-01/04-01/06-679, 8 November 2008; ICC, *Prosecutor v. Thomas Lubanga Dyilo,* Trial Chamber I, Decision Regarding the Practices Used to Prepare and Familiarise Witnesses for Giving Testimony at Trial, ICC-01/04-01/06-1049, 30 November 2007.

[108] ICC, *Prosecutor v. Jean-Pierre Bemba Gombo*, Trial Chamber III, Decision on the Unified Protocol on the practices used to prepare familiarise witnesses for giving testimony at trial, ICC-01/05-01/08-1016, 18 November 2010, para 34; ICC, *Prosecutor v. Laurent Gbagbo and Charles Blé Goudé*, Trial Chamber I, Decision on Witness Preparation and Familiarisation, 2 December 2015, ICC-02/11-01/15-355, para 19; ICC, *Prosecutor v. Dominic Ongwen*, Trial Chamber IX, Decision on Protocols to be Adopted at Trial, ICC-02/04-01/15-504, 22 July 2016.

[109] ICC, *Prosecutor v. William Samoei Ruto and Joshua Arap Sang*, Trial Chamber V, Decision on Witness Preparation, ICC-01/09-01/11-524, 2 January 2013, para 50; ICC, *Prosecutor v. Bosco Ntaganda*, Trial Chamber VI, Decision on Witness Preparation, ICC-01/04-02/06-652, 16 June 2015, para 18.

but they had to refrain from holding substantive discussion with witnesses about the topics to be dealt with during their evidence.[110]

At the STL, the Prosecution can either directly contact the dual status victim or go through the LRV. The Defence at the STL has thus far contacted dual status victims through the LRV, rather than contacting the participating victim directly.[111]

9.4.4 Disclosure or Notification of Dual Status Victims' Application Forms

As with the calling of any witness, the courts require the disclosure of certain material to the (other) parties when a participating victim is called to provide evidence.

At the ICC, where a participating victim gives evidence an issue arises regarding the access by the parties to the victim's application form. This is most clearly the case where the victim is called as a witness for the Prosecution, and the Prosecution is in possession of an unredacted version of the victim's application form, while the Defence is not.[112] In these circumstances, it is clear that disclosure is required as part of the Prosecution's usual obligations under Rules 76 (Pre-trial disclosure relating to prosecution witnesses) and 77 (Inspection of material in possession or control of the Prosecutor), and where relevant under Article 67(2) (which relates to exculpatory material) of the ICC RPE.[113] In the *Lubanga* case, Trial Chamber I held that this should be accomplished by normal Prosecution disclosure procedures, and not by having the Registry reclassify the unredacted applications so as to provide access to the Defence.[114] The Chamber required that prior to disclosing information relevant to the dual status victims, the Prosecution

---

[110] See, for example: ICC, *Prosecutor v. Thomas Lubanga Dyilo*, Trial Chamber, Transcript 16 January 2009, ICC-01/04-01/06-T-104-ENG, 16 January 2009, p. 25; ICC, *Prosecutor v. Jean Pierre Bemba Gombo*, Registrar, Victims and Witnesses Unit's Unified Protocol on the practices used to prepare and familiarise witnesses for giving testimony at trial, ICC-01/05-01/08-972-Anx, 22 October 2010, para 33; ICC, *Prosecutor v. Laurent Gbagbo and Charles Blé Goudé*, Trial Chamber I, Annex to Decision on witness preparation and familiarization, ICC-02/11-01/15-355-Anx, 2 December 2015, para 32; ICC, *Prosecutor v. Bosco Ntaganda*, Trial Chamber VI, Annex A to the Decision on the protocol on witness familiarization, ICC-01/04-02/06-656-AnxA, 17 June 2015, para 34.

[111] Written correspondence with Kinga Tibori-Szabó, former associate legal officer, Legal Representative of Victims, STL, 28 September 2016 (notes on file with editor).

[112] See Chap. 2.

[113] ICC, *Prosecutor v. Thomas Lubanga Dyilo*, Trial Chamber I, Decision on the defence application for disclosure of victims applications, ICC-01/04-01/06-1637, 21 January 2009, paras 12–13.

[114] Ibid., para 13.

must seek the views of the relevant legal representatives, and bring any objections to the attention of the Chamber for resolution.[115] A similar approach was followed in the *Ruto and Sang* case, where the Chamber authorised the Prosecution to disclose lesser redacted versions of dual status victims' application forms on the basis that the material which had been redacted was material to the preparation of the Defence.[116] Redactions were permitted to be maintained in respect of contact information of the dual status victims and third parties, which was not argued by the Defence to be relevant to the case.[117] This approach has also been followed in some subsequent cases.[118]

A slightly different situation arises where the parties already possess the same (redacted) versions of the dual status victims' application forms.[119] This was the situation in the *Bemba* case. On first considering the issue, the Trial Chamber endorsed the position taken in the *Lubanga* case as set out above.[120] It went on to note that because both parties were in possession of the same (redacted) versions of the victim application forms, an obligation of disclosure would only fall on the Prosecution were it to come into possession of additional information not in the possession of the Defence.[121] In a passing reference in the *Ntaganda* case, Trial Chamber VI mentioned an obligation on the Prosecution to *obtain* any disclosable information which might be included in the application forms of dual status witnesses, referring to Article 54(1)(a) of the ICC Statute which obliges the Prosecutor to investigate 'incriminating and exonerating circumstances equally'.[122] However it is not clear what the content of this obligation would involve in practice: it may be limited to seeking such information from the dual status victims themselves in the context of witness interviews, rather than attempting to access unredacted or lesser redacted versions of victim applications.

A slightly different approach was taken in the *Abu Garda* case. There, the Prosecution already possessed unredacted versions of three dual status

---

[115] Ibid., para 13.

[116] ICC, *Prosecutor v. William Samoei Ruto and Joshua Arap Sang*, Order authorising disclosure of lesser redacted versions of victims' applications, ICC-01/09-01/11-826, 24 July 2013, para 5.

[117] Ibid., para 6.

[118] ICC, *Prosecutor v. Bosco Ntaganda*, Trial Chamber VI, Decision on victims' participation in trial proceedings, ICC-01/04-02/06-449, 6 February 2015, para 40; ICC, *Prosecutor v. Laurent Gbagbo*, Trial Chamber I, Decision on victim participation, ICC-02/11-01/11-800, 6 March 2015, para 56.

[119] See Chap. 2.

[120] ICC, *Prosecutor v. Jean-Pierre Bemba Gombo*, Trial Chamber III, Decision on the participation of victims in the trial and on 86 applications by victims to participate in the proceedings, ICC-01/05-01/08-807, 30 June 2010, paras 58–59.

[121] Ibid., para 59.

[122] ICC, *Prosecutor v. Bosco Ntaganda*, Trial Chamber VI, Decision on victims' participation in trial proceedings, ICC-01/04-02/06-449, 6 February 2015, para 40.

applications. Rather than requiring the Prosecution to provide these to the Defence via normal disclosure procedures, Pre-Trial Chamber I required the Registry to provide unredacted versions of the applications to the Defence.[123]

Where it is the legal representative, rather than the Prosecutor, who requests that participating victims give evidence, a similar approach has been taken in practice. The Appeals Chamber in *Katanga and Ngudjolo Chui* held that participating victims do not have a general disclosure obligation.[124] However, the Appeals Chamber also held that when legal representatives are permitted to call evidence, disclosure must be made to the parties sufficiently in advance of the evidence being called, as determined by the chamber.[125] Furthermore, any victim authorised to give evidence must relinquish his or her anonymity.[126]

At the STL, Rule 112*bis* of the STL RPE provides that if the participating victims are granted the right to call evidence, the chamber shall decide on the corresponding disclosure obligations. It remains to be seen how the Trial Chamber interprets this rule in the *Ayyash* et al. case. It should be noted, however, that, to date, in *Ayyash* et al., application forms are not shared with the parties in any form, and victims are not permitted to participate anonymously.[127]

Similarly at the ECCC, no special disclosure issues have arisen where a civil party gives evidence.

9.4.5 Protective Measures for Victims Giving Evidence

The ICC, STL, and ECCC all provide for protective measures for participating victims or civil parties who testify in court.[128] Both the ICC and the STL have

[123] ICC, *Prosecutor v. Bahar Idriss Abu Garda*, Pre-Trial Chamber I, Decision on the 34 Applications for Participation at the Pre-Trial Stage of the Case, ICC-02/05-02/09-121, 25 September 2009, para 102 and p. 32.

[124] ICC, *Prosecutor v. Germain Katanga and Mathieu Ngudjolo Chui*, Appeals Chamber, Judgment on the Appeal of Mr Katanga Against the Decision of Trial Chamber II of 22 January Entitled "Decision on the Modalities of Victim Participation at Trial", ICC-01/04-01/07-2288, 16 July 2010, para 71.

[125] Ibid., para 55.

[126] ICC, *Prosecutor v. Germain Katanga and Mathieu Ngudjolo Chui*, Trial Chamber II, Corrigendum to Directions for the conduct of the proceedings and testimony in accordance with Rule 140, ICC-01/04-01/07-1665-Corr, 1 December 2009, para 22; ICC, *Prosecutor v. Germain Katanga and Mathieu Ngudjolo Chui*, Trial Chamber II, Decision on the Modalities of Victim Participation at Trial, ICC-01/04-01/07-1788-tENG, 22 January 2010, para 92. In the *Bemba* case, Trial Chamber III ordered, however, that the identity of victims did not need to be disclosed to the parties unless and until the Chamber granted them permission to testify. ICC, *Prosecutor v. Jean Pierre Bemba Gombo*, Trial Chamber III, Second order regarding the applications of the legal representatives of victims to present evidence and the views and concerns of victims, ICC-01/05-01/08-2027, 21 December 2011, para 19.

[127] See Chaps. 2 and 6.

[128] See ICC RPE, Rules 68, 87; ECCC Internal Rules, Rule 29; STL RPE, Rule 133.

specifically recognised the potential additional complications and risks associated with a participating victim who is granted the opportunity to testify in court.[129] For all three courts alike, the measures available to these victim-witnesses or civil parties are similar to those granted to witnesses, require that consent be obtained (where possible) from the person for whom protective measures is sought,[130] and are administered and facilitated by the respective victims and witnesses units of these courts.[131]

9.5 Risk of Participating Victims Expressing Views and Concerns or Giving Evidence

Legal representatives should give careful consideration to the risks and benefits involved in having their clients appear in person to provide view and concerns or give evidence. These go beyond the potential psychological impact of the appearance. Chambers at both the ICC and the ECCC have revoked the status of participating victims or civil parties following the provision of evidence by these individuals.[132] The chambers in these instances determined that the testimony by these participating victims or civil parties was unreliable or inaccurate and called into doubt the information on the basis of which victim status had been granted. This risk could also arise in relation to victims presenting views and concerns in person, especially where they relate to facts before the chamber.

Given the potentially significant risks associated with participating victims or civil parties expressing views and concerns or testifying, victims' lawyers should clearly assess the precise modality of participation for their clients. Participating

---

[129] See ICC, *Prosecutor v. Thomas Lubanga Dyilo,* Trial Chamber I, Decision on certain practicalities regarding individuals who have the dual status of witness and victim, ICC-01/04-01/06-1379, 05 June 2008, para 52. See also ICC, *Prosecutor v. Jean-Pierre Bemba Gombo*, Trial Chamber, Decision on the participation of victims in the trial and on 86 applications by victims to participate in the proceedings, ICC-01/05-01/08-807, 30 June 2010, para 54; STL, *Prosecutor v. Ayyash* et al., Pre-Trial Judge, Decision on the VPU's Access to Materials and the Modalities of Victim' Participation in the Proceedings before the Pre-Trial Judge, STL-11-01/PT/PTJ, para 61.

[130] See Article 1.5 of the Practice Direction on Protective Measures, ECCC/03/2007/Rev.1.

[131] See ICC RPE, Rule 87 (the Victims and Witnesses Unit); STL RPE, Rule 133 (Victims and Witnesses Unit); ECCC Internal Rules, Rule 29(3) (Witness and Expert Support Unit). See Chap. 6.

[132] ICC, *Prosecutor v. Thomas Lubanga Dyilo,* Trial Chamber I, Judgment pursuant to Article 74 of the Statute, ICC-01/04-01/06-2842, 14 March 2012, para 484; ICC, *Prosecutor v. Germain Katanga and Mathieu Ngudjolo Chui*, Trial Chamber, Decision relative au maintien du statut de victime participant à la procédure des victimes a/0381/09 et a/0363/09 et à la demande de Me. Nsita Luvengika en vue d'être autorisé à mettre fin à son mandat de représentant Légal desdites victimes, ICC-01/04-01/07-3064, 7 July 2011; ECCC, *Case 001,* Trial Chamber, Trial Judgment, 26 July 2010, para 647. See also Chap. 14.

victims should be carefully advised by LRVs of the potential risks involved in expressing views and concerns in person or providing testimony.

9.6 Key Points

- Participating victims are granted *in-person* participatory rights to varying degrees at the ICC, the STL, and the ECCC.
- The most important distinction in respect of participating victims is between an appearance to provide *views and concerns* in person, and an appearance in person to provide *evidence*. Where victims appear in person to provide evidence, at the ICC and the STL, they are usually referred to as 'dual status' victims. Different rules and procedures may apply to dual status victims depending on whether the victim is called by a party or appears at the request of the LRV.
- At the ECCC, civil parties can be called by the Civil Party Lead Co-Lawyers, by the Prosecution, or by the Defence to provide evidence before the court. They can also provide statements of suffering after their testimony or at a so-called impact hearing.

Participating victims presenting views and concerns in person

- To date, the possibility for victims to present their views and concerns in person has only been identified at the ICC, and to date has only occurred in the *Bemba* case.
- *Exceptional submissions*: Although only three victims in the *Bemba* case have appeared in person to present views and concerns before the ICC, other chambers of that court have discussed this modality of participation. Chambers have thus held that the presentation of views and concerns by victims were essentially considered submissions, rather than evidence and that an appearance for such purpose was to be authorised on an exceptional basis.
- *Scope*: In the *Bemba* case, Trial Chamber III requested that the three victims focus their 'views and concerns' on the harm suffered and on the impact of the alleged crimes on their lives.
- *Procedure*: Requests to present views and concerns in person must be made in writing. The specific information required to be included in such a request has varied among chambers. Views and concerns were presented in *Bemba* without requiring the victims to take an oath, and without any possibility for questioning by the parties.
- *Timing*: In the *Bemba* case, the three victims who presented their views and concerns in person did so between the Prosecution and Defence cases, and after the Court had heard from two participating victims who gave evidence. In contrast, Trial Chamber I in the *Lubanga* case appeared to have in mind the possibility that such views and concerns might be more appropriately heard after the conclusion of evidence in the case.

- *Disclosure obligations*: In the *Bemba* case, Trial Chamber III found that the disclosure obligations incumbent on the victims presenting their views and concerns were the same as for those giving evidence. It also held that victims granted authorisation to appear in person to present views and concerns had to first relinquish their anonymity and have their identities disclosed to the parties.

Participating victims giving evidence

- The ICC, the ECCC and the STL, all allow for victims to give evidence, whether they are called by the Prosecution or the Defence, by their own representative, or by the relevant chamber.
- At the ECCC, civil parties do not need to meet any special requirements in order to call a civil party to give evidence, other than the ordinary requirements applicable to witnesses. It is the Trial Chamber's decision who would ultimately be allowed to take the stand.
- At the ICC, no special conditions apply if one of the parties wants to call a participating victim as a witness. Where an LRV wishes to call evidence from a participating victim, certain specific conditions apply, elaborated in Chap. 8.
- At the STL, Rule 150(D) of the STL RPE provides that a participating victim may be permitted to give evidence if a Chamber decides that the interests of justice so require. It remains to be seen how this provision will be applied in the *Ayyash* et al. case.
- *Disclosure obligations*: As with the calling of any witness, the courts require the disclosure of certain material to the (other) parties when a participating victim is called to provide evidence.
  - At the ICC, participating victims do not have a general disclosure obligation, but when they are permitted to call evidence, disclosure must be made to the parties sufficiently in advance of the evidence being called, as determined by the chamber. Additionally, application forms may be subject to various degrees of disclosure. Any victim authorised to give evidence must relinquish his or her anonymity.
  - At the STL, if the participating victims are granted the right to call evidence, the chamber decides on the corresponding disclosure obligations. Victim application forms are not shared with the parties in any form, and victims are not permitted to participate anonymously.
  - At the ECCC, no special disclosure issues have arisen where a civil party gives evidence.
- *Protective measures*: The ICC, STL and ECCC all provide for protective measures for participating victims or civil parties who testify in court.
- Participating victims should be carefully advised by LRVs of the potential risks involved in expressing views and concerns in person or providing testimony.

Reference

STL (2012) Summary of Accepted Rule Amendments and some key rejected Rule Amendment Proposals pursuant to Rule 5(1) of the Special Tribunal for Lebanon's Rules of Procedure and Evidence (Fourth Plenary of Judges, February 2012)

Chapter 10
Victims in the Witness Stand: Socio-Cultural and Psychological Challenges in Eliciting Victim Testimony

Ellie Smith

Abstract Victim testimony does not occur in a legal vacuum. This chapter explores socio-cultural and psychological barriers that inhibit testimony for victims of international crimes. These barriers can arise at the time of the crime, during the period between the perpetration of the crime and testimony, and during testimony itself, where the psychological impact of trauma has affected the ability of the victim to recall or coherently articulate their experiences. While many of these barriers stem directly from the abuse suffered, actions of the courts, including collective approaches to victim representation, the use of interpreters and intermediaries, and the nature and style of questioning, also have the potential to mediate or inhibit individual testimony. These barriers pose challenges not only for the victim themselves, but also for Prosecution and Defence counsel, victims' lawyers, victim support personnel and judges in the attainment and assessment of victim evidence.

Keywords International Criminal Court · Testimony · Credibility · Trauma · Psychological impact · Memory · Sexual violence · Rape · Contaminated testimony · Composite narrative · Collective representation

---

Dr. Ellie Smith is a consultant and trainer specialising in medico-legal and psychological issues affecting victims of international crimes within the justice process.
Elements of this chapter have their origins in an earlier presentation relating specifically to the investigation and prosecution of crimes of sexual violence given at the International Criminal Court Student Network conference, *The Lubanga Trial: Lessons Learned,* The Hague, 8th–9th March, 2012, which was subsequently published in *Issues in International Criminal Justice*, Special Volume, 2012, 99–112.

E. Smith (✉)
Newcastle, UK
e-mail: elliesmith.research@yahoo.co.uk

K. Tibori-Szabó and M. Hirst (eds.), *Victim Participation in International Criminal Justice*, International Criminal Justice Series 11,
DOI 10.1007/978-94-6265-177-7_10

Contents

10.1 Introduction: The Need for an Understanding of Socio-Cultural and Psychological Impacts

The last two decades have seen the advent of a new wave of international criminal justice mechanisms which strive not only to investigate and punish perpetrators of mass and wide-spread international crimes, but also to provide an additional and more inclusive, restorative role for victims in proceedings through the granting of participatory rights. Victims of international crimes now appear before these international or internationalised courts in differing capacities—as witnesses or as participants. In doing so, victims, legal officers and judges are likely to have a diverse range of expectations and understandings as to the function of testimony, be it the attainment of evidence for the furtherance of the Prosecution's case, the elucidation of the nature and scale of the harm suffered or the cathartic empowerment of the victim, all of which respond to legitimate goals of the new breed of court.

While victim testimony remains an important feature of international criminal justice processes, the specific nature of the offences which those courts are designed to consider poses additional difficulties in terms of victim evidence and testimony. In particular, the ability of victims of international crimes to recall and construct a cogent and coherent account of events or to otherwise publicly articulate abusive episodes may be affected by a number of factors. These factors include socio-cultural barriers, which operate upon the victim to consciously inhibit testimony, and the victim's psychological traumatic response to the events in question, which may operate beyond the conscious control of the victim to disrupt their memory and articulation of the event. In practice, these factors arise in response to (i) practical and contemporaneous aspects of the abuse itself, (ii) intervening barriers which arise subsequent to the abuse and which discourage articulation, and (iii) the clinical consequences of trauma, including those which arise contemporaneously with the abuse, and those responses which develop in the abuse aftermath.

This chapter therefore examines those socio-cultural and psychological factors which have the potential to affect the content, nature and quality of victim testimony, the judicial perception of victim credibility and ultimately, the victim's experience of engaging with the court. Sexual violence as an additional, exacerbating factor is considered, and attention is then given to the potential impact of clinical trauma on the perceived credibility of the narrated account. Finally, the allied issue of contaminated testimony is considered with particular reference both to collective approaches to victim participation and representation, and victim engagement with professional therapeutic services, and some concluding thoughts offered.

Notably, while posttraumatic stress disorder (PTSD) is one of the most commonly diagnosed mental health disorders in victims of atrocities,[1] the diagnosis itself comprises a collection of symptoms which can vary as between victims, and hence it is difficult to draw any specific and overarching conclusions about the impact of PTSD upon the ability of victims to recall and articulate their experiences during testimony. Reference in this chapter is therefore to specific symptoms of trauma rather than to clinical diagnoses, although some of the symptoms identified will form part of the diagnostic criteria for PTSD.[2]

Significantly, the socio-cultural and psychological impacts identified and explored in this chapter apply irrespective of the court in which the victim may be testifying. While many of the findings in the clinical literature have arisen in the human rights context, they are of direct and equal applicability to the international

[1] See, for example, Modvig and Jaranson 2004, p. 43.

[2] For full diagnostic criteria and features, see American Psychiatric Association (APA) 2013, pp. 271–276.

criminal context. The response of the court to those impacts may, however, vary depending upon the specific exigencies of the court and its respective constitutive and governing documents.

The primary focus of this chapter is on the experience of the International Criminal Court (ICC), although where similar provisions or practices exist in other international or internationalised criminal justice mechanisms, reference is made to them.

The trauma responses referred to in this chapter, and the corresponding challenges in eliciting testimony, have the potential to affect all victims of international crimes. Notably, trauma responses may be heightened or otherwise exacerbated where the abuse(s) suffered consisted of, or included, the perpetration of sexual violence, thereby posing additional challenges in eliciting cogent and coherent testimony. Exacerbating elements allied to experiences of sexual violence are identified in the text where appropriate.

For the purpose of this chapter, the term "trauma" refers to an adverse psychological response to an overwhelming experience of sudden or catastrophic events.[3] "Clinical" is used in the medical sense to refer, in the specific context, to psychological theory, practice and approaches.

10.2 Barriers to Testimony Arise at the Time of the Abuse, and May Stem from the Nature or Context of the Abuse Suffered

The nature and form of abuse suffered, together with the context within which crimes were perpetrated, may affect the ability of a victim to provide a full, detailed and coherent testimony of events.

In particular, legal practitioners on all sides and judges alike should be alert to the possibility of an incomplete account of events where the victim has experienced any form of sensory deprivation. This might include blindfolding or hooding, the occurrence of attacks during the hours of darkness, and lapses of consciousness in the victim. Practitioners should also be aware that any difficulties encountered by the victim in constructing a complete testimony may be exacerbated by feelings of disorientation, confusion and extreme stress experienced during the particular episode.

Specific attention is also required in situations where victims have been held by perpetrators or have otherwise been under their sole control for a significant period of time—such as when children are forced to act as child soldiers or where girls

[3] A similar, although not identical definition is used in Caruth 1996, p. 91. The definition is adjusted here to the specific context.

and women are held as domestics and/or sex slaves. In these circumstances, the victim's ability to accurately recount the specifics of individual events can be affected by factors such as drugging, as well as repeated or similar abuse experiences involving multiple perpetrators. In the latter case, practitioners should be alert to the possible unintentional generation by the victim of a composite narrative, which combines elements from any number of similar abuse experiences into a single and specific event.[4]

The broader context of the crime may also be relevant to the cogency of victims' testimony, and should be borne in mind. Where, for example, crimes have been committed within a context of prevailing malnutrition—where conflict has interrupted domestic agricultural activity, where livestock and/or crops have been destroyed or stolen, or where victims have been forced to leave their homes to seek safety and food is not readily available—issues such as starvation or vitamin deficiency can impair neuro-psychiatric memory, and again, this can affect the cogency and completeness of testimony.[5]

Finally, practitioners should be aware of any significant head injury suffered by the victim, as this can produce forms of neuro-psychiatric memory impairment.[6] Where practitioners are unsure about the potential impact of a head injury or otherwise want to protect evidence against any counter-claim that the victim's memory is impaired, a medical examination, with the victim's informed consent, is appropriate.

10.3 Factors Arising After the Abuse but Before Testimony May Affect the Willingness of the Victim to Speak in Public About Their Experiences: Shame, Lack of Trust and the Role of Interpreters

Intervening factors arise in the period between the perpetration of the crime under consideration by the court and the planned testimony of the victim. A number of intervening factors have the potential to discourage the articulation by the victim of the abusive episode in the formal, public context of the court. In particular, practitioners should be alert to the potential impact of shame and the issue of trust on testimony. In addition, factors which arise out of the use of interpreters and intermediaries can also affect a victims' willingness to speak in full about their experiences of the crimes charged, and so should also be borne in mind. These factors are outlined in more detail below.

4 Herlihy et al. 2002, p. 326.

5 International Rehabilitation Council for Torture Victims (IRCT) 2007, p. 16.

6 IRCT 2007, p. 16.

10.3.1 Social, Cultural and Familial Barriers to Full Testimony: The Impact of Shame

While shame operates as an intervening factor to discourage articulation of abuse experiences in a wide variety of trauma situations, its impact is particularly inhibiting in cases involving rape and other forms of sexual violence.[7]

In many societies sex remains a taboo subject. For male victims, rape may be interpreted as a diminution of masculinity and is rarely articulated.[8] For women victims, the disclosure of sexual violence to the victim's family or community may have devastating consequences for her marriage, leading to ostracism from the family, destitution and impoverishment, as well as social exclusion within the victim's community.[9] In cases of unmarried rape victims, sexual violence may reduce a victim's prospects of marriage. Social ostracism or cultural isolation may, in turn, heighten the trauma response of the victim, thereby further exacerbating difficulties in testifying about her experiences.[10] Moreover, while there is clinical evidence of a link between shame and the non-disclosure of experiences of rape, evidence shows an even stronger link between shame and the non-disclosure of resulting clinical symptoms,[11] which may be a significant consideration for victims' lawyers in the establishment of the nature and extent of harm suffered. In particular, a failure of the court's judgment to reflect the extent of harm experienced by victims of sexual violence may operate not only to deny victims the acknowledgment and validation that many seek, but also to affect the consequent crafting of appropriate reparations awards for victims of rape and other forms of sexual violence, including the provision of appropriate rehabilitative services.

---

[7] Clinical research with victims of trauma shows that those with a history of sexual violence experience greater levels of shame when compared with victims of non-sexual violence, assessed by reference to a 25-item scale investigating characterological, behavioural and bodily shame, and considering experiential, cognitive and behavioural components of shame within each of the three identified domains: Andrews et al., reported in Bogner et al. 2007, pp. 75–81. See also Herlihy and Turner 2006, p. 85.

[8] See, for example, Peel 2004, pp. 61–70.

[9] See, for example, United Nations Division for the Advancement of Women, Toronto, 9th–12th November 1997, Gender-Based Persecution: UN Report of Expert Group Meeting, UN Doc. EGM/GBP/1997/Report, para 41.

[10] According to the Istanbul Protocol, the UN-endorsed manual for the effective investigation and documentation of torture, 'psychological consequences…occur in the context of personal attribution of meaning, personality development, and social, political and cultural factors', Office of the United Nations High Commissioner for Human Rights (OHCHR) (2004), Manual on the effective investigation and documentation of torture and other cruel, inhuman or degrading treatment or punishment, www.ohchr.org/Documents/Publications/training8Rev1en.pdf. Accessed 30 July 2014. See also IRCT 2007, p. 24.

[11] Hook and Andrews 2005, p. 434.

While, therefore, victims of rape and other forms of sexual violence may have been able to disclose their experience(s) within the private and confidential context of discussion with their lawyer or gender-appropriate victim group, public testimony may be a very different prospect for them. While this undoubtedly poses problems for victims in testifying about their experiences, it also represents a significant obstacle for Prosecution counsel in the investigation and prosecution of offences of sexual violence, as well as for victims' lawyers in establishing the extent and nature of harm encompassed by the charges, and the party calling the victim to give evidence should consider the use of specific and appropriate procedural measures to facilitate full testimony.[12]

For the purpose of determining an appropriate sentence for a convicted defendant, the ICC has shown a willingness to hear expert evidence of trauma, including in relation to the long-term and intergenerational impacts of sexual violence, where such information has not already appeared in the Court's evidentiary record.[13] Such an approach negates, to some extent, the need for individual victims of sexual violence to testify in depth to the impact of the abuse suffered, and might also prove helpful in the crafting of reparations awards, particularly where individual testimony is difficult for victims or otherwise problematic.

10.3.2 Trust and the Existential Dilemma

Victims of international crimes may experience what is termed in psychological literature the "existential dilemma", by which a victim's core beliefs about the world as a just place have been challenged. The victim's "guiding paradigms"—their fundamental assumptions by which they interpret and make sense of the world around them—may be undermined by the traumatic event, producing an intense psychological crisis.[14] As a result, victims may experience severe difficulties in trusting others, and this is particularly so in the case of those who are asking them to relate painful or traumatic experiences.[15]

[12] See ICC, Protocol on vulnerability assessment and support procedure, ICC-01/05-01/08-974-Anx2 (2010).

[13] See, for example, the decision to permit expert evidence at the sentencing hearing of in ICC, *Prosecutor v. Jean-Pierre Bemba Gombo,* Trial Chamber III, Decision on requests to present additional evidence and submissions on sentence and scheduling the sentencing hearing, ICC-01/05-01/08-3384, 4 May 2016, para 12.

[14] For a detailed exploration of the notion and nature of personal core assumptions and their role in the formation of traumatic response, see Janoff-Bulman 1992, pp. 3–25.

[15] Herlihy and Turner 2006, p. 84.

In such circumstances, victims may find testifying an uncomfortable, upsetting and potentially hostile experience, while counsel may encounter problems in eliciting the anticipated testimony. Although it is possible that these difficulties will arise in participating victims, they are likely to be more pronounced where the victim is appearing as a Prosecution witness or while being cross-examined by Defence counsel, where parties do not represent the interests of the victims, pursue a different agenda to the victims and are perceived to manipulate the victim's testimony for the adversarial purpose.[16] In such a situation, liaison with the court's victim and witness support personnel may be appropriate.

10.3.3 The Use of Interpreters and Intermediaries

Practitioners from all sides should be particularly sensitive to the fact that victims may seek to interact with the court anonymously, or otherwise try to avoid drawing attention to their involvement with the court in their home countries, and this is particularly likely where victims either wish to prevent their families or communities from learning of their experiences of sexual violence, or where victims fear retaliatory action against themselves or their families because of their engagement with the court.

In light of the limited ground presence of most international courts and the relative lack of familiarity of many court officials with the region where the international crimes took place, recourse is often had to local intermediaries to provide both links and access to potential victims and witnesses. On the use of intermediaries more generally see also Chap. 4.

While intermediaries clearly provide courts with beneficial access to victims and witnesses in many cases, concerns about confidentiality and fear of retaliation may inhibit other potential victims and witnesses from coming forward. Moreover, in cases of sexual violence in particular, victims who are concerned about the possibility of their families or communities learning of their experiences may limit their reporting solely to their non-sexual experiences of abuse, and so exacerbate pre-existing difficulties in the prosecution of crimes of sexual violence.

In addition, if the court is working through interpreters in the production of testimony, difficulties may arise where the interpreter is from the same community as the victim and there is a fear of a lack of confidentiality, leading to a reluctance on the part of the victim to provide the testimony expected of them by the Prosecutor or their lawyers.

[16] See, for example, Doak 2011, p. 272.

10.4 The Clinical Impact of Trauma on the Victim May Prevent Them from Producing a Complete, Coherent, Chronological and Credible Account of Their Experiences

The construction and articulation of a full, coherent testimony of events can also be hampered by the psychological impact that trauma can have on the memory of victims. Proper evaluation of testimony therefore requires some degree of understanding of the quality of the witness' memory, and the decision of the ICC to hear expert evidence of the potential impacts of trauma on victims' memories in the *Ntaganda* trial is a promising step in this direction.[17]

Notably, not all witnesses and participating victims will be suffering from trauma at the time of testimony, although a substantial number of victims are likely to have suffered a trauma response at the time of the event, and as a result may experience difficulties in remembering the event in its entirety and with a sufficient degree of coherence. Moreover, it is also clear that a significant number of victims may be suffering ongoing trauma, at some level, at the time of testimony, and again, this will affect the quality and nature of the testimony they are able to give.[18] The trauma response, and so corresponding memory levels, may differ between witnesses, and will be influenced not only by the nature, extent and duration of the trauma suffered, but also by the personality of the victim and the degree to which they have been able to integrate the trauma.[19]

Significantly, the ICC Statute requires the Office of the Prosecutor to take specific measures to protect victims' psychological well-being during its

[17] ICC, *Prosecutor v. Bosco Ntaganda*, Office of the Prosecutor, Prosecution's list of expert witnesses and request pursuant to regulation 35 to vary the time limit for disclosure of the report of one expert witness, ICC-01/04-02/06-560, 16 April 2015; ICC, *Prosecutor v. Bosco Ntaganda*, Trial Chamber VI, Decision on Defence Preliminary Challenges to Prosecution expert witnesses, ICC-01/04-02/06-1159, 9 February 2016. For transcripts of the expert testimony, see ICC, *Prosecutor v. Bosco Ntaganda*, Transcript 21 April 2016, ICC-01/04-02/06-T-84-ENG; ICC, *Prosecutor v. Bosco Ntaganda*, Transcript 22 April 2016, ICC-01/04-02/06-T-87-ENG.

[18] A cross-sectional survey of a population-based sample of over 1,300 victims conducted in the Former Yugoslavia ten years after the conflict there found that a third of those sampled had suffered from PTSD, with 22% of the study sample experiencing current PTSD symptoms (Basoglu et al. 2005, p. 585). In a randomised study into the mental health status of 400 victims of the Rwandan genocide, researchers found that over half of the victim population still had PTSD symptoms ten years later, while 60% suffered from major depression (Brouneus 2010, pp. 419–420).

[19] See, for example, the evidence of expert clinical witness John Yuille, in ICC, *Prosecutor v. Bosco Ntaganda,* Trial Chamber VI, Transcript 21 April 2016, ICC-01/04-02/06-T-84-ENG, and in particular, pp. 13–19.

investigation.[20] In the case of the International Criminal Court at least, potential witnesses are assessed by a court-funded psychologist before being interviewed by an investigator, and those deemed insufficiently mentally robust may be excluded from the formal investigative process.[21] As a result, the number of Prosecution witnesses suffering from a significant degree of ongoing trauma is likely to be relatively small. It remains a possibility, however, that even though Prosecution witnesses may not be suffering from any ongoing trauma, they may have experienced a trauma reaction at the time of the event, and this has the potential to affect their recollection of it. As a result, the potential impact of trauma on testimony is still a live issue even as concerns Prosecution witnesses at the ICC.

Notably, the constituent documents and procedural rules of both the Extraordinary Chambers in the Courts of Cambodia (ECCC) and the Special Tribunal for Lebanon (STL) are silent on the issue of the psychological well-being of victims at the investigation stage. In the absence of any practice to exclude psychologically vulnerable victims from the Prosecution's investigations at the STL and ECCC, it is likely that victim witnesses will include amongst them those who have experienced or continue to experience trauma symptoms. As a result, prosecuting lawyers should be aware that witnesses may be vulnerable during testimony, and may also have difficulties in constructing a full and detailed account of events as a result of their trauma.

There is no statutory obligation on victims' lawyers at the ICC, STL or ECCC to protect the psychological well-being of participating victims, and as a result, representatives do not receive any assistance from a court-funded psychologist during their evidence gathering and evidence-testing activities, including in their consideration of which victims should appear in person before the court, whether to testify or in a similar capacity. Moreover, while participating victims' lawyers undoubtedly seek to act in the best interests of victims, they are not equipped to assess a victim's psychological readiness for formal testimony.

[20] See Article 68(1) of the Rome Statute of the International Criminal Court, A/CONF.183/9 (2010) (the 'ICC Statute').

[21] Private communication with OTP psychologist, 9 March, 2012 (records on file with the author). The approach is also referenced in para 70 of the ICC Office of the Prosecutor's Policy Paper on Sexual and Gender-based Crimes (2014), http://www.icc-cpi.int/iccdocs/otp/OTP-Policy-Paper-on-Sexual-and-Gender-Based-Crimes--June-2014.pdf. Accessed 17 May 2016. Notably, while such an approach might be believed to better protect both the emotional safety of the victim and the integrity of the evidence when it is placed before the Court, there has been no psychological assessment, follow-up or research conducted into the psychological impact on the victim of rejection by the Office of the Prosecutor's investigators. There is, however, some evidence at least that a denial of justice may be experienced as psychologically detrimental by victims already suffering a degree of trauma, and this may be particularly relevant where engagement with the investigative and prosecutorial process was perceived by the victim as an aspect of justice; see, for example, Danieli 2009, p. 352; Sveaass and Lavik 2000, pp. 42–44, noting that in psychological terms the denial of justice represents a continuation of violence; Rauchfuss and Schmolze 2008, p. 40.

As a result, it is reasonable to assume that the body of victim participants appearing before the court in person are likely to include amongst them individuals who are psychologically vulnerable or those whose memory of events is affected by trauma. Moreover, victims' lawyers should be particularly alert to the fact that while participation was designed with a specific victim focus, the potential nature of engagement, including testifying as to the form, impact and extent of harm suffered, also means greater exposure to the trauma story and hence greater potential difficulties during testimony, and the possibility of psychologically disadvantageous engagement.

In the context of the ICC, the Victims and Witnesses Section (VWS) is mandated to provide protective and supportive measures to ensure the security, physical and psychological well-being of victims and witnesses once they are physically before the court.[22] A similar service is provided at the STL,[23] while psychological support for individuals giving testimony before the ECCC is provided through the Witness and Experts Support Unit.[24] In light of the potential vulnerability of some victims, liaison with these units by all parties is essential, and victims themselves, or their lawyers or calling party, may ask for special measures to facilitate testimony, including the attendance of a psychologist during testimony and/or a psychological debriefing following testimony.[25]

During questioning and testimony itself, counsel from all parties and officials of the court itself should be particularly conscious of the potential impacts of trauma on both the victim and the evidence they are able to provide. While legal practitioners do not need to be experts in trauma, they should be alert to the fact that past or current trauma reactions may play a significant role in the content and nature of any evidence that victims are able to provide. As a result, awareness, at least, of possible trauma responses and their potential impact on testimony is required. A greater appreciation of these will better enable both judges and legal representatives of victims (LRVs) to understand and interpret victim testimony in their consideration of the credibility of evidence given. These responses are broad and wide-ranging. Those of particular relevance to the judicial process of eliciting testimony can include issues of avoidance, dissociation and auto-biographical memory impairment, and are outlined below.

22 ICC Statute, Article 43(6).

23 Article 12(4) of the Statute of the Special Tribunal for Lebanon, S/RES/1757 (2007) (the 'STL Statute'), together with Rule 50 of its Rules of Procedure and Evidence, STL-BD-2009-01-Rev.7-Corr.1., (2015). See also Chap. 6.

24 Although services are hugely under-resourced, and in practice, the Court provides psychological support via agreements with two clinical NGOs. See in particular, Leang and Williams 2010, p. 160.

25 Provided for explicitly in the case of the ICC, Rules 88(1) and (2) of the Rules of Procedure and Evidence, ICC-ASP/1/3-Corr.1 (Part.II-A) (2002).

10.4.1 Avoidance

Avoidance strategies in victims of international crimes can include not only voluntary tactics, such as trying not to think about past experiences, or avoiding places or events that might trigger painful memories, but also involuntary avoidance responses. These involuntary responses can include forms of psychogenic amnesia, which involve a disruption of memory or perception. These in turn can lead to gaps in the victim's memory, particularly in relation to the traumatic event.[26] As a result, aspects of the traumatic event, or the event in its entirety, may simply be unavailable to the victim so long as he or she continues to experience avoidance symptoms.

10.4.2 Dissociation

Dissociation is understood as 'a disruption of and/or discontinuation in the normal integration of consciousness, memory, identity, emotion, perception, body representation, motor control, and behaviour', leading to gaps in recall and problematic perception in relation to the traumatic event.[27]

Dissociation can arise as a coping mechanism at the time of the traumatic event itself,[28] producing a psychogenic amnesia for some or all of the traumatic event.[29] In addition, dissociation may occur after the traumatic event, with memories of the event and during times of stress or high arousal, including in situations where a victim is questioned about their experiences and, significantly, during testimony.[30] This in turn can affect the ability of the individual to construct and articulate a full and coherent account of the event.[31]

10.4.3 Autobiographical Memory Impairment

Autobiographical memory (otherwise known as declarative or explicit memory) refers to the ability to recall events in our own lives. These memories are recorded and stored chronologically, can be retrieved voluntarily, and it is possible to

[26] Herlihy and Turner 2006, pp. 85–87.

[27] APA 2013, p. 291.

[28] Weiss et al., cited in Bogner et al. 2007, p. 75.

[29] Known as peritraumatic dissociation. See Weiss et al., ibid., p. 75.

[30] This has been noted, for example, in the context of the UK domestic asylum system during the conduct of asylum interviews by Home Office representatives, Bogner et al. 2007, pp. 77–78.

[31] Ibid.

construct a chronological and coherent narrative of them.[32] A critical feature of autobiographical memory is an accompanying awareness that the events concerned occurred in the past.[33]

There is a growing consensus in clinical literature that traumatic memories are of a different character.[34] During deeply traumatic events, it is believed that greatly heightened emotional arousal interferes with the processing and storage of information in explicit memory, and the process essentially fails. As a result, autobiographical memory of the event is fragmentary or non-existent.[35]

While explicit memory fails, however, non-declarative (implicit) memory, which includes emotional responses, habits and reflexive actions, appears to be unaffected by trauma. As a result, while a victim may not be able to access a coherent narrative memory of the event, he or she may be aware of sensory perceptions and behavioural re-enactments emanating from it.[36] These may in turn be experienced as images, smells, sensations or emotional states.[37] Such memories are accessed through qualitatively different 'pathways', and rather than arising voluntarily or consciously in the victim, respond to triggers or reminders of the event. Significantly, from the point of view of the legal practitioner, these triggers can include being questioned or cross-examined about the event. Because these memories are subject to triggers, different aspects may arise, depending upon the questions posed. As a result, Prosecution and Defence counsel as well as victims' lawyers will require a particularly considered and specific strategy to their questioning. In addition, where victims are able to retrieve memories, these are often not chronological and are fragmented. As a result, testimony may be both incomplete and potentially lacking in coherence.

Notably, unlike autobiographical memory, implicit memories are not perceived by the victim as occurring in the past, but instead are experienced in the present, at the time that the memory is recalled.[38] As a result, accessing implicit memories can be a highly distressing and potentially re-traumatising experience for the victim. Retrieval of memories of this nature during testimony can therefore pose significant difficulties for counsel of all parties, and prior liaison with available victim psychological support services within the court, together with judicial sensitivity to the issue, is needed in order to ensure a rapid and targeted response to victims' psychological needs, should they arise.

---

[32] Herlihy and Turner 2006, p. 86.

[33] Ibid.

[34] Brewin 2003, cited in Herlihy and Turner 2006, p. 86; Herlihy et al. 2002, p. 86.

[35] Herlihy and Turner, for example, observe that 'when someone is interviewed and asked about an experience that was traumatic, and has only, or largely, memories of this fragmented type, they are unlikely to be able to produce a coherent verbal narrative, quite simply because no complete verbal narrative exists.' Herlihy and Turner 2006, p. 86.

[36] Janet 1925, p. 660, and cited in van der Kolk and Risler 1995, p. 511; Bremner et al. 1998, pp. 379–380; Van der Kolk and Van der Hart 1995, p. 160.

[37] Van der Kolk 1996, in Herlihy and Turner 2006, p. 86.

[38] Hellawell and Brewin 2004, pp. 1144 and 1148. See also Brewin 2015, pp. 1–2.

10.4.4 Additional Intrusive Phenomena

In addition to the symptoms referred to above, intrusive memories and flashbacks relating to the traumatic event might also arise at the time that a victim is giving an account of his or her experiences during interview or testimony, affecting both their ability to focus on the question posed and to construct a full and coherent account of events.[39]

10.5 Sexual Violence May Exacerbate the Difficulties Experienced by Victims[40]

Victims of international crimes who have experienced rape and other forms of sexual violence are particularly prone to difficulties in speaking about and producing a coherent and complete testimony of their experiences.

While trauma can affect the quality and nature of testimony in all victims, practitioners should be especially alert to the possibility of problems in testimony where victims are survivors of sexual violence. In addition to issues surrounding shame, which have already been discussed, avoidance symptoms are significantly more evident in victims of rape and other forms of sexual violence than in victims of non-sexual trauma.[41] Victims of sexual violence also experience more dissociation symptoms, a higher PTSD symptom count and greater difficulty in disclosure when compared to victims of non-sexual trauma,[42] all of which further militate against the ability of victims to recall and coherently articulate their abuse experiences during judicial testimony.

Finally, in the South African context at least, there is evidence that women giving testimony before the Truth and Reconciliation Commission had a tendency to talk about the experiences of their male relatives rather than their own abuse experiences,[43] indicating a potential differential between the willingness of women and men to testify to their own experiences, and again, a factor which Prosecution and Defence counsel as well as victims' lawyers should bear in mind. Notably, it is not clear whether the tendency identified in the South African study was due to a reluctance on the part of the women to talk about experiences of sexual violence in particular, or was due more broadly to a lack of prioritisation of victims' own experiences, and hence potentially alternatively rooted, to some extent, in cultural norms relating to the status of women.

---

[39] Bogner et al. 2007, p. 78.

[40] And see in particular, Smith 2012, which deals specifically with this issue, pp. 99–112.

[41] Van Velsen et al. 1996, p. 188.

[42] See, generally, Bogner et al. 2007; Ramsay et al. 1993, pp. 5–58; see also Lecic-Tosevski and Bakalic 2004, p. 97.

[43] Duggan and Abusharaf 2008, p. 639.

10.6 The Impact of Trauma May also Affect Perceptions of Credibility in the Victim

In addition to clinical issues which affect the ability of victims of international crimes to recall and articulate their experiences, a number of factors emanating from the trauma itself or arising as a consequence of it may affect legal perceptions of credibility in relation to victims' testimony, and so warrant the particular attention of practitioners and judges alike. In general, for many survivors, relating traumatic events can be a deeply upsetting and distressing experience. Victims may feel they lack the language to fully describe traumatic episodes, and high levels of emotion can hamper both recall and coherent articulation. Where victims deport themselves poorly in the witness stand, speak quickly, sweat, tremble or show other signs of nervousness, these are not necessarily signs that the witness is lying, but instead may indicate normal reactions to speaking about highly distressing events. To date, recourse to psychological evidence as an aid to better understanding the impacts of trauma on the way in which testimony is given has been relatively limited within international criminal justice mechanisms. Notably, however, the ICC, in the *Lubanga* case, did hear expert evidence of possible psychological impacts of child soldiering on testimony and victims' deportment in the witness stand.[44] In addition, particular factors associated with trauma have the potential to affect perceptions of credibility in the victim, and should be borne in mind by judges and LRVs. These include issues of central and peripheral detail, emotional numbing and the potential impact of engagement by victims with rehabilitative services.

10.6.1 Central v. Peripheral Detail

Central details of an event are those factors that, from the perspective of the individual, constitute the primary details or elements of the event, and which are typically directly related to the source of the traumatic experience. Peripheral details are, from the perspective of the victim or witness, ancillary or irrelevant to the stressful event.

Essential to the legal understanding of credibility is the idea that while details which are central to an event might be constructed by reference to historical and publicly-available data, such as through the media, specific details and features,

[44] The Office of the Prosecutor obtained a report from an expert psychologist to this end, see, http://www.ijmonitor.org/2010/10/lubanga-trial-highlights-plight-of-child-soldiers/. Accessed 19 May 2016.

including peripheral detail, cannot. As a result, recall by victims of the latter in testimony is considered to be indicative of credibility in the witness.[45]

This approach, however, is at odds with the way in which details of an event are perceived, interpreted and stored in the memory of victims during a traumatic episode. In particular, memories of traumatic events tend to focus on central events, to the detriment of peripheral detail, and hence the inability of victims to provide a detailed testimony beyond the central elements of a traumatic episode should not automatically operate to impugn the nature and quality of the evidence that they are able to provide. While, for example, a victim who was raped at knife point might be able to describe the weapon in detail, she may not be able to describe the perpetrator's clothing, because it was not a central issue or key element of the attack.

In addition, depressive symptoms, which might arise in the aftermath of the traumatic event, have been shown to have a direct, negative impact on the ability of victims to recall both central and peripheral detail, while for individuals with high levels of post-traumatic stress symptoms, discrepancies in accounts are known to arise in peripheral detail in particular with the increase of time between interviews or the length of court proceedings.[46]

10.6.2 Emotional Numbing

Emotional numbing is a trauma response associated with avoidance, and results in the victim having little or no emotional connection to his or her experiences. This means that while victims are able to articulate and describe a traumatic event during testimony, they experience no feelings in relation to it. This lack of any range of affect impacts upon the victim's demeanour when giving testimony, leading potentially to perceptions of "coldness" which may not accord with lay assumptions of how a victim of international crimes is expected to behave, and hence can be interpreted negatively and erroneously to impugn the credibility of the victim.[47]

10.6.3 Victims Who Have Received Rehabilitative Treatment

Where victims have engaged in a relatively lengthy formal therapeutic process within which the trauma experience has been repeatedly narrated, this can affect the way in which testimony is given, and in turn, the degree of credibility ascribed to the resulting account.

---

[45] Cameron 2010, pp. 483–486. See also Herlihy and Turner 2007, p. 3.

[46] Herlihy et al. 2002, p. 326.

[47] See Smith and Boyles 2009, p. 13. See, generally, Baillot et al.

In particular, many victims who have become used to speaking about their experiences will find narrative less upsetting,[48] and as a result, their emotional response to their experiences may not accord with lay perceptions of how a victim should act when testifying about difficult events. In addition, repetition of the trauma narrative may mean that any judicial testimony might appear in some way "rehearsed" or otherwise lacking in spontaneity, again impacting upon perceptions of credibility in relation to the victim's account.

10.7 There Is Potential for the Emergence of a Composite Narrative in Testimony

In certain situations, a victim's testimony may comprise a composite of experiences rather than a single experience that is directly related to the event(s) under consideration by the court.

As noted above, where the victim has experienced multiple attacks of a similar nature, such as the perpetration of rape in situations where women and girls have been held captive for a period, an unintentional, composite account of events might emerge in cases where the victim is unable to discern between specific incidents of abuse.

In addition, Prosecution and Defence counsel as well as victims' lawyers should be particularly alert to other factors which have the potential to produce a composite narrative in the victim. These factors include the specific forensic focus of legal charges, and a divergence between Western and non-Western approaches to the conception of the self, and are outlined in more detail below.

10.7.1 The Limits of Legal Charges, Prosecutorial Discretion and the Psychological Need for Narrative

While the investigative and prosecutorial remit of international criminal justice institutions is theoretically broad, in practice, resource limitations, prosecutorial priorities and the availability of evidence will mean that the number of cases brought will be relatively small. In particular, the exercise of prosecutorial discretion will necessarily affect not only the selected target of a prosecution but also the nature of charges brought, and a number of offences, including in particular, offences of sexual violence, are more challenging to establish, and, in the context of the International Criminal Court at least, remain under-represented.[49] As a

[48] Herman 1997, p. 195.

[49] See, for example, Women's Initiative for Gender Justice, Gender Report Card on the International Criminal Court 2014, p. 66.

result, the charges brought in any one case are unlikely to reflect in full the experiences of victims in terms of the abuses suffered.

At the same time, the need for victims of atrocities to tell their stories to an engaged listener and to receive formal and objective acknowledgment and condemnation of those experiences is widely recognised in both psychological[50] and restorative and transitional justice literature,[51] as well as in the writings of victims themselves.[52] Within this context, the limited, forensic focus of the court can clearly be a source of frustration for some victims,[53] and a composite account incorporating elements of a number of trauma experiences or events may be consciously produced as a means for victims to relate in full their abuse experience.[54]

10.7.2 A Non-Western Understanding of the Self: Collective Identity

The potential for the emergence of a composite account in this context is best explained by recourse to psychological literature on the development of trauma in the aftermath of atrocities. Within Western psychological literature, the self is characterised as 'an autonomous, individualised, volitional, and independent entity having control over one's existence and environment through rational means.'[55] By contrast, some non-Western societies, including potentially societies or communities which might, at some point, form the subject of international criminal investigation, may conceptualise the self in relation to the environment and/or emphasise interdependence, group identity and collectivist views of suffering over more Western notions of the individual self.[56] Moreover, it is apparent that where persecutory or abusive actions, such as genocide or ethnic cleansing, are directed at entire ethnic or cultural populations, the sense of group identity and allegiance is further heightened,[57] producing or increasing pre-existing collective notions of identity.[58]

---

[50] Janoff-Bulman 1992, p. 108; Felman and Laub 1992, p. 78; Herman 1997, p. 175; Hamber 1995, p. 3. It is not suggested here that testifying in court is necessarily therapeutically beneficial for victims.

[51] Zehr 2005, p. 191; Stover et al. 2011, pp. 521–522; Kirchenbauer et al. 2013, pp. 19–20.

[52] Levi 1979, pp. 15–16.

[53] Kelsall and Stepakoff 2007, pp. 372–373.

[54] There is primary clinical evidence of this occurring, for example, during the course of narrowly-focused psychological investigations; see Igreja et al. 2004, p. 256.

[55] De Jong 2004, p. 164.

[56] Ibid.

[57] See, for example, Aroche and Coello 2004, p. 56.

[58] Modvig and Jaranson 2004, p. 37.

This collective notion of identity might in turn prove problematic for counsel, victims' lawyers and the court itself from an evidential point of view, where individual victims fail to distinguish between abuses suffered collectively or by other members of the group, and those which the victim suffered personally. As a result, victims might give testimony as to what is in effect a "collective" experience, presented as personal experience. In doing so, victims are not deliberately deceiving or otherwise seeking to mislead the court, but instead are displaying fundamentally different assumptions about individual identity and the self.

Notably, psychological exploration of non-Western responses to traumatic stress is constantly evolving and developing, and it is not clear to what extent the issue of a collective testimony in such circumstances might pose a problem in practice. An awareness of the area, however, is important for lawyers working with victims in order to ensure the integrity of evidence contained within victim testimony. In particular, specific questioning or briefing of witnesses would be appropriate to establish either that the testimony given is limited to the personal and individual experiences of the victim, or that distinctions are clear between harm suffered by the victim and that inflicted upon others within the group.

10.8 Testimony of Victims May Be Deemed Contaminated or Otherwise Mediated by Their Engagement with Therapeutic Services or by Aspects of Collective Approaches to Victim Representation

Prosecution and Defence counsel as well as victims' lawyers should be aware of the possibility for victims' testimony to become moderated or contaminated through their interaction with others, or at least, for their evidence to be attacked on that basis. Contaminated testimony can take various forms. The specific focus of this section is on the perceived contaminating impact of formal therapeutic engagement and the potentially mediating effect of collective approaches to victim participation and representation.

10.8.1 The Impact of Formal Therapeutic Engagement

For many victims of traumatic experiences, natural recovery responses, which arise spontaneously in the aftermath of a stressful and upsetting event, will mean that any formal therapeutic intervention is unnecessary. However, many other victims continue to experience severe trauma symptoms years after the abuse took place, and for these individuals, rehabilitation will most likely require some level of engagement with professional clinical services.[59] It is therefore appropriate to consider briefly how formal therapeutic approaches might interact with victim testimony.

Notably, clinical rehabilitation processes are known to reduce the desire for vengeance in victims. In contrast, poor psychological health is associated with low levels of forgiveness.[60] Psychological recovery therefore arguably serves the pro-societal goal of contributing to the maintenance of peace and security and hence responds to a legitimate function of the court.[61] Moreover, there is some limited, anecdotal evidence that where victims have been through a therapeutic process, their testimony is more coherent as a result,[62] and hence beneficial for both the victim and the court.

Despite these benefits, however, there is initial evidence that in the case of the ICC, the Office of the Prosecutor chooses not to use as witnesses victims who have been through a formal therapeutic process, due to fears that the therapeutic process itself has contaminated the integrity of any evidence they are able to provide.[63] As yet, there is no indication that individuals engaging with the ICC as participating victims have been excluded from providing evidence or from testifying where they had previously benefitted from rehabilitative services. Notably, there is no evidence of a similar practice of excluding witnesses on the basis of engagement with therapeutic services at either the STL or ECCC. As a result, there is the potential, at least, that the evidence of victims appearing before the ICC or the STL either as witnesses or participating victims, might be discredited where their testimony is deemed contaminated by the therapeutic process.

The impugning or exclusion of evidence from victims who have benefited from rehabilitative services is seemingly based upon a fundamental misunderstanding of the nature and function of the modern therapeutic process, and may well stem from historical legal difficulties involving the 'retrieval' of memories of childhood sexual abuse. While it is true that the provision of therapeutic support is

---

[59] Notably, full rehabilitation in this context is likely impossible, and the concept of rehabilitation in the aftermath of atrocities is therefore a relative one. The aim of therapeutic engagement in such circumstances is to achieve as full rehabilitation as possible; see 1984 UN Convention against Torture, and Other Cruel Inhuman or Degrading Treatment of Punishment 1465 UNTS 113, Article 14. For a detailed exploration of the notion of rehabilitation in the context of gross human rights violations, see Smith et al. 2010, pp. 12–18.

[60] See Kaminer et al. 2001, p. 375; Rauschenbach and Scalia 2008, p. 445; Herman 1997, p. 190.

[61] In the case of the ICC, the broad, societal goal of peace is contained in the Preamble to the ICC Statute.

[62] Agger et al. 2009, p. 215. Notably, the suggestion is anecdotal and requires further empirical investigation and verification.

[63] Private conversation with psychologist for the ICC Office of the Prosecutor, 9 March, 2012 (records on file with the author).

potentially transformative of the victim's narrative, this transformation is limited only to the extent that the account is contextualised and made more "real" to the victim,[64] and the therapist makes no assumptions as to the facts of the story.[65]

Notably, the number of victims seeking to engage with the courts as either witnesses or participants, who have benefitted from formal therapeutic support, is unknown, and it may be, at this stage at least, that the problem is a theoretical rather than a practical one. With the introduction by the ICC's Trust Fund of rehabilitative services in countries where the Prosecutor's investigations remain active and ongoing, however, the issue may arise if it has not done so already, and an awareness of the issue amongst prosecutors and victims' lawyers is therefore required.

10.8.2 Mediation Through Collective Approaches to Victim Representation

In light of the scale of crimes which fall within the remit of the modern international criminal justice mechanism and the correspondingly significant number of participating victims engaged in any one case, a collective approach to victims' legal representation has been adopted across the various judicial bodies where victims' participation is permitted. While this approach aims to render the victim participation endeavour of these courts operational in practice, they also arguably introduce the potential for a mediated testimony, which victims' lawyers in particular should bear in mind.

Notably, during group meetings or forums for participating victims, victim narrative, by which participating victims relate their own experiences to the group of fellow participants, can arise spontaneously, at the direct instigation of the victims themselves.[66] While spontaneous narrative may occur as a result of victims' restorative and rehabilitative needs to relate their stories to an engaged listener, narrative in such circumstances also risks the development and emergence of a shared, group understanding or narrative of traumatic events which may become the dominant narrative. This in turn can have the effect of stifling or silencing individual narrative that does not fit or is otherwise inconsistent with the emergent shared

64 Herman 1997, p. 181.

65 Herman 1997, p. 179. Notably, the impact of any determination by the court that a victim lacks competence to testify to their own experiences and has instead been the victim of implanted memories is potentially disempowering, and hence contrary to the court's restorative aim. The area therefore requires further investigation and detailed consideration by the court.

66 Private communication with the Case Manager for the Legal Representative of Victims in ICC, *Prosecutor v. Uhuru Muigai Kenyatta*, 5 September 2013 (records on file with the author).

narrative,[67] as well as the narratives of less dominant groups, including women victims of sexual violence.

Moreover, there are potential risks to the integrity of evidence that is produced following participation in meetings where numerous narratives emerge, whereby 'shared meaning so derived may overshadow individual memory of what happened, and thus complicate any forensic/evidentiary processes that will follow subsequently.'[68]

It is unclear to what extent testimony produced in such circumstances might be mediated or otherwise contaminated by the narrative of others or the perception of a group consensus around certain events, the nature and extent of harm suffered or responsibility for the harm experienced, and the impact might be quite individual. There is, however, a clear need for lawyers, as well as the courts more generally, to be conscious of the potential for the mediation of individual testimony in such circumstances.

What is clear now, however, is that narrative in this context emerges in the absence of any available professional psychological support for potentially vulnerable victims, and hence risks psychologically detrimental engagement. The development of collective approaches to representation has therefore expanded the locus of victim testimony beyond the courtroom, warranting a re-examination by courts of the geographical scope of their duties to protect the well-being of the victim through the provision of therapeutic support.

10.9 Key Points

- A number of factors, including those which relate to the socio-cultural context of the abuse as well as the clinical impact of the abuse on the individual, can affect the ability of the victim to recall and articulate a coherent, chronological, credible and complete account of events.
- These factors will undoubtedly pose problems for victims in the realisation of restorative aims and ultimately may impact upon the extent to which victims' regard their experience of engaging with the court as a positive one.
- Such factors present particular difficulties for Prosecution and Defence counsel, victims' lawyers and the court itself in terms of the quality and nature of evidence that victims may be able to provide, requiring creative and thoughtful approaches to how testimony is obtained.
- Such approaches might include adjustments to the mode of questioning, the manner in which evidence is elicited or presented to the court, the pursuit of

[67] This is particularly so where the dominant narrative is a heroic one; see in relation to truth commission processes, Grunebaum and Henri 2003, pp. 103–104. In such circumstances, issues of shame might arise to inhibit personal testimony.

[68] See, generally, Raphael 2003, pp. 146–161.

additional lines of questioning or investigation and a significant degree of liaison with clinical staff within the court's victim and witness support services in order to ensure both the psychological safety of the victim and the integrity of evidence before the court.

- The appropriate use, interpretation and application of victim testimony in situations where the victim has suffered or continues to experience trauma symptoms requires greater legal awareness of and engagement with issues of trauma,[69] and in particular, the potential impacts of trauma on testimony evidence and the perceived credibility of victims in the various capacities in which they might appear before the court.
- Engagement might entail not only dedicated and targeted training activities for judicial staff but also recourse to expert clinical witnesses in specific cases. The 2016 decision of the ICC to hear evidence of the impact of trauma on evidence is a step in the right direction, and should be replicated in other situations where a need is indicated. In addition, a greater recognition of the various contexts for potentially detrimental interaction with the court is needed, and a corresponding re-examination, reassessment and expansion of how psychological support is currently made available to victim participants is appropriate.

References

Agger IS et al (2009) Testimonial therapy: A pilot project to improve psychological wellbeing among survivors of torture in India. Torture 19(3):204–217

American Psychiatric Association (APA) (2013) Diagnostic and statistical manual of mental disorders, 5th edn. American Psychiatric Publishing, Washington

Aroche J, Coello MJ (2004) Ethnocultural considerations in treatment of refugees. In: Wilson J, Drozdek B (eds) Broken spirits: The treatment of traumatized asylum seekers, refugees, war and torture victims. Brunner-Routledge, New York, pp 53–80

Baillot H et al [undated] Research briefing: Rape narratives and credibility assessment (of female claimants) at the AIT. http://www.nottingham.ac.uk/law/documents/briefing-papers/research-briefing-rape-narratives-and-credibility-assessment-(of-female-claimants)-at-the-ait.pdf. Accessed 25 July 2014

Basoglu M et al (2005) Psychiatric and cognitive effects of war in former Yugoslavia: Association of lack of redress for trauma and posttraumatic stress reactions. J Am Med Assoc 294(5):580–592

Bogner D et al (2007) Impact of sexual violence on disclosure during Home Office interviews. Br J Psychiatry 191:75–81

69 Some, albeit limited, progress has already been made in this regard in the International Criminal Tribunals for the former Yugoslavia and Rwanda, the former of which has concluded that PTSD would not necessarily affect the credibility of a victim/witness; see ICTY, *Prosecutor v. Furundzija*, Trial Chamber, Judgment, IT-95-17/1-T, 10 December 1998, paras 108–109; ICTY, *Prosecutor v. Kunarac* et al., Appeals Chamber, Judgment, IT 96-23-I & IT 96-23/1-An, 12 June 2002, para 324; ICTR, *Prosecutor v. Bagilishema*, Trial Chamber, Judgment, ICTR 95-1A-T, 7 June 2001, para 24. Statements to date, however, have been limited to PTSD diagnoses as opposed to symptomology, or otherwise make vague reference to "trauma", without consideration of specific sequels.

Bremner JD et al (1998) Trauma, memory and dissociation: An integrative formulation. In: Bremner JD et al (eds) Trauma, memory and dissociation. American Psychiatric Press, Washington, p 365
Brewin C (2003) Posttraumatic stress disorder: Malady or myth? Yale University Press, London
Brewin C (2015) Re-experiencing traumatic events in PTSD: new avenues in research on intrusive memories and flashbacks. European Journal of Psychotraumatology 6:1–16
Brouneus K (2010) The trauma of truth telling: Effects of witnessing in the Rwandan Gacaca Courts on psychological health. J Conflict Resolut 54(3):408–437
Cameron HE (2010) Refugee status determinations and the limits of memory. Int J Refugee Law 22(4):469–511
Caruth C (1996) Unclaimed experience: Trauma, narrative and history. John Hopkins University Press, Baltimore
Danieli Y (2009) Massive trauma and the healing role of reparative justice. J Trauma Stress 22(5):351–357
De Jong J (2004) Public mental health and culture: Disasters as a challenge to western mental health care models, the self, and PTSD. In: Wilson J, Drozdek B (eds) Broken spirits: The treatment of traumatized asylum seekers, refugees, war and torture victims. Brunner-Routledge, New York, pp 159–178
Doak J (2011) The therapeutic dimension of transitional justice: Emotional repair and victim satisfaction in international trials and truth commissions. International Criminal Law Review 11:263–298
Duggan C, Abusharaf M (2008) Reparation of sexual violence in democratic transitions. In: De Greiff P (ed) The handbook of reparations. Oxford University Press, Oxford, pp 623–649
Felman S, Laub D (1992) Testimony: Crises of witnessing in literature, psychoanalysis, and history. Routledge Press, New York
Grunebaum H, Henri Y (2003) Re-membering bodies, producing histories: Holocaust survivor narrative and Truth and Reconciliation Commission testimony. In: Bennett J, Kennedy R (eds) World memory: Personal trajectories in global time. Palgrave Macmillan, Basingstoke, pp 101–118
Hamber B (1995) Do sleeping dogs lie? The psychological implications of the Truth and Reconciliation Commission in South Africa. Paper presented at the Centre for the Study of Violence and Reconciliation, Seminar No. 5 (Johannesburg 26 July 1995)
Hellawell SJ, Brewin CR (2004) A comparison of flashbacks and ordinary autobiographical memories of trauma: content and language. Behav Res Ther 42:1–12
Herlihy J, Turner S (2006) Should discrepant accounts given by asylum seekers be taken as proof of deceit? Torture 16(2):81–92
Herlihy J, Turner S (2007) Asylum claims and memory of trauma: sharing our knowledge. Br J Psychiatry 191:3–4
Herlihy J et al (2002) Discrepancies in autobiographical memories - implications for the assessment of asylum seekers: repeated interviews study. Br Med J 324:324–327
Herman J (1997) Trauma and recovery: The aftermath of violence—from domestic abuse to political terror. Basic Books, New York
Hook A, Andrews B (2005) The relationship of non-disclosure in therapy to shame and depression. Br J Clin Psychol 44:425–438
Igreja V et al (2004) Testimony method to ameliorate post-traumatic stress symptoms: Community-based intervention study with Mozambican civil war survivors. Br J Psychiatry 184:251–257
International Criminal Court (ICC) (2010) Protocol on the vulnerability assessment and support procedure used to facilitate the testimony of vulnerable witnesses. http://www.icc-cpi.int/icc-docs/doc/doc957719.pdf. Accessed 26 January 2015
International Rehabilitation Council for Torture Victims (IRCT) (2007) Psychological evaluations of torture allegations: A practical guide to the Istanbul Protocol—for psychologists. 2nd edn. http://www.irct.org/Files/Filer/publications/psychological_en_web_red.pdf. Accessed 30 July 2014

Janet P (1925) Psychological healings vols 1–2. Macmillan, New York
Janoff-Bulman R (1992) Shattered assumptions: Towards a new psychology of trauma. The Free Press, New York
Kaminer D et al (2001) The Truth and Reconciliation Commission in South Africa: Relation to psychiatric status and forgiveness among survivors of human rights abuses. Br J Psychiatry 178:373–377
Kelsall M, Stepakoff S (2007) 'When we wanted to talk about rape': silencing sexual violence at the Special Court for Sierra Leone. Int J Trans Justice 1:355–374
Kirchenbauer et al (2013) Victims' participation before the Extraordinary Chambers in the Courts of Cambodia: Baseline study of the Cambodian Human Rights and Development Association's Civil Party Scheme for Case 002. http://www.eccc.gov.kh/sites/default/files/Victims-participation-before-ECCC-Baseline-Study-Jan-2013.pdf. Accessed 28 July 2014
Leang C, Smith W (2010) The early experience of the Extraordinary Chambers in the Court of Cambodia. In: Bellilli R (ed) International criminal justice: Law and practice from the Rome Statute to its review. Ashgate Publishing, Surrey, pp 143–160
Lecic-Tosevski D, Bakalic J (2004) Against torture—The road to a healthy individual and society. In: Spiric Z, Knezevic G, Jovic V et al (eds) Torture in war: Consequences and rehabilitation of victims—Yugoslav experience. International Aid Network, Belgrade, pp 95–105
Levi P (1979) If this is a man: The truce. Abacus Publishers, London
Modvig J, Jaranson JM (2004) A global perspective of torture, political violence, and health. In: Wilson J, Drozdek B (eds) Broken spirits: The treatment of traumatized asylum seekers, refugees, war and torture victims. Brunner-Routledge, New York, pp 33–52
Office of the United Nations High Commissioner for Human Rights (OHCHR) (2004) Manual on the effective investigation and documentation of torture and other cruel, inhuman or degrading treatment or punishment. http://www.ohchr.org/Documents/Publications/training8Rev1en.pdf. Accessed 30 July 2014
Peel M (2004) Men as perpetrators and victims. In: Peel (ed) Rape as a method of torture. Medical Foundation for the Care of Victims of Torture, London, pp 61–70
Ramsay R et al (1993) Psychiatric morbidity in survivors of organised state violent including torture. A retrospective series. The British Journal of Psychiatry 162:55–59
Raphael B (2003) Early intervention and the debriefing debate. In: Ursano RJ, Fullerton CS, Norwood AE (eds) Terrorism and disaster: Individual and community mental health interventions. Cambridge University Press, Cambridge, pp 146–161
Rauchfuss K, Schmolze B (2008) Justice heals: The impact of impunity and the fight against it on the recovery of severe human rights violations' survivors. Torture 18(1):38–50
Rauschenbach M, Scalia D (2008) Victims and international criminal justice. International Review of the Red Cross 90:441–459
Smith E (2012) Investigating rape at the International Criminal Court: The impact of trauma. Issues in International Criminal Justice, Special Volume, pp 99–112
Smith E, Boyles J (2009) Justice denied: The experiences of 100 torture surviving women of seeking justice and rehabilitation. Medical Foundation for the Care of Victims of Torture, London
Smith E et al (2010) A remedy for torture survivors in international law: Interpreting rehabilitation. Medical Foundation for the Care of Victims of Torture, London
Stover E, Balthazard M, Koenig KA (2011) Confronting Duch: Civil party participation in Case 001 at the Extraordinary Chambers in the Courts of Cambodia. International Review of the Red Cross 93:503–546
Sveaass N, Lavik NL (2000) Psychological aspects of human rights violations: The importance of justice and reconciliation. Nordic Journal of International Law 69(1):35–52
Van der Kolk BA (1996) Trauma and memory. In: Van der Kolk B, MacFarlane A, Weisaeth L (eds) The effects of overwhelming experiences on mind, body and society. Guildford Press, New York, pp 279–302

Van der Kolk BA, Fisler R (1995) Dissociation and the fragmentary nature of traumatic memories: Overview and exploratory study. J Trauma Stress 8(4):505–525

Van der Kolk BA, Van der Hart O (1995) The intrusive past: The flexibility of memory and the engraving of trauma. In: Carruth C (ed) Trauma: Explorations in memory. John Hopkins University Press, London, pp 158–182

Van Velsen C et al (1996) Survivors of torture and organized violence: demography and diagnosis. J Trauma Stress 9:181–193

Women's Initiative for Gender Justice (2014) Gender report card on the International Criminal Court 2013. http://www.iccwomen.org/documents/Gender-Report-Card-on-the-ICC-2013.pdf. Accessed 30 July 2014

Zehr H (2005) Changing lenses: A new focus for crime and justice, 3rd edn. Herald Press, Scottsdale

Chapter 11
Victims' Attendance in the Courtroom to Observe Proceedings

Elizabeth A. Turchi

Abstract The foundational texts of the STL, ICC, and ECCC are silent as to whether victims' are permitted to observe proceedings in person when otherwise not testifying or participating. Nor has the courts' jurisprudence expressly clarified whether victims' participatory rights encompass the observation of proceedings in person. Despite this, observational attendance has evolved through practice at the STL and the ECCC.

Keywords Right to be present throughout trial · Observational attendance · Meaningful participation · Victim-centred justice

Contents

Ms. Elizabeth A. Turchi is a Legal Officer with the United Nations in New York serving within the peacekeeping headquarters with a focus on victims' assistance and the United Nations' response to sexual exploitation and abuse in conflict and post-conflict states. The views expressed herein are those of the author(s) and do not necessarily reflect the views of the United Nations.

E.A. Turchi (✉)
United Nations, New York, USA
e-mail: ElizabethTurchi@gmail.com

K. Tibori-Szabó and M. Hirst (eds.), *Victim Participation in International Criminal Justice*, International Criminal Justice Series 11,
DOI 10.1007/978-94-6265-177-7_11

11.1 Introduction

The international criminal justice mechanisms preceding the ICC did not accord special status to victims. Rather, the statutes, and relevant rules and regulations of such bodies focused support and services on those testifying as witnesses. Thus, victims not testifying as witnesses were largely treated without distinction from members of the public. This generally meant that resources were dedicated to facilitating the appearance of witnesses in court by way of preparing travel logistics, ensuring security, and supporting witness's psychosocial needs. Practice and procedures within Registries by in large did not facilitate non-testifying victims' attendance at proceedings. One of the consequent forms of frustration expressed by many victims was their inability to engage with these institutions for the purpose of observing court proceedings first hand. An incident emblematic of this problem occurred on 26 October 2009, when over 200 representatives of the victims' associations from Bosnia and Herzegovina including the Association of Mothers of Srebrenica arrived by bus at the ICTY to observe the start of the trial against the former President of Republika Srpska, Radovan Karadžić.[1] Then Head of the Psychosocial Support Unit within the Victims and Witnesses Section of the ICTY, recalled that,

> The victims' groups arrived with the intention to observe the trial from the public gallery, but the public gallery could not fit that many people. Usually the general public is unable to enter once the gallery reaches maximum occupancy, however, they were not really members of the general public—they were victims' groups. It was challenging. At the request of the ICTY Outreach and Communications Section, we offered logistical support by way of organizing viewing rooms for the victims' groups to watch the trial's opening statements through closed circuit television set up in overflow rooms beyond the public gallery. The VWS was in charge of ensuring that protected witnesses and confidential information were not exposed while large quantities of victims' groups were transported through the halls of the ICTY in areas beyond the public gallery. This occurrence stretched VWS's resources as the necessary attention to this situation came in addition to the VWS's primary responsibility of supporting and facilitating the appearance of the victims and witnesses present that day to testify in the multiple concurrent trials also in session.[2]

As discussed elsewhere in this book, some of the international criminal institutions established after the ICTY have provided an autonomous role for victims in their proceedings either as "civil parties" at the ECCC or as participating victims such as at the ICC and STL.[3] This evolution has allowed for the dedication of staff

---

[1] Sense News Agency, Karadzic Trial to Start on Monday, With or Without Him, (22 October 2009), www.sense-agency.com. Accessed 16 February 2015.

[2] Interview with Helena Vranov Schoorl, Head of Psychosocial Support Unit within the Victims and Witnesses Section, ICTY, 15 February 2015 (records on file with the author).

[3] See ECCC Internal Rules (Rev. 9), 16 January 2015, Rule 23; Statute of the Special Tribunal for Lebanon, S/RES/1757 (2007) (the 'STL Statute'), Article 17; STL Rules of Procedure and Evidence (Rev. 7) (the 'STL RPE'), Rule 86(B); Rome Statute of the International Criminal court (A/CONF.183/9 (2010)) (the 'ICC Statute'), Article 68(3); ICC Rules of Procedure and Evidence (the 'ICC RPE') Rule 90(1) and (2).

and financial resources to facilitate victims' participation at these courts. Despite this evolution, however, there has been relatively little attention given to the facilitation of victim attendance for the purpose of *observing* proceedings in person. Most of these judicial bodies broadcast the proceedings on livestream via the internet or other web mechanism so the public may watch the proceedings from anywhere in the world. Although proceedings are broadcast, victims also often wish to observe the proceedings in person. The courts are finding that their jurisprudence and internal procedures are not adequately developed to provide for this. In this regard, the law and practice are in their infancy and whether such concepts are to mature at all remains unknown. To date, none of these judicial bodies have carved out an express right of victims to observe proceedings or to do so in person; but they have not expressly excluded this possibility either. This chapter sets out the extent to which such observational attendance has been realised in law and practice at the ICC, STL and ECCC.

11.2 The Rationale for Victims' Observational Attendance

While many academics have speculated as to the impact on victims of their participation in international criminal tribunals, only minimal empirical research has been conducted in this area to date. Furthermore, to date, no study has specifically examined victims' attendance in person at such trials for the purpose of observing. Consequently, information available on why victims request in-person observation is currently limited to anecdotal reports from those working with victims in the courts.

The foundational texts of the STL, the ICC, and the ECCC are silent as to whether observational attendance is part of victims' participatory rights. The matter is also not significantly clarified by jurisprudence. In the absence of specific legal bases supporting victims' observational attendance, practitioners may find it useful to derive arguments in favour of such attendance from established principles of international human rights law.

Nonetheless, even where justifications can be provided for observational attendance, judges and/or Registries may still determine that practical limits constrain observation. Tribunal resources are limited and likely unable to support victims' observational attendance for lengthy periods. The strain on staffing and finances is compounded by trials that involve large numbers of participating victims. Logistical realities also frustrate the ability for large numbers of victims to attend and observe. Public galleries have limited seating, courtrooms are likewise limited, and most tribunals' premises are not equipped with other viewing spaces.

11.2.1 Possible Arguments Advancing a Legal Rationale for Victims' Observational Attendance

Legal representatives of victims (LRVs) might consider arguing that the meaningful exercise of victims' rights to truth and justice involves the effective observation of the proceedings in the body of the court.[4] In order to achieve the right to truth, one could argue that victims should be afforded the opportunity to observe the entirety of the proceedings (subject to confidentiality and security matters). Observation also seems a necessary component to victims' perceptions of justice and the "experience of justice" which in turn might be argued to contribute to the healing process, at least for some victims. Since observing proceedings in person (from inside the courtroom, the public gallery, or a private viewing room), provides a more complete, unfettered access to the proceedings, it affords victims the greatest fulfilment of this right. Observational attendance is therefore arguably a derivative right to the right to know and the right to truth.

Victims' lawyers might argue that victims should be granted observational attendance as it orients victims to the larger context of the trial providing for more meaningful participation. It is undeniable that observation of the *entire* trial, at least in person at the seat of the tribunal, would be a difficult feat. Trials at international courts are complex and almost always span several years. It is likely not possible for victims to spend continuous years away from their homes and/or livelihoods to be present to observe an entire trial. In a complex trial like those at the STL, ICC and ECCC, observing one or two days of proceedings may not actually enhance victims' ability to attain the truth or clarify the facts. The most effective way for victims to understand the overview of complex proceedings, and to clarify facts, undoubtedly rests with the effective representation of victims by legal representatives who understand the particular proceedings in light of the totality of the trial and evidence. Nonetheless, when undertaken in the context of such representation and the information it provides, attending part of the trial to observe proceedings may very well contribute to victims' understanding of the proceedings.

---

[4] For sources on and common understanding of victims' rights for truth and justice, see: 1985 Declaration of Basic Principles of Justice for Victims of Crime and Abuse of Power, U.N. doc. A/RES/40/34 (Nov. 29, 1985); Commission on Human Rights, Promotion and Protection of Human Rights Study on the Right to the Truth, 2006, Report of the Office of the United Nations High Commissioner for human Rights, U.N. Doc. E/CN.4/2006/91, paras 12, 21; SaCouto and Cleary 2008, pp. 76–84; Commission on Human Rights, Questions of the Impunity of Perpetrators of Human Rights Violations (Civil and Political), 1997, Final Report prepared by Mr. Joinet pursuant to Sub-Commission Decision 1996/119 UN Doc. E/CN.4/Sub.2/1997/20, pp. 5–8; United Nations Office of the High Commissioner for Human Rights, Report of Diane Orentlicher, independent expert to update the Set of principles to combat impunity (18 February 2005), https://documents-dds-ny.un.org/doc/UNDOC/GEN/G05/111/03/PDF/G0511103.pdf?OpenElement. Accessed 2 August 2016, para 21; United Nations Commission on Human Rights, Study by the Office of the UN High Commissioner for Human Rights on the right to the truth, U.N. Doc. E/CN.4/2006/91 (2006), pp. 14–15.

Furthermore, victims' lawyers might also argue that observation does not disrupt the common scheme of representation nor measurably delay trial. The passive nature of observation does not in and of itself interrupt proceedings as observing proceedings in person is passive and does not in itself imply a request to present views, as might occur in other forms of participation. Only negligible delay might arise when victims are required to exit the courtroom for a closed session. Essentially, observation may be achieved without measured interference with the proceedings or impact on the overall trial duration. In short, the benefits to participating victims would outweigh any negative impact on the speedy flow of trial.

11.2.2 Possible Arguments Advancing an Interest-Based Rationale for Victims' Observational Attendance

As said above, victims' lawyers might also argue that attendance for the purpose of observing the proceedings contributes to victim empowerment, validation, and a sense of recognition by the court and international community. In the Victims and Witnesses Section of the ICTY, many victim witnesses expressed feeling a duty to testify as a way to honour their deceased relatives and the other victims of their communities. Victims also expressed feeling compelled to testify to gain closure and to contribute to justice.[5] Whether victims want to observe proceedings in person also for cathartic or psychosocial reasons, such as a yearning for connectedness, the need to "see to believe," for closure, or just due to plain curiosity, is speculative. As previously noted there is little empirical data to support an assertion that observation has reparative attributes or that observation in person has an impact different from viewing via live broadcast from a distance. Likewise, victims' own desires to observe proceedings are not direct evidence that observation has reparative attributes. It is plausible that the nature and context of what victims observe may fall short of their expectations of justice, proving to be a disappointing, traumatic, or neutral experience.

Victims' motivations to observe proceedings vary. A member of the Legal Representative for Victims' team at the Special Tribunal for Lebanon explained the reasons why victims participating before that tribunal have wanted to observe proceedings from inside the courtroom:

> In the beginning, before we had any victims in the courtroom, the main reason for attending the proceedings was that our clients wished to see the court and see how it functions. Sitting in the courtroom as such was not necessarily a specific wish. Most victims were quite afraid of the idea, even though [their identities] were public. This all changed once the first victims sat in the courtroom at the opening of the trial. These victims all felt empowered, in some way "acknowledged" by the judges and the entire court. Some of these victims met others in Lebanon and told them about their experience and this led to a higher number of victims

[5] Interview with Helena Vranov Schoorl, Head of Psychosocial Support Unit within Victims and Witnesses Section, ICTY, 15 February, 2015 (records on file with the author).

> wishing to attend the proceedings. Others have seen the victims on television and told us that they felt their presence sent a very powerful message and they wanted to be part of that message. So for most victims, now, after some have already attended the hearings, it is about acknowledgement, about the confirmation of their victim status. I must say that the unanimous effect of these attendances is a feeling of empowerment.[6]

At the STL, "protected" or "confidential" victims are unable to observe the proceedings from inside the courtroom for security reasons. The STL has accommodated them by providing a private viewing room overlooking the courtroom—that is not viewable from the public gallery or from inside the courtroom. On this matter the LRV team member explained the victims' general sentiment as follows:

> As for the confidential victims who sat in the private room, most of them wished in the end to be in the courtroom and experience the empowering moment, but because of their status they were not allowed to do that. Although these victims may have had a slight feeling of regret that they are not public, they all conveyed to us that watching the proceedings made them understand how seriously the case was taken by all parties concerned. This feeling was also expressed by the public victims sitting in the courtroom, but their major feeling was acknowledgment; empowerment.[7]

The significance of victims' presence inside the courtroom to observe proceedings also impacts the judicial process and the atmosphere of the proceedings. The former Spokesperson[8] of the STL reflected upon seeing victims present in the courtroom to observe the opening statements of the STL's first trial, as follows:

> It is sometimes easy in a legal process to focus so much that one gets lost in the legal procedure, deadlines, filings; but the victims' presence inside the courtroom serves as a steadfast reminder why everyone is there. It also reminds those watching the broadcast and the world at large that justice is a victims-centered process.

11.3 Victims' Observational Attendance at Proceedings—Overview of Law and Practice

As stated above, the question of whether victims have a *right* to observe in their capacity as either civil parties (ECCC) or participants in the proceedings (STL, ICC) is not clearly established or excluded in the current jurisprudence. Despite this, some practice has developed, at least at the ECCC and STL allowing for observational attendance. Observational attendance at these courts have occurred either from inside the courtroom, public viewing galleries, from private viewing rooms, or another location on court premises.

---

6 Written correspondence with Kinga Tibori-Szabó, former associate legal officer, Legal Representative of Victims, STL, 15 February 2015 (records on file with the author).

7 Written correspondence with Kinga Tibori-Szabó, former associate legal officer, Legal Representative of Victims, STL, 15 February 2015 (records on file with the author).

8 Interview with Marten Youssef, former Spokesperson, STL 15 February 2015 (records on file with the author).

Unless otherwise decided by the chamber, international court proceedings are generally conducted publically or in "open session." Open sessions aim to maximise public access by broadcasting and/or streaming via the internet (either a livestream or on a minimal delay). In addition, the public and members of the press usually may enter the premises to observe live proceedings from a public gallery.[9] With public access to these trials either on the premise or via broadcast, it may not be readily apparent why victims' observation of proceedings should be a matter different from observation as a member of the public at large. The international criminal justice bodies have thus been faced with the question of whether (and if so why) victims need specific accommodation to facilitate their observation of proceedings. At first glance, one might conclude that victims could simply observe proceedings in the same manner as the general public by showing up to the public gallery using their own time, money, and travel arrangements. Victims, however, are not part of the general public in the same sense as other persons—they have a special relationship with the proceedings of the court, having been personally affected by the alleged crimes. If international criminal justice intends to bring justice to victims, a true victim-centred approach dictates accommodation for observational attendance.

In many national jurisdictions the body of the courtroom itself—the place where judges, prosecutor and the defence appear—is open for public entry and seating for the public is provided in this area. However, this is not the case in most international courtrooms. Rather the public and members of the press may observe live proceedings only from a specific viewing room separate from the courtroom, known as the public gallery. The public galleries at these bodies are of a similar design to each other—they are external to the courtroom often attached via a glass partition and are equipped with audio interpretation equipment and television monitors.

The tribunals have taken varying approaches to victims' observational attendance. Civil parties at the ECCC have been permitted to observe from inside the courtroom, subject to space restrictions. The STL has devised a scheme to accommodate victims' observation of proceedings either inside the courtroom, in a private viewing room, or in the public gallery. At the time of writing, the ICC has not yet developed a practice whereby participating victims attend the seat of the court solely for the purpose of observing.

11.3.1 Observation from the Public Gallery

The ECCC, STL, and ICC all have public galleries. As their name suggests, the public galleries at the courts are open to the public. This means victims may arrive at the seat of the tribunal on their own initiative and observe proceedings while

9 STL RPE, Rule 136 "Open Session," and Rule 137 "Closed Session"; ICC RPE, Rule 87.

sitting amongst the general public. Victims whose identities are not concealed from the public (public victims) may generally do so without compromising their security and well-being. However, arriving to the public gallery unbeknownst to the courts leaves little guarantee the victims will be ensured seating in the public gallery as it is usually first-come first-serve and the space is limited.

While the ECCC public gallery has 482 seats[10] and the new ICC galleries accommodate approximately 342 visitors,[11] the STL only accommodates 75 visitors.[12] Key hearings such as opening and closing arguments, verdicts and sentencing announcements often attract numerous observers and priority seating is often reserved for journalists and diplomats. This significantly reduces the likelihood that victims will be able to enter and observe without tribunals being aware of their attendance and reserving seats for victims. Lawyers of those victims who wish to observe key hearings from the public gallery should seek to make arrangements in advance wherever possible.

Observing proceedings from the public gallery will generally be inadvisable for victims who have been granted protective measures. Presence of such victims in the public gallery may risk the disclosure of their concealed identity. Victims' lawyers should therefore advise protected victims of the risks involved in observing the proceedings from the public gallery and advise against doing so where this may expose the victims' identities. If the victims nevertheless decide to attend the hearing from the public gallery, the lawyers may consult the court's witness and/or victim protection unit for professional advice. Their opinion should also be communicated to the victims.

11.3.2 Observation from Within the Courtroom

The nature of international trials necessitate that courtrooms are controlled environments to ensure security and the protection of sensitive information dealt with in proceedings. At times entire proceedings or portions of proceedings are conducted in "closed session" on account of their confidential subject matter. When a witness whose identity is protected testifies, the view from the public gallery is blocked by partitions or screens so that persons seated there cannot see the witness. For the pubic watching proceedings via broadcast, image distortion technology is used to conceal the witness's image.

[10] ECCC, Visitor information for public hearings, http://www.eccc.gov.kh/en/about-eccc/visitor-info/public-hearings. Accessed 2 Aug 2016.

[11] The new ICC premises have 3 courtrooms in total. The larger courtroom (Courtroom I) has 142 seats in the public gallery and the other two (II and III) have 100 seats each. Written correspondence with ICC Public Affairs Unit, 9 September 2016 (notes on file with the editors).

[12] STL, Written correspondence with the Chief of Public Affairs, 19 May 2015 (records on file with the author).

Permission to enter the courtroom is usually a judicial determination since presence in the courtroom may result in access to confidential information. Because they are designed to accommodate participants only and not observers, the courtrooms of international tribunals tend to have limited seating. Furthermore, given that participating victims are not generally permitted to access confidential information (see Chap. 7), it follows from these restrictions on courtroom access that participating victims would not automatically be entitled to observe proceedings from inside the courtroom without a chamber's permission.

The ECCC was the first court to permit participating victims (civil parties) to attend proceedings and to establish a system for supporting and facilitating observational attendance. At the ECCC, there is no express jurisprudence establishing a right for civil parties to sit inside the courtroom. There is also no expressly devised protocol or standard operating procedure governing civil party observation in the courtroom. Nonetheless, civil party presence inside the courtroom for most proceedings is permitted, restricted only by space and logistics. The number is limited to ten based on the amount of space for seating, which is behind the location designated for the lawyers. On some days, additional civil parties sit in the public gallery. There is a general consensus that the civil parties may be present inside the courtroom during proceedings in so far as space permits.[13] NGOs and the Victims Support Section (VSS) pooled funding in *Case 001* to ensure that the seats reserved for civil parties were filled every day of trial hearings. The VSS continued this practice in *Case 002*.[14]

Civil parties observing inside the courtroom are also permitted to remain in the courtroom during closed session proceedings and can see the protected witnesses testifying. Civil parties observing from the public gallery, however, are not able to observe closed sessions. The selection of which victims sit inside the courtroom, and which in the public gallery, is based on a rotation with victims taking turns on continuous loop on a daily basis.[15]

The presence of civil parties inside the courtroom throughout the trial proceedings has thus become an important feature of the hearings at the ECCC.[16]

The STL has likewise developed a practice for permitting and facilitating victims to observe proceedings in person including inside the courtroom. In the *Ayyash* et al. case, participating victims have been permitted to sit with their legal representatives inside the courtroom in order to observe proceedings. This is done subject to judicial control whereby victims' legal representatives must formally request permission for their clients to be present in the courtroom during specified

[13] Interview with Eleonor Fernandez, Senior legal consultant in the Civil Party Lead Co-Lawyers Section, ECCC, 3 June 2015 (records on file with the author).

[14] Written correspondence with Christoph Sperfeldt, PhD. Scholar, Australian National University, 20 August 2016 (records on file with the editors).

[15] Interview with Eleonor Fernandez, Senior legal consultant in the Civil Party Lead Co-Lawyers Section, ECCC, 3 June 2015 (records on file with the author).

[16] Written correspondence with Christoph Sperfeldt, PhD. Scholar, Australian National University, 20 August 2016 (records on file with the editors).

hearings and a case-by-case decision is taken by the Trial Chamber.[17] The conditions under which attendance may be allowed by the Trial Chamber were set out in an oral order, following a submission by the LRV.[18] In their request, the LRV categorised the purpose and importance of in-courtroom attendance as follows:

> [T]he attendance of VPPs in the courtroom is not intended to nor in fact does erode the principle of common legal representation [...] the participating victims will continue to express their views and concerns via their common legal representatives [...] their attendance is a corollary of their status as participants [...] and only meant to make their participation as victims more meaningful [...].[19]

On November 18, 2014, the Trial Chamber issued its Oral Order and held:

> With regard to the clarification sought on the conditions more generally under which participating victims may attend proceedings, the Trial Chamber reiterates [...] that it will deal upon request and on a case-by-case basis with requests for individual victims who attend in the courtroom. The reason for this is the following. The Statute of the Special Tribunal provides that the views and concerns of victims may be presented in court by their legal representatives [...] They in this case present the views and concerns of some 70 victims, but physical and logistical considerations, and notably the Tribunal's limited resources and the size of the courtroom impose limitations on the number of victims who can be present in the courtroom at any one time. These factors taken together mean that the victims' presence in the courtroom is not ordinarily required or is possible, and is therefore, exceptional.[20]

The Trial Chamber further explained it would also consider:

> [...] whether the proceedings at which attendance is requested will be held in a public session, whether the testifying witness has any protective measure, and whether the victims has dual status pursuant to Rule 150(D) [...] that is they are a victim and a witness at the same time.[21]

Based on the Trial Chamber's oral rulings, there is no *right* on the part of victim participants to attend the proceedings within the courtroom for the purpose of observation. Instead, the Chamber deemed observation not "ordinarily required" on grounds that the LRV represent their views and concerns. The rulings do however seem to reveal an inclination to permit the VPPs to observe inside the courtroom provided it is 'possible'. Whether attendance is possible appears to be based principally on physical and logistical limitations such as the size of the courtroom. The Chamber has distinguished observational attendance from inside the courtroom

---

[17] STL, *Prosecutor v. Ayyash* et al., Trial Chamber, Public Official Transcript 14 October 2014, STL-11-01/T/TC, pp. 8–9; STL, *Prosecutor v. Ayyash* et al., Trial Chamber, Oral Order, Public Official Transcript 18 November 2014, STL-11-01/T/TC, pp. 1–3.

[18] STL, *Prosecutor v. Ayyash* et al., LRV, Public Redacted Version of the "Request of the Legal Representatives of Victims for Clarification of the Conditions under Which Participating Victims May Attend Proceedings", STL-11-01-T/TC, 4 November 2014.

[19] Ibid., para 10.

[20] STL, *Prosecutor v. Ayyash* et al., Trial Chamber, Oral Order, Official Public Transcript 18 November 2014, STL-11-01/T/TC, pp. 1–3.

[21] Ibid.

from observation in the private viewing room or public gallery. Whether a victim may observe from inside the courtroom is a matter reserved for judicial determination. If observation is to occur from the public gallery or private viewing room, the Chamber need not receive submissions and it remains a matter for the Registry to facilitate. To date, no requests for in-court attendance have been denied, so it is difficult to predict the circumstances in which that might occur. So far, victim attendance in the courtroom of the STL has been limited to adult participating victims with public status attending during public court sessions. Victims observing from inside the courtroom are required to sit next to or immediately behind their legal representatives. As at October 2016, 18 public participating victims attended the proceedings in the courtroom. The first nine attended the opening of the *Ayyash* et al. trial in January 2014.[22] Subsequent attendances involved one or two victims per occasion.[23] The Trial Chamber has also allowed the presence of dual status victims in the courtroom if their testimony or statement was already in evidence.[24] At each attendance, the LRV seeks leave to introduce the victim to the court by stating their name and offering some information, previously agreed with the victim(s), pertaining to the harm they suffered.[25]

Additional complexities would be introduced if protected victims wished to observe proceedings from within the courtroom. Trial proceedings are filmed for broadcast and it would therefore be difficult to avoid publicising the identity of confidential victims seated inside the courtroom. For these reasons, the STL provides a separate private room from which protected victims may view proceedings, as described below.

The ICC does not have a system accommodating victims' observational attendance in The Hague. Although to date ICC jurisprudence has not expressly limited such attendance at proceedings, several factors render it particularly challenging. First, although the ICC Statute permits the Court to sit in locations other than The Hague,[26] to date all hearings have occurred in The Hague. This places the hearings at considerable distance from the victims, who are mostly located in various countries throughout Africa and often in remote locations. The cases at the ICC have to date also been such that they involve very large victim populations. The costs and

---

[22] STL, *Prosecutor v. Ayyash* et al., Transcript 29 October 2013, STL-11-01/PT/TC, p. 31.

[23] Written correspondence with Kinga Tibori-Szabó, former associate legal officer, Legal Representative of Victims, STL, 19 May 2015 (records on file with the author).

[24] STL, *Prosecutor v. Ayyash* et al., Trial Chamber, Decision Allowing Two Participating Victims to Attend Courtroom Proceedings, STL-11-01/T/TC, 4 October 2016; STL, *Prosecutor v. Ayyash* et al., Legal Representative of Victims, Request to Allow Two Participating Victims to Attend Proceedings in the Courtroom, 4 October 2016, para 6; STL, *Prosecutor v. Ayyash* et al., Decision Allowing Two Participating Victims to Attend Courtroom Proceedings, STL-11-01/T/TC, 21 September 2016; STL, *Prosecutor v. Ayyash* et al., Legal Representative of Victims, Request to Allow Two Participating Victims to Attend Proceedings in the Courtroom, 20 September 2016, para 6.

[25] See, for instance, STL, *Prosecutor v. Ayyash* et al., LRV, Transcript 18 June 2014, STL-11-01/T/TC, pp. 31–32.

[26] ICC Statute, Article 3(3).

logistical challenges involved in attendance would be sizeable on a per-victim basis, and potentially enormous if the very large number of participating victims is considered. Further challenges would be introduced by the fact that a large portion of victims participate in ICC proceedings anonymously or confidentially, meaning that special consideration would need to be given to protective measures if victims were to attend proceedings in The Hague.

The ICC does however hold screenings of the proceedings in situation countries in locations accessible to victims. Such screenings are overseen by the ICC's outreach unit without involvement from chambers. In addition, outreach staff travel to the various situation countries and victimised communities to conduct small face to face informational sessions about the trials. In addition, the ICC outreach has created a Tumblr blog whereby outreach staff provides informational updates about case progression and inform communities of outreach staff locations so they are able to meet and discuss proceedings. The ICC Outreach unit updates its Tumblr blog with notes from their community outreach endeavours. These efforts include partnering with entities such as the United Nations Organization Stabilization Mission in the Democratic Republic of the Congo and the UN Joint Human Right Office to broadcast live proceedings in Kinshasa and Goma and to bring video footage of proceedings played via generators in remote villages.[27]

11.3.3 Private Viewing Rooms

The STL has made a private gallery available for those victims who wish to attend and observe hearings without revealing their identity to the public. While typically victims granted protective measures use this private gallery, public victims may also opt for it. The LRV in the *Ayyash* et al. case need not file a submission to request attendance by protected victims who will observe from the private room. However, the Trial Chamber ordered that the LRV must keep the Trial Chamber legal officer informed of the planned presence of victims in the private room. Furthermore, the LRV must comply with requirements that the attending victims not observe a protected witness testimony and so where such testimony will be heard victims are escorted out of the private viewing room.[28]

[27] See ICC Outreach Blog, http://iccoutreach.tumblr.com/. Accessed 12 October 2015.

[28] STL, *Prosecutor v. Ayyash* et al., Trial Chamber, Oral Order, Official Public Transcript 18 November 2014, STL-11-01/T/TC, p. 3.

11.3.4 Logistical Considerations to Facilitate Victim Observation

As discussed in other chapters, each court provides various forms of financial, logistical and psychosocial support to victims to facilitate their participation in proceedings. Tribunals have limited staff and resources, which as a matter of priority may first need to be allocated to testifying witnesses and participating victims in accordance with the mandate of these units. Even leaving legal issues aside, victims' observation at these institutions require thoughtful coordination at a practical and logistical level with due consideration for limited court resources, security, privacy, confidentiality, victim well-being, and compliance with host-state agreements. Participating victims who attend proceedings in person, whether from a private gallery, inside the courtroom, or in the public gallery, may be able to receive some fiscal, logistical, and psychosocial assistance from the tribunals for this purpose.

At the ECCC, logistical support to civil parties is provided by the VSS (in the early years NGOs provided such support as well). This includes support in traveling to and from the court, security and protection if granted protective measures, psychosocial support if requested, and fiscal support if this is determined to be warranted.[29] The VSS provides for the travel and accommodation involved in civil party observation, however, the funding does not come from an allocation in the central ECCC budget. During the early years, earmarked funding came from the German Ministry of Foreign Affairs, channelled through the Deutsche Gesellschaft für Internationale Zusammenarbeit (GIZ). More recently, German funding has continued through the Federal Ministry for Economic Cooperation and Development (BMZ). The ECCC also received funding from UN Trust Fund to End Violence against Women.[30] It is only when a civil party testifies that the travel, accommodation, and other expenses are paid from ECCC funds.

At the STL some observational attendance by participating victims is funded from the STL's budget. Fiscal and logistical support such as transportation, accommodation, allowance of accompanying support persons etc., is reviewed and financed by the Registry's Victims' Participation Unit (VPU) and Victims and Witnesses Unit (VWU). These two units are guided by an internal standard operating procedure establishing parameters for assessing and granting fiscal support such as financing a victim's travel to and accommodation at the seat of the tribunal. Based on an internal agreement between the VPU and the VWU, the travel and accommodation of accompanying persons can also be reimbursed under certain conditions. LRVs lodge a request of attendance of one or more VPPs with the

---

[29] Interview with Eleonor Fernandez, Senior legal consultant, Civil Party Lead Co-Lawyers, ECCC, 29 May 2015 (records on file with the author).

[30] Written correspondence with Christoph Sperfeldt, PhD. Scholar, Australian National University, 20 August 2016 (records on file with the editors).

VPU. The VPU will then liaise with the VWU to inquire on the logistical feasibility of the request and any special protection or support needs which might arise in respect of the request. If the request is approved by the VPU, after consulting with the VWU, arrangements will be made for travel and accommodation by the latter, in consultation with the VPU and the LRV. If the attendance is planned to take place in the courtroom, the LRV submits its request to the Trial Chamber only after the administrative approval of the VPU and when the dates of the planned attendance are set. Likewise, the LRV informs the Trial Chamber's legal officer of the attendance of VPPs in the private room after the approval of the VPU and when the dates of the planned visit are fairly certain. The VPU liaises with the VWU and Court Management Services Section in order to ensure all arrangements are in place for the facilitation of victims' attendances.[31]

Victims' observational attendance must also be viewed in light of the various host-state agreements. These include clauses pertaining to the ability of victims to enter the host-state's territory, something which is usually contemplated to be for purposes of testifying. In many scenarios the host-state is agreeable to accepting the determination of the court as to whether presence of a witness or victim is in furtherance of the judicial process.

11.4 Key Points

- The foundational texts of the STL, the ICC, and the ECCC are silent as to whether observational attendance is part of victims' participatory rights. The matter is also not clarified by jurisprudence.
- In the absence of specific legal bases supporting victims' observational attendance, practitioners may find it useful to derive arguments in favour of such attendance from established principles of international human rights law. Legal representatives of victims might consider arguing that the meaningful exercise of victims' rights to truth and justice involves the effective observation of the proceedings in the body of the court. Likewise, it could be argued that victims should be granted observational attendance as it orients them to the larger context of the trial providing for a more meaningful participation. Victims' lawyers might also argue that observation does not disrupt the common scheme of representation nor measurably delays trial.
- Additionally, invoking the victims' personal interests, lawyers might argue that attendance for the purpose of observing the proceedings contributes to victim empowerment, validation, and sense of recognition by the court and the international community.

[31] Written correspondence with Kinga Tibori-Szabó, former associate legal officer, Legal Representative of Victims, STL, 19 May 2015 (records on file with the author).

- Chambers and/or Registries may, however, determine that practical limits constrain observation as tribunal resources are limited and likely not able to support victims' observational attendance for a long duration.
- Victims whose identities are not concealed from the public (public victims) may generally attend proceedings in the public gallery, but without the involvement of the lawyers representing victims there is little guarantee that seating will be ensured, as it is usually first-come first-serve and the space is limited.
- Observing proceedings from the public gallery will generally be inadvisable for victims who have been granted protective measures. The presence of such victims in the public gallery may risk the disclosure of their concealed identity.
- The ICC does not have a system accommodating victim's observational attendance at the court in The Hague. It does, however, hold screenings of the proceedings in situation countries in locations accessible to victims.
- The ECCC was the first court to permit participating victims (civil parties) to attend proceedings and to establish a system for supporting and facilitating observational attendance. At the ECCC, there is currently no express jurisprudence establishing a right for civil parties to sit inside the courtroom. Nonetheless, civil party presence inside the courtroom for most proceedings is permitted, restricted only by space and logistics. Moreover, civil parties observing inside the courtroom are also permitted to remain in the courtroom during closed session proceedings and can see the protected witnesses testifying.
- The STL has also developed a practice for permitting and facilitating victims to observe proceedings in person. Although there is no *right* on the part of participating victims to attend the proceedings in the courtroom for the purpose of observation, in the *Ayyash* et al. case, participating victims have been permitted to sit next to or behind their legal representatives to observe proceedings. This is done subject to judicial control whereby victims' legal representatives must formally request permission for their clients to be present in the courtroom during specified hearings and a case-by-case decision is taken by the Trial Chamber.
- The STL has made a private gallery available for those victims who wish to attend and observe hearings without revealing their identity to the public. While typically victims granted protective measures use this private gallery, public victims may also opt for it. The LRV in the *Ayyash* et al. case need not file a submission to request attendance by protected victims who will observe from the private room. However, the LRV must keep the Trial Chamber legal officer informed of the planned presence of victims in the private room.
- At the STL, whether proceedings are observed in the courtroom or from the private room, the LRV must comply with requirements that the attending victims not observe a protected witness testifying.
- At the ECCC, the VSS provides for the travel and accommodation involved in civil party observation; however, the funding does not come from the ECCC budget, but from external sources.

- At the STL, observational attendance is funded from the STL's budget. Fiscal and logistical support such as transportation and accommodation, is reviewed and financed by the Registry's Victims' Participation Unit (VPU) and Victims and Witnesses Unit (VWU).

References

Commission on Human Rights (1997) Questions of the impunity of perpetrators of human rights violations (civil and political), 1997, Final Report prepared by Mr. Joinet pursuant to Sub-Commission Decision 1996/119 UN Doc. E/CN.4/Sub.2/1997/20

Commission on Human Rights (2005) Resolution, U.N. Doc. E/CN.4/2005/L.48 (July 25 2005) adopted April 13, 2005. U.N. Doc. E/CN.4/2005/102/Add.1, 8 Feb 2005

Commission on Human Rights (2006) Promotion and protection of human rights: Study on the right to the truth. Report of the Office of the United Nations High Commissioner for Human Rights, U.N. Doc. E/CN.4/2006/91

G.A. Res. 40/34, U.N. GAOR, 40th Session, Supp. No. 53, at 213, U.N. doc. A/RES/40/34 (29 Nov 1985)

Report of the UN Secretary General (2006) STL President's Explanatory Memorandum of the Rules of Evidence and Procedure, S/2006.893, 15 Nov 2006

SaCouto S, Cleary K (2008) Victims' participation in the investigations of the International Criminal Court. Trans Law Contempo Prob 17:74–105

Sense News Agency (2009) Karadzic Trial to Start on Monday, With or Without Him, The Hague, October 22, 2009. www.sense-agency.com. Accessed 16 Feb 2015

U.N. Commission on Human Rights, Sub-Committee on Prevention of Discrimination and Protection of Minorities (1997) The administration of justice and the human rights of detainees, U.N. Doc. E/CN4/Sub.2/1997/20/Rev/1, 2 Oct 1997, prepared by Special Rapporteur Louis Joinet

Chapter 12
The Rights of Participating Victims to Appeal and Participate in the Appeal Against Interlocutory Decisions and Trial Judgments

Kinga Tibori-Szabó

Abstract Appeals against decisions at international criminal courts can generally be classified into appeals against interlocutory decisions (rulings made by a court before rendering a judgment in the case) and appeals against judgments, of acquittal, conviction, sentencing and reparations. All three courts analysed in this chapter—the Extraordinary Chambers in the Courts of Cambodia (ECCC), the International Criminal Court (ICC) and the Special Tribunal for Lebanon (STL)—provide victims participating in the proceedings with varying degrees of entitlements in respect to such appeals. This chapter provides an overview of these rights. First, it addresses the rights of participating victims to lodge interlocutory appeals in their own right. Then it looks at the extent to which victims can participate in the interlocutory appeals of the (other) parties and the procedure that must be followed. On this basis, it provides a comparative table of the different approaches adopted by the three courts as regards victims' rights in interlocutory appeals. Secondly, the chapter reviews the rights of participating victims to appeal judgments on acquittals, conviction, sentencing and reparations as well as their entitlement to participate in such appeals. The comparative conclusions as to the rights of participating victims in appeals against judgments are also organised into a table for better clarity. Finally, the chapter highlights the key points to be remembered in relation to victims' rights in interlocutory and final appeals.

Keywords Interlocutory appeals · Participating victims · Appeal against convictions · Appeals against acquittals · Appeals against sentencing

---

Kinga Tibori-Szabó is legal officer for the Kosovo Specialist Chambers. She has previously worked for the Legal Representative of Victims at the Special Tribunal for Lebanon. The views expressed herein are those of the author and do not necessarily reflect the views of the employing organisations.

K. Tibori-Szabó (✉)
The Hague, The Netherlands
e-mail: kingatibori@gmail.com

K. Tibori-Szabó and M. Hirst (eds.), *Victim Participation in International Criminal Justice*, International Criminal Justice Series 11,
DOI 10.1007/978-94-6265-177-7_12

Contents

12.1 Introduction

Appeals against decisions at international criminal courts can generally be classified into appeals against interlocutory decisions (that is, against rulings made by a court before rendering a judgment in the case) and appeals against judgments, which usually relate to decisions regarding acquittal, conviction, sentencing and reparations. All three courts analysed in this chapter—the Extraordinary Chambers in the Courts of Cambodia (ECCC), the International Criminal Court (ICC) and the Special Tribunal for Lebanon (STL)—differentiate between appeals against interlocutory decisions and appeals against judgments. Likewise, at all three courts, victims participating in the proceedings have varying degrees of entitlements in relation to such appeals. This chapter provides an overview of these rights. First, it addresses the rights of participating victims to lodge interlocutory appeals in their own right. Then it looks at the extent to which victims can participate in the interlocutory appeals of the other parties and the procedure that must be followed. Following that, the chapter reviews the rights of participating victims to appeal final judgments on acquittals, conviction, sentencing and reparations as well as their entitlement to participate in such appeals.

This chapter does not touch upon the rights of applicant victims to appeal decisions rejecting their participation in the proceedings, nor does it elaborate on the rights of participating victims in relation to appeals against reparation orders, as these issues are addressed elsewhere in this book.[1]

The term 'interlocutory appeal' will be used to denote appeals against decisions prior to a judgment of conviction or acquittal. It must be noted, however, that the term is not ordinarily used at the ECCC.

[1] See Chaps. 2 and 13.

12.2 Interlocutory Appeals

12.2.1 The Right of Participating Victims to Lodge Interlocutory Appeals

At the ECCC, appeals[2] can be lodged both at the investigative and the trial phase. During the **investigative phase**, the Pre-Trial Chamber hears motions and appeals against orders and decisions issued by the Co-Investigating Judges.[3] According to Internal Rule 74, Co-Prosecutors have a general right to appeal all orders of the Co-Investigating Judges, while the accused and the civil parties only have limited entitlements in this respect. In particular, Internal Rule 74(4) permits civil parties to appeal the following orders of the Co-Investigating Judges:

(a) refusing requests for investigative action allowed under these Rules;
(b) declaring a civil party application inadmissible;
(c) refusing requests for the restitution of seized property;
(d) refusing requests for expert reports allowed under these IRs;
(e) refusing requests for further expert investigation allowed under these IRs;
(f) a Dismissal Order where the Co-Prosecutors have appealed;
(g) refusing an application to seize the Chamber for annulment of investigative action;
(h) relating to protective measures; or
(i) reducing the scope of judicial investigation under Rule 66*bis*.

In particular, an appeal of the civil parties in *Case 002* against the refusal of the Co-Investigating Judges to interview several persons in relation to allegations of forced marriage was rendered by the Pre-Trial Chamber admissible, as it determined that such requests qualified as requests for investigative action pursuant to Internal Rule 55(10) and that the impugned order amounted to an order refusing requests for investigative action under Internal Rule 74(4)(a).[4] Conversely, the Pre-Trial Chamber found inadmissible an appeal by the civil parties against the refusal of the Co-Investigating Judges to conduct a full investigation into the properties owned by the charged person, take measures to preserve any properties for reparation purposes, and identify properties transferred to family members of the charged persons to determine the origins of the properties and whether they had been obtained as a result of the position of the accused in the Khmer Rouge

---

[2] At the ECCC, the term 'interlocutory appeals' is not ordinarily used.

[3] ECCC Internal Rules, Rule 73(a).

[4] ECCC, *Case 002,* Pre-Trial Chamber, Decision on Appeal of Co-Lawyers for Civil Parties Against Order Rejecting Request to Interview Persons Named in the Forced Marriage and Enforced Disappearance Requests for Investigative Action, 21 July 2010.

regime.[5] The Pre-Trial Chamber found that since the Co-Prosecutors had not expanded the scope of their investigations to cover such requests, civil parties had no right to expand investigative actions themselves and therefore the appeal was not admissible under Internal Rule 74(4)(a).[6]

During the **trial phase** at the ECCC, it is the Supreme Court Chamber that decides appeals made by the accused, the civil parties, or the Co-Prosecutors against the decisions of the Trial Chamber.[7] Interlocutory appeals against decisions of the trial court are known at the ECCC as 'immediate appeals'. According to Internal Rule 104, an immediate appeal against a decision of the Trial Chamber may be based on a discernible error in the exercise of the Trial Chamber's discretion which resulted in prejudice to the appellant.

The following decisions of the Trial Chamber are subject to immediate appeal:

(a) decisions which have the effect of terminating the proceedings;
(b) decisions on detention and bail under Internal Rule 82;
(c) decisions on protective measures under Internal Rule 29(4)(c); and
(d) decisions on interference with the administration of justice under Internal Rule 35(6).[8]

No other decisions may be appealed during the trial proceedings. In *Case 001*, the Supreme Court Chamber found inadmissible an appeal by civil parties against the Trial Chamber's decision barring them from making submissions on sentencing issues. In the same decision, the Supreme Court Chamber also found inadmissible another appeal of the civil parties against a decision of the Trial Chamber precluding them from posing questions to witnesses and the accused in relation to the character of the accused. The Supreme Court Chamber cited the content of Internal Rule 104(4) and concluded that decisions on sentencing or on limits of examination were outside the scope of the Rule and thus not subject to an immediate appeal.[9]

The parties can, however, appeal other decisions when they appeal against the judgment on the merits.[10]

At the ICC, the rights of participating victims in relation to interlocutory appeals are much more restricted. According to current jurisprudence, participating victims at the

[5] ECCC, *Case 002*, Pre-Trial Chamber, Decision on Appeal of Co-Lawyers for Civil Parties Against Order on Civil Parties' Request for Investigative Actions Concerning All Properties Owned by the Charged Persons, 4 August 2010, para 1.

[6] ECCC, *Case 002*, Pre-Trial Chamber, Decision on Appeal of Co-Lawyers for Civil Parties Against Order on Civil Parties' Request for Investigative Actions Concerning All Properties Owned by the Charged Persons, 4 August 2010, para 16.

[7] ECCC, Law on the Establishment of the Extraordinary Chambers, with inclusion of amendments as promulgated on 27 October 2004 (NS/RKM/1004/006), Article 36 new.

[8] ECCC Internal Rules, Rule 104(4).

[9] ECCC, *Case 001*, Supreme Court Chamber, Decision on the Appeals Filed by Lawyers for Civil Parties (Groups 2 and 3) against the Trial Chamber's Oral Decisions of 27 August 2009, 24 December 2009, paras 10–12.

[10] ECCC Internal Rules, Rule 104(4).

ICC can only appeal orders for reparations. Article 82(4) of the ICC Statute provides that a legal representative of the victims (LRV), the convicted person or a *bona fide* owner of property adversely affected by an order under Article 75 may appeal against the order for reparations. This provision has been interpreted restrictively, in the sense that participating victims at the ICC cannot initiate an appeal in their own right against any other decision negatively affecting victim participation.[11] In any case, to date, this specific issue has not been addressed conclusively by the ICC Appeals Chamber.

At the STL, Article 17 of the Statute establishes that where the personal interests of victims are affected, the STL shall permit their views and concerns to be presented and considered at stages of the proceedings determined to be appropriate by the Chamber and in a manner that is not prejudicial to or inconsistent with the rights of the accused and a fair and impartial trial. Moreover, Rule 87 of the Rules of Procedure and Evidence (RPE) elaborates on the modes of participation of victims at all stages of the proceedings. Although Rule 87(D) provides that participating victims may participate in the appeal stage subject to the authorisation of, and in a manner deemed appropriate by the Appeals Chamber, the Rule does not explicitly address the right of the participating victims to initiate or participate in interlocutory appeals. At the STL, interlocutory appeals are not available as of right; the parties must apply for certification before the chamber that issued the decision.[12] Rule 126 setting out the conditions for requesting the certification of a decision makes it clear that only a "party" may appeal to the Appeals Chamber once certification is given. The LRV in the *Ayyash* et al. case nevertheless applied for the certification of the Pre-Trial Judge's decision to deny participating victims the right to remain anonymous in the proceedings.[13] The Pre-Trial Judge partly granted the request for certification.[14] On appeal, the LRV argued that Rule 126

---

[11] ICC, *Prosecutor v. Thomas Lubanga Dyilo*, Trial Chamber I, Decision on two requests for leave to appeal the "Decision on the request by DRCDOl-WWWW-0019 for special protective measures relating to his asylum application" (Reclassified as public), ICC-01/04-01/06-2779, 4 August 2011, paras 10–24; ICC, The Office of Public Counsel for Victims, Representing Victims before the International Criminal Court, A Manual for Legal Representatives Manual, 2014, pp. 23–24.

[12] STL RPE, Rule 126. Some decisions can be appealed without certification, e.g.: decisions regarding jurisdiction (Rule 11(D) and (F)), decisions regarding deferral to Lebanon (Rule 17(H)), orders of safe conduct (Rule 81(C)), decisions denying victim participation (Rule 86(C)), orders on provisional detention (Rule 88(B)), decisions on motions challenging jurisdiction (Rule 90(B)(i)), decisions regarding exceptional gathering of evidence (Rule 92(D)), decision on release (Rule 102(C)), decisions on the appearance of the accused during in absentia proceedings (Rule 108(C)), certain decisions on non-disclosure (Rule 116(D) and Rule 118(K)), decisions on special counsel (Rule 119(D)), and state request for review (Rule 178).

[13] STL, *Prosecutor v. Ayyash* et al., LRV, Motion of the Legal Representative of Victims Seeking Certification of the "Decision on the Legal Representative Of Victims' First, Second And Third Motions for Protective Measures for Victims Participating in the Proceedings", STL-11-01/PT/PTJ, 21 December 2012.

[14] STL, *Prosecutor v. Ayyash* et al., Pre-Trial Judge, Decision on the Motion of the Legal Representative of Victims Seeking Certification to Appeal the Decision of 19 December 2012 on Protective Measures, STL-11-01/PT/PTJ, 30 January 2013.

should be construed as encompassing the possibility for participating victims to seek and receive certification to appeal a decision if such a decision relates to their personal interests.[15] The Appeals Chamber, by majority, found that Rule 126(E) was exceptionally applicable to allow for a narrow right to an interlocutory appeal of the participating victims in strictly confined circumstances and only after obtaining certification.[16] The Appeals Chamber noted that if the drafters of the Rules had believed that participating victims did not have a general right to file interlocutory appeals, the express prohibition on appeals of Rule 86(D)—in relation to dividing victims into distinct groups for representation purposes—would not have been necessary. Accordingly, the Appeals Chamber concluded that the Rules did not contain any general prohibition of interlocutory appeals by participating victims.[17] In this respect, the Appeals Chamber discerned three specific situations in which victims may request interlocutory appeals, subject to certification:

- Decisions on applications for status as a participating victim (a right of appeal is already provided for under Rule 86(C)),
- Decisions on the modalities of victims' participation in the proceedings (such as decisions concerning access of the LRV to documents and decisions on whether victims may call evidence and make submissions),
- Decisions on protective measures for participating victims and the variation of such measures.[18]

As at October 2016, no other request for certification had been submitted by the LRV in the *Ayyash* et al. case.

12.2.2 Participation of Victims in Interlocutory Appeals

Although the ECCC Internal Rules limit the right of civil parties to lodge appeals at both the investigative and trial phases of the proceedings, case-law has

---

[15] STL, *Prosecutor v. Ayyash* et al., LRV, Appeal of the Legal Representative of Victims Against the Decision of the Pre-Trial Judge Refusing Protective Measures, STL-11-01/PT/AC/AR126.3, 8 February 2013, para 22.

[16] STL, *Prosecutor v. Ayyash* et al., Appeals Chamber, Decision on Appeal by Legal Representative of Victims Against Pre-Trial Judge's Decision on Protective Measures, STL-11-01/PT/AC/AR126.3, 10 April 2013, para 10.

[17] STL, *Prosecutor v. Ayyash* et al., Appeals Chamber, Decision on Appeal by Legal Representative of Victims Against Pre-Trial Judge's Decision on Protective Measures, STL-11-01/PT/AC/AR126.3, 10 April 2013, para 13.

[18] STL, *Prosecutor v. Ayyash* et al., Appeals Chamber, Decision on Appeal by Legal Representative of Victims Against Pre-Trial Judge's Decision on Protective Measures, STL-11-01/PT/AC/AR126.3, 10 April 2013, para 15.

repeatedly provided for their participation in the appeals of the other parties. In particular, while Internal Rule 74(4) does not allow civil parties to appeal an order of the Investigating Judge that relates to provisional detention or bail of the accused (as this right is reserved to the Prosecution and the charged person only),[19] the Pre-Trial Chamber in *Case 002* allowed civil parties to participate in the appeal of the other parties against such orders. The Chamber held that according to Internal Rule 23, a civil party, once admitted, can participate in all stages of the proceedings, and that there was no need to show any special interest of the civil parties to participate in said proceedings.[20] The same approach was followed at the trial phase.

Early ICC case-law required participating victims to apply to participate in the interlocutory appeals of the parties. However, in 2015, the Appeals Chamber found that participating victims should not be required to ask leave to participate in interlocutory appeals, provided that the victims in question participated in the proceedings that gave rise to the appeal.[21] The development of this jurisprudence is elaborated below.

The Appeals Chamber has consistently held that Article 68(3) of the Statute did not draw a distinction between the different stages of the proceedings before the Court, therefore the Article could fairly be construed to allow victims to submit observations at all stages, i.e. in respect of proceedings in a situation, or in a case, whether at the pre-trial, trial or appeals stage of proceedings.[22]

[19] ECCC Internal Rules, Rules 74(2) and 74(3)(f).

[20] ECCC, *Case 002,* Pre-Trial Chamber, Decision on Civil Party Participation in Provisional Detention Appeals, 20 March 2008, para 49.

[21] ICC, *Prosecutor v. Laurent Gbagbo and Charles Blé Goudé*, Appeals Chamber, Reasons for the "Decision on the 'Request for the recognition of the right of victims authorized to participate in the case to automatically participate in any interlocutory appeal arising from the case and, in the alternative, application to participate in the interlocutory appeal against the ninth decision on Mr. Gbagbo's detention (ICC-02/11-01/15-134-Red3)'", ICC-02/11-01/15-172, 31 July 2015, para 16.

[22] ICC, *Situation in Darfur, Sudan,* Appeals Chamber, Decision on Victim Participation in the appeal of the Office of Public Counsel for the Defence against Pre-Trial Chamber I's Decision of 3 December 2007 and in the appeals of the Prosecutor and the Office of Public Counsel for the Defence against Pre-Trial Chamber I's Decision of 6 December 2007, ICC-02/05-138, 18 June 2008, para 20; ICC, *Situation in the Democratic Republic of the Congo*, Appeals Chamber, Decision on Victim Participation in the appeal of the Office of Public Counsel for the Defence against Pre-Trial Chamber I's Decision of 7 December 2007 and in the appeals of the Prosecutor and the Office of Public Counsel for the Defence against Pre-Trial Chamber I's Decision of 24 December 2007, ICC-01/04-503, 30 June 2008, para 89. See also ICC, *Prosecutor v. Joseph Kony* et al., Appeals Chamber, Decision on the participation of victims in the appeal, ICC-02/04-01/05-324, 27 October 2008, paras 7–8; ICC, *Prosecutor v. Omar Hassan Ahmad Al Bashir*, Appeals Chamber, Decision on the Second Application by Victims a/0443/09–a/0450/09 to Participate in the Appeal against the "Decision on the Prosecution's Application for a Warrant of Arrest against Omar Hassan Ahmad Al Bashir, ICC-02/05-01/09-70," 28 January 2010, para 9; ICC, *Prosecutor v. Abdallah Banda Abakaer Nourain and Saleh Mohammed Jerbo Jamus,* Appeals Chamber, Decision on the participation of victims in the appeal, ICC-02/05-03/09-470, 6 May 2013, para 11.

Article 82 of the ICC Statute permits the parties to appeal the following decisions:

(a) decisions regarding jurisdiction or admissibility;
(b) decisions granting or denying release of the person being investigated or prosecuted;
(c) decisions of the Pre-Trial Chamber to act on its own initiative under Article 56, para 3;
(d) decisions that involve an issue that would significantly affect the fair and expeditious conduct of the proceedings or the outcome of the trial, and for which, in the opinion of the Pre-Trial or Trial Chamber, an immediate resolution by the Appeals Chamber may materially advance the proceedings.

The first three types of decisions can be appealed by the parties without leave from the Pre-Trial or Trial Chamber, whereas decisions under Article 82(1)(d) can only be appealed if leave is granted by the court that issued the impugned decision.

Participating victims can, in principle, participate in these interlocutory appeals, if their personal interests are affected and the Appeals Chamber considers their participation to be appropriate. It is for the Appeals Chamber to ensure that the manner of their participation is not prejudicial to or inconsistent with the rights of the accused and a fair and impartial trial.[23]

The question of victim participation in interlocutory appeals was first addressed by the Appeals Chamber in the *Lubanga* case. In that case, participating victims submitted a response to the appeal of the Defence against the Trial Chamber's decision on interim release without any prior application to participate in the appeal.[24] The Appeals Chamber exceptionally granted the victims' right to participate in the appeal, as it was 'aware that this is the first time that it has considered the manner in which victims can participate in interlocutory appeals.'[25] It stated, however, that an application for participation in interlocutory appeals was obligatory, because the requirement under Article 68(3) of the Statute that victim participation shall be permitted 'at stages of the proceedings

---

[23] ICC, *Prosecutor v. Thomas Lubanga Dyilo*, Appeals Chamber, Judgment on the appeal of Mr. Thomas Lubanga Dyilo against the decision of Pre-Trial Chamber I entitled "Décision sur la demande de mise en liberté provisoire de Thomas Lubanga Dyilo", 01/04-01/06-824, 13 February 2007, para 55.

[24] ICC, *Prosecutor v. Thomas Lubanga Dyilo*, Appeals Chamber, Response of Victims a/0001/06, a/0002/06 and a/0003/06 to the appeal of the Defence from the Decision on the application for interim release of Thomas Lubanga Dyilo, ICC-01/04-01/06-704-tEN, 16 November 2006.

[25] ICC, *Prosecutor v. Thomas Lubanga Dyilo*, Appeals Chamber, Judgment on the appeal of Mr. Thomas Lubanga Dyilo against the decision of Pre-Trial Chamber I entitled "Décision sur la demande de mise en liberté provisoire de Thomas Lubanga Dyilo", 01/04-01/06-824, 13 February 2007, para 37.

determined to be appropriate by the Court' mandated a specific determination by the Appeals Chamber that the participation of victims was appropriate in the particular interlocutory appeal under consideration. The Appeals Chamber could not automatically be bound by the previous determination of the Pre-Trial Chamber that it was appropriate for the victims to participate before the court of first instance. As the Appeals Chamber explained, the Pre-Trial Chamber could not, at that stage, have had any mandate which could grant the victim participants the right automatically to participate in any interlocutory appeal that could arise.[26]

Consequently, an application from victims seeking leave to participate was required in order to enable the Appeals Chamber appropriately to make that determination.[27] The Appeals Chamber's decision in the *Lubanga* case was confirmed by subsequent decisions in other cases.[28]

---

[26] ICC, *Prosecutor v. Thomas Lubanga Dyilo,* Appeals Chamber, Judgment on the appeal of Mr. Thomas Lubanga Dyilo against the decision of Pre-Trial Chamber I entitled "Décision sur la demande de mise en liberté provisoire de Thomas Lubanga Dyilo", 01/04-01/06-824, 13 February 2007, paras 40 and 43.

[27] ICC, *Prosecutor v. Thomas Lubanga Dyilo,* Appeals Chamber, Judgment on the appeal of Mr. Thomas Lubanga Dyilo against the decision of Pre-Trial Chamber I entitled "Décision sur la demande de mise en liberté provisoire de Thomas Lubanga Dyilo", 01/04-01/06-824, 13 February 2007, para 40.

[28] ICC, *Situation in the Democratic Republic of the Congo,* Appeals Chamber, Decision of the Appeals Chamber on the OPCV's request for clarification and the legal representatives' request for extension of time and Order of the Appeals Chamber on the date of filing of applications for participation and on the time of the filing of the responses thereto by the OPCD and the Prosecutor, ICC-01/04-450, 13 February 2008, para 1; *Prosecutor v. Thomas Lubanga Dyilo,* Appeals Chamber, Decision, in limine, on Victim Participation in the appeals of the Prosecutor and the Defence against Trial Chamber I's Decision entitled "Decision on Victims' Participation", ICC-01/04-01/06-1335, 16 May 2008, paras 13, 37–50; ICC, *Situation in Darfur, Sudan,* Appeals Chamber, Decision on Victim Participation in the appeal of the Office of Public Counsel for the Defence against Pre-Trial Chamber I's Decision of 3 December 2007 and in the appeals of the Prosecutor and the Office of Public Counsel for the Defence against Pre-Trial Chamber I's Decision of 6 December 2007, ICC-02/05-13, 18 June 2008, paras 49 and 51; *Prosecutor v. Jean Pierre Bemba Gombo,* Appeals Chamber, Reasons for the "Decision on the Participation of Victims in the Appeal against the "Decision on the Interim Release of Jean-Pierre Bemba Gombo and Convening Hearings with the Kingdom of Belgium, the Republic of Portugal, the Republic of France, the Federal Republic of Germany, the Italian Republic, and the Republic of South Africa"", ICC-01/05-01/08-566, 20 October 2009, paras 13–14; *Prosecutor v. Germain Katanga and Mathieu Ngudjolo Chui,* Appeals Chamber, Decision on the Participation of Victims in the Appeal of Mr. Katanga Against the "Decision on the Modalities of Victim Participation at Trial", ICC-01/04-01/07-2124, 24 May 2010, para 5; ICC, *Prosecutor v. Thomas Lubanga Dyilo,* Appeals Chamber, Decision on the Participation of Victims in the Appeal against Trial Chamber I's Decision to Stay the Proceedings, ICC-01/04-01/06-2556, 18 August 2010, para 9; *Prosecutor v. Laurent Gbagbo,* Appeals Chamber, Decision on the application by victims for participation in the appeal, ICC-02/11-01/11, 27 August 2013, para 9; *Prosecutor v. Uhuru Kenyatta,* Appeals Chamber, Decision on the victims' request to participate in the appeal proceedings, ICC-01/09-02/11, 24 April 2015, para 8.

Until recently, the majority of the Appeals Chamber consistently held that participating victims were required to apply to participate in interlocutory appeals, and that each application had to be examined on the basis of the following criteria:

(i) whether the individuals seeking participation are victims in the case,
(ii) whether they have personal interests which are affected by the issues on appeal,
(iii) whether their participation is appropriate and lastly,
(iv) that the manner of participation is not prejudicial to or inconsistent with the rights of the accused and a fair and impartial trial.[29]

In relation to the first criterion, the Appeals Chamber required that the application be made on behalf of already participating victims and that they should be specifically referred to.[30] It also invited reference to the decisions which granted partici-

[29] ICC, *Prosecutor v. Thomas Lubanga Dyilo,* Appeals Chamber, Decision, in limine, on Victim Participation in the appeals of the Prosecutor and the Defence against Trial Chamber I's Decision entitled "Decision on Victims' Participation", ICC-01/04-01/06-1335, 16 May 2008, paras 35–36; ICC, *Prosecutor v. Thomas Lubanga Dyilo,* Judgment on the appeal of Mr. Thomas Lubanga Dyilo against the decision of Pre-Trial Chamber I entitled "Décision sur la demande de mise en liberté provisoire de Thomas Lubanga Dyilo", Appeals Chamber, 01/04-01/06-824, 13 February 2007, paras 43–44; See also *Situation in Darfur, Sudan*, Appeals Chamber, Decision on Victim Participation in the appeal of the Office of Public Counsel for the Defence against Pre-Trial Chamber I's Decision of 3 December 2007 and in the appeals of the Prosecutor and the Office of Public Counsel for the Defence against Pre-Trial Chamber I's Decision of 6 December 2007, ICC-02/05-138, 18 June 2008, para 23; *Situation in the Democratic Republic of the Congo,* Appeals Chamber, Decision on Victim Participation in the appeal of the Office of Public Counsel for the Defence against Pre-Trial Chamber I's Decision of 7 December 2007 and in the appeals of the Prosecutor and the Office of Public Counsel for the Defence against Pre-Trial Chamber I's Decision of 24 December 2007, ICC-01/04-503, 30 June 2008, paras 88–98; *Situation in the Democratic Republic of the Congo,* Appeals Chamber, Decision of the Appeals Chamber on the OPCV's request for clarification and the legal representatives' request for extension of time and Order of the Appeals Chamber on the date of filing of applications for participation and on the time of the filing of the responses thereto by the OPCD and the Prosecutor, ICC-01/04-450, 13 February 2008, para 1; *Situation in Darfur, Sudan,* Appeals Chamber, Decision of the Appeals Chamber on the OPCV's request for clarification and Order of the Appeals Chamber on the date of filing of applications for participation and on the time of the filing of the responses thereto by the OPCD and the Prosecutor, ICC-02/05-129, 29 February 2008, para 1; *Prosecutor v. Callixte Mbarushimana, Decision on the "Requete tendant à obtenir autorisation de participer à la procédure d'appel contre la 'Décision relative à la confirmation des charges' (ICC-01/04-01/10-465-Conf-tFRA)"*, Appeals Chamber, ICC-01/04-01/10-509, 2 April 2012, paras 6–9.

[30] ICC, *Prosecutor v. Thomas Lubanga Dyilo*, Appeals Chamber, Judgment on the appeal of Mr. Thomas Lubanga Dyilo against the decision of Pre-Trial Chamber I entitled "Décision sur la demande de mise en liberté provisoire de Thomas Lubanga Dyilo", 01/04-01/06-824, 13 February 2007, para 45; *Prosecutor v. Thomas Lubanga Dyilo,* Decision, in limine, on Victim Participation in the appeals of the Prosecutor and the Defence against Trial Chamber I's Decision entitled "Decision on Victims' Participation", ICC-01/04-01/06-1335, 16 May 2008, paras 16, 37–40; *Prosecutor v. Laurent Gbagbo,* Appeals Chamber, Decision on the application by victims for participation in the appeal, ICC-02/11-01/11, 27 August 2013, para 10.

pant status to the victims on whose behalf the application was made.[31] On more than one occasion, the Appeals Chamber rejected applications that did not list the participating victims.[32]

As to the second criterion, the Appeals Chamber held that 'any determination […] of whether the personal interests of victims are affected in relation to a particular appeal will require careful consideration on a case-by-case basis'.[33] Furthermore, in seeking to demonstrate that their personal interests were affected by the interlocutory appeal, victims had to ensure, *inter alia*, that express reference was made to the specific facts behind their individual applications, and the precise manner in which those facts were said to fall within the issue under consideration on appeal.[34] The Appeals Chamber also held that the facts or issues underlying one appeal may be different from another and thus it was necessary for victims to demonstrate with sufficient particularity and clarity the link between the specific issues on appeal and the effect of such issues on their personal interests.[35]

---

[31] ICC, *Prosecutor v. Germain Katanga and Mathieu Ngudjolo Chui,* Decision on the Participation of Victims in the Appeal of Mr. Katanga Against the "Decision on the Modalities of Victim Participation at Trial", ICC-01/04-01/07-2124, 24 May 2010, para 6.

[32] ICC, *Prosecutor v. Jean Pierre Bemba Gombo,* Appeals Chamber, Decision on the Participation of Victims in the Appeal against the "Decision on Applications for Provisional Release" of Trial Chamber III, ICC-01/05-01/08-1597, 14 July 2011, paras 13–14; Appeals, Chamber, Decision on "Application of Legal Representative of Victims Mr. Zarambaud Assingambi for leave to participate in the appeals proceedings following the Defence appeal of 9 January 2012 and addendum of 10 January 2012", ICC-01/05-01/08-2098, 1 February 2012, para 12.

[33] ICC, *Prosecutor v. Thomas Lubanga Dyilo,* Appeals Chamber, Decision of the Appeals Chamber on the Joint Application of Victims a/0001/06–a/0003/06 and a/0105/06 concerning the 'Directions and Decision of the Appeals Chamber' of 2 February 2007, ICC-01/04-01/06-925, 13 June 2007, para 28; See also ICC, *Prosecutor v. Callixte Mbarushimana,* Appeals Chamber, Decision on the "Requete tendant à obtenir autorisation de participer à la procédure d'appel contre la 'Décision relative à la confirmation des charges' (ICC-01/04-01/10-465-Conf-tFRA)", ICC-01/04-01/10-509, 2 April 2012, para 9; *Prosecutor v. Germain Katanga and Mathieu Ngudjolo Chui,* Appeals Chamber, Decision on the Participation of Victims in the Appeal of Mr. Katanga Against the "Decision on the Modalities of Victim Participation at Trial", ICC-01/04-01/07-2124, 24 May 2010, para 7; *Prosecutor v. Laurent Gbagbo,* Appeals Chamber, Decision on the application by victims for participation in the appeal, ICC-02/11-01/11, 27 August 2013, para 11.

[34] ICC, *Prosecutor v. Joseph Kony* et al., Appeals Chamber, Decision on the participation of victims in the appeal, ICC-02/04-01/05-324, 27 October 2008, paras 11–14; *Prosecutor v. Jean Pierre Bemba Gombo,* Appeals Chamber, Reasons for the "Decision on the Participation of Victims in the Appeal" against the "Decision on the Interim Release of Jean-Pierre Bemba Gombo and Convening Hearings with the Kingdom of Belgium, the Republic of Portugal, the Republic of France, the Federal Republic of Germany, the Italian Republic, and the Republic of South Africa", ICC-01/05-01/08-566, 20 October 2009, para 15; ICC, *Prosecutor v. Callixte Mbarushimana,* Appeals Chamber, Decision on the "Requete tendant à obtenir autorisation de participer à la procédure d'appel contre la 'Décision relative à la confirmation des charges' (ICC-01/04-01/10-465-Conf-tFRA)", ICC-01/04-01/10-509, 2 April 2012, para 9.

[35] ICC, *Prosecutor v. Jean Pierre Bemba Gombo,* Appeals Chamber, Decision on the Participation of Victims in the Appeal against the "Decision on the review of the detention of Mr. Jean-Pierre Bemba Gombo pursuant to Rule 118(2) of the Rules of Procedure and Evidence" of Trial Chamber III, ICC-01/05-01/08-857, 18 August 2010, para 10.

The Appeals Chamber consistently found that interlocutory appeals related to the interim release of the accused,[36] stay of proceedings,[37] the form of individual criminal responsibility of the accused,[38] and modalities of victim participation,[39] could affect the personal interests of the participating victims. Conversely, the Appeals Chamber found that the scope of the Prosecutor's disclosure obligations under Rule 77 of the RPE was an issue that was unrelated to the personal interests of the victims, as it related solely to the relationship between the accused and the Prosecutor, and victims' participation in the appeal was thus not warranted.[40] A request for participation in the determination of the admissibility of a Defence appeal against the confirmation of charges was also rejected, as the Appeals Chamber was not convinced that the personal interests of the victims were affected by a preliminary consideration of whether the appeal was correctly brought under Article 82(1)(b) of the Statute.[41]

---

[36] ICC, *Prosecutor v. Thomas Lubanga Dyilo,* Appeals Chamber, Judgment on the appeal of Mr. Thomas Lubanga Dyilo against the decision of Pre-Trial Chamber I entitled "Décision sur la demande de mise en liberté provisoire de Thomas Lubanga Dyilo", 01/04-01/06-824, 13 February 2007, para 54; *Prosecutor v. Jean Pierre Bemba Gombo,* Appeals Chamber, Reasons for the "Decision on the Participation of Victims in the Appeal against the "Decision on the Interim Release of Jean-Pierre Bemba Gombo and Convening Hearings with the Kingdom of Belgium, the Republic of Portugal, the Republic of France, the Federal Republic of Germany, the Italian Republic, and the Republic of South Africa", ICC-01/05-01/08-566, 20 October 2009, para 17; ICC, *Prosecutor v. Thomas Lubanga Dyilo,* Decision on the Participation of Victims in the Appeal against Trial Chamber I's Oral Decision of 15 July 2010 to Release Thomas Lubanga Dyilo, Appeals Chamber, ICC-01/04-01/06-2555, 17 August 2010, para 18; *Prosecutor v. Laurent Gbagbo,* Appeals Chamber, Decision on the application by victims for participation in the appeal, ICC-02/11-01/11, 27 August 2013, para 11.

[37] *Prosecutor v. Thomas Lubanga Dyilo,* Appeals Chamber, Decision on the Participation of Victims in the Appeal against Trial Chamber I's Decision to Stay the Proceedings, ICC-01/04-01/06-2556, 18 August 2010, para 9; *Prosecutor v. Uhuru Kenyatta,* Appeals Chamber, Decision on the victims' request to participate in the appeal proceedings, ICC-01/09-02/11-1015, 24 April 2015, para 11.

[38] ICC, *Prosecutor v. Germain Katanga,* Appeals Chamber, Decision on the application of victims to participate in the appeal against Trial Chamber II's decision on the implementation of regulation 55 of the Regulations of the Court, ICC-01/04-01/07-3346, 17 January 2013, paras 6, 7, 9.

[39] ICC, *Prosecutor v. Germain Katanga and Mathieu Ngudjolo Chui,* Appeals Chamber, Decision on the Participation of Victims in the Appeal of Mr. Katanga Against the "Decision on the Modalities of Victim Participation at Trial", ICC-01/04-01/07-2124, 24 May 2010, para 7.

[40] ICC, *Prosecutor v. Abdallah Banda Abakaer Nourain and Saleh Mohammed Jerbo Jamus,* Appeals Chamber, Decision on the participation of victims in the appeal, ICC-02/05-03/09-470, 6 May 2013, paras 12.

[41] ICC, *Prosecutor v. Thomas Lubanga Dyilo,* Appeals Chamber, Decision of the Appeals Chamber on the Joint Application of Victims a/0001/06 to a/0003/06 and a/0105/06 concerning the 'Directions and Decision of the Appeals Chamber' of 2 February 2007, ICC-01/04-01/06-925, 13 June 2007, paras 24–28.

As regards the third and fourth criteria, the Appeals Chamber has consistently rendered them met, if the first two conditions were fulfilled. In such cases, the Appeals Chamber found that the victims' participation was appropriate and not prejudicial to or inconsistent with the rights of the accused and a fair and impartial trial.[42]

Notwithstanding the consistent case-law in this respect, some of the members of the Appeals Chamber expressed dissenting opinions on this issue. Accordingly, Judge Sang-Hyun Song repeatedly dissented from the Appeals Chambers' decisions regarding participation of victims in interlocutory appeals. In his view, participating victims should not be required to ask leave to participate in interlocutory appeals, provided that the victims in question participated in the proceedings that gave rise to the appeal. According to Judge Song, 'this results from Regulation 64(4) and (5) of the Regulations of the Court, pursuant to which participants may file a response to the document in support of the appeal within five days of the notification of that document. There is no reason why the word "participant" in these provisions should not include all participants to the proceedings that gave rise to the appeal, including victims.'[43] Another member of the Appeals Chamber,

[42] ICC, *Prosecutor v. Joseph Kony* et al., Appeals Chamber, Decision on the participation of victims in the appeal, ICC-02/04-01/05-324, 27 October 2008, para 14; ICC, *Prosecutor v. Callixte Mbarushimana,* Appeals Chamber, Decision on the "Requete tendant à obtenir autorisation de participer à la procédure d'appel contre la 'Décision relative à la confirmation des charges' (ICC-01/04-01/10-465-Conf-tFRA)", ICC-01/04-01/10-509, 2 April 2012, para 9.

[43] ICC, *Prosecutor v. Thomas Lubanga Dyilo,* Appeals Chamber, Judgment on the appeal of Mr. Thomas Lubanga Dyilo against the decision of Pre-Trial Chamber I entitled "Décision sur la demande de mise en liberté provisoire de Thomas Lubanga Dyilo", 01/04-01/06-824, 13 February 2007, Dissenting Opinion of Judge Sang-Hyun Song Regarding the Participation of Victims, para 3. See also: *Prosecutor v. Thomas Lubanga Dyilo,* Appeals Chamber, Decision, in limine, on Victim Participation in the appeals of the Prosecutor and the Defence against Trial Chamber I's Decision entitled "Decision on Victims' Participation", ICC-01/04-01/06-1335, 16 May 2008, Dissenting opinion by Judge Song, paras 3–7; ICC, *Situation in Darfur, Sudan,* Appeals Chamber, Decision on Victim Participation in the appeal of the Office of Public Counsel for the Defence against Pre-Trial Chamber I's Decision of 3 December 2007 and in the appeals of the Prosecutor and the Office of Public Counsel for the Defence against Pre-Trial Chamber I's Decision of 6 December 2007, ICC-02/05-138, 18 June 2008, Partly dissenting opinion by Judge Song, para 3; ICC, *Situation in the Democratic Republic of the Congo,* Appeals Chamber, Decision on Victim Participation in the appeal of the Office of Public Counsel for the Defence against Pre-Trial Chamber I's Decision of 7 December 2007 and in the appeals of the Prosecutor and the Office of Public Counsel for the Defence against Pre-Trial Chamber I's Decision of 24 December 2007, ICC-01/04-503, 30 June 2008, Partly dissenting opinion by Judge Song, paras 1–2; ICC, *Prosecutor v. Jean Pierre Bemba Gombo,* Appeals Chamber, Decision on the Participation of Victims in the Appeal against the "Decision on the Interim Release of Jean-Pierre Bemba Gombo and Convening Hearings with the Kingdom of Belgium, the Republic of Portugal, the Republic of France, the Federal Republic of Germany, the Italian Republic, and the Republic of South Africa", Appeals Chamber, ICC-01/05-01/08-623, Dissenting opinion by Judge Song, 27 November 2009, paras 3–4; ICC, *Prosecutor v. Germain Katanga and Mathieu Ngudjolo Chui,* Appeals Chamber, Decision on the Participation of Victims in the Appeal of Mr. Katanga Against the "Decision on the Modalities of Victim Participation at Trial", ICC-01/04-01/07-2124, 24 May 2010, Separate opinion of Judge Song, p. 8.

Judge Christine Van den Wyngaert, adopted a similar position.[44] The Office of Public Counsel for Victims (OPCV) shares this view.[45]

Moreover, on 31 July 2015, in the *Gbagbo and Blé Goudé* case, the Appeals Chamber found merit in the request of the OPCV to revisit its interpretation of the conditions under which victims could participate in an interlocutory appeal and found itself to be persuaded by the interpretation first espoused by former Judge Song.[46] First, the Appeals Chamber found that, in light of Article 21(2) of the ICC Statute, it was not obliged to follow its previous interpretations of principles and rules of law through binding *stare decisis*; rather it was vested with discretion as to whether to do so.[47] Then, it held that the practice of requiring victims to seek authorisation to participate in an interlocutory appeal had resulted in considerable delays in the proceedings given the added procedural steps involved. These included the time spent in: (i) deciding on the applications for participation in each appeal; (ii) waiting for the victims to file their substantive observations on the appeal; and (iii) waiting for the parties to file their responses thereto. In view of the delay occasioned by these procedural steps and the need for more efficient proceedings, the Appeals Chamber was persuaded that a modification of its interpretation of the relevant provisions was necessary in order to make the participation of victims in interlocutory appeals more efficient.[48] The Appeals Chamber noted, however, that in the event that it considers that the personal interests of victims are not affected by the issues arising in a particular appeal or that the participation of victims would be inappropriate, it could issue an order to that effect.[49] It remains to be seen how the case-law of the Appeals Chamber will develop after this decision.

---

[44] ICC, *Prosecutor v. Thomas Lubanga Dyilo,* Appeals Chamber, Judgment on the appeals of Mr. Lubanga Dyilo and the Prosecutor against the Decision of Trial Chamber I of 14 July 2009 entitled "Decision giving notice to the parties and participants that the legal characterisation of the facts may be subject to change in accordance with Regulation 55(2) of the Regulations of the Court", ICC-01/04-01/06-2205, Separate opinion of Judge Song and Judge Van den Wyngaert, 8 December 2009, p. 42.

[45] ICC, *Prosecutor v. Thomas Lubanga Dyilo,* LRV, Application by the OPCV in its Capacity as Legal Representative of Victims a/0047/06, a/0048/06, a/0050/06, and a/0052/06 to Participate in the Interlocutory Appeal Lodged by the Prosecution Challenging the Oral Decision of Trial Chamber I of 15 July, ICC-01/04-01/06-2535-tENG, 23 July 2010.

[46] ICC, *Prosecutor v. Laurent Gbagbo and Charles Blé Goudé*, Appeals Chamber, Reasons for the "Decision on the 'Request for the recognition of the right of victims authorized to participate in the case to automatically participate in any interlocutory appeal arising from the case and, in the alternative, application to participate in the interlocutory appeal against the ninth decision on Mr. Gbagbo's detention (ICC-02/11-01/15-134-Red3)'", ICC-02/11-01/15-172, 31 July 2015, para 16.

[47] Ibid., para 14.

[48] Ibid., paras 15–17.

[49] Ibid., para 18.

In the *Ayyash* et al. case at the STL, the LRV was granted legal standing to respond to an interlocutory appeal lodged by the Defence of three accused against a Trial Chamber decision denying access to confidential information for a Defence expert consultant.[50] The Appeals Chamber held that participating victims had a right to respond to interlocutory appeals of the parties within the same limits as those applicable to their right to lodge an interlocutory appeal (i.e. against decisions on applications for status as a VPP, decisions on the modalities of victims' participation in the proceedings and decisions on protective measures for VPPs and the variation of such measures).[51] The Appeals Chamber found that the Defence appeal related to the modalities of victims' participation during trial proceedings as well as to protective measures afforded to participating victims:

> In the proceedings before us, the matter on appeal affects the VPPs' personal interests in two ways. First, a Defence request to grant Mr Nashabe access to confidential information could potentially result in his receiving information concerning the identity of VPPs. Second, the Trial Chamber crafted a system under which the LRV has to be consulted in all cases where the Defence makes requests that could lead to such information being made available to Mr Nashabe.[footnote omitted] The Trial Chamber therefore regulated the modalities of the VPPs' participation in the proceedings.[52]

The Appeals Chamber thus held that the LRV had standing to respond to the appeal, to the extent that the response concerned Defence arguments relating to issues that significantly affected the personal interests of the participating victims.[53]

In the same case, the LRV was also granted leave to respond to a Defence appeal against the Trial Chamber's decision regarding the probative value of the evidence on the death of one of the accused.[54] The Appeals Chamber found that the matter on appeal clearly affected the personal interests of the participating victims, as the potential termination of the proceedings against the accused could affect their right to claim compensation at the national level pursuant to Article 25 of the STL Statute.[55]

---

[50] STL, *Prosecutor v. Ayyash* et al., Appeals Chamber, Decision on Interlocutory Appeal against the Trial Chamber's Decision Regarding the Conditions of Assignment of Defence Expert Consultant, STL-11-01/T/AC/AR126.10, 3 May 2016, paras 16–17. The interlocutory appeal was lodged after a four-year long debate regarding the conditions of assignment of a defence expert consultant. For a detailed procedural background see the cited Appeals Chamber decision, paras 2–11.

[51] STL, *Prosecutor v. Ayyash* et al., Appeals Chamber, Decision on Interlocutory Appeal against the Trial Chamber's Decision Regarding the Conditions of Assignment of Defence Expert Consultant, STL-11-01/T/AC/AR126.10, 3 May 2016, para 16.

[52] Ibid., para 17.

[53] Ibid., para 18.

[54] STL, *Prosecutor v. Ayyash* et al., Appeals Chamber, Decision on the Request of the Legal Representative of Victims Seeking Leave to Respond to the Badreddine Defence Interlocutory Appeal, STL-11-01/T/AC/AR126.11, 17 June 2016.

[55] Ibid., paras 3, 5.

12.2.3 Procedure for Interlocutory Appeals

At the ECCC, as said above, during the investigative phase, it is the Pre-Trial Chamber that hears all appeals against orders and decisions of the Co-Investigating Judges. The procedure for interlocutory appeals applies to all parties equally.

Except if otherwise provided in the Internal Regulations, a notice of appeal must be filed to the Pre-Trial Chamber within 10 days from the date that notice of the decision or order was received.[56] According to Internal Rule 75(2), the notice of appeal must be made in writing to the Greffier of the Co-Investigating Judges, who will immediately inform the Co-Investigating Judges and keep a record of all pre-trial appeals. As soon as a notice of appeal is received, the Greffier of the Pre-Trial Chamber shall be immediately informed. The submissions on the merit of the appeal must be filed by the appellant with the Greffier of the Pre-Trial Chamber within 30 days from the date on which notice of the decision or order was received. Internal Rule 75(3) allows, under exceptional circumstances, the extension of the time-limit.

As for the content of the submissions on appeal, Internal Rule 75(4) provides that the submissions must contain the reasons of fact and law upon which the appeal is based together with all supporting documents. If an appeal hearing is held, the appellant may not raise any matters of fact or law not set out previously in the written submissions.

As discussed elsewhere in this book, appeals regarding the admissibility of a civil party application are considered expeditiously by the Pre-Trial Chamber, on the basis of written submissions alone.[57]

During the trial phase at the ECCC, when deciding on an immediate appeal, the Supreme Court Chamber may itself examine evidence and call new evidence to determine the relevant issue. Usually, an immediate appeal does not stay the proceedings before the Trial Chamber, but the Supreme Court Chamber may decide otherwise.[58] When lodging an immediate appeal, civil parties will have to follow the same procedure as the other parties in the case. According to Internal Rule 107, an immediate appeal shall be filed within 30 days of the date of the decision or its notification. An immediate appeal will have to set out the grounds of appeal and arguments in support thereof. For each ground of appeal, the written submission will have to:

(a) specify an alleged error on a question of law and demonstrate how it invalidates the decision; or

[56] ECCC Internal Rules, Rule 75(1).

[57] See Chap. 2.

[58] ECCC Internal Rules, Rule 104(4).

(b) specify a discernible error in the exercise of the Trial Chamber's discretion which results in prejudice to the appellant; or
(c) specify an alleged error of fact and demonstrate how it occasioned a miscarriage of justice.[59]

If the immediate appeal relates to a decision on detention, bail or protective measures, the time-limit for filing is 15 days from the date of the decision or its notification, as appropriate.[60] Nonetheless, if the immediate appeal relates to a decision of the Trial Chamber ordering release from provisional detention, the appeal must be filed within 24 h of the notification of the decision to release.[61]

When lodging an immediate appeal, civil parties need to be represented by the Lead Co-Lawyers, who will have to sign the written submission and file it with the Greffier of the Trial Chamber.[62]

At the ICC, the filing of appeals under Article 82 of the ICC Statute is governed by Rules 154 and 155 of the RPE. An appeal under Article 82(1)(a) or (b) of the Statute can be filed not later than five days from the date upon which the party filing the appeal is notified of the decision.[63] An appeal under Article 82(1)(c) can be filed not later than two days from the date upon which the party filing the appeal is notified of the decision.[64] When a party wishes to appeal a decision under Article 82(1)(d), or Article 82(2) it must make a written application to the Chamber that gave the decision within five days of being notified of that decision, setting out the reasons for the request for leave to appeal.[65] Participating victims can apply to participate (or directly participate, if the Appeals Chamber's decision in the *Gbagbo and Blé Goudé* case discussed above is followed)[66] in these appeals as soon as possible after the appeal is filed.[67] In any event, victims have to submit

---

[59] Ibid., Rule 105(2).

[60] Ibid., Rule 107(2).

[61] Ibid., Rule 107(3). See also Internal Rules, Rule 82(6) for the procedure for release from provisional detention.

[62] ECCC Internal Rules, Rule 106(2)–(4).

[63] ICC RPE, Rule 154(1).

[64] ICC RPE, Rule 154(2).

[65] ICC RPE, Rule 155(1).

[66] ICC, *Prosecutor v. Laurent Gbagbo and Charles Blé Goudé*, Appeals Chamber, Reasons for the "Decision on the 'Request for the recognition of the right of victims authorized to participate in the case to automatically participate in any interlocutory appeal arising from the case and, in the alternative, application to participate in the interlocutory appeal against the ninth decision on Mr. Gbagbo's detention (ICC-02/11-01/15-134-Red3)'", ICC-02/11-01/15-172, 31 July 2015, paras 14–18.

[67] ICC RPE, Rule 156(1) and (2). ICC, *Situation in Darfur, Sudan,* Appeals Chamber, Decision on Victim Participation in the appeal of the Office of Public Counsel for the Defence against Pre-Trial Chamber I's Decision of 3 December 2007 and in the appeals of the Prosecutor and the Office of Public Counsel for the Defence against Pre-Trial Chamber I's Decision of 6 December 2007, ICC-02/05-138, 18 June 2008, para 26.

their request before the date of filing of the response to the document in support of the appeal,[68] or, following the *Gbagbo and Blé Goudé* case, they can file a response to the document in support of the appeal pursuant to Regulation 64(4) and (5) of the Regulations of the Court.[69]

The Appeals Chamber also determined that the procedures adopted in respect of interlocutory appeals pursuant to Article 82(1)(b) of the Statute should be equally applicable to interlocutory appeals arising under Article 82(1)(d) of the Statute.[70]

According to the case-law before *Gbagbo and Blé Goudé*, the request for participation in an appeal has to be in writing and should include a statement from the LRV in relation to whether and how the victims' personal interests are affected by the particular interlocutory appeal, as well as why it is appropriate for the Appeals Chamber to permit their views and concerns to be presented.[71] The Appeals Chamber also noted that submissions as to why victims' participation would not be prejudicial to or inconsistent with the rights of the accused and a fair and impartial trial would also be considered by the Appeals Chamber in making its determination.[72] If the application for participation is granted, participating victims will be allowed to present their views and concerns solely in relation to the

[68] ICC, *Situation in Darfur, Sudan,* Appeals Chamber, Decision on Victim Participation in the appeal of the Office of Public Counsel for the Defence against Pre-Trial Chamber I's Decision of 3 December 2007 and in the appeals of the Prosecutor and the Office of Public Counsel for the Defence against Pre-Trial Chamber I's Decision of 6 December 2007, ICC-02/05-138, 18 June 2008, para 26; ICC, *Situation in the Democratic Republic of the Congo,* Appeals Chamber, Decision on Victim Participation in the appeal of the Office of Public Counsel for the Defence against Pre-Trial Chamber I's Decision of 7 December 2007 and in the appeals of the Prosecutor and the Office of Public Counsel for the Defence against Pre-Trial Chamber I's Decision of 24 December 2007, ICC-01/04-503, 30 June 2008, para 39.

[69] ICC, *Prosecutor v. Laurent Gbagbo and Charles Blé Goudé,* Appeals Chamber, Reasons for the "Decision on the 'Request for the recognition of the right of victims authorized to participate in the case to automatically participate in any interlocutory appeal arising from the case and, in the alternative, application to participate in the interlocutory appeal against the ninth decision on Mr. Gbagbo's detention (ICC-02/11-01/15-134-Red3)'", ICC-02/11-01/15-172, Appeals Chamber, 31 July 2015, para 21.

[70] ICC, *Prosecutor v. Thomas Lubanga Dyilo,* Appeals Chamber, Decision, in limine, on Victim Participation in the appeals of the Prosecutor and the Defence against Trial Chamber I's Decision entitled "Decision on Victims' Participation", ICC-01/04-01/06-1335,16 May 2008, para 13.

[71] ICC, *Prosecutor v. Jean Pierre Bemba Gombo*, Appeals Chamber, Reasons for the "Decision on the Participation of Victims in the Appeal against the 'Decision on the Interim Release of Jean-Pierre Bemba Gombo and Convening Hearings with the Kingdom of Belgium, the Republic of Portugal, the Republic of France, the Federal Republic of Germany, the Italian Republic, and the Republic of South Africa'", ICC-01/05-01/08-566, 20 October 2009, para 15.

[72] ICC, *Prosecutor v. Thomas Lubanga Dyilo,* Appeals Chamber, Judgment on the appeal of Mr. Thomas Lubanga Dyilo against the decision of Pre-Trial Chamber I entitled "Décision sur la demande de mise en liberté provisoire de Thomas Lubanga Dyilo", 01/04-01/06-824, 13 February 2007, para 44.

issues raised on appeal. Observations by the victims must be specifically relevant to the issues arising in the appeal and to the extent that their personal interests are affected by the proceedings.[73]

In line with the above-mentioned decision of the Appeals Chamber at the STL, if participating victims are granted leave to appeal an interlocutory decision, the procedure applicable to the other parties will have to be followed. In any event, the right of participating victims to seek appellate review in the limited circumstances set out by the Appeals Chamber should not prejudice the Accused.[74]

12.2.4 Comparative Conclusions

Figure 12.1 contrasts the different approaches adopted by the three courts as regards participating victims' rights in interlocutory appeals. The ICC seems to be adopting the most restrictive approach, by not permitting victims to appeal interlocutory decisions in their own right. The ECCC and the STL provide limited rights of interlocutory appeal to victims. All three courts allow the participation of victims in the interlocutory appeals of the other parties.

12.3 Right to Appeal or Participate in the Appeal Against Trial Judgments

The extent to which participating victims may appeal or participate in the appeal of a judgment differ across the three courts analysed herein, depending on whether the appeal concerns the acquittal or conviction of the accused, the sentencing of the convicted person or reparations.

12.3.1 Appeals Against Convictions or Acquittal

At the ECCC, an appeal against the judgment of the Trial Chamber may be filed by the Co-Prosecutors, the Accused and also the civil parties before the Supreme

---

[73] ICC, *Prosecutor v. Thomas Lubanga Dyilo,* Appeals Chamber, Decision, in limine, on Victim Participation in the appeals of the Prosecutor and the Defence against Trial Chamber I's Decision entitled "Decision on Victims' Participation", ICC-01/04-01/06-1335,16 May 2008, para 50.

[74] STL, *Prosecutor v. Ayyash* et al., Appeals Chamber, Decision on Appeal by Legal Representative of Victims Against Pre-Trial Judge's Decision on Protective Measures, STL-11-01/PT/AC/AR126.3, 10 April 2013, para 16.

Court	Ability to appeal interlocutory decisions	Ability to participate in (other) parties' interlocutory appeal
ECCC	Civil parties can appeal a limited number of decisions: - Internal Rule74(4) during the investigation phase - Internal Rule 104(4) during the trial phase	Yes In line with Internal Rule 23, a civil party, once admitted, can participate in all stages of the proceedings, and that there is no need to show any special interest of the civil parties to participate in said proceedings
ICC	No, but this specific issue has not been addressed conclusively by the ICC Appeals Chamber	Before 31 July 2015: Yes, but only if it is shown by leave that (i) the individuals seeking participation are victims in the case, (ii) they have personal interests which are affected by the issues on appeal, (iii) their participation is appropriate and lastly, (iv) the manner of participation is not prejudicial to or inconsistent with the rights of the accused and a fair and impartial trial After 31 July 2015: In the *Gbagbo and Blé Goudé* cases, participating victims were permitted to participate in the interlocutory appeals of the parties if the victims in question participated in the proceedings that gave rise to the appeal
STL	Participating victims may request to appeal decisions on (i) applications for status as a participating victim, (ii) modalities of victims' participation in the proceedings, and (iii) protective measures for participating victims and the variation of such measures.	Participating victims may respond to an interlocutory appeal of a party, if that appeal relates to issues that significantly affect the personal interests of the victims within the same limits as those set for lodging an interlocutory appeal (i.e. applications for status as a participating victim, modalities of victims' participation in the proceedings, and protective measures for participating victims and the variation of such measures)

Fig. 12.1 The rights of participating victims to appeal and participate in appeals against interlocutory decisions

Court Chamber,[75] but the latter's right of appeal is limited. Accordingly, civil parties may appeal the verdict of conviction or acquittal only if the Co-Prosecutors have appealed it.[76]

The Internal Rules are silent on whether civil parties may respond to the submissions of the other parties on appeal. Nonetheless, the Supreme Court Chamber ruled on this issue in *Case 002/01*. On 7 August 2014, the Trial Chamber issued its judgment in *Case 002/01* convicting both accused of the crimes against humanity and sentencing them each to life imprisonment.[77] Both accused filed notices of appeal, while the Co-Prosecutors submitted a notice of appeal on the sole ground that the Trial Chamber allegedly erred in deciding to exclude consideration of the third form of joint criminal enterprise as a mode of liability.[78] Civil parties did not lodge any appeal against the Trial Judgment, nonetheless, following a number of motions from the appellant parties, the civil parties submitted a request to respond to the prospective Defence appeal briefs on the basis that civil parties are a 'distinct rights-bearing party', and that a significant number of arguments encapsulated in the Defence appeal briefs relate directly to evidence provided by the civil parties during the trial stage.[79] The Supreme Court Chamber noted that where the applicable regulations generically entrusted the "parties" with a procedural prerogative, such prerogative had to be presumed available to all parties to the trial, provided that it was not functionally party-specific, and had not been explicitly limited.[80] On this basis, it agreed with the Lead Co-Lawyers in that their right to rebut the Defence appeal briefs, inasmuch as the arguments contained therein affected civil parties' interests, flowed logically from the prerogatives afforded to civil parties at the investigative, trial and appeal stages.[81] The Supreme Court Chamber further noted that, in accordance with Internal Rules 92 and 104*bis*, "[t]he parties" were entitled to make written submissions before the competent

---

[75] ECCC, Law on the Establishment of the Extraordinary Chambers, with inclusion of amendments as promulgated on 27 October 2004 (NS/RKM/1004/006), Article 36 new.

[76] ECCC Internal Rules, Rule 105(c).

[77] ECCC, *Case 002/01,* Trial Chamber, *Case 002/01* Judgment, Case No. 002/19-09-2007/ECCC/TC, 7 August 2014.

[78] ECCC, *Case 002/01,* Defence for Nuon Chea, Notice of Appeal against the Judgment in *Case 002/01*, Case No. 002/19-09-2007/ECCC/SC, 29 September 2014; ECCC, *Case 002/01,* Defence for Khieu Samphan, Declaration d'appel de la Defense de M KHIEU Samphan contre le jugement rendu dans le proces 002/01, Case No. 002/19-09-2007/ECCC/SC, 29 September 2014; ECCC, *Case 002/01,* Office of the Co-Prosecutors, Co-Prosecutors' Notice of Appeal of a Decision in *Case 002/01*, Case No. 002/19-09-2007/ECCC/SC, 29 September 2014.

[79] ECCC, *Case 002/01,* Civil Parties, Civil Party Lead Co-Lawyers' Requests Relating to the Appeals in *Case 002/01*, Case No. 002/19-09-2007-ECCC/SC, 24 November 2014, paras 2, 13–18.

[80] ECCC, *Case 002/01,* Supreme Court Chamber, Decision on Civil Party Lead Co-Lawyers' Requests Relating to the Appeals In *Case 002/01*, Case No. *002/19-09-2007-ECCC/SC,* 26 December 2014, para 14.

[81] Ibid.

chamber up until the closing submissions. The authorisation to submit written applications and pleadings reasonably incorporated the right to respond and reply to other parties' submissions. As such, the Court found that it would be discordant with civil parties' powers relating to their overall role in all phases of proceedings to disavow their right to respond to the Defence appeal briefs.[82] This said, the Supreme Court Chamber also noted that the civil parties' right to respond to the Defence appeal briefs had to be subject to limitations. First, the arguments set out in the proposed response had to relate to grounds directly affecting civil parties' rights and interests. Secondly, the Lead Co-Lawyers had to endeavour to avoid repetitiveness and overlap with issues already covered by the Co-Prosecutors' projected response to the Defence appeal briefs.[83]

As regards the general appeal procedure, civil parties are bound by the same rules as the other parties.[84]

At the ICC, participating victims have no right of their own to appeal a judgment of acquittal or conviction. Article 81(1) of the ICC Statute vests the right to appeal acquittals or convictions in the Prosecution and convicted person alone.

Nonetheless, participating victims can participate in the appeal of the other parties. The trial judgment in the *Lubanga* case was rendered on 14 March 2012, convicting Thomas Lubanga Dyilo of committing war crimes.[85] On 10 July 2012, Mr. Lubanga was sentenced to 14 years' imprisonment.[86] Mr. Lubanga appealed against both the conviction and the sentence, while the Prosecutor appealed against the sentence only.[87] Relying on Article 68(3) of the Statute, which provides that the Court shall permit victims to present their views and concerns at stages of the proceedings determined to be appropriate, the Appeals Chamber authorised the participation of victims in these appeals.[88] The Appeals Chamber determined that the legal representatives of victim groups V01 and V02 could present the victims' views and concerns with respect to their personal interests in the issues on appeal

---

[82] Ibid.

[83] Ibid., para 17.

[84] ECCC Internal Rules, Rules 105–111.

[85] ICC, *Prosecutor v. Thomas Lubanga Dyilo*, Trial Chamber, Judgment pursuant to Article 74 of the Statute, ICC-01/04-01/06-2842, 14 March 2012.

[86] ICC, *Prosecutor v. Thomas Lubanga Dyilo,* Trial Chamber, Decision on Sentence pursuant to Article 76 of the Statute, ICC-01/04-01/06-2901, 10 July 2012.

[87] ICC, *Prosecutor v. Thomas Lubanga Dyilo,* Defence for Thomas Lubanga, Notice of Appeal lodged by the Defence for Mr. Thomas Lubanga against Trial Chamber I's Judgment pursuant to Article 74 of the Statute of 14 March 2012, ICC-01/04-01/06-2934, 3 October 2012; Defence for Thomas Lubanga, Notice of Appeal lodged by the Defence for Mr. Thomas Lubanga against Trial Chamber I's Decision on sentence pursuant to Article 76 of the Statute of 10 July 2012, ICC-01/04-01/06-2935, 3 October 2012; Office of the Prosecutor, Prosecution's Notice of Appeal against Trial Chamber I's "Decision on Sentence pursuant to Article 76 of the Statute", ICC-01/04-01/06-2933, 3 October 2012.

[88] ICC, *Prosecutor v. Thomas Lubanga Dyilo,* Appeals Chamber, Decision on the participation of victims in the appeals against Trial Chamber I's conviction and sentencing decisions, ICC-01/04-01/06-2951, 13 December 2012.

by filing consolidated observations on the three submitted appeals. The Defence and the Prosecutor could each file a consolidated response to the victims' observations.[89] The legal representatives for victims V01 filed their consolidated observations on 4 February 2013, while the LRV for V02 filed their observations on 7 February 2013.[90] On 4 April 2013, the Prosecutor and the Defence filed their consolidated responses to the victims' observations.[91] The Defence therein requested that the observations that did not relate to the personal interests of the victims, be rejected *in limine*.[92] In particular, the Defence submitted that only the Prosecutor was permitted to submit observations regarding any ground related to alleged violations of his fair trial rights and the participating victims did not have this right.[93] The Appeals Chamber found it unnecessary formally to dismiss any observations for exceeding the personal interests of the victims, it held, however, that the observations of the legal representatives of victims would only be considered to the extent that the issue under consideration affected the victims' personal interests.[94]

Participating victims were also allowed to participate in the Prosecution's appeal against Trial Chamber II's acquittal of Mathieu Ngudjolo Chui under conditions similar to those stipulated in the *Lubanga* case.[95]

---

[89] ICC, *Prosecutor v. Thomas Lubanga Dyilo,* Appeals Chamber, Decision on the participation of victims in the appeals against Trial Chamber I's conviction and sentencing decisions, ICC-01/04-01/06-2951, 13 Dec. 2012, para 5.

[90] ICC, *Prosecutor v. Thomas Lubanga Dyilo,* LRV, Observations on the appeals against the decisions pursuant to Articles 74 and 76 of the Rome Statute, ICC-01/04-01/06-2966-Corr-Anx1-tENG, 4 February 2013, with a Corrigendum filed on 11 February 2013; ICC, *Prosecutor v. Thomas Lubanga Dyilo,* V02 LRV, Public Redacted Version Corrigendum Consolidated observations of the V02 team of Legal Representatives of Victims on the Defence and Prosecution appeals against the judgment and sentence pursuant to Articles 74 and 76 of the Rome Statute, ICC-01/04-01/06-2976-Corr-Red-tENG, 7 February 2013 with a Corrigendum filed on 8 February 2013.

[91] ICC, *Prosecutor v. Thomas Lubanga Dyilo,* Office of the Prosecutor, Prosecution's Response to the Observations of Legal Representatives Group V01, ICC-01/04-01/06-3004, 4 April 2013; Réplique de la Défense aux observations des Représentants légaux des groupes de victimes V01 et V02 sur les appels de la Défense relatifs au Jugement et à la Décision sur la peine et sur l'appel du Procureur relatif à la Décision sur la peine, ICC-01/04-01/06-3005-Red, 4 April 2013.

[92] ICC, *Prosecutor v. Thomas Lubanga Dyilo,* Defence for Thomas Lubanga Dyilo, Réplique de la Défense aux observations des Représentants légaux des groupes de victimes VOl et V02 sur les appels de la Défense relatifs au Jugement et à la Décision sur la peine et sur l'appel du Procureur relatif à la Décision sur la peine, ICC-01/04-01/06-3005-Red, 4 April 2013, para 7.

[93] ICC, *Prosecutor v. Thomas Lubanga Dyilo,* Defence for Thomas Lubanga Dyilo, Réplique de la Défense aux observations des Représentants légaux des groupes de victimes VOl et V02 sur les appels de la Défense relatifs au Jugement et à la Décision sur la peine et sur l'appel du Procureur relatif à la Décision sur la peine, ICC-01/04-01/06-3005-Red, 4 April 2013, para 6.

[94] ICC, *Prosecutor v. Thomas Lubanga Dyilo,* Appeals Chamber, Public redacted Judgment on the appeal of Mr. Thomas Lubanga Dyilo against his conviction, ICC-01/04-01/06-3121-Red, 1 December 2014, para 36.

[95] ICC, *Prosecutor v. Mathieu Ngudjolo Chui,* Appeals Chamber, Decision on the participation of anonymous victims in the appeal and on the maintenance of deceased victims on the list of participating victims, ICC-01/04-02/12-140, 23 September 2013.

The abandonment of the cross appeals by the Prosecution and the Defence in the *Katanga* case, also rendered the victims' participation in the appeal moot.[96] Legal representatives of both victim groups filed observations submitting that they were neither consulted on nor notified of the Prosecution's decision to discontinue the appeal against the judgment.[97] The legal representative of the group of child soldier victims also submitted that this course of action would close all hope for reparations for the victims of the crime of using child soldiers.[98] The Prosecutor responded to both submissions stating that its decision to discontinue its appeal took into account all of the relevant factors, including sensitivity to the interests of victims in the *Katanga* case.[99] The Appeals Chamber confirmed the parties' discretion to discontinue the appeals and terminated the proceedings.[100] Because Mr. Katanga was acquitted of the charges of using child soldiers to participate actively in hostilities as a war crime under Article 8(2)(e)(vii) of the Statute, and that decision remained final, the group of victims comprising former child soldiers lost any opportunity to participate in reparation proceedings.[101]

At the STL, the Statute and the Rules are silent on whether participating victims have a right of their own to appeal convictions or acquittals. Rule 177(A) of the RPE vests the Prosecutor with the right to appeal a judgment of acquittal, whereas the second paragraph of the same Rule stipulates that 'a Party' can appeal a judgment of conviction or the sentence.

---

[96] ICC, *Prosecutor v. Germain Katanga,* Appeals Chamber, Decision on the victims' requests to participate in the appeal proceedings, ICC-01/04-01/07-3505, 24 July 2014.

[97] ICC, *Prosecutor v. Germain Katanga,* Legal Representative of Victims, Observations des victimes sur le désistement d'appel du Procureur contre le jugement concernant G. Katanga, ICC-01/04-01/07-3499, 26 June 2014, para 3; ICC, *Prosecutor v. Germain Katanga,* Legal Representative of Victims, Communication du Représentant légal des victimes enfants soldats relative au double désistement d'appel dans le dossier Le Procureur c. Germain Katanga et Annexe publique, ICC-01/04-01/07-3501, 30 June 2014, Annex I, p. 2.

[98] ICC, *Prosecutor v. Germain Katanga,* Legal Representative of Victims, Communication du Représentant légal des victimes enfants soldats relative au double désistement d'appel dans le dossier Le Procureur c. Germain Katanga et Annexe publique, ICC-01/04-01/07-3501, 30 June 2014, Annex I, p. 3.

[99] ICC, *Prosecutor v. Germain Katanga,* Office of the Prosecutor, Prosecution's Response to the Observations of the Legal Representative of the main group of Victims filed on 26 June 2014, ICC-01/04-01/07-3500, 27 June 2014, para 8; ICC, *Prosecutor v. Germain Katanga,* Office of the Prosecutor, Prosecution's Response to the Communication of the Legal Representative of the child soldier group of victims, ICC-01/04-01/07-3502, 2 July 2014, para 3.

[100] ICC, *Prosecutor v. Germain Katanga,* Appeals Chamber, Decision on the victims' requests to participate in the appeal proceedings, ICC-01/04-01/07-3505, 24 July 2014.

[101] On 7 March 2014, Trial Chamber II acquitted Germain Katanga of the charges of sexual slavery, rape and using child soldiers (*Jugement rendu en application de l'article 74 du Statut,* ICC-01/04-01/07-3436). In its initial notice of appeal, the Prosecution appealed only the acquittals for rape and sexual slavery and not that for using child soldiers. *Prosecution's Appeal against Trial Chamber II's "Jugement rendu en application de l'article 74 du Statut"*, ICC-01/04-01/07-3462, 9 April 2014.

As regards participation in the appeal proceedings, Rule 87(D) of the STL RPE provides that participating victims may participate in the appeal stage, subject to the authorisation of and in a manner deemed appropriate by the Appeals Chamber. The STL has not yet commenced appeal proceedings in the *Ayyash* et al. case, and it thus remains to be seen how the rights of the participating victims will be interpreted at that stage.

12.3.2 Appeals Against Sentencing

The rights of participating victims to appeal a sentencing judgment are even more restricted than those regarding acquittals or convictions. At the outset, none of the three courts analysed herein allow participating victims to appeal, in their own right, the sentence of the convicted person.[102]

The ECCC does not permit civil parties to make submissions on the sentencing of the accused,[103] thus their participation in any form in an appeal against sentence is also barred.

The ICC adopted a more permissive approach in this respect. The Appeals Chamber in the *Lubanga* case allowed participating victims to make observations on the sentence in the appeal proceedings and it held that such observations would only be considered to the extent that the issue under consideration affected the victims' personal interests.[104]

Rule 87(C) of the STL RPE states that participating victims, subject to the authorisation by the Trial Chamber, may be heard or permitted to file written submissions relating to the personal impact of the crimes at the sentencing stage. This could be construed as an indication that participating victims may be allowed to make submissions in appeal proceedings regarding sentencing as well. This, however, remains to be seen if and when the STL entertains appeal proceedings.

12.3.3 Appeals Against Reparation Orders

Both the ECCC and the ICC allow victims to appeal, in their own right, reparation orders. Since this issue is addressed elsewhere in this book, only the relevant

---

[102] ECCC Internal Rules, Rule 105(c); ICC Statute, Article 81(2)(a); STL RPE, Rule 177(B).

[103] ECCC, *Case 001,* Trial Chamber, Decision on Civil Party Co-lawyers' joint request for a ruling on the standing of Civil Party lawyers to make submissions on sentencing and directions concerning the questioning of the accused, experts and witnesses testifying on character, Case No. 001/18-07-2007/ECCC/TC, 9 October 2009.

[104] ICC, *Prosecutor v. Thomas Lubanga Dyilo,* Appeals Chamber, Judgment on the appeals of the Prosecutor and Mr. Thomas Lubanga Dyilo against the "Decision on Sentence pursuant to Article 76 of the Statute", 1 December 2014, ICC-01/04-01/06-3122, para 94.

provisions will be briefly touched upon.[105] Accordingly, Internal Rule 105(2) at the ECCC and Article 82(4) of the ICC Statute allow civil parties and participating victims, respectively, to appeal decisions on reparations regardless of the other parties' appeals. Both courts also allow participating victims to respond to the other parties' appeal against reparation decisions. The STL does not provide possibilities for participating victims to pursue reparations before it.

12.3.4 Comparative Conclusions

Figure 12.2 summarises the different approaches adopted by the ECCC, ICC and the STL in relation to participating victims' rights at the appeal stage. All three courts allow for some form of participation of victims in appeals against acquittals and convictions, although only the ECCC permits civil parties to appeal such decisions, but only if the Co-Prosecutors do so. None of the three courts seem to allow participating victims to appeal decisions on sentencing, although the ICC has allowed victims to make observations on sentence at the appeal stage. Both the ICC and the ECCC allow victims to appeal orders on reparations.

12.4 Key Points

Interlocutory appeals

- Only the ECCC and the STL currently allow participating victims to appeal interlocutory decisions, under strict limitations.
- Pursuant to current case-law, participating victims at the ICC cannot initiate an appeal in their own right against an interlocutory decision, but this issue has not been specifically addressed by the ICC Appeals Chamber.
- All three courts allow some form of participation of victims in the interlocutory appeals of the (other) parties.
- The ICC Appeals Chamber has set out strict criteria on the basis of which participating victims may apply to participate in interlocutory appeals, but a recent Appeals Chamber decision seems to be adopting the view that participating victims can participate in the interlocutory appeals of the parties if the victims in question participated in the proceedings that gave rise to the appeal.

Appeals against final judgments

- Civil parties at the ECCC may appeal the verdict of conviction or acquittal only if the Co-Prosecutors have appealed it, but they are generally allowed to participate in the other parties' appeal.

[105] See Chap. 13.

Courts	Appellate Rights	Appeals against Acquittals and Convictions	Appeals against Sentencing	Appeals against Reparation orders
ECCC	Appeal in own right	Only if Co-Prosecutors appeal	No	Yes
	Participation in appeal	Yes – *Cases 001, 002/001*	No	Yes
ICC	Appeal in own right	No	No	Yes
	Participation in appeal	Yes – *Lubanga*; *Ngudjolo Chui* cases	Yes – *Lubanga* case	Yes – *Lubanga* case
STL	Appeal in own right	Rules indicate no right; case-law will decide	Rules indicate no right; case-law will decide	Not applicable
	Participation in appeal	Yes – Rule 87(D)	Probably yes – spirit of Rule 87(C)	Not applicable

Fig. 12.2 Rights of participating victims to appeal and participate in appeals against final judgments

- At the ICC, participating victims have no right of their own to appeal a judgment of acquittal or conviction, but the Appeals Chamber has allowed their participation in the appeal of the parties.
- The STL has not yet commenced appeal proceedings in a case with participating victims, it thus remains to be seen how their rights will be interpreted at that stage.
- None of the three courts allow participating victims to appeal, in their own right, the sentence of the convicted person.
- The ICC Appeals Chamber has, however, allowed participating victims to make observations on sentence in the *Lubanga* appellate proceedings.
- The ECCC and the ICC allow victims to appeal, in their own right, decisions on reparations.
- The STL does not provide possibilities for participating victims to pursue reparations before it.

Reference

International Criminal Court, The Office of Public Counsel for Victims (2014) Representing victims before the International Criminal Court, A manual for legal representatives, December 2014. https://www.icc-cpi.int/iccdocs/opcv/OPCVManual-4-Eng.pdf. Accessed 29 Sept 2016

Chapter 13
Reparations, Assistance and Support

Carla Ferstman

Abstract Reparations, assistance and support are relatively new features in international criminal law, and the practice remains in a state of flux. Victims' lawyers can play an important role in shaping and further developing the evolving practice for the ultimate benefit of victims. This chapter focuses on the mandates, rules and procedures, and practice of international criminal courts, in relation to reparations, assistance and support. These aspects are analysed from the perspective of victims' active engagement with these mandates. At the Extraordinary Chambers in the Courts of Cambodia (ECCC), only those victims that are admitted to participate in the proceedings as civil parties are entitled to apply for and obtain reparations. In contrast, at the International Criminal Court (ICC), victims' participation and reparations requests are treated distinctly; a victim may apply for and/or obtain reparations without having participated in the proceedings. The Special Tribunal for Lebanon (STL) does not afford reparations to victims. The chapter is split in two parts: (i) reparations and (ii) assistance and support. Each part begins by providing an overview, comparing and contrasting the statutory frameworks, rules and procedures of the various courts. An analysis is then provided of how victims and their lawyers may access their entitlements to reparations and assistance and support, the challenges that have arisen in the practice, as well as the various steps that victims' lawyers may take to enhance access, bearing in mind the jurisprudence and other relevant factors.

Keywords Reparations · Assistance and support · Provisional measures · Assets · Harm · Eligibility · Criminal liability · Restitution · Compensation · Rehabilitation

---

Carla Ferstman is the Director of REDRESS. The views expressed herein are those of the author and do not necessarily reflect the views of the organisation. This chapter contains updates until November 2016.

C. Ferstman (✉)
London, UK
e-mail: carla@redress.org

K. Tibori-Szabó and M. Hirst (eds.), *Victim Participation in International Criminal Justice*, International Criminal Justice Series 11,
DOI 10.1007/978-94-6265-177-7_13

Contents

13.1 Introduction

This chapter focuses on the mandates, rules and procedures, and practice of international criminal courts, in relation to reparations, assistance and support. In keeping with the orientation of this book, these aspects are analysed from the perspective of victims' active engagement with these mandates. Thus, while the various systems of victims' participation operating before some of these courts do not form the focus of this chapter, these are relevant nonetheless, insofar and to the extent that victims' participation in international criminal proceedings and the advocacy carried out by victims' lawyers may impact on the extent to which victims' may access reparations, assistance and support. At the Extraordinary Chambers in the Courts of Cambodia (ECCC), only those victims who are admitted to participate in the proceedings as civil parties are entitled to apply for and obtain reparations. In contrast, at the International Criminal Court (ICC), victims' participation and reparations requests are treated distinctly; a victim may apply for and/or obtain reparations without having participated in the proceedings. The Special Tribunal for Lebanon (STL) does not afford reparations to victims, so it will not be discussed in this chapter.

Given that victims' participation is treated in other chapters in this volume, this chapter considers only aspects of victims' participation that impact, or have the potential to so impact, victims' access to reparations, assistance and support.

The chapter is split into two parts: (i) reparations and (ii) assistance and support. Each part begins by providing an overview, comparing and contrasting the statutory frameworks, rules and procedures of the various courts. An analysis is then provided of how victims and their lawyers may access their entitlements to reparations and assistance and support, the challenges that have arisen in the practice, as well as the various steps that victims' lawyers may take to enhance access, bearing in mind the jurisprudence and other relevant factors.

Reparations, assistance and support are relatively new features in international criminal law, and the practice remains in a state of flux. Victims' lawyers can play an important role in shaping and further developing the evolving practice for the ultimate benefit of victims. Therefore, this chapter explains both the current state of affairs and where relevant, posits ways in which victims' lawyers can potentially extend access to victims in these crucial areas.

13.2 Reparations

13.2.1 Overview and Comparisons of the Legal Frameworks

As will be described, both the ICC and ECCC include provisions in their legal frameworks relating to reparations for victims. Before these frameworks were adopted, there was little by way of precedent. Neither the Nuremberg[1] or Tokyo[2] tribunals, nor the *ad hoc* tribunals for Rwanda and the former Yugoslavia, nor the Special Court for Sierra Leone (SCSL), allowed for victims of the crimes under the jurisdiction of those tribunals to seek reparations before the tribunals. The statutes and rules of the latter three tribunals made clear that the judgments issued by them could be used by victims to pursue compensation before domestic courts.[3] Additional provisions outlined that as part of the penalty, the Trial Chambers could order one or more States to adopt provisional measures to freeze the assets of the accused, without prejudice to the rights of third parties,[4] or order the return to their rightful owners of any property and proceeds acquired by criminal conduct, including by means of duress.[5] In practice however, these provisions did not result in victims realising reparations.[6]

The initial draft of what became the ICC Statute made no provision for reparation either.[7] This draft, prepared by the International Law Commission, proposed that the Court be empowered to order that fines paid be transferred to a trust fund established by the UN Secretary-General for the benefit of victims of crime,

---

[1] See Article 28 of the Charter of the International Military Tribunal: 'In addition to any punishment imposed by it, the Tribunal shall have the right to deprive the convicted person of any stolen property and order its delivery to the Control Council for Germany' (1945 Charter of the International Military Tribunal 82 UNTS 280). Discussed in Moffett 2012, pp. 256–257 who indicates that the provision was never applied. The Tokyo tribunal had no such provision.

[2] The Potsdam Declaration made reference to reparation in Article 11: 'Japan shall be permitted to maintain such industries as will sustain … allow of the exaction of just reparations.' (The Potsdam Declaration, Proclamation By Heads of Governments, United States, United Kingdom, and China, 26 July 1945). However, this was not taken forward in the framework for the Tokyo Tribunal. See Charter of the International Military Tribunal for the Far East, Adopted at Tokyo, Japan, 19 January 1946.

[3] See Rule 106 common to the Rules of Procedure and Evidence of the International Criminal Tribunal for Rwanda (ITR/3/Rev. 1, (2015) (the 'ICTR RPE')) and the International Criminal Tribunal for Former Yugoslavia (IT/32/Rev. 49, (2013) (the 'ICTY RPE')), which provides that judgments establishing guilt are to be binding as to the criminal responsibility of the convicted person for the purpose of an action for compensation, which might be brought by victims in national courts. See also Rule 105 of the SCSL Rules of Procedure and Evidence, Rev. 14 (2012) (the 'SCSL RPE') and Statute of the STL, S/RES/1757 (2007) (the 'STL Statute'), Article 25.

[4] See ICTR and ICTY RPE, Rule 61(d). A similar provision is found in STL Rules of Procedure and Evidence STL-BD-2009-01-Rev.7-Corr. 1 (2015) (the 'STL RPE'), Rule 82(c).

[5] See ICTR and the ICTY RPE, Rule 105; SCSR RPE, Rule 104(c).

[6] Malmström 2001, pp. 373–384; De Brouwer 2005, pp. 394–400.

[7] See, International Law Commission, Draft Code of Crimes against the Peace and Security of Mankind, Report of the International Law Commission covering its 46th Session, 2 May–22 July 1994 49 UN Doc. A/49/10, Article. 47(3)(c).

foreshadowing in part the ICC's Trust Fund for Victims.[8] There was no independent role for victims to seek reparations before the Court. Similarly, the ECCC founding texts did not include provisions for reparations.[9] However in their final incarnations, the notion of reparations was incorporated into the mandates of these courts and armed with some of the hindsight of what were perceived as failings to victims at the *ad hoc* tribunals, thanks to strong advocacy, a growing awareness and acceptance of victims' rights in criminal proceedings.[10] Provisions on reparations were incorporated into the ICC Statute agreed in Rome and the Internal Rules eventually adopted by the ECCC.[11] In both of these courts, victims are able to apply for reparations for the harm they suffered as a result of the criminal acts for which a perpetrator has been convicted. The ICC may award reparations to or in respect of victims, following a conviction, including restitution, compensation and rehabilitation.[12] This award must be made against a convicted person or where appropriate, it may be made through a separately established Trust Fund for Victims.[13] At the ECCC, the chambers may award collective and moral reparations to civil parties, to be paid by the convicted person, or by recognition of an externally funded project.[14]

The trajectory of international criminal courts in the area of reparations appears to be one of slow recognition of the need to incorporate reparations into the mandates and procedures of these bodies. However, it is not a simple or neat trajectory. The Special Tribunal for Lebanon (STL) provides no possibilities for victims to pursue reparations before the Tribunal, despite the fact that the ability to seek reparations before criminal courts features in Lebanon's domestic criminal law. And, as will be described, in both the ICC and ECCC, the mandate to afford reparations has been applied with restraint, with the reparations afforded failing to approximate even remotely the internationally recognised standards for reparations relating to proportionality, adequacy and effectiveness.[15]

While the jurisprudence remains in its early stages, thus far judges have felt constrained by a combination of factors which have all impacted on the

---

[8] Ibid.

[9] Law on the Establishment of the Extraordinary Chambers in the Courts of Cambodia for the Prosecution of Crimes Committed during the period of Democratic Kampuchea, NS/RKM/1004/006 (2004).

[10] For an analysis of the negotiations leading to the inclusion of these provisions see, in relation to the ICC, Muttukumaru 1999, pp. 262–264; Donat-Cattin 1999, pp. 965–978; Ferstman 2002, p. 667. In relation to the ECCC, see Sperfeldt 2012, pp. 457–489; McGonigle 2009, pp. 127–149.

[11] See Rome Statute of the International Criminal Court, A/CONF.183/9 (2010) (the 'ICC Statute'), Article 75; ECCC Internal Rules, Rev. 9 (2015) (the 'ECCC Internal Rules'), Rule 23.

[12] ICC Statute, Article 75.

[13] Ibid., Article 79.

[14] ECCC Internal Rules, Rule 23*quinquies*.

[15] These standards are set out in a range of texts, including the UN Basic Principles and Guidelines on the Right to a Remedy and Reparation for Victims of Gross Violations of International Human Rights Law and Serious Violations of International Humanitarian Law, UN Doc. A/RES/60/147 (2005).

procedures and decisions they have chosen to adopt. First, the immense scale of the harm has underpinned judges' concerns about the manageability of the process. There is fear that the necessarily vast numbers of persons who will have suffered harm as a result of the crimes within the jurisdiction of these courts could make anything other than a restrained reparations process and its implementation unwieldy. Second, the approaches taken reflect an overriding concern about limited resources. Judges worry that awards should be capable of implementation bearing in mind convicted perpetrators' usual indigence and the limited additional sources to fund reparations. Third, judges are conscious of the limits of their mandates and the need not to overstep these in the reparations phase. There is concern to avoid even the slightest inference of State or other forms of responsibility in courts with mandates limited to determining individual criminal responsibility. This is despite the fact that it will often be collectives or other groupings (e.g. governments, rebel movements, criminal enterprises, companies) that have benefited financially from the commission of crimes carried out by the individual perpetrators.

13.2.2 Key Aspects of Reparations Before International Criminal Courts

This section focuses mainly on the ECCC and ICC, as the key bodies with an ability to award reparations to victims.

13.2.2.1 Provisional Measures: Assets

Most international criminal courts recognise the ability for the courts themselves, or States collaborating with them, to locate, freeze and seize assets of accused persons on a precautionary or provisional basis. In most instances, such procedures are designed to help secure custody over suspects who remain at large. The property and assets may eventually be used to contribute to the costs of defence, property may be returned to the rightful owners and in some instances the assets may be used to fund reparations to victims. Thus far, however, the various courts have had only minimal success with the recovery of assets, for a combination of reasons.

One of the main reasons for this failure is that property or assets of accused persons have not been located because the persons are impecunious, or States have not adequately cooperated with requests for the location and freezing of assets. A second reason is that in those tribunals where victims do not have the ability to participate directly in the proceedings, they have been forced to rely on the Prosecution to make requests, and due to the competing work priorities, investigations into the location of assets have invariably not been prioritised. Even where victims can participate directly in the proceedings, the Prosecution is tasked with carrying out investigations into assets and it is usually for it to engage the relevant chamber with a view to encouraging it to issue a request for cooperation. Despite the utility of so doing, victims' lawyers have rarely had the wherewithal to carry out their own investigations into assets and armed with such data, to press the Prosecution in its own investigation and/or to engage the Court directly to issue orders relating to the location and freezing of assets. A third reason is that not all courts have seen it is as their role to engage in efforts to locate and seize assets, or request States to cooperate in such endeavours. A fourth reason is that the provisions on precautionary measures tend to focus on such proceeds and instrumentalities of crime, and thus some courts have recognised that only such assets could be the subject of seizure orders, and/or the procedures put in place by States to cooperate with such requests have narrowly focused on such proceeds and instrumentalities of crime.

Some of these issues have arisen before the ICC and the ECCC. Many of the filings and orders issued by the Court remain confidential and it can therefore be difficult to piece together a clear picture of courts' practices in this regard. However, there is an increasing trend of de-classifying documents once the need for their confidentiality ceases. Albeit with some delay, the approach to precautionary assets and property orders is thus slowly becoming more apparent. Article 57(3)(e) of the ICC Statute provides that the Pre-Trial Chamber may 'seek the cooperation of States pursuant to Article 93, para 1(k), to take protective measures for the purpose of forfeiture, in particular for the ultimate benefit of victims.' Rule 99(1) of the ICC Rules of Procedure and Evidence[16] specifies that: 'the Pre-Trial Chamber, pursuant to Article 57, para 3(e), or the Trial Chamber, pursuant to Article 75, para 4, may, on its own motion or on the application of the Prosecutor or at the request of the victims or their legal representatives who have made a request for reparations or who have given a written undertaking to do so, determine whether measures should be adopted.' These provisions are of critical importance to the realisation of reparations awards, in those instances where there are assets and they are traceable. However, the wording of Article 93(1)(k) speaks about 'the identification, tracing and freezing or seizure of proceeds, property and assets and instrumentalities of crimes for the purpose of eventual forfeiture, without prejudice to the rights of *bona fide* third parties.' This would at first sight suggest that the precautionary measures focus on proceeds of crime, not simply assets for eventual victims, which differs from post-conviction enforcement.[17]

The interpretation of Article 57(3)(e) arose in *Kenyatta*. In that case, in 2011, Pre-Trial Chamber II had ordered the Registrar to prepare and transmit a request for cooperation to the competent authorities of the Republic of Kenya for

[16] ICC Rules of Procedure and Evidence, ICC-ASP/1/3 Corr.1 (Part.II-A) (2002) (the 'ICC RPE').

[17] See also ICC Statute, Article 75(4). See Discussion by Donat-Cattin 1999, p. 966.

purposes of identifying, tracing and freezing or seizing the property and assets belonging to or under the control of Mr. Kenyatta.[18] At a much later stage, the Registry brought to the attention of Trial Chamber V(b) the Kenyan Government's refusal to execute the Pre-Trial Chamber's request on the basis that Article 93(1)(k) of the Statute only applies at the post-conviction phase and then only to assets that could be considered to be the proceeds or instrumentalities of the crime. Trial Chamber V(b) held that the statutory framework does not require a nexus to be established with the proceeds or instrumentalities of the crime when ordering protective measures under Article 57(3)(e).[19] It further held that the term "forfeiture" may carry a broader meaning which encompasses an award for reparations.[20] Referring to a teleological interpretation of Article 57(3)(e) of the Statute, and to ensure that the relevant Trial Chamber will have recourse to such assets for the purpose of an eventual order for reparations, Trial Chamber V(b) held that it is necessary that protective measures are implemented at the earliest opportunity prior to the commencement of trial, after the issuance of a warrant of arrest or a summons to appear.[21] Judge Henderson, in his dissent, took the view that Article 57(3)(e) of the ICC Statute and Rule 99(1) of the ICC RPE do not authorise a chamber to request a State to take protective measures under Article 93(1) of the Statute for the purposes of an order for reparations. In his view, protective measures can be taken for the purposes of eventual forfeiture, which in appropriate circumstances can be transferred to the Trust Fund and thereafter used for the benefit of the victims in an award for reparations. Under Judge Henderson's analysis therefore, the forfeiture requirements (of the assets being linked to the proceeds and instrumentalities of crime) would appear to apply to protective measures.[22] It is unclear how other Trial Chambers will interpret Article 57(3)(e) or whether the issue will in future be decided more resolutely by the Appeals Chamber. The decision of the majority, if it holds, is a progressive interpretation of the statutory framework which should encourage victims' lawyers to actively engage with the Prosecution and the relevant chambers on the issue of asset orders, for the ultimate benefit of victims.

[18] ICC, *Prosecutor v. Uhuru Muigai Kenyatta*, Pre-Trial Chamber II, Decision Ordering the Registrar to Prepare and Transmit a Request for Cooperation to the Republic of Kenya for the Purpose of Securing the Identification, Tracing and Freezing or Seizure of Property and Assets of Francis Kirimi Muthaura, Uhuru Muigai Kenyatta and Mohammed Hussein Ali, ICC-01/09-02/11-42, 5 April 2011.

[19] ICC, *Prosecutor v. Uhuru Muigai Kenyatta*, Trial Chamber V(b), Decision on the implementation of the request to freeze assets, ICC-01/09-02/11-931, 8 July 2014, para 12.

[20] Ibid., para 12.

[21] Ibid., para 14.

[22] ICC, *Prosecutor v. Uhuru Muigai Kenyatta*, Trial Chamber V(b), Decision on the implementation of the request to freeze assets, Dissenting opinion of Judge Henderson, ICC-01/09-02/11-931-Anx, 8 July 2014, para 7.

Before the ECCC, lawyers representing civil parties had sought the Pre-Trial Chamber's assistance with the investigation of the location, tracing and implementing measures for the preservation, of accused persons' assets. However, the Pre-Trial Chamber adopted a restrictive analysis of the ECCC mandate.[23] It determined that there was no provision under applicable law or interest of a civil party or any other party that permits the Co-Investigating Judges to undertake investigative action for a matter that is not within the scope of the investigation as delimited by the Co-Prosecutors. In other words, the investigation was not focused on the assets of suspects; it was focused on the commission of crime. Given that the matter was not within the ongoing investigation, the civil parties could not, under the law of the ECCC, request that an investigation into the assets of suspects be undertaken. Notwithstanding the Pre-Trial Chamber's understanding that such provisions for provisional measures exist before other international courts, and despite the fact that the ECCC judges are the authors of their own limited provisions[24] (and thus could have presumably amended the Internal Rules should they have seen fit), the Pre-Trial Chamber held that:

> Contrary to the assertions of the Appellants, Internal Rule 113 does not give the Civil Parties the right to initiate enforcement of reparations at the pre-trial stage of a criminal proceeding. Internal Rule 23*quinquies* specifies that reparations can only be awarded against a convicted person. As reparations can only be awarded against a convicted person, reparations cannot be *enforced* against an unindicted, untried and unconvicted person. It is outside the jurisdiction of this Chamber to take measures to enforce a potential award of reparations prior to such time as the competent chamber has determined guilt following a trial upon indicted charges, recorded a conviction and determined an award of reparations, if any. While, as described below, the Civil Parties have an interest in the assets of the charged persons, neither the interest itself nor any right in respect of such interest has crystallised. Pursuant to the framework of this Court, the fact that no interest or right has crystallised is dispositive. Granting the requested relief would place the Pre-Trial Chamber and the Co-Investigating Judges in the position of acting beyond our collective jurisdiction.[25]

13.2.2.2 The Scope of Beneficiaries of Reparations

Given the nature of crimes within the jurisdiction of international criminal courts, there is potentially a very wide scope of beneficiaries who may be eligible to receive reparations. But resource constraints will necessitate that prosecutors and investigative judges be selective in their approach to international prosecutions.

---

[23] ECCC, *Case 002*, Pre-Trial Chamber, Decision on Appeal of Co-Lawyers for Civil Parties against Order on Civil Parties' Request for Investigative Actions Concerning all Properties Owned by the Charged Persons, Case No. 002/19-09-2007-ECCC/OCIJ (PTC 57), 4 August 2010.

[24] Ibid., paras 25 and 32.

[25] Ibid., para 23.

The mandate for courts to award reparations stems from their jurisdiction to consider and decide charges brought before them; there is no independent possibility for courts to determine reparations without a prior finding of guilt in respect of a particular accused person. It is therefore clear that not all victims of crimes within the jurisdiction of the relevant courts will fall within the potential class of beneficiaries for reparations awards, for the simple reason that no charges have been brought and/or proven which relate to their victimisation.

The approach to the issue of "scope" therefore has a profound impact on the realisation of reparations and in this respect is highly sensitive to, and critical for victims. Some of the determinations on the size and scale of the beneficiary class will be influenced by the approach taken by prosecutors or investigating judges in deciding what conduct to investigate and the charges to be brought. Victims, civil parties or their lawyers as the case may be, in practice do not have much ability to influence which cases are selected for prosecution.

If a perpetrator is not apprehended, reparation can be years away, if it is received at all, such as the situation in Sudan before the ICC. If, as happened with *Case 002* at the ECCC, there is a decision to sever a case into sub-cases with different charges to be heard in consecutive trials, the civil parties whose victimisation relates to the second sub-case may be forced to have a lengthy wait before their reparations claims can be determined.[26] Similarly, if there is an acquittal on all or some of the charges, and the Prosecutor decides not to appeal, as was the case in the *Katanga* case before the ICC,[27] the victims of those crimes will lose their opportunity for court-ordered reparations. The limited eligibility of victims can create further problems between victims who receive reparations and those who do not, thus creating a "reparation gap" and risking further victimisation or discontent by recognising only certain victims and not others.

Whilst victims and others have the possibility to inform prosecutors and investigators about the commission of crimes and tender evidence, they have no automatic standing to oblige that certain leads or lines of inquiry are pursued, nor an ability to appeal a decision not to pursue certain lines of enquiry, though they can have the right to be informed of such developments and to submit views and concerns.

In accordance with the ICC Statute, victims may be able to present their "views and concerns" should the Prosecutor decide not to initiate an investigation or not to prosecute.[28] However those with the main interest in ensuring that the

[26] Heindel 2013.

[27] ICC, Office of the Prosecutor, Statement of the Prosecutor of the International Criminal Court, Fatou Bensouda, on Germain Katanga's Notice of Discontinuance of his Appeal against his Judgment of Conviction, 25 June 2014, http://www.icc-cpi.int/en_menus/icc/press%20and%20media/press%20releases/pages/otp-statement-25-06-2014.aspx. Accessed 1 June 2015.

[28] See ICC Statute, Article 53(1)(c), (2)(c) and 3(b); ICC RPE, Rules 93 and 107.

Prosecutor undertakes full investigations that correspond with the nature, scale and gravity of the crimes are not able to invoke the Article; they have no standing to address the Court if the circumstances of their victimisation lie outside of the charges already before the Court.[29] Furthermore, if the Prosecutor decides to suspend an investigation or prosecution as opposed to ending it, it may not be sufficient to trigger a hearing before the relevant chamber, as it is always open to the Prosecution to revive the charges.[30] In certain circumstances, there may be scope for counsel to argue that a suspension constituted a *de facto* end to proceedings, however to date the ICC has not seen fit to limit or appear to limit the Prosecution's discretion in this way.

At the ECCC, civil parties have a greater role in contributing evidence to the Investigating Judges. In accordance with Rule 55(10), civil parties can request that the Co-Investigating Judges order or carry out a particular investigation. If the latter reject the request, civil parties may appeal. Civil parties can also appeal the Closing Order issued by the Co-Investigating Judges at the conclusion of the investigation, setting out an indictment or dismissing the case, so long as the Co-Prosecutors have also appealed.[31]

As part of any reparations award, judges must determine how closely connected the beneficiary class must be to the crimes for which perpetrators have ultimately been convicted.

Before the ICC, there was opportunity to consider this issue in the *Lubanga* case. In its decision establishing the principles and procedures to be applied to reparations,[32] Trial Chamber I did not provide a clear answer, holding more generally that 'a wholly flexible approach to determining factual matters is appropriate, taking into account the extensive and systematic nature of the crimes and the number of victims involved.'[33] On appeal, the Appeals Chamber determined that in the decision on reparations it was incumbent on the Court to go beyond the articulation of mere principles. It must go one step further and derive from these principles specific determinations and findings based on those principles which would form part of the order on reparations in the case.[34] The Appeals Chamber also made clear that an order for reparations, whether for individual or collective forms

---

[29] See Ferstman 2012, p. 801.

[30] ICC, *Prosecutor v. Thomas Lubanga Dyilo*, Pre-Trial Chamber I, Decision on the Requests of the Legal Representative for Victims VPRS 1–6 regarding "Prosecutor's Information on further Investigation", ICC-01/04-399, 26 September 2007.

[31] ECCC Internal Rules, Rule 67(5) and 74(4)(f).

[32] ICC, *Prosecutor v. Thomas Lubanga Dyilo*, Trial Chamber I, Decision establishing the principles and procedures to be applied to reparations, ICC-01/04-01/06-2904, 7 August 2012.

[33] Ibid., para 254.

[34] ICC, *Prosecutor v. Thomas Lubanga Dyilo,* Appeals Chamber, Judgment on the appeals against the "Decision establishing the principles and procedures to be applied to reparations" of 7 August 2012 with AMENDED order for reparations (Annex A) and public Annexes 1 and 2, ICC-01/04-01/06-3129, 3 March 2015, para 55.

of reparation or both, and irrespective of whether the award is to be made through the Trust Fund for Victims, must necessarily be made against the convicted perpetrator.[35]

Reparations 'must reflect the context from which they arise, which, at the Court, is a legal system of establishing *individual* criminal liability for crimes under the Statute. In the view of the Appeals Chamber, this context strongly suggests that reparation orders are intrinsically linked to the *individual* whose criminal liability is established in a conviction and whose culpability for those criminal acts is determined in a sentence.'[36] The Appeals Chamber in the *Lubanga* case stuck firmly to this principle. It made clear that because they were not included in the sentence, sexual and gender-based violence cannot be defined as a *harm* resulting from the crimes for which Mr. Lubanga was convicted.[37] This underscores the importance for victims' lawyers to take all possible steps to encourage the Prosecutor to bring charges relating to the full scale of victimisation; as held by the Appeals Chamber, the failure of the Prosecutor to do so cannot be remedied at the reparations stage:

> [T]he Appeals Chamber considers that the Trial Chamber's finding that the acts of sexual violence could not be attributed to Mr Lubanga amounts to concluding that the Trial Chamber did not establish that harm from sexual and gender-based violence resulted from the crimes for which Mr Lubanga was convicted, within the meaning of rule 85 (a) of the Rules of Procedure and Evidence. The Appeals Chamber is of the view that, having made the above-mentioned finding in the Sentencing Decision, the Trial Chamber was required to explain in the Impugned Decision how it nonetheless considered that Mr Lubanga should be liable for reparations in respect of the harm of sexual and gender-based violence. It did not do so. The Appeals Chamber therefore considers that Mr Lubanga cannot be held liable for reparations in respect of such harm and accordingly amends the Impugned Decision in this respect.[38]

Trial Chamber I in the *Lubanga* case noted that in its view, it would be inappropriate to limit reparations to the relatively small group of victims that participated in the trial and those who applied for reparations. It noted that in accordance with Rule 85 of the ICC RPE which defines the term 'victims', reparations *may* be granted to direct victims, who suffered harm resulting from the crimes of enlisting, conscripting and using children under the age of 15 in Ituri in the Democratic Republic of Congo (DRC), from 1 September 2002 to 13 August 2003; indirect victims, including family members of direct victims, along with individuals who intervened to help the victims or to prevent the commission of these crimes. Indirect victims need to demonstrate a close personal relationship between them

[35] Ibid., paras 69–76, 115.

[36] Ibid., para 65. See also, para 99.

[37] Ibid., para 196.

[38] Ibid., para 198.

and a direct victim, for instance as exists between a child soldier and his or her parents; and legal entities, such as NGOs or hospitals.[39] This aspect of the Trial Chamber's decision was affirmed on appeal.

Before the ECCC, this issue was canvassed in the *Case 001* reparations decision and the appellate decision. The approach to the nexus question has been much more narrowly construed by the ECCC, where only civil parties (who must demonstrate that they suffered physical, material or psychological injury as a direct consequence of at least one of the crimes alleged against the Charged Person),[40] are entitled to apply for and obtain reparations. The Trial Chamber held that the injury suffered by a civil party must result directly from the criminal conduct of the Accused. This requirement of a direct link between the crime and the injury suffered by the victim does not restrict the right to reparations to the target of the criminal act. As such immediate family members, and in exceptional circumstances members of a victim's extended family, who also suffered harm as a result of the crimes may be eligible.[41]

The requirement of a direct link between the crime and injury suffered was upheld in the appeal judgment. The Supreme Court Chamber noted however that 'absent any limiting provision, the category of indirect victims is not restricted to any specific class of persons such as family members. It may encompass common law spouses, distant relatives, friends, *de facto* adopters and adoptees, or other beneficiaries, provided that the injury on their part can be demonstrated. On the other hand, persons who did not suffer injury will not be considered indirect victims even if they were immediate family members of the direct victim.'[42]

13.2.2.3 The Relationship Between Victims' Participation in the Criminal Procedure and Reparations

Victims' participation affects reparation in a number of ways. The right to the truth, as a form of reparation,[43] is one way in which reparation can be assured; unveiling the truth is a form of reparation, and victims' participation is integral to that end. In addition, victims' participation may allow eliciting information on harms caused by the accused, which can positively impact victims' claims for

[39] ICC, *Prosecutor v. Thomas Lubanga Dyilo*, Trial Chamber I, Decision establishing the principles and procedures to be applied to reparations, ICC-01/04-01/06-2904, 7 August 2012, paras 187, 194–195.

[40] ECCC Internal Rules, Rule 23*bis*.

[41] ECCC, *Case 001*, Trial Chamber, Judgment, Case No. 001/18-07-2007/ECCC/TC, 26 July 2010, paras 642–643.

[42] ECCC, *Case 001*, Supreme Court Chamber, Appeal Judgment, Case No. 001/18-07-2007/ECCC/SC, 3 February 2012, para 418.

[43] UN Basic Principles and Guidelines on the Right to a Remedy and Reparation for Victims of Gross Violations of International Human Rights Law and Serious Violations of International Humanitarian Law, UN Doc. A/RES/60/147 (2005), para 22(b).

reparation. Victim participants or civil parties have been accorded certain rights throughout the trial proceedings such as the right to review evidence, adduce new evidence, call witnesses, put questions to witnesses, and to raise more generalised views and concerns. These can be an opportunity to contribute actively to the trial process which can itself enhance victims' sense of agency and can also help substantiate their eventual claims for reparations. Even though there may be a formal hearing on reparations at the end of a trial, reparations proceedings should not be understood as isolated from the trial proceedings.

At the ICC, Regulation 56 of the Regulations of the Court stipulates that '[t]he Trial Chamber may hear the witnesses and examine the evidence for the purposes of a decision on reparations in accordance with Article 75, para 2, at the same time as for the purposes of trial.' Whether it will do so will depend on whether 'it is in the interests of individual witnesses or victims, or if it will assist with the efficient disposal of issues that may arise for determination.'[44] While the participation of a victim at the trial is not a prerequisite for claiming reparations, the finding that reparations issues may possibly be considered during the trial underscores the need for victims' interests to be protected during this phase.[45] At the ECCC, civil parties' ability to engage in the trial process is more extensive, even taking into account the limitations introduced with the revisions to the Internal Rules in 2008, according to which civil parties' interests are represented by the Civil Party Lead Co-Lawyers.

13.2.2.4 Victim Applications for Reparations and the Determination of the Award

The ECCC Internal Rules, as well as the ICC Statute and RPE set out ways in which victims may apply for reparations.

At the ECCC, this is one of the rights within the civil party system. Victims may apply to become civil parties and once they are granted this status, they are entitled to submit claims for reparations in accordance with Rule 23. As such there is no further need to demonstrate the harm suffered by the individual and its nexus to the crimes, as this will have already been proven as part of the civil party application process. The ECCC have interpreted its mandate narrowly, and the judges have only incorporated into their Internal Rules the possibility to award collective and moral reparations; no individual awards and no monetary payments are allowed under the Internal Rules. These restrictions are at the heart of the ECCC's arguably underrated understanding of its role. The Supreme Court Chamber has

---

[44] ICC, *Prosecutor v. Thomas Lubanga Dyilo*, Trial Chamber I, Decision on Victims' Participation, ICC-01/04–01/06, 18 January 2008, para 122.

[45] Ferstman and Goetz 2009, pp. 336–338.

said that '[o]n the policy level, it should be emphasised that ECCC criminal proceedings ought to be considered as a contribution to the process of national reconciliation, possibly a starting point for the reparation scheme, and not the ultimate remedy for nation-wide consequences of the tragedies during the DK. As such, the ECCC cannot be overloaded with utopian expectations that would ultimately exceed the attainable goals of transitional justice.'[46] These limitations have influenced the application process, as has the desire for efficiency and strong prospects for implementation.

The procedure for applications has evolved from *Case 001* to *Case 002*. In *Case 001*, in order to be granted, reparations awards needed to qualify as collective and moral reparations and be sufficiently certain or ascertainable to give rise to an enforceable order against the Accused.[47] The Trial Chamber made it clear that it did not see it as its role, nor did it believe it had the mandate, to determine itself, or indeed to award, adequate and effective reparations awards. Instead, it could only assess and approve, as appropriate, the necessarily constrained proposals made by civil parties:

> The Chamber is, additionally, unable to issue orders where the object of the claim is uncertain or unascertainable, and which are incapable of enforcement. Accordingly, a prerequisite to the grant of an award is the clear specification of the nature of the relief sought, its link to the harm caused by the Accused that it seeks to remedy, and the quantum of the indemnity or amount of reparation sought from the Accused to give effect to it. Placing the burden on the Chamber to substitute its own decision in these areas is inconsistent with a mechanism that is claimant-driven, and is also irreconcilable with the need for a fair and expeditious trial, the envisaged duration of the ECCC and the resources at its disposal.[48]

This *laissez-faire* approach, while privileging the wishes of civil parties, also proved problematic, in that very little guidance was provided to civil parties in advance of their filings of the level of precision expected by the Trial Chamber to be considered 'sufficiently certain or ascertainable.' Consequently, the bulk of the requests were rejected by the Chamber on the grounds of lack of specificity or that they fell outside the mandate of the ECCC. The Trial Chamber agreed to the civil parties' request that their names and those of the immediate victims be included in the final judgment, including a specification as to their connection with the crimes committed at S-21 and to the compilation and publication of all statements of apology made by the convicted Kaing Guek Eav during his trial. These rulings were confirmed on appeal.

For *Case 002* and subsequent cases, as a result of an amendment that came into force subsequent to *Case 001*, the Internal Rules now indicate that the Civil Party

---

[46] ECCC, *Case 001*, Supreme Court Chamber, Appeal Judgment, Case No. 001/18-07-2007/ECCC/SC, 3 February 2012, para 655.

[47] ECCC, *Case 001*, Trial Chamber, Judgment, Case No. 001/18-07-2007/ECCC/TC, 26 July 2010, para 651.

[48] Ibid., para 665.

Lead Co-Lawyers must collect from the civil party lawyers the reparations proposals pertaining to their clients and consolidate these into a single submission put forward to the chambers:

> Reparations shall be requested in a single submission, which may seek a limited number of awards. This submission shall provide:
>
> (a) a description of the awards sought;
> (b) reasoned argument as to how they address the harm suffered and specify, where applicable, the Civil Party group within the consolidated group to which they pertain; and
> (c) in relation to each award, the single, specific mode of implementation described in Rule 23*quinquies*(3)(a)–(b) of the ECCC Internal Rules sought.[49]

At the ICC, Article 75(1) of the ICC Statute provides that the Court shall 'establish principles relating to reparations to, or in respect of, victims.' Based on these principles, the Court may 'determine the scope and extent of any damage, loss and injury to, or in respect of, victims.' Article 75(2) authorises the Court either to 'make an order directly against a convicted person specifying appropriate reparations to, or in respect of, victims, including restitution, compensation and rehabilitation' or, where appropriate, to 'order that the award for reparations be made through the Trust Fund provided for in Article 79.' The provision does not specify whether such principles should be determined within the context of a particular situation or case before the Court or by the plenary of judges outside of the context of any case. Thus far, the judges have taken a case-by-case approach. At the time of writing, the *Lubanga* case had reached the reparations phase, and as indicated earlier, in that case the Trial Chamber judges delegated the task of determining reparations to the Trust Fund for Victims. On appeal, the Appeals Chamber made clear that 'a convicted person's liability for reparations must be proportionate to the harm caused and, *inter alia*, his or her participation in the commission of the crimes for which he or she was found guilty, in the specific circumstances of the case.'[50]

There are two ways in which reparation claims may be considered by the ICC.

First, victims may submit applications for reparations. Rule 94 of the ICC RPE sets out the particulars that applicants must provide to substantiate their reparations claims, which include *inter alia* a description of the injury, loss or harm and where restitution of assets, property or other tangible items is sought, a description of them as well as supporting documentation. The Registry has incorporated a list

[49] ECCC Internal Rules, Rule 23*quinquies*(2).

[50] ICC, *Prosecutor v. Thomas Lubanga Dyilo,* Appeals Chamber, Judgment on the appeals against the "Decision establishing the principles and procedures to be applied to reparations" of 7 August 2012 with AMENDED order for reparations (Annex A) and public Annexes 1 and 2, ICC-01/04-01/06-3129, 3 March 2015, para 118.

of questions for victims, who may be individuals or organisations, in its standard application forms for a request for participation in the proceedings and reparations at the ICC. These include open-ended questions about the harm, loss and/or injury suffered, what the victim is seeking, and who the benefit should go to (the victim, his or her family and/or community).[51] In the *Lubanga* case, at the time of the issuance of the Trial Chamber's decision on reparations, 85 applications for reparations had been received.

Second, the Court may determine reparations on its own initiative *proprio motu*, regardless of whether any application has been made by victims. The ability for the Court to determine reparations *proprio motu* recognises that not all individuals who may be deserving of reparations will be in a position to apply to the Court, and that this should not prevent the Court from determining reparations in a general or specific way. It is made clear that these powers should be exercised on an exceptional basis only,[52] though the criteria for determining what may constitute such an exceptional situation are not spelt out and are likely to be considered on a case-by-case basis by the Court. As indicated, Trial Chamber I in the *Lubanga* case made reference to the importance of not restricting reparations awards to those who apply:

> All victims are to be treated fairly and equally as regards reparations, irrespective of whether they participated in the trial proceedings. Notwithstanding the submissions of the defence and the legal representatives of victims, it would be inappropriate to limit reparations to the relatively small group of victims that participated in the trial and those who applied for reparations.[53]

Under Rule 95 of the ICC RPE, should the Court decide to utilise these *proprio motu* powers, it shall request the Registrar to notify this intention to the defendant(s) (i.e. the person(s) against whom the Court is considering making a determination), and to the extent possible, to victims and other interested persons or interested States.

The ICC Statute provides that reparations may be awarded on an individualised basis or, where it is deemed appropriate, on a collective basis or both. In the decision on reparations in the *Lubanga* case, despite the fact that a number of individuals submitted applications for individualised reparations, Trial Chamber I favoured collective reparations in that case, and considered as appropriate the Trust Fund for Victims' recommended 'community-based' approach, which, it held 'would be more beneficial and have greater utility than individual awards, given the limited

---

[51] These forms are available on the website of the Court, here: http://www.icc-cpi.int/en_menus/icc/structure%20of%20the%20court/victims/Pages/forms.aspx. Accessed 1 June 2015.

[52] Article 75(1) of the ICC Statute refers to 'on its own motion *in exceptional circumstances*' (emphasis added).

[53] ICC, *Prosecutor v. Thomas Lubanga Dyilo*, Trial Chamber I, Decision establishing the principles and procedures to be applied to reparations, ICC-01/04-01/06-2904, 7 August 2012, para 187.

funds available and the fact that this approach does not require costly and resource intensive verification procedures.'[54] The Appeals Chamber affirmed Trial Chamber I's approach to the extent that the harm suffered by members of the community meets the eligibility standard for reparations.[55] It held that 'when only *collective* reparations are awarded pursuant to Rule 98(3) of the ICC Rules, a Trial Chamber is not required to rule on the merits of the individual requests for reparations.'[56] It determined that applicants did not have an intrinsic right to have their applications considered individually. In reaching its decision, it made note of the fact that the applicants had included in their applications submissions relating to both individual *and* collective awards: 'through their Legal Representatives, the victims who had filed requests for individual reparations also supported reparations being awarded on a collective basis and made submissions relevant to the design and nature of any eventual collective reparation award.'[57] The reference by the Appeals Chamber to such 'in the alternative' submissions appears somewhat disingenuous, and is a lesson to counsel to take care with the making of such submissions. At the time of writing, the reparations implementation procedure is still ongoing in the *Lubanga* case, with Trial Chamber II recently issuing its order approving the symbolic reparations project proposed by the Trust Fund for Victims.[58]

The Statute further sets out that reparations may include restitution, compensation and/or rehabilitation.[59] In the decision on reparations in the *Lubanga* case, Trial Chamber I makes clear that 'this list is not exclusive. Other types of reparations, for instance those with a symbolic, preventative or transformative value, may also be appropriate. As set out above, a gender-sensitive approach should be applied when determining the manner in which reparations are to be applied.'[60] In coming to a decision on the appropriate form(s) and scope of reparations, the provisions allow for the appointment of appropriate experts to assist the Court in determining the scope, extent of any damage, loss and injury to, or in respect of victims and to suggest various options concerning the appropriate types and modalities of reparations. The Court is also obligated to invite, as appropriate,

---

[54] Ibid., para 274.

[55] ICC, *Prosecutor v. Thomas Lubanga Dyilo*, Appeals Chamber, Judgment on the appeals against the "Decision establishing the principles and procedures to be applied to reparations" of 7 August 2012 with AMENDED order for reparations (Annex A) and public Annexes 1 and 2, ICC-01/04-01/06-3129, 3 March 2015, para 214.

[56] Ibid., para 152.

[57] Ibid., para 156.

[58] ICC, *Prosecutor v. Thomas Lubanga Dyilo*, The Trust Fund for Victims, Public redacted version of the Filing regarding symbolic collective reparations projects, ICC-01/04-01/06-3223-Red, 19 September 2016, para 13; ICC, *Prosecutor v. Thomas Lubanga Dyilo*, Trial Chamber II, Order approving the proposed plan of the Trust Fund for Victims in relation to symbolic collective reparations, ICC-01/04-01/06-3251, 21 October 2016. For details on these developments, see Chap. 1.

[59] ICC Statute, Article 75(1).

[60] ICC, *Prosecutor v. Thomas Lubanga Dyilo*, Trial Chamber I, Decision establishing the principles and procedures to be applied to reparations, ICC-01/04-01/06-2904, 7 August 2012, para 222.

victims or their legal representatives, the convicted person as well as interested persons and interested States to make observations on the reports of the experts.[61]

Rule 98(1) provides that 'individual awards for reparations shall be made directly against a convicted person', and paras 2–4 detail modalities for using the Trust Fund for Victims to allocate or distribute the reparations awards made by the Court to victims. Paragraph 2 provides that the Court may order that awards for reparations against a convicted person be deposited with the Trust Fund where at the time of making the order it is impossible or impracticable to make individual awards directly to each victim, whereas paras 3 and 4 provide that awards for reparations be made through the Trust Fund, 'where the number of the victims and the scope, forms and modalities of reparations makes a collective award more appropriate,' or when made 'to an intergovernmental, international or national organization approved by the Trust Fund.' Paragraph 5 provides that 'other resources of the Trust Fund may be used for the benefit of victims subject to the provisions of Article 79.' In the decision on reparations in the *Lubanga* case, Trial Chamber I decided to make the award of reparations through the Trust Fund.[62]

13.2.2.5 Appeals

Both the ICC and ECCC allow victims to appeal reparations orders. At the ICC, this is the only time in the trial process when victims can lodge on their own motion an appeal,[63] whereas before the ECCC, the opportunity to appeal reparations orders is part of the wider set of procedural rights afforded to civil parties.

At the ECCC, the reparations order issued in the course of the judgment on *Case 001* was appealed. The Supreme Court Chamber of the ECCC issued its decision on 3 February 2012.

At the ICC, in the *Lubanga* case, the Appeals Chamber issued its decision on 3 March 2015. Despite the fact that the ICC RPE indicates that appeals 'shall be heard as expeditiously as possible',[64] it took two and a half years for the Appeals Chamber to issue its decision. In a preliminary decision on procedural matters concerning the conduct of the appeal,[65] the ICC Appeals Chamber determined that

---

[61] ICC Statute, Article 75(3); ICC RPE, Rule 97(2).

[62] ICC, *Prosecutor v. Thomas Lubanga Dyilo*, Trial Chamber I, Decision establishing the principles and procedures to be applied to reparations, ICC-01/04-01/06-2904, 7 August 2012, paras 269–275.

[63] Article 82(4) of the ICC Statute provides that 'A legal representative of the victims, the convicted person or a bona fide owner of property adversely affected by an order under Article 75 may appeal against the order for reparations, as provided in the Rules of Procedure and Evidence.'

[64] ICC RPE, Rule 156(4).

[65] ICC, *Prosecutor v. Thomas Lubanga Dyilo*, Appeals Chamber, Decision on the admissibility of the appeals against Trial Chamber I's "Decision establishing the principles and procedures to be applied to reparations" and directions on the further conduct of proceedings, 14 December 2012.

the convicted person has an unencumbered right to appeal orders for reparations, regardless of whether the convicted person is adversely affected by the decision.[66] Furthermore, the Appeals Chamber decided that the individuals who are allowed to appeal an order for reparations are a wider group than just those victims who participated in the trial proceedings or sentencing phase. They may also include other persons who claim to have suffered harm as a result of the crimes in relation to which the accused was convicted and who request reparations.[67] This is thus significantly wider than the ECCC framework where only those victims who were recognised as civil parties may lodge an appeal. The ICC Appeals Chamber also indicated that while persons not yet identified as victims may have valid concerns which might appropriately be taken up in the course of the appeal, those individuals do not have the right, exercised through counsel, to bring an appeal.[68]

13.2.2.6 Enforcement of Awards

A central concern to those international criminal courts that have the possibility to award reparations is how these awards will be enforced. If awards are made against convicted perpetrators and these persons are indigent, there is a likelihood that the awards would remain incapable of enforcement. At the domestic level, most courts have the practice of making reparation awards that correspond to the harm that claimants suffer, irrespective of whether these awards are capable of being enforced. Successful claimants would need to take separate and additional measures to enforce domestic damage awards, which might consist of orders to freeze assets, garnishing orders or the like. Some would argue that awarding damages that correspond to the level of harm irrespective of the capacity for enforcement is an important acknowledgement by courts of the significance, both in terms of quality and quantum, of the harm victims suffered. Neither the ICC Trial Chamber I in the *Lubanga* case nor the ECCC have taken this approach. The ECCC Supreme Court Chamber has articulated that

> [c]onsidering the *sui generis* and dual private/public character of the ECCC reparations regime, this Chamber holds that an award that, in all probability, can never be enforced, i.e., is *de facto* fictitious, would belie the objective of *effective* reparation and would be confusing and frustrating for the victims. Unlike in the civil action, where seeking a title of execution against an indigent defendant is based on a choice and private interest of the plaintiff, in proceedings that have elements of reparations, the effectiveness requirement mandates that there be a tangible availability of funds.[69]

[66] Ibid., para 66.

[67] Ibid., para 69.

[68] Ibid., para 72.

[69] ECCC, *Case 001,* Supreme Court Chamber, Appeal Judgment, Case No. 001/18-07-2007/ECCC/SC, 3 February 2012, para 667.

Before the ICC, Trial Chamber I determined that Mr. Lubanga's indigence was relevant to whether he should be liable for any reparations awarded. However, the Appeals Chamber overruled this approach. It determined that indigence is not an obstacle to the imposition of liability for reparations on the convicted person, because assets of the convicted perpetrator may in principle be located and seized at some future date.[70]

Both the ICC and ECCC provide that reparations awards are to be made against convicted perpetrators. In the case of the ICC, a framework is established for the cooperation of States in the search and seizure of assets and other property of the accused, as described in Sect. 13.2.2.1 above. In addition, States parties are obliged to give effect to fines and forfeitures ordered by the Court, as well as reparations orders. Rule 217 of the ICC Rules provides that: 'the Presidency shall, as appropriate, seek cooperation and measures for enforcement [...] as well as transmit copies of relevant orders to any State with which the sentenced person appears to have direct connection by reason of either nationality, domicile or habitual residence or by virtue of the location of the sentenced person's assets and property or with which the victim has such connection.' Rule 218(3) further provides that:

> In order to enable States to give effect to an order for reparations, the order shall specify:
>
> (a) The identity of the person against whom the order has been issued;
> (b) In respect of reparations of a financial nature, the identity of the victims to whom individual reparations have been granted, and, where the award for reparations shall be deposited with the Trust Fund, the particulars of the Trust Fund for the deposit of the award; and
> (c) The scope and nature of the reparations ordered by the Court, including, where applicable, the property and assets for which restitution has been ordered.

States would not have the ability to modify the reparations orders specified by the Court.[71] The correct procedure is instead for persons affected by reparations orders to appeal the Court's reparations decision. In accordance with these provisions, it is envisioned, at least as a matter of principle, that the Trial Chamber may order reparations without having previously identified the assets. Clearly however, it is most advantageous for assets to be identified much earlier in the process so that there is less chance of dissipation and they can be frozen and made available to enforce reparations orders following a conviction. The ECCC Internal Rules have no comparable provisions for securing the assets of accused persons either on

[70] ICC, *Prosecutor v. Thomas Lubanga Dyilo*, Appeals Chamber, Judgment on the appeals against the "Decision establishing the principles and procedures to be applied to reparations" of 7 August 2012 with AMENDED order for reparations (Annex A) and public Annexes 1 and 2, ICC-01/04-01/06-3129, 3 March 2015, paras 102–105.

[71] ICC RPE, Rule 219.

a protective basis or following conviction. The Internal Rules simply provide that after the final judgment is delivered, 'the enforcement of reparations shall be made at the initiative of a Civil Party.'[72]

States parties clearly have the obligation to enforce reparations orders emanating from the ICC. However, it is not evident how national courts will deal with the competing claims for assets, or how they will assign priorities in order to adjudicate between these claims. For instance, reparations orders against former heads of State or senior officials may give rise to competing claims against the perpetrator for corruption or misappropriation of State. There may also be additional creditors and/or victims who did not apply through the ICC reparations process, whose claims would need to be adjudicated by national courts. In certain cases, assets belonging to perpetrators may have been frozen pursuant to Security Council or other sanctions regimes, and the ability of the ICC to obtain control of those assets for the purposes of reparations is untested. As a matter of principle, States' obligations pursuant to Article 103 of the UN Charter would trump any obligations they have to cooperate with the Court, however the ability of the Security Council to order the transfer of assets to the Court is also untested. The Relationship Agreement between the International Criminal Court and the United Nations[73] provides no guidance.

In the event that property or assets are located and frozen, a question arises as to the circumstances and modalities in which they will be made accessible for the purposes of reparations. The ICC will have a number of uses for the assets which go beyond reparations, such as for instance, the payment of defendants' legal costs that had, prior to the location of the assets, been covered by legal aid. In accordance with Rule 221(1) of the ICC RPE, the Presidency is mandated to decide on the disposition or allocation of such assets. Of note, Rule 221(2) specifies that the Presidency 'shall give priority to the enforcement of measures concerning reparations to victims.' In the *Lubanga* case, this Rule was inapplicable given the absence of assets in the custody of the Court. The Regulations of the Court provide no further clarity,[74] though Regulation 117 affirms that the Presidency shall monitor the financial situation of the sentenced person on an ongoing basis, even following completion of a sentence of imprisonment.[75] The Appeals Chamber made reference to this provision when determining that the indigence of a convicted perpetrator at the time of issuance of the reparations order should not

[72] ECCC Internal Rules, Rule 113(1).

[73] ICC, Negotiated Relationship Agreement between the International Criminal Court and the United Nations, ICC-ASP/3/Res.1 (2004).

[74] See Regulation 116(2) of the ICC Regulations of the Court, ICC-BD/01-03-11 (2011).

[75] ICC Regulations of the Court, Regulation 117.

impede the Trial Chamber from determining his or her liability.[76] However, the Appeals Chamber did not address the issue as to what will happen to assets which come into the Court's possession after the closure of reparations phase of a case. On the one hand, the possible eventuality of such a late receipt of assets could be an important rationale for victims' legal representatives to encourage the Court to order reparations that are adequate and effective, even if the means to enforce such reparations are not immediately available to the Court. As indicated, this was not the approach taken by Trial Chamber I in the *Lubanga* case, where the decision to make the award through the Trust Fund was largely based on the absence of immediately available assets. However, it is consistent with the approach taken by the Appeals Chamber. On the other hand, the Statute does not provide a clear avenue for victims' legal representatives to seek to re-open reparations proceedings after the close of a case.

Both the ICC and the Special African Chambers make reference to trust funds, which could be used to enforce court-ordered reparations. The ICC Trust Fund for Victims has been established for some time whereas no trust fund has been established yet in connection with the work of the Special African Chambers.

As will be further described, the ICC Trust Fund has a dual mandate. It may use the voluntary funds it collects to provide assistance to victims and their families outside the context of a case. The Court may also award court-ordered reparations through the Trust Fund where it is most practicable to do so. These court-ordered reparations are funded by fines and forfeitures, but particularly where there have been none, the Court has clarified that the voluntary funds collected by the Trust Fund may be applied to the enforcement of reparations awards. In the decision on reparations in the *Lubanga* case, Trial Chamber I held that:

> [W]hen the convicted person has no assets, if a reparations award is made 'through' the Trust Fund, the award is not limited to the funds and assets seized and deposited with the Trust Fund, but the award can, at least potentially, be supported by the Trust Fund's own resources. [...] Regulation 56 of the Regulations of the TFV imposes an obligation on the TFV's Board of Directors to complement the resources collected from a convicted person with 'the other resources of the Trust Fund', providing [sic] the Board of Directors make all reasonable efforts to manage the Fund taking into consideration the need to provide adequate resources to complement payments for awards under Rule 98(3) and (4) of the Rules. In the Chamber's view, the wording of Regulation 56 of the Regulations of the TFV suggests that the 'need to provide adequate resources' includes the need to fund reparation awards. In circumstances when the Court orders reparations against an indigent convicted person, the Court may draw upon 'other resources' that the TFV has made reasonable efforts to set aside.[77]

---

[76] ICC, *Prosecutor v. Thomas Lubanga Dyilo*, Appeals Chamber, Judgment on the appeals against the "Decision establishing the principles and procedures to be applied to reparations" of 7 August 2012 with AMENDED order for reparations (Annex A) and public Annexes 1 and 2, ICC-01/04-01/06-3129, 3 March 2015, para 104.

[77] ICC, *Prosecutor v. Thomas Lubanga Dyilo*, Trial Chamber I, Decision establishing the principles and procedures to be applied to reparations, ICC-01/04-01/06-2904, 7 August 2012, para 71.

The Trial Chamber considered this interpretation to be consistent with the approach adopted by Pre-Trial Chamber I, according to which, 'the responsibility of the Trust Fund is first and foremost to ensure that sufficient funds are available in the eventuality of a Court reparation order pursuant to Article 75 of the Statute.'[78]

This holding was reversed on appeal. In particular, the Appeals Chamber made clear that it was for the Trust Fund for Victims, in the exercise of its full discretion, to apply its voluntary funds towards the implementation of a reparations award against an indigent convicted perpetrator. The Court did not have the power to oblige the Trust Fund for Victims to apply its voluntary resources in this way.[79]

The ECCC has not established a Trust Fund, even though this could arguably have been established by the judges as part of their revision of the Internal Rules. Amidst the calls from civil society to establish some form of fund or related mechanism to ensure that reparations awards could be implemented, the ECCC judges instead took the decision to allow the Lead Co-Lawyers to identify specific projects that appropriately give effect to reparations. In order for these specific projects to be recognised by the Trial Chambers as reparations awards, they will need to have been 'designed or identified in cooperation with the Victims Support Section and have secured sufficient external funding.'[80] In essence, this places the burden on civil parties to determine and agree on projects which amount to collective and moral reparations and seek independent funding for such projects. Thereafter the Trial Chamber may 'recognise' these projects as reparations. This limits to the greatest possible extent the role of the ECCC Trial Chamber, to rubber-stamping projects developed with external funding by the civil parties.[81]

13.3 Assistance and Support to Victims

Some of the *ad hoc* tribunals and the International Criminal Court have, over time, developed programmes of assistance and support to witnesses, which go beyond the witness support provided to those coming to testify for the Prosecution in court hearings.

---

[78] Ibid., para 272. See also *Situation in Democratic Republic of* Congo, Pre-Trial Chamber I, Decision on the Notification of the Board of Directors of the Trust Fund for Victims in accordance with Regulation 50 of the Regulations of the Trust Fund, 11 April 2008, ICC-01/04-492, p. 7.

[79] ICC, *Prosecutor v. Thomas Lubanga Dyilo*, Appeals Chamber, Judgment on the appeals against the "Decision establishing the principles and procedures to be applied to reparations" of 7 August 2012 with AMENDED order for reparations (Annex A) and public Annexes 1 and 2, ICC-01/04-01/06-3129, 3 March 2015, paras 111–114.

[80] ECCC Internal Rules, Rule 23*quinquies*(3)(b).

[81] The development of this narrow 'recognition' mandate is explored in Sperfeldt 2012, p. 457.

At the ICTR, there was concern that witnesses' basic needs were not being met, nor were they benefiting from physical and psychological rehabilitation. This was in contrast to the extensive measures in place to support accused persons in custody. It was understood that these gaps, if left unaddressed, had the potential to undermine the positive impact of justice before the Tribunal. A Trust Fund support programme for witnesses and potential witnesses was established in 2000 to provide measures of support to 'ensure that [witnesses] receive relevant support, including physical and psychological rehabilitation, especially counselling in cases of rape and sexual assault; and to develop short term and long term plans for the protection of witnesses who have testified before the Tribunal and who fear a threat to their life, property or family.'[82] The ICTR has also provided medical support and counselling to mainly sexual violence witnesses via a clinic it established in Kigali, Rwanda, including HIV-AIDS diagnosis and treatment. Important as a matter of principle, the mandate of the programme significantly evolved over time. However, it suffered from a range of controversies and insufficient funding has limited its effectiveness.[83] The SCSL RPE has taken on board many of the ICTR's rehabilitative goals. For instance, pursuant to Rule 34 of the SCSL RPE, the Witnesses and Victims Section of the SCSL is mandated to support witnesses, victims who appear before the Court, and others who are at risk on account of testimony given by such witnesses, in accordance with their particular needs and circumstances. As part of this mandate, the Section is mandated to provide them with 'adequate protective measures and security arrangements and develop long- and short-term plans for their protection and support' and 'ensure that they receive relevant support, counselling and other appropriate assistance, including medical assistance, physical and psychological rehabilitation, especially in cases of rape, sexual assault and crimes against children.'[84] The ICTY's mandate is more limited; it can provide counselling and support, however there is no reference in its RPE to physical and psychological rehabilitation or the long term protection of victims.[85]

The ICC Trust Fund for Victims also has a support mandate. The main difference between the ICTR or SCSL and the ICC models is that the former focus on support to witnesses—mainly those who testified at trial, whereas the latter's assistance mandate is geared to the much wider constellation of victims of crimes within the jurisdiction of the court, the majority of whom will have very little interaction with the ICC. It is also highly discretionary; thus far, the Trust Fund has not carried out activities in all or most active 'situation' countries, but has chosen to concentrate its activities mainly in DRC and Uganda. Victims' lawyers, civil society groups working with victims and others may alert the Trust Fund to needy

[82] ICTR RPE, Rule 34.

[83] See generally, Haslam 2007, pp. 57, 66–69; De Brouwer 2007, pp. 216–217.

[84] SCSL RPE, Rule 34(A)(ii) and (iii).

[85] See ICTY RPE, Rule 34.

victims however they have little opportunity to insist on a shift to the Trust Fund's orientation, other than through general public reporting. For instance, victims and civil society in Kenya have sought for many years to encourage the Trust Fund to become active in that country, though at the time of writing, no activities had been planned.

In accordance with Rule 98(5) of the ICC RPE, the emphasis of the Trust Fund's assistance mandate is on victims and their families who have suffered physical, psychological and/or material harm as a result of crimes within the jurisdiction of the Court.[86] The Trust Fund can entertain such assistance when the Trust Fund considers that it is necessary to provide such support[87] and outside of the boundaries of any ongoing criminal case and irrespective of any conviction.

This assistance and support mandate operates outside of and distinct from any role that the Trust Fund has to enforce court-ordered reparations. One worry of the drafters was the potential for the assistance mandate of the Trust Fund to negatively impact, or appears to so impact, on the impartiality of ongoing court proceedings. In order to avoid those potentialities, the Regulations of the Trust Fund set out a procedure whereby, when the Trust Fund wishes to engage its assistance mandate, it is obligated to notify the Court of its intention to undertake specified activities, and provide an opportunity for the relevant chamber to determine that a specific activity or project, would pre-determine any issue to be determined by the Court.[88]

At the ECCC, the Victims' Support Section (VSS) was given in 2010, a mandate to implement so-called 'non-judicial measures', which consisted in developing and implementing 'new programs and measures occurring outside of formalised court proceedings' to address 'the broader interests of victims'.[89] The VSS was thus vested with two mandates relating to restorative measures for victims: (i) identifying, designing and later implementing judicial reparation projects, in cooperation with the Civil Party Lead Co-Lawyers; and (ii) developing and implementing non-judicial measures.[90] The non-judicial measures mandate remains, however, under-utilised, with only few projects being implemented to date.

[86] See Regulations of the Trust Fund for Victims, Resolution ICC-ASP/4/Res.3 (2005) (the 'ICC Regulations of the Trust Fund'), Regulation 48.

[87] ICC Regulations of the Trust Fund, Regulation 50(a).

[88] ICC Regulations of the Trust Fund, Regulation 50(a)(ii) and (iii).

[89] ECCC, 7th Plenary Session of ECCC concludes, 9 February 2010. https://www.eccc.gov.kh/en/articles/7th-plenary-session-eccc-concludes. Accessed 30 September 2016.

[90] Sperfeldt, Christoph, 'Collective Reparations at the Extraordinary Chambers in the Courts of Cambodia', 12 *International Criminal Law Review* (2012), 466–467.

13.4 Key Points

- In conclusion, the practice of the *ad hoc* and internationalised tribunals as well as the International Criminal Court relating to the issues of reparations and support and assistance remain relatively new and novel.
- With respect to reparations, it is not possible to say that there is a clear or emerging trend in relation to the way in which the ECCC and ICC have approached their reparation mandates, given the emphasis of those bodies on their *sui generis* status and their particularised legal frameworks.
- Both bodies have felt constrained by what they appear to perceive as the weight of their mandates and the boundless numbers and complex needs of the victims, however the ways in which they have approached their fears of the mandate differ.
- There is a sense that the reparations mandate ought to be easier to implement; that the difficulties make the mandate a nuisance, annoying, a stain on the otherwise 'more straightforward' work of international investigations and prosecutions. Yet, in contrast, the 'difficulties' of the reparations mandate are the challenges that judges and other court officials must progressively embrace. It is part and parcel of the unique opportunity they have to mete out justice for the most serious crimes under international law. Victims' lawyers need to employ a great deal of creativity to push back against the constrained approaches to reparations by both the judges and ordinary court officials.
- In the areas of support and assistance, whilst there have been a number of important developments before the *ad hoc* tribunals and the ICC, the main challenge for victims and their lawyers is to progressively change the dynamic before these bodies.
- Rehabilitation and assistance are not simply charitable gifts that may be afforded should the budgets be present and should court officials be sufficiently motivated or interested in a particular country situation or form of victimisation. They should be part and parcel of the service these bodies provide, which should be a service that is accountable and transparent not only to States parties but to the end-users themselves.

References

De Brouwer A-M (2005) Supranational criminal prosecution of sexual violence: The ICC and the practice of the ICTY and the ICTR. Intersentia, Antwerp–Oxford

De Brouwer A-M (2007) Reparation to victims of sexual violence: Possibilities at the International Criminal Court and at the Trust Fund for Victims and Their Families. Leiden J Int Law 20:207–237

Donat-Cattin D (1999) Article 75. In: Triffterer O (ed) Commentary on the Rome Statute of the International Criminal Court. Observers' notes, article by article, 1st edn. Nomos, Baden -Baden, pp 965–978

Ferstman C (2002) The reparation regime of the International Criminal Court: practical considerations. Leiden J Int Law 15:667–686

Ferstman C (2012) Limited charges and limited judgments by The International Criminal Court—Who bears the greatest responsibility? Int J Hum Rights 16:796–813

Ferstman C, Goetz M (2009) Reparations before the International Criminal Court: The early jurisprudence on victim participation and its impact for reparation proceedings. In: Ferstman C, Goetz M, Stephens A (eds) Reparations for genocide, crimes against humanity and war crimes: Systems in place and systems in the making. Martinus Nijhoff Publishers, Leiden, pp 313–352

Haslam E (2007) Law, civil society and contested justice at the International Criminal Tribunal for Rwanda. In: Dembour M-B, Kelly T (eds) Paths to international justice: Social and legal perspectives. Cambridge University Press, Cambridge, pp 57–82

Heindel A (2013) Impact of severance on individual civil parties' legal status and right to reparations. http://www.cambodiatribunal.org/wp-content/uploads/2013/08/commentary_130223-english.pdf. Accessed 20 May 2015

Malmström S (2001) Restitution of property and compensation to victims. In: May D (ed) Essays on ICTY procedure and evidence. Kluwer Law International, The Hague, pp 373–384

McGonigle B (2009) Two for the price of one: Attempts by the Extraordinary Chambers in the Courts of Cambodia to combine retributive and restorative justice principles. Leiden J Int Law 22:127–149

Moffet L (2012) The role of victims in the international criminal tribunals of the Second World War. Int Crim Law Rev 12:245–270

Muttukumaru C (1999) Reparations to victims. In: Lee RS (ed) The International Criminal Court: The making of the Rome Statute: issues, negotiations, results. Kluwer Law International, The Hague, pp 262–270

Sperfeldt C (2012) Collective reparations at the Extraordinary Chambers in the Courts of Cambodia. Int Crim Law Rev 12.457–489

Chapter 14
Termination of Victim Participation

Megan Hirst

Abstract Minimal guidance exists in the texts of the International Criminal Court (ICC), Special Tribunal for Lebanon (STL) and Extraordinary Chambers in the Courts of Cambodia (ECCC) regarding the ways by which a victim's participation in proceedings can be brought to an end. Developing case-law, however, reveals that participation can be ended by a voluntary withdrawal of participation, by the death of a participating victim, or where a chamber decides that the evidence in support of the victim's status has been negated. The narrowing of charges in a case can also result in the termination of some victims' participation. This chapter examines these circumstances and considers when participation will be ended. It then considers associated questions such as whether a victim's participation can be carried on after the victim's death by a successor. The chapter addresses the possibilities for withdrawal or termination where an application for participation has been submitted but not yet judicially determined. Finally, consideration is given to the obligations which follow or survive the end of a victim's participation, including those falling on the victim's lawyers, the Registry and the victim him or herself.

Keywords Withdrawal of application · Withdrawal of participation · Death (of a participating victim) · Resumption of participation · Revocation of participation · Standard of proof

---

Megan Hirst is a barrister at Doughty Street Chambers in London and a member of an LRV team in *Prosecutor v. Dominic Ongwen*. She has previously worked on victims' participation in the Registries of the ICC and the STL.

M. Hirst (✉)
London, UK
e-mail: m.hirst@doughtystreet.co.uk

K. Tibori-Szabó and M. Hirst (eds.), *Victim Participation in International Criminal Justice*, International Criminal Justice Series 11,
DOI 10.1007/978-94-6265-177-7_14

Contents

14.1 Introduction

In most cases, a victim's participation in international criminal proceedings will continue until those proceedings reach their final conclusion. In addition, at the Extraordinary Chambers in the Courts of Cambodia (ECCC), where victims participate not only *in* the proceedings, but also as 'civil parties' making a claim for reparations against one or more accused, civil party participation *vis-à-vis* a particular accused will be ended by the death of that accused.[1]

However, in some instances the participation of particular victims may be ended sooner. This chapter sets out the law and practice relating to such cases of early termination of victim participation. It covers early termination of victim participation in the following circumstances:

- Termination of a victim application *prior to* the grant of participation:
  - Voluntary withdrawal of a victim application
  - Narrowing of the scope of the charges in the case
- Termination of victim participation *after* it has been granted:
  - Voluntary withdrawal by a participating victim
  - Involuntary termination of a victim's participation
  - Death of a participating victim
  - Narrowing of the scope of the charges in the case

[1] See Rule 23*bis*(6) of the ECCC Internal Rules, Rev. 9 (2015) (the 'ECCC Internal Rules').

14.2 General Comments

A striking feature of this area is the dearth of statutory guidance. Few provisions deal with early termination of participation. The International Criminal Court (ICC) Regulation 101 of the Regulations of the Registry[2] deals with withdrawal of an application prior to its acceptance; while Rule 91(1) of the ICC RPE[3] and Rule 23*bis*(5) of the ECCC Internal Rules deal with forms of termination or withdrawal after victim participation begins. However, for the most part little detail is provided regarding the principles and procedures which regulate such early termination. As a result, judges faced with issues relating to the early termination of victim participation have largely been forced to derive their approach from more general principles. In particular, the voluntary nature of victim participation may be understood as the theoretical basis for voluntary victim withdrawal,[4] while the pre-conditions for victim participation provide guidance on the situations in which participation may be terminated without a request or consent from the victim.[5]

However, relatively few instances of early termination have arisen at the courts to date. As a result, minimal jurisprudence exists. This compounds the lack of clarity regarding the principles and procedures relating to the early termination of victim participation.

14.3 Termination of Participation at the Application Stage

14.3.1 Voluntary Withdrawal of an Application not yet Determined by a Chamber

The legal texts of the Special Tribunal for Lebanon (STL) and the ECCC make no express provision for the possibility of victims withdrawing an application for participation which has yet to be considered by a chamber. Nor do the more important

[2] ICC Regulations of the Registry, ICC-BD/03-03-13 (2013).

[3] Rules of Procedure and Evidence of the ICC, ICC-ASP/1/3 Corr.1 (Part.II-A) (2002), (the 'ICC Rules').

[4] STL, *Prosecutor v. Ayyash* et al., Pre-Trial Judge, Decision on the Duty Legal Representative's Motion for Review of the Registrar's Decision of the Lead Legal Representative for Victims, STL-11-01/PT/PTJ, 27 September 2012, para 48; STL, *Prosecutor v. Ayyash* et al., Pre-Trial Judge, Decision Relating to the Request of the Legal Representative of Victims to Authorise Two Victims to Withdraw Their Participation, STL-11-01/PT/PTJ, 19 December 2012, para 5.

[5] In general terms these requirements are set out in Rule 85 of the ICC Rules, Rule 23*bis*(1) of the ECCC Internal Rules, and Rule 86(B) of the STL Rules of Procedure and Evidence, STL-BD-2009-01-Rev.7-Corr. 1 (2015) (the 'STL Rules'). For detail on these requirements see Chap. 3.

texts of the ICC. Only the ICC Regulations of the Registry, in Regulation 101, refers to this possibility.

Regulation 101 distinguishes between two situations.

Where the application has not yet been presented to the chamber, the Registry shall retain the application in its records.[6] This provision resulted from a 2013 amendment to the Regulations of the Registry, before which such applications were required to be transmitted to the chamber with information about the withdrawal. The result of this amendment is that these applications will ordinarily never be presented to a chamber, in effect meaning that victims have the power to unilaterally withdraw their application for participation prior to its transmission to a chamber.

Where an application has already been presented by the Registry to the chamber but has not yet been decided, Regulation 101 requires that the Registry 'present the withdrawal' to the chamber, along with any reasons given for the withdrawal.[7] No text of the ICC, however, regulates how a chamber should deal with this situation and it appears that this process has not yet been used in practice.

14.3.2 Narrowing of the Charges in the Case

As explained elsewhere in this book, victims can only participate in a case where the harm they have suffered is linked to at least one of the charges in that case.[8] Consequently, where the charges in a case are narrowed, this can result in the termination of some victims' participation. This applies not only to victims already participating in proceedings, but also any victims whose applications are pending with the Registry or before a chamber. Indeed, the impact on applicants is equivalent to the impact on already participating victims, which is considered below.

14.4 Termination of Participation Following the Acceptance of an Application

14.4.1 Voluntary Withdrawal of Participation

Only the legal texts of the ECCC expressly state that a victim may voluntarily withdraw his or her participation in proceedings once it has begun.[9] However, it is clear from the case-law of the ICC and STL that this is also possible before those

6 ICC Regulations of the Registry, Regulation 101(1).

7 ICC Regulations of the Registry, Regulation 101(2).

8 See Chap. 3.

9 ECCC Internal Rules, Rule 23*bis*(5).

courts.[10] It is worth noting that even under the model of participation used in the Kenya cases,[11] in which Trial Chamber V treated the legal representatives of victims (LRVs) as representing 'all victims [of the case], regardless of whether they have registered or not,'[12] it was possible for victims to voluntarily withdraw their 'procedural status', with the consequence that they were removed from the Registry's database of victims.[13]

While it is clear that voluntary withdrawal from proceedings is possible, less clear is what procedure must be followed, and whether any requirements must be met by the withdrawing victim. In particular: who may communicate a participating victim's request for withdrawal to the court? Is a signed statement from the participating victim necessary or sufficient? Must a reason for the withdrawal request be given?

Rules of general application in this area cannot yet be derived from ICC case-law. In one apparently straightforward case, the legal representative in the *Katanga* case, filed a 'notification' of the withdrawal of one of his clients.[14] The LRV provided a written and signed statement from the victim indicating the latter's decision to withdraw.[15] That the Chamber issued no subsequent decision appears to suggest that it considered this notification document sufficient in itself to effect the victim's withdrawal.

In a separate and somewhat more complex example, in the *Ruto and Sang* case, an intermediary sent a letter to the ICC which was purportedly signed by a large number of participating victims and requested their withdrawal from the

[10] ICC, *Prosecutor v. William Samoei Ruto and Joshua Arap Sang*, Trial Chamber V(a), Decision on the Legal Representative's Report on the Withdrawal of Victims, ICC-01/09-01/11-1098-Red2, 14 November 2013, para 15; STL, *Prosecutor v. Ayyash* et al., Pre-Trial Judge, Decision on the Duty Legal Representative's Motion for Review of the Registrar's Decision of the Lead Legal Representative for Victims, STL-11-01/PT/PTJ, 27 September 2012, para 48; STL, *Prosecutor v. Ayyash* et al., Pre-Trial Judge, Decision Relating to the Request of the Legal Representative of Victims to Authorise Two Victims to Withdraw Their Participation, STL-11-01/PT/PTJ, 19 December 2012.

[11] See Chap. 2.

[12] ICC, *Prosecutor v. William Samoei Ruto and Joshua Arap Sang*, Trial Chamber V, Decision on victims' representation and participation, ICC-01/09-01/11-460, 3 October 2012, para 53; ICC, *Prosecutor v. Francis Kirimi Muthaura and Uhuru Muigai Kenyatta*, Trial Chamber V, Decision on victims' representation and participation, ICC-01/09-01/11-498, 3 October 2012, para 52.

[13] ICC, *Prosecutor v. William Samoei Ruto and Joshua Arap Sang*, Trial Chamber V(a), Decision on the Legal Representative's Report on the Withdrawal of Victims, ICC-01/09-01/11-1098-Red2, 14 November 2013, para 15.

[14] ICC, *Prosecutor v. Germain Katanga*, Legal Representative of the main group of victims, Notification du désistement d'une victime (a/0317/09), ICC-01/04-01/07-3509, 31 October 2014.

[15] ICC, *Prosecutor v. Germain Katanga*, Legal Representative of the main group of victims, Annexe 2 A la Notification du désistement d'une victime (a/0317/09), ICC-01/04-01/07-3509-Anx2-Red, 31 October 2014.

proceedings.[16] Trial Chamber V(a) refused to treat the letter as sufficient in itself to effect the withdrawal of those victims. In doing so it was influenced by the fact that some signatories to the letter later informed their LRV that they did not want to withdraw, as well as other circumstances suggesting that the letter was not a reliable indicator of its signatories' intent. The Trial Chamber held that participating victims would only be treated as having withdrawn where they had 'individually and freely communicated their wish to withdraw from the proceedings to the [Legal Representative of Victims] and/or the Court.'[17] Thus those signatories to the letter whom the LRV was subsequently unable to contact (for the purpose of verifying their intent) were treated as continuing their participation.

This decision may be taken to indicate a victim's withdrawal must be communicated to the Court by the LRV or an officer of the court who must have received the request directly from the victim. It also supports the proposition that the request conveyed through the LRV or court official need not be made in writing by the victim. No requirement for a written request is mentioned in the decision, and the Trial Chamber granted some 20 withdrawals although it is not clear from the LRV's report (at least in redacted form) whether he received the requests in writing. This contrasts with the requirement in Rule 89(1) that victim applications must be made in writing. However, it appears to be a sensible approach in the ICC context, given the circumstances and numbers of ICC victims, the possibility for their withdrawal to be conveyed through a court-recognised LRV, and the fact that the risk of abuse of process through a voluntary withdrawal is negligible (as discussed further below).

However, it is clearly possible to overstate the precedential value of this decision. Despite a request from the LRV in the *Ruto and Sang* case for the Trial Chamber to issue guidelines on when and how a participating victim shall be considered to have withdrawn from the proceedings, Trial Chamber V(a) declined to do so.[18] Given the divergent approaches of the ICC chambers, it is also possible that an entirely different approach could be taken in another case. Practitioners are therefore advised to obtain a written statement of the victim's desire to withdraw where it is possible and safe to do so.

At the STL, victims have been permitted to withdraw from proceedings where this wish was communicated to the Tribunal by their LRV. The Pre-Trial Judge

---

[16] ICC, *Prosecutor v. Silliam Samoei Ruto and Joshua Arap Sang*, Common Legal Representative for Victims, Common Legal Representative for Victims' Comprehensive Report on the Withdrawal of Victims from the Turbo area by Letter dated 5 June 2013, ICC-01/09-01/11-896-Corr-Red, 5 September 2013.

[17] ICC, *Prosecutor v. William Samoei Ruto and Joshua Arap Sang*, Trial Chamber V(a), Decision on the Legal Representative's Report on the Withdrawal of Victims, ICC-01/09-01/11-1098-Red2, 14 November 2013, para 16.

[18] ICC, *Prosecutor v. William Samoei Ruto and Joshua Arap Sang*, Trial Chamber V(a), Decision on the Legal Representative's Report on the Withdrawal of Victims, ICC-01/09-01/11-1098-Red2, 14 November 2013, para 23.

required in general terms that 'it must be ensured that the request for withdrawal formulated by the victim in question is a voluntary one, and was made with full knowledge of the facts,'[19] but did not provide specific procedural measures directed to ensuring this. In fact, the two victims requesting withdrawal had made their requests in writing, through their LRV (one by email, one by signed statement).[20] This was considered sufficient by the Pre-Trial Judge, although no independent proof had been provided that the victims' requests had been made 'with full knowledge of the facts.'

At the ECCC, the Internal Rules permit civil parties to 'waive the right to request reparation, and abandon a Civil Party action' at any time during the pre-trial stage.[21] During trial stage 'and beyond', civil parties may 'withdraw from the consolidated group.' No guidance is provided in the Internal Rules or the Practice Direction on Victim Participation regarding the procedure for withdrawal. In practice it appears that the chambers have simply been informed of the withdrawal (or 'waiver') by the civil party's legal representative in writing or orally during a hearing, and no formal decision of the chamber has been required.[22] No requirement appears to exist that the civil party has expressed his or her request for withdrawal in writing.[23]

The courts have not yet been confronted with a situation in which voluntary withdrawal appears to have been undertaken as an abuse of process or in order to avoid obligations otherwise falling on a participating victim (e.g. in respect of disclosure). This question was raised in a filing by the STL Registrar, who argued that although victim withdrawal must be possible, it 'must also be judicially controlled. This is necessary given that by acquiring the status of [victim participating in the proceedings], victims also acquire obligations in the proceedings.'[24] The Registrar expressed the concern that withdrawal might conceivably be used to avoid such obligations, and submitted that before authorising a withdrawal, the

[19] STL, *Prosecutor v. Ayyash* et al., Pre-Trial Judge, Decision Relating to the Request of the Legal Representative of Victims to Authorise Two Victims to Withdraw their Participation, STL-11-01/PT/PTJ, 19 December 2012, para 5.

[20] Ibid., para 6.

[21] Rule 23*bis*(5) of the ECCC Internal Rules.

[22] See ECCC, *Case 001*, Trial Chamber, Judgment, Case No. 001/18-07-2007/ECCC/TC, 26 July 2010, para 638; ECCC, *Case 001*, Civil Party Co-Lawyers Group 3, CPG3—Lettre d'abandon de droit de la constitution de la partie civile au près des chambres extraordinaires au sein des Tribunaux Cambodgiens, Case No. 001/18-07-2007/ECCC/TC, 15 September 2009; ECCC, *Case 001*, Transcript of Trial Proceedings, Case No. 001/18-07-2007/ECCC/TC, 27 August 2009, pp. 7–8.

[23] Indeed, in one instance the civil party lawyer had received the withdrawal request through a family member of the civil party: see ECCC, *Case 001*, Transcript of Trial Proceedings, Case No. 001/18-07-2007/ECCC/TC, 27 August 2009, pp. 7–8.

[24] STL, *Prosecutor v. Ayyash* et al., Registrar, Registrar's Submissions in Response to the Duty Legal Representative's Motion for Review of Designation, STL-11-01/PT/PTJ, 21 August 2012, para 49.

Pre-Trial Judge should, *inter alia*, assess whether the withdrawal would have an impact on the fairness of the proceedings or the rights of the accused.[25] To date such an approach has not been taken, but neither has a case arisen where withdrawal may raise questions of fairness to an accused.

To date no instance has arisen at any of the courts in which a victim requests to participate again following a voluntary withdrawal. However at least at the ICC it is clear that this is possible, and that a victim who has voluntarily withdrawn his or her participation may still request reparations.[26]

14.4.2 Death of Participating Victims

A victim's participation in proceedings may end with the victim's death. However, this is not always the case.

At the ECCC a deceased victim's participation may be continued by a family member or successor, consistent with Article 16 of the Cambodian Code of Criminal Procedure.[27] It provides that 'in case of death of a victim, a civil action may be started or continued by his successor.' In order to permit the resumption of a civil party action under this provision, the ECCC required that the deceased must have been recognised as a civil party, as well as proof that the person seeking to continue the action is the successor of the deceased. In practice, the chambers have required the presentation of a death certificate for the deceased civil party, and a statement and identification document from the successor.[28]

The position at the ICC is somewhat less clear. At least three chambers of the ICC have also taken the view that deceased victims may participate, by having their previously stated views and concerns expressed to the Court by a close family member.

This position was first advanced in the *Katanga and Ngudjolo Chui* case. Trial Chamber II permitted the 'resumption' of participation by a 'close relative' where

---

[25] Ibid., paras 49–50.

[26] ICC, *Prosecutor v. William Samoei Ruto and Joshua Arap Sang*, Trial Chamber V(a), Decision on the Legal Representative's Report on the Withdrawal of Victims, ICC-01/09-01/11-1098-Red2, 14 November 2013, paras 15 and 18.

[27] ECCC, *Case 001*, Trial Chamber, Decision on Motion Regarding Deceased Civil Party, Case No. 001/18-07-2007/ECCC/TC, 13 March 2009, paras 10–13.

[28] ECCC, *Case 002*, Trial Chamber, Memorandum: Succession of deceased Civil Parties in *Case 002*, Case No. 002/19-09-2007/ECCC/TC, 21 May 2013; ECCC, *Case 002*, Trial Chamber, Memorandum: Succession of deceased Civil Party MAO Son in *Case 002*, Case No. 002/19-09-2007/ECCC/TC, 23 January 2014.

a victim already participating died during the course of proceedings.[29] The Chamber stipulated that the family member could only continue the participation 'on behalf of the deceased victim and within the limits of the views and concerns expressed by the victim in his or her initial application.'[30] Given that the application form is intended largely to solicit information relevant to the requirements of Rule 85, and that detailed information is rarely provided on those forms regarding the victim's views and concerns about the conduct of proceedings, it appears that any such 'resumed' participation is likely to be largely symbolic in nature. Trial Chamber II required persons wishing to resume participation in this way to provide proof (i) of the death of the participating victim (usually by death certificate), (ii) of the family relationship between the deceased and the person wishing to resume the participation, and (iii) that the deceased victim's family have specifically mandated the person to continue the deceased victim's participation before the ICC.[31]

---

[29] ICC, *Prosecutor v. Germain Katanga and Mathieu Ngudjolo Chui*, Trial Chamber II, Motifs de la deuxième decision relative aux demandes de participation de victimes à la procedure, ICC-01/04-01/07-1737, 22 December 2009, para 30; ICC, *Prosecutor v. Germain Katanga and Mathieu Ngudjolo Chui*, Trial Chamber II, Decision on the applications to resume action submitted by the family members of deceased Victims a/0025/08, a/0051/08, a/0197/08 and a/0311/09, ICC 01/04-01/07-3018-tENG, 14 June 2011, para 20; ICC, *Prosecutor v. Germain Katanga*, Trial Chamber II, Decision on the application to resume action, submitted by a family member of deceased Victim a/0253/09, ICC-01/04-01/07-3383-tENG, 10 June 2013, para 6.

Note that in contrast, in the same case Trial Chamber II had refused to grant participation status to applicants seeking to act on behalf of their family members who had died before the submission of an application for participation: ICC, *Prosecutor v. Germain Katanga and Mathieu Ngudjolo Chui*, Trial Chamber II, Grounds for the Decision on the 243 Applications for Participation in the Proceedings Submitted by Victims, ICC-01/04-01/07-1491-Red-tENG, 23 September 2009, paras 49–56. See also Chap. 3.

[30] ICC, *Prosecutor v. Germain Katanga and Mathieu Ngudjolo Chui*, Trial Chamber II, Motifs de la deuxième decision relative aux demandes de participation de victimes à la procedure, ICC-01/04-01/07-1737, 22 December 2009, para 30; ICC, *Prosecutor v. Germain Katanga and Mathieu Ngudjolo Chui*, Trial Chamber II, Decision on the applications to resume action submitted by the family members of deceased Victims a/0025/08, a/0051/08, a/0197/08 and a/0311/09, ICC-01/04-01/07-3018-tENG, 14 June 2011, para 20; ICC, *Prosecutor v. Germain Katanga*, Trial Chamber II, Decision on the application to resume action, submitted by a family member of deceased Victim a/0253/09, ICC-01/04-01/07-3383-tENG, 10 June 2013, para 6.

[31] ICC, *Prosecutor v. Germain Katanga and Mathieu Ngudjolo Chui*, Trial Chamber II, Motifs de la deuxième decision relative aux demandes de participation de victimes à la procedure, ICC-01/04-01/07-1737, 22 December 2009, paras 31–32; ICC, *Prosecutor v. Germain Katanga and Mathieu Ngudjolo Chui*, Trial Chamber II, Decision on the applications to resume action submitted by the family members of deceased Victims a/0025/08, a/0051/08, a/0197/08 and a/0311/09, ICC-01/04-01/07-3018-tENG, 14 June 2011, paras 21–29; ICC, *Prosecutor v. Germain Katanga and Mathieu Ngudjolo Chui*, Trial Chamber II, Décision relative aux demandes de reprise d'instance formées par les proches des victimes décédées a/0025/08 et a/031/09, ICC-01/04-01/07-3185, 21 October 2011; ICC, *Prosecutor v. Germain Katanga*, Trial Chamber II, Decision on the application to resume action, submitted by a family member of deceased Victim a/0253/09, ICC-01/04-01/07-3383-tENG, 10 June 2013, paras 7–8.

However, in September 2013 the Appeals Chamber rejected the possibility for deceased victims to participate in this way in the appeal against the *Ngudjolo* case judgment.[32] The Chamber held that '[v]ictims who are deceased can no longer be said to be participating.'[33] It noted that the views and concerns of these victims 'remain a part of the case record under review' even though the deceased victims would no longer be participating, and for this reason considered the resumption of their participation by a successor inappropriate.[34] The Chamber accordingly ordered the Registry to update its list of participating victims, removing reference to deceased victims and any person previously authorised to resume their participation.[35]

Depending on the interpretation given to its scope, the Appeals Chamber's decision could be taken to contradict and therefore potentially to overrule the approach in *Katanga and Ngudjolo Chui* as well as in some previous decisions at the application stage whereby deceased victims were permitted to participate through a representative. (The latter decisions are discussed in Chap. 3.) A consideration of the nature of victim participation at the ICC, in contrast to civil party participation at the ECCC, appears to support the Appeals Chamber's position, and would suggest that it should apply in all ICC proceedings. At the ECCC a request for civil party participation implicitly involves a request for reparations. As any entitlement to reparations should be transferrable through succession, it is logical that succession operates in respect of civil party actions. In contrast, victim participation at the ICC does not *per se* involve a request for reparations, but rather only the possibility for victims to have their views and concerns heard on matters affecting their *personal* interests. As these interests, and the views and concerns responding to them, are *personal* to the victim, it is less clear that they can be transferred on death. It is significant to note in this context that the ICC Appeals Chamber specifically noted that its decision rejecting the resumption of proceedings in the event of a victim's death was without prejudice to the position in reparations proceedings.[36] This distinction could have explained why Trial Chamber II was subsequently willing to permit further resumptions following the deaths of victims participating in reparations proceedings in the *Katanga* case.[37]

Despite this, two separate trial chambers have since followed the approach taken in *Katanga* regarding the possibility for a deceased victim's participation to be resumed *outside* the context of reparations proceedings. In *Prosecutor v. Bosco*

---

[32] ICC, *Prosecutor v. Mathieu Ngudjolo Chui*, Appeals Chamber, Decision on the participation of anonymous victims in the appeal and on the maintenance of deceased victims on the list of participating victims, ICC-01/04-02/12-140, 23 September 2013.

[33] Ibid., para 25.

[34] Ibid., paras 25–26.

[35] Ibid., para 26.

[36] Ibid., footnote 48.

[37] ICC, *Prosecutor v. Germain Katanga*, Trial Chamber II, Decision on the applications for resumption of action submitted by the family members of deceased victims a/0170/08 and a/0294/09, ICC-01/04-01/07-3547-tENG, 11 May 2015.

Ntaganda Trial Chamber VI did so apparently without considering the potentially contradictory jurisprudence from the Appeals Chamber.[38] In contrast, when Trial Chamber III considered the issue in *Bemba*, the Defence had specifically relied on the Appeals Chamber's decision. However the Trial Chamber emphasised that the latter decision 'relates to appellate proceedings' and was in any event without prejudice to the position in reparations proceedings.[39] Since judgment had been handed down in the case, the Trial Chamber noted that the resumed participation related only to sentencing and reparations, and therefore considered that its approach was 'not inconsistent with the Appeals Chamber's decision.'[40] The Chamber did not explain on what basis sentencing could be equated or assimilated to reparations proceedings.

In terms of the requirements for the resumption of a deceased victim's participation, Trial Chamber III effectively adopted the requirements laid down by Trial Chamber II,[41] namely that proof must be provided of: (i) the death of the participating victim; (ii) the familial or similarly close relationship between the deceased victim and the successor; and (iii) a mandate authorising the successor to continue the participation of the deceased victim.[42] Trial Chamber VI developed slightly further this last requirement, indicating that it would require positive proof of this only where 'the applicant cannot easily be presumed to be entitled to continue the action or represent the family' and explaining that such a presumption exists where the applicant is 'the spouse of a deceased victim; an only surviving child of a deceased victim, where the child has reached the age of eighteen and the deceased victim was either unmarried or the victim's spouse is already deceased; or the parents of an unmarried deceased victim who either has no children or whose children are below the age of eighteen.'[43]

Trial Chambers III and VI both established a formal procedure using a standard application form, by which applications for resumption would be submitted by LRVs and processed by the Registry.[44]

---

[38] ICC, *Prosecutor v. Bosco Ntaganda*, Trial Chamber VI, Fourth decision on victims' participation in trial proceedings, ICC-01/04-02/06-805, 1 September 2015.

[39] ICC, *Prosecutor v. Jean-Pierre Bemba Gombo*, Trial Chamber III, Decision on "Requête relative à la reprise des actions introduites devant la Cour par des victims décédées", ICC-01/05-01/08-3346, 24 March 2016, para 22.

[40] Ibid.

[41] See above and the decisions cited in *supra* footnote 31.

[42] ICC, *Prosecutor v. Jean-Pierre Bemba Gombo*, Trial Chamber III, Decision on "Requête relative à la reprise des actions introduites devant la Cour par des victims décédées", ICC-01/05-01/08-3346, 24 March 2016, para 23.

[43] ICC, *Prosecutor v. Bosco Ntaganda*, Trial Chamber VI, Fourth decision on victims' participation in trial proceedings, ICC-01/04-02/06-805, 1 September 2015, para 8 and footnote 10.

[44] Ibid, paras 12–13; ICC, *Prosecutor v. Jean-Pierre Bemba Gombo*, Trial Chamber III, Decision on "Requête relative à la reprise des actions introduites devant la Cour par des victims décédées", ICC-01/05-01/08-3346, 24 March 2016, para 49.

Interestingly, despite the very large numbers of victims participating in some cases before the ICC, there remains relatively little practice whereby chambers have been notified of the death of participating victims. It may be that some legal representatives have not been able to adequately maintain contact with all clients and are simply not aware when clients die.

At the STL, no question has been raised regarding the possibility for a deceased victim's participation to be continued by a family member. However neither has it been assumed that the death of a victim automatically terminates his or her participation. In the *Ayyash* et al. case, the LRV requested that one of his clients be considered withdrawn from the proceedings because of his death.[45] However, before the victim could be withdrawn from the proceedings, the Pre-Trial Judge required that documentation be provided proving that the victim had died.[46]

14.4.3 Involuntary Termination of Participation

Participating victims may have their participation revoked by a judge or chamber where new information calls into question whether the person is indeed a victim of the crime charged.

This has occurred most commonly at the time of the trial judgment, based on a chamber's consideration of the evidence led at trial.

At the ECCC, the original Internal Rules required that the Trial Chamber rule, in its judgment, on the admissibility and substance of each civil party's claim against the convicted accused.[47] This effectively required a review of each individual civil party's status.[48] In *Case 001,* the Trial Chamber terminated the civil party status of 22 persons in its judgment.[49] In most cases this was because their civil party applications were found to be insufficiently supported by evidence; in some it resulted from inconsistencies between the civil party application and other material before the Chamber. Civil parties were able to appeal these decisions, and indeed ten of those whose status was terminated in the judgment were later

---

45 STL, *Prosecutor v. Ayyash* et al., Legal Representative of Victims, Request of the Legal Representative of Victims to Withdraw one Participating Victim from the Proceedings, STL-11-01/PT/PTJ, 29 May 2013.

46 STL, *Prosecutor v. Ayyash* et al., Pre-Trial Judge, Decision on the Request of the Legal Representative of Victims to Authorise the Withdrawal of a Victim Participating in the Proceedings, STL-11-01/PT/PTJ, 5 December 2013.

47 See Rule 100(1) of the original ECCC Internal Rules (and up to Revision 4).

48 On the correctness of the Trial Chamber's approach in applying Rule 100(1) see ECCC, *Case 001*, Trial Chamber, Judgment, Case No. 001/18-07-2007/ECCC/TC, 26 July 2010, paras 494–495.

49 ECCC, *Case 001*, Trial Chamber, Judgment, Case No. 001/18-07-2007/ECCC/TC, 26 July 2010, paras 644–650.

re-admitted on appeal.[50] In this process civil parties bore the burden of proving their eligibility for the status to the civil standard of 'a preponderance of the evidence.'[51]

However, owing to changes in the Internal Rules, the Trial Chamber is no longer required to undertake a systematic review of all civil party applications at the judgment stage.[52] This does not appear to remove the possibility for the Trial Chamber to terminate a civil party's status on an *ad hoc* basis if new evidence calls that status into question.

At the ICC the approach taken has been similar to that now in place at the ECCC as described in the preceding paragraph. Thus, while the Trial Chamber does not systematically reconsider each participating victim's status, it will terminate the status of a victim where evidence calls into question whether the requirements of Rule 85 have in fact been met.

In the *Lubanga* case the status of nine participating victims was revoked at the judgment stage. All nine had given evidence during the course of trial. Six were dual status victims who testified for the Prosecution. Three were given permission by Trial Chamber I to give evidence in their capacity as a participating victim, following the request of their LRV. The credibility of all nine victims was forcefully attacked by the Defence. It revealed inconsistencies within the victims' own accounts, and produced contrary evidence from witnesses whom the Chamber found to be credible. In its Judgment the Trial Chamber first considered whether each victim's testimony could be relied upon by it in determining the guilt of the accused, finding that they could not. It then turned to the question of the impact that these findings had on the status of the victims. The majority said that:

> In general terms, if the Chamber, in investigation, concludes that its original *prima facie* evaluation [of a victim's application to participate] was incorrect, it should amend any earlier order as to participation, to the extent necessary. It would be unsustainable to allow victims to continue to participate if a more detailed understanding of the evidence has demonstrated they no longer meet the relevant criteria.[53]

Judge Odio Benito partly dissented on this point (see further below), finding that the participation of the six dual status victims should continue,[54] though not opposing the termination of the other three victims' participation.

---

[50] ECCC, *Case 001,* Supreme Court Chamber, Appeal Judgment, Case No. 001/18-07-2007/ECCC/SC, 3 February 2012, paras 537–623.

[51] ECCC, *Case 001*, Trial Chamber, Judgment, Case No. 001/18-07-2007/ECCC/TC, 26 July 2010, paras 428, 522–531.

[52] ECCC, *Case 002*, Trial Chamber, *Case 002/01* Judgement, Case No. 002/19-09-2007/ECCC/TC, 7 August 2014, para 1110.

[53] ICC, *Prosecutor v. Thomas Lubanga Dyilo*, Trial Chamber I, Judgment pursuant to Article 74 of the Statute, ICC-01/04-01/06-2842, 14 March 2012, paras 484 and 502.

[54] ICC, *Prosecutor v. Thomas Lubanga Dyilo*, Trial Chamber I, Judgment pursuant to Article 74 of the Statute, Separate and Dissenting Opinion of Judge Odio Benito, ICC-01/04-01/06-2842, 14 March 2012, paras 22–35.

These developments raise a number of issues, both legal and practical.

First, it is worth noting the timing of the Chamber's decision to terminate. Although in some cases serious questions about some of the victims' credibility may have been apparent from the time they gave evidence, the Chamber did not take steps to terminate the victims' participation at that time. It rather waited until it conducted its evaluation of all the evidence in the context of its judgment. It could be argued that this approach was necessary, since the veracity of the victims' accounts had become a matter to be determined in the context of its final judgment, and should therefore not be determined until that time.

Secondly, the court records give no indication that the participating victims were afforded an opportunity to be heard through their LRVs on the question of whether their status should be revoked.

Thirdly, as victims may not appeal from judgments at the ICC,[55] no recourse was available to these victims from the decision. The Office of Public Counsel for Victims (OPCV), which had been appointed LRV for four of the victims in question, recognised this difficulty and filed a request for reconsideration in relation to the revocation of those victims' status.[56] The Trial Chamber rejected the request, holding that it was without any legal basis in that it failed to advance any arguments capable of meeting the test for reconsideration.[57] Indeed a further question might conceivably have been raised (but was not), as to whether the OPCV even retained standing on this matter following the Chamber's decision to revoke the status of the victims in question.

Fourthly, the approach adopted by the Trial Chamber left unresolved the important questions of the standard and burden of proof where questions arise during proceedings about a victim's participation status. Judge Odio Benito, in her Separate and Dissenting Opinion, criticised the majority approach, which in her view applied the 'beyond reasonable doubt' standard when determining the victims' status.[58] Indeed, the majority did not explain what it considered to be the appropriate standard of proof, or where the burden of proof lay. Rather, it appears to have assumed that simply because the victims' evidence was not reliable for the purpose of determining the accused's criminal responsibility (i.e. in light of the 'beyond reasonable doubt' standard), it immediately followed that their accounts

[55] Article 81 of the Rome Statute of the International Criminal Court, A/CONF.183/9 (2010).

[56] ICC, *Prosecutor v. Thomas Lubanga Dyilo*, Request for reconsideration of Trial Chamber I's decision to withdraw the status of participating victims in the proceeding to a/0047/06, a/0048/06, a/0050/06 and a/0052/06, ICC-01/04-01/06-2845, 23 March 2012.

[57] ICC, *Prosecutor v. Thomas Lubanga Dyilo*, Trial Chamber I, Order refusing a request for reconsideration, ICC-01/04-01/06-2846, 27 March 2012.

[58] ICC, *Prosecutor v. Thomas Lubanga Dyilo*, Trial Chamber I, Judgment pursuant to Article 74 of the Statute, Separate and Dissenting Opinion of Judge Odio Benito, ICC-01/04-01/06-2842, 14 March 2012, para 35.

were also insufficient for supporting the status of victim.[59] In relation to the three victims who had given evidence in person, the majority stated that there was a 'real possibility' that these victims had lied about their victimhood, and that 'material doubts' exist as to their identities.[60] This language does appear to suggest that the Chamber applied the beyond reasonable doubt standard.

In contrast, Judge Odio Benito advocated for a more nuanced approach. In respect of the six dual status victims she agreed with the majority that their evidence was unreliable (for what she considered good reasons, given the lapse of time and the effects of trauma) and should not be used to determine the accused's criminal responsibility. However, she nonetheless considered it possible that these individuals were victims meeting the requirements of Rule 85. Judge Odio Benito did not specify the standard of proof she considered relevant in this determination, however the language she used suggests a low threshold: 'could well have been [the victim of the crime charged]',[61] 'could have been [the victim of the crime charged]',[62] and 'a real possibility exists that [the person was a victim of the crime charged].'[63] Moreover she considered it to be 'unfair and discriminatory' that dual status victims should have their status determined according to a more onerous standard of proof than all other victims.[64] This suggests that she considered the appropriate standard to be the *prima facie* standard applied at the application stage.[65]

It is interesting that Judge Odio Benito was silent on the question of the three participating victims who had given evidence in person before the Chamber. On the termination of these persons' victim status she did not dissent. It could be that this was because she considered their accounts to have been so thoroughly undermined that they no longer even met the *prima facie* standard of proof. Or alternatively, it may be that she took into account the different capacity in which they came before the Chamber: was it relevant that they had at their own request been subjected to questioning and a heightened level of judicial scrutiny?

Whether or not that is the case, the decision certainly highlights the practical risks involved for a victims' lawyer in having his or her clients appear before a chamber to give evidence. The provision of evidence at trial is likely to involve a much more detailed account than that provided in the victim's original application form, a factor that in itself opens the possibility for internal inconsistencies. This risk compounded by the additional scrutiny added by cross-examination

---

[59] ICC, *Prosecutor v. Thomas Lubanga Dyilo*, Trial Chamber I, Judgment pursuant to Article 74 of the Statute, ICC-01/04-01/06-2842, 14 March 2012, paras 484 and 505.

[60] Ibid., para 502.

[61] ICC, *Prosecutor v. Thomas Lubanga Dyilo*, Trial Chamber I, Judgment pursuant to Article 74 of the Statute, Separate and Dissenting Opinion of Judge Odio Benito, ICC-01/04-01/06-2842, 14 March 2012, para 25.

[62] Ibid., para 28.

[63] Ibid., para 29.

[64] Ibid., para 35.

[65] See Chap. 3.

and judicial questioning. Moreover, once a victim contributes *evidence*, the party against whose interest it is given (usually the Defence) is given a clear incentive to carry out investigations and to lead evidence intended to undermine the victim's credibility and thereby potentially his/her victim status.

Victims at the ICC may in many cases be convinced that they meet the requirements for victim status, but have little concrete evidence to support this. These circumstances can withstand the *prima facie* review at the application stage, but may not withstand a greater level of scrutiny, particularly if a high standard of proof is applied. Unless a victim's lawyer is confident that his or her client account cannot plausibly be challenged, a cautious approach is advisable. Participating victims may in many cases be eager to give evidence at trial. However, victims' lawyers should advise their clients of the risks inherent in that step.

The above advice is relevant where a lawyer believes his clients are victims, but in circumstances where the supporting evidence may be meagre. But what if a lawyer becomes aware of information demonstrating that one of his clients is not entitled to victim status?

In the *Katanga and Ngudjolo Chui* case, a legal representative was interviewing two clients ahead of their presentation of evidence before the Chamber, when he became aware of information which called into question the accounts given in their applications for participation. The LRV requested that the Chamber terminate his mandate to represent the two victims, stating that the relationship of trust between lawyer and client had broken down as a result of his investigations into the matter.[66] He also argued that was unable to report to the Chamber on the information known to him about the victim status of the two individuals, because professional obligations prevented him from disclosing such information without his clients' agreement. It was suggested that the Registry, as a neutral organ, investigate and report to the Chamber.

Trial Chamber II responded to the situation by simply revoking the victim status of the two individuals in question.[67] The Chamber was willing to do so without a report provided by the LRV or the Registry. Instead, it inferred from the circumstances that the information provided to the LRV by his clients was not sufficient 'to assuage [his] doubts' as to the veracity of their accounts. Like Trial Chamber I in *Lubanga*, Trial Chamber II provided no examination of the appropriate standard of proof to apply in this decision, or where the burden of proof should fall. However, the decision seems to suggest that where any doubt comes to the Chamber's attention about a correctness of a victim's participation, the victim

[66] ICC, *Prosecutor v. Germain Katanga and Mathieu Ngudjolo Chui*, Rapport du représentant legal conformé à la decision ICC-01/04-01/07-2699-Conf et demande de pouvoir mettre fin à son mandat concernant deux victimes (Article 18 du Code de conduite professionnel), ICC-01/04-01/07-2782, 18 March 2011.

[67] ICC, *Prosecutor v. Germain Katanga and Mathieu Ngudjolo Chui*, Trial Chamber II, Decision on the maintenance of participating victim status of Victims a/0381/09 and a/036/09 and on Mr Nsita Luvengika's request for leave to terminate his mandate as said victims' Legal Representative, ICC-01/04-01/07-3064-tENG, 7 July 2011.

bears the burden of dispelling those doubts and will otherwise have his or her status revoked.

In contrast to the approach of Trial Chamber I in *Lubanga*, Trial Chamber II did not wait for its deliberations and judgment to issue its terminations of victim status. This may be because the doubts about the victims' status arose before they could appear to give evidence before the Chamber. As a result, the veracity of their accounts was not a matter relevant to the Chamber's final judgment and could be decided earlier. While this reasoning may well explain the different approaches taken in the two cases, it nonetheless leads to an anomalous result. Victims who have given evidence would thereby be protected until judgment from an involuntary termination of their participation, while other victims could have their status terminated at any time.

14.4.4 Narrowing of the Charges in the Case

Victims may only participate in proceedings where the harm they suffered was caused by conduct which forms part a charge in the case before the court.[68] Where the charges originally included in an arrest warrant (at the ICC) or an indictment (at the STL and ECCC) are subsequently narrowed, participating victims will be excluded as a result if the harm suffered was caused by a crime which is no longer part of the case. This may occur if the Prosecution withdraws certain charges, if they are removed as a result of a 'no case to answer' motion, or (at the ICC) if the charges are narrowed at confirmation stage.

14.5 Obligations Following or Arising from Early Termination

14.5.1 Obligations on the Registry and/or Victims' Lawyers

Wherever a victim's status is terminated, the victim should be notified of this fact. Whether this is to be done by the victim's lawyer or the court itself is not made clear by the rules of the different courts. Technically, the relationship of representation between the victim and his or her lawyer may have ended at the point of termination, however it is also probable that the victim's lawyer retains some obligations in relation to this termination itself, including notification.[69] At both the ICC and the STL, chambers have required a legal representative to provide

[68] See Chap. 3.

[69] See Chap. 5.

notification to former clients who have voluntarily withdrawn.[70] In contrast, where the ICC terminated victims' status against their will during proceedings, Trial Chamber II ordered that the Registry notify the victims of this fact.[71]

The notification should not only include the fact of the decision, but also include related information such as the continuing obligations (if any) of the victims,[72] and whether or not they may seek participation and/or reparations again in the future.[73] These factors will vary depending on the court and the reason for early termination.

14.5.2 Obligation on the Previously Participating Victim

Only the STL has concerned itself to date with the obligations which fall on a victim who has ceased to participate in the proceedings. The Pre-Trial Judge in the *Ayyash* et al. case has made clear that the obligations of confidentiality imposed on victims by virtue of their participation do continue after the withdrawal of the victim's status.[74] It is not clear whether a victim's disclosure obligations (which exist at least at the STL)[75] survive the withdrawal or termination of a victim's status.

14.6 Key Points

- Registry staff and victim's lawyers should endeavour to make clear to victims the circumstances in which their participation can be ended, whether voluntarily or otherwise.

---

[70] ICC, *Prosecutor v. William Samoei Ruto and Joshua Arap Sang*, Trial Chamber V(a), Decision on the Legal Representative's Report on the Withdrawal of Victims, ICC-01/09-01/11-1098-Red2, 14 November 2013, paras 18, disposition; STL, *Prosecutor v. Ayyash* et al., Pre-Trial Judge, Pre-Trial Judge, Decision Relating to the Request of the Legal Representative of Victims to Authorise Two Victims to Withdraw Their Participation, STL-11-01/PT/PTJ, 19 December 2012, disposition.

[71] ICC, *Prosecutor v. Germain Katanga and Mathieu Ngudjolo Chui*, Trial Chamber II, Decision on the maintenance of participating victim status of Victims a/0381/09 and a/036/09 and on Mr Nsita Luvengika's request for leave to terminate his mandate as said victims' Legal Representative, ICC-01/04-01/07-3064-tENG, 7 July 2011, disposition.

[72] STL, *Prosecutor v. Ayyash* et al., Pre-Trial Judge, Pre-Trial Judge, Decision Relating to the Request of the Legal Representative of Victims to Authorise Two Victims to Withdraw Their Participation, STL-11-01/PT/PTJ, 19 December 2012, disposition.

[73] ICC, *Prosecutor v. William Samoei Ruto and Joshua Arap Sang*, Trial Chamber V(a), Decision on the Legal Representative's Report on the Withdrawal of Victims, ICC-01/09-01/11-1098-Red2, 14 November 2013, para 18.

[74] ICC, *Prosecutor v. Ayyash* et al., Pre-Trial Judge, Pre-Trial Judge, Decision Relating to the Request of the Legal Representative of Victims to Authorise Two Victims to Withdraw Their Participation, STL-11-01/PT/PTJ, 19 December 2012, para 7.

[75] See Chap. 7.

- Where an application for participation has been submitted to the relevant court but not yet determined by a chamber, it may be terminated either by voluntary withdrawal or by the narrowing of the charges in the case.
- All three courts permit victims to voluntarily withdraw their participation once it has begun.
- Where victims seek to withdraw voluntarily, none of the courts has clearly required that this be done in writing by the victim him/herself. However, where possible victims' lawyers are advised to seek a written request for withdrawal from their clients to avoid doubt as to the voluntary nature of the withdrawal.
- At the ECCC a deceased civil party's participation may be continued by a family member or other successor.
- At the ICC the possibility of a deceased victim's participation being continued varies depending on the chamber with carriage of the case. Three chambers have to date permitted this.
- In any event victims' lawyers should establish systems to the extent possible to enable them to maintain communications with clients and their families and to ensure they are aware of the death of any clients. In any case where a participating victim dies this should be brought to the attention of the relevant chamber. Where it is possible for participation to be resumed by a successor, victims and their family members should be made aware of this, and steps taken to ensure where appropriate that a successor can be identified.
- Participating victims may have their role terminated by a chamber where new information calls into question whether the person is indeed a victim of the crime(s) charged. This has most often occurred at the time of trial judgment. At the ICC it has particularly affected dual status victims whose witness testimony has called into doubt their victim status.
- Lawyers of participating victims should carefully consider the risks involved in having their clients appear in person before a court to give evidence, and where appropriate should discuss any matters relevant to these risks with the Prosecution if it proposes to call a participating victim as a witness. Participating victims wishing to appear before a chamber to give evidence should be made aware of the increased risk of having their participation withdrawn if apparent inconsistencies in their accounts arise through cross-examination.
- Victims' lawyers and Registry officials should together ensure that victims who have had their participation terminated are appropriately notified of this fact and of its legal and practical implications.

Chapter 15
Communication Between Victims' Lawyers and Their Clients

Kinga Tibori-Szabó, Barbara Bianchini, Anushka Sehmi and Silke Studzinsky

Abstract This chapter looks at the goals and framework of communication between lawyers representing victims and their clients, with a view to offering specific and practical advice for initiating, maintaining and improving that communication. It will first look at the goals and framework of communication between representatives and victims, and how such goals can be set. Then it will address the content of the communication from lawyers to victims and *vice versa*, namely how victims should be informed, consulted and involved throughout their representation. Thirdly, the chapter will elaborate on the manner and methods through which communication should be achieved. Practical examples based on past ECCC, ICC

Kinga Tibori-Szabó is legal officer for the Kosovo Specialist Chambers. She has previously worked for the Legal Representative of Victims at the Special Tribunal for Lebanon. Barbara Bianchini, Clinical psychologist, Victims and Witnesses Unit of the Special Tribunal for Lebanon. Anushka Sehmi, lawyer, former Legal Assistant and Case Manager for the Legal Representative for Victims in the case of *The Prosecutor v. Uhuru Muigai Kenyatta* before the International Criminal Court and former Field Officer for the Victims Participation and Reparations Section at the ICC. Silke Studzinsky, Head of Victims Participation Office at the Kosovo Specialist Chambers, former Legal Adviser to the Trust Fund for Victims at the International Criminal Court and former international civil party lawyer before the ECCC. The views expressed herein are those of the authors and do not necessarily reflect the views of the employing organisations.

K. Tibori-Szabó (✉) · B. Bianchini · A. Sehmi · S. Studzinsky
The Hague, The Netherlands
e-mail: kingatibori@gmail.com

B. Bianchini
e-mail: resiliencebeyondborders@gmail.com

A. Sehmi
e-mail: anushkasehmi@gmail.com

S. Studzinsky
e-mail: silke.studzinsky@gmail.com

K. Tibori-Szabó and M. Hirst (eds.), *Victim Participation in International Criminal Justice*, International Criminal Justice Series 11,
DOI 10.1007/978-94-6265-177-7_15

and STL experience will be offered throughout the chapter. Although its main purpose is to address communication between victims' lawyers and their clients, the chapter can also be useful to registry officials, Prosecution and Defence lawyers, as well as judges and legal officers involved in the victim participation process.

Keywords Communication · Non-verbal communication · Verbal communication · Information · Consultation · Trauma

Contents

15.1 Introduction

Meaningful victim participation in international criminal justice depends on adequate and effective legal representation. One of the most important elements of adequate and effective legal representation is maintaining proper communication between victims' lawyers and their clients.

Lawyers representing civil parties before the Extraordinary Chambers in the Courts of Cambodia (ECCC) are bound by the Code of Ethics for Lawyers Licensed with the Bar Association of the Kingdom of Cambodia, which contains general provisions requiring lawyers to respect the obligations of their oath and the principles of conscience, humanity, and tact. The Code does not contain specific provisions related to the manner and methods of communication between lawyer and client.

The Code of Professional Conduct of the International Criminal Court (ICC) states that 'Counsel shall provide the client with all explanations reasonably needed to make informed decisions regarding his or her representation.'[1]

[1] ICC, Code of Professional Conduct for Counsel, Resolution ICC-ASP/4/Res.1 (adopted at the 3rd plenary meeting on 2 December 2005, by consensus), Article 15.

The Code of Professional Conduct for Defence Counsel and Legal Representatives of Victims at the Special Tribunal for Lebanon (STL) is the most detailed in this respect. Article 8(F) provides that a legal representative must 'exercise professional judgment, render open and honest advice to his Clients and act at all times with fairness, integrity and candour towards his Clients' and that he or she should 'consult to the extent possible with all his Clients regarding the substantial aspects of their representation and their views and concerns on questions arising in or related to the proceedings.'[2] Moreover, Article 33(B) of the same code of conduct provides a list of factors on the basis of which the effectiveness of representation can be assessed. Next to attendance at court, motion practice, knowledge of the law, knowledge of the facts relevant to the case, development of case theory and other factors, communication with clients is also provided as a criterion on the basis of which effective representation can be assessed. Accordingly, Article 33(B)(xi) offers the following details in relation to communication with clients.

A legal representative should:

(a) To the extent permitted by obligations of confidentiality pursuant to relevant judicial rulings, advise the Clients with complete candour concerning all aspects of the case, inform them objectively of the possible outcomes and keep them regularly informed of the material developments in the case;
(b) Meet regularly with the Clients;
(c) Obtain the observations of the Clients concerning any statements they might previously have made to the Office of the Prosecutor, the Defence, law enforcement, government agencies, tribunals, international bodies or the media;
(d) Consult the Clients regularly regarding the overall objectives of representation and whether they have views or concerns regarding specific issues or motions which are before, or likely to come before, the Pre-Trial Judge or Trial Chamber;
(e) Maintain a full and contemporaneous record of the substance of any oral communication with the Clients and maintain a full record of all written communication;
(f) Execute the instructions of the Clients in conformity with the strategy adopted and the interests of the Clients; and,
(g) Undertake all activities, including meetings, communications and other interactions with Clients, in a way which takes into account any vulnerabilities or special needs of the clients and does not prejudice the privacy, security or well-being of the Clients.

Notwithstanding the details provided in the STL code of conduct as regards the duty of victims' lawyers to communicate with their clients, not much is said about the manner and methods through which such communication should take place.

The purpose of this chapter is therefore to elaborate on the goals and framework of communication between representatives and victims, the content of the communication from lawyers to victims and *vice versa*, and the manner and methods through which communication should be achieved. Given some of the differences between the universe of victims at the three courts analysed (i.e. the number of victims in particular cases, the trauma they suffered, their educational and cultural background), the various limitations and difficulties that may arise can be

[2] STL, Code of Professional Conduct for Defence Counsel and Legal Representatives of Victims appearing before the Special Tribunal for Lebanon, STL/CC/2012/03 (adopted 14 December 2012), Article 8(F).

quite different and the most important ones will be tackled in this chapter in the relevant sections.

Although this chapter primarily focuses on how victims' lawyers can improve communication with their clients, the overall message can be useful to all legal practitioners (Prosecution and Defence lawyers, legal officers, judges as well as Registry officials) whose work entails dealing with victims having participant or party status at the relevant courts.

15.2 Goals of Communication with Victims

At the earliest phases, even before a legal representative or civil party lawyer is appointed, those familiar with the victims or groups of victims play a crucial role in advising them to apply for participation.[3] Such individuals include not only (local or foreign) lawyers, but also intermediaries, NGO employees, or Registry officials working for the relevant international court.

At the ECCC, the vast majority of victims who decided to apply for civil party status did so through outreach activities conducted by local NGOs. More than 80% of victim information forms at the ECCC were submitted through intermediary NGOs, with the main NGOs being the Cambodian Human Rights and Development Association (ADHOC), the Documentation Center of Cambodia (DC-Cam) and the Khmer Institute for Democracy (KID). As a result of the adoption, in 2007, of the Internal Rules allowing for victim participation, major NGOs began including in their outreach activities the collection of applications for civil party status. In 2007, in the absence of a victims' unit, such applications were submitted to the Office of the Co-Investigating Judges. In January 2008, the Victims Unit formally came into being, but it had no budget for operations until the beginning of 2009. So during 2007–2008 initial contact with survivors was handled by NGOs as part of their outreach activities. During this phase, little was known about the Court's scope of investigations, so for applications submitted during 2007–2008, it made little sense to distinguish between *Case 001* and *Case 002*. It was only during the second half of 2008 that the rudimentary Victims Unit began to review the forms received, in order to identify potential civil parties for the upcoming *Case 001* and to prioritise their processing. The Victims Unit, later renamed the Victims Support Section (VSS), played a more active outreach role in the months leading up to the application deadline in *Case 002* (end of 2009—beginning of 2010).[4]

---

[3] REDRESS (2005) Ensuring the Effective Participation of Victims before the International Criminal Court. Comments and Recommendations Regarding Legal Representation for Victims, http://www.redress.org/downloads/publications/REDRESS%20-%20Legal%20Representation%20for%20Victims%2023%20May%202005.pdf. Accessed 26 August 2016, p. 2.

[4] Written correspondence with Christoph Sperfeldt, Ph.D. Scholar, Australian National University, 27 September 2015 and 5 October 2015 (records on file with the authors).

At the ICC, while it is usually the Victims Participation and Reparations Section (VPRS) and/or the Public Information and Outreach Section (PIOS) that first make contact with victims for the purpose of informing them of their right to participate in the proceedings, it is the intermediaries who usually bear the greatest burden in the task of explaining participation to the affected communities. For this reason, the VPRS endeavours to train intermediaries both on the participatory rights of victims and on assisting victims to fill out application forms for participation and reparations. Despite the best of intentions of intermediaries and of the VPRS,[5] the task of explaining the judicial process at the ICC and the concepts of participation and reparations is a difficult one. This situation can be made even more complex when intermediaries or local lawyers who have not received any training from the VPRS or are not familiar with the application process, assist victims in the completion of application forms.[6]

For these reasons, upon meeting their clients for the first time, victims' lawyers appointed by the relevant court should not assume that the victims have clearly understood their rights. The initial contact between lawyer and victim should aim to clarify the basic tenets of the victims' participation in the proceedings. In a more general sense, if managed in a respectful and compassionate way, the first contact can help create an effective and trustful working relationship between lawyer and victim.[7] The initial contact will also greatly inform the case strategy and allow the lawyer to ascertain the goals and framework of future communication with clients.

It is essential that a lawyer meet with clients for the first time in person in order to introduce himself or herself, and in order to allow the victims to introduce themselves to him or her. With smaller groups of victims, it is easier to undertake one-on-one introductions. However, when working with larger groups of victims this is much more difficult. Depending on the types of crimes suffered by the victims, the initial meeting may require more effort on the part of the lawyer in order to ensure that the victims are comfortable to speak with him or her. Of course with an increased frequency of contact between client and lawyer, it is easier to establish a true relationship of trust and allow for more candid discussions.

In preparation for the first meeting, a newly appointed legal representative should review all the information available to him or her regarding the particular victim(s). As it will be discussed in Sect. 15.5.1, this preparation will provide

[5] It is also worth noting that the ICC Registry does not have a field presence in all situation countries, which can make the task of conveying messages to victims difficult. In many cases security concerns mean that the VPRS and PIOS cannot operate in such situation countries, leaving a wide information gap.

[6] For a more detailed consideration of the challenges involved in working with intermediaries, see Chap. 4.

[7] Personal notes and experience of co-author Barbara Bianchini.

the lawyer with some basic ideas on what to expect from and how to conduct the initial meeting. The legal representative should identify the goals of the first communication. Ideally, these goals will encompass all of the following: meet the clients, hear their story, identify their needs and concerns, explain the justice process and the role the victim or civil party plays in it, help them understand their rights, highlight the limitations of the process and of participation, explain the role of the legal representatives in this process, explain the possible forms of reparation, the existing limitations thereof, and ascertain and follow the development of any security risk in order to protect the victims. Moreover, lawyers should also inquire about the frequency and extent of the communication expected by the victim from the lawyer.

For this purpose, the legal representative may consider drawing up a check list in advance (see Fig. 15.1), putting down all the questions to be asked from the client and all the issues he or she wishes to discuss with the particular individual, together with some basic reminders on how to conduct the meeting. Needless to say, it will seldom be the case that all these issues could be discussed during the first meeting with the client, especially if the first encounters are with a group of victims rather than an individual victim. Nonetheless, the checklist should be an exhaustive one, as it can then be adjusted based on the initial contact with the victims.

The legal representative should find a suitable method to create a record of the initial and ensuing conversations. Such a record will serve as a reminder of the pertinent issues related to the victim or the group or representatives of victims. The identified and adjusted set of goals together with a system of recording the main elements of the initial and subsequent contacts can create a basic framework for communication between lawyer and victims.

In this respect, at the STL, the legal representatives meet new participating victims as soon as practicable after the Victim Participation Unit (VPU) notifies the applicants that their participating victim status has been granted.[8] The legal representatives in the *Ayyash* et al. trial have developed a practice in relation to initiating contact with the victims granted participant status. Before meeting them, the representatives consult the application forms and supporting materials relevant to each victim to reach an initial familiarity with the particular person. Where relevant, the LRV also consults the VPU liaison officer who helped the victims fill out their application forms. In some cases, the legal representatives will know a victim in advance, as the victim may be a relative or acquaintance of already participating

[8] See, for instance: STL, *Prosecutor v. Ayyash* et al., STL-11-01/PT/PTJ, Decision on Victims' Participation in the Proceedings, 8 May 2012, *Dispositif*; Second Decision on Victims' Participation in the Proceedings, 3 September 2012, *Dispositif*; Third Decision on Victims' Participation in the Proceedings, 28 November 2012, *Dispositif*; Fifth Decision on Victims' Participation in the Proceedings, 18 July 2014, *Dispositif*; Sixth Decision on Victims' Participation in the Proceedings, 6 November 2014, *Dispositif*.

Sample Check-List for First Contact with the Victims

- Introduce yourself and everyone present
- Listen to the victim (his or her story)
  - Do not interrupt the victim when he or she is recalling significant events
- Explain the justice process (establishment of the court, organs, place of the victims' lawyers within the structure)
- Explain the role the victims play in the justice process
- Explain the rights and duties that come with their status
- Highlight the limitations of their participant or party status
- Explain the role of the victims' lawyers
- Explain the possible forms of reparation, and the existing limitations thereof
- Ask questions to identify the needs and concerns of the victim(s)
  - Ask what the victim(s) expect(s) from the proceedings
  - Ask how often the victim(s) wish(es) to see the lawyers
  - Ask about the frequency and content of the information the victim(s) wish(es) to receive about the proceedings
  - Ask whether and to what extent the victim(s) wish(es) to be consulted about the case
  - Elicit and be sensitive to any special needs or concerns
  - Ascertain any security risk the victim is facing
- Provide the victim(s) with contact details of the lawyers
- Create a record of the meeting (when and where was it held, who was present, what was said, the demeanour of the victim and any other relevant information).

Fig. 15.1 Sample Check-List for First Contact with the Victims (Adapted from Sample Check-List used by the *Ayyash* et al. LRV team. Also relying on personal notes and experience of co-author Barbara Bianchini. See also: Ministry of Justice (2011) Achieving Best Evidence in Criminal Proceedings Guidance on interviewing victims and witnesses, and guidance on using special measures, London (UK))

victims, who put them in contact with the LRV. In any case, the LRV conducts the initial meeting with the victim on the basis of a standard checklist used with every client. If the LRV is aware of specific issues relating to a particular victim, he or she will bring those up during the first meeting. After the initial contact, the LRV holds individual meetings with the victims 3–4 times a year and maintains regular contact with them via other means (phone calls, emails, access to secured website, messaging applications). The written record of the first meeting (comprising summaries of what was said to the victim, what questions, concerns, wishes the victim expressed and any other issue discussed) will serve as basis for the "LRV Notes" supplemented each time there is a contact between the representatives and the victim. This ensures that the legal representatives are easily reminded of the main issues for every victim before meeting them again. It is also a very efficient way of recording changes in the personal situation, attitude, wishes or concerns of the victims. This practice was gradually developed by the legal representatives in the *Ayyash* et al. trial, and some of the notes were later supplemented to construct a consistent, homogenous system of notes, but given the relatively small number of victims and recentness of participation, such adjustment was feasible. To complete the framework, the LRV also tracks separately the date and place of contact for each victim, including face-to-face, phone, email or messaging.[9]

As said above, it will often take more than one meeting to touch upon all the pertinent issues related to the victims' participation. For instance, at the ECCC, in *Case 001*, the group of victims (mainly relatives of deceased victims and only a few direct victims) were regularly meeting well before the establishment of the VSS, so the significance of a first contact with their lawyers was not so prominent. Given the relatively low number of civil parties in *Case 001* (approximately 90) these regular meetings proved to be a successful medium for keeping the civil parties informed and, in time, build a strong sense of community.

There will be cases, however, where the number of victims is so large that it is impossible to meet with everybody individually or collectively on a continuous basis. In such cases, other options need to be developed, such as selecting, from the group of victims, one or more representatives with whom the lawyers can meet. This is not necessarily the ideal solution, but in some cases it is the only available option.

In this respect, as said above, most lawyers representing civil parties at the ECCC initially relied on NGOs to communicate with their clients. This is especially true with regards to *Case 001*, where most communication with civil parties was facilitated by NGOs. This only changed after 2009, when the VSS began to organise its own provincial forums (which continue today), then mainly focusing on *Case 002*.[10] Initially, the VSS provided general information to the participating civil parties. Later on, a part of the one-day forums was reserved for meetings with the lawyers of the civil parties.[11] Small localised community-style meetings offer more opportunities for two-way communication. The ADHOC civil party representative scheme was perhaps the most innovative communication model around the ECCC.[12] In this scheme, civil parties met by provinces and selected or elected representatives who regularly met with the civil party lawyers. The meetings between victims' lawyers and representatives lasted on average 1.5–2 days. During these meetings, the lawyers informed the representatives of the ongoing proceedings, answered their questions and discussed specific topics. Once back in their district, the representatives, with the assistance of ADHOC, organised regular meetings at the district or community level where they transmitted the acquired

[9] Personal notes and experience of co-author Kinga Tibori-Szabó.

[10] Written correspondence with Christoph Sperfeldt, Ph.D. Scholar, Australian National University, 27 September 2015 and 5 October 2015 (records on file with the authors).

[11] Personal notes and experience of co-author Silke Studzinsky.

[12] Sperfeldt 2013, p. 360; Written correspondence with Christoph Sperfeldt, Ph.D. Scholar, Australian National University, 27 September 2015 and 5 October 2015 (records on file with the authors).

information to their fellow civil parties.[13] KID was also able to maintain its own scheme until 2011, after which it ran into difficulties and eventually ceased operations. Today the few VSS provincial forums and trial attendance of civil parties facilitated by the VSS are among the few remaining communication channels, together with some smaller NGO outreach projects targeting specific sub-groups among the civil parties. Overall, communication patterns vary greatly across the different civil party lawyers' groups at the ECCC. Legal teams with smaller numbers of civil parties and well established links to local intermediary NGOs tend to be best in communicating with clients. Many other civil parties may hear rarely (or never) from their lawyers, especially from those based outside the country. Almost all models rely on certain focal persons (often better educated, and in possession of a mobile phone) able to facilitate communication with other civil parties living in the same area.[14]

Likewise, the large number of participating victims in some of the ICC cases makes it very difficult to hold individual or even collective meetings.[15] In the *Bemba* case, 5,229 victims were granted participatory rights. As at November 2016, this is the greatest number of victims participating in any case before the ICC.[16] The legal representative's team[17] at trial consisted of 5–6 people, who were responsible for the representation of over 5000 victims. Moreover, a large number of participating victims have suffered from sexual violence and as such it was not always possible to meet with such victims in a group setting. Therefore, it was often the case that the team conducted individual meetings with the victims. Additionally, the security situation in the Central African Republic prevented the victims' lawyers from regularly meeting with their clients. Cumulatively, the sheer number of participating victims, the local security situation and the small size of the representatives' team made it impossible to hold regular individual or even

[13] Personal notes and experience of co-author Silke Studzinsky.

[14] Written correspondence with Christoph Sperfeldt, Ph.D. Scholar, Australian National University, 27 September 2015 and 5 October 2015 (records on file with the authors).

[15] As at April 2015, there were 839 participating victims in the *Prosecutor v. Uhuru Muigai Kenyatta* case, 850 in the *Prosecutor v. William Samoei Ruto and Joshua Arap Sang* case. Furthermore, as at April 2015, the Office of the Public Counsel for Victims (OPCV) represented, among others, 1120 participating victims in the *Prosecutor v. Bosco Ntaganda* case, 729 in the *Prosecutor v. Laurent Gbagbo and Charles Blé Goudé* case, and 512 in the *Prosecutor v. Simone Gbagbo* case. In total, the OPCV represents over 3000 victims across eight cases and situations. As at April 2015, it was composed of 11 members of staff.

[16] Interview with Carine Pineau and Virginie Roche, legal assistants to Ms. Douzima Lawson, Legal Representative for Victims in *Prosecutor v. Jean-Pierre Bemba Gombo*, ICC, March 2015 (records on file with the authors).

[17] Initially, two groups of participating victims were constituted in the *Bemba* case, each represented by one legal representative and a small team. After the 2014 death of Mr. Assingambi Zarambaud, one of the legal representatives, the court merged the two victims' groups who have since then been represented by a single larger team under Me Douzima Lawson.

effective collective meetings.[18] Communication was much more frequent and effective in the *Kenyatta* and *Ruto and Sang* cases, where the LRV teams were locally based and employed several field assistants. Communication with victims usually took place through in-person meetings every 6–8 weeks. In addition, the field assistants maintained telephone communication with the victims. Most of the victims either had their own mobile telephone or had access to a phone of a relative or neighbour. Victims had the contact details of the field staff, and those who were able to speak English could also contact the LRV directly.

Whether communication takes place during individual conversations, group meetings or meetings with selected representatives of the victims, victims' lawyers need to have a set of goals in mind. Communication should always be a two-way process: information provided by the lawyer to the victim(s) and information shared by the victim(s) with the lawyer. As said above, a relatively low number of participating victims will permit holding regular individual meetings and the detailed discussion of topics related to victim participation. Group meetings and meetings with group representatives will have to follow an adjusted agenda, depending on the size and composition of the group as well as the logistical implications of holding such meetings. In any case, victims' lawyers should work on the basis of a check-list (as sampled above) that they can continually adjust, in order to keep track of the set goals of communication between lawyer and client. Setting and adjusting the goals of this contact, recording the series of communication and, as it will be discussed below, adequately providing information, consulting and involving the victims and paying attention to the manner of communication will create an overall framework in which this two-way process will function effectively. Needless to say, many limitations and difficulties arise when communicating with victims and some of the most important ones will be discussed in this chapter. The need, however, to achieve communication with victims based on identified goals and within a particular framework is unequivocal regardless of the difficulties that may arise in this process.

15.3 Informing the Victims

In the two-way process of communication providing accurate, adequate and helpful information to the victims is essential not only because of the ethical duty every lawyer has towards his or her client, but also because this is one of the fundamental rights that participation entails for the victims.[19]

[18] Interview with Carine Pineau and Virginie Roche, legal assistants to Ms. Douzima Lawson, Legal Representative for Victims in *Prosecutor v. Jean-Pierre Bemba Gombo*, ICC, March 2015 (records on file with the authors).

[19] It is important to note here that the right to information is not a privilege of participating victims or civil parties only. Victims of crimes prosecuted before the ECCC, ICC and STL in general ("affected populations" in ICC parlance) have a right to information that is usually the responsibility of the relevant outreach sections.

Depending on the proceedings in question, victims' lawyers should prepare in advance the information that needs to be provided to victims throughout the representation process. Preparation can take the form of a check-list, or any other, more open-ended or flexible form of *aide-memoire*. The overall purpose is to aid the lawyer in conveying the information in an understandable manner and not to leave out inadvertently essential details. The extent, specificity and nature of information as well as the frequency with which it is shared may be attuned to the particular victim or group of victims, but the "hard" data related to the proceedings and the status of the victim in those proceedings needs to be conveyed to the clients. Some of this information may be more important during the initial contact with the victim(s), whereas other issues will arise later. In any case, a legal representative or a lawyer representing civil parties should never assume that explaining an issue once to a victim will preclude recurring questions on the same issue. On the contrary, lawyers should be prepared to give explanations to the same questions and topics as many times as needed.

The content of information that needs to be provided to the victim(s) will depend on many factors: the court or tribunal itself, the particular case, the form of victim participation, the plethora of rights accorded to victims, the stage of the proceedings, the rules of procedure and evidence, decisions taken by the judges, the manner in which evidence is presented by the Prosecution and other matters related to the justice process. Likewise, the way in which the court or tribunal is perceived in the community of the victim(s), the overall security situation in the area, the particular security situation of the victim, his family or community, the personal situation of the victim or the characteristics of the group of victims are just some of the factors that will influence the content of the information to be provided to them.

Notwithstanding the multitude of factors continuously shaping the content of the information to be provided, victims' lawyers should keep in mind certain basic themes that will aid them in sharing information (Fig. 15.2).

There are two very important, overarching issues that need to be kept in mind by lawyers when providing information to the victims.

First, legal representatives and lawyers representing civil parties should always explain, as clearly as possible, the limitations of participation—whether these are true barriers against achieving some of the needs of victims, substantive limitations of their rights, or temporal, logistical or procedural conditions that qualify certain aspects of participation. For instance, if the specific needs of the victims cannot be achieved by becoming a participant or a party in an international criminal proceeding, this needs to be explained clearly to the victim. Further, for those victims who are familiar with a domestic civil party system, understanding the different nature of victim participation at the ICC or STL may be cumbersome and needs to be addressed by the legal representatives as early as possible. Likewise, limitations of a judicial process need to be clarified to victims. For example, at the STL, the legal representatives in the *Ayyash* et al. case had to justify repeatedly the delayed start of the trial to their clients and to explain the procedure through which trial proceedings may start at the tribunal. In other words, victims' lawyers need

Basic themes to keep in mind when providing information

- Explain how the respective court or tribunal works (where it is, why it was set up, what its purpose is, who works there, etc.)
- Explain the roles of the relevant units of the court or the tribunal (especially those with which the victim may come in contact)
- Explain the roles of parties and participants (who does what)
- Explain the role of the victims' lawyers in the judicial process
    - Outline the composition of the victims' lawyers' team (who does what)
- Explain the meaning and content of their rights as participating victims or civil parties
- If and when relevant, explain that the meaning and content of their rights may be interpreted in various ways by the court (more restrictive or more permissive approaches)
- Highlight developments in the proceedings (explain the stage and state of proceedings; justify longer recess periods; explain the order of case presentation, etc.)
- Explain decisions taken by the judges and their effects (especially if they impact on the victims)
- Summarise important testimonies and tendered documents
- Highlight and discuss the potential need for protective measures

Fig. 15.2 Basic Themes to Keep in Mind when Providing Information

to be prepared to explain to their clients what an international criminal trial can really serve to achieve and whether the needs of victims can be met or approximated by such proceedings.

Secondly, legal representatives and lawyers representing civil parties need to be aware that the information provided can greatly influence the opinion and perspective of their clients. They need to reflect on what is said and how it is said. Whereas it is nearly impossible to convey successfully all information related to their participation, victims should be adequately informed, so that they can take informed decisions regarding their status. Reflecting on the selection of the information conveyed, while remaining honest and transparent is an absolute condition of effective victim representation.

15.4 Consulting the Victims

Often lawyers may assume that their duty is simply to relay information regarding case proceedings and developments to their clients. As said above, however, communication between lawyers and victims is a two-way process, comprising not only information provided by lawyers to their clients, but also information shared by the victims with their lawyers. Listening to what the victims have to say and building a relationship of trust is equally important. Moreover, this second prong of the process also means consulting the client on the amount and form of information they wish to receive as well as on pertinent issues related to the case with a view to involving them actively in decision-making.

15.4.1 Consulting Victims on the Amount and Form of Information They Wish to Receive

At the outset, victims' lawyers should determine what the victims' respective wishes are with regard to the amount of information that they want to receive from their lawyers (see Fig. 15.1). For example, it should be clarified whether the victim or group of victims prefers to receive a copy of a particular decision, a brief summary of the ruling or simply a notification of the outcome. Some victims will wish to be sent daily information regarding the proceedings or read decisions themselves. Others would want to receive weekly or regular updates with a summary of decisions and proceedings. Yet others would only want to be informed of the most significant decisions that impact on their participation.

Likewise, victims' lawyers should determine the form in which their clients want to receive the information. The manner and methods of communication will be detailed below, but for the purpose of this section it is helpful to note that conveying the right information in the wrong form is almost equivalent to not conveying any information to the client. For instance, sending emails to a victim or group of victims while knowing that the particular individuals do not check their emails is impractical. Likewise, providing leaflets or other written information to illiterate victims is inappropriate.

For instance, at the ECCC, providing most civil parties with written information through e-mail or leaflets has not been an option, as many were illiterate or were not used to read and understand complex legal matters. The main medium of communication has been the face-to-face meeting, where relevant information is summarised and explained. A secondary means of communication has been via the phone; usually a Cambodian team member would call the civil parties reachable by phone in order to inform them about a particular decision.[20]

At the ICC, depending on the case, individual and collective meetings, as well as other forms of communication are used. In the *Bemba* case, the LRV team met their clients 3–4 times a year; other forms of communication were not necessarily fruitful.[21] In the Kenya cases, both individual and collective meetings, as well as phone contact was used.[22] The OPCV reports that it resorts to individual meetings, collective meetings, phone calls, email, Skype and distributes information sheets to maintain communication with participating victims.[23] In the *Banda* case, many of the victims lived in poor rural areas and many were illiterate, and thus in-person communication was the only way to keep in contact. For those few victims who

[20] Personal notes and experience of co-author Silke Studzinsky.

[21] Interview with Carine Pineau and Virginie Roche, legal assistants to Ms. Douzima Lawson, Legal Representative for Victims in *Prosecutor v. Jean-Pierre Bemba Gombo*, ICC, March 2015 (records on file with the authors).

[22] Personal notes and experience of co-author Anushka Sehmi.

[23] Interview with Paolina Massidda, Principal Counsel, Office of Public Counsel for Victims, ICC, November 2014 (records on file with the authors).

were able to use the internet, the LRV team has sent out informative letters with case updates including any developments, as well as explanations regarding the slow progress on the case every quarter. In addition, some victims were also informed of the proceedings and the forthcoming informative letter through phone calls.[24] In the *Lubanga* case, the LRV team strived to hold regular individual meetings, but it also relied on telephone communication as well as intermediaries.[25]

At the STL, the LRV team in the *Ayyash* et al. case has developed a dynamic communication plan relying on both more traditional and innovative media of communication. Individual meetings, mail or email correspondence, phone calls and phone messaging have been the original methods through which the LRV team communicated with its clients. Nonetheless, in the last two years, due to a growing need on behalf of the victims to proliferate contact methods and as a result of the LRV's resolve to create some cohesion within the group of public victims, additional tools of communication were introduced. First, the LRV team set up a bi-annual newsletter, distributed to the victims, in which the trial proceedings and other events of the STL are summarised, staff members of the court are introduced, legal concepts are explained and through which the LRV directly speaks to the group of victims. Second, the LRV set up a secure website that contains information similar to the newsletter, but which serves the needs of those victims who regularly use the internet and would prefer to receive information more often than a bi-annual newsletter permits. Thirdly, the LRV decided to hold "town-hall meetings" for the public victims, which are dinners organised by the LRV and the Victim Participation Unit (VPU), where victims are invited to receive a brief update of the proceedings, ask questions from the representatives, and share thoughts and mingle with the other victims. Lastly, as a result of repeated requests from its clients and after careful consideration of the security risks involved, the LRV team now accepts contact initiatives from its clients via messaging applications (Whatsapp, Viber). This decision was preceded by careful considerations regarding: the availability of more secure forms of communication, the willingness of the victims to use such forums, and, ultimately, the content of information shared through these messaging applications. Since it became evident that the victims were not interested in switching to more secure messaging environments and that the content of the information shared via these messages was non-confidential and trivial (brief greetings, holiday wishes), the LRV accepted to have restricted communication with its clients via these applications. This decision opened the door to frequent, *ad hoc* communication between clients and the LRV members, which helped create a more cordial, trustful relationship with individual victims. These four methods have greatly enhanced the capacity of a small team to communicate with 72, geographically remote victims. All these contacts are tracked by

[24] Interview with Hélène Cissé, Legal Representative of Victims, *Prosecutor v. Abdallah Banda*, ICC, November 2014 (records on file with the authors).

[25] Interview with Luc Walleyn, Legal Representative for Victims, *Prosecutor v. Thomas Lubanga Dyilo*, ICC, October 2014 (records on file with the authors).

the LRV team in a spreadsheet that notes the pseudonym of the victim, the date of contact, the LRV member in contact and the medium of contact. This record also helps the LRV realise which are those victims with whom it has only occasional or rare contact and act upon this observation.

While it will not be always possible to meet victims' preferences regarding communication media, lawyers should strive to follow the suggestions and wishes expressed by the victims as regards the amount and form of information they ought to receive.

15.4.2 Consulting Victims About Their Views and Concerns

Typically, the amount and form of information victims wish to receive will also allow the lawyers to draw conclusions on the extent to which their clients wish to be consulted about issues related to their participation. There will always be more active victims who wish to be consulted on strategic and procedural issues alike, while others will only want to be asked for an opinion if the matter directly impacts on them. In general, victims' lawyers should be prepared to consult their clients on: the different strategic issues related to participation, building and developing the representation strategy together, selecting the type of evidence to be presented to the court, employing experts to carry out scientific research for the victims' case, if applicable, and the importance of various procedural matters related to the proceedings. If relevant, victims' lawyers should maintain discussions regarding the possible forms of reparation and regularly consult their clients on probable reparation requests.

Consulting clients will apprise the legal representatives and lawyers representing civil parties on the views of the victims, their evolving attitude and interests. Victims can be involved in taking decisions on strategic issues related to representation, but also on questions related to the particular phase of the proceedings.

At the ICC, both chambers in the *Ruto and Sang* and the *Kenyatta* cases requested information from the legal representatives as to the victims' view on where the trial should take place.[26] In the *Kenyatta* case, 155 victims were consulted on the possible venue of the trial.[27] The legal representatives' team took

[26] For academic views on the benefits of having trials take place close to the location where the crimes were committed and/or where the surviving victims are see: Kamatali 2005, pp. 90–93; Clark 2011, pp. 521–545. Nonetheless, the same commentators also emphasise that security and the impartiality of the judicial process are essential factors to be taken in consideration.

[27] ICC, *Prosecutor v. Uhuru Muigai Kenyatta,* LRV, Victims' Observations in relation to the "Defence Application for change of place where the Court shall sit for Trial", ICC-01/09-02/11-629, 7 February 2013, para 5.

steps to ensure that a broad cross-section of the victims was consulted from the perspective of gender, ethnicity and geographic location.[28] At first, the legal representative's field staff consulted the majority of the victims by telephone. Thereafter, the legal representative raised the issue with several other victims in person. After brief explanations regarding the possibility of having the ICC trial proceedings take place in The Hague, Arusha or Kenya, the victims were asked their preference as to where the trial should take place.[29] The overwhelming majority of the victims expressed a preference that the trial be held in The Hague. Only two respondents stated that the trial should take place in Nairobi as they would be able to observe the hearings in person.[30] The vast majority of the consulted victims had serious security- and fairness-related concerns regarding the judicial process if the trial were to be held in either Arusha or Kenya.[31] On this basis, the legal representative in the *Kenyatta* case submitted that the trial should take place in The Hague.[32] In the *Ruto and Sang* case, the LRV consulted 94 victims on this issue.[33] First, the LRV informed the victims of the Chamber's order, in particular about the three possible venues (The Hague, Arusha, and Kenya) that were possible options for the trial. The LRV then explained to the victims the issues (pros and cons) regarding each of the three locations, including victim and witness security, logistics and delay in commencement of the trial. In order not to influence the responses, it was clearly spelt out that the issues were non-exhaustive, and the victims were also given the opportunity to give freely their views.[34] Of those consulted, 50 participants gave their views whilst the rest chose to abstain or were not ready to give their opinion.[35] The results of the victims' views were provided in an annex to the LRV's submission. Public Annex I showed that 82% of the victims considered that the trials should continue to be held at The Hague, 16% thought that the trials should be held in Arusha, Tanzania and 2% opined that the trials should be held in Kenya.[36] In Public Annex II, the LRV provided a

[28] ICC, *Prosecutor v. Uhuru Muigai Kenyatta,* LRV, Victims' Observations in relation to the "Defence Application for change of place where the Court shall sit for Trial", ICC-01/09-02/11-629, 7 February 2013, para 6.

[29] Ibid., para 7.

[30] Ibid., paras 8–9.

[31] Ibid., para 12.

[32] Ibid., para 13.

[33] ICC, *Prosecutor v. William Samoei Ruto and Joshua Arap Sang,* LRV, Common Legal Representative for Victims' Observations in Relation to the "Joint Defence Application for Change of Place Where the Court Shall Sit for Trial", ICC-01/09-01/11-620, 22 February 2013, para 3.

[34] Ibid., para 4.

[35] Ibid., para 3.

[36] Ibid., para 5 and Annex I (public).

breakdown of the reasons given by the victims on their preferred venue for the trial. Accordingly, the main reasons provided related to the security of the victims and the fear of interference with the judicial process.[37] Notwithstanding these views, the LRV submitted that the demands of affected communities in general, and the views and concerns of the victims of the case in particular, would be better served by holding the trial at a venue closer to where the crimes were committed, from where the victims could follow the proceedings more closely.[38] Cognisant that a majority of the victims preferred the case to be held at The Hague, the LRV nevertheless submitted that the trial should take place in Arusha, Tanzania.[39] It is beyond the purpose of this chapter to comment on the LRV's decision to submit his own observation in addition to those of the victims. It is important to note, however, that the purpose of consulting the victims is to seek their instructions and ensure this way that they play a sufficiently central role in decision-making. This is very much dependent on the form of participation, the form of representation and the pool of clients to which lawyers can reach out. Involving the victims in the decision-making process ensures that their lawyers are truly "representatives" and that the victims are thereby meaningfully participating in the proceedings.

Where relevant, victims could be involved in deciding whether various requests should be lodged in the pre-trial phase. In this respect, in April 2013, as a result of media reports publishing the personal data of purported STL Prosecution witnesses, the legal representatives of victims in the *Ayyash* et al. case lodged a request with the Pre-Trial Judge for the initiation of contempt proceedings. Although the ensuing filing did not elaborate on the victims' instructions, it was maintained that the media reports negatively affected the victims' personal interests, especially in relation to their safety.[40]

Furthermore, in the trial phase, victims could be involved in deciding on evidence to be tendered or witnesses to be called on behalf of the participating victims.

For example, at the ECCC, deciding which civil parties should testify in their own case is a decision that needs to be discussed and explained to all other civil parties, who may wish to testify, but who, for one reason or another, are not selected by the civil party lawyers. The final selection is made by the Civil Party Lead Co-Lawyers after consultation with the civil party lawyers.[41] Their decision is final and cannot be challenged.[42]

---

[37] Ibid., Annex II (public).

[38] Ibid., para 17.

[39] Ibid., paras 27–29.

[40] STL, *Prosecutor v. Ayyash* et al., LRV, Public Redacted Version of the Request on Behalf of the Legal Representative of Victims to the Pre-Trial Judge to Refer Certain Facts to the President Under Rule 60*bis*(D), STL-11-01/PT/PTJ, 15 April 2013, para 34.

[41] Written correspondence with Eleonor Fernandez, Senior legal consultant, Civil Party Lead Co-Lawyers Section, 28 September 2015 (records on file with the authors).

[42] Personal notes and experience of co-author Silke Studzinsky.

Additionally, a corollary of involving victims in the decision-making process is giving them feedback regarding the outcome of their choices: what could be achieved, what failed to produce the desired results and what are the reasons for the success or failure.

Whether consulting victims on pertinent issues or involving them in the decision-making process, the ultimate responsibility for a successful representation strategy rests with the legal representative. For that reason, it is the victims' lawyers' responsibility to explain the legal issues to the victims in such a manner as to allow them to take an informed decision. In most instances and to the extent possible, victims' lawyers should explain all relevant legal issues to their clients and seek instructions. There will be instances, of course, when the highly technical nature of certain procedures will make it difficult for the legal representatives to elicit an informed decision from their clients. In such cases, the lawyers should explain the principles and interests involved and consult the victims on their opinions. If lack of time prevents the legal representatives from involving their clients in particular decisions, they should nevertheless inform them about the actions taken at the earliest possibility. Generally, however, most issues will greatly benefit from getting the victims' instructions on the matter. Lawyers should thus continually reflect on their own role, their openness towards accepting a variety of views expressed by their clients, the ease or reticence with which they involve the victims in their decisions and, ultimately, their power to influence victims. Such reflection should be undertaken with professional peers and through feedback from the clients.

15.5 Manner and Methods of Communication

Whether it is an initial contact or a subsequent meeting, the manner and methods through which information is shared with and elicited from victims is very important. Victims' lawyers should keep in mind that every aspect of an initial or subsequent contact with a victim or a group of victims can have important repercussions on the individual(s), the lawyer-client relationship and the effectiveness of the representation before the court. Communication is both verbal and non-verbal, and lawyers need to be adequately prepared and aware of the potential effects of what they say and how they say it.

Whether speaking to an individual victim or a group of victims, legal representatives should be guided by certain fundamental parameters. First, it is imperative to be aware of the victims' backgrounds and understand the potential barriers to communication. Secondly, lawyers should have some basic understanding of the possible impact of trauma on their clients and how that may affect communication with them. Thirdly, lawyers should know how to employ methods to enhance their communication with the victims. This includes being accustomed to active listening and properly using both verbal and non-verbal signs thereof. Lastly, lawyers should be able to observe the behaviour of their clients during meetings based on some basic guidelines of non-verbal communication.

15.5.1 Understanding the Backgrounds of the Victims and the Potential Barriers to Communication

As said above, lawyers need to prepare for their first contact with the victims. Apart from drawing up a check-list of what needs to be discussed with their clients, lawyers should also look at the personal backgrounds of the victims. "Profiling" the victims would allow their lawyers to anticipate their potential needs, identify the most suitable manner of communication and develop a trustful relationship with them.[43]

While circumstances will often limit what can be elicited about a victim prior to the first contact, as much as possible of the following information should be obtained:

- Age
- Preferred name or form of address
- Ethnicity and race
- Religion, cultural perspective, traditions and beliefs
- Sexual orientation or gender identity (in particular for those offences where the crime is motivated by hostility towards the victim)
- Educational background, level of literacy, knowledge of languages
- Physical or mental ability, the nature of the victim's disability, if any, and the implications for the process of communication
- Current emotional state (including trauma, distress, shock, depression, fears of intimidation and recent significant or stressful events experienced)
- The likely impact of recalling traumatic events on the behaviour of the victim
- The relationship of the victim with the alleged perpetrators, if any
- Military, veteran or civilian status
- Lifestyle and domestic circumstances, including whether the victim is currently in a "safe" environment
- Political affiliation
- Socio-economic status
- Geography (urban or rural)[44]
- Precarious legal status (e.g. immigration difficulties, outstanding court orders, etc.)

Obtaining (some of) this information can provide lawyers with important tools on how to communicate efficiently with the victim[45] as well as an initial assess-

---

[43] Personal notes and experience of co-author Barbara Bianchini.

[44] Adapted from National Victim Assistance Academy 2007, Chapter 5: Communication with Victims and Survivors, V-16; Ministry of Justice 2011. Personal notes and experience of co-author Barbara Bianchini.

[45] Personal notes and experience of co-author Barbara Bianchini.

ment of potential vulnerabilities. By becoming aware of cultural communication styles (i.e. how people express themselves, how they display emotions, and how they deal with crisis and conflict), victims' lawyers can adapt their own communication style to accommodate that of the victims when speaking to them.[46] Additionally, lawyers can use this information to select appropriate team members, including field staff, to facilitate communication with the victims.

At the STL, the LRVs' team in the *Ayyash* et al. case maintains a "fact-sheet" of the participating victims as a group listing their gender, age, religion, level of education, knowledge of languages and location. This information is drawn from the application forms and application summaries submitted by the VPU to the Pre-Trial Judge as well as from the representatives' team's subsequent contact with the participating victims. On the basis of the "fact-sheet" several decisions were taken on how to enhance communication with the victims. For instance, since most of the victims have high-school education and use internet, the *Ayyash* et al. LRVs' team set up a secured website, accessible only to victims, through which it shares weekly information. Likewise, the LRVs' team began organising "town-hall meetings" where public victims are invited to have dinner with their lawyers and discuss the case. These decisions were taken thanks to the representatives' awareness of the characteristics of the group they are representing. In the *Ayyash* et al. case, because of the relatively small number of participating victims (72 as at November 2016), the above-mentioned parameters can also be observed on an individual level and communication with each victim personalised. For instance, the representatives' team took note of the knowledge of foreign languages among the victims (especially English and French), so as to assess which members of the representatives' team can communicate with each victim.

Victims' lawyers should also keep in mind that individual factors (personal traits, attitudes, habits, expectations, physical disabilities, etc.), interpersonal factors (differences in perceptions, language and cultural differences, prejudices and biases) and communication factors (lack of attention, interest or irrelevance to the receiver, etc.) play an important role in the likelihood of the message being appropriately communicated to the victim with its original meaning transferred accordingly.[47]

The specificity of communications involving legal proceedings and the particular vulnerability of the victims participating in such proceedings may create further, more specific barriers to communication.[48]

The main types of communication barriers that victims' lawyers may come across are:

- physical barriers (geographical remoteness, victims' isolation);

[46] National Victim Assistance Academy 2007, Chapter 5: Communication with Victims and Survivors, V-16.

[47] Personal notes and experience of co-author Barbara Bianchini.

[48] Personal notes and experience of co-author Barbara Bianchini.

- cultural barriers (cultural differences between victims, lawyers and other relevant individuals, such as interpreters, gender differences in communication,[49] stereotypes and expectations in communication);
- perceptual barriers (cognitive filters, false assumptions, stereotypes and stigmas of the lawyer towards the victim, or of the victim towards the lawyer/justice system, or towards the type of crime);
- semantic and language barriers;[50]
- psychological barriers (the psychological state of both the lawyer and the victim, if not recognised and managed, can indirectly influence how the message is sent, received and perceived);[51]
- past/present trauma barriers (some victims may communicate deficiently, especially once on the witness stand, due to both past trauma events and the way in which they are subjected to the questioning process);[52]
- barriers due to disabilities of the victim (including physical, cognitive and mental health related disabilities); and
- programmatic barriers (e.g. lack of adequate training on behalf of the lawyers to deal with the victim or with traumatised individuals,[53] limited skills of the lawyer(s) in interviewing techniques to minimise trauma and to assist the victim's testimony).[54]

For instance, at the ICC, some of the legal representatives' teams struggle with significant physical barriers due to geographical remoteness and the overall state of the country of residence. In particular, the precarious security situation in the Central African Republic, the recurring fighting in the north and west of the

[49] Kloch 2000, pp. 45–58.

[50] Words are symbols and may be used in several ways and have different meaning. These barriers appear when victims and lawyers do not share the same semantic context, do not assign the same meaning to a particular word or symbol, or interpret the same word with a different level of understanding. A language barrier may also occur when the lawyer uses words which are too technical for the victim, or simply they do not speak a common language, and interpreters are not available. Personal notes and experience of co-author Barbara Bianchini.

[51] For example, when someone is in distress or upset, he or she will often have difficulty in hearing, understanding, remembering and retaining information. See Henckens et al. 2009, pp. 10111–10119. Also, a stressed victim may not be as receptive to the message as if (s)he was calm, or lawyers who feel frustrated because of the negative outcome of the first meeting with the client might react emotionally to clients' requests for generic explanation.

[52] Without an appropriate explanation to the victims about direct and cross-examination techniques as well as witness preparation or in-court dynamics, those who have been intimidated or subjected to severe abuse may be more suggestible or prone to give erroneous answers to leading questions. The Crown Prosecution Service 2002, para 9.5, http://www.cps.gov.uk/publications/prosecution/pretrialadult.html. Accessed 23 February 2015.

[53] National Victim Assistance Academy 2007, Chapter 5: Communication with Victims and Survivors, V-17 to V-22.

[54] Gazurek and Saris 2002.

country and an increase in violence in the country's capital Bangui has rendered meetings with victims in the *Bemba* case virtually impossible.[55] Likewise, in the *Banda* case, the fact that participating victims are located in five different countries within the African continent presents the LRV team with a significant physical barrier.[56] In the *Lubanga* case, many of the victims are former child soldiers who do not wish to reveal their participant status in their communities, so specific security arrangements need to be put in place before meeting them. Moreover, the trauma suffered because of their past engagement has led many to succumb to drug abuse, and as such, maintaining the interest of such victims in participating before the ICC can require extra effort on the part of the LRV.[57]

The relevance of these barriers for the particular victim can be elicited by gaining an in-depth understanding of the victims' backgrounds and being adequately prepared for communicating with them.

15.5.2 Verbal Communication

All guidelines on the goals, framework, content and manner of communication will go to waste if victims' lawyers do not know how to speak to their clients. The importance of using clear, simple and logical language cannot be overstated. Victims' lawyers should be able to explain complex and difficult legal or technical matters in plain, simple terms, tailored to their clients' understanding. In this respect, it might be helpful to create a glossary of key terms: it could remind the lawyer how to explain certain concepts and, distributed to the clients, it would help them understand the more difficult terms.

At the initial meeting, victims' lawyers need properly to introduce themselves and their team. Sometimes such introductions will also be necessary at subsequent meetings, for instance, when a long time has passed from the initial contact, or when the composition of the team changes or if the mental state of a victim is such that a reminder or confirmation is needed of the identity of his or her interlocutors.

If the contact is with one or a handful of victims, it is helpful to ask how they prefer to be addressed. This question can avoid misunderstandings stemming from cultural differences and also signals to victims thoughtfulness on the part of their lawyer.

Communication between lawyers and victims cannot be effective and adequate if the two sides do not fully understand each other's spoken words. It will often be

---

[55] Interview with Carine Pineau and Virginie Roche, legal assistants to Ms. Douzima Lawson, Legal Representative for Victims, *Prosecutor v. Jean-Pierre Bemba Gombo*, ICC, March 2015 (records on file with the authors).

[56] Interview with Hélène Cissé, Legal Representative of Victims, *Prosecutor v. Abdallah Banda*, ICC, November 2014 (records on file with the authors).

[57] Interview with Luc Walleyn, Legal Representative for Victims, *Prosecutor v. Thomas Lubanga Dyilo*, ICC, October 2014 (records on file with the authors).

the case that the lawyers and their clients will not speak a common language or that they can only partially understand each other. In such cases, it is very important to have either qualified field assistants or professional interpreters available. The added value of a qualified field assistant is that, in addition to the required language skills, such a person could also have the necessary experience, cultural awareness and communication skills to connect effectively with the victims. While field assistants are indeed the optimal choice for legal representatives' team, in cases where such staff members are not provided by the court, the engagement of professional interpreters is the next best option. Lawyers and support staff understanding the victim's language should only engage in their own interpretation if the information to be conveyed is short and simple or if because of the urgency of the situation, finding a qualified interpreter is impracticable.

When eliciting information from the victim, lawyers should properly use open-ended or close-ended questions. For instance, if they wish to hear the story or parts of the story of the victim, they should ask open-ended questions, such as 'Can you tell me about…', 'Is there anything else you wish to tell me?' or 'How has this affected you and your family?'. Conversely, if what is sought is a specific piece of information or the clarification of a specific point of discussion, then close-ended questions are more appropriate. Examples of close-ended questions include: 'When did you find out what happened to your husband?', 'How many days did you spend in the hospital?', 'Would you like to attend the trial in The Hague next year?', etc.[58]

To ensure that the questions have been effectively used, lawyers should always cross-check whether they understood what their clients said and whether their clients understood what was said to them. This requires lawyers to be accustomed to active listening: listening with a purpose, paying attention to the narrative, asking for clarifications or repetitions of statements to understand what the victim is saying, and taking notes.[59]

Active listening not only means focusing fully on the speaker, but also entails using both verbal and non-verbal signs of listening.

Some of the most important verbal signs of active listening are also very useful techniques to improve communication with the victims:[60]

- *Minimal encouragers*: conversational speech fillers used to indicate that one is paying attention to someone during a conversation. When communicating with a victim, minimal encouragers consist of short utterances and questions that let the victim know that his or her interlocutor is listening, but does not interfere with the narrative flow. Examples include: 'Oh?', 'I see', 'Yeah', 'Uh-huh', 'When?', 'And?', 'Really?', 'You do?', or 'She did?'.[61]

---

[58] Lewis and Jaramillo 2007, Chapter 5, v-14 to v-15.

[59] Lewis and Jaramillo 2007, Chapter 5, v-4 to v-5.

[60] The list is adapted on the basis of the personal notes and experience of co-author Barbara Bianchini.

[61] Miller 2008, p. 89.

- *Emotional labelling*: helps the victim clarify what he or she is feeling. It contributes to a state of calmness by reducing internal confusion. This technique is particularly useful with victims as it gives power and acknowledges their state of mind. Examples of emotion labelling phrases are: 'You sound [angry, happy, confused]', 'You seem [*ibidem*]', 'I hear [anger, happiness, confusion…]'.[62]
- *Affirmation*: statements that recognise and validate the strengths of a victim or a group of victims. They include acknowledgment that the victim has been harmed and help build the victim's confidence in his or her ability to persist. Affirmations must be congruent and genuine to be effective and they must avoid sounding patronising.[63] Examples of affirmations include: 'It must have been very hard for you to decide to…', 'That must have been very difficult for you…', 'You and your family are very strong…'. Needless to say, these are mere examples and a standard list of affirmations cannot be put together, for many reasons. First, affirmations should be genuine; if they are mechanically repeated, they will sound false and will offend the victims. Secondly, each situation is unique and the victims' lawyers will have to find those aspects of their client's narrative which can be highlighted and affirmed in order to help the victims understand and acknowledge their strengths. Thirdly, affirmations which would be wholly appropriate in one situation, may sound patronising or ridiculous in other, though very similar situations, for the simple reason that people are different and what helps one person does not necessarily assist another.
- *Remembering*: recalling facts, thoughts and other details from previous conversations proves that attention was kept and is likely to encourage the victim to become more trustful towards his or her representative.
- *Summarisation*: providing a summary of the main points of the received information and reiterating it in a logical and clear manner, giving the victim the chance to correct it, if necessary.
- *Paraphrasing*: stating in one's own words what was understood that the victim was saying. Paraphrasing usually begins with phrases such as 'So what I understood you are saying is…', 'If I hear you correctly then…'.[64] It enables the victim to feel heard and to clarify anything lawyers may have misunderstood.
- *Silence and pause*: apart from buying time, silence can be used strategically. In a relatively active conversation, silence on the part of the lawyer may encourage the victim to fill the gaps and keep him or her talking. Nonetheless, too much silence can create a perception of mistrust or lack of interest in the victim.[65]

Non-verbal signs of active listening are equally important and also constitute important techniques to enhance communication with victims:[66]

62 Miller 2005, pp. 277–298.

63 Lewis and Jaramillo 2007, Chapter 5, v-7.

64 Ibid.

65 Miller 2008, p. 89.

66 The list is adapted on the basis of the personal notes and experience of co-author Barbara Bianchini.

- *Eye contact*: generally encourages the listener to look at the speaker. It can, however, be intimidating, especially for introverted speakers. It should be within the victims' control to initiate direct eye-contact if desired. Lawyers need also to keep in mind that the appropriateness and the amount of eye contact may vary from one culture to another.
- *Posture*: those perceived as attentive listeners tend to lean slightly forward or sideways whilst sitting. Other signs of active listening may include a slight slant of the head or resting the head on one hand.
- *Encouraging nods*: nodding, if combined with small smiles, can be very useful in affirming that the victim is being listened to and understood.
- *Mirroring*: matching or mirroring techniques contribute to creating a climate of familiarity by empowering the "comfort zone" of the victim. A victim's lawyer can mirror the victim's kinesics (i.e. display the same sort of body language and posture as the victim). For example, lawyers could smile when the victim smiles, or use similar words, phrases, and expressions as the victim; lawyers could also follow the victim's paralanguages, such as using a similar rate, volume and pitch of speech.[67]
- Ask *open-ended questions* as they allow lawyers to get more information and expand the discussion, they typically begin with 'How', 'When', 'What', 'Where'.[68]

It should be kept in mind, however, that not all verbal or non-verbal signs of active listening are appropriate in all circumstances and with all cultures. The type of physical or personal contact that is appropriate may vary from person to person and across cultures and social groups. For example, how close to stand to someone, how much eye contact to make or how acceptable it is to touch someone may vary from culture to culture. Victims' lawyers should be informed about cultural norms to understand what the various gestures mean in the relevant culture, and to identify those acts that are taboo.

Victims' lawyers may also consider bringing together smaller working groups to have victims share their story, their worries and their wishes with each other. This technique can also have a significant empowering and cohesive effect. Nonetheless, lawyers should be mindful of the dynamic of the particular groups and abandon or adjust this method if they notice negative developments (uneasy power relations; brewing conflicts, etc.).

15.5.3 Observation of Behaviour and Non-verbal Communication

Enhancing communication and building trust with clients also entails an active effort in observing the behaviour of victims during communication. Observation

---

67 Dreeke and Navarro 2009, pp. 1–10.

68 Lewis and Jaramillo 2007, Chapter 5, v-14.

of behaviour could help identify potential reactions by the client, which then could be used to assess more accurately the needs of the victims and the manner in which the victims' lawyers could respond or adapt to those needs. Paying attention to non-verbal communication can also personalise the interaction between the lawyer and the victims, by enhancing the latter's sense of confidence and trust.

Some of the more important aspects of non-verbal communication to pay heed to are:

- *Position of the body and body orientation*: proximity between a victim and his lawyer is critical to successful communications, both verbal and non-verbal. A victim should always be given the choice to sit and the option of choosing the seat. The lawyer's posture should promote a clear interest and decide proximity with the client based on victim's verbal/non-verbal indications.[69]
- *Facial expressions or micro-expressions*: provide a rich source of non-verbal information, particularly in conveying emotion.
- *Physical contacts with victims*: generally not recommended unless the victim specifically invites such a gesture. Moreover, culture weighs heavily on a person's comfort with personal touch, so victims' lawyers should exercise caution in this regard.[70]
- *Considering the impact of community trauma*: how the community interprets a particular event, who are considered "victims", perception about the perpetrators of the crime, availability of social support services, the importance of traditional healing processes, etc. can help the legal representatives reframe the impact of the event within a larger perspective than the individual's one.[71]

All in all, when it comes to the right manner in which to communicate with victims, victims' lawyers should keep in mind that building a workable communicative relationship with their clients takes time, that often, despite the best of efforts, there will be failures and drawbacks. Nonetheless, as long as it is seen as a learning process for everyone involved, the manner and methods of communication can improve and can produce positive results.

15.5.4 Understanding the Impact of Trauma on the Victims

In the overwhelming majority of cases, lawyers do not possess specialised knowledge on how to deal with clients traumatised by past events. Nonetheless, lawyers will often have to deal with the impact such trauma caused on the victim. As put by Winick:

> 'How should we as lawyers deal with these problems? We, of course, are going to deal with their legal problems. But in the process, let us understand that our clients are people

[69] Ibid., v-9.

[70] Ibid.

[71] The list is adapted on the basis of the personal notes and experience of co-author Barbara Bianchini. See also Chap. 10.

who possess the full range of human emotions that inevitably interrelate with the legal problems they are encountering. [...] We need to understand that the client is a person, a fellow human being. It is our role to understand their emotional problems, as well as their legal ones, and to minister to the whole person. As lawyers, we inevitably are therapeutic agents'.[72]

First and foremost, communication needs to unequivocally show respect and understanding toward the victims, even though at times conducting a conversation may prove to be difficult and distressing.

Furthermore, legal representatives and lawyers representing civil parties must be able to communicate effectively in order to reduce the possibility, through poor communication, of further traumatising or re-victimising the victim.[73]

Lawyers should also keep in mind that the experience of being victimised has the potential to turn every aspect of a victim's life into chaos and disarray. A common feeling reported by victims is one of loss of control, which can persist long after the event and affect areas of life not related to the traumatic experience. Victims tend to be suspicious; they mistrust others, including judicial procedures.[74] In this context, developing trust also refers to the ability of lawyers to provide clients with timely, reliable, congruent and accurate information, in a secure environment, supported by a compassionate understanding of the history of the individual.[75]

For this reason, it is very important for victims' lawyers to have some knowledge about trauma, its forms, symptoms, consequences and ways of dealing with it. Surely, most lawyers are not professionally qualified to deal with traumatised individuals and, indeed, they are not required to turn into psychologists, psychotherapists or social workers. Nonetheless, lawyers need to listen to their clients and assist them the best they can. For this purpose, it is recommended that, if practicable, victims' lawyers attend trainings to learn how to deal with trauma and how to improve their communication with traumatised victims. Likewise, victims' lawyers should work closely with qualified professionals: trauma counsellors, psychologists, psychotherapists, victimologists or social workers—preferably local ones, if available, or those familiar with the particular conflict and/or the traumas suffered by the victims.

Professionals can then set guidelines for the victims' lawyers on how to communicate with traumatised victims, how to recognise symptoms of trauma and how to best deal with them. Nonetheless, there will be many situations in which the victims' lawyer will have to rely on his or her common sense and intuition when communicating with a traumatised victim. In these cases, the following basic guidelines should be kept in mind:[76]

---

[72] Winick 2009, pp. 536–544. Personal notes and experience of co-author Barbara Bianchini.

[73] Personal notes and experience of co-author Barbara Bianchini.

[74] Lewis and Jaramillo 2007, Chapter 5, v-2.

[75] Personal notes and experience of co-author Barbara Bianchini.

[76] These guidelines are adapted from: Justice Solutions 2001; See also, generally: Foa et al. 2010; personal notes and experience of co-author Barbara Bianchini.

- *Privacy*: Invite the victim to sit, try to ensure some level of privacy for the conversation, and give the person your full attention. Speak softly and calmly. Refrain from looking around or being distracted; explain your organisation's *confidentiality* policies and how collected information may be used during the proceedings.
- *Allow the victim to speak freely*: Permit victims to tell their story uninterrupted, especially at the initial meeting; offer opportunities for victims to provide input into the case.
- *Respect*: Avoid making assumptions about the victims' experience, avoid patronising them. Do not assume all victims are traumatised.
- *"Every victim is unique"*: It is essential to individualise each victim, each crime, and each victim's reaction to that crime.[77]
- *Being impartial*: Do not judge, contradict, or correct what victims say about their personal beliefs. Follow the lead of the victim in discussing the event. Do not judge the quality of the communication based on a victim's traits and habits (i.e. different political/personal/ideological affiliation between client and lawyers). Make no discrimination as to gender, nationality, race, ethnicity, rich and poor, religious beliefs, sex, class or political opinions.
- *"Reminders"*: Bear in mind when talking to the victim that questions related to the traumatic event ("trauma reminders") can evoke upsetting thoughts and feelings about what happened. Questions about consequences of the event ("loss reminders") can bring to mind the loss of a beloved one and questions comparing past and current opinions ("change reminders") might trigger thoughts related to how the victim's life changed as a result of certain events.[78]
- *Remain calm, even in a very difficult situation*: Lawyers should not become flustered by the victim's anxiety or urgency and they should always remember that their anxiety can easily be transmitted to the victim. Lawyers should never become defensive or arrogant, or get into an argument with a victim. They should also refrain from making explicit or implicit disapproving comments.[79] Lawyers will often find themselves in situations—especially when communicating with groups of victims—that test not only their communication skills, but also their patience and impartiality. For instance, individual victims may have differing views about a certain topic and an open argument or conflict may arise during the collective meeting with their lawyer. In such a situation it is essential that the lawyer shows equal respect to the points of views expressed and, if possible, provides information that helps solving the difficulty. In any case, even if a resolution of the argument is not possible, the communication needs to be transparent and sincere, so that the victims are allowed to build trust towards their lawyer.
- Lawyers should not be discouraged if the first (few) meeting(s) are unsatisfactory. Some victims need more time to build trust.

[77] Justice Solutions 2001.

[78] See, generally: Foa et al. 2010.

[79] See, generally: Justice Solutions 2001.

At the STL, the LRVs' team in the *Ayyash* et al. case works together with a qualified victimologist, who has met most of the participating victims and who provides advice to the lawyers on an ongoing basis. The LRV also cooperates with the Victims and Witnesses Unit (VWU) psychologist for the purpose of sharing information about vulnerable witnesses testifying at the tribunal or victims attending the proceedings. In this direction, it might be relevant for LRVs, where possible, to provide victims with referrals to a full range of social support services, such as crisis counselling, safety planning, and domestic legal assistance.

The ECCC did not offer any services to victims with regard to their traumatisation. Nonetheless, the NGO 'Transcultural Psychosocial Organization' (TPO) assisted civil parties with face-to-face and telephone counselling on how to deal with trauma and also participated and supported group meetings of civil parties. Additionally, TPO provided training to members of the VSS and the Witness Expert Support Unit (WESU). TPO also organised self-help groups for victims of sexual and gender-based violence, mainly forced marriage. Likewise, in cooperation with the VSS and the Cambodian Defenders Project (CDP), TPO implemented a program focusing on equal access to justice for female survivors of the Khmer Rouge and fostered participation and standing for female civil parties and victims of sexual and gender-based violence.

At the ICC, the OPCV reports that it has used the services of Victims and Witnesses Section (VWS) psychologists to interact with some of its clients. Psychological expertise indeed exists in the VWS, but is principally used for supporting witnesses. Most of the time, however, victims may benefit from this in-house support, which includes psychological assistance, when they face a threat as a result of their status as participating victims and are referred to the VWS. In addition, dual-status victims (victims who may be called to testify as witnesses), may also benefit from VWS assistance, however the vast majority of victims do not have any such access. To date, LRVs have not been provided with legal aid funds in order to engage independent expert assistance in this field, in the way that has occurred at the STL.

15.5.5 A Word of Caution: "Secondary Traumatisation" as a Side-Effect of Communicating with Victims of Crime

While it is important for victims' lawyers to learn how to communicate with traumatised victims, it is equally important to recognise the reciprocal impact that traumatic stories might have on those who are listening to them.

Secondary traumatisation, also known as "vicarious traumatisation",[80] "compassion fatigue",[81] and "secondary traumatic stress disorder",[82] happens when

[80] McCann and Pearlman 1990.

[81] Joinson 1992, pp. 116–122.

[82] Figley 1995.

thoughts about a victim's experience begin to intrude on a professional's daily life.[83] It is defined as 'the stress resulting from helping or wanting to help a traumatised person'[84] and all providers of a service addressing traumatised individuals are affected to some degree by it.

Secondary traumatisation happens as a result of communicating with victims for the recollection of relevant events. During this process, victims' lawyers and staff assisting them indirectly become witnesses to the crime(s) and harm the victim(s) suffered. Absorbing these narratives may have insidious impacts. Personal balance can be lost for a brief or longer period. Confusion, apathy, isolation, anxiety, sadness and/or illness can often result from exposure to such narratives.[85]

Secondary trauma reactions include:

- Sleeping problems;
- Nightmares;
- Intrusive thoughts, memories and flashbacks;
- Hyper-vigilance;
- General anxiety and anxiety attacks;
- Isolation and disconnection;
- Substance abuse and high risk behaviours;
- Changes in appetite and sex drive;
- Irritability and depression;
- Cynicism, negativity, and apathy about life and the world.[86]

Because of the common tendency to underestimate this phenomenon, it is important for victims' lawyers (and legal professionals dealing with victims) to be aware of the impact communication with victims can have on their own professional and personal life. Various models have been developed to assist legal professionals in recognising and dealing with secondary traumatisation symptoms.[87] Most of these models share some basic principles, such as the importance of self-awareness (e.g. detecting signs of excessive stress), the need to identify personal triggers (e.g. what are the situations which cause stress, vulnerability, etc.), as well as competent supervision (managers should encourage brainstorming and/or debriefing sessions in case of difficult clients).

Victims' lawyers must always be very receptive about their personal level of vulnerability and should be keen to develop personal strategies to strengthen their own resilience in order to avoid becoming victims of their own professional commitment.

Guarding against secondary traumatisation cannot be considered as an individual responsibility, but rather an organisational duty. To ensure that victims' lawyers

---

[83] Sushelsky 2011.

[84] Ibid.

[85] Richardson 2001, p. 7.

[86] Faith Community Professional Education Initiative 2002.

[87] Williams and Sommer 1999, pp. 230–246; Pearlman 1999, pp. 51–64; Fischman 2008, pp. 107–115.

can communicate effectively with their clients without being affected, LRVs and their team members should be educated about secondary traumatisation and its potential implications. Victims' lawyers should not shy away from requesting that such training be provided. Needless to say, this also applies to other legal professionals or tribunal staff working closely with victims of international crimes.

15.6 Key Points

- Upon meeting their clients for the first time, victims' lawyers appointed by the relevant court should not assume that the victims are already fully familiar with their rights.
- The initial contact between lawyer and victim should aim to clarify the basic tenets of the victims' participation in the proceedings.
- In preparation for the first meeting, a newly appointed victims' lawyer should review all the information available to him or her regarding the particular victim(s).
- The victims' lawyer should identify the goals of the first communication. For this purpose, he or she may consider drawing up a check list in advance (see Fig. 15.1), putting down all the relevant issues to be discussed with the client(s).
- It will seldom be the case that all these issues could be discussed during the first meeting with the client(s). Nonetheless, the checklist should be an exhaustive one, as it can then be adjusted based on the initial and the ensuing contacts with the victims. The lawyer should find a suitable method to create a record of the initial and ensuing conversations.
- Whether communication takes place during individual conversations, group meetings or meetings with selected representatives of the victims, victims' lawyers need to have a set of goals in mind. Communication between the two sides will always be a two-way process: information provided by the lawyer to the victim(s) and information shared by the victim(s) with the lawyer.
- Before every contact with the victim(s), victims' lawyers should prepare in advance the information that needs to be provided. Preparation can take up the form of a check-list, or any other more open-ended or flexible form of aide-memoire.
- Notwithstanding the multitude of factors continuously shaping the content of the information to be provided, victims' lawyers should keep in mind certain basic themes that will aid them in sharing information (Fig. 15.2).
- Victims' lawyers should determine what the victims' respective wishes are with regard to the amount and form of information that they want to receive from their lawyers.
- The amount and form of information victims wish to receive will also allow the lawyers to draw conclusions on the extent to which their clients wish to be consulted about issues related to their participation throughout the proceedings.

- The obvious reason for consulting victims on pertinent issues regarding their participation is to seek their instructions and ensure this way that they play a sufficiently central role in decision-making. This is very much dependent on the form of participation, the form of representation and the pool of clients to which lawyers can reach out.
- It is imperative to be aware of the victims' background and understand the potential barriers to communication (cultural, physical, psychological, programmatic, language, barriers due to disabilities).
- Victims' lawyers should have some basic understanding of the possible impact of trauma on their clients and how that may affect communication with them. They should attend relevant trainings and work closely with professionals.
- Victims' lawyers should know how to employ methods to enhance their communication with the victims. This includes being accustomed to active listening and properly using both verbal and non-verbal signs thereof.
- Victims' lawyers should be able to observe the behaviour of their clients during meetings based on some basic guidelines of non-verbal communication.
- Secondary traumatisation happens as a result of communicating with victims for the recollection of relevant events. During this process, victims' lawyers and staff assisting them indirectly become witnesses to the crime(s) and harm the victim(s) suffered.
- Victims' lawyers must always be very receptive about their personal level of vulnerability and should be keen to develop personal strategies to strengthen their own resilience in order to avoid becoming victims of their own professional commitment.
- To ensure that victims' lawyers can communicate effectively with their clients without being affected, international courts should educate victims' lawyers and their team members about secondary traumatisation and its potential implications.

References

Clark JN (2011) Peace, justice and the International Criminal Court: Limitations and possibilities. J Int Crim Justice 9:521–545

Dreeke RK, Navarro J (2009) Behavioral mirroring in interviewing. FBI Law Enforc Bull 78(12):1–10

Faith Community Professional Education Initiative (2002) Vicarious trauma. http://fcpei.denverda.org/Classroom/UnitNine.htm. Accessed 22 Dec 2015

Figley CR (1995) Compassion fatigue: Coping with secondary traumatic stress disorder in those who treat the traumatized. Brunner/Mazel, Levittown

Fischman Y (2008) Secondary trauma in the legal professions, a clinical perspective. Torture 18(2):107–115

Foa EA et al (2010) Effective treatments for PTSD: Practice guidelines from the International Society for Traumatic Stress Studies. Guilford Press, New York

Gazurek A, Saris A (2002) The protection of women as witnesses in the ICTR. Coalition for Women's Human Rights in Conflict Situations. https://www.atria.nl/epublications/2002/Protection_of_Women_as_Witnesses_ICTR.PDF. Accessed 22 Dec 2015

Henckens MJAG, Hermans EJ, Pu Z, Joels M, Fernandez G (2009) Stressed memories: How acute stress affects memory formation in humans. J Neurosci 29(32):10111–10119
International Criminal Court (2005) Code of Professional Conduct for Counsel, ICC-ASP/4/Res.1
Joinson C (1992) Coping with compassion fatigue. Nursing 22(4):116–122
Justice Solutions (2001) Communicating with victims: The do's and don'ts. http://justicesolutions.org/art_pub_communicating_with_victims.pdf. Accessed 22 Dec 2015
Kamatali JM (2005) From the ICTR to ICC: Learning from the ICTR experience in bringing justice to Rwandans. N Engl J Int Comp Law 12:89–103
Kloch Z (2000) Language and gender: Social and psychological determinants in communication. Psychol Lang Commun 4(2):45–58
Lewis N, Jaramillo A (2007) Communication with victims and survivors. National Victim Assistance Academy, Track 1, Foundation-Level Training, Chapter 5, v-14 to v-15
McCann IL, Pearlman LA (1990) Psychological trauma and the adult survivor: Theory, therapy, and transformation. Brunner/Mazel, New York
Miller L (2005) Hostage negotiation: Psychological principles and practices. Int J Emerg Ment Health 7(4):277–298
Miller L (2008) Counseling crime victims: Practical strategies for mental health professionals. Springer, Berlin/Heidelberg
Ministry of Justice (2011) Achieving best evidence in criminal proceedings: Guidance on interviewing victims and witnesses, and guidance on using special measures. London
National Victim Assistance Academy (2007) Track 1, Foundation-Level Training, Chapter 5: Communication with victims and survivors, 1–28. http://www.ccvs.state.vt.us/sites/default/files/resources/VVAA%20Ch%205%20Communications.pdf. Accessed 26 Aug 2016
Pearlman LA (1999) Self-care for trauma therapists. Ameliorating vicarious traumatization. In: Stamm BH (ed) Secondary traumatic stress. Self-care issues for clinicians, researchers & educators. Sidran Press, Maryland, pp 51–64
Redress (2005) Ensuring the effective participation of victims before the International Criminal Court: Comments and recommendations regarding legal representation for victims. http://www.redress.org/downloads/publications/REDRESS%20-%20Legal%20Representation%20for%20Victims%2023%20May%202005.pdf. Accessed 26 Aug 2016
Richardson J I (2001) Guidebook on vicarious trauma: Recommended solutions for anti-violence workers. http://www.mollydragiewicz.com/VTguidebook.pdf. Accessed 22 December 2015
Special Tribunal for Lebanon (2012) Code of Professional Conduct for Defence Counsel and Legal Representatives of Victims appearing before the Special Tribunal for Lebanon, STL/CC/2012/03
Sperfeldt C (2013) The role of Cambodian civil society in the Victim Participation Scheme of the Extraordinary Chambers in the Courts of Cambodia. In: Bonacker T, Safferling C (eds) Victims of international crimes: An interdisciplinary discourse. Springer, Berlin/Heidelberg
Sushelsky M (2011) Secondary trauma and burnout in lawyers and what to do about it. Lawyers Journal. http://www.massbar.org/publications/lawyers-journal/2011/december/secondary-trauma-%E2%80%A8and-burnout-in-lawyers-and-what-to-do-about-it. Accessed 26 Aug 2016
The Crown Prosecution Service (2002) Provision of therapy for vulnerable or intimidated adult witnesses prior to a criminal trial—Practice guidance. http://www.cps.gov.uk/publications/prosecution/pretrialadult.html. Accessed 23 Feb 2015
Williams MB, Sommer JF (1999) Self-care and the vulnerable therapist. In: Stamm BH (ed) Secondary traumatic stress. Self-care issues for clinicians, researchers & educators. Sidran Press, Maryland, pp 230–246
Winick BJ (2009) Therapeutic jurisprudence, perspectives on dealing with victims of crime. Nova Law Rev 33:536–544

Chapter 16
International Criminal Proceedings—An Adequate Tool for Victims' Justice?

Rianne Letschert

Abstract This chapter discusses six factors, addressed throughout the book, that stand out as crucial for rendering victim participation in criminal justice meaningful: cultural awareness, accessible application mechanisms, effective communication, effective protective measures, accessible psychological assistance and reparations. The chapter also puts international criminal proceedings in the greater context of transitional justice. With a sharp lens, it highlights the shortcomings of such proceedings and advises on the way forward.

Keywords Victimological perspectives · Transitional justice

Victim participation in international criminal justice has been both hailed as milestone in the development of victims' rights and criticised for failing to address the particular needs of victims of mass crimes. A crucial question that must be asked is whether existing theories and concepts developed within mainstream victimology are adequate to address issues pertaining to mass victimisation resulting from such international crimes. The relationship between victims of crime and criminal justice in the domestic sphere is complicated, because many victims experience their interaction with criminal justice actors as a burden rather than a

Rianne Letschert is Rector Magnificus of the University of Maastricht. Between 2011 and 2016, Dr. Letschert was professor of victimology and international law at Tilburg University. She also served as director of the International Victimology Institute Tilburg (INTERVICT). Dr. Letschert has authored and edited several book publications and articles in national and international journals.

R. Letschert (✉)
University of Maastricht, Maastricht, The Netherlands
e-mail: R.Letschert@maastrichtuniversity.nl

K. Tibori-Szabó and M. Hirst (eds.), *Victim Participation in International Criminal Justice*, International Criminal Justice Series 11,
DOI 10.1007/978-94-6265-177-7_16

benefit; but this complexity and its associated nuances are largely lost in the transition to the international level.[1]

Responding to victimisation through international crimes comes with its own problems. These stem from the very nature of these particular crimes, relating mainly to their magnitude, often inherent to them. Enormous challenges lie in developing victimological approaches to the complexities of victimisation by international crimes.[2] The fact that international criminal justice is largely accompanied by triumphant rhetoric about its impact on war-torn societies suggests that one of the basic lessons of victims' rights in the criminal justice system has yet to be learned: that the benefits of victim participation are as much related to practice as to principle.[3] Victims' rights will only benefit victims when their implementation in practice is secured. The notion that anything is better than nothing when it comes to victims' procedural rights has been repeatedly refuted by research.[4] Allowing victims to participate and then disrespecting them or flagrantly failing to meet their expectations will lead to secondary victimisation.[5] It has been well said that a key principle of victims' procedural rights is 'do no further harm'.[6]

Victim participation, when meaningful, can contribute to the acknowledgement of one's status as a victim and may also have an empowering effect. The extent to which participation is meaningful is ordinarily decided by the victims themselves. In this sense, even mere symbolic acknowledgement of victim status may have an empowering effect. As elaborated in Chap. 11, observational attendance in the courtroom can have a positive impact on individual victims. But the needs of victims vary and change over time, and symbolic gestures may not always be an adequate answer. As victims themselves become more informed regarding their rights, more sophisticated forms of participation in international criminal proceedings become desirable. Besides the generally shared needs for truth, justice and reparations, victims may have particular desires when it comes to the daily practice of their participation. In particular, victims may have differing expectations as to the content and frequency of information they receive, the length of proceedings, the procedural principles adopted (e.g. whether trials *in absentia* are permitted), the possibility to give evidence, available protective measures and the various forms of reparations to be awarded, if any. Various chapters of this book highlight shortcomings in the practice of the three courts in this respect. To name a few, Chap. 6 highlights that the legal concept of anonymity has only been accepted at the ICC, while victims wishing to participating in proceedings before ECCC

1 Pemberton et al. 2015, p. 357.

2 Letschert 2010, p. 2.

3 Pemberton and Letschert 2012, pp. 298, 302–303; Groenhuijsen and Pemberton 2009, pp. 48–51.

4 See, generally: Herman 2003; Davis and Smith 1994; Laxminarayan 2012.

5 See, generally: Orth 2002.

6 Groenhuijsen and Pemberton 2011, p. 27.

and the STL will have to disclose their identity to all parties in the proceedings. Closely related to this enforced exposure, the lack of well developed, adequate and continuous psychological assistance to victims—regardless of their status as witnesses—may lead to secondary victimisation. Likewise, factors that can have a fundamental impact on the testimony of a traumatised victim, thoroughly discussed in Chap. 10, are largely overlooked in proceedings before the three courts and lawyers of all parties often examine vulnerable witnesses (including victims) in ways that may exacerbate their suffering.

The variety of these needs coupled with the substantial numbers of victims participating in some cases present a true challenge to international criminal courts, especially where financial and logistical resources are less than adequate. Therefore, with the benefits of participation come risks as well. At worst, victims can experience international criminal justice as another traumatic event, leading to secondary victimisation. Even in cases where the effect is not that extreme, victims' sentiment that impunity prevails may be confirmed by slow, apparently ineffective proceedings that produce no meaningful effects for them.

There are a multitude of factors that influence the effectiveness of victim participation. While current practice has a few common threads, the three courts have adopted differing approaches to many elements of victim participation. It is thus very difficult to list all factors that need to be taken in consideration to effect one or more schemes of meaningful victim participation. Nonetheless, six such factors, addressed throughout this book, stand out.

First and foremost, cultural awareness as regards the background of the victim and his or her community is crucial. Such awareness informs decision making regarding essential aspects of victim participation. For instance, as discussed in Chap. 3, setting strict evidentiary standards (in the sense of requiring documentary proof of harm suffered) may exclude many victims from participation. Such standards should take into consideration the society the victims originate from. As elaborated in Chap. 15, cultural awareness will also inform the manner of communication with victims. It will also play a significant role in assessing the (psychological) assistance needed by particular individuals. Chapter 10 also examines the way in which social, cultural and familial barriers affect testimony of victims. This also shows how important cultural awareness is when dealing with victims.

Secondly, the mechanisms by which victims are identified and granted status by the respective tribunals must be accessible. Such mechanisms must not become a bureaucratic obstacle to participation. This is particularly susceptible to happening where individual written procedures are used and tight deadlines are imposed. While maintaining the integrity and credibility of the process is important, this should not become a reason to create a procedure which defeats its own intended purposes and also runs the risk of creating added burdens for the Prosecution and Defence. The challenges involved in finding an appropriate balance in this area, particularly where courts grapple with crimes involving tens or hundreds of thousands of victims, are touched upon in Chaps. 2 and 3.

Also closely related to the first factor, effective communication with victims is crucial to meaningful participation. Chapter 15 thoroughly discusses this topic.

Significantly, the chapter also delves into technologically progressive methods of communication. As the large number of participating victims is often mentioned as the main reason for ineffective representation, the question must be asked why courts do not exert more effort in creating technologically progressive methods for more inclusive participation. Similarly, there is a need to ensure that funding available for victims' legal representation adequately reflects the practical challenges which are involved in maintaining communication with large numbers of participating victims, as discussed in Chap. 5.

Two further interrelated factors are the provision of protection and psychological assistance. Participation of victims in international criminal proceedings exposes them to new risks, including threats to personal safety and security and secondary victimisation. Chapter 6 elaborates on the protective measures available for victims, but also on the divergent trends at the three courts in this respect. Chapters 10 and 15 elaborate on the various risks of secondary victimisation that victims participating in international criminal proceedings may face. It is important to adopt adequate measures to address both of these factors.

Lastly, the importance of reparations cannot be understated. At the outset, any effective model of victim participation should include reparations, in the broad sense of the concept. Even if reparations are not envisaged as a direct result of proceedings (as with the STL), all courts contemplating or entertaining victim participation schemes should have realistic options for reparations being awarded directly or indirectly. Compensation is only one form of reparation and may be impossible when dealing with large number of victims. In addition, the lengthy nature of procedures of international criminal justice implies that those most acutely in need of compensation run a real risk of receiving it when it is much too late, which is particularly true when compensation is needed to cover for instance health care costs.[7] Other forms of reparations may be more effective, for example the establishment of rehabilitation or reintegration services, symbolic measures such as enabling commemorations, setting up memorialisation monuments, or offering official apologies. At the same time, care should be taken not to discount too quickly the potential benefits of individual compensation for victims where this can be practically achieved in a given case.

Commentators have suggested that participating in court may positively contribute to reducing trauma that victims may suffer from. It is possible that this effect is overestimated, particularly given that a courtroom does not resemble a therapeutic environment.[8] However, therapeutic benefits can be viewed in conjunction 'with the symbolic aspects of participation, or in other terms what the procedural rights signal *to* and *about* the victim.'[9] This means in particular that the victim should perceive the procedure to be about what happened to him or her and its results to be a reaction to the wrongs visited on him or her. Granting

7 See generally Pemberton et al. 2015, p. 364.

8 Doak 2011, pp. 281–282.

9 See generally Pemberton et al. 2015, p. 361.

information rights to victims of crime is therefore an important measure to prevent secondary victimisation, as it recognises the special interest of victims in following the case and contributes to the perception that the criminal justice actors are acting on their behalf.

With regard to more far-reaching involvement (voice) in the criminal justice procedure, the same motives—acknowledgement, assuring the self-relevance of criminal justice reactions—apply, with participating victims seeing added value in asserting them *in person*. The latter raises an important complexity in the translation of these findings from the domestic to the international sphere. Getting information across to victimised populations and offering effective participation is therefore crucial. As stated in a previous publication, 'signalling to victims that international criminal justice is a reaction to what was done to them, in their name, acknowledging their interest through the provision of information and allowing for victim participation in the process geared to emphasising these goals are without a doubt a *greater* rather than a *smaller* concern.'[10] Nevertheless, for international criminal justice institutions, the idea of a multitude of victims asserting their right to participate is a daunting one.[11] The trials of many of the top-level accused persons could last forever if each of the tens of thousands of victims voiced his or her experience in detail. Seeing the large-scale nature of victimisation in international crimes, some might be tempted to propose collective modes of participation as a viable and more feasible solution. However, international crimes are planned and performed by individuals against individuals and thus remain rooted in perceptions of interpersonal meaning.[12] An important aspect of the perpetration of international crimes involves the de-individualisation of its victims, who are lumped together in their subhuman or inhuman status, which in turn implies that re-individualisation should ideally be a feature in the criminal justice reaction.

Although there is no easy solution, a firm focus on the importance of symbolic goals in victims' participation, while connecting collective and individual modes of participation is recommended. To be more concrete, apart from strengthening the participation possibilities at international criminal justice institutions for those victims who wish to participate in the trials,[13] one could imagine a combination of, for instance, truth commissions in which victims can individually speak out on their experiences, a compilation of which is subsequently and explicitly used as a base for collective input in international criminal justice procedures.

To conclude, justice is seen to be done when it is seen in the eyes of the victimised population. Simply put, it is the victims who determine whether victim participation works. Victim participation should not merely be about a few additional provisions in the texts of courts, a few additional lawyers sitting in the courtroom and overall positive-image building. For international criminal justice

[10] Pemberton et al. 2015, p. 362.

[11] See generally Wyngaert 2011; Vasiliev 2009.

[12] Haldemann 2011, pp. 273–276.

[13] Pena and Carayon 2013, p. 535.

truly to embrace victim participation, more needs to be done to impact individual victims. This also entails that international criminal justice can be strengthened by acknowledging its limitations and communicating to victims what it can and cannot offer. This is in part due to the specific problems that international crimes cause for criminal justice, but also due to the victimological insight identified at the outset, namely that the relationship between victims and criminal justice in general is always complicated. No justice reaction can undo the harm and the recurrent and awful memories of suffering through international crimes. However, international criminal justice, at best, can and should put more effort into reaffirming the human dignity of the victims of these crimes, to recognise their individuality and treat victims with respect and recognition during the proceedings.

References

Davis RC, Smith BE (1994) Victim impact statements and victim satisfaction: An unfulfilled promise. J Crim Justice 22(1):1–12

Doak J (2011) The therapeutic dimension of transitional justice: emotional repair and victim satisfaction in international trials and truth commissions. Int Crim Law Rev 11:263–298

Groenhuijsen MS, Pemberton A (2009) The EU framework decision on victims. Does hard law make a difference? Eur J Crime, Crim Law Crim Justice 17:43–59

Groenhuijsen MS, Pemberton A (2011) Genocide, crimes against humanity and war crimes: a victimological perspective. In: Letschert R, De Brouwer AM, Haveman R, Pemberton A (eds) Victimological approaches to international crimes. Intersentia, Antwerp, pp 7–34

Haldemann F (2011) Drawing the line: amnesty, truth commissions and collective denial. In: Letschert R, Haveman RH, Brouwer AM, Pemberton A (eds) Victimological approaches to international crimes: Africa. Intersentia, Antwerp, pp 265–288

Herman JL (2003) The mental health of crime victims: impact of legal intervention. J Trauma Stress 16(2):159–166

Laxminarayan MS (2012) The heterogeneity of crime victims: Variations in procedural and outcome preferences. Intervict, Tilburg

Letschert R (2010) Protecting and empowering victims of international crimes through the human security concept—A new challenge for victimologists? Social Science Research Network (SSRN), https://papers.ssrn.com/sol3/papers.cfm?abstract_id=1594250. Accessed 1 Nov 2016

Orth U (2002) Secondary victimization of crime victims by criminal proceedings. Soc Justice Res 15(4):313–325

Pemberton A, Letschert R (2012) Global justice and global criminal laws. The importance of Nyaya in the quest for justice after international crimes. Tilburg Law Rev: J Int Comp Law 17(2):296–303

Pemberton A, Letschert R, De Brouwer AM, Haveman RH (2015) Coherence in international criminal justice, a victimological perspective. Int Crim Law Rev 15(2):339–368

Pena M, Carayon G (2013) Is the ICC making the most of victim participation? Int J Trans Justice 7:518–535

Van den Wyngaert C (2011) Victims before international criminal courts—Some views and concerns of an ICC trial judge. Case West J Int Law 44:475–496

Vasiliev S (2009) Article 68(3) and personal interests of victims in the emerging practice of the ICC. In: Stahn C, Sluiter G (eds) The emerging practice of the International Criminal Court. Martinus Nijhoff Publishers, Leiden

Table of Cases

ECCC

ICC

K. Tibori-Szabó and M. Hirst (eds.), *Victim Participation in International Criminal Justice*, International Criminal Justice Series 11,
DOI 10.1007/978-94-6265-177-7

STL

Index

A

K. Tibori-Szabó and M. Hirst (eds.), *Victim Participation in International Criminal Justice*, International Criminal Justice Series 11,
DOI 10.1007/978-94-6265-177-7

MIX
Papier aus verantwortungsvollen Quellen
Paper from responsible sources
FSC® C105338

FSC
www.fsc.org

If you have any concerns about our products,
you can contact us on
ProductSafety@springernature.com

In case Publisher is established outside the EU,
the EU authorized representative is:
Springer Nature Customer Service Center GmbH
Europaplatz 3, 69115 Heidelberg, Germany

Printed by Libri Plureos GmbH
in Hamburg, Germany